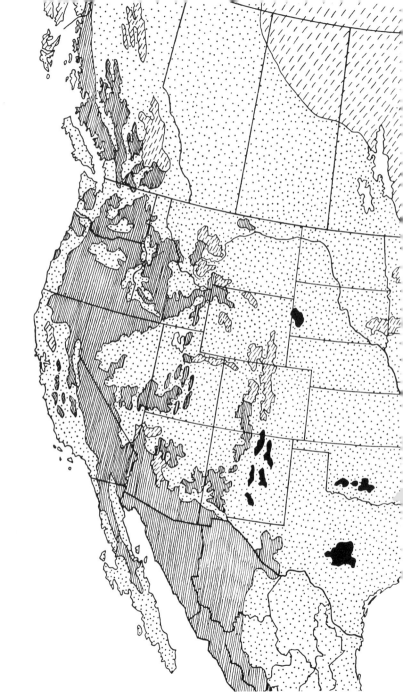

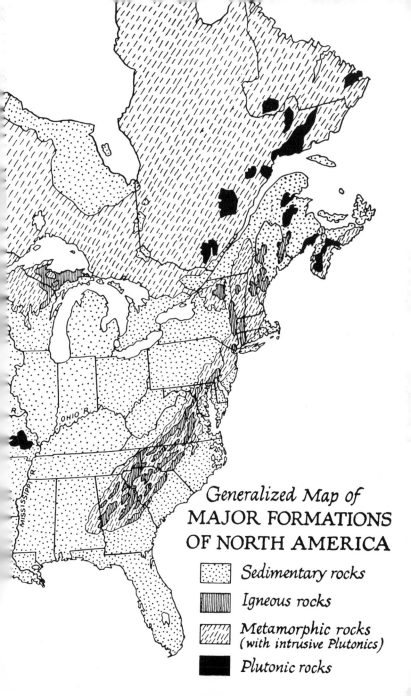

Generalized Map of
MAJOR FORMATIONS
OF NORTH AMERICA

Sedimentary rocks

Igneous rocks

Metamorphic rocks
(with intrusive Plutonics)

Plutonic rocks

THE PETERSON FIELD GUIDE SERIES®
Edited by Roger Tory Peterson

A Field Guide to
Rocks and Minerals

FREDERICK H. POUGH

Photographs by
JEFFREY SCOVIL

Fifth Edition

*Sponsored by the National Audubon Society,
the National Wildlife Federation, and
the Roger Tory Peterson Institute*

HOUGHTON MIFFLIN COMPANY
Boston   New York

For information about permission to reproduce selections from this book, write to
trade.permissions@hmhco.com or to Permissions, Houghton Mifflin Harcourt
Publishing Company, 3 Park Avenue, 19th Floor, New York, New York 10016.

Library of Congress Cataloging-in-Publication Data

Pough, Frederick H.
A field guide to rocks and minerals / by Frederick H. Pough—5th ed. /
illustrations by Jeff Scovil..
p. cm. — (The Peterson field guide series ; 7)
"Sponsored by the National Audubon Society, the National
Wildlife Federation, and the Roger Tory Peterson Institute."
Includes bibliographical references and index.
ISBN 0-395-91097-8   ISBN 0-395-91096-X (pbk.)
ISBN 978-0-395-91096-2 (pbk)
1. Mineralogy—Determinative.   2. Rocks   I. Title.   II. Series.
QE367.2.P68   1995
549'.1—dc20 94-49005

Visit our Web site: www.hmhco.com

Printed in China

SCP 25 24

4500796192

PREFACE

In the 46 years that have elapsed since the first edition of this Field Guide, there have been great changes of emphasis in mineral collecting and an unforeseen growth in the number of collectors. Mineral specimens have won popular recognition as objects of beauty and merit, and colorful crystal clusters are now regarded as decorative accessories for elegant homes; their prices have skyrocketed. At the same time, many sources have been depleted, and seemingly inexhaustible deposits have given out, particularly once-promising Mexican sources. New areas in Russia, Africa, and Asia have become significant sources. An increasing recognition of investment values in fine specimens, supplementing the popular demand for colorful accents (usually, and fortunately, examples of little worth to the mineral professional), has driven prices to levels that older collectors find shocking. New species have been described by the dozens in recent decades, but today's novelties are seldom large and colorful and require sophisticated instrumentation for the determination of their individuality. Well over 3,500 species are known, and nearly all are rare and very limited in distribution. Most of the minerals herein are relatively common. You will find that some are rare but are included because of their popularity among collectors, especially at shows frequented by competitively minded collectors. Often despite general rarity, one or two sources may produce in abundance and beaut some special examples, giving them enough general interest and making them sufficiently available in attractive specimens to justify their inclusion. Diaspore and boracite, new to this edition, are examples.

The rise in interest and cost of minerals has also had the fringe benefit of enormously improving the quality of specimens. Once their preservation was a matter of chance. Now, many are obtained by professional collectors who have researched old localities known for their attractive specimens and who then, often at some risk, have succeeded in obtaining outstanding examples that they have carefully preserved to arrive on a dealer's shelf in an unblemished state. Would that the old-time miners, who had far greater chances of obtaining good specimens, had also the incentive, the knowledge, the ability, and the skills of the present generation, who search through their leavings. What wonders we would now have!

Sadly we must concede that the attitude of the general public toward mineral collecting has changed more than the attitude of those responsible for most mineral production. The majority of the mines still officially discourage collecting by workers. The wonders formed by nature are unique, and ore veins represent seeps from cubic miles of magma. Ownership of a few acres on the apex of a vein, although it gives a company the right to mine, should not be taken as justification for barbaric destruction of unique objects of beauty for their few cents' worth of metal. Mines that encounter specimens of great artistic and scientific merit should feel obliged to preserve a part for the world to view. Some who appreciate fine minerals have formed groups, hoping to apply pressure—through the press, simple conscience and good will, or as stockholders—to encourage mine operators to arrange for specimen preservation in one way or another. To a collector, it matters little how a mining company might arrange this. Ideally, the mine could collect and sell specimens and thereby make more profits for the stockholders. If the mine owners consider this too trivial, they can close their eyes to the miners' thefts, as many fortunately do, and avoid getting a bad name. Or they could allow qualified collectors to do the collecting under supervision in a profit-sharing agreement when the mine is not working. Surely with goodwill and understanding something could be worked out, any required insurance coverage arranged, and any extra costs repaid.

The important thing is to save the specimens, and that must be done while the mine is working and still in the shallower levels where pockets abound in which secondary minerals have formed. Salvage cannot be postponed for a more convenient time. We must hope that the regrettably common can't-be-bothered attitude can be replaced by an enlightened recognition of the operators' public obligation to this and future generations. The mining engineers of the next decades could easily be people inspired in their youth by specimens thoughtfully saved today. The author pleads for coordinated action in this respect on the part of collectors organized into groups. Such are the Friends of Mineralogy, who have made a good start. In view of all that must be done, their efforts are only a beginning. Surely there must be some lawyers and insurance agents among the world's rock hounds who could develop some sort of insurance coverage for the protection of the mine and quarry operators.

The writer wishes to express his appreciation to many who have helped in the preparation of the book. First and foremost, to the authorities of the American Museum of Natural History who, many years ago, gave the writer the position that commenced the familiarity, experience, and access to collections so essential to the original work and to many of the illustrations. To Guenever Pendray Knapp and Walter Holmquist, responsible for the major part of the work on the crystal drawings; to Eunice Robinson Miles, now a legend of the Gemological Institute of America, who in the fifties assisted with some tedious black and white photographic chores. In this edition, we are primarily indebted to Jeff Scovil for the new mineral photographs. Many collectors and some institutions granted permission for their specimens to be portrayed. They include: Diane Baine, Ross Behnke, David Bunk, Ralph Clark, The Collector, Maha DeMaghgio, De Natura, Edward David, Harold Dibble, Paul Geffner and Angel Martinez, O. B. Gerthelsen, Grant Gibson, Cal and Kerith Graeber, Ray Grant, Jack Halpern, Lance Hampel, Heliodor, Pat Hendrick, William Hunt, Bruce Jarnot, Rukin Jelke, Evan Jones, Keeper of the Earth, Kristal Keller, Marvin Kilgore, John Koivula, William Larson, Betty Llewellyn, John Lucking, Jim Mann, Eugene Meiran, Bill Mickols, James and Dawn Minette, Mingeo, Barbara Moore, Mountain Minerals International, Bill Moller, Paulo Orlandi, Louis Perloff, Preferrred Jewelry, Lester and Paula Presmyk, Marvin Rausch, Carter Rich Minerals, George Robertson, David Shannon, Manfred Schwartz, Silverhorn, Tim Sherbun, Steve Smale, Bill and Carol Smith, Marshall Sussman, Syntaxis, Wayne Thompson, Tyson's, Utah Mineral and Fossil Co., Jimmy Vacek, Valadares Minerals, Les Wagner, Jr., Zeolites India, Marty Zinn, and Zuni Mining and Minerals. Institutions providing specimens include the American Museum of Natural History, the Arizona Mining and Mineral Museum, the Arizona Bureau of Mines, the Arizona Sonora Desert Museum, the Canadian Museum of Nature, Yale's Peabody Museum, the Houston Museum of Natural Science, the A. E. Fersman Museum of Moscow, the

Royal Ontario Museum, the Gemological Institute of America, the Geologisk Museum of Copenhagen University, the U.S. National Natural History Museum, Stefano Merlini of the University of Pisa, Italy, and Father J. W. Skehan of Boston College. For all and any we failed to note, the author apologizes and will try to do better in the 6th edition. Jane Kessler Hearn aided by checking the blowpipe and chemical tests, and editors Harry Foster, Lisa White, and Susan Kunhardt of Houghton Mifflin Company put in many extra hours on the tedious copyediting job. Countless friends and local collectors have helped through the loan of specimens and indirectly with locality information. They have helped to determine the minerals included, with a constant stream of specimens for identification and with displays at the numerous shows, which have shown where emphasis should be placed.

Since this is a practical work, intended to be of the greatest possible value to the amateur, the author will always appreciate additional observations on tests and mineral occurrences that can be included in later editions of this Field Guide. This request is more urgent than ever because of the excessively protective government attitude that makes it difficult for the consumer to obtain some of the chemicals needed for even the simplest and most traditional testing. We need new tests that require only household products available in stores: ammonia, Quikdip, Drano caustic soda, white vinegar (acetic acid), and swimming pool muriatic acid—all just as hazardous as some of the chemicals we find difficult to buy. As with anything we do, use common sense. When we proposed to drop entirely the descriptions of blowpipe and chemical testing from the book, the response was that we should not, that some book in print should preserve some of the laboratory tradition, for to the serious collector the satisfaction of determining a mineral for yourself is half the fun.

CONTENTS

ILLUSTRATIONS

Endpapers: Generalized Map of Major Formations of North America (front); Rock and Mineral Environments (back)

ABOUT THIS BOOK

The compilation of a pocket Field Guide to mineral identification that is both comprehensive enough for the serious collector and basic enough for the beginner involves choices of what to include and what to omit; no selection can please everyone. More than 3,500 different minerals have been described to date, with annual additions. Yet 97 or 98 percent of the total number of different minerals of the earth's rocks are made up of less than a dozen species, with two, quartz and feldspar, coming in at about 90 percent. All the important minerals are described here, as well as a selection of rare and more intriguing ones that collectors may not encounter outdoors, but which, when they do, will be far more thrilling than the usual find.

In preparing this guide an attempt has been made to simplify the identification of minerals and give as much information as possible to help the beginner form the habit of observing and testing. A certain minimum of mental application and special equipment is prerequisite, as for other nature-study hobbies. A hammer, a lens, some testing equipment, and a few chemicals are as essential to the serious study of minerals as a pair of field glasses is to the birder.

On the other hand, the book is not intended to be a textbook of mineralogy. A Field Guide aimed primarily at identification is not the place for a complete course in crystallography or the details of analytical chemistry. This is a practical book, with as much firsthand observational information as possible in a limited space.

Identification

Tests: This guide departs from descriptions of tests, procedures, and physical properties used in other books. The traditional tests given here have been repeated and observed by the writer, and many interesting observations are included that have been forgotten in the century since blowpipe and chemical testing was our primary recourse. This aspect has been retained and the presently customary electron microscope and x-ray structural methods of testing omitted because the latter are unsuited to the training and accessible facilities of the average amateur, and their inclusion can only have a discouraging effect on the beginner. The significant minerals of today hardly differ from the significant minerals of Pliny, Agricola, and Goethe.

New emphasis has been placed on the use of the ultraviolet light. Now a relatively common piece of equipment for the pursuit of mineralogy, it provides an extremely rapid means of distinguishing between some otherwise similar species. Used in this way, ultraviolet light becomes an essential addition to the collector's equipment. The use of a solution of cobalt nitrate is also emphasized in this Field Guide, for when we have to distinguish between only two minerals by some special type of behavior, as we do in this book, slight differences in reaction are immediately apparent.

The failure of today's professionals to think in terms of traditional testing, together with a lack of initiative among the amateurs, has reduced home testing and identification of minerals to its present secondary status. Some suggestions for new tests will be found in the testing section of the mineral descriptions; they are particularly appropriate to a book in which no attempt is made to distinguish by blowpipe tests one mineral from 3,499 others. Here, on the contrary, the problem has been reduced, eliminating most similar compounds, with the aid of common sense to eliminate all dissimilar compounds—to the determination of which one of two or three similar species is in question.

Illustrations: For this edition the plates are grouped at the center of the book and stem from multiple sources. An attempt has been made in the main to select specimens typical of those that might be found by the amateur and to illustrate to the best possible advantage the characteristic appearance, size, and associations of each mineral. The crystal drawings on the legend pages opposite the plates usually show two different crystal habits: the left-hand, or top drawing when they are vertically arranged, is the more common one; the right-hand (or lower) is a less frequent but still important habit. Occasionally there is a sketch to emphasize a manner of growth.

Measurements: Metric equivalents are given to supplement the traditional U.S. inches and feet. However, minerals are not limited to exact dimensions, so they do not require the same statistics important in the identifying of living organisms that mature to standard sizes. All measurements are approximations: translating 1 in. into 2.54 cm, the exact equivalent, would imply a precision that is unintended and misleading. So the policy in this book is to say 1–2 in. (2.5–5 cm) for average conditions; or, when the tendency in the crystals is on the large size, to convert it to 3–6 cm, or, if on the smaller size as an average, to 1–3 cm. The purpose of all dimensions mentioned is only to give an order of magnitude. Some minerals normally form only minute crystals, others have crystals in the 1–6 in. (2–15 cm) range, and some crystals may be enormous and measurable in yards (meters). As a rule, the rarest minerals (rare because the combination of conditions for their formation is seldom present, with a consequent infrequency of occurrence) tend to form smaller crystals. Common minerals (common because they can form under a wide range of conditions) are more likely to be large. Often collectors are interested in obtaining the largest crystals possible; such crystals frequently come from one exceptional locality.

For Field Guide purposes it has been helpful to indicate the normal dimensions. Reference to the average sizes given will also assist the show-specimen collector in realizing just how notable a particular specimen is — at least in respect to the size of the crystals. Along the inside edge of the back cover of the book is a longer conversion rule than the one given below:

PART I

AN INTRODUCTION TO THE STUDY OF ROCKS AND MINERALS

1

YOUR MINERAL COLLECTION

Rocks and minerals are fundamental introductions to the study of all natural history, leading to a greater appreciation of nature. They are tangible, often beautiful, enduring objects that can be preserved in collections. They do not fade and lose their beauty, unlike flowers; their preservation in a collection harms neither the environment nor any living thing. Unlike many other objects of nature that may be assembled in collections, their gathering from the field actually conserves them for future generations. Often, particularly in recent years, such accumulations from old collections have served useful purposes for scientific and economic studies of inaccessible and abandoned mines. Someday many old mines may come again to life, reopened because studies of specimens that were saved when the mines were running have indicated that other minerals found there now have value, though they were once thought worthless.

A general collection of the common and important mineral species is best for beginners, to familiarize them with the overall principles of geology and mineralogy. Later they may wisely choose some narrower specialty. A goal of having an example of every described species is unrealistic. If mineral specimens are sufficiently large, pure, and typical, their definitive characteristics are more easily observed than in small, impure samples. They should be large enough in size and except for the crystals we cherish and shield, be freshly broken to show a characteristic surface.

Read several books, observe, and learn all there is to know about each mineral, so that you will recognize each the next time you encounter it, even though it may appear in a different guise. Attend shows, cultivate the acquaintance of other collectors in your vicinity and see their collections. You will thereby learn faster what good specimens look like. When you collect, keep a careful record of where you obtained each example.

Before entering private property, ask permission, if you can, and be considerate when collecting in ore piles you may find at a mine or quarry. Even a few pounds of some minerals (such as beryl) can be valuable, and the quarry owner is not likely to be pleased to find a week's production decimated on a Monday morning after leaving it unguarded over a weekend. When you have the owner's permission, do not abuse the privilege granted you; one bad experience will put all mineral collectors in a bad light and close the site to others. Do not clean out a locality or beat up crystals you cannot take out yourself; other, perhaps more adept, collectors will follow you. Encourage others to join you in the hobby; from today's collectors come tomorrow's professionals. Join local mineral societies and work to improve their meetings. Study some specialized phase of mineralogy and make yourself its master; you will get as much out of your hobby as you put into it. Visit museums and see what they have from your localities. Take pride in the museums and give to them, because they cannot exist without your support. Their principal funds for the purchase of specimens may be your financial contributions. In the basic sciences there is no more educational hobby than mineralogy. It combines chemistry, physics, and mathematics. A lifetime of study will not make you the master of every phase.

Care of the Collection

Collect specimens that are the right size for the space you have available. Crystallized specimens, when obtainable, should be the goal of the collector. When collecting, wrap each specimen carefully and label the wrapper at once if you plan to visit several localities on a single trip.

When you arrive home, wash specimens carefully to remove dirt and stains. Persistent iron stains can be removed by soaking in a strong oxalic acid solution to dissolve the limonite, but try it first on an inferior specimen to make sure that the acid does not attack the mineral itself. (Oxalic acid comes as a white poisonous powder so be careful. A saturated solution of oxalic acid crystals that has later been diluted slightly is best: first dissolve in a water-filled glass or plastic vessel all the dry acid crystals that will go into solution, then dilute it a little.) When you are out collecting do not overlook calcite-filled veins, since calcite can be dissolved in acid to expose a surface studded perhaps with insoluble sulfide, oxide, or silicate minerals. This is done by soaking specimens in dilute acetic acid (the acid of vinegar) or hydrochloric acid in a plastic or glass container. Here, too, try out a small specimen first, to see whether the mineral you want to save is also attacked by the acid. Acetic acid is far safer than hydrochloric; dioptase, for example, can be ruined by hydrochloric acid, but has a fine luster after a brief, weak acetic acid soak to remove calcite. Also, talk with chemists; there are many milder acids that some have found useful. It is a field full of possibilities for original discoveries by amateurs.

Plan some sort of catalog and numbering system. A personally modified Dana number system is good.* Give the Dana number and then your own. Your first pyrite specimen might be 85–1, your sixth pyrite would receive the number 85–6. Paint a neat white rectangle in an inconspicuous place on the back of the specimen, and when the paint is dry, write the number in India ink. The added protection of a thin coat of clear nail polish will keep it from rubbing off when the specimen is handled or washed.

Assemble your collection in shallow drawers or on shelves in a nice and not too crowded display, and plan on some definite arrangement: locality, Dana order, groups of the ores of one metal, crystal systems, etc. Discard poorer specimens as you find better ones. Do not let your collection become dirty and overcrowded, and as far as practical and reasonable, without going to extremes, avoid broken and bruised crystals.

Finally, since for most of us both space and resources are limited, consider specializing in a selected aspect: one mineral, one group, one locality, a crystal system, or the like. You cannot rival the overawing accumulations of the museums, but you can easily excel in some specialized category.

Collecting Equipment

The tools needed for the collecting of minerals are easily obtained and inexpensive. With more experience at specific

---

*The Dana numbers will be found in the 7th edition of the classic mineralogy text used by all professional mineralogists: Dana's *Systems of Mineralogy*. (Three of the planned four volumes have been published, and the fourth volume is well along, but while we've waited for the last, so much new information has been found that the already-published parts now need revising and updating!)

collecting localities, you will add or adapt aids as you need. Improvisation and originality are the mark of the experienced collector, who may scorn the commonplace but more expensive tools.

The first fundamental is a *hammer*. Any hammer will do, though for most hard rocks the prospector's pick works well. (Fig. 1). The widely sold one has a fairly small tapered head and the back is drawn out to a long point. (It needs redesigning: often, especially for layered rocks, one is better off with the chisel end of a bricklayer's hammer.) Adventuresome souls who temper their own hammers should not make them too hard, for steel splinters are likely to fly off a very hard head. The best plan is to make the center the hardest point and the edges fairly soft; this can be achieved by heating the head and carefully dropping single water drops on the center of the striking surface, thus cooling the outer edges more slowly.

Fig. 1 Prospector's pick

The pick or chisel end, in contrast, should be very hard or it will soon become dull; use it cautiously.

Lighter hammers and sledgehammers may be needed for special tasks; a light, long-handled sledge is a useful thing to carry about in the car if one usually drives when collecting. Short-handled, small sledges wield more authority than a mineral pick and are often useful. Cold chisels are also useful for carefully working crystals out of solid rock, where they are apt to be shattered by vibrations set up by a repetition of heavy blows. Very light hammers and the picks your dentist has discarded are well adapted for finishing the trimming of the specimen or for opening crystal pockets after a mass has been brought home.

Next in utility to the collector is some sort of *magnifying glass*. For field work the inexpensive ones are ordinarily as useful as the highly corrected lenses. In using them we generally look at selected small crystals and so do not really require the larger field of sharp focus provided by more expensive lenses. Do not get too high a power, 8× to 10× is usually sufficient; a trained observer can see more with a 10-power lens than the beginner with double the magnification. A 20× lens has too small a field, with too little of it sharp, to have much use in ordinary field work.

A *collecting sack* or container of some sort stuffed at the start with enough wrapping paper to protect all the specimens collected is desirable on prolonged trips. Usually it is wise not to start wrapping the day's haul until toward the end of the day—a careful review may reveal that the first specimens, which initially looked promising, are not worth keeping.

If one is collecting residual heavy minerals in loose gravel on slopes or in streambeds, a *shovel*, a *sieve*, and a *rake* will be useful. Many collectors like to carry a *gold pan* and wash for gold "colors." Long deep pockets in solid rock cannot be brought home, but a short *stove poker* is ideal for freeing inaccessible crystals tightly frozen on the walls. A *car jack* will turn over boulders too heavy to turn by hand. All sorts of adaptations to overcome special difficulties are part of the fun of collecting. A portable *ultraviolet light*, which permits collecting fluorescent minerals at night, and a portable *Geiger counter*, for prospecting among radioactive minerals, are two more specialized tools that can give good results. Metal detectors have turned up lots of tin cans and a few gold nuggets.

Once in the laboratory, specimens should be trimmed, washed, and, if necessary, cleaned up before they are cataloged and shelved (see Care of the Collection, p. 2).

Testing Equipment

The laboratory of the mineral collector may contain many of the basic reagents and equipment of the chemist. Though the testing methods of today's professional mineralogist require expensive high-tech equipment, the traditional blowpipe and chemical tests of the amateur (tools of the last generation's professionals) are still perfectly satisfactory and effective. As mentioned earlier, they could profitably be supplemented by experimentation, using new equipment, new reagents, and new techniques. (Please report to the author any practical and simple discoveries involving Drano, Clorox, and the like.)

The *Bunsen burner* is the fundamental piece of equipment when gas is available. Bottled gas can be obtained in many places where piped gas is out of the question. Small disposable cans of pressurized bottled gas with a needle flame are now available and can often replace the breath-activated blowpipe (try jewelers' supplies). Failing that, for field testing, an alcohol flame, a cigarette lighter, or a paraffin candle can be used, though none is as satisfactory as the gas flame. The air inlet of the Bunsen burner (named for a 19th-century German chemistry professor at Heidelberg) should be adjusted so that the flame is blue-violet, with a bright inner cone of blue unburned gas. The pressure should be kept low, so that the flame burns quietly, without a roaring sound (Fig. 2). There are two parts to this flame. The hottest place is just above the center, where there is often a slight yellow touch. The lower part of the flame, just at the tip of the blue cone, has gas

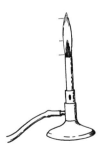

Fig 2. Bunsen Burner

in excess and takes oxygen from anything placed within it. For this reason it is called the reducing flame, and oxidized compounds placed here will lose any removable oxygen — in chemistry terminology, they will be reduced.

At the far tip of the flame, where the last of the gas is being burned, oxygen is now in excess, so objects heated in this part of the flame, like the gas itself, are free to take oxygen from the air and oxidize if they can; this part of the flame is known as the oxidizing flame.

For certain tests (the bead tests discussed in Chapter 6) these two parts of the flame are important, and beginners should practice with easily oxidized and reduced compounds in the borax beads (iron, for instance) to see where they get the best results. Practice will show how long it takes to change the color completely from that of the oxidized bead to that of the reduced bead and back again to the oxidized bead. The blue inner cone is relatively cool, so the bead should be held near its top, high enough in the flame to keep it red-hot, for if it becomes too cool it cannot react.

In conjunction with the Bunsen burner, the lungs are used on a *blowpipe*, an equally fundamental piece of equipment (Fig. 3). Blowpipes are of two types. One is a simple curved tube whose tip is held near the edge of the Bunsen burner flame, pointing slightly downward so that a needlelike blast of air goes across the top of the burner to direct a jet of flame horizontally or slightly downward onto a block of charcoal held on the other side of the flame. In this way bits of the unknown mineral can be heated in a pit on the charcoal (Fig. 4). This reaction is the one that mineral texts de-

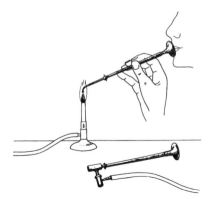

Fig. 3. Blowpipes

nominate as "B.B.," or "before blowpipe." By varying the strength of the blast and the position of the flame, an oxidizing or a reducing flame may be applied to the test piece. A continuous air blast can be managed by breathing steadily with the cheeks puffed out; cheeks exhaling air as the lungs are taking in their next breath. A little practice in this technique is all that is needed to become an expert in blowpiping, capable of maintaining a uniform unbroken blast for several minutes at a time. For minerals difficult to fuse and for reductions of compounds to metal, such continued heating may be necessary. Thin frag-ments held in forceps give better re-sults when trouble is encountered in the fusion. A far better blowpipe, but one that is not widely used or general-ly available, has a gas connection leading directly to it (Fig. 3). When not in use it gives a yellow flame and can safely be set directly on the table. When it is in use, the charcoal block can be left on the tabletop—which

Fig. 4. Blowpipe test

should be of some acid- and heat-resistant type such as soap-stone—and the danger of scorched fingers is eliminated.

A pair of *tweezers*, preferably with stainless steel tips and double-ended (one end designed to hold itself closed) is es-sential for testing the fusibility of splinters of minerals that melt only with some difficulty in the Bunsen flame. Forceps that must be held together can become too hot near the tip, where they must be held to keep them tight.

Charcoal blocks about $^3/_4$ x 1 x 4 in. (2 x 3 x 10 cm) are the most important bases for the support of test minerals. If charcoal cannot be obtained, a wood splinter can be charred deeply by working the blowpipe flame over the area in which the test mineral is to be placed. This will do for an occasional test, but if any considerable work is planned, try to obtain charcoal blocks from a chemical supply house. A small pit, $\frac{1}{4}$ in. (6 mm) across and about as deep, should be made at one end before the test is started. The mineral grain placed in this pit for blowpiping will be less likely to blow away. A *mortar*, preferably of solid iron with a close-fitting ring and pestle, will be useful for crushing mineral grains. A *magnet* of any common type is essential for the recognition of many iron compounds. A very sensitive test can be made with a magnetized needle hanging by a thread.

Test tubes from chemical supply houses are glass tubes 6 or 8 in. (15 or 20 cm) long, and about $\frac{3}{4}$ in. (2 cm) in diameter. They are made of ordinary glass or Pyrex glass. Pyrex or Vycor tubes cost a little more but are less likely to break and are preferable. They are used for all the acid-solution tests and for all liquid reactions.

Glass tubes (cut off from hollow glass rods), about $\frac{1}{4}$ in. (6 mm) in diameter, are occasionally of value in testing minerals using the open and closed-tube tests. Ordinary glass tubes of this diameter, bought by the foot or yard, are broken into shorter lengths. Use a sharp-edged triangular file to groove the place where the glass is to be broken; then a quick snap with the fingers breaks the tube off in a clean sharp line without trouble. When a closed tube is desired, cut the glass to twice the final length, about 9 in. (23 cm). Use the Bunsen flame to melt it at the middle, concentrating the flame at a single point as the tube is turned to heat it uniformly all around. Quickly draw the tube apart and melt back the short drawn-out ends with a rapid dip in the flame to resemble the bottom of a minute test tube and form a rounded closure. Before using either open or closed glass tubes (in cases where you wish to determine the presence of moisture), heat them a bit before inserting the mineral grain to drive out any moisture from the air in the tube. The tube should be long enough so that the fingers can hold it in the Bunsen flame without its becoming too hot. If the tube should finally get too hot, a fold of paper wrapped around it and held together at the ends, like a cup handle, will insulate the fingers. This trick is also useful for holding test tubes if a metal holder is not available.

Since the amount of air in the closed tube has a negligible

effect, the closed-tube test is used for noting the response of the sample to heat. The open tubes, which should be held on a slant, permit a constant stream of air to pass over the hot sample. The deposits from this oxidizing treatment may be very different from those resulting from simple heat decomposition. (See Tube Tests in Chapter 6.)

A *platinum wire,* shaped around the tip of a sharpened pencil into a small loop, is also essential in testing. It is used in flame tests; the platinum wire is dipped into chemical solutions of the unknown and then run through a flame to observe the color given to the flame. It usually takes the form of a quick flash as the liquid volatilizes. Also, the wire becomes a frame for beads of melted borax, salt of phosphorus and sodium or lithium fluoride. (See Bead Tests in Chapter 6.)

The mineral collector is well advised to purchase some sort of ultraviolet light. It has value as a testing tool and makes an impressive spectacle for friends. Grossly overpriced expensive ones have little merit other than for large displays; the pocket ones are fine. (See Fluorescence and Phosphorescence in Chapter 6.)

Reagents

The following substances can be obtained from chemical supply houses. The dry powder reagents that will be needed include a few ounces of sodium carbonate (Na_2CO_3), lithium fluoride (LiF), borax ($Na_2B_4O_7 \cdot 10H_2O$), sodium fluoride (NaF), and salt of phosphorus $HNa(NH_4)(PO_4) \cdot 4H_2O$]. Other dry compounds include cobalt nitrate [$Co(NO_3)_2 \cdot 6H_2O$], silver nitrate ($AgNO_3$), potassium iodide (KI), dimethylglyoxime (dissolve in ethyl or grain alcohol, a little at a time, until no more will dissolve), tin (Sn) metal in granules (this was formerly obtainable from toothpaste tubes but is not today, and the tin on tin-coated cans may be too thin to use), and zinc (Zn) metal (this can be obtained easily, since it is the outer metal in ordinary flashlight batteries).

In addition there are several common liquid chemicals, all generally available from chemical supply houses. Most important is hydrochloric acid (HCl), usually sold concentrated, by the pound (kg), although it is a liquid. Buy the minimum quantity you can (swimming pool suppliers usually have a commercial grade which will do for solution of calcite and the like). Dilute for use in two strengths: 2 parts acid to 3 of water and 1 part acid to 5 of water. Add the acid to the water and avoid splashing. Before discarding, completely neutralize by leaving a piece of marble or limestone in the container for a few days. In most localities it is desirable but not necessary to use distilled water for all dilutions. Nitric acid (HNO_3) is also used for testing; the same precautions and dilutions apply as for hydrochloric acid. Purchase the minimum quantity available. Aqua regia, not often used, is a mixture of one part concentrated nitric acid to three parts concentrated hydrochloric acid. Sulfuric acid (H_2SO_4), diluted 1 to 6, is not often used and can be omitted. For gypsum precipitate test determinations of Ca in specimens, battery acid might provide you a few drops. It is more hazardous than the others and will boil up violently when it is diluted unless one remembers: **ALWAYS ADD THE ACID TO THE WATER; NEVER, NEVER ADD WATER TO ACIDS.** This is especially true of sulfuric acid, which boils up violently when water is added.

Ammonia, or ammonium hydroxide (NH_4OH), diluted 1 to 2 parts of water, is the opposite of acids and neutralizes them. It is available as is, in grocery stores. Weak acetic acid is also available in grocery stores as white vinegar.

Testing Supplies Required for Laboratory Mineral Identification

Equipment
    Blowpipe
    Charcoal blocks about 4 x 1 x $^3/_4$ in. (about 10 x 3 x 2 cm)
    Glass tubes $^1/_4$ in. and $^3/_8$ in. (6 mm and 8 mm) in diameter
    Small triangular file
    Bunsen burner (alcohol lamp, compressed gas torch, or paraffin candle)
    Balance or scale arranged for determining specific gravity
    Platinum wire (27-gauge)
    Forceps
    Magnet
    Unglazed white tile
    Set of hardness points or minerals of the Mohs scale
    Ultraviolet light—best of all, two; one for longwave and one for shortwave ultraviolet
    Mortar (diamond mortar of iron, or agate)
    Test tubes (12), holders, and rack

Reagents
  Wet
    Hydrochloric acid (HCl)—in two dilutions
    Nitric acid (HNO$_3$)—in two dilutions
    Sulfuric acid (H$_2$SO$_4$) is of minor usefulness. Dilute 1
      to 6 of water. **REMEMBER: ALWAYS ADD THE
      ACID TO THE WATER; never add water to this acid.**
    Ammonium hydroxide (ammonia)—dilute 1 to 2 of water
    Weak acetic acid—white vinegar
    Ethyl alcohol—to dissolve dimethylglyoxime
    Calcium chloride solution—calcite dissolved in hydro
      chloric acid
  Dry (buy smallest quantities obtainable, usually an
      ounce or so [30g], except for borax)
    Borax—for bead tests
    Sodium carbonate—flux in charcoal block fusibility
      tests
    Salt of phosphorus—for bead tests
    Cobalt nitrate—dissolve in water
    Ammonium molybdate
    Dimethylglyoxime—dissolve in ethyl alcohol
    Oxalic acid: dissolve in water to make solution for
      cleaning iron stain from specimens; buy 5 lb. (about
      2 kg) at a time
    Potassium iodide—for testing for lead and phosphorus
    Silver nitrate—for testing for chlorine
    Zinc—from flashlight battery casings
    Tin—you are on your own; maybe a thick tin can

2

ROCKS AND MINERALS
AND WHERE TO FIND THEM

Minerals are the building stones of the earth's crust. They are stony or metallic mixtures of one or more of the 92 relatively stable elements that have been found in the earth's rocks. They have pretty definite formulas and the elements that go into them are usually the same, no matter where they are found, even on the Moon. The quartz sand of Coney Island has one part of silicon and two parts of oxygen (SiO_2 in chemical shorthand), just like the quartz sand of the Sahara Desert.

In scientists' attempts to cover all possible alternatives, the definition of a mineral has become so complex that it sounds almost meaningless to the beginner. In general, a *mineral* can be considered as a naturally occurring inorganic compound with a structure and composition confined within fixed parameters and consistently exhibiting a characteristic range of physical properties. Within a mineral's accepted chemical formula, iron and magnesium may replace each other, as do sodium and calcium, molybdenum and tungsten, antimony and arsenic, sometimes completely and sometimes up to a fixed limit. Unless one replacing element overwhelms its partner, drastically changing physical properties, the compound is regarded as the same mineral. These substitutional variations are indicated in the formulas as $(Mg,Fe)_x$. Albite may contain no lime (calcium) and 11.8 percent soda (sodium), or, alternatively, it may contain 4 percent lime and 9.5 percent soda. Albite is one end member of what is known as an isomorphous series, a specific group of minerals in which two or more elements can replace each other without greatly changing the appearance of the mineral crystals. At the other end of this series is anorthite, in which calcium (lime) has almost completely replaced the sodium; in between the two end members lie several named intermediate species. Minerals can be recognized by their appearance plus a synthesis of various physical properties that are characteristic for each element combination.

Rocks, on the other hand, can be defined as extensive solid stony bodies, usually composed of a small assortment of minerals present in varying proportions, constituting a significant part of the earth's crust. To be positively identified — as a granite, a basalt, a schist, or a limestone — rocks require more than a simple series of tests. Field identifications must be made on the basis of appearance and geography: where you are, what you know, and what you see of the geological environment. For the average amateur collector this is enough. The professional petrographer (a geologist who specializes in rock recognition) needing to know detailed differences will slice a rock, cement it to a glass slide, grind it thin enough to see through, and examine the assembly under the microscope. Studying the pattern and nature of grains found in one or more slices from a single rock exposure (known as the *outcrop*) can reveal the exact mix and average mineral makeup of the rock. Such detailed analysis is required to classify rocks according to the 3,500 or so names used by professional petrographers. But several dozen standard names such as granite, basalt, gneiss (pronounced "nice"), and schist are all the amateur needs to know. Broadly speaking, as with minerals, those few dozen make up about 95 percent of the earth's surface. The rarer and newer names are so little used that even a geologist may find it necessary to look up their meaning each time. Common sense favors mineralogically descriptive terms in most cases. The handful of rock species listed here under Rock Classifications (p. 15) are old, universally accepted and understood, and usually recognizable on outcrops. It should be remembered that one cannot expect to do more than guess at the name of any igneous or plutonic rock sample in the absence of detailed laboratory work determining its precise mineral makeup.

Geographical Distribution

For the collector, the first indication about the nature of a rock specimen comes from the region where it was collected. In the field, knowing where you are is the fundamental step in recognizing any rock outcrop. The different sections of the United States can be broadly divided on the basis of the rocks that occur in them (see front endpaper). Volcanoes and their rock products, the lava flows and near-surface intrusions, abound in the West. Here and there, mountainous masses of deeper-seated rocks that solidified more slowly and grew coarser in grain project above the surface. These are now separated in classifications from the lava rocks and are called plutonic rocks. They too solidified from a liquid, or were so changed by heat, pressure, and gases at considerable depth that they have the crystalline granular texture and uniformity of grain and grain size which could only have formed in this manner. In places, as in the Sierra Nevada of California and in the Rocky Mountains, great bodies of these rocks are exposed at the surface.

To the east, the underlying plutonic rocks are buried beneath deposits of rubbish from the bounding mountain masses, carried down and spread out over low plains or sunk in seabeds as the mountains decayed and were worn away. Only here and there in the Central States, as in the Black Hills, in the Ozarks, in Arkansas and Minnesota, do crystalline rocks rise above this great mantle of sediments so that the collector in the Midwest can see them and get samples. Occasionally we find indications that the millions of years have not been wholly uneventful as these sediments were laid down and raised again. In various places, later igneous activity has melted some lava (called *magma* when it is well below the surface of the earth) and let it eat its way up. Here and there in sedimentary beds we find streaks of a fine-grained dark rock that cut through the strata, giving isolated occurrences of igneous rocks in a great sedimentary terrain.

As we work farther east, past Ohio to Pennsylvania, we come to the place (all along the Appalachian mountain chain) where we again have an indication that the sedimentary rocks have been squeezed into great arches and basins, called *anticlines* and *synclines*, until we reach the area where the pressure has been great enough to change the sediments to a new type of rocks, the metamorphic rocks. In some places the burial, with the pressure, has been enough to restore completely the original igneous minerals, and in a few places even to melt the sediments into a new magma, which then squeezed upward to form another plutonic rock. This would have an unusual composition, because it was formed from sorted-out sediments instead of the complex original mixture of elements which went to make up the earliest igneous rocks. Here and there along the East Coast we have intrusions of magma to bring granite near the present surface with its associate, the very coarse variety known as pegmatite (see Pl. 6, entry 5).

The rock collector's variety will be as limited as that of the mineral collector if he or she is unable to visit other regions (see rear endpaper). Areas in which all types of rocks meet are relatively few. Except for glacial boulders, the Midwestern collector is likely to be limited to sedimentary rocks and the minerals that occur in them. Californians or New Englanders are lucky, for they can collect plutonic, some igneous, and many metamorphic rocks, with their host of related minerals and veins. Even a few sediments may be picked up, such as the Maine limestones and the red sandstones of the Connecticut Valley with their dinosaur tracks and ripple marks, or the lightly consolidated, sometimes fossiliferous Recent West Coast sediments.

Rock Classifications

Igneous Rocks

Rock types are classified into three major groups—igneous, sedimentary, and metamorphic—and then subdivided into several divisions. Those that formed from a molten state (lava or subsurface magma) are either *igneous* or *plutonic;* those words are used loosely and often interchangeably. To be more specific, igneous rocks are small grained and form when *extrusive* lava spills out onto the surface (a lava flow) or when a thin sheet of *intrusive* lava fills a crosscutting seam and cools quickly (a dike). Plutonic rocks, cooled and solidified at great depths, thus much more slowly, develop larger grains. They surface only after erosion has stripped away their cover. What this has meant to mineral formation we shall see later. Igneous rocks are characterized by a uniformly fine-grained texture (except for *porphyries*, where larger already-started crystals rise with the lava and are embedded in a fine-grained base called the groundmass.) Lava that has flowed out onto a surface forms extrusive igneous rock. Today, lava flows are usually basalt; less fluid lava may be explosive and brittle.

Extrusive Igneous Rocks

Obsidian (Pl. 5): Obsidian is a comparatively rare black glassy rock that has not crystallized, a high-silica lava that cooled too quickly for any of its atoms or ions to group into the regular structures of minerals. Obsidian is locally abundant in the western United States (California and Oregon), but does not occur in the East. It will be found only where volcanic activity has taken place in relatively recent times, for with time obsidian tends to slowly crystallize into a fine-grained rock or to regroup into analcime or its like, by taking on moisture and trading some elements. No obsidians can be very old in the geologic sense.

Freshly broken obsidian looks black and glassy; thinner bits are translucent against light, and sawn slices look smoky. Sometimes it is streaked with brownish red and black, called "mahogany obsidian." Like color-flowed glass marbles, broken obsidian surfaces often exhibit a texture of streaks and swirls. In sunlight, some bits reflect a pastel iridescence of violet, yellow, green, or gold, caused by microcrystals frozen along different planes of flow. Lapidaries call such varieties "rainbow obsidian," "silver sheen," and "gold sheen," the latter two filled with coarser flakes resembling mica. White crystallite clusters with tiny, rudimentary crystals suggest another name: "snowflake obsidian." "Fire obsidian," with curved opaque planes of iridescent hues, remains unexplained. At Glass Buttes, Oregon, a mélange of all the types of obsidian seems to have pushed up in volcanic plugs, embedded in partially broken down and crystallized shards, forming a brecciated obsidian neck (diatreme).

Old obsidian flows can take up water, causing their glassy luster to dull. Dull, partially altered obsidian is known as *pitchstone*. The moisture trapped in this altered rock can make it puff like a breakfast cereal when heated, turning it into a glass froth. This roasted substance, sold as "perlite," resembles natural *pumice*, which forms in midair as gas-filled, sometimes lightweight globs of lava are hurled from a volcano; it shows a shattered crust, picturesquely named "bread crust" bombs. Gas bubbles trapped in glassy lava expand before it hardens to make a light, glassy froth that floats on water, sometimes for months.

Sometimes a network of cracks develops in the obsidian, along which alteration extends, leaving a series of rounded, fresh glassy cores in a natural *perlite*. When such a flow is mechanically eroded before the change has run its course, translucent smoky pebbles survive, littering the surface. Resembling smoky quartz and known to collectors as "Apache tears," they are often faceted by amateurs.

The volcanic belt of the western United States, with its obsidian formations, continues into Mexico. Obsidian was a valued raw material of the American Indians, the Aztecs, and Mayans for weapons, tools, and decorative objects. At many western sites the unsuccessful "seconds" of their arrowheads and spear points are abundant. In composition, obsidian is high in silica; it is the quick-cooled, uncrystallized equivalent of rhyolite or granite. Outcrops are always stacked into conchoidally or convexly bounded boulders. Generally, outcrops are not very showy; weathering dulls the surfaces, giving them thin, matte, white or gray-white surfaces. Only fresh fractures have a glassy look. However, glassy flakes generally abound in good exposures and if a driver slows, somewhere in a brittle outcrop glass will shine. Although there are places where obsidian appears to have formed an actual flow or a dike, it is more often found as an intrusive rhyolite plug, which on a cliff exposure looks like a series of lava injections, with obsidian dikes bisecting rhyolitic domes. Some localities are noted on road maps (Glass Butte in central Oregon, halfway between Burns and Bend, Glass Road off California Route 95, just north of Mammoth Mountain).

Felsite: "Felsite" is a usefully ambiguous general name for professionals and amateurs alike. It can apply to any light-hued fine-grained igneous rock. For want of a better term, fine-grained darker gray and greenish gray igneous rocks, commonly found in the West, have long been called felsite. There is not much a field collector can do with felsite. With textures so fine, it is not possible to see the individual grains; they cannot be recognized without a microscope. (See the quartz hardness test under Rhyolite, below.)

The texture called felsitic is generally free of the larger crystal units (phenocrysts) common in fine-grained rhyolitic flows or in dark basalt formations. Outcrops weather darker, they show no layered type of structure, and generally break into flat-surfaced, angular blocks. In general they appear to be featureless and unexciting intrusive masses rather than flows. Just keep driving past them in road cuts!

Rhyolite (Pl. 6): The microgranular igneous equivalent of granite is known as rhyolite. It is often filled with vesicles and may be very white to light gray, but more often is pinkish to reddish brown. However, unless one has a real reason for naming a specimen rhyolite, caution suggests a less specific term such as felsite. In microgranular rocks no more precise identification can be made without examining the grains in thin slices under the microscope. Still, rhyolite is a common volcanic rock, both in flows and as an intrusive, especially in the West. At an earlier time of thickening crust, tremendous volumes of rhyolitic lavas seem to have been intruded or extruded; many a mountainous Arizona mile is mantled with rhyolite. Several of today's low-grade Western copper pits were once rhyolite mountains. In the East, rhyolite is rare.

Felsites and rhyolites can be confused with compact, very fine-grained and firmly cemented sandy sediments. Unless one knows the source of a specimen and the type of rock common in the region, it may be impossible to make a positive identification on the basis of a hand specimen alone. An average hardness equal to or less than that of quartz can be determined by trying to scratch a quartz crystal face—proving the presence of quartz in the sample (which would make it rhyolite).

Recognizing the look of rhyolite beside your route comes with experience. It appears far more viscous than basalt. Unlike the steam and gases carried by and freed from fluid flows, the volatile vapors within viscous rhyolite were trapped. The trapped vapors created centers of froth, areas within formations with holes and pits that erode into grotesque peaks and forms which park rangers and touring children love to name. A looming, sunset red and menacing rhyolite mass flanks the Las Vegas approach to the Hoover Dam.

Basalt (Pl. 4): The earth's crust is now so thick that present-day lavas rise from great depths, bearing more of the heavier elements: sodium and calcium instead of potassium; more iron and magnesium with less silicon and aluminum, spawning more dark minerals. Most recent volcanoes produce flows of blacker lava that hardens into a fine-grained black stone known as basalt. Composed largely of microscopic grains of calcium-sodium (plagioclase) feldspars, iron-magnesium silicates (pyroxene and olivine), and no quartz, basalt is commonly quarried when found near any city. Slightly coarser and often intrusive old sheets of basalt, usually partially altered but still fundamentally black, are popularly known from an old German term as "traprock" (*treppen stein*) or simply "trap." In New Jersey, a basaltic sheet, a *sill* squeezed between sandstone beds, has made the Palisades. Nearby in Paterson and beyond the bridge, on

Watchung Mountain, are extensive quarries of stone used in concrete foundations for the city. Traprock is a stone with no particular directional weaknesses; for construction, it can be crushed to fairly uniform shapes and sizes.

Across the West, multiple flows of basalt have piled up; along great fault scarps in California, Washington, and Oregon, we see layering that might be mistaken for sedimentary strata. Lava flows cap many mesa tops, with vertical cliffs sometimes alternating with gentler slopes succeeded, perhaps, by another wall of basalt. Close-up, in road cuts through a flow, we see tightly fitted walls of deep gray or black boulders, conchoidally or convexly split, many with surface deposits of white caliche. Tightly piled as an Incan wall, the blocks may cover or underlie sheets of loose sandy material, ash falls hinted at by the gentler slopes in the distance from explosive eruptions that followed or preceded outflows of lava. In the lava band, there is often a hint of uniform boulder sizes within each separate, tight-fitting curving surface. While driving down a valley, beyond the road and out across the landscape, one will usually see monstrously contorted black tongues of frozen lava, and often it is easy to discern the cone from which each came. In a tremendous trip behind the Sierra Nevadas and down the Owens Valley, from Mono Lake to Independence, California (U.S. Route 395), one can feast on views of cinder cones and lava flows that leaked from faults that bound the graben valley floor.

In places (usually intrusive sills) where cooling shrinkage cracks worked downward from the top, six-sided lava columns grew. Less-than-perfect examples can be seen in the Hudson River's Palisades. They are very sharp and very perfect in California's Devil's Postpile and make up the whole of Wyoming's Devil's Tower. Basalt columns make a path of paving block hexagonal tops at Ireland's Giant's Causeway, and in quarries along the banks of the scenic Rhine, they are piled like cords of wood.

The temperature at which basalt melts and solidifies is much lower than that of rhyolite, so basalt lava is more fluid. Basalt flows will be longer and thinner than flows of rhyolite. Fluidity varies greatly; the higher the proportion of silica, the slower the lava spreads. For many years, basalt piled up in multiple lava sheets along Oregon's Columbia River. Very fluid *pahoehoe* (a type of lava characterized by glassy, ropy-surfaced flows) build sloping lava sheets that can eventually reach great heights in gently sloped mound volcanoes like Hawaii's Mauna Loa. The most viscous flows form *aa* lava flows, characterized by blocky, fractured, impassable surfaces. Bombs are explosively ejected, football-shaped, plastic lumps of lava that have already cooled to solid when they land. These pile up in cinder cones; even they, over time and interlaced with periodic flows, can still build cones of great height, such as Fuji in Japan.

Lower silica content makes oceanic lavas very fluid. Hawaiian lava torrents dash like mountain brooks. Oceanic low-silica lava from one fissure source in Iceland was so liquid it formed no cone but instead flowed for 40 miles. The lava of continental andesitic volcanoes, on the other hand, very stiff, gas-saturated, and with a high silica content, can literally be explosive. Tugged by gravity but suspended friction-free en route, buoyed by repeated explosive releases of its brittle, gas-saturated lava, pyroclastic flows travel miles in minutes. With ancient eruptions producing quantities of *tephra* and *lapilli*, unsorted angular blocks, glass shards, and tiny felsite fragments settle on the surface as a tuff. Vast areas in the West were buried, sometimes under mantles of comminuted rock fragments hundreds of feet thick, which weather in a readily recognizable fashion into tall "hoodoo" pinnacles.

Not uniformly spread over the landscape, lahars or pyroclastic flows, following gravity, tend to fill pre-existing valleys with thick deposits of unsorted fragmented stone and rock powder. They gradually harden into what are known as welded tuffs. Drainage patterns may not change, rivers will normally resume their flow down pre-eruption valleys. Wearing away at a poorly cemented jumble of rocks, tuffs tend to leave clustered pinnacles of random brecciated fragments and cemented ash, some still topped by the perched boulder whose protection clearly started them, picturesque tuff spikes revealing a record of innumerable violent eruptions of the past, tuff formations many times greater than that of Mount St. Helens. It must have been rough on the dinosaurs.

Intrusive Igneous Rocks

Magma does not always reach the surface to build a volcano or pour out in a lava flow. It may be too viscous; it may cool too rapidly and be trapped below the surface. Cooling beneath the surface, magma can freeze in thin dark seams that cut through other rock. We call those thin bands dikes when they cut across other formations. Sheets and sills are larger bodies of molten rock injected parallel to the layering of the overlying rocks. When weak and relatively light overlying beds swell upward as magma is injected, the lens-shaped body created is called a laccolith. (Devil's Tower, earlier admired for its columnar jointing, has been thought to be the residual central portion of an eroded laccolith.) When cooling takes place at greater depths, the magma may already be partly solid; perhaps it moved as a mush of crystals floating in a liquid, like half-frozen milk. In rising magma, some crystals could have formed en route, somewhere on the upward journey, possibly even starting to grow in the magma chamber itself. Even when no crystals have a head start, the cooling of deeply buried magma proceeds slowly, and the mineral grains get a chance to grow larger than in lava-flow basalts.

Porphyry (Pl. 6): We can think of porphyries as an intermediate stage, like frozen mush, with isolated crystals of some mineral, commonly feldspar, floating about in magma. The liquid part of the mush consists of slower-to-crystallize minerals and the remaining magma mix. When the liquid eventually hardens, it forms a finer-grained base called the groundmass. Some well-developed porphyritic magmas reach the surface and spread out as lava flows studded with feldspar crystals. Others fail to reach the surface and harden as dikes or as small plutonic intrusions. A broken white or pink orthoclase feldspar phenocryst (large crystal) often shows signs of growth over a long period of time, with successive bands of slightly changing hue. The colors are the result of the alkali ratios changing slightly as the mother liquor, the magma, selectively loses one or more of its starting elements to growing crystals. Such zoned crystals are helpful in tracing the history of rocks, giving support to the theory that all igneous rocks can be derived from a single magma, if still-molten residues escape at any cooling stage. Theoretically, starting with one original magma, it is possible that fractions leaking at intervals can grossly differ, since each leak can only involve those elements that are molten and thus still able to move out of the hardening mass. Feldspar, quartz, pyroxene, and olivine, in one place or another, have all been found as phenocrysts in porphyritic lava. With no leaks, the final product may be a uniformly textured rock. But if fractions of magma leak out and freeze quickly, we find a fine-grained matrix studded with larger crystals. The final rock may be known as a rhyolite porphyry, dacite porphyry, or a basalt porphyry. Older and intrusive porphyry feldspars in reddish rhyolite, the material of many Egyptian statues, are opaque and may show zonal banding; their feldspar is usually orthoclase. Drachenfels on the Rhine (see the stone of the Romanesque church in Bonn), and Puy de Dôme in France have wonderful sanidine feldspar phenocrysts in a gray andesitic matrix.

Diabase: Usually, in a cooling crystallizing sequence, dark minerals (olivine, magnetite, pyroxenes) separate first, feldspar and mica next, and any remaining uncombined silica (as quartz) finally fills in the crannies. Sometimes, however, the feldspar may start forming first, growing in small lathlike crystals. Then the dark minerals are forced to fit themselves in among the lathlike feldspar as best they can. This texture, seen best in microscope-thin sections, is described as diabasic and can be a common trap-rock grain pattern. The rocks of the Palisades along the Hudson River, which are themselves further zoned from base to top, are a prominent example. There is nothing very distinctive about outcrops of diabase; one would have to stop and chip to see the feldspar pattern.

Plutonic Rocks

We cannot always positively distinguish between coarse-textured rocks that were once actually molten and similar-appearing rocks that many geologists now think were formed by an atom-by-atom replacement of continuously solid (though possibly plastic) rocks. So it is safer to group the coarser-textured ones under the term plutonic rocks. Many, probably most, were completely molten, for some granites very clearly have squeezed into spaces in other rocks. For example, there are outcrops spotted like a marble cake, where light and dark granitic magmas have mixed but remained discrete. This phenomenon can be seen in some great exposures on California's Highway 50, just west of Twin Bridges and also not too far east of San Diego, as well as at Vittoria de Conquista in Bahia, Brazil. The word *exposures* describes visible plutonic formations better than *outcroppings*, because unlike extrusive formations, plutonic rock only reaches the surface after eons of erosion have passed, permitting mountain roots to see the sky and feel the rain.

Plutonic rocks such as granite are generally found in batholiths, the bottomless cores of mountain ranges, often very old magma masses that underlie all metamorphic and sedimentary strata. The chemical and mineral compositions of plutonic rocks naturally parallel those of the extrusive rocks described above. Chemically identical, the groups differ only in grain size. There are many more named variations among the plutonic rocks without a specific fine-grained extrusive equivalent for each, but in the field it matters not, for we cannot recognize a host of differences if we cannot see the grains.

Granite (Pl. 6): This, with all its closely related species, is the most common of the coarse-grained group. It gives its name to the coarse-grained granitic texture. Granite proper is fundamentally only quartz and potash feldspar, usually peppered with a few (or many) specks of mica or a darker mineral. All are granite, though grain size may range from a millimeter to a centimeter and more. Pegmatite is the name for a very coarse granite in which a grain, a single crystal unit, may be feet or yards across. Quartz content should average about 27 percent, the mica and/or dark mineral (amphibole or pyroxene), 3 to 10 percent. If albite feldspar is also present and more abundant than the potash feldspar, the rock is called a soda-granite. Should the soda feldspar, albite, have more than a 10 percent content of the calcium feldspar molecule, anorthite, (see feldspar in the Mineral Descriptions), it becomes a different plagioclase feldspar, and we call the rock a quartz monzonite. It is neither necessary nor desirable, however, for the collector to learn all these specialized varietal names. With a hammer and lens, and without detailed microscopic study, "granite" is sufficient.

Granites are usually light in color, with readily visible individual mineral grains. They may be gray, white, pink, black, and yellow-brown. (For architectural or monumental use, they should contain no pyrite, or they will develop rust marks. Because they resist erosion, they frequently form prominent landscape features (Stone Mountain, Georgia; Mt. Rushmore, South Dakota). Monumental and building stone quarries often extract granite, and the mineral collector should look in such quarries for small pegmatites, crystal-lined cavities (miarolitic cavities), and joint surfaces coated with quartz, epidote, fluorite, feldspar, stilbite, and even micaceous uraniferous green torbernite, all minerals formed during the final stages in the crystallization of the granite. Rarer syenite is like granite, except that it lacks the free silica (quartz) and finds less use as a building stone.

Granite outcrops are distinctive and the easiest to recognize of the plutonic family. Under Iowa, Indiana, and Illinois, they probably are the basic continental crust, just lying there and supporting a mile or so of sediments so deep we will never see them. It is different in the East and in the West, continent margins where cruising crustal plates collide and buckle, where earthquakes are more frequent and granite is found on the surface.

It appears that during batholith emplacement, pressure exerted by the overburden on the almost frozen magma and final adjustments in the chamber create stress and directional weaknesses in the granite, creating easier ways of splitting, joints that can be exploited to ease extraction of building blocks from quarries. Nature also finds zones of weakness, where air and water sink into the stone, while frost and sun warm, cool, and crack exfoliating sheets of stone developing in time great domes of granite, like Yosemite's Half Dome, Georgia's Stone Mountain, and politically crowded Mt. Rushmore. Once we thought of dome formation by exfoliation as purely weathering, but slabs too thick for thermal warming are now believed to be due in part to emplacement stress, indicative perhaps of close proximity to the original sedimentary roof.

Differential expansion and contraction of unlike grains, quartz and feldspar, weakens bonds and encourages crumbling of the granite without great chemical destruction. Freed grains tend to wash from great rounded granite mountains. From a distance, a vista of Sierra Nevada peaks commonly look less tree-clad than residual remnants of a metamorphic roof.

Where erosion has just reached the batholith roof it seems often to have been crowned here and there by cupolas, which, thanks to jointing, create bizarre boulder piles that rise above the granite plain. Boulder wildernesses result: Texas Canyon, east of Tucson (Highway 10); Missouri's Elephant Rock (Stone Mt., near Belleview); the jumble east of Yuma, Arizona (Gila Mountains, Highway 10); another jumble south of Kingman, Arizona (Highway 93); and scattered boulder pyramids (Sherman Mountains, Highway 80) west of Cheyenne, Wyoming.

With round-cornered boulder piles like those, granite outcrops are unmistakable. Half-buried in granite gravel tumbling from the joints, the individual grains are often remarkably fresh. As explained above, the bonding between grains has weakened, so frequently the filling in crevices between the boulders, like the gravel at their base, is just fresh feldspar and quartz. Near Wausau, Wisconsin; Loomis, California; and the Lovejoy Pits in Maine are gravel pits that extract granite gravel, leaving here and there a few harder fresher boulders and standing dikes with pegmatitic pockets. In highway cuts all through the mountainous West, round-cornered granite boulders bulge from crumbling slopes of fresh-looking granite gravel; go east from San Diego (Highway 10) or thread your way on Lake Tahoe's western shores (Route 89).

Diorite: Diorite is darker than granite, with similar grains and history but richer in heavier minerals. Like granite, diorite is a group name for granite-textured rocks containing plagioclase feldspar, and almost no quartz. Soda-diorite has more of the albite molecule in its feldspar and lime-diorite has more of the anorthite molecule. Anorthosite is the name given to a dioritic rock composed almost entirely of feldspar; occurrences in the Adirondacks, in Finland, and in Labrador of labradorite feldspar rocks are important examples of this type of rock. Quartz content may be negligible, perhaps 3 percent, feldspar 75 percent or more, and any dark minerals, usually amphiboles, are less than 20 percent.

Gabbro: Gabbro is even lower in silica and darker in hue than diorite. Chemically it is the coarse, plutonic equivalent of diabase. Its feldspar is a plagioclase with a higher lime content than the feldspars of diorite, and the more abundant dark mineral is often a pyroxene rather than an amphibole. Olivine may be present. Gabbro weathers like granite but is softer and lacks the boulder jumble. This darker, more rapidly weathered rock does not occur in giant batholithic masses like granite, and we cannot generalize about the appearance of outcrops as we can with granite and rhyolite.

Peridotite or Pyroxenite: This is a dark rock composed almost entirely of dark minerals: olivine or olivine and pyroxene. A pure olivine rock, such as the sandy olivine formation at Webster, North Carolina, is a dunite, and a rock of pure pyroxene is a pyroxenite.

Darker rocks such as peridotite, rich in the ferromagnesian ("femag" or iron-magnesium) minerals, are more vulnerable to chemical weathering. They are often altered to serpentine, a name for both a rock type and a light greenish gray to green to black mineral (see entry under Mineral Descriptions). Pyroxenites or amphibolites meet their first challenge before they are cool, attacked by residual water and volatile compounds that initiate alteration while the magma is still hardening. So dark rock outcrops, except for greenish, glistening, oily, conchoidal serpentine blocks (common in California's Coast Range), are usually undistinguished and often much decayed. One cannot miss the soapy sheen of curving, concave-convex surfaces of green serpentine along the coast and Mother Lode on California roads. Serpentine rock is often host to mercury as cinnabar.

The most famous peridotites are the pyroxene-olivine mixtures called kimberlite in South Africa. These fill the necks of cylindrical bodies that fed long-gone volcanoes, and their peridotite is now largely changed to a serpentine. It is the matrix of diamonds, the rock of the "blue ground" pipes. It weathers very readily, so it will never make a prominent landscape feature nor form an impressive outcrop. The surface of the pipe may not be recognizable because it may be buried under "yellow ground." Peridotite dikes have also proved to be diamond sources in Botswana.

Sedimentary Rocks

As rocks of any sort are exposed on the surface of the earth, sun and rain, air and frost launch joint attacks, breaking them down and turning stone to soil. The jagged mountains of the moon, which has no atmosphere, stand as high and sharp today as when they formed, because heat and cold alone are not enough to tear them down. It takes the oxygen in the air and the water that falls as rain to break down the minerals, with wind and rain transporting the rubble. In high mountain regions where temperature change is rapid and drastic, fracturing of rocks by freezing and thawing is a major cause of rock disintegration. In tropical lowlands temperatures change less, so, in contrast, chemical alteration by water, oxygen, and vegetation acids proceeds at a steady pace. In high mountains, feldspars are freed but little altered, as we saw with mountain granite. In the valleys and the tropics, where humidity is high and temperatures less extreme, rock-making minerals more often take in water and change to clay, unshackling the quartz grains. Rain and groundwater dissolve some silica and any metallic elements and carry them away in the water that seeps through the rocks. Streams running over these disintegrating rocks pick up the clay and sand and transport both to lower land.

Soon the streams slow and drop their loads. The slower rivers run, the finer the grains they can carry. In the end only what has been dissolved will add its salty quota to the sea. As we go outward from a river's mouth, we find that each successive bed of sediments shows a concentration of like-sized finer particles. In valleys, in lake beds, or on sea floors, wherever rivers spread, we find horizontal layers of grains, alike in size and nature. Within each sedimentary layer, times of flood and times of drought are recorded by minor changes in the horizontal sheets, a sequence known as stratification. Sedimentary rocks gradually form as these deposits become ever thicker, and time and burden finally weld them into a rigid mass. Loose grains crushed together become interlocked by pressure as solutions of silica, rust, or calcite glue them together. Sedimentary rocks spread out in thick sea-floor beds, one layer above another, often forming deposits thousands of feet thick. Much of the North American continent is mantled by old sedimentary rocks, layered formations later uplifted from former sea and estuary floors.

Banded sediment deposits may be laid by water, wind, or ice. Recent glaciation has covered the northern parts of North America with thin skins of unconsolidated mixtures of rocks and clay. Layered sand and clay deposits formed in northern lakes from the water that ran from the melting glacier. None of this debris, such as the mixture of clay and boulders known as till or the varved clays of glacier-fed lake beds, would be considered a rock by the collector, because it is not cemented together into a solid mass. Older sediments, however, have become cemented and now are rocks in the usual sense. In general sediments are layered and all once lay flat. Crustal movements tilt and bend the layers. Inclined rock structures are known as synclines (basined), anticlines (arched) and monoclines (slanted). When a slanting set is overlain by a horizontal set slicing off some tilting layers, it is known as an unconformity.

Arkose: Arkose is a sedimentary rock derived by mechanical disintegration (fragmentation predominantly by freezing and warming) of a granitic rock. It may form when disintegration in a granite outcrop has disrupted the bonds between the grains but has not turned the feldspar into clay. In texture it amounts to a coarse sandstone, its grains both quartz and feldspar. In the hand specimen, without evidence of banding (and of the secondary origin), arkose is readily mistaken for the far harder primary rock, the original granite. But arkose outcrops do not mimic granite's; arkose just crumbles again. Jointless "granite" should evoke suspicion.

Conglomerate (Pl. 7): Conglomerate is a rock composed of rounded water-worn pebbles, usually of quartz, cemented by the mass of finer material filling in the spaces between.

Often there is a color contrast between pebbles and matrix, which makes appropriate the name "puddingstone" applied to colorful conglomerates found on Mount Tom and in Roxbury, Massachusetts. Glacial boulders from that Bay State outcrop have been recognized as far away as the terminal moraine, which is now Long Island, New York. Tight-held pebbles pimpling a stony slope make recognition of this uncommon sediment easy.

Breccia: Breccia is almost the same as conglomerate, except that its pebbles are more angular in outline because they have not been rounded by water. Breccias can form under the surface, when buried beds are shattered by fault movements of the crust. The weight of overlying rock crushes the fragments together and in time they are reunited into a solid mass.

Sandstone (Pl. 7): This common rock is composed principally of sand grains cemented more or less firmly together. Depending upon the character of the cement, the rock may be white, gray, yellowish, or dark red. More frequently than not, the cementing material is stained with iron.

Iron oxide gives the color to the brown sandstone of New York City's famed "brownstone fronts." This facing stone came from almost horizontal sandstone beds lying on the Connecticut Valley floor. Dinosaur footprints have been found in the broad planes of large sandstone quarries worked for this stone bordering the river at Portland, Connecticut.

There are two sorts of conditions under which sandstone forms. To the Easterner, the obvious one is beaches, familiar to us all. Sand deposited in this way once was wet, thoroughly stratified, and easily quarried, some layers marked by footprints, ripple marks, and raindrops. It is not a great source of marine fossils, though in some bands in the West, fossilized bones of larger land animals are often found. More prominent there are wind-deposited formations. Today, here and there in the West, there are great sand dune areas, such as White Sands, in New Mexico; Sand Mountain in Nevada; Palm Springs in California; and in Africa, the Sahara and the Kalahari. Cemented mountains of wind-blown sand in the West show interestingly layered structures, with thin set after set truncating similar streaks from below, demonstrating that the sand was moved along in wind-blown dunes, each day's breeze pushing loose grains up and over a ridge, constantly advancing the crest, only to cut it off again. Giant, wind-sculpted and cross-bedded sand formations like the Great White Throne in Zion Park display these eolian (wind) patterns to perfection.

Sandstone's most common color is reddish brown. Enormous reddish sandbeds in western Colorado, Utah, and Arizona tend to crumble, creating buttes and mesas, such as those of Monument Valley, Utah, wind-cut arches, cliff dweller caves, and sculpted amphitheaters. The cliffs surrounding the prehistoric pueblos of Mesa Verde, Colorado, are an example of the effects of rain and wind, which erodes outcrops, making their surfaces round rather than angled and sharply pointed. The water-laid strata of the East are thinner, with more shale and limestone. St. Peters sandstone, a white and friable sandbed, extends from Minnesota to Missouri, an inexhaustibly thick glass-quality sand formation that surfaces again in Crystal City, Missouri, a town just off historic Highway 66.

Shale (Pl. 8): Shale is a layered rock composed principally of clay particles, often intermixed with sand from some long-forgotten flood that created stratification. Stream-buoyed mud will obviously be deposited farther offshore than stream-carried sand. Shale bands build successive layers of the finer particles that traveled farther in a quietly flowing stream before settling to the bottom. Proceeding deeper on the floor of a continent's shallow inland sea, we would expect a sedimentary sequence of sandstone beds, overlain by shale, with that in turn mantled by the still finer material from clearer water. Shale is soft; seen in a road cut it makes slanting banks and multiple layers. On a larger scale, unprotected by harder caps it makes a landscape of low hills. In harsh environments it may be bare of vegetation and sometimes shows colorful layers of greens and reds.

Multiple layers often at a slant are frequent in sedimentary road cuts. Between eastern Ohio or Denver and Cheyenne, we thread our way through multiple-sediment road cuts, some sand, some lime, some shale; each bed has its own strengths and ability to make a wall, a slope, or just a pile of mud. Well-cemented sand may allow a solid cliff, a whiter wall with brittle bedding is likely to be limestone, and a gentle sheeted slope above the next cliff may betoken a bed of shale. Clams and snails interred in shale may be fossilized, and then stand out on weathered slopes, awaiting you or eternity.

Limestone (Pl. 9): This sedimentary rock is composed of calcium carbonate (calcite) in a very fine microgranular texture. Some lime is chemically precipitated on deep sea floors as chalky marl. Other limestone beds represent a secondary accumulation of lime first removed from seawater by living organisms. In Bermuda, fragmented shell masses make a stone that is called coquina, from which blocks are hewn and houses built. Older beds of purer lime form farther out to sea in deep waters, beyond the spread and depth that stream-born clay and sand can move. Remains of extinct life in seas of the era of the lime deposition are included in the beds. Pure tiny spherules of chemically formed lime carbonate have built a structurally useful quarry bed in what is now Bedford, Indiana. Not nearly as insoluble as quartz sand or clay, the watery environment reworks the marly sludge into a hardened limestone or dolomitic bed, recrystallizing tiny crystals of calcite into large units (perhaps with added magnesium to make it dolostone, see below).

Limestone sometimes forms outcrops of thin-bedded layers, a yard or less layered with particulate sediments. Precipitated as a thick marl mush, then hardened below long-static seas, it can also form a great white and solid bed, with perhaps a line or two of stratification, caused by some Paleozoic cataclysm. Since limestone is susceptible to solution weathering, fracture edges are rounded rather than sharp. It usually weathers into darker, grayer colors; a fresh fracture will be buff to white in most outcrops.

Dolomite (or **Dolostone,** as some now call the rock to avoid confusion with the mineral of which its formed): This rock resembles limestone, except that its chemistry has changed. The original calcium has been partially replaced with magnesium. It forms under the same conditions as limestone and probably represents later alteration of the original marl by seawater. Indistinguishable in the field and in the quarries from limestone, it is white to gray to buff. It, too, finds use as building stone and in cement manufacture, and both are widely quarried. Pockets in Ohio, New York, Indiana, south Michigan, and elsewhere in the Midwest contain various minerals such as calcite, dolomite, quartz, fluorite, and celestite.

Salt, Coal (Pl. 7), Oil: Salt is an economically valuable substance associated with sedimentary deposits resulting from some special set of conditions. We have seen in the last decade how the level of Great Salt Lake can change as the water source floods or fails. In time, if it wholly evaporates and then becomes buried by later river sediments, it would form a typical bed of rock salt. Protection by a windblown mantle of sand, clay, or mud prevents subsequent re-solution. Coal represents the compaction and partial carbonation of plant remains buried in the same way. Oil probably results from similar burial of animal remains in sediments. Adjacent sand formations, with faults and folds, beneath tight shale caps, provide closed reservoirs into which oil can seep. Seekers of oil hunt buried structures and formations that might have trapped gas and a pool of oil in rock types known to be oil-rich.

Special Features of Sedimentary Rocks

From their manner of formation by deposition along the shore in mudflats, and on the floor of the sea, sedimentary rocks are likely to enclose traces of life and characteristic markings that in time will be preserved in rock when sediments are hardened. These included surface irregularities such as ripple marks, raindrop dents, and perhaps the footprint of a dinosaur; for waves washed shores and rain made dents in sand or mud millions of years ago, just as it does today. Teeth, skulls, and skeletons, along with shells and plant remains, became entrapped and were preserved, often to their finest detail, in the sediments. Such fossils are characteristic of sedimentary rocks and are best preserved in shales and limestones. The geologist uses them as the guide to tell the age of the rocks; scientists can determine from the kind of fossils found whether a formation has been there for three million or three billion years. The study of fossils, a science known as paleontology, can be as complex and as fascinating to the amateur as mineralogy. Over and over, animals evolved and then died out. The species a paleontologist finds tell when the beds were formed. Those who live where sediments reign may find fossil hunting just as challenging as mineralogy. Be sure you collect with permission and on private land.

Metamorphic Rocks

The pressure and heat that accompany deep burial of sedimentary rocks will in time make unstable the oxidized and hydrated minerals that formed on the surface as the primary rocks decomposed and decayed. Heat and pressure create an environment like the original one deep under the crust or in volcanoes, where the primary rock minerals first formed. Eventually the moisture, oxygen, and carbon dioxide that came from the air will again be pressed out of the rocks. The sediments making up the shale, sandstone, and limestone will begin to change. Some minerals—the more drastically changed ones, such as the clay of shales—will revert completely to the ancestral mica and feldspar. However, despite the mineral change the rocks still preserve the banding created by their water-laid origin. Sediments are usually a concentration of one or two minerals, in contrast to the heterogeneous character of the original rock. So, though the high-temperature minerals of the crystalline rocks are reborn, the original mixture of minerals has been destroyed. This manifests itself in the new mineral makeup and arrangement of the regionally metamorphosed ("changed form") rocks.

Slate (Pl. 10): Slate resembles shale, except it is a first stage in a progressive reversion of clay back to mica. Tiny mica flakes have grown along new cleavage surfaces. Their flakes impart to the compacting stone a new and brighter luster not found on earthy shales. The tiny growing mica flakes tend to arrange themselves so that their flat sides lie across the direction of the pressure, with the result that the cleavage of the slate follows the new mica plate direction; that is, at right angles to the squeezing. The result is ready cleavage in the slate reflecting the new mica plate direction. Often the flakes and fracture surface of the slate cut sharply across stratified shale bed, whose layering was the prominent structural feature of the sediments.

Slate is used for several things; in old or costly homes, it makes a heavy but truly long-lived and fireproof roofing material. Slate hearths and stepping stones add aesthetic value and durability to homes and gardens. Outcrops are easily recognized—sharp shards with thin edges lie all about slanting roadside outcrops; on the outcrop, shale cascades in a shower of flat and lustrous chips. From the fields behind rise "tombstone" slabs. A band of slate follows the California Mother Lode along Highway 49, raising its monuments here and there in fields.

Phyllite (Pl. 10): This rock is not very different from slate, except that metamorphism has progressed further, so the mica flakes are larger and their change more evident. Slate's tiny mica flakes have merged and spread, giving a shining silver surface to the phyllite rock. It is hard to draw a line between the slates on the one hand and the phyllites on the other. By the time we choose to call it phyllite it has started to show a wavy rather than a flat surface, though it is anybody's call when the mica flakes on the cleavage face have coarsened enough to warrant a new name. Fresh phyllite (from Greek for "leafy") is greenish or grayish, like slate. It is primarily a foothill rock, an occupant of regions of low-grade metamorphism where crustal buckling is still slight. It will not be found in the flat areas, where unaltered sediments prevail, nor is it likely in schistose associations. Less brittle than slate, outcrops are more rounded and the jutting "tombstones" rare, for mica bends and wears, while slate just chips to ever smaller sharp-edged bits.

Schist (Pl. 10): The final stage of metamorphism. Just short of actual remelting, mica schist is the penultimate product of alteration, by heat, volatile gases, and pressure, of the mixture of the hydrated and oxidized minerals in shale and muddy sandstones. Sandy shales, on complete recrystallization, will be compressed and will recrystallize to a final rock that appears to be predominantly mica. Mica becomes especially conspicuous on the surface of the easy fracture, so in a flat-cleaved bit of schist, mica looks more abundant than it really is, covering the fracture surface. As in the initial phyllite and slate stages, the mica crystals have arranged themselves so that the flat plates have grown at right angles to the crustal pressure affecting the rock. Volatile compounds introduced in the most intense metamorphism encourage the growth of recognized high-pressure minerals, such as garnet, staurolite, andalusite, and kyanite, which can grow in the mica despite surrounding interference. Micaceous banding and the dominance of one mineral makes schist distinct from any primary rock, even though the principal minerals may be identical. When sliced across, as in a microscope thin section, we may find more bits of quartz and feldspar than expected, but the weakest plane of cleavage makes mica more conspicuous.

Manhattan Island is largely underlain by schist. In road cuts and bordering cliffs, schist and gneiss (described next) are often interlayered. They can show highly contorted differing bands, arched and folded; here a band of schist right beside a band of gneiss. Entering the Rockies out of Denver, one encounters striking gneiss and schist formations, as well as in the Alleghenies, in Massachusetts, and in Connecticut. Gneiss and schist tend to alternate in rapidly changing, barely different layers, unlike thick contrasting walls and slopes we may see in tilted sedimentary sheets.

Gneiss (Pl. 10) (pronounced "nice"): Gneiss represents the same intensity of metamorphism as schist, but in its mineral makeup, mica, or black hornblende (which can substitute for mica to make an amphibole schist), is less abundant. More quartz was in the sedimentary ancestor, which may have been a sandy shale or a very shaly sandstone. Unaltered fresh granite subjected to metamorphic pressures in its closing crystallization stages can be changed to gneiss through simple pressure realignment of its mica, so that the plates are all aligned in one direction in place of the less conspicuous structure of an ordinary granite. Gneisses, which may be gray to almost white, resemble granites very closely except for their structural pattern. An exact line of distinction between gneiss and schist is difficult to draw, for when split on a rich mica plane, many gneisses look far richer in mica than they truly are. A very popular building stone is a red granite with gneissic streaks and patches of pegmatitic mosaics from St. Cloud, Minnesota, architecturally known as granite-gneiss. Lacking the jointing of granite, gneiss outcrops are not dotted with boulders, but they can form great domed *roches moutonée* ("sheep backs") in glaciated New England, and expose contorted banding.

Quartzite (Pl. 11): Formed by the metamorphism of sandstone. Since quartz grains, large or small, hot (to 573°C) or cold, are about the same, heating and squeezing does little to sandstone except make a very hard rock. With deep burial and further cementation, the sand grains eventually become so tightly welded that any fracture breaks across the grains, instead of around, as in the loosely bound surfaces of a sandstone. Quartzites are among the hardest and the most resistant of all rocks. They show the same colors as sandstones: brown, yellow, gray, reddish, or white. While quartz has no conspicuous cleavage, under pressure it does tend to develop parting planes. When silica cements sand grains together, the cementing unit is usually large enough to enclose a group of sand grains (poikilitic texture). Fractures of poor cleavage cross whole units, reflecting patterns of larger surfaces than a single sand grain. of a sandstone. Resistant to weathering, hard and brittle, outcrops lack the mellow rounding of sculptured sandstone or the fluting of soluble limestones, so they are not too hard to recognize, though they can easily be confused with felsite.

Marble (Pl. 11): Like quartzite, marble forms during regional metamorphism from another single-mineral sedimentary rock, either limestone or dolostone. Like sandstone, limestone and dolostone are rocks in which (without mineralizing infusions from the depths) no major change can take place other than growth and cementation of the individual crystal units. If the original sediments are fairly pure carbonates, their metamorphic successor becomes a coarsely crystalline white or varicolored marble, valued for decorative uses. Crustal squeezing and heat of regional metamorphism are not always necessary for the recrystallization of a limestone. Some architectural marbles grew coarse grains that will take a polish with their fossils still intact. Time and burial with ample circulating groundwater solutions apparently can also do the work of heat and pressure. In those exceptional marbles, the fossil shells and crinoid stems caught in the original lime sediments survive in the decorative, usually buff-hued, marbles with fossils standing out as whiter sections of pure calcite. Polished black Moroccan baculites fossil rock is widely sold as specimens and table tops.

Contact Metamorphism

Sometimes pressure and heat are not the sole factors in the metamorphism of earlier rocks. Intrusions of magma with the various accompanying gases can alter rocks in advance of the magma's arrival. Fluid magma and a panoply of volatile and metallic elements—fluorine, salt, and silica in solution—will soak into simple sediments and create a new type of rock, with different silicate minerals, such as garnet and epidote, replacing the original assortment. Ore and gangue minerals—metal sulfides and sulfosalts, calcite, barite, quartz, and fluorite—frequently replace the original assembly in this contact metamorphism. Impure limestones are the most interesting and most easily altered formations, while quartzite, igneous rocks, and gneiss are the least altered and the least interesting. The latter are also the least likely hosts for ore deposits.

Hornfels: This compact fine-grained black rock forms near the line of contact of sedimentary country rocks with an invading magma *stock* (a small magma intrusion, often bringing ore solutions) where there are usually roughly circular zones of lessening alteration with distance from the source of heat, solutions and gas. The affected rock rims, the *skarns*, are usually compact and fine-grained mixtures of dark minerals, mica, and silica. Under unusual conditions, particularly in limestone or marble, coarse new mineral crystals may form, and some of the finest of all mineral collecting localities are such coarsely crystalline contact-metamorphic zones. Typically they may host garnet, epidote, vesuvianite pyrite, sphalerite, and scheelite. Though not typical, since they are loose blocks of stone, altered limestone blocks from the slopes of Monte Somma, the classic predecessor of Vesuvius, are fine examples since they so well illustrate the process. Monte Somma's rising lava plucked limestone blocks along the walls of its rise, and as it bore its loot upward, the limestone chunks were marinated in volcanic gases and solutions, one element substituting for another, taking a little from this and adding a little to that all the way up. Fully cooked and tossed, well done, on the surface, they are honeycombed with crystal cavities in which typical contact-metamorphic minerals such as vesuvianite, garnet, scapolite, spinel, and all their pressure- and heat-loving brethren grew. Collecting localities of such contact metamorphosed bombs are few, with Monte Somma and Germany's Eifel District (around the Laacher See) preeminent sites. Contact-metamorphic zones around an intrusion may be rewarding for easily freed silicate crystals such as vesuvianite, epidote, garnet, and wollastonite. Zoning often occurs around a small intrusion with, perhaps, an ore deposit close to its flanks and a succession of lower-temperature metamorphic minerals extending outward from the epicenter.

Summary of Rock Characteristics

Igneous
> *Volcanic:*
>> Fine-grained, a mixture of unrecognizable minerals; their only inherent structure that of the flow lines in obsidians and rhyolites.
>
> *Plutonic:*
>> Coarse-grained, without any noticeable structures in the hand specimen, and composed of common identifiable primary minerals (quartz, feldspar, mica, dark minerals).

Sedimentary
> Mainly a single, low-temperature mineral; banded, stratified, and often fossiliferous.

Metamorphic
> High-temperature minerals, like those of the plutonic rocks, but banded, stratified, and, as a general rule, with a concentration of a single mineral in a formation.

Mineral Environments

From this review of the earth's rocks and their environments, it should be obvious that the earth's mineral factories and furnaces are enormously varied. We have only to regard an exploding volcano to contrast the conditions in its throat with those of a cool and quiet, water-dripping cavern. Minerals of infinite variety are forming in both places. Certain species are the product of recognized, but grossly differing surroundings. For example, a prominent group of possibly warm-water deposited minerals is commonly associated with older volcanic rocks, a group of hydrous silicates called *zeolites* (from the Greek word meaning "to boil," because before the blowpipe they melt into a frothy mass).

Close around active volcanoes we may find water-soluble minerals that form at gas vents. In hot-spring regions near recent volcanism we find silica deposits (geyserite) and minerals composed of more volatile elements (mercury, arsenic, and antimony) that remain dissolved longer (in cooler solutions), so are likely to travel farther from their plutonic source. Near the surface they finally separate from the water at low temperatures and pressures. Stibnite, cinnabar, and the arsenic sulfides are the best known.

Other elements remain close to their plutonic source, elements whose volatility and solubility are low. Nevertheless, since all magma has some accompanying gases they often migrate short distances into the surrounding rocks and fill fissures with ore, forming deep-seated veins. Temperature sensitive, they make associated groups in vertical zones. Best developed and studied are the ores of Cornwall, England. The earliest minerals to form, found in deep-seated veins close to plutonic intrusion, are any of several high-temperature minerals, such as cassiterite and wolframite. Elsewhere, in Spain, Portugal, and South Africa, the very deepest of such veins are not very different from a fluid magma, light-colored, relatively thin rock-splitting sheets comprising the coarsest closing stage of granite rock formations, and known as pegmatite dikes. At that final stage all the volatile elements, and all the still-uncombined rare elements, are concentrated in a residual magmatic-liquid phase. We surmise that this hard-to-visualize residue is very fluid, watery enough so the remaining rock-making minerals (quartz, feldspar, and mica) can crystallize into coarse units, often accompanied by rare associated minerals that could only combine here, in the presence of enough of a rare element. Beryllium, tin, tungsten, tantalum, fluorine, and boron are such residual elements. We find minerals containing them in the granite pegmatites.

Sometimes we find that these pegmatites *(simple pegmatites)* have later been attacked by watery and gaseous solutions containing other rare and more volatile elements. The units of the early and usual pegmatite minerals (grains of granite, as a rule), recombine to produce feldspars richer in sodium (albite), lithium joins the potassium in mica (lepidolite in place of muscovite), and minerals with beryllium and boron grow. Later, sparse cesium may replace some of the beryllium in beryl, changing its blue to pink. A simple pegmatite has now become a *complex pegmatite,* a home for many rarer minerals. Pegmatite dikes are commonly quarried for feldspar (the "hasn't scratched yet" abrasive, also used in ceramic glazes) and for by-products: mica, tantalum, niobium ore, beryllium ore, and yet rarer metals. With their enormous mineralogical variety, they are favorites sites of the mineral collector.

In addition to the pegmatite dikes there are two more examples of late concentrations of water and other volatile compounds that are likely mineral sources. One is *miarolitic cavities* in granite, openings where gases, instead of escaping out of the magma through a crack, have stayed and cooled in great trapped bubbles, preserved in the cold granite as small pegmatitic-textured gashes, with their central open cavities lined with crystals. Still later, as contraction cooling splits solidified granite joints and seams to let the last of the gases escape, we sometimes find thin crevices sparkling with small and perfect crystals of late pegmatite minerals—apatite, fluorite, quartz, and epidote. Seam faces of a granite quarry always merit attention. Sometimes we may even find intersecting sets with different assemblages of minerals in each: high-temperature compounds such as topaz, beryl, and fluorite on one set, low-temperature epidote and zeolites in another, and with luck, even calcite and sulfides in a third.

When a batholithic magma has really cooled and hardened, and all the high-temperature minerals have separated, there may still be considerable quantities of gas and watery solutions. In this broth are dissolved metals, sulfur, silicon, and other elements. As the liquid moves into the surrounding strata, dissolved elements combine to make mineral deposits along the walls of the fissure through which the cooling mineral soup is leaking. The mineral-filled fissures are *veins*, and often the mineral filling in these veins is a valuable ore. Even the bordering rocks may be attacked by the solutions escaping from the fissures, and ore minerals are commonly deposited in the *country rock*, replacing more soluble substances such as calcite which have been dissolved to make room.

Experience has shown us that certain minerals are found in veins that must have been very hot, formed close to the magma and at great depth. Tin and tungsten ores, for example, are confined to the hottest seams, accompanied sometimes even by pegmatite minerals such as topaz and beryl. By contrast, other elements (antimony, arsenic, and mercury ores) travel great distances and are deposited near the surface and at low temperatures. Because it will help in identifications, it is desirable to remember which are the early high-temperature minerals and which are the late low-temperature vein fillers.

The usual occurrence and association is noted in the paragraph headed **Environment** for each of the detailed species descriptions. Knowledge of the type of occurrence you visit helps to eliminate minerals that might be confused with others similar in appearance, but which would not occur in the same environment.

Veins and their mineral-enriched borders, like rocks, are affected by exposure to the work of the air and weather. Sulfides may oxidize into water-soluble sulfates. Some of these are carried away in solution; some sink into the vein and react with fresh sulfides, perhaps enriching them by taking iron in exchange for copper and driving out other elements. As alteration proceeds further, air and water exposure can change sulfides to carbonates, silicates, oxides or hydroxides and can react as well with the surrounding wall rocks. A whole new group of secondary, more stable ore minerals can form, or alternatively, the surface exposure (outcrop) may be leached of everything but iron oxide (limonite) or aluminum oxide (bauxite). Residual deposits of this sort are *laterites* (broad) and *gossans* (capping just the vein). On the surface, a pyrite vein may be oxidized and leached to form an "iron hat" or limonite gossan. Any gold originally in the pyrite will have been freed and perhaps remains in the gossan unless removed by erosion.

As rocks crumble and wear, we find harder, tougher grains, such as quartz, surviving. Heavier minerals, gold and diamonds, may settle close to their source. They will lag behind when running water carries off the lighter and smaller particles; ultimately, they may accumulate into a *placer* deposit (a deposit of heavy mineral residues in stream gravels). A low-grade deposit (one whose mineral deposits are too scattered for mining to be economical) can produce a workable placer, when streams remove the lighter-weight minerals with no economic value, leaving a river bed enriched with an accumulation of the heavy minerals. Grains once sparsely distributed through a great thickness of rock are heaped together and left behind during thousands of years of erosion. Diamond-bearing gravels in several parts of the world (the Amazon and Orinoco basins in South America and the Orange River delta off the Namibian coast) are thought to have been concentrated and reconcentrated in this way, perhaps through millions of years, perhaps through more than one erosion cycle.

When we say outcrops have "weathered," we recognize that some of the elements in the magma, then in the rock minerals, and finally in the rock debris, go into solution and ultimately reach the sea. They may separate from the seawater by precipitation and be concentrated in sediments piling up on the sea floor. They may be differentially removed by marine life, in need of calcium for shells or iodine for fronds. Trapped seawater saturates the sediments, reworking and cementing the grains and helping to harden lime muck into rock. Later, when raised above the sea, rainwater seeping through them, dissolves and carries away selected elements. Metals in solutions may concentrate as solutions slowly migrate along layers sometimes finding a bit of sulfur or a breath of carbon dioxide eventually separating out in cavities or in crevices to form ore veins.

Sulfides, carbonates, and insoluble sulfates are common low-temperature minerals of such cavities in lime-rich sedimentary rocks, making some quarries good collecting localities. In places, we find great beds of chemical precipitates formed, like rock salt and gypsum, by the direct evaporation of cut-off estuaries of saltwater. Local reactions in the ocean appear sometimes to have precipitated, either by bacteria or chemical supersaturation, beds of iron ore, calcium phosphate, and limestone. Boron-enriched lakes may evaporate to form beds of borax ores; we can only speculate on the source of the boron.

With cracks, crevices, and caverns in sedimentary rocks serving as centers for more mineral precipitation far from plutonic sources, we expect veins to be filled with low-temperature minerals such as quartz and calcite, as well as low-temperature sulfides. In caves we get calcite stalactites and gypsum rosettes. In fossils we may find quartz or pyrite linings.

Lastly, as sediments on continental plate margins plunge below other crustal plates and are reheated, remelted, and compressed, hydrated sea-floor minerals reverse their course and revert to high-temperature minerals. But conditions of stress, the heat and pressure that created schists and gneisses, also favor the formation of a new group of minerals. A small number have come to be recognized as characteristic of highly metamorphosed rocks; they include garnets and the kyanite-staurolite series of the schists. These regionally metamorphosed rocks usually contain mica and other minerals with a flattened structure. As the rocks are folded, sometimes sharply, arches and tension crevices develop; into these gaps may migrate scattered elements, some perhaps rare, once disseminated through the bordering layers. This is the origin of the famous *alpine crevices* that yield so many beautifully crystallized specimens.

As magma fluids, enriched with quantities of rare elements, penetrate a compressed mass of metamorphosed rocks, additional changes in the original composition come about with the introduction of silica, boron, or magnesium. A new series of contact-metamorphic minerals develops, especially during the reworking of impure limestones, providing still another special mineral-forming environment. These in turn may decay and join the oxidized group, making a different hydrated set of minerals in yet another environment.

The important thing to remember is that there are a great many mineral-forming environments, and each is characterized by its own set of species. Some are mutually exclusive. For example, beryl will not be found in sedimentary rock in Ohio any more than celestite will be found in a New England pegmatite. So the finder of a blue mineral in each of those states can immediately dismiss at least one of the alternatives. If this lesson is clearly understood, and the reader observes the environment of each specimen before trying to identify it, the problem will be much simpler (see rear endpaper).

3

PHYSICAL PROPERTIES OF MINERALS

The identification of minerals by their physical properties alone is entirely practical for many of the minerals included in this book. It is, however, utterly impossible to distinguish the majority of the newer species, whose recognition as new and different was only made possible by a microprobe, an electron microscope, or an x-ray analysis of their structure. As beginners become more advanced it is likely that sometime they will encounter some respectable compound not mentioned here. (Over 3,000 of the 3,500 known minerals are wholly insignificant to most collectors.) In such cases it is necessary to enlist the aid of a trained mineralogist, with suitable instruments, or to learn some of the advanced methods of the professional. The utility of the physical properties discussed below varies, and their respective importance varies with the interest, the breadth of experience, and the dedication of each collector.

Distinguishing Characteristics

Color: The ability to interpret the clues provided by various hues in minerals is the most significant by-product of experience. Color is the first property noted when we look at a mineral. To the novice it is immediately discouraging to learn that in many cases color is only a result of accidental impurities, an indication of the presence of trace amounts of pigmenting elements of no significance to a mineral's composition, and widely variable. On the other hand, with the accumulated knowledge of a professional, reliance on color is basic; the experienced eye recognizes nuances of tint and shade characteristic of a particular species.

In some cases color may be a fundamental property, directly related to the composition. The blue of azurite and the green of malachite are typical hues of copper minerals, so typical that the discovery of blue and green stains on rock outcrops are the best possible indications to the prospector that the somewhere in a vein below lie copper sulfides. For sulfide minerals with metallic luster, color is fundamental, constant, and—on fresh fractures—invariable. In light-colored, transparent, and translucent minerals, of which we find so many, color is often of no help at all. For the very experienced, it can be a valuable guide, for some minerals never occur in some colors and hence can be eliminated in the pursuit of a label.

Luster: Luster permits a division of minerals into two main classes, the *metallic* and the *nonmetallic* lusters. Metallic minerals really look metallic with invariable hues: golden, silver, bronze, pink, or blue. Some may be naturally occurring, or native, metals, the rest are primarily metal sulfides and sulfosalts. The range of describable metallic lusters is not great.

Nonmetallic lusters have been given many names, most of which are obvious and found in any dictionary. A *vitreous* luster means that the mineral looks like glass; "glassy" is an equally suitable term. One or two truly hard minerals with tight-linked elements, and some soft minerals containing certain elements such as lead, mercury, and antimony, have a brilliant, almost metallic look, as do diamonds. They are said to have an *adamantine* luster. A *greasy* luster is a little less brilliant and less hard-looking than diamond. A still less brilliant luster is known as a *resinous* luster. A *silky* luster describes a finely fibrous substance with many parallel needles. A pearly (shining, silvery) luster resembles the reflections from the flat surfaces of an iridescent shell, and is to be noted in minerals with real and incipient cleavage cracks, micaceous cracks paralleling a reflecting surface.

Hardness: The scale of hardness in use among mineralogists is one that was set up by a German mineralogist, Friedrich Mohs, in 1822. Although imprecise, it is so practical that it has been followed ever since. It is now recognized that there is no exact mathematical relationship: 10 on the scale is merely a lot harder than 9, while 9 is somewhat harder than 8, and so on. For this reason fractional hardness, even when expressed in decimals, will only be an approximate determination. To suggest this ambiguity, we prefer here to use fractions rather than decimals. There are instruments that give accurate hardness tests, and they indicate that if diamond is 1,000 on a scale reading from 0 to 1,000, corundum (9 on Mohs scale) is about 250 and topaz (8) is 160.

The Mohs Hardness Scale

1	Talc	6	Feldspar
2	Gypsum	7	Quartz
3	Calcite (rhomb face)	8	Topaz
4	Fluorite	9	Corundum
5	Apatite	10	Diamond

The mineral with the higher number can scratch anything beneath it or equal to it in hardness. In other words, glass will scratch glass or anything softer. If we can scratch something with quartz but not with feldspar, and that something will scratch feldspar (and naturally not scratch quartz), we say it has a hardness of 6.

Hardness is often different in different crystal directions; diamonds are at their hardest parallel to the octahedron face, and cutters cannot grind that plane. In some softer minerals this difference is equally pronounced but more determinable by a collector: calcite's base plane can be scratched with the fingernail ($2\frac{1}{2}$ on the Mohs scale) while the rhombohedral cleavage face is 3 and too hard. Phosgenite's prism direction can be scratched with the fingernail (about 2) though the cross direction appears to be about 3. Best known in literature is kyanite, whose elongation direction can be scratched with a knife (about 5), while the direction across is too hard.

A few handy implements can help us if a hardness set is not available. The fingernail is a little over 2, a copper penny about 3, a steel knife just over 5, glass about $5\frac{1}{2}$, and a good steel file about $6\frac{1}{2}$.

Specific Gravity or Density: This is a determinable and pretty constant mathematical figure, meaning the weight of a substance in relation to the weight of the same volume of water. A substance said to have a specific gravity of 2.5 would be 2.5 times as heavy as the same volume of water. "Heft," a simple estimation of density, is an important observation. It becomes evident when we handle many specimens and come to think of them individually as heavy or light in relation to others of about the same size that we have held.

More definite gravity determinations are made by weighing

Fig. 5 Arrangement for determining specific gravity

a substance in air and then weighing it again suspended in water. Reliability depends on the care observed in making sure that the mineral is pure and not mixed with any other substance. It would be well to practice with a scale and make a suspension arrangement for weighing in water with a few known pure samples before attempting an unknown.

To make the calculation, we weigh the substance first in air with a scale set up so that a second lower pan is already in water and properly balanced before anything is put on either side. We then weigh the substance again, now in the pan that is under water, and get a second and lesser figure (Fig. 5). The lowered weight, in water, is then subtracted from the first weight, that in air. This gives us a number that represents the weight of the water that was pushed out of the way by the stone as it was submerged. This is of course the volume of the stone x 1—the specific gravity of water. If we divide the weight of the whole stone by the weight of the water that represented its volume (in other words, the loss of weight in the second weighing), we get the specific gravity, or the number of times more the stone weighs than the same amount of water. For example:

Weight in air	23.67 grams	
Weight in water	16.95 grams	
Loss of weight	6.72 grams	
Weight in air	23.67	
Divided by	6.72 the loss of weight	
Equals	3.52 the specific gravity	

There are various other methods for determining specific gravity. High-density liquids can match the density of an unknown. Special scales or water-filled bottles called pycnometers may be used, but all are more complicated or more expensive than the simple balance the amateur can rig up, or graduated beams designed for such determinations.

Streak is the color of a powdered mineral. It is best seen on an unglazed white porcelain tile, obtainable from any source that sells tile. Since the tile has a hardness of about 7, minerals of higher hardness will not make a colored streak. However, for these minerals, particularly black ones, it is possible to see the color of a powder on bruised edges, or actually to crush some into powder. It will be found that lighter hues often show up in the powder of many seemingly black minerals (many are not truly black and opaque but only seem so because of their grain size and opacity).

Fracture: An unimportant term describing the appearance of a broken surface. Most minerals have an *uneven* fracture, an irregular *grainy* fracture, or a curving, shelly, glasslike break known as a *conchoidal* fracture. Most substances have one or the other as a constant property, with most glassy minerals having a conchoidal fracture.

Native metals distributed through rock tend to tear apart leaving jagged points to catch the flesh as a hand is brushed across. This infrequent event is known as a *hackly* fracture. It is usually well shown in copper specimens of the Michigan Upper Peninsula type (copper disseminated in rhyolite) and could happen with silver and gold. Minerals with a pronounced elongation and cleavage are said to have a *splintery* fracture, which is rather obvious.

Cleavage: The tendency of a mineral to break in smooth flat planes is known as cleavage and is obviously a fundamental property of a mineral, since it is related to the atomic arrangement within the crystal. It is, of course, also related to the symmetry of the mineral: a cubic mineral, such as sphalerite or fluorite, may have a dodecahedral (12-sided) or octahedral (8-sided) cleavage, while a monoclinic or triclinic crystal will probably have only *pinacoidal* (one plane of smooth fracture) or prismatic (two planes) cleavages. Cleavage is one of the more important properties for identification.

Parting: This resembles cleavage in producing flat surfaces, except that it is present only in some specimens and on some planes of some species. Parting is possible only in certain parallel, but structurally spaced, locations. They are planes of weakness in the crystal because of the presence of a disoriented sheet of atoms displaced into a mirror ("twinned") orientation. Often visible in Iceland spar calcite (though not an obvious parting plane) and observable as an actual easy fracture plane in ruby corundum (where it is a lapidary hazard) and diopside.

Tenacity: Crystalline masses vary in their resistance to fracture, and various terms have been applied to describe this. If a mass is very resistant to a separation of the individual grains it is called *compact*. This may be carried to the extreme that we find in quartzite, the metamorphosed sandstone, in which cementation between the grains is such that in breaking, the fracture actually splits the sand grains rather than going around their surfaces. In granite, fracture is always through the grains, which are so tightly interlocked that they cannot easily be separated. Other granular rocks, such as schist, may crumble more readily. Some marbles break easily into little individual cleavage rhombohedrons, and for this reason prove worthless for long-term building stones. Olivine rocks (dunites) are particularly *friable* or *crumbly*; as in some sandstones, falling apart in a shower of sand grains when a finger is rubbed across them. Massive minerals with elongated or flattened crystals may be brittle, breaking easily into a pile of splinters or plates, while nephrite, one of the jades that could also be regarded as a rock, is tough and hard to break. *Sectile* is the term used to describe the tenacity of several of the softer metals; it refers to the ability to be cut cleanly by a knife.

Clarity: Minerals range from transparent to opaque. Almost any translucent mineral can, under ideal circumstances, be nearly or entirely transparent. Hence, though we frequently do, it is redundant to say that a mineral is transparent to translucent; obviously if it is transparent under some conditions, it will, since inclusions or flaws are more the rule than the exception, more often be translucent at best. Completely opaque minerals, on the other hand, include only the sulfides and oxides as a general group; even in black silicates, thin enough splinters will usually show some light transmission. It is related to streak—to the color of the powder, which will be truly black only in the case of truly opaque minerals. Truly transparent minerals are described as *gemmy* because of their resemblance to gemstones.

Fluorescence and Phosphorescence: The property of changing invisible ultraviolet light or x-ray beams into visible

Fig. 6 Piezoelectricity testing device. For best results, puff gently, from a distance of several inches.

light is a property known as *fluorescence*. In some cases light emission persists for an interval after the stimulating source is turned off. This is *phosphorescence*. Phosphorescence is rarer than fluorescence and may be brief. Not all specimens of a fluorescent mineral will fluoresce; it depends upon the impurities present. Some localities are noted for having an abundance of fluorescent minerals (Franklin, New Jersey; Langban, Sweden).

Several other intriguing luminescent effects are shown by minerals. Some species give small flashes of light when hit with a hard point: sphalerite and corundum may show this *triboluminescence*, as it is called. Orange pseudo-sparking is seen in rock crystal in the slit as it is sawed, and we have heard it can be produced at night by throwing rocks at a quartz-veined face.

Thermoluminescence, a phosphorescent glow appearing when low heat is applied, is a property shown by fluorite and some calcite. Try it for a few seconds, by placing a chip on warming electric stove coils in the dark.

Other Phenomena: *Pyroelectricity* and *piezoelectricity* are phenomena shown by some minerals, notably tourmaline and quartz. Temperature or pressure changes cause the minerals to acquire an electrical charge, positive and negative poles on the c-axes, as they are warmed, cooled, or compressed. The charge may be colorfully demonstrated by dusting a cooling or warming crystal with a powder of red lead and sulfur puffed through a thin silk or nylon screen. A simple bellows and screen can be made by placing two layers of a stocking over the end of a rubber bulb filled with a mixture of about 2 parts of red lead to 1 of sulfur. The dust particles receive electrical charges as they pass through the screen and settle on the appropriate ends of the charged crystals, the sulfur becoming negatively charged and settling on the positive end of the crystal while the red lead, recipient of a positive charge, goes to the negative end of the crystal. Though rarely made by amateur collectors, the demonstration is so spectacular that it should be tried as an intriguing mineral property. The apparatus pictured is inexpensive and simple to make (Fig. 6).

Percussion figures are 6-rayed stars shown by the micas when they are struck a light single blow by a sharp-pointed needle. Naturally, the rays of the star follow crystal directions in the mica.

Asterism is the 4- or 6-rayed star shown by some minerals when they are polished so that a point source of light can be seen through them, or when they are cut into a sphere to reflect light from microscopic inclusions paralleling crystal directions. Rose quartz, some grayish pegmatite quartz, and corundum (star sapphires) are the best examples of this phenomenon. It may often be seen on looking at a distant light through a cleavage sheet of phlogopite mica (especially "books" from Bancroft, Ontario).

Adularescence or *labradorescence* is a bluish sheen seen in some feldspars (moonstone and labradorite) when the light is reflected at the correct angle. It is caused by a submicroscopic scale intergrowth of light-disturbing planes of different composition (feldspar) and refractive index.

Schiller is an almost metallic sheen with a different cause. Schiller reflections come from almost visible, aligned particles, which characterize some pyroxenes. The word is a reference to a turbid German wine.

Pleochroism is shown by colored transparent or translucent crystals of any of the noncubic symmetry groups. Light vibrating and transmitted in one direction is absorbed differently from light following a different route, with absorption creating differences in the color seen in the two directions. In a few minerals such as tourmaline, cordierite, and andalusite, this color change may be so pronounced that it alone is a useful guide to identity. Frequently it is a help in identification, since any color change when a mineral is rotated over a Polaroid sheet before a light shows that the mineral cannot belong to the cubic system, even though no crystals are present. A small splinter might be held in front of a divided Polaroid sheet, one that has been cut and mounted, in a way that places their two polarizing (vibration) directions at right angles to each other. As the translucent splinter is moved back and forth across the dividing line the change in color will be apparent.

Mineral Textures and Outlines of Aggregates

Mineral Surfaces

When minerals solidify in open cavities with no interference from other solids or each other, most assume the angular, flat-faced shapes known as crystals, shapes discussed in the next chapter. The rate at which crystals grow, the abundance and distribution of their growing centers, and the richness and nature of the solutions from which they are forming determine whether a single mineral or a mixture of minerals will crystallize, how large the crystals will be, and whether they will form isolated individual crystals or produce continuous crusts. A crystallized crust is known as a *druse*; it is composed of numerous points or surfaces studded with a few larger crystals. Solid-quartz druses are very common, so quartz should first and always be considered the most likely substance whenever a shining crystal crust is seen. When it is quartz, only terminal points of the crystals may show; prism faces do not develop well under these conditions.

Sometimes the crystals are smaller, needlelike, and compact. Then they may not end in crystal planes but in a smoothly rounded surface, which may be described under various names, depending upon the size of the individual domes. The term *botryoidal* (grapelike) is used when the knobs are rather small. *Reniform* (kidneylike) and *mammillary* are equally descriptive terms for larger rounded surfaces (see hematite, Pl. 25).

Various, but always obvious, terms are used to describe other growth habits that may be encountered in minerals. A branching treelike growth may be called *dendritic*; such a pattern is seen in moss agates and in manganese oxide stains on rock seams, often mistaken for fossil plant impressions. Small spheres are called *globular*, slender hairs are *acicular*, hanging masses are *stalactitic*, and jointed rods like bridge girders are *reticulated*.

Rock and Mineral Textures

When it does crystallize, in the mass of solidifying minerals (beneath a possibly freely grown and drusy surface), each grain is competing with its neighbors. The coarseness of the texture will depend upon factors similar to those determining the appearance of the free-growing surface. Since we are often dealing here with direct crystallization of a molten mass, the viscosity of the solidifying liquid and the rate of cooling are both very important. Molten magma that comes to the surface as lava cools quickly and solidifies rapidly. Deep underground the same magma cools and solidifies much more slowly. Fewer centers of crystallization develop with slow cooling, so each crystal has a longer chance to grow before encountering interference from a neighbor.

Crystalline textures develop a granularity that may be fine or coarse, depending on its speed of cooling and growth environment. When large enough, individual grains can be seen on a broken face. Many minerals break more easily in one direction than in another; a fractured surface is an uneven plane produced by the interaction between the cleavage and easy fracture directions of each of the constituent grains. When we examine such a broken surface we can see if the individual grains are coarse or fine: if it is *coarsely crystalline* or *finely crystalline.* We can also note if the individual crystals are uniform in size or grossly different, if they are more or less equal in their length and breadth, or if they are rods elongated in one direction. Various terms have been applied to such crystalline masses, descriptive of the characteristics of the grains. They may be *foliated, micaceous,* or *lamellar* if they are tabular in habit and have micaceous cleavages. Needles may be *rodlike, fibrous, acicular,* or *hairlike.* If the needles have no parallel arrangement but interlock, like the hairs that make up felt and the fibers in paper, we call the texture *felted;* this texture in jade explains its unusual strength.

Sometimes, often in fact, the crystalline structure is so fine that the individual grains cannot be seen with the naked eye. In this case we call it *microcrystalline* or *cryptocrystalline.* That does not mean that the substance is not crystallized; though built of structures undetectable except by x-ray or microscope, the atomic structure of each grain is the same as that of the mineral in the coarsest aggregates or in a monumental crystal. The chalcedony division of quartz has such a cryptocrystalline texture. When a substance is really not crystallized, and gives no regular pattern of stripes even in an x-ray diffraction film, we call it *amorphous* (without form). Some minerals—but surprisingly few—fall in this group, which include opal, chrysocolla, and some of the hydrous silicates and oxides. Many substances long considered to be amorphous have been found, since the advent of x-ray studies, to be crystalline after all. Volcanic glass (obsidian) is made of lava that cooled too quickly for any crystals to develop; it, too, is amorphous.

4

CRYSTAL CLASSIFICATIONS

Note: *If this section seems complicated and difficult at first, skip it and come back later. All you really need is a familiarity with the six systems.*

The smooth-faced angular shape assumed by a chemical compound in solidifying from a molten state or in separating from a solution in an open space, where it is free to adopt any shape normal to it, is known as a *crystal*. The external shape traditional for the solid reveals its internal arrangement of atoms. The smooth surfaces that bound a crystal, called its *faces*, are directly related to the internal sheets of aligned atoms and their importance in the different planes. All the distinctive properties of minerals discussed in Chapter 3, such as cleavage, hardness, and light absorption are related to this three-dimensional internal atomic pattern.

Physicists need but a fragment to define a crystal unit; the presence of external faces means nothing to an x-ray beam, which pierces a crystal like a stream of water striking a picket fence, bouncing off, like the water, from sets of planes. A physicist studying crystal structure concentrates deflected beams of the x-ray stream onto a negative, creating a pattern of exposed spots from which the internal atomic distribution can be deduced. To a mineral collector, expert in sight identification, however, the external form and faces of the crystal are of paramount importance, and well-developed crystals of significant species are usually sufficiently characteristic to allow identification from their shape alone. The angles between pairs of crystal faces are unique for all species of minerals. Identifications can be, and once were, made by the careful measurement of the angles with an instrument called a *goniometer*. With easier methods now at hand, this time-consuming technique is no longer used as a tool for identification.

Many amateurs find *crystallography* the most difficult aspect of mineral study. The memorizing of all of the *crystal classes* would, indeed, be rather tedious; but it should be remembered that naturally occurring representatives of many of the 32 classes are rare or unknown. The *crystal system* alone is usually enough for identification when considered along with the physical properties. The crystal system will be one of six, and only six, mathematical possibilities. Each system is defined by the relative lengths and angular intersections of three (four in the hexagonal system) imaginary internal lines that run from opposite face centers, paralleling intersecting edges of faces and crossing in a center. For a discussion of the elements of a crystal, let us start with a simple cube and seek all of its inner connections. As it is the shape with the highest symmetry, the cube is the easiest to visualize.

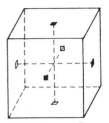

Fig. 7 Cube with 3 principal axes

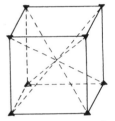

Fig. 8 Corner axes of threefold symmetry

Axes are imaginary lines (we can visualize them as threads) running from the center of each face to the center of the face exactly opposite. As we see, in a cube there are three such lines: each parallel to the cube's corner edges, intersecting in the center at right angles, and all equal in length (Fig. 7). These are the fundamental axes that define a system. Next we could run similar imaginary lines to the corners. These are not parallel to the cube

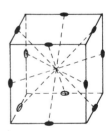

Fig. 9 Axes of twofold symmetry

edge intersections, so they are not the definitive crystal axes. However, should we pick a cube up by two opposite corners and turn it one-third of the way around, we see the cube with its six faces in exactly the same place as they were before we turned it. Another third of a rotation repeats this experience, and following the third turn of 120 degrees we have the top back where it started. So, though we may not

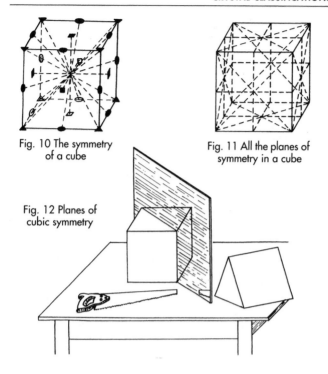

Fig. 10 The symmetry of a cube

Fig. 11 All the planes of symmetry in a cube

Fig. 12 Planes of cubic symmetry

be turning it on a crystal axis, it certainly is an axis on which the crystal can be turned to repeat itself without changing its true appearance; in other words, it, too, is an *axis of symmetry* (Fig. 8), in this case, an axis of *threefold* symmetry. Were we to pick up the crystal between fingers placed in the center of opposite edges, instead of corners, we would find that we would have to give a full half turn before the crystal appeared to reassume its original position. These, then, would be axes of *twofold* symmetry (Fig. 9). In a cube there would be six of these, with four of threefold symmetry and the three principal crystal axes, which have fourfold symmetry (Fig. 10).

Now, if our cube is of wood and we were to saw it diagonally through the center, we would have two halves, each of which, if placed upon a mirror, would give us back the appearance of the whole cube (Fig. 12). We could also divide the cube in the middle of the face and get the same effect.

Fig. 13 Cube with octahedral corner truncations

Fig. 14 Octahedron, related to same axes as the cube

Fig. 15 Tetrahexahedron

Fig. 16 Trigonal trisoctahedron, or trapezohedron

These are *planes of symmetry,* and in a cube there are nine of these (Fig. 11). Lines connecting the centers of any like pairs of faces would intersect at a central point. As long as there are opposing pairs of faces on several sides you would have an intersection of connecting lines and the crystal would be said to have a *center of symmetry.*

We have now reviewed all the symmetry elements of a cube, the crystal system that has the largest number of these elements and the highest symmetry. To sum up, then, we call the system in which this type of symmetry is found the *cubic system.* It is characterized by three *equal axes at right angles* to each other. These three *fourfold* crystal axes are the basis of the systems; the other elements are not invariable. The fundamental cube has, in addition, four axes of *threefold* symmetry, six axes of *twofold* symmetry, nine planes of symmetry, and a *center* of symmetry. There are some modifications we can now impose on our fundamental cube. We might cut off each corner of the cube, a little at first (Fig. 13) then all the way to the center of each face (Fig. 14). Now we find ourselves with an eight-faced form, a double pyramid, but it still has all the symmetry elements it had when it was a cube. So we can infer that a crystal shaped like this eight-faced form also belongs in the cubic system. This is called an octahedron. Suppose we were to erect a low four-faced pyramid on each of the faces of the cube, we would then have a 24-faced form, a tetra(4)-hexa(6)hedron (Fig. 15). In the same way we can imagine three faces on the octahedron, a trisoctahedron (Fig. 16). So all of these different-looking crystals (and we can get combinations of them, too) still fit into our simple cubic system, all with three axes of equal length at right angles to each other.

Having seen all the possibilities with this description of the cube symmetry elements, we can go on. There are six crystal systems, and the 32 crystal classes are subdivisions of these. The names of the systems refer to their appearance and their axes, and once learned are easy to remember. The classes depend upon other symmetry elements. In some crystals, for example, the top and bottom of the crystal are different, so there is no center of symmetry or horizontal plane of symmetry. Some of the axes of symmetry will also be missing, though the crystal axes must remain.

The symbols, known as Hermann-Mauguin symbols, pinpoint the class and are derived from the symmetry axes of each class. The amateur collector may find them of little use; we list them only as a ready reference.

The Crystal Systems

A. Cubic or Isometric System (Greek for "equal measure")

In this group the axes are equal in length and at right angles to each other. There are various symmetry classes, keeping the same equal axial ratio but losing some of the elements of symmetry:

1. Hexoctahedral (common in galena, halite, fluorite, garnet, many more)

$\dfrac{4}{m} \ \bar{3} \ \dfrac{2}{m}$

3 (crystal) axes of fourfold symmetry
4 (diagonal) axes of threefold symmetry
6 (diagonal) axes of twofold symmetry
9 planes of symmetry
center of symmetry

2. Diploidal (pyrite, cobaltite)

$\dfrac{2}{m} \ \bar{3}$

4 (diagonal axes) of threefold symmetry
3 (crystal) axes of twofold symmetry
3 axial planes of symmetry
center of symmetry

3. Tetrahedral (Hextetrahedral; tetrahedrite, sphalerite)

$\bar{4} \ 3 \ m$

4 (diagonal) axes of threefold symmetry
3 (crystal) axes of twofold symmetry
6 diagonal planes of symmetry

4. Gyroidal (cuprite, sal ammoniac)

	3 (crystal) axes of fourfold symmetry
4 3 2	4 (diagonal) axes of threefold symmetry
	6 (diagonal) axes of twofold symmetry

5. Tetartohedral (Tetartoidal; rare in nature)

| | 4 (diagonal) axes of threefold symmetry |
| 2 3 | 3 (crystal) axes of twofold symmetry |

B. Tetragonal System (*tetra,* Greek for "four," refers to the square cross section)

This system resembles the cubic except that one of the axes, one that is always placed vertically as we look at (orient) the crystal, is longer or shorter than the other two. This change in the axes means that the vertical direction is now fixed and the crystal may not be turned equally well to bring a side up, as in the cubic system. The definitive forms are the upright ones—the prisms—which are vertical and are said to be *first* or *second order,* depend-

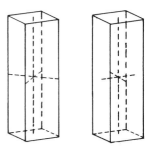

Fig. 17 Tetragonal systems prisms

ing on whether a face cuts one horizontal axis and is parallel to the other or whether each face cuts both horizontal axes at an equal distance from the center (Fig. 17). The top and bottom faces are known as the *basal pinacoids.* Intermediate slanted and truncating faces are bipyramids (in the classes that are alike at top and bottom with a center of symmetry; otherwise simply pyramids), and they too may be first or second order. Eight-faced prisms are known as *ditetragonal prisms,* when the adjoining angles in a cross section are unlike, which helps to distinguish them from a combination of first- and second-order prisms. When only one of a ditetragonal pair is preserved, as in Class 8 (or Class 15 in the hexagonal system), it is known as a *third-order form* (see Fig. 19).

6. Ditetragonal bipyramidal (zircon, vesuvianite, cassiter
ite, rutile)

$\dfrac{4}{m}\dfrac{2}{m}\dfrac{2}{m}$
1 vertical axis of fourfold symmetry
4 horizontal axes of twofold symmetry
1 horizontal plane of symmetry
4 vertical planes of symmetry
center of symmetry

7. Ditetragonal pyramidal (no common mineral)

4 m m
1 vertical axis of fourfold symmetry
4 vertical planes of symmetry

8. Tetragonal bipyramidal (scheelite, scapolite)

$\dfrac{4}{m}$
1 vertical axis of fourfold symmetry
1 horizontal plane of symmetry
center of symmetry

9. Tetragonal pyramidal (wulfenite)
4 1 vertical axis of fourfold symmetry

10. Ditetragonal alternating (Tetragonal scalenohedral;
chalcopyrite)

$\overline{4}$ 2 m
3 axes of twofold symmetry
2 vertical diagonal planes of symmetry

11. Tetragonal trapezohedral (phosgenite)

4 2 2
1 vertical axis of fourfold symmetry
4 horizontal axes of twofold symmetry

12. Tetragonal alternating (Tetragonal bisphenoidal; no
common mineral)

$\overline{4}$
1 vertical axis of twofold symmetry

C. Hexagonal System

This system with a star of three horizontal axes intersected
at right angles by one vertical axis is the most complicated
of all because of the confusion that results from the very
common subdivision in which alternate faces have not
formed. This results in a threefold instead of a sixfold symmetry. It is known as the *rhombohedral division* of the hexagonal system, and has sometimes been placed in a separate
group called the *trigonal system* with axes that parallel the
rhombohedron edges. Since the relationship of the rhombo-

hedral division to the hexagonal system is the same as the sphenoidal or tetrahedral classes in the first two systems, it does not seem logical to follow the trigonal system further. For mathematical reasons it is sometimes preferred, but it only makes the subject unnecessarily difficult.

In the hexagonal system we visualize three horizontal axes of equal length, intersected by an upright fourth that is longer or shorter. The fully developed forms would be six-sided prisms or bipyramids of either a first or second order, as

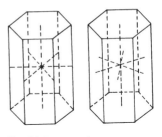

Fig. 18 Hexagonal system axes

in the tetragonal system, depending upon whether two or three of the horizontal axes were cut (Fig. 18).

As we find an eight-faced form in the tetragonal system, we expect and find a 12-faced form in the hexagonal, which is merely a doubling of the six faces, called the *dihexagonal prism* (or dihexagonal bipyramid). By alternate development and suppression of one side or the other of these dihexagonal faces, we get a skewed six-faced form (as in apatite), called the third order, just as in the tetragonal system (Fig. 19).

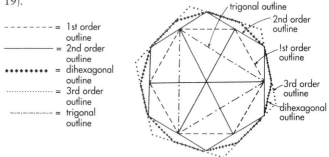

- - - - - - - = 1st order outline
―――――― = 2nd order outline
✦✦✦✦✦✦✦✦ = dihexagonal outline
················ = 3rd order outline
–·–·–·–·– = trigonal outline

trigonal outline
2nd order outline
!st order outline
3rd order outline
dihexagonal outline

Fig. 19 Hexagonal system

13. Dihexagonal bipyramidal (beryl)

$$\frac{6}{m}\frac{2}{m}\frac{2}{m}$$

1 vertical axis of sixfold symmetry
6 horizontal axes of symmetry
6 vertical planes of symmetry
1 horizontal plane of symmetry
center of symmetry

14. Dihexagonal pyramidal (zincite, greenockite)

6 m m   1 vertical axis of sixfold symmetry
          6 vertical planes of symmetry

15. Hexagonal bipyramidal (apatite, pyromorphite, vana
    dinite)

$\frac{6}{m}$ vertical axis of sixfold symmetry
        horizontal plane of symmetry
        center of symmetry

16. Hexagonal pyramidal (nepheline)

6   vertical axis of sixfold symmetry

17. Hexagonal trapezohedral (quartz—high temperature)

6 2 2   vertical axis of sixfold symmetry
       6 horizontal axes of twofold symmetry

In the two trigonal classes of the hexagonal division, the vertical axis has a threefold rather than a sixfold symmetry, but, unlike the rhombohedral division in the ditrigonal bipyramidal class there is a horizontal plane of symmetry. The trigonal pyramidal class, which lacks the horizontal plane of symmetry, is logically placed in the rhombohedral group; but since there is no known mineral with this class of symmetry, argument here about its proper position in a classification is purely academic.

18. Ditrigonal bipyramidal (benitoite)

$\overline{6}$ m 2   1 vertical axis of threefold symmetry
       3 horizontal axes of twofold symmetry
       3 vertical planes of symmetry
       horizontal plane of symmetry

19. Trigonal bipyramidal (no mineral representative)

$\overline{6}$ 1 vertical axis of threefold symmetry
    1 horizontal plane of symmetry

The rhombohedral division may be likened to the tetrahedral class of the cubic system and the sphenoidal classes of the tetragonal system; for the rhombohedron—the major form of the division—is developed by the dominant growth of every other face, alternating from top to bottom of the crystal. A simple rhombohedron has six faces. With 90° angles it would be a cube stood on its corner, the vertical axis coming out the point, if external form were the only criterion for crystal classification. In the normal orientation of the rhombohedral division the horizontal axes are regarded as coming out the center of each of the equatorial edges (Fig. 20). Because of the alternate-face growth, it differs from the trigonal class (seen in the mineral benitoite) by lacking the horizontal plane of symmetry even in the classes with like faces above and below the center.

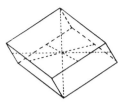

Fig. 20 Rhombohedral axes

20. Rhombohedral holohedral (Hexagonal scalenohedral; calcite, hematite, corundum, etc.)

$\overline{3} \frac{2}{m}$
    1 vertical axis of threefold symmetry
    3 horizontal axes of twofold symmetry
    3 vertical planes of symmetry (not on the horizontal axes but between them)

21. Rhombohedral hemimorphic (Ditrigonal pyramidal; tourmaline)

3 m
    1 vertical axis of threefold symmetry
    3 vertical diagonal planes of symmetry

22. Rhombohedral tetartohedral (Rhombohedral; phenak ite, willemite, dioptase, dolomite)

$\overline{3}$
    1 vertical axis of threefold symmetry
    center of symmetry

23. Trapezohedral (Trigonal trapezohedral; quartz, cinna bar)

3 2
    1 vertical axis of threefold symmetry
    3 horizontal axes of twofold symmetry

24. Rhombohedral tetartohedral (Hemimorphic = Trigonal pyramidal; no common mineral)

3
    1 vertical axis of threefold symmetry

D. Orthorhombic System

This system is a return to our uncomplicated three axes at right angles to each other, now with the variant that all are of unequal length. Obviously there must be a longest, a shortest, and an intermediate axis. To set up properly (orient) an orthorhombic crystal, we place vertically what is commonly the longest direction (the *c*-axis), and direct the shortest axis (the *a*-axis) toward us. The intermediate axis extending from left to right then becomes the *b*-axis (Fig. 21). As with bases in the tetragonal and hexagonal systems, the face pairs paralleling each other at opposite ends of the axes are the pinacoids, known respectively as basal, front, and side or *basal, macro-,* and *brac-hypinacoids.* (Remember: *b*-pinacoid equals the brachypinacoid). Vertical sets of four faces cutting the two horizontal axes are the *prisms* (they are often striated parallel to their length), and similar but horizontal sets of 4 faces cutting the vertical axis and one or the other horizontal axis (like a roof) are the *macro-* and *brachydomes.* As in the other systems, faces cutting all three are pyramids and bipyramids.

Fig. 21 Orthorhombic system axes and pinacoids

25. Orthorhombic bipyramidal (barite group, sulfur, topaz, staurolite, andalusite, olivine, etc.)

$\dfrac{2}{m}\dfrac{2}{m}\dfrac{2}{m}$

3 perpendicular axes of twofold symmetry
3 axial planes of symmetry
center of symmetry

26. Orthorhombic pyramidal (hemimorphite, bertrandite)

m m 2

1 vertical axis of twofold symmetry
2 vertical planes of symmetry

27. Orthorhombic sphenoidal (Rhombic bisphenoidal; no common mineral)

2 2 2   3 perpendicular axes of twofold symmetry

E. Monoclinic System

Having exhausted the possible variations of three axes at right angles, the next mathematical possibility is to reduce the symmetry by inclining one of the axes slightly toward the plane of the other two, which remain at right angles. The setting up of such a crystal inclines the tilted axis toward the observer; this is the clinoaxis or *a*-axis (Fig. 22). The other two axes lie in a vertical plane at right angles to that defined by the *a* and *c* axes. Either the *b*-axis or the *c*-axis may be the longer, but the *b*-axis will be one of twofold symmetry and the *a–c* plane will be the only plane of symmetry. The forms are the same as those of the orthorhombic system, except that the macrodomes become *clinodomes*. The pyramids will be "front" or "back" pairs, however, so there are only 4 faces in the bipyramid of the full symmetry class.

Fig 22. Monclinic system and axes

28. Monoclinic normal (Pris matic; gypsum, spodumene, orthoclase, chondrodite, epidote, etc.)

$\frac{2}{m}$

1 horizontal axis of twofold symmetry
1 vertical plane of symmetry (with 2 crystal axes)
center of symmetry

29. Monoclinic hemimorphic (Sphenoidal; no common mineral)

2

1 horizontal axis of twofold symmetry

30. Monoclinic hemihedral (Domatic; no common mineral, but sucrose—sugar, rock candy—is a familiar example)

m

1 vertical plane (with *a–c* axes) of symmetry

F. Triclinic System

The last possible variation we can imagine with our three unequal axes is to have all three inclined at some angle other than 90° (Fig. 23). Since an asymmetrical set of axes such as this can have symmetry only with pairs of faces, the domes, prisms, and pyramids of the other systems are now represented by two faces only, which are top and bottom, front and back, or to the right and the left. The center of symmetry is the only element of symmetry left, and when it is present it makes the triclinic crystal of the normal class. The triclinic system is the most difficult to calculate mathematically. Lacking in its hemihedral class any element of symmetry at all, it is from the standpoint of the mathematician the easiest and most simply understood system. On the other hand, since the recognition of symmetry and the prop-

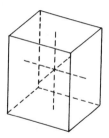 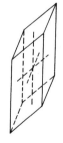

Fig. 23 Triclinic system axes and pinacoids

er setting up of crystals is the chief joy of the study of this aspect of minerals, it is the least rewarding to the collector. The names of forms revert to those of the orthorhombic system. Since all are inclined, there would be no distinction between a clinodome or clinopinacoid in this system. Any axis can be made the vertical one. Only the x-ray crystallographer can finally determine the proper orientation of the group, though the axial ratios determined by the older methods often coincide with those of the modern x-ray crystallographer.

31. Triclinic normal (Pinacoidal; axinite, pyroxenes, and plagioclase feldspars)

$\overline{1}$ center of symmetry

32. Triclinic hemihedral (Pedial; no common mineral)

1   no symmetry

Other Forms and Phenomena

Twinning in Crystals

Since crystals often grow close together, an intergrowth of two individuals is common. Sometimes the contact plane is a prominent plane in both crystals, and the two individuals are symmetrically arranged along either side of it. When this is suspected and the plane is a frequently observed face, or when we find many identical intergrowths paired on a less common plane, we speak of the doubling as *twinning*. Twins are often marked by re-entrant angles between the two halves. Common types of twinning are sometimes known under the name of a mineral that often intergrows in this fashion. Twinning involves a different orientation of the crystal segments and should not be confused with stepped, parallel growths.

In the cubic system we have the contact twinning on an octahedral face, which produces a crystal with a flattened triangular outline known as *spinel twinning*—frequent in spinel (Fig. 24), of course, and in diamond.

Two individuals may penetrate each other and corners of one may protrude from faces of the other individual. This is

Fig. 24
Spinel twin

Fig. 25
Penetration twin
of fluorite

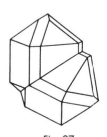

Fig. 26 Rutile
"sixling"

known as *penetration twinning,* often present in cubic fluorite (Fig. 25) and pyrite.

In the tetragonal system we find a repeated twinning in rutile which may make a complete wheel of geniculated ("kneelike") twins (Fig. 26). Cassiterite intergrows in the same fashion so that the re-entrant angle is a good guide to the mineral (Fig. 27).

In the hexagonal system we find calcite contact twins in many different arrangements, and cinnabar in penetrations like those of fluorite. We also find attractive penetration twinning in phenakite.

Fig. 27
Cassiterite twin

The orthorhombic system commonly has a penetration twinning of three individuals on a prism plane (trilling), so that the impression of a hexagonal crystal is developed. This is typical in aragonite and chrysoberyl (see Pls. 29 and 26).

Monoclinic crystals often form contact twins on the back pinacoid, as in the fishtail gypsum crystals (Fig. 28). Repeat-

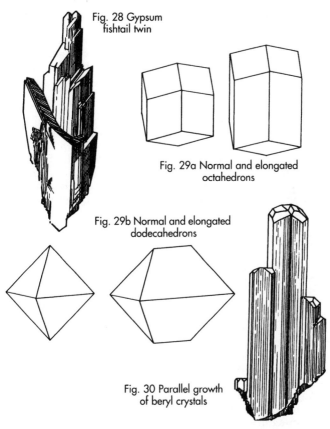

Fig. 28 Gypsum fishtail twin

Fig. 29a Normal and elongated octahedrons

Fig. 29b Normal and elongated dodecahedrons

Fig. 30 Parallel growth of beryl crystals

ed twinning of the triclinic feldspar is common enough to serve as an identification characteristic when the parallel lines are observed on the cleavage faces (see oligoclase, Pl. 47).

Distorted Crystals

The development of crystals is seldom perfectly symmetrical, and we often find greatly elongated crystals of one system resembling those of another. Experience in setting up crystals is the only guide to the recognition of these distorted crystals; an elongated dodecahedron may look like a rhombohedral mineral with a combination of the prism and rhombohedron (Figs. 29a, b). A study of face surfaces — striations, low symmetrical mounds, etched pits — will help in this respect. Prism faces are often striated differently from the terminal faces. If both have the same luster and markings, a distorted crystal should be suspected, and a higher symmetry considered.

Parallel Growths

It is easy to confuse stepped and parallel growths with twinnings. Unless a definite re-entrant is seen, with simultaneous reflections from the two individuals on *unlike* faces, the probability is that the group in question is a parallel growth rather than a twin (Fig. 30). This single distinction probably elicits more disagreements among collectors than any other aspect of crystallography.

Crystal Habit

Crystals usually show several different sets of crystal faces, sets called "forms" in the crystal discussion. Any crystal can only show forms of its system. Corner-cutting on cubic-system minerals can only be cubes, octahedrons, dodecahedrons, tetrahexahedrons, trapezohedrons, and the like. They cannot have pinacoids, pyramids, or prisms, which are the forms of other systems. Commonly crystals show a combination of several forms—such as a cube with its corners cut by the octahedron faces, and/or its edges cut by dodecahedrons (Fig. 31). However, all the crystals of the same mineral on a specimen from one locality may be dominantly cubic (Fig. 32), while the same mineral from another source is predominantly octahedral (Fig. 33). This is known as *habit*. We speak of low-temperature (of formation) fluorite as having a cubic habit and high-temperature fluorite as having an octahedral habit. High-temperature calcite is commonly tabular. The study of the significance of crystal habit is still in its fundamental stages but is a fascinating branch of crystallography. Temperature, pressure, composition of the mineral-depositing solutions, and variations in their concentration may all play a part in determining the final outline of the crystal. We also find, from the study of ghostlike earlier growth stages delineated by a band of impurities within the crystal (known as phantoms) that the habit of a crystal may have changed during its growth (Fig. 34).

Fig. 31
Combination
crystal (fluorite)

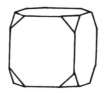

Fig. 32
Crystal habit
dominantly cubic

Fig. 33
Crystal habit domi-
nantly
octahedral

Pseudomorphs

Occasionally we encounter the confusing situation of one mineral taking the place of another as a result of chemical alteration, and preserving the shape of the earlier crystal. The simplest way in which this can happen is a change from simple weathering. In the phenomenon known as secondary enrichment, a downward leaching of metal (often copper) can remove iron, for example, and substitute copper in a crystal, which retains the original shape but is now a different mineral with a higher copper content. A common change resulting from rainwater weathering is that from pyrite (iron sulfide) to limonite (hydrous iron oxide). Garnets may be similarly altered, through a more complex change that occurs at greater depths: hot solutions beneath the crust alter the garnet to chlorite. Altered crystals are known as *pseudomorphs* (*pseudo* from "false," *morph* meaning "form").

There are several types of such pseudomorphs, and a rather complex series of names has been developed to specify the type of change in each case. Those first described are simple alterations. Crusts may form over unchanged crystals; some

Fig. 34 Phantom calcite showing habit change with later growth: a prismatic habit replaced an earlier scalenohedral termination

call these coatings "pseudomorphs by incrustation." Sometimes an entirely new substance may take the place of the old mineral, as in the serpentine casts of quartz from Bavaria, nephrite jade in Wyoming, and Cuban quartz alterations of fluorite.

Paramorphs are special cases in which there is no real change in composition, but the mineral has simply rearranged its atoms into a different configuration that no longer coincides with the original crystal outline. Rutile paramorphs after brookite are common at Magnet Cove, Arkansas.

More often we have a slight substitution of elements, as in the change of the blue copper carbonate (azurite) to the more stable green copper carbonate (malachite), or of hydrous gypsum replacing water-free anhydrite.

Lastly, we have a case of a mineral simply filling in a space left by the disappearance of the earlier mineral, as in the quartz casts of glauberite at West Paterson, New Jersey. They may appear to be angular objects, but they have no orientable shape since they are not regimented by crystal laws: they have preserved only the form of an empty space lined by crystals. Though often mistaken for crystal pseudomorphs themselves, they are really are only pseudo-pseudomorphs! A locality in Brazil has hundreds of angular agate fill-ins between calcite plates.

5

THE CHEMICAL CLASSIFICATION
OF MINERALS

Through science we have come to know that a sandy speck of stone can be divided and subdivided into tiny, uniform building blocks called atoms. Throughout the universe, atoms occur in 92 different forms, specific combinations of neutrons and protons surrounded by orbiting electrons, smaller-than-microscopic solar systemlike units we call elements. Few atoms exist as pure and single elements; most have joined with atoms of complementary elements to make soil, sand, and rocks. Though stable and solid as the building blocks of the crust on which we live, beneath us in the earth's furnace, hot elements still move about to join, rejoin, and separate. The weight of the earth's crust creates pressure and heat to melt rock into water-thin magma, a state in which elements are fugitive and mobile, free to make and quick to break any elemental liason. Convection stirs the still-molten magma below the crust, and at continent margins beds of sorted sediments worn off the continents are thrust below the earth's crust into a remelting environment. These processes assure a continuous redistribution of the elements throughout the planet.

All 92 elements are sparsely distributed through the earth's material; a teaspoon of sea water or a pebble of granite is said to have a few atoms, at least, of every one of the elements. But probably only a handful of elements make up better than 95 percent of the total, and the minerals they build combine into almost 99 percent of the surface rocks. Locally, rare elements enriched beyond their average abundance permit improbable element combinations when they volatilize or dissolve in hot liquids. As they are carried up to form overlying rocks, they separate out as rarer minerals and add new numbers to species brought near the surface and within human grasp.

Chapter 2 discussed the nature of minerals and what a mineral is: a naturally occurring chemical compound, one differing from others in its unique combination and pattern of elements. One of the most familiar of these chemical compounds, ordinary table salt, will serve as an example. Found in nature, table salt is a mineral known as halite; great beds of halite form when sea water or salt lakes dry up. Table salt contains but two elements, sodium and chlorine. Like calcium and potassium, sodium is an unstable metallic element, and chlorine is gaseous at normal temperatures. The refined and purified metal, sodium, is an oddly active silvery substance, impossibly quick to combine with something—even water—so the unprotected element cannot survive as a metal. Sodium can combine with many different elements, though not with all. Nor, fortunately, do we often find pure, poisonous chlorine gas, which is likewise ever in search of a companion. Both of these elements are always joined, together in salt, or separately with something else. Table salt is not manufactured but made from halite by freeing it of various impurities that commonly associate with it in nature.

Metallic elements customarily combine with nonmetallic elements to form what are known as salts. "Salt-forming" elements form acids with hydrogen, such as those used for testing. With hydrogen, chlorine forms hydrochloric acid, written in chemical shorthand as HCl. But in the acid, some metals will seize the chlorine and free the hydrogen; copper dissolves to a solution of copper chloride as hydrogen bubbles away. Consequently, aside from a few native elements (gold, silver, platinum, arsenic, antimony, and iron) that can exist in nature either because of their relative stability in a native state, or in unusual conditions, most minerals are salts of one sort or another.

Since there are now some 3,500 recognized minerals, of which almost 300 are described here, it is necessary to arrange them in some kind of classification. Several approaches to this goal of simplification have been tried. Despite attempts to arrange them by crystal structure without using composition as the traditional determining criterion, the chemical classification to be found here has best stood the test of time. With modifications and qualifications it is still generally accepted by professional mineralogists. The present sequence follows that used in the seventh edition of Dana's *Systems of Mineralogy,* which places the silicates last.

The predictable properties of significant elements in natural chemical compounds frequently give their compounds telltale characteristics, greatly simplifying the identification of the particular species. A true expert can usually guess the chemical group to which a mineral belongs from its associates in the field, and back endpaper) and from the obvious physical properties described below and in the group summaries introducing each chemical class in Part II of this book. In other cases it may be necessary to make a single test—perhaps a drop of acid, perhaps a chemical reaction—to distinguish two groups that sometimes look alike and occur together, as for example the carbonates and the sulfates. In general the following rules for the recognition of chemical classes will prevail.

The Elements

Native elements—elements existing free and uncombined—are not common. With a few exceptions they are not found as natural minerals. Among *nonmetallic* solid elements we have sulfur and two forms of carbon (diamond and graphite). These are fairly unmistakable, even though in appearance they have little in common. There are a few more elements, known as *semimetals*, which have some properties (such as chemical activity) but not others (such as malleability) in common with the metals. The *metals* are the most numerous of the native elements. It is their malleability—that is, the way they can be flattened and shaped by hammering—together with their metallic appearance, that makes them easy to recognize. A yellow native metal that can be flattened by hammering can only be gold.

Sulfides and Sulfosalts

Most of these look metallic and all but one or two are soft. The appearance of the few nonmetallic sulfides is so consistent that they should give little difficulty. In addition, they are usually associated with metallic-looking relatives in ore veins. Practically all are brittle, except for molybdenite; all the commoner metallic sulfide crystals shatter to a dark or black powder when struck by a hammer. All are heavy. The nonmetallics may have a white or light-hued powder (streak). Gold flattens, but "fool's gold" (pyrite) crushes.

Oxides and Hydroxides

The very unlike minerals that fall into this category can be further grouped by common characteristics. There are some that are original rock minerals which, since they are oxides, are very resistant to further change by the air's oxygen ("weathering"). The group includes some very heavy rock and ore-vein minerals; those free from water (anhydrous) are relatively hard. Water-free species are usually primary— formed directly from molten rocks, a melt, or from hot, watery (hydrothermal) solutions. Other oxides, those that form on the surface by weathering and many of which contain water, are more likely to be soft. Often they are red, brown, or black, the typical iron and manganese oxide colors. Because of their great variation in appearance and the inert nature of the primary oxides, minerals of the oxide group are among the more difficult ones to identify, resembling some silicates which also are hard.

Halides

This small group comprises compounds of a few metals with fluorine, chlorine, bromine, and iodine, a group known as the halogen elements. Many halides, such as rock salt, are water-soluble, so they occur as natural minerals only under special conditions. All are light in color when fresh (some of the silver and mercury compounds will darken on exposure to light), and many are transparent or translucent. None is hard. Like salt, several crystallize in the cubic system.

Carbonates

Most of these are translucent to transparent. None is hard; two major groups, the calcite group and dolomite group, grow rhombohedral crystals and have a pronounced rhombohedral cleavage (see Chapter 4). All are more or less readily soluble in acid, freeing bubbles of carbon dioxide as they dissolve.

Nitrates and Borates

Like the halides, most members of this group are very soluble in water and are soft. The conspicuous exceptions are a few remarkably hard, but very rare, anhydrous borates; several occur in pegmatites. Because of their high solubility, the common hydrous borates, sources of borax, are restricted to dry regions. They are mainly white, and many are transparent.

Sulfates

This group can be split into very soluble and rather insoluble ones. Many of the latter contain no water, so are called anhydrous. Both types commonly form in the upper and oxidized portions of sulfide veins. Anhydrous and rather insoluble sulfates such as barite, anhydrite, and celestite, have little or no economic value. (Compounds and minerals with little value in an ore vein are known as gangue.) Copper sulfates are typically colorful, usually greens and blues. All sulfates—even the less soluble—are soft and translucent, sometimes transparent. Many of the group are extremely stable and insoluble. Rapid formation of hydrous calcium sulfate (gypsum) needles in a nitric or hydrochloric acid solution indicates the presence of a sulfur atom, when we are testing unknown minerals.

Phosphates, Vanadates, and Arsenates
This group includes numerous secondary species generally taking the form of thin crusts or as scattered, often colorful, crystals. Many are chemically and physically somewhat alike. All are soft, and many are uncommon. Commonly bright-hued, most vanadates and arsenates develop in upper, oxidized zones of ore bodies, formed secondarily as alteration products from air and water attacks on earlier minerals. However, apatite (calcium phosphate), occurs as a primary mineral; it is disseminated in small crystals through the feldspars of many granites and considered the likely source of the phosphorus for a plethora of secondary phosphates. Most are fairly soluble in acid, and all can be dissolved after fusion with sodium carbonate. The solution then gives a good phosphorus test.

Tungstates, Molybdates, and Uranates
This catchall group of soft, heavy, and often colorful near-surface ores has few individual members. Each common one has a distinctive appearance and a characteristic paragenesis, making recognition easy. Like the previous group, many are secondary minerals (products of weathering).

Silicates
This group, which includes over half of all known minerals, is the most difficult to distinguish. Silicates are not easily or rapidly soluble in acid or in molten solvents (beads on platinum wire loop or hanging on a pencil lead). Some leave a silica ghost of the grain when the fragment is dissolved in a salt of phosphorus bead. Some silicates are very hard, infusible in a blowpipe flame and insoluble in the safer acids. Their specific gravity ranges from fairly light to intermedi-

ate, because silicon is a lighter element. Their luster is commonly glassy; most crush to a light or white powder even though the specimen appears black. They occur chiefly as components of rocks, as segregations in rocks, or as druses of crystals lining cavities in rocks. The greater number of the hard silicates are primary minerals—formed in magma or during powerful metamorphism, not softer secondary products from weathering. Secondary silicates are usually hydrous (contain water) and many of them will form a gel in a small quantity of hydrochloric acid, particularly after the blowpipe fusion that results when we heat hydrous silicates such as zeolites.

The Chemical Elements and Their Symbols

Aluminum . Al	Holmium. . Ho	Rhodium . . . Rh
Antimony. . . Sb	Hydrogen. . H	Rubidium. . . Rb
Argon . . . . . . A	Indium. . . . In	Ruthenium . Ru
Arsenic . . . . . As	Iodine. I	Samarium . . Sm
Barium . . . . . Ba	Iridium . . . Ir	Scandium. . . Sc
Beryllium . . . Be	Iron . . . . . . Fe	Selenium . . . Se
Bismuth . . . . Bi	Krypton . . . Kr	Silicon . . . . . Si
Boron . . . . . . B	Lanthanum La	Silver . . . . . . Ag
Bromine . . . . Br	Lead . . . . . . Pb	Sodium. . . . . Na
Cadmium . . . Cd	Lithium . . . Li	Strontium . . Sr
Calcium . . . . Ca	Lutecium. . Lu	Sulfur . . . . . . S
Carbon C	Magnesium Mg	Tantalum . . . Ta
Cerium . . . . . Ce	Manganese Mn	Tellurium. . . Te
Cesium . . . . . Cs	Mercury. . . Hg	Terbium . . . . Tb
Chlorine Cl	MolybdenumMo	Thallium . . . T
Chromium . . Cr	NeodymiumNd	Thulium. . . . Tm
Cobalt. . . . . . Co	Neon . . . . . Ne	Tin . . . . Sn
Columbium . Cb*	Nickel . . . . Ni	Titanium . . . Ti
Copper . . . . . Cu	Nitrogen . . N	Thorium. . . . Th
Dysprosium . Dy	Osmium . . Os	Tungsten . . . W
Erbium . . . . . Er	Oxygen . . . O	Uranium . . . U
Europium . . . Eu	Palladium . Pd	Vanadium. . . V
Fluorine . . . . F	Phosphorus P	Xenon. . . . . . Xe
Gadolinium . Gd	Platinum . . Pt	Ytterbium . . Yb
Gallium . . . . Ga	Potassium . K	Yttrium . . . . Y
Germanium . Ge	PraseodymiumPr	Zinc . . . . Zn
Gold . . . . Au	Radium . . . Ra	Zirconium . . Zr
Hafnium . . . . Hf	Radon . . . . Rn	
Helium . . . . . He	Rhenium . . Re	

*In Europe, columbium is known as niobium and its symbol is Nb.

Many of the element symbols are derived from Latin so their symbols are not as inappropriate as they might seem. Sodium is Na from *Natrium*, lead is Pb from *Plumbum*, and potassium is K from *Kalium*. Other elements retain symbols from other older names; tungsten is W from *Wolfram* (see Wolframite entry).

6

TESTS, TECHNIQUES, AND TIPS

When the first intelligent interest in metal ores and eye-catching rocks was taken by scientists, they searched for a way to recognize the useful crystals and nuggets they found in mines and placers. Handling look-alikes with superficial similarities, rocks sharing properties such as color, hardness, weight, and luster proved confusing. Early investigators relied upon responses to fire and acid, upon ease of scratching and resistance to blows. One could be distinguished from another if it melted, if a flake fused with ease into a small black ball, while its look-alike remained impervious to the torch.

Of necessity, since there was little else to call upon, only the simplest equipment was enlisted. The number of identifiable species in Agricola's time (A.D. 1556) was few, possibly in the hundreds; now we know of thousands. Today's technicians with the most sophisticated state-of-the-art equipment find a dozen species in what was once thought one. Unfortunately, the corollary is that their equipment requires investments of time, money, and education far beyond the interest or the resources of the amateur collector. No matter how primitively alchemical it seems today, time-honored observations of fusibility, solubility, streak, hardness, density, fracture, and cleavage are still paramount. The person who has everything except professional training, the serious amateur, is still in need of shrewdness. In the field, in the shop, in the cellar, the only recourse for self-reliant hobbyists are the same tools their ancestors used. The simple tests and techniques described here require only the basic equipment described in Chapter 1: blowpipes, hammers, platinum wire loops, Bunsen burners, hammers, chisels, and the like.

Field work and field identification still have their uses. Greenland and the frozen Antarctic are far from most elections, even the professionals need to look at properties, those alike and those unlike, as we always have.

Use common sense when carrying out any of the procedures described. Always wear eye protection; safety goggles are available from any science supply house or hardware store. Breaking rocks may send a rock splinter flying, and several mineral species fly apart when heated in a flame. Always keep any flammable materials well out of the reach of the Bunsen burner or alcohol lamp. Make sure you have a stable, flame-proof surface on which to work, and clear it of any flammable clutter before you begin. If you use a regular table—or your favorite workbench—as a testing site, clamp a sheet of Formica or plywood over the top to protect the surface. Keep the area well ventilated; smoke and fumes (such as the rotten-egg smell of hydrogen sulfide gas) are unpleasant as well as unhealthy.

Handle acids carefully. Even dilute acids can burn skin and eat holes in clothing, so wear old clothing and wash skin immediately with generous quantities of water if acid spills on you. If you follow the advice to always *add acid to water*, rather than the other way around, you will prevent drops of pure acid from splashing up on you (if something splashes, it will just be water, or water with only small amounts of acid). Store acids and other reagents out of the reach of children, and dispose of all chemicals responsibly.

Fusibility

These tests involve the blowpipe or the jeweler's torch. The ease with which different minerals melt, and the route that fusion follows, is the basis for the beginner's primary tests. Most of the sulfides melt easily; some will yield a malleable bead. Members of the other groups are usually less fusible and the results accordingly less satisfactory. The first test of an unknown sulfide is to place a grain in a pit on a charcoal block and, with the blowpipe, try to melt it. With the other groups (especially silicates, where melting is not ordained by inspection), a sometimes easier method is to hold a flake or a splinter in the flame with forceps, and see if even the thinnest edge will round.

With so many variably fusible minerals, a scale of fusibilities has been propounded which assigns a sequence of numbers, up to six for bronzite (a variety of pyroxene whose splinters barely melt on the edge in the hottest flame).

Many minerals could rate infinity, for they are quite infusible. Because the numbers are ill defined, only simple descriptive terms have been used in the text, such as "fuses easily," "with some difficulty," "with great difficulty," and so on. In fusing, a flake may melt quietly to a clear glass, or froth to a bubbly glass. It may turn black, and may become magnetic. For the minerals considered here, an attempt has been made to give descriptions of distinctive performances for any with an unusual or characteristic behavior. Sometimes the mineral may swell, or send up little horns like a Fourth of July "snake," or open out like leaves of a book (exfoliate). A few minerals glow (phosphoresce) in characteristic hues long before they are hot enough for incandescence. Sometimes the flame around the melted grain will be colored by the vapor of an element. This coloration can often be intensified if a drop of acid is added to the fused mass; a flash of color will be seen as the flame next hits the mass.

The technique is easily acquired. Readily fused minerals, particularly ones that are suspected of being sulfides, rest in a split-pea-sized depression dug in a charcoal block, where they are blasted with the blowpipe. Many of the sulfides will give off fumes and deposit colored rings around the grain. Details of the tests will be found in the mineral descriptions; the phenomena to be observed include such things as a garlic smell (arsenic) or, around the edge of the heated area, a yellow coating that turns white on cooling (zinc). Inhaling arsenic and mercury fumes involves some hazard; need one suggest that the blowpiper avoid any excess inhalation of such fumes?

Often a metal bead can be recovered by intensely heating the fused mineral grain in the reducing flame. Sometimes this can be obtained directly; at other times something to aid the separation—a flux (like sodium carbonate), which removes the sulfur and keeps the metal from oxidizing—must be added to the mineral grain. The glassy ball contains the metal, which is recovered by pounding up the fused mass, and the color of the metal (copper, lead, gold, or silver) will usually show what the metallic element was. The malleability or flattening of the bead by the pounding shows it to be a metal. When the presence of iron is suspected, test the bead for magnetism.

If the mineral tends to fly apart as the flame hits it (decrepitates) and will not stay on the charcoal, overcome that difficulty by crushing the mineral to a powder and then blowpiping the powder. It may sometimes be necessary to slightly moisten the powder with our ever-ready paste, saliva, to help the particles adhere. Sometimes a splinter can first be held in the Bunsen flame for a gentle heating to overcome the tendency to decrepitate, before putting the mineral on the charcoal for final melting. The grain, or powder, can also be heated in a Pyrex test tube, or closed tube, until it stops popping. Single crystal fragments are more likely to decrepitate than fine-grained masses of the same mineral. Crushing is best accomplished in the mortar; the most suitable type, often called a "diamond mortar," consists of a steel cup with a piston nested in a steel ring that fits closely into the hole. Hammer this with some force and the loose steel collar will prevent the mineral grains from flying off to limbo. An agate mortar and pestle will serve for more easily crushed grains; here, too, a small, loose metal collar surrounding the pestle and confining the grains as they break is recommended.

In some cases our source of heat is insufficient, and fusion eludes us. For zinc we can still make tests on roasted fragments. Sphalerite, for example, does not fuse, but if touched with a cobalt nitrate solution after heating and heated again, it will develop a dusty greenish color that is indicative of the zinc it contains.

Flame Tests

Flame tests are indirect companions of the melting tests, for blowpipe flame colorations are often seen during the fusion of such minerals as the copper sulfides. An added drop of acid will free a brief bright flash of color. The usual flame-test colors are better seen in other ways. The most frequent procedure is to insert the platinum wire in a powder of the unknown mineral that has been moistened with nitric acid. Introduce this carefully at the edge of the Bunsen flame, where it will flare in a distinctive skyrocket color flash. Copper colors the flame blue-green, strontium red, calcium orange-red, potassium light violet, lithium red, and so on (see Table 1, p. 89). Concentrated solutions of the minerals in acid into which the platinum wire is dipped will also give the typical flame colors.

There are two hazards for the tester in these pyrotechnics. Arsenic in a mineral reacts with the platinum of the wire to make a brittle compound. If there is any possibility that arsenic is present, the unknown grain should be heated for a long time by the blowpipe ("roasted") before crushing it for use on the platinum wire (arsenic readily volatilizes as white fumes). Secondly, the sodium in the salts melted in bead tests is very persistent on the wire, and for minutes gives a yellow flame. Burn it for a time, until the yellow color disappears. It may be in the mineral, too, and can mask the color of another element present. (Blue filter glasses cancel out the yellow sodium light and transmit the other colors, but their value hangs on a user's experience.) Flame colors are best observed in low light.

Bead Tests

These are made with a platinum wire bent at the end into a small loop. Small containers with borax ($Na_2B_4O_7 \cdot 10H_2O$), salt of phosphorus (microcosmic salt, $HNaNH_4PO_4 \cdot 4H_2O$), sodium fluoride (NaF), or lithium fluoride (LiF) are most convenient. The wire is heated in the flame until red and dipped, still hot, into the reagent. Some powder clings to the wire, which is then returned to the flame to melt the white powder to a clear glass bead. It may be necessary to return to the powder well several times before the loop is filled out into a plump bead. Borax swells into writhing "worms" as it melts, finally shrinking to almost nothing as it clears to glass.

The unknown mineral, or the residue of a bead fused on the charcoal, is crushed in the steel mortar and spilled out onto a convenient, flat, nonflammable surface. The glowing liquid in the loop is pressed onto one or two of the grains, which cling to it, and is returned to a flame (a blowpipe is usually the most efficient method of heating). As the bead melts again, glowing grains dissolve in the clear red liquid; swirling and twisting as in a glass marble, they soon disappear. On cooling, if enough of the mineral has been added and if it contains an element that gives a good color, a beautifully tinted bead will be seen.

Often the bead hue depends upon the location of the bead in the flame during the heating; it may be held either in the oxidizing tip or the reducing basal region. Both hues should be observed. A few minutes of reheating in one or the other part of the flame is enough to reverse the oxidized or reduced state of the metal.

As usual, a few cautions should be observed. We have noted before that if there is any possibility of arsenic being present the mineral should be thoroughly heated on the charcoal to drive out the last arsenic traces before it is placed on the platinum wire. It is easy to get too much of the unknown powder in the bead and end with a black mass. This can be corrected by crushing the oversaturated, opaque bead on the mortar's edge and introducing a small fragment into a new bead. This usually reduces the concentration down to a point where the bead is transparent and colored. The overdarkened bead can also be removed from the wire loop by heating it red-hot and quickly whipping it off onto the table top. The hot bead will burn anything it strikes, so be careful not to let it fall on anything that can be damaged. The residue left on the wire will probably tint a new bead enough to give a good test. When the test is finished, the wire can be cleaned by flipping it off in the same way. Ideal cleaning results from producing successive fresh beads until they come out completely colorless. The platinum wire used for the beads should probably be restricted to bead tests without trying to use it also in flame tests, since the sodium in the borax and salt of phosphorus is very persistent and is difficult to remove completely from the wire. So it is better to have two wires for the different tests. Bead hues are given in Tables 2 and 3 (pp. 90–91).

Often silicates only partially dissolve in the salt of phosphorus, leaving within a ghostly outline of their original grain. A silica ghost is a good indication of the silicate group.

Tube Tests

Open and closed glass tubes made from slender hollow glass rods have some, but not great, use in blowpiping, mainly in testing the sulfides. Discoveries depend upon the deposition of sublimed oxides or of the separated films of the unknown metals or compounds on higher, cooler walls of the container. Hold some grains in the open tube over the flame at a slight slant that permits the passage of a current of air over the grain being tested. Coatings of sublimates will be deposited on the glass above the mineral grains in cooler areas, and in some cases several successive bands of increasingly volatile compounds can be observed. The diameter of the glass tubing used for open tubes may very profitably be somewhat greater than that of the closed tubes, perhaps by $5/16$ in. (8–9 mm) to ensure a good current of air. Pyrex glass is useful but not essential; glass-melting heat is not needed.

Open-tube heating should not be hastened, or the air supply may be insufficient and the films obtained would resemble those of the closed tube.

The technique of closed-tube testing is similar, though a different type of sublimate is usually obtained. Water drops may indicate a hydrous mineral. Etching of the glass may suggest the presence of fluorine. If moisture is sought, it is wise first to heat the tube enough to dry out the air that is in it before looking for water in the mineral. The typical sublimates of the open and closed tube are listed in Tables 4 and 5 (p. 92).

Wet Tests in Test Tubes

As a last resort it sometimes becomes necessary to dissolve some of the unknown fragments, or some of the charcoal block residue, in an acid, then try to identify some elements (qualitative analysis). A few reactions are critical, and chemical tests may be essential with minerals for which blowpipe tests will not work. The titanium in ilmenite, for example, must be identified by first dissolving the mineral on the charcoal block in a slaggy fusion of sodium carbonate, and then dissolving the mixture in concentrated hydrochloric acid. When this solution is boiled with zinc or tin (a small sliver of the metal dropped in the test tube will do), the solution turns blue-violet when titanium is present. Copper gives acid solutions a greenish color, which, on the addition of ammonia, turn blue. Silver in nitric acid solutions precipitates in a curdy white mass if hydrochloric acid is added. When sulfur is suspected, the addition of a few drops of a solution of calcite dissolved in hydrochloric acid to the nitric acid solution, induces small needles of hydrous calcium sulfate (gypsum in nature). The addition of a grain of potassium iodide to a weak nitric acid solution of a lead mineral will cause sparkling yellow flakes to form. Phosphorus and arsenic may also show up as amorphous yellow grains, but the shiny spangles of the lead salt are unmistakable. These and other special tests will be found under the appropriate mineral descriptions.

Fluorescence and Phosphorescence

A glow of visible light during a bombardment of invisible rays such as x-rays and ultraviolet light (fluorescence) or glowing in the dark after exposure to a source of such invisible radiation or to sunlight (phosphorescence) are mineral properties that have long intrigued mineral collectors. Brightly glowing colorful fluorescence is a property with which television viewers are quite familiar. Development of ultraviolet sources has resulted in special fluorescence displays in many museums and in fluorescence becoming a spectacular toy of the amateur. It had little practical application until ultraviolet was used in prospecting for scheelite, a blue-fluorescing ore of tungsten. Many other minerals are fluorescent and phosphorescent, but usually this property is not consistent enough for it to have much value in actual testing.

Nonetheless, the ultraviolet light can in some cases be of real testing value, with fluorescence first developing after roasting or blowpiping of an earlier unresponsive specimen. Further work along these lines should be done; the amateur collector has an opportunity here to make a real contribution to mineral-testing techniques by investigating fluorescence in a serious way along the lines suggested throughout the mineral descriptions. Much celestite is naturally fluorescent yellow-green; it was found by experiment that even unresponsive celestite became brilliantly fluorescent and phosphorescent yellow-green after roasting. Barite is only occasionally fluorescent, but all barite tested was found to be fluorescent yellow-orange after roasting. Hence, with the two similar minerals we have only to briefly roast an edge in the flame until red hot, allow it to cool, and observe, in ultraviolet. The yellow-green one will be celestite, the yellow-orange one barite. Several tests of this type are included in the mineral descriptions.

The serious mineral collector should by all means purchase one or two ultraviolet lights. Small, inexpensive, battery-operated pocket ones are available. The ultraviolet spectrum is a long one, ranging from light with wavelength just beyond the wavelength of visible light to very short rays near the x-ray end of the light spectrum. Different sources of ultraviolet light produce either shortwave (SW) ultraviolet or longwave (LW) ultraviolet, with both types available in the format mentioned above. Some minerals respond to one or the other; some respond to both long- and shortwave ultraviolet light, with differing hues. Sicilian aragonite accompanying sulfur, for instance, is a beautiful brilliant pink under the longwave ultraviolet, with a weak greenish phosphorescence persisting after the exposure; it is a medium-intensity greenish white with a bright greenish white phosphorescence under and after the shortwave ultraviolet light. Scheelite is negative under longwave ultraviolet and bright blue under shortwave.

Shortwave ultraviolet light is said to have a wavelength of about 2500 angstrom units (or Å, a measure of wavelength of light: 6700 angstrom units is the wavelength of red light; around 4300 angstrom units is the wavelength of visible violet light). Shortwave ultraviolet is best produced by a mercury-vapor light, operating in an evacuated fused-quartz tube and covered by a filter that shuts out the visible light. Longwave ultraviolet lights, 3000 to 4000 angstrom units, are available in many forms, though the very cheapest, like the "black lights" (photoflood bulbs in a deep purple filter glass) have little value except for very fluorescent minerals such as some of the uranium compounds.

A Suggested Testing Procedure

The substance of mineralogy occurs throughout the universe. Aside from those with a specific regional emphasis, any mineralogical text is international, even intergalactic, in scope. The broad laws of physics and chemistry are international; under like geological conditions, the same compounds result. So, instead of the hundreds of thousands of species with which the entomologist must concern himself, the mineral collector has only about 3,500 natural compounds, and of these fewer than 200 can be considered at all common. For the average collector with a book listing only common minerals and likely finds, the problem simmers down to which one of 200 possibilities is any particular specimen. The environment and ordinary physical description (color, hardness, and crystal shape) eliminate nine-tenths of what is left, so in reality there are only half a dozen or fewer likelihoods. Beginning collectors really do not want to face 600 choices; in their lifetimes, two-thirds of them will never come to to their attention, much less their hammer.

Intelligent observation followed by a simple test or two is often sufficient for a likely guess. Since the real problem is only that of separating one out of two or three possibles, instead of one from 3,500, it is still most practical to adapt grandfather's simple tests, such as the addition of a drop of cobalt nitrate to the surface of a melted mass, an activity not usually suggested in current books for beginners.

For more advanced collectors, identification by sight of the common minerals becomes a matter of habit. Collectors who reach this stage are ready for one of the more complete books listed in the Bibliography at the back of this Field Guide.

Since a professional cannot, the collector should not expect to be able to identify by observation every specimen. In the first place, there are twenty times as many known minerals as are included here. Inevitably even a complete beginner will stumble on some of the rarities when collecting at a rich locality. For these occasions he should have no hesitation about enlisting the aid of an expert. In the second place, all minerals are not under every circumstance identifiable by simple means. The botanist does not try to identify new plants without a bloom. The mineral collector must recognize that mineralogy, too, has limitations. A poor, uncrystallized grain or rock may not be identifiable when it reveals few of its physical properties. (Nor has such an ill-defined specimen any merit in a collection, unless one begins to truly specialize and wishes, for example, to collect all possible mineral species from a particular locality.)

Let us assume, then, that you have been out collecting somewhere and have secured an attractive specimen that seems worth adding to your collection. You are uncertain of its identity. How can you go about finding out what it is with the help offered in this book?

Many of the specimens you find will be crystallized. After you have worked with minerals for a while you will come to know crystals so well that you will be able to orient them and recognize their crystal system with very little trouble. In fact, with sophistication, in many cases you will not regard a specimen as worth preserving unless it exhibits well-formed, distinctive crystals.

Even beginning collectors should note in what type of deposit they have been collecting—a limestone quarry, bands of schist or gneiss in a road cut, near a volcano, a pegmatite, a metal mine, or a granite quarry. Certain mineral groups are more likely found in one type of deposit than another. In biology we speak of ecology; in mineralogy we call it paragenesis, which refers to the geological conditions in which a mineral formed and its associated species. If there is any doubt of this, one has only to read over the first entry under each mineral species: **Environment**. Even when you have not collected the specimen yourself, for all but loose crystals with no matrix, you can often guess by the associated minerals from what kind of formation it comes. This bonus of information provided by the associated species makes matrix specimens much more valuable scientifically than orphan crystals, no matter how lovely their sparkle.

The first step, then, is to look at the specimen carefully, and to determine what you can of its environment Next, if possible, determine its crystal system. You will incidentally observe other physical properties such as color, luster, cleavage, and (should the unknown constitute the major part of the specimen) its specific gravity (or, loosely, its "heft").

The next step is to make some tests: commencing with the least destructive and the simplest, one perhaps that gives the chemical class as readily as possible. Probably the very first test you will want to make is for hardness, trying the specimen with a knife to see whether it can be scratched. If it cannot be scratched you might immediately assign it as most likely a silicate; if it can be scratched it probably belongs to one of the other groups. (There are a few hard oxides and other compounds, but they are comparatively few and you will soon come to know them.)

If you can scratch it, you note whether or not there is a good cleavage. If there is a good rhombohedral cleavage, or something that looks as if it might be rhombohedral, you should suspect a carbonate and try the mineral with a drop of hydrochloric acid (cold first, then warmed). When this test is positive (releasing bubbles), you can easily run down the individual mineral from the carbonate mineral descriptions in the book. If it is negative, you should suspect a sulfate first and make the blowpipe tests (and test for resultant fluorescence if you have an ultraviolet light) and other tests suggested previously in this chapter. If it is highly colored, look among the phosphates and arsenates. If it is metallic in luster, look for it among the sulfides. To speed your identifications, memorize the outstanding characteristics of each mineral group that you find summarized in Chapters 5 and 6 under the group names and in introductory group descriptions throughout Part II.

If the mineral is too hard to scratch, or can be scratched only with difficulty, you have a hard oxide or a silicate. The hard oxides are few in number and are easily recognized by the crystals, which are usually present. If it is a silicate, the problem is much more difficult, for many silicates do not fuse readily, and the elements usually contained in them—calcium, magnesium, iron, potassium, sodium, and others—often give no simple chemical or blowpipe reactions. Fusion, or attempted fusion on charcoal, is recommended. Many of your final determinations will be made by a process of elimination; you will just have to try tests for suspected minerals suggested under the subheading **Tests** in the mineral descriptions, and then see how they work out.

The well-qualified amateur whose background includes a chemical course can work out an analytical procedure that will enable almost any mineral to be run down. Once the material is put into solution the analytical procedure is much like that followed in a good chemistry course in high school. O. C. Smith's *Identification and Qualitative Chemical Analysis of Minerals* (out of print, but look for one second-hand) gives an excellent analytical procedure, though this type of mineral identification is usually a later step in the study of minerals. It must be confessed that most mineral identification is done by sight, experience, reading, examination of collections of others, and one or two simple and definitive tests; perhaps the hardness, or streak test, or fluorescence gives the answer. Running a mineral down by a long series of tests, like the identification of a plant by botanical keys, is difficult, time-consuming, and sometimes successful. But such a procedure is not necessary for the collector who has had a little experience.

Table 1: Flame Tests

Flame Coloration or Flash	Element
Violet red	strontium
Bright red	lithium
Orange-red	calcium
Yellow-orange	sodium
Yellow-green	barium
Green	boron
Emerald green (intense)	copper
Bluish green (pale)	phosphorus
Greenish blue	antimony
Bluish white	arsenic
Blue	tellurium
Violet	potassium

Table 2: Borax Bead Tests

Oxidizing Flame Color		Reducing Flame Color		Element
Hot	*Cold*	*Hot*	*Cold*	
pale yellow	colorless to white	brown	brown to black	molybdenum
pale yellow	colorless to white	gray or yellow	brownish	titanium
yellow to orange	yellow to brown	pale green	green	uranium (fluorescent)
yellow	green	green	green	chromium
yellow	green	brown to gray-green	yellow to green	vanadium
green	blue	colorless to green	opaque red-brown	copper
blue	blue	blue	blue	cobalt
yellow to orange	greenish to brown	bottle green	paler bottle green	iron
violet	reddish brown	opaque gray	opaque gray	nickel
violet	reddish violet	colorless	colorless	manganese

Table 3: Salt of Phosphorus Bead Tests

Oxidizing Flame Color		Reducing Flame Color		Element
Hot	*Cold*	*Hot*	*Cold*	
yellowish to green	colorless	dirty green	yellow-green	molybdenum
pale yellow	colorless	yellow	pale violet	titanium
yellow	yellow-green	light gray-green	green	uranium (fluorescent)
reddish to gray-green	yellowish green to green	red to gray-green	green	chromium
yellow	greenish yellow	brown to gray-green	green	vanadium
dark green	greenish blue	brownish green	opaque red	copper
blue	blue	blue	blue	cobalt
yellow to brown-red	brownish yellow	red or yellow to green-yellow	pale violet	iron
reddish to brown-red	yellow to reddish yellow	reddish to brownish red	yellow to reddish yellow	nickel
pale yellow	colorless	greenish to dirty blue	greenish blue	tungsten
insoluble white ghost in clear bead				silica

Table 4: Open-Tube Tests

Sublimate(s)	Gases	Element
white powder (yellowish when hot)	dense white fumes	antimony
white minute sparkling crystals	garlic odor	arsenic
brown (hot) and yellow (cold)		bismuth (oxide)
white powder that fuses to yellow drops, nonvolatile		bismuth (sulfide)
white powder that fuses to yellow drops		lead
silver droplets (or gray film) (rub with needle to make into droplets)		mercury
network of slender crystals, yellow (hot) and white (cold)		molybdenum
white powder that fuses to yellow drops		tellurium

Table 5: Closed-Tube Tests

Sublimate(s)	Element (compound)
white needle crystals that will melt	antimony oxide
black (hot) and reddish brown (cold) film	antimony sulfide and sulfosalt
brilliant black; gray and crystalline at lower end	arsenic: metal and arsenides
white, crystalline	arsenic oxide
deep red to black liquid (hot); reddish yellow solid (cold)	arsenic sulfides and sulfosaslts
black, turning red when rubbed	mercury sulfide
water drops on cool part	hydrous mineral

Table 6: Fusibility

Typical Minerals	Standard Scale	Behavior	Description in Mineral Text Section
Stibnite	1	melts easily in any flame	fuses very readily
Natrolite Chalcopyrite	2	melt in any flame	fuse easily
Almandine	3	melts with difficulty in alcohol flame	fuses
Actinolite	4	no fusion in alcohol flame, thin splinters melt to globule in gas flame	fuses with some difficulty
Orthoclase	5	gas flame rounds thin edges	almost infusible
Bronzite	6	gas flame barely rounds thinngest edges	melts only on thinnest edges in gas flame
Topaz	infusible	no rounding	infusible

PART II
MINERAL DESCRIPTIONS

MINERAL DESCRIPTIONS

■ ELEMENTS

Few elements are found in their uncombined or pure state. Usually there are too many other unattached or promiscuous elements in the magma, solution, or vapor at the time of their formation with which they can combine. Most of the elements found in a "native" state either do not combine with oxygen (to form oxides) or do so only at high temperatures. They form three major groups: the metals, the semimetals, and nonmetals.

◆ METALS

The metals are most readily identified by their color and malleability (which means that they can be deformed by pounding without crumbling).

GOLD   Au   Cubic — hexoctahedral $\frac{4}{m}\,\overline{3}\,\frac{2}{m}$ **Pl. 13**

Environment: In quartz veins and in stream deposits. **Crystal description:** Most often in octahedral crystals, with or without other faces. However, clusters of parallel growths distorted into feathery leaves, wires, or thin plates are common. **Physical properties:** Rich yellow to silvery yellow. *Luster* metallic; *hardness* $2\frac{1}{2}$–3; *specific gravity* 19.3. Very malleable and ductile. **Composition:** Gold, usually alloyed with silver. The higher the silver content, the paler the color. **Tests:** Fuses readily on charcoal, drawing into golden button. Pure gold is soluble in aqua regia (1 part concentrated nitric acid to 1 part concentrated hydrochloric acid); silver-rich gold is soluble in other acids.
Distinguishing characteristics: Confused with metal sulfides,

particularly pyrite ("fool's gold"), but distinguished from them by softness and malleability. Microscopic, soft brown mica flakes, which may be seen in stream beds or in mica schist, are distinguished by the blowpipe test or by simply crushing the mica plates with a needle.

Occurrence: The inertness of gold and its high density causes it to concentrate in streambeds, either in small flakes or in larger nuggets, from which it may be recovered by panning. It is of very wide occurrence, originating most often in quartz or sulfide veins, from which it is freed by the destruction of the enclosing rock in the weathering process. Nuggets are more rounded the farther they have traveled from their source. Mines in quartz veins often produce rich specimens of the quartz-gold mixture, "picture rock." Sometimes cavities yield well-crystallized pieces. Gold residues are also found in brown iron-stained rock, freed from associated sulfides that have oxidized, dissolved, or weathered away. Some gold deposits can be worked profitably even when yielding only a few dollars in gold to the ton. Hence, any specimen showing visible gold can be regarded as rich. Beautifully crystallized gold specimens have been found all over the world. California, Australia, and Hungary are famous for specimens, but in all likelihood some of the best were smelted for their metal; when intrinsic values are high it is rare to find minerals in their natural state, be they metal or gemstones. A revival of gold mining has made fine California specimens again available. However, more gold is recovered from ores so low in grade that no metal is discernible; the minute specks are leached from ore piles with a cyanide solution and then recovered from the solution.

SILVER Ag Cubic — hexoctahedral $\frac{4}{m} \overline{3} \frac{2}{m}$ **Pl. 13**

Environment: In ore veins. **Crystal description:** In cubic or octahedral crystals, but either is uncommon; more often it forms long contorted wires. However, the cubic Kongsberg (Norway) crystals—among the best—may be pseudomorphs formed from the sulfide mineral argentite (acanthite at room temperature). **Physical properties:** Fresh surface bright white, usually blackened by tarnish. *Luster* metallic; *hardness* $2\frac{1}{2}$–3; *specific gravity* 10.0–11.0. Very malleable and ductile. **Composition:** Silver, usually fairly pure. **Tests:** Pure silver fuses readily on charcoal to a white button. Impurities tend to make melting more difficult. Dissolves in nitric acid, producing a white curdy precipitate on the addition of hydrochloric acid.

Distinguishing characteristics: No other white malleable metal, soluble in acid, is likely to be encountered in its native state. Lead is softer and grayer; platinum is harder and insoluble; the silvery sulfides are brittle.

Occurrence: In Mexico and Norway in veins with calcite and silver sulfides; often in wires and in good crystals. In n. Canada (Great Bear Lake) and Czechoslovakia with uranium ores (pitchblende). In Michigan in pure masses appended to copper sheets and forming aggregates known as "half-breeds." Native silver is not an important source of silver; lead and silver minerals with which it is commonly associated, as at Cobalt, Ontario, and in Idaho, are richer in silver. Lead ores that formed at higher temperatures than the sedimentary deposits of the Mississippi Valley are more likely to contain significant percentages of silver.

COPPER   Cu   Cubic — hexoctahedral $\frac{4}{m}\,\overline{3}\,\frac{2}{m}$ **Pl. 13**

Environment: In the upper levels of copper sulfide veins and in some types of volcanic rock. **Crystal description:** Usually in distorted, often rounded, complex crystals, with cubes, dodecahedrons, and octahedrons predominant. Often in hackly masses (Michigan) and in sheets without recognizable crystal forms. **Physical properties:** Copper color. *Luster* metallic; *hardness* $2\frac{1}{2}$–3; *specific gravity* 8.9. Malleable and ductile. **Composition:** Fairly pure as a rule, often alloyed with small amounts of silver, arsenic, iron, etc. **Tests:** Small bits fuse on charcoal to black-coated copper button; malleable, soluble in acids, giving greenish solutions. Colors flame blue-green.

Distinguishing characteristics: Almost inescapable green and blue stains on rock outcrops, known as "copper blooms," are a guide to deposits of copper and its associated minerals. The malleability and the color are distinguishing characteristics.

Occurrence: Since weathering processes free copper from its primary ore, chalcopyrite ($CuFeS_2$), it is likely to be found in the cap rock (the gossan) of copper-bearing sulfide veins, particularly in arid climates. Native copper is also found in ancient lava flows, where iron and oxygen have robbed the magma of sulfur. It is abundant in this form in Michigan's Upper Peninsula, where copper has been deposited in a thick series of flows, and this is the only economic source where all the copper is in the native state. Great masses found in these deposits were hard to remove because of their size and the difficulty of breaking them up. Nuggets from this deposit carried south by the glacier were scattered across the north-central states and were manufactured by the Indians into copper artifacts. Native copper was once found in Chessy, France, and Cornwall, England. Today it is abundant in some of the Arizona mines still working in the upper levels, like Morenci and Ajo. Surprisingly, it is not a major mineral in Chile, though that country contains rich sources of the metal.

MERCURY Hg Hexagonal — rhombohedral $\overline{3}$ **Pl. 13**
Environment: Often in or close to volcanic regions, in low-temperature veins. **Crystal description:** Mercury is the only metal that is liquid at normal temperatures. It does not become solid until the temperature falls to $^-40°F$ (which equals $^-40°C$). Hence, we find it in nature only in the form of liquid metallic drops or as thin metallic films on small cavities and surfaces of rocks. **Physical properties:** Silvery white. *Luster* metallic; *specific gravity* 13.6. Liquid, whence the name "quicksilver." **Composition:** Mercury, sometimes with a little silver. Poisonous and instantly amalgamates with gold, so caution is recommended in any utilization or testing. Avoid breathing any fumes. **Tests:** Volatilizes (disappears as fumes) under a blowpipe; dissolves in nitric acid.
Distinguishing characteristics: The liquid droplets cannot be confused with anything else. The silvery films are more confusing but can easily be burned off with a blowpipe. The usual association with cinnabar (HgS) helps in identification.
Occurrence: Native mercury is almost invariably associated with the red sulfide of mercury, cinnabar. It is often found in cavities and cracks in cinnabar-impregnated rocks and sometimes forms as a result of the weathering of cinnabar, which leaves little holes lined with drops and films of mercury. Mercury and cinnabar will be found in rocks of regions where there has been some volcanic or hot-spring activity, though the deposits may lie some distance from any obvious source.
Remarks: Found in the U.S. in California, Oregon, Texas, and Arkansas. The most notable occurrences are the Almadén (Spain) and the Idrija, in the former Yugoslavia, cinnabar mines. It is never an ore alone, but often enriches the mercury sulfide ores.

PLATINUM Pt Cubic — hexoctahedral $\frac{4}{m}\overline{3}\frac{2}{m}$ **Pl. 13**

Environment: Originally a placer mineral in grains and nuggets in sands and gravels. Now mined from a mafic rock in South Africa and one of the sought-after metals in the Sud-

bury, Ontario, nickel complex, where tiny crystals of the arsenide sperrylite $(PtAs_2)$ are found. **Crystal description:** Crystals (octahedrons and cubes) are rare. Usually it is found in the form of thin scales or grains. **Physical properties:** Light gray-white. *Luster* metallic; *hardness* 4–4$\frac{1}{2}$; *specific gravity* 14.0–19.0 (the pure metal is 21.5); *fracture* hackly; *cleavage* none. Malleable and ductile; sometimes magnetic. **Composition:** Usually very impure, most commonly mixed with iron, also alloyed with several members of its chemical group: iridium, osmium, rhodium, and palladium (hence the wide range in specific gravity). **Tests:** The high gravity, color, and malleability are characteristic, coupled with its infusibility and its insolubility in acid.
Distinguishing characteristics: Few substances will be confused with it. The magnetism of the iron-rich nuggets would confuse the finder if it were not for platinum's high gravity, its malleability, and insolubility.
Occurrence: Once common as nuggets in placer deposits, sometimes associated with gold. Its primary occurrence is with other metal ores associated with basic igneous rocks; commonly in olivine-rich rocks known as dunites, olivine pyroxenites, or gabbros. The best crystals have come from the Urals, in slightly waterworn shapes. Colombia and Alaska are other important placer sources.
Remarks: A very important metal for laboratory use because of its insolubility and high melting point, as in gemstone synthesis. Valued for its catalytic characteristic of promoting chemical reactions without entering into the reaction itself. It is used in this way in the manufacture of sulfuric acid and in automobile antipollution devices. It also finds use in jewelry, though it is much harder to work than white gold.

IRON Fe Cubic — hexoctahedral $\frac{4}{m}\overline{3}\frac{2}{m}$ **Pl. 13**

Environment: In meteorites and rarely in basalt. **Crystal description:** Practically unknown in crystals, and rare except in meteorites. Sometimes found in large masses in basalt or smaller disseminated grains, rarely in placers in nuggets (as josephinite, a nickel-iron alloy). **Physical properties:** Steel gray. *Luster* metallic; *hardness* 4–5; *specific gravity* 7.3–7.8; *fracture* hackly; *cleavage* cubic, also has distinct partings parallel to the cube and dodecahedron. Magnetic. **Composition:** Iron, usually with some nickel. In meteorites nickel may be abundant. **Tests:** Magnetic, easily soluble in acids with rusty residue on evaporation.
Distinguishing characteristics: Native iron is so rare that its few

sources are well known, one in Germany, and one on an island in the Arctic. Masses of iron from slag are often mistaken for meteorites. A suspected meteorite should be tested for nickel (see millerite, p. 117), after the presence of iron has been shown by a magnet or a compass. A polished surface is then acid-etched to bring out a crystal pattern, known as Widmanstaetten lines, for final confirmation.

Occurrence: Because of its easy oxidation (rust), native iron is naturally most uncommon. It has been found in disseminated grains in a basalt in Bühl, northwest of Kassel, Germany, and in masses of considerable size once thought to be meteorites at Disko I., Greenland. Iron-nickel alloy nuggets are found in gold placers in New Zealand, Oregon, and British Columbia. Native iron is found in meteorites, which range from pure metal to stone with small percentages of metal. The nickel content roughly determines the crystal texture and the pattern that is brought out by etching with dilute nitric acid.

Remarks: Tremendous numbers of meteorites fall, though most burn up in the sky. Few reach the earth, and fewer yet are found. Fewer in number, iron meteorites are more often recognized than the stones. There is usually a crust on a fresh meteorite from the dissipation of heat on the surface during its fall. In their passage through the air, meteorites are never actually melted; they never contain cavities, enclose pebbles, or make casts of objects they hit. They are most often confused with concretions of various sorts, with pyrite balls, and with corroded rocks; but none of these is ever magnetic.

◆ SEMIMETALS

This small group of native elements is distinguished from the true metals because its members are not malleable and ductile like the metals. It includes, among other elements, arsenic, antimony, and bismuth.

ARSENIC   As   Hexagonal — scalenohedral $\overline{3}\,\dfrac{2}{m}$ **Pl. 14**

Environment: In ore veins in crystalline rocks. **Crystal description:** Crystals, which are almost unknown, are rhombohedrons resembling cubes. The commonest appearance is in rounded mammillary or botryoidal crusts or granular masses. **Physical properties:** White. *Luster* metallic; *hardness* $3^1/_2$;

specific gravity 5.7; *fracture* uneven; *cleavage* basal (rarely seen, since crystals are rare). Brittle. **Composition:** Arsenic, usually relatively pure, sometimes with a little antimony. **Tests:** It is tin-white in color, brittle, and volatilizes completely under the blowpipe, giving off a garlic odor and not melting.

Distinguishing characteristics: Can be confused with antimony (which melts) and with the antimony-arsenic compound allemontite (which gives off white arsenic fumes and forms a metallic globule that takes fire and burns). The color and total volatilization distinguish it from most other similar substances.

Occurrence: In metal ore veins, but not common. Most collection specimens are ancient botryoidal crusts from Saxony. In France it has been found at Sainte-Marie-aux-Mines, Alsace. It has been found in masses in Arizona. Small balls of crystals are found in a decomposed rhyolite in the Akadani Mine, Fukui Prefecture, s. Honshu, Japan. Allemontite (AsSb) occurs in similar veins and brittle, white, metallic grains have been found in pegmatites.

TELLURIUM Te   Pl. 14

Hexagonal — Trigonal trapezohedral   3 2

Environment: Medium-temperature veins, often associated with the gold tellurides, though sometimes alone. **Crystal description:** Massive, often in large segregations with columnar structure, occasionally in free-growing slender crystals. **Physical properties:** Tin-white. *Luster* metallic; *hardness* 2–2$\frac{1}{2}$; *specific gravity* 6.1–6.3; *fracture* uneven; *cleavage* prismatic good, basal poor. Brittle. **Composition:** Native tellurium, sometimes with a little selenium, iron, and, in telluride occurrences, gold and silver. **Tests:** Volatilizes rapidly and completely on charcoal under blowpipe flame, with a light blue flame coloration, unlike copper's blue-green.

Distinguishing characteristics: Its behavior on the charcoal is distinctive; sylvanite would leave a golden bead.

Occurrence: Masses and veins of tellurium have been found in n. Mexico, where it has altered to form, among other minerals, poughite (yellow, crumbly), $Fe_2(TeO_3)2(SO_4)\cdot3H_2O$; and in Lincoln Co., Nevada. The best American crystals are from Colorado, where tellurium and tellurides has been found at Cripple Creek in Teller Co. and in several other Colorado gold-mining areas.

◆ NONMETALS

SULFUR S Orthorhombic — bipyramidal $\frac{2}{m}\frac{2}{m}\frac{2}{m}$ **Pl. 14**

Environment: Associated worldwide with volcanic rocks, though the major commercially developed deposits are in sedimentary formations having been freed through the breakdown of sulfates such as gypsum or freed from H_2S. **Crystal description:** All low-temperature natural crystals are orthorhombic. Remelted sulfur crystallizes in an unstable structure in the monoclinic system. Well-formed, translucent orthorhombic crystals are common in the developed sedimentary occurrences, usually as steep bipyramids, though sometimes tabular. Irregular cavernous and skeletal crystals are characteristic of the volcanic localities, where sulfur often sublimates from escaping volatile compounds, usually at temperatures lower than those condensing sal ammoniac and the like. Often in crusts without individualized crystals. **Physical properties:** Light yellow when pure, sometimes amber when stained with hydrocarbons; some slag-like volcanic specimens are reddish from selenium contamination or grayish from arsenic contamination. *Luster* resinous; *hardness* 2; *specific gravity* 2.0–2.1; *fracture* conchoidal; *cleavage* basal, prismatic, and pyramidal. Brittle; translucent. **Composition:** Sulfur, but often contaminated with clay or bitumen. Volcanic sulfur may contain selenium, arsenic, etc. **Tests:** Melts at 108°C and burns with a blue flame and acrid fumes of SO_2. Insoluble in water and acids, dissolves in carbon disulfide. Not really fun to play with as the fumes are noxious and its acid (sulfuric, H_2SO_4) very corrosive. Sulfur's physical states are interesting, for it melts to an amber liquid and, as it gets hotter, turns black, then yellow again when still hotter. However, it is not recommended that such experiments be undertaken outside of a well-equipped laboratory; chemists' laboratories keep fumes under a vented hood.

Distinguishing characteristics: There are few minerals with which it would be confused. The ease of melting and the burning with noxious smell will readily distinguish it from any other substance.

Occurrence: Sulfur is a characteristic deposit of the later stages of volcanic activity. In New Zealand, and Middle and South America it has been quarried from the craters of volcanoes that are, or have been thought to be, extinct. Tiny sulfur crystals are found in cavities in some weathered sulfides. In galena it is associated in cavities with anglesite. It is constantly forming in crusts of small crystals at a fumarolic deposit south of San Felipe, Baja California, and in Steamboat Springs and elsewhere in Nevada. Masses were mined for the copper smelter at the Leviathan Mine on the California-Nevada border near the Yerington, Weed Flat, Nevada, copper mine.

However, the economically important deposits in Sicily, Spain, Poland, and along the Gulf Coast appear to have formed from gypsum (calcium sulfate) through a chemical reaction. The best specimens come from the Italian sulfur mines, where well-formed crystals up to 6 in. (15 cm) or more in length are found. Probably comparable ones occur in Louisiana and Texas, but because of the method of mining (the Frasch process of melting the sulfur in deeply buried rocks with superheated steam, and piping the amber liquid to the surface), the only American crystals available from the Gulf area come from 8-inch diamond-drill well cores. Large amounts of sulfur are extracted from high-sulfur fuel oils in the refining process and fumes for acid are recovered from smelters. Crystals have also been found in an asphaltic deposit in n. Italy, in a sulfur deposit in France at Malvesi, near Narbonne, with gypsum at Bex, Switzerland, near Cadiz, Spain, and in limestone in Michigan.

Remarks: Sulfur is of great economic importance in fungicidal plant sprays, the vulcanization of rubber, and the production of sulfuric acid. It is a poor conductor of electricity and with friction becomes negatively charged. The warmth of the hand will cause crystals to expand at the surface and crack. Specimens should be kept out of sunlight, out of severe cold, and handled as little as possible.

DIAMOND C Cubic — hextetrahedral $\overline{4}\ 3\ m$ **Pl. 14**
Environment: Formed at great depths in subcrustal iron-magnesium magmas, and ferried to the surface in volcanic lavas. Thanks to their toughness and density, now commonly residual in alluvial deposits derived from the disintegration of dark plutonic rocks. **Crystal description:** Most often in brilliant, commonly well-formed, triangularly pitted octahedrons. The cube faces are never smooth; though the crystal is unmistakably dicelike, its faces are always uneven but still lustrous. Smooth and shiny hexoctahedrons are usually almost spherical, marked by curved faces. Also in translucent balls with a radiating structure, known as "ball bort" or ballas, and in irregular hard black compact masses known as carbonado. Flat triangular crystals are usually spinel-

twinned octahedrons known in the diamond trade as "macles." **Physical properties:** White, or tinted all hues, gray to black. *Luster* adamantine; *hardness* 10; *specific gravity* 3.52; *fracture* conchoidal; *cleavage* perfect octahedral, poor dodecahedral; brittle; often fluorescent and phosphorescent; blue stones often electrically conducting. **Composition:** Carbon; a little nitrogen makes for yellower crystals. **Tests:** Infusible, insoluble. Burns at high temperatures (about 500°C). At slightly lower temperatures the surface frosts (can be repolished, if disaster strikes).

Distinguishing characteristics: The submetallic (adamantine) luster is unmistakable when combined with the crystal form and hardness. The quartz pebbles with which diamond is most often confused by hopeful dreamers (because quartz too will scratch glass) are wholly different in luster and fly apart with heat.

Occurrence: In alluvial deposits the harder and heavier diamonds survive when parent rock weathers and is worn away. They are mined from the original rocks only in Siberia, South Africa, Australia, and in Arkansas. They usually occur in a basic plutonic rock in cylindrical, more or less vertical, volcanic plugs known as "pipes." In Canada many suitably located pipes (and glacial deposit finds) indicate that there is a possibility of economic diamond-bearing formations in the north. Alluvial localities, perhaps reweathered with their prime source long gone, are numerous. Sporadic diamonds are found in gold placers in the eastern U.S. and in California. In recent decades Siberia has become an important source. Brazil, New Guinea, India, Namibia, and other African states have many localities, though none has proved notably large or abundant.

Remarks: Though promotions claim that only about 20 percent of the diamonds found are suitable for gem use, in fact the percentage is far higher, with Indians proving adept at obtaining small stones from what was long considered hopeless bort (poor-quality diamond material). Industrial diamonds are used for tools and dies, with the lowest grades crushed to a fine abrasive powder. The difference in hardness between diamond (10) and corundum (9) is said to be great, with diamonds almost twice as hard as their nearest Mohs neighbor. Synthetic diamonds are now an enormous business, but as of 1996, it is not believed that gem material production is economically practical. Cuttable crystals have been grown, but their cost is great, and their hue not of gem quality.

Irradiation (cyclotron, nuclear reactor pile, or electrons) produces greenish hues; heat then changes the greenish to yellow, golden, or chestnut. Long treatment makes them black. Zircon blues come from electron treatment followed by light heating. Fancier hues are unpredictable and usually minute.

GRAPHITE   C   Pl. 14

Hexagonal — Dihexagonal bipyramidal $\dfrac{6}{m}\dfrac{2}{m}\dfrac{2}{m}$

Environment: Mainly in metamorphic rocks, possibly in pegmatites. **Crystal description:** Isolated crystals are thin plates, usually in marbles, with rhombohedral faces on the edges. Commercial deposits are strange veinlike masses of solid material, or abundant plates disseminated through rock. **Physical properties:** Black. *Luster* submetallic; *hardness* 1–2; *specific gravity* 2.3; *streak* black; *cleavage* perfect basal. Flexible inelastic flakes; greasy feel; stains the fingers; completely opaque. **Composition:** Carbon. **Tests:** Infusible, insoluble.

Distinguishing characteristics: Can only be confused with molybdenite, which shares its softness and greasy feel but is soluble in nitric acid and gives off fumes under the blowpipe flame.

Occurrence: Most frequently found in isolated, well-formed but tiny black crystals in an impure marble, associated with other minerals such as spinel, chondrodite, and pyroxene; apparently one product of the metamorphism of the organic contaminants of limestone. Around Ticonderoga, New York—where it was once mined for use in lead pencils—it also occurs in thin veins. Madagascar and Sri Lanka (Ceylon), where it forms large pure masses in thick veins, are the most important (and unusual) occurrences. European localities have included Bohemia, Bavaria, and Styria (Austria); but the most important were those in Siberia. There is no U.S. occurrence of this type.

Remarks: Its Old World name, plumbago (black lead) comes from its use in lead pencils. It is also used as a lubricant and as a refractory in crucibles. It is an outstanding example of the effect of the internal atomic arrangement on a mineral's physical properties. Carbon, with an open and sheeted spacing that gives it a specific gravity of 2.3, is opaque and one of the softest minerals. The diamond, the same element in a tighter spacing with a consequent specific gravity of 3.5, is transparent and the hardest substance known.

■ SULFIDES AND SULFOSALTS

This group of compounds of the metallic and submetallic elements with sulfur is economically of the highest importance because many of the metal ores belong to this group. Most of them are easily recognized by their metallic luster. Brittleness (they crush to a powder) distinguishes most from the native metals. Usually they occur in primary deposits, but few are able to resist atmospheric weathering once erosion strips away their cover. Sulfides soon oxidize or hydrate into secondary ore minerals. Sulfides do not dominate in such mines until the lower levels are reached. The group is subdivided into the simple compounds of one or two metal elements with sulfur, the *sulfides,* and into compounds of metal elements with sulfur plus a semimetal (arsenic, antimony, or bismuth), known as the *sulfosalts.* The former are deposited under a variety of temperature states, from high (hypothermal), through medium (mesothermal), to low (epithermal). The latter are usually meso- and epithermal and consequently are found near the start of a mining operation, disappearing at greater depths. (See discussion of secondary enrichment under Chalcocite.)

◆ SULFIDES

ARGENTITE Ag_2S Cubic — hexoctahedral $\frac{4}{m} \, \overline{3} \, \frac{2}{m}$ **Pl. 15**

Environment: In fairly low-temperature ore veins formed at some distance from the primary source. **Crystal description:** Frequently occurs in poorly formed, dull black crystals, usually cubic but often so distorted and branching that it is difficult to recognize their faces. Commonly massive. **Physical properties:** Dark lead gray. *Luster* metallic, usually tarnished to dull black; *hardness* 2–2$\frac{1}{2}$; *specific gravity* 7.3; *fracture* subconchoidal; *cleavage* poor cubic and dodecahedral. Like lead, can be cut by a knife (sectile). **Composition:** Silver sulfide (87.1% Ag, 12.9% S). **Tests:** Blowpipe fuses it into a bead on charcoal, which in an oxidizing flame gives silver button. Tests for silver then apply.

Distinguishing characteristics: Sectility distinguishes it from other sulfides, particularly galena (which shows far better brittle cleavage). Grayer color distinguishes it from very white native silver; colorless nitric acid solution distinguishes it from chalcocite; copper nitrate solution is green.

Occurrence: Argentite is the most important primary ore of silver. Of common occurrence in veins with native silver. It seems to have catalytic power, with wire silver appearing to rise from argentite crystal surfaces. Fine crystals are found in Mexico, in Saxony, at Kongsberg, Norway, and at Cobalt, Ontario. Encountered near the surface of ore veins; there are no good commercial occurrences remaining in the U.S.

Remarks: Argentite has a cubic structure only at temperatures above 180°C, so its presence indicates that the vein formed at temperatures higher than 180°C. Actually all Ag_2S specimens are structurally rearranged into acanthite (orthorhombic Ag_2S) at room temperature and are now pseudomorphs after the original cubic argentite.

CHALCOCITE Cu_2S **Pl. 15**

Orthorhombic — bipyramidal $\frac{2}{m} \frac{2}{m} \frac{2}{m}$

Environment: Usually secondary, altered by later, cooler solutions in ore veins and by near-surface enrichment of chalcopyrite in disseminated deposits. **Crystal description:** Commonly massive; crystals are usually small and are infrequent. With edge face angles close to 60°, many crystals look six-sided from twinning. Elongated prisms are often twinned in geniculated (kneelike) pairs. **Physical properties:** Dark lead gray (some specimens in collections become coated with a soft brown-black sooty film; see discussion under marcasite, p. 126). *Luster* metallic; *hardness* $2\frac{1}{2}$–3; *specific gravity* 7.2–7.4; *fracture* conchoidal; *cleavage* poor prismatic. Moderately sectile. **Composition:** Cuprous sulfide (79.8% Cu, 20.2% S). **Tests:** Powder, moistened with hydrochloric acid on platinum wire, colors flame bluish green (copper). Careful blowpiping with gas flame will produce a copper bead. Soluble in nitric acid, giving green solution that becomes blue on addition of ammonia.

Distinguishing characteristics: Usually associated with copper minerals, it is less sectile than argentite and gives easy copper tests. The gray color distinguishes it from the related copper sulfides.

Occurrence: Chalcocite is an important ore of copper. It is sometimes primary and sometimes secondary (when associated with chalcopyrite, bornite, and covellite). A higher-temperature, and primary, cubic form of Cu_2S is known as digenite and was once abundant at Butte, Montana. Chalcocite's most frequent development results from a process known as secondary enrichment. Solutions descend through oxidizing copper iron sulfides (typically chalcopyrite) near the surface. Because iron sulfate is more soluble than copper sulfate, lower-grade copper iron sulfides are enriched in copper as more of their iron goes into solution. The sequence commences with primary chalcopyrite ($CuFeS_2$), becoming bornite (Cu_5FeS_4), then covellite (CuS), and finally chalcocite (Cu_2S).

Chalcocite was found in fine crystals in sulfide veins in Cornwall, England, in an ancient mine in Bristol, Connecticut (the best American occurrence), and at Butte, Montana, where digenite also occurs in 1–2 in. (2.5–5 cm) crystals. French localities included Cap Garonne in Var, Garde-en-Oisans (Isère), Giromagny (Belfort), and Framont (Alsace). Its French name is chalcosine. New specimens were briefly found in a new mine in Ladysmith, Wisconsin, but the prospect of finding more is largely a memory at present.

BORNITE Cu_5FeS_4 Pl. 16

Cubic — hexoctahedral $\quad \frac{4}{m} \; \bar{3} \; \frac{2}{m}$

Environment: Commonly disseminated in igneous intrusives as a primary mineral. Also in copper ore veins, both as a primary and secondary mineral. See discussion under chalcocite. **Crystal description:** Crystals rare and poor, usually in intergrown clusters and seldom over 1 in. (2–3 cm). As a rule, bornite is massive and compact. **Physical properties:** Bronze. *Luster* metallic (but this tarnishes rapidly to purple after a freshly broken surface is exposed); *hardness* 3; *specific gravity* 4.9–5.4; *fracture* uneven; *cleavage* poor octahedral. Brittle. **Composition:** Sulfide of copper and iron (63.3% Cu, 11.1% Fe, 25.6% S). **Tests:** Fuses to a brittle magnetic globule on charcoal. Dissolves in nitric acid, giving a copper coloration to the solution.

Distinguishing characteristics: Could be confused with pyrrhotite (which is weakly magnetic), but it gives the copper tests, and requires roasting to become magnetic. Niccolite is similar in color, but is nonmagnetic and remains so despite roasting. The rapid development of a purple tarnish is characteristic. Bornite occurs with the other copper sulfides and as such is an important ore of copper. It has been found in fair crystals at Cornwall, England, at Charrier, near La Prugne, France, and at Bristol, Connecticut. However, at the economically important localities in Arizona it is generally massive and/or disseminated, and intimately intergrown with chalcopyrite and chalcocite.

Remarks: A characteristic and colorful tarnish has given rise to the old miner's term "peacock ore" and is responsible for its French name, erubescite. Most dealers' "peacock ore" actually is not bornite but chalcopyrite treated to produce a colorful iridescence simulating true "peacock ore."

GALENA   PbS   Cubic — hexoctahedral $\frac{4}{m}\,\overline{3}\,\frac{2}{m}$ **Pl. 15**

Environment: In medium- to low-temperature ore veins, in igneous and sedimentary rocks, and disseminated through sediments. **Crystal description:** Crystals are very common, usually cubic, sometimes octahedrons. They may also show combinations of several forms of the cubic system. Frequently in granular masses, often very fine-grained or fibrous. **Physical properties:** Lead-gray. *Luster* metallic; *hardness* $2^1/_2$–$2^3/_4$; *specific gravity* 7.4–7.6; *fracture* even (rarely seen); *cleavage* perfect cubic, with occasional octahedral parting. Brittle. **Composition:** Lead sulfide (86.6% lead, 13.4% sulfur). Often contains silver, arsenic, antimony, and other impurities. **Tests:** Fuses on charcoal, with yellow coating around the bead, and can be reduced to lead. Makes cloudy solution in nitric acid, with sulfur and lead sulfate separating out.
Distinguishing characteristics: The ready cubic cleavage, with the lead gray metallic color and luster, is characteristic. Might be confused with dark sphalerite, in which case the light streak of the latter would permit a distinction. Other similar sulfides have good cleavages in a single direction, but not in three directions. The blowpipe reactions will help in very fine-grained (and deceptive) varieties.
Occurrence: The chief ore of lead, commonly found in shallow ore veins in which open cavities are frequent; hence, crystals are common and well developed. Unfortunately, their faces are usually dull. Commonly associated with the sulfides sphalerite, pyrite, and chalcopyrite, and with quartz, siderite, dolomite, fluorite, calcite, or barite as worthless associates (gangue minerals). The same mineral association occur in both sedimentary rocks and igneous rocks.

Fine distorted crystals have been found in Germany, and good examples in France, the former Yugoslavia, and elsewhere in Europe. The Joplin District of Missouri, Kansas, and Oklahoma is notable for its crystals, usually cubes, sometimes cubo-octahedrons with octahedral growths on the faces. Cen. Missouri is a recent source of relatively shiny cubic crystals, as is a mine in Madan, Bulgaria. Uncommon flattened and shiny spinel-twinned cubo-octahedral crystals seem to be characteristic of a good Mexican (Naica) occurrence. There are many occurrences of fine examples of this mineral.

Remarks: Through near-surface alteration, particularly of the finer-grained examples, galena produces many other lead minerals such as anglesite, cerussite, and phosgenite. It often contains enough silver to make it an important source of that metal. It is commonly thought that galena with flaky curving cleavage planes—irregular rather than smooth, often slightly tarnished—is likely to be higher in the silver impurity.

SPHALERITE ZnS Cubic — hextetrahedral $\overline{4}\ 3\ m$ **Pl. 15**
Environment: In sulfide ore veins in all rock classes, under the same conditions responsible for galena. **Crystal description:** Tetrahedral crystals very common, sometimes so completely developed as to look octahedral. Cube, dodecahedron, and tristetrahedron faces also present, the latter often rounded so that it is difficult to distinguish the faces. Also stalactitic, granular, and massive. **Physical properties:** Colorless (very rare) through yellow and green to red-brown and black. *Luster* adamantine to resinous; *hardness* $3\frac{1}{2}$–4; *specific gravity* 3.9–4.1; *streak* white to cream; *fracture* conchoidal; *cleavage* perfect dodecahedral. Brittle; transparent (even gemmy) to opaque; interesting luminescent effects (see below); occasionally fluorescent. **Composition:** Zinc sulfide (67.0% Zn, 33.0% S with varying amounts of cadmium, iron, manganese, and other elements). **Tests:** Practically infusible on charcoal, but develops a coating on and around a chip that is yellow when hot and white when cold. Touched with cobalt solution, the yellow coating becomes green in the reducing flame (the addition of Na_2CO_3 powder facilitates this test). Dissolves reluctantly in hydrochloric acid with bubbles of hydrogen sulfide (rotten-egg smell).

Distinguishing characteristics: When it is very black its high luster and easy cleavage gives it a resemblance to galena, but the light streak, the powder, and any blowpipe test suffice for this distinction. Resembles some siderite, but can be distinguished by remaining nonmagnetic after roasting and by its higher gravity. The characteristic luster and association with pyrite and galena generally serve to identify sphalerite. **Occurrence:** Same as galena, with which it is usually associated. Localities are almost too numerous to mention, but the gemmy, transparent light yellow to red Santander (Spain) masses are notable. Joplin District (Missouri, Kansas, and

Oklahoma) crystals range from black and dull irregular giants to minute red ("ruby jack") incrustations. The palest U.S. specimens are light yellow-green crystals from Franklin, New Jersey, and colorless in Balmat, New York. Trepça, in the former Yugoslavia, has become an important source of good "black jack" specimens, as has the Nicolaj Mine, Dolnegorsk, Russia, and a mine in Madan, Bulgaria.

Remarks: Sphalerite is the principal ore of zinc. It alters to hemimorphite, smithsonite, and willemite. Impurities recovered in smelting—gallium, indium, and cadmium—make it also the chief ore of those metals. Its cleavage and luminescent responses make it of particular interest to mineral collectors. It is the best mineral example of dodecahedral cleavage, and with care perfect dodecahedrons can be cleaved out. Sometimes it fluoresces orange in ultraviolet light. Fluorescent sphalerite also shows the infrequent phenomenon of triboluminescence; that is, it emits flashes of orange light on being firmly stroked with a hard substance such as a knife or a stone. Though too soft for use, rare-gem collectors treasure the fiery brilliants that may be cut from the light-hued Picos de Europa, Santander (Spain) specimens.

CHALCOPYRITE $CuFeS_2$ Pl. 16

Tetragonal — scalenohedral $\overline{4}$ 2 m

Environment: Common in multitemperature sulfide veins, and often disseminated through porphyritic igneous rocks. **Crystal description:** Though tetragonal, the characteristically sphenoidal crystals of chalcopyrite resemble tetrahedra. Crystals of 2–3 cm are common; often they are even larger, with faces usually somewhat uneven and tarnished from black to brilliant iridescent hues. Usually massive, often making up golden sulfide mixtures of several minerals. Structurally close to sphalerite, it often makes oriented intergrowths, with small crystals studded over sphalerite surfaces. **Physical properties:** Golden. *Luster* metallic, often with iridescent tarnish; *hardness* $3\frac{1}{2}$–4; gravity 4.1–4.3; *fracture* uneven; *cleavage* 1 poor (and rarely noted). Brittle. **Composition:** Sulfide of copper and iron (34.5% Cu, 30.5% Fe, 35% S). **Tests:** On charcoal, fuses to magnetic black globule; touched with HCl, tints flame with blue flash. Solution with strong nitric acid is green; ammonia precipitates red iron hydroxide and leaves a blue solution.

Distinguishing characteristics: Confused with gold, but is brittle, crushes to a green-black powder, gives black streak, and dissolves in acid. Distinguished from pyrite by ease of scratching and by copper tests. The color is a richer yellow than pyrite. Also, obviously hard and shiny pyrite will frequently show smooth flat surfaces, striated cubes or pyritohedrons, whereas chalcopyrite, when not massive, is in characteristic sphenoidal crystals.

Occurrence: The basic copper ore. Widely distributed and may be found in all types of primary occurrences. Often associated with other copper minerals: pyrite, sphalerite, galena, and pyrrhotite. The economically important "porphyry coppers" of Bingham, Utah; Ely, Nevada; and Ajo, Arizona; are representative of open-pit–mined, worldwide low-grade (1–3 percent) copper disseminations through igneous rocks. Some of the best crystals are from Cornwall, England; Akita and Tochigi prefectures, Japan; French Creek, Pennsylvania; and several Colorado localities. Often crystallized in the parallel growths on and through crystals of sphalerite in the Joplin District of Missouri, Kansas, and Oklahoma. Giant 6-in. (15 cm) crystals were found in Freirina, n. Chile. Abundant in n. Mexico, another good source of large crystals.

Remarks: Chalcopyrite is the generic copper ore that, by alteration and successive removals of iron, produces a series starting with chalcopyrite and going through bornite (Cu_5FeS_4), covellite (CuS), and chalcocite (Cu_2S), and ending (rarely) as native copper (Cu). (See discussion of secondary enrichment under chalcocite.)

GREENOCKITE CdS   Pl. 16

Hexagonal — Dihexagonal pyramidal   6 m m

Environment: In traprock cavities and in ore veins. **Crystal description:** Crystals small to minute, complex, and interesting as examples of an infrequent symmetry class: hemimorphic hexagonal. Crystals are very rare, however; greenockite usually manifests as a yellow, pollenlike dusting over other minerals, especially sphalerite and calcite and even in smithsonite, staining it yellow. **Physical properties:** Yellow to brown or red. *Luster* adamantine to resinous; *hardness* 3–$3^{1}/_{2}$; *specific gravity* 4.9–5.0; *streak* yellow; *fracture* conchoidal; *cleavage* good prismatic and poor basal. Brittle; transparent to translucent. **Composition:** Cadmium sulfide (77.8% Cd, 22.2% S). **Tests:** In closed glass tube the yellow powder turns red when hot and back to yellow or brown when cool. Gives a reddish brown coating on charcoal in the reducing flame. Soluble in hydrochloric acid, releasing hydrogen sulfide gas (rotten-egg smell).

Distinguishing characteristics: Likely to be mistaken for sphalerite when in crystals, but can be distinguished by its crystal form and by the closed-tube test. The yellow films might be confused with uranium minerals, but the association with zinc minerals should suffice for correct identification.

Occurrence: Crystals are very rare, and were first found at Greenock, Scotland, in cavities in traprock, associated with prehnite. Even the largest are not much over $1/4$ in. (6 mm) long. A few distorted crystals have been found in the Paterson, New Jersey, traprock area. Orange-red microscopic crystals have been described from Llallagua, Bolivia, associated with pyrite and tin ores. Yellow films are common in the Joplin District (Missouri, Kansas, and Oklahoma) and in the Illinois-Kentucky fluorite region.

Remarks: It is the only "ore" of cadmium, but that metal is actually recovered only as a by-product of lead and zinc refining. The cadmium is separated in the purification of the other metals. Because of its hemimorphic symmetry, unusual electronic properties make laboratory manufacture of some interest.

PYRRHOTITE $Fe_{1-x}S$ **Pl. 16**

Pseudohexagonal (several polymorphs)

Environment: Widespread in many types of occurrences, mostly those formed at higher temperatures. **Crystal description:** Crystals usually tabular, their most common form being piles of hexagonal plates with sides that have deep horizontal striations. Its major occurrences, however, are massive and granular. **Physical properties:** Bronze. *Luster* metallic; *hardness* 4; *specific gravity* 4.6–4.7; *fracture* subconchoidal; *cleavage* none, but crystals commonly show a basal parting. Brittle; magnetism varies from strong to negligible. **Composition:** Ferrous sulfide (approximately 60.4% Fe, 39.6% S). There is a slight deficiency of Fe in this mineral, which makes it somewhat unstable and easily decomposed. The x in its formula ranges from 0.0 to 0.2. **Tests:** Fuses easily to black magnetic mass, dissolves readily in hydrochloric acid, producing hydrogen sulfide (rotten-egg smell).

Distinguishing characteristics: The magnetic nature of its powder is usually sufficient to distinguish it from anything similar in color (fresh bornite and niccolite) and from pyrite and chalcopyrite.

Occurrence: Pyrrhotite is a common mineral of magmatic sulfide segregations and high-temperature ore veins. It also occurs in pegmatites and in contact-metamorphic deposits.

Good crystals have been found in Romania, exhibiting the laminated vertical development (the deep, discontinuous, horizontal grooving mentioned under Crystal description) and somewhat concave basal faces. The largest crystals of good form have come from the San Antonio mine at Aquiles Serdán (formerly Santa Eulalia), Chihuahua, Mexico. Well-formed platy crystals were found in a pegmatite at Standish, Maine. Morro Velho, Brazil's deep gold mine in Minas Gerais, is the source of small sharp hexagonal plates that are perched on calcite rhombohedrons. The main ore body at Sudbury, Ontario, is pyrrhotite, and the ore minerals pentlandite (an iron-nickel sulfide), sperrylite (a hard, white, cubic crystallized platinum arsenide), and chalcopyrite are embedded in it. A bit unstable, some pyrhotites tend to crumble in collections.

Remarks: Meteorites contain the closely related nonmagnetic mineral troilite (FeS), which is regarded as a charge-balanced ferrous sulfide. Pyrrhotite's structure has been repeatedly studied, and most examples prove to be mixtures of hexagonal and monoclinic lattices. Those with less sulfur are likely to be hexagonal; those with great sulfur excesses, monoclinic. Heating to 350°C rearranges the structure to full hexagonal symmetry.

NICCOLITE NiAs   **Pl. 16**

Hexagonal — Dihexagonal bipyramidal $\dfrac{6}{m}\dfrac{2}{m}\dfrac{2}{m}$

Environment: Uncommon, probably middle-temperature. In ore veins with silver; also copper, nickel, and cobalt arsenides and sulfides. **Crystal description:** Crystals rare, poor, and small, usually in hexagonally studded crusts. Also massive and in reniform crusts. **Physical properties:** Copper-colored. *Luster* metallic, tarnishing black; *hardness* 5–5$\frac{1}{2}$; *specific gravity* 7–8; *fracture* uneven; *cleavage* none. Brittle. **Composition:** Nickel arsenide (43.9% Ni, 56.1% As). Arsenic sometimes replaced in part by antimony (nickel antimonide is breithauptite). **Tests:** On charcoal gives fumes with faint arsenic (garlic) odor and fuses to bronzy, metallic globule. Gives nickel test with dimethyl-glyoxime (pink needles in ammonia-neutralized acid solution). Dissolves in nitric acid to form clear green solution with black residue.

Distinguishing characteristics: The copper color is characteristic. It may be confused only with the related breithauptite (NiSb), from which it can hardly be distinguished, especially since niccolite often contains some antimony. Most fre-

quently associated with silvery white, massive skudderite.
Occurrence: Niccolite is relatively rare and usually associated
with other nickel and copper minerals. Because of its accompanying related species, it too is valuable. Usually massive
in layered veins with the silvery minerals, it is best observed
in polished specimens where niccolite stands out because of
its copper hue.

Free-growing crystal crusts are rare and usually represented in collections only in old specimens from Germany, either from Reichenbach or Eisleben, and recently in small
crystal balls from near Freiberg. Niccolite and breithauptite
occur in large masses at Cobalt, Ontario, usually intimately
associated with skudderite and silver.
Remarks: This mineral, known to the old German miners as
Kupfernickel ("copper nickel"), gave the element its name.
Nickel was a disparaging name for underground imps (see
cobaltite).

MILLERITE   NiS   Pl. 16

Hexagonal — Rhombohedral holohedral $\overline{3}$ m

Environment: In limestone and dolomite, sometimes in ore
veins. **Crystal description:** Its common name, "capillary py-
rites," aptly describes the cobwebby crystals. Very rarely
does it become coarse enough to show individual hexagonal
outlines across any rod in parallel bundles of needles. Also
in crusts with columnar fracture. **Physical properties:** Brass
yellow. *Luster* metallic; *hardness* 3–3$\frac{1}{2}$; *specific gravity* 5.3–
5.6; *fracture* uneven; *cleavages* 2 rhombohedral. Brittle, but
cobweb threads flexible. **Composition:** Nickel sulfide (64.7%
Ni, 35.3% S). **Tests:** Fuses easily on charcoal in the reducing
flame to a black magnetic bead. Gives nickel test (pink needles in ammonia-neutralized nitric acid solution) with dimethylglyoxime.
Distinguishing characteristics: The capillary crystals could only
be confused with capillary tourmaline or rutile, neither of
which would fuse on charcoal, nor would they be found in
the same associations. The nickel test would distinguish it
from similarly colored sulfides.
Occurrence: Millerite is sometimes valued as an ore of nickel
when present in minor quantities in association with other
metallic sulfides in middle-temperature veins, as in Germany and the massive Sudbury, Ontario, sulfide complex.
Locally it is sparsely distributed through limestones in central Mississippi Valley limestone quarries, particularly near

St. Louis, Missouri, and Keokuk, Iowa. At these places long millerite hairs are found in cavities lined with crystals of calcite, dolomite, and fluorite. (An interesting, if improbable, speculation suggests the original source of this nickel might be a heavy Paleozoic meteor shower.) Coarser millerite needles have been found with hematite in Antwerp, New York, and in Alamos, Mexico.

COVELLITE CuS   Pl. 17

Hexagonal — Dihexagonal bipyramidal $\frac{6}{m} \frac{2}{m} \frac{2}{m}$

Environment: In enriched portions of copper sulfide veins. **Crystal description:** Sheaves and bundles of thin, platy hexagonal crystals, usually standing on edge. Often the basal pinacoids are coated with a golden secondary chalcopyrite or have become so tarnished that the blue surface does not show. Also in veins filled with loosely intergrown plates, and in tight masses with the space between filled in with chalcocite. **Physical properties:** Blue, usually tarnished purple to black. *Luster* metallic; *hardness* $1\frac{1}{2}$–2; *specific gravity* 4.6; *cleavage* basal; plates flexible but not elastic. Sectile; translucent blue-green in very thin plates. **Composition:** Cupric sulfide (66.4% Cu, 33.6% S). **Tests:** Blue flakes catch fire and burn with blue flame before melting. Further blowpiping melts them to a bead, following some boiling and bubbling.

Distinguishing characteristics: Platy appearance, often with some crumpling of the edges, is characteristic. The blue color and dichroism should not be confused with the iridescent film common on chalcopyrite and bornite. Always associated with other copper minerals.

Occurrence: A rare mineral whose crystals are sought after by major collectors. Possibly always a secondary alteration product except for a sublimate occurrence of small crystals around a fumarole at Vesuvius, Italy, found by N. Covelli. The largest sheets have come from Sardinia, but their edges were poorly formed. The sharpest, best-developed, unmistakably hexagonal plates are those from the Leonard Mine in Butte, Montana. Thin, fresh, scattered metallic very blue plates have been found in Colorado. At Kennicott, Alaska, it has formed rich blue masses exhibiting a lathlike diabasic texture on polished surfaces. Lately, from some source, there have been specimens solid enough for carvings to be found at shows.

Remarks: With other sulfides, infrequent covellite can be a valuable ore of copper, but good specimens are relatively rare. The Kennicott occurrence has provided the most beautiful examples for the study of polished specimens in polarized light under the microscope. Laths are intergrown in a felted mass; as the specimen is rotated, the color of each plate edge changes from light to dark blue and back again.

CINNABAR HgS   **Pl. 17**

Hexagonal — Trapezohedral   3 2

Environment: In shallow veins and rock impregnations, very often in a quartzite (Almaden, Spain) or serpentine (California). **Crystal description:** Well-individualized crystals are rare, crystallized crusts and complex intergrowths fairly common. Twinned intergrowths of steep rhombohedrons found at several localities. Also massive, powdery, and granular, sometimes in capillary needles. **Physical properties:** Bright red to brick red to almost black. *Luster* adamantine; *hardness* $2^{1}/_{2}$; *specific gravity* 8.1; *fracture* subconchoidal; *streak* red; *cleavage* very perfect prismatic. Easily bruised and crushed; translucent to transparent. **Composition:** Mercuric sulfide (86.2% Hg, 13.8% S). **Tests:** Volatilizes completely on charcoal. In open tube produces sulfur fumes; forms black ring and above this a thin deposit of metallic droplets. This "mercury mirror" can be resolved into drops by scratching over its surface with a needle.

Distinguishing characteristics: Likely to be confused with realgar, cuprite, and possibly "ruby jack" sphalerite or hematite. Easily distinguished by the open-tube test.

Occurrence: Cinnabar, the only ore of mercury, is deposited by epithermal ascending solutions (those near surface and not too hot) far removed from their igneous source. It is associated with native mercury, stibnite, realgar, opal, quartz, and barite. The richest occurrences are on Mt. Avala, Idria, near Belgrade, Serbia; Almadén, Spain; Italy; and Mexico. Historically, the best crystals, including the penetrating rhombohedron type, have been found as scattered individuals up to 2 in. (4–5 cm) in a white calcite matrix in Hunan Province, China. Loose 1–2 in. (3–6 cm) crystals come from the Nikitovka Mine in Ukraine. Briefly, in the late 1920s, the Kirby Mine, Pike Co., Arkansas, had good twins on an iron-stained quartz matrix and enclosed in quartz crystals with hairs of stibnite. Waterworn cinnabar nuggets are found in the Tempati River, Surinam. American deposits are not extensive; the best are in California, with one in Alaska. Smaller quantities have been found in Nevada.

REALGAR   AsS   Monoclinic — prismatic $\frac{2}{m}$ **Pl. 17**

Environment: In low-temperature veins. **Crystal description:** Good crystals fairly common, usually prismatic; also massive. **Physical properties:** Orange-red. *Luster* resinous; *hardness* $1^1/_2$–2; *specific gravity* 3.4–3.5; *streak* red-orange; *fracture* subconchoidal; *cleavage* perfect side and fair basal. Sectile; translucent to transparent. **Composition:** Arsenic sulfide (70.1% As, 29.9% S). **Tests:** Fuses easily, melting to shiny mass, spreading and completely volatilizing with the characteristic arsenic (garlic) odor. Makes red deposit shading to orange and yellow on walls of closed tube, while yellow fumes escape from the end.

Distinguishing characteristics: It could be mistaken for cinnabar; blowpipe and closed-tube tests would show the differences. Often associated with yellow orpiment.

Occurrence: Not a common mineral, but an important ore of arsenic. Usually in rich veins, as at the Getchell gold mine in Nevada, with calcite and yellow, micaceous orpiment. Like stibnite and cinnabar, it is a late magmatic mineral associated with cooler solutions such as those at hot springs. It is often associated with colemanite, as at Boron, California, and Bigadiç, Turkey. Isolated single 1-in. (2–3 cm) crystals have been found in marble pockets in Carrara, Italy, and in Binnatal, Switzerland. Excellent old-time crystal specimens have come from Transylvania, Romania. Rich masses and well-developed crystal pockets are found in the U.S. at the Getchell gold mine, Nevada, and very fine singles come from the Reward Mine, King Co., Washington. Hunan, China, is now producing the finest realgars of this generation in rich-hued crystals of 2 in. (5 cm) and more.

Remarks: Realgar is a very unstable mineral, affected by exposure to light. Most museum specimens quickly become disgraceful on the shelf, rimmed with a crumbled orange dust (but still structurally realgar) after a few years of display. Storage in darkness delays the inevitable deterioration, but even this does not indefinitely preserve specimens. Other factors, such as exposure to air or release of pressure, may play a part in their breakup.

The ancient Chinese apparently admired its red hue and cemented small fragments into chunks for carvings, though all these artifacts are now badly affected by time, light, and air. Most good American specimens are obtained from Getchell Mine material by dissolving in hydrochloric acid the calcite from filled veins to expose the arsenic sulfide crystals (realgar and orpiment) lining the walls.

ORPIMENT As_2S_3 Monoclinic — prismatic $\dfrac{2}{m}$ **Pl. 17**

Environment: Nearly always associated with realgar in low-temperature veins, occasionally alone. **Crystal description:** Almost always well crystallized, though often in compact masses characterized by micaceous yellow flakes. Free-growing crystals relatively rare; usually they form as crystalline crusts, with individuals being difficult to orient. Elongated rodlike crystals are found in Hunan, China. **Physical properties:** Orange-yellow to yellow to brown and greenish black on crystal surfaces other than the flaky cleavage direction; tends to blacken on dumps. *Luster* resinous to pearly; *hardness* $1^1/_2$–2; *specific gravity* 3.4–3.5; *streak* micaceous golden flakes; *cleavage* perfect micaceous, side pinacoidal. Sectile; flexible but inelastic cleavage flakes; translucent to transparent. **Composition:** Arsenic trisulfide (61% As, 39% S). **Tests:** Same as for realgar (above).

Distinguishing characteristics: Unlikely to be taken for any other mineral. Strikingly brilliant cleavage faces distinguish it from sulfur with no need of blowpipe tests. An almost inescapable association with realgar and stibnite eliminates often fluorescent yellow minerals such as uranium compounds (autunite) and greenockite.

Occurrence: In Russia and Macedonia, orpiment sometimes forms large micalike cleavable masses. Good crystals from Rumania and Luceram (s. France), and unusually large isolated ones at Mercur, Utah. Rich masses, mixed with realgar, lie all about the dumps at the Getchell gold mine, Nevada; their weather-affected surfaces look dark greenish yellow, while the crumbling realgar dust is orange. Fine brownish resinous crystal crusts have been found in Peru, in Iran at Valilo, and at Ahar, in Azerbaijan. Yellow hairs in calcite crevices at Manhattan, Nye Co., Nevada, long thought to be orpiment, are now identified as a newer mineral, also found in Japan, named wakabayashilite $(As,Sb)_{11}S_{18}$.

Remarks: Less light sensitive than realgar, though old specimens do deteriorate. In collections and light orpiment tends to dull and develop a white film, presumably a response to exposure and oxidation. The usual color of the front and top crystal faces is a brownish orange, very different from the golden color and high luster of a fresh cleavage surface. The red and yellow arsenic sulfide mixture is very decorative, but the poisonous character of the oxide coupled with its tendency to disintegrate make it unsatisfactory, and perhaps even unwise, for interior design use, though it is widely sold for such uses.

STIBNITE Sb_2S_3 **Pl. 17**

Orthorhombic — bipyramidal $\dfrac{2}{m}\dfrac{2}{m}\dfrac{2}{m}$

Environment: In low-temperature, often open, veins and rock impregnations. Associated with arsenic and antimony minerals. **Crystal description:** Usually in well-formed crystals, sometimes very large and solid (Japan, China); at other times stocky and short, slender and fragile, or fibrous, massive, bladed, or granular. **Physical properties:** Steel gray. *Luster* metallic; *hardness* 2; *specific gravity* 4.5–4.6; *streak* black; *fracture* subconchoidal; *cleavage* perfect side pinacoid. **Composition:** Sulfide of antimony (71.7% Sb, 28.3% S). **Tests:** Melts to a liquid, spreads out and completely volatilizes on charcoal, making a white coating around grain and weakly coloring the blowpipe flame white. Dissolves in hot concentrated HNO_3 and slowly forms a white precipitate on addition of water.

Distinguishing characteristics: Distinguished from lead-bearing sulfosalts by the lack of a yellow (lead oxide) coating on the surrounding charcoal and by its complete volatility. Distinguished from bismuthinite by lower gravity, more fluid fusion on charcoal, and more rapid volatilization.

Occurrence: An ore of antimony. Like realgar and orpiment, a late low-temperature deposit of hot solutions, often associated with the arsenic minerals and cinnabar. The finest crystals ever found were brilliant needles over a foot long (30 cm) from the Ichinokawa Mine, Iyo Province (now Ehime Prefecture), n. Shikoku I., Japan. Almost their equal are those of Xikuangshan Antimony Mine in Hunan, China. Stubbier, bluntly terminated, fine 1–2-in. (2.5–5 cm) crystals in crusts and radiating clusters come from Baia Sprie (Felsöbanya), Romania. The best U.S. crystals have been found at Manhattan, Nye Co., Nevada. A few large crystals, nearly like those of China, have been found in Huarás, Peru.

Giant ocherous pseudomorphs, now two Sb oxides—cervantite (Sb_2O_4) and stibiconite ($Sb_3O_6[OH]$)—give hope for some eventual fine stibnites from sources near Oaxaca, Mexico.

Remarks: Stibnite is the outstanding example of a mineral showing the phenomenon of well-developed gliding planes. Slipping directions are so well developed that many of the crystals found in nature are bent, or soon become bent, without fracturing. The atoms will glide a definite distance in the basal plane and then stop. (See calcite and vivianite.)

BISMUTHINITE Bi_2S_3 Pl. 17

Orthorhombic — bipyramidal $\frac{2}{m} \frac{2}{m} \frac{2}{m}$

Environment: Pegmatites and high-temperature ore veins.
Crystal description: Rare in free-growing slender crystals. More often in embedded masses with a bladed or fibrous structure. Large altered crystals in pegmatites show that it can grow larger, but no unaltered giants have been found.
Physical properties: Steel gray. *Luster* metallic; *hardness* 2; *specific gravity* 6.4–6.5; *streak* black; *fracture* brittle or splintery; *cleavage* perfect side pinacoid. Slightly sectile.
Composition: Sulfide of bismuth (81.2% Bi, 18.8% S). **Tests:** Fuses easily but volatilizes slowly, forming dark gray globules surrounded by thin yellow sublimates. The powder dissolves easily in hot concentrated nitric acid, leaving a yellow spongy insoluble residue (sulfur).
Distinguishing characteristics: Masses can be confused with stibnite and the sulfosalts. Complete volatilization under the blowpipe separates it from the sulfosalts, and the formation of a spherical globule instead of a watery liquid distinguishes it from stibnite.
Occurrence: Bismuthinite is a by-product source of bismuth. It looks much like stibnite when associated with other ores, as in Bolivian tin mines. Unlike stibnite, however, also found in pegmatites as single crystals, not associated with any arsenic-antimony suite. Minute ribbonlike crystals found around fumaroles in the Lipari Is., Italy, are in part bismuthinite and part galenobismutite ($PbBi_2S_4$), first named cannizarite when the flexible ribbonlike needles were all thought to be a new mineral. The richest bismuthinite occurrences are in Bolivia, in the tin-tungsten veins. A frequent pegmatite mineral, large masses have been found in quarries at Bedford, Westchester Co., New York, and in Boulder Co., Colorado. Pseudomorphs of bismuthinite crystals up to 2 ft. (61 cm) long and 1 in. (3 cm) thick of an often greenish-stained, earthy white bismuth carbonate (bismutite, $Bi_2[CO]_3O_2$) have been found associated with cyrtolite in northern Brazil.

PYRITE FeS_2 Cubic — diploidal $\frac{2}{m} \overline{3}$ Pl. 18

Environment: Ubiquitous; in all classes of rocks and all types of veins. **Crystal description:** Often crystallized, most frequently in striated cubes, less commonly in octahedrons. Massive pyrite is common. **Physical properties:** Light yellow. *Luster* metallic; *hardness* 6–6$\frac{1}{2}$; *specific gravity* 5.0; *streak* powdery greenish black; *fracture* conchoidal; *cleavage* none. Brittle. **Composition:** Iron sulfide (46.6% Fe, 53.4% S). **Tests:** Fuses easily, becoming magnetic and giving off sulfur dioxide (SO_2) fumes. Insoluble in hydrochloric acid, but a fine powder will dissolve in concentrated nitric acid (HNO_3).

Distinguishing characteristics: The tarnished sulfide might be confused with chalcopyrite, but its great hardness is distinctive. It is slightly yellower and more slowly soluble in nitric acid than marcasite, giving a clear solution. It is harder than gold, and very brittle.

Occurrence: Any weathered rock formation that appears rust-stained probably contains—or contained—pyrite, a frequent associate of all sorts of metal ores. In addition, it forms concretionary masses in sedimentary rocks, which then frequently alter to very compact limonite balls. Golden discs called "pyrite dollars" are found in an Illinois coal formation, and more spherical concretions with brown oxidized skins are common in clays, slates, and other metamorphic rocks. Daisylike golden crystal disks with coarse cubic "petal" rims were found during the Dallas–Fort Worth airport construction. So often mistaken for gold it is popularly known as "fool's gold." Fine specimens have been found throughout the world. Particularly notable in the past were the large well-formed crystals from Leadville, Colorado, and well-developed crystal groups from Park City, Utah. Misshapen octahedral crystals containing 0.2 percent arsenic were found at French Creek, Pennsylvania. "Cathedral" pyrite was a name given to the large cubes with Gothic arch growth patterns on their faces. Many-faced complex and perfect crystals come from Rio Marina on the island of Elba, Italy. Quiruvilca and Cerro de Pasco, both in Peru, now yield outstanding octahedral crystals and pyritohedral groups. Many Mexican occurrences have been reported. Highly modified crystals in fine clusters are typical of Oruro and Colavi, Bolivia. Falun, Sweden, yielded a pyrite rich in cobalt. Fantastic groups of sharp cubes are broken from a limestone in Spain and reconstructed into startling staircases with cubes of up to 5 cm or more.

Remarks: Pyrite was once important as a source of sulfur for the manufacture of sulfuric acid, and could be again. Invisible specks of gold between the grains frequently provide value to seemingly worthless but cyanide-leachable deposits, so it may be an important ore of gold.

COBALTITE CoAsS Cubic — tetartohedral 2 3 **Pl. 18**

Environment: Very uncommon, in sulfide veins with other cobalt and nickel ores. Well-developed single crystals stud some metamorphic rock. **Crystal description:** Silvery crystals, well formed, in cubes and pyritohedrons resembling pyrite. Also granular, massive. **Physical properties:** Tin-white. *Luster* metallic; *hardness* 5$^1/_2$; *specific gravity* 6–6.3; *fracture* uneven; *cleavage* good cubic. Brittle. **Composition:** Cobalt sulfarsenide (35.5% Co, 45.2% As, 19.3% S). **Tests:** After powdering, fuses on charcoal with difficulty, giving off sulfur and faint arsenic (garlic) fumes and forming magnetic granules. Grains partially dissolve in warm nitric acid giving clear pink to red solution; residue remains metallic in luster.

Distinguishing characteristics: The tin-white color, coupled with the cubic or pyritohedral crystal form, is unmistakable. Cobaltite is harder and has a less perfect cleavage than galena. It is historically rare.

Occurrence: An insignificant ore of cobalt with two unusual crystal occurrences. Large, 1-in. (2.5 cm) or more, well-formed pyritohedral crystals were found at Tunaberg, Sweden, and Skutterud, Norway. Unexciting granular masses are found in veins at Cobalt, Ontario, mixed with (and hard to distinguish from) several white cobalt and nickel arsenides.

Remarks: Cobalt gets its name from the word *kobold* (German, *Kobalt*) given to imps that were imagined to live underground and thwart the miners; today we might call them gremlins.

LOELLINGITE FeAs$_2$

Orthorhombic — bipyramidal $\frac{2}{m}\frac{2}{m}\frac{2}{m}$

Environment: Silvery metallic crystals in rare pegmatites. Otherwise mingled with cobalt and/or nickel in high-temperature and medium-temperature veins. **Crystal description:** In pegmatites it forms small crystals of a prismatic habit. Otherwise observed only in polished study specimens, identified by microscope in massive or thin veins of cobalt-nickel ores. **Physical properties:** Tin-white. *Luster* metallic; *hardness* 5–5$^1/_2$; *specific gravity* 6.2–8.6; *fracture* uneven; *cleavage*: basal.

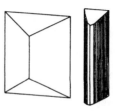

Composition: Diarsenide of iron, sometimes (in vein manifestations) with antimony, cobalt, and nickel. The presence of small quantities of nickel and cobalt make variously named varieties. Arsenic plus antimony totals about 68% (about 32% Fe, As + Sb about 68%). **Tests:** Fuses with difficulty into a magnetic globule, giving off white arsenic oxide fumes (garlic odor) on charcoal. Dissolves in nitric acid to form a clear yellow solution, which may be colored pink or pale green when notable quantities of cobalt or nickel are present. See other tests under skutterudite (p. 130).

Distinguishing characteristics: This brittle silvery sulfide is difficult to distinguish from arsenopyrite, which it resembles in appearance. However, loellingite gives no sulfur test (see arsenopyrite, p. 127). In vein occurrences, indistinguishable from skutterudite, safflorite ([Co, Fe]As$_2$), and rammelsbergite without x-ray tests (but these are all present only in the rare nickel-silver-cobalt (Ni-Ag-Co) ore suites and give most collectors no problem, because they are not found in pegmatites).

Occurrence: In the U.S., loellingite is a rare mineral, except in some of the New England pegmatites, where it forms silvery metallic stringers in garnet or phosphates. Crystals were found at Franklin, New Jersey. Massive loellingite or rammelsbergite (NiAs$_2$) was one of the cobalt ores at Cobalt, Connecticut, in a briefly worked high-temperature vein. It has been reported from Gunnison Co., Colorado (an ore vein), and Alexander Co., North Carolina. It is more abundant abroad; good crystals were found in Norway, Sweden, and Finland in nonlithia-type pegmatites.

MARCASITE FeS$_2$ **Pl. 18**

Orthorhombic — bipyramidal $\dfrac{2}{m} \dfrac{2}{m} \dfrac{2}{m}$

Environment: Sedimentary rocks and low-temperature veins. **Crystal description:** Crystals tabular, parallel to a horizontal axis. However, usually grown together in curving or cockscomblike groups. Also in concretionary masses with radiating structure and botryoidal or reniform crusts. **Physical properties:** Light brass yellow. *Luster* metallic; *hardness* 6–6^1/$_2$; *specific gravity* 4.9; *fracture* uneven; *cleavage* poor prismatic. Brittle. **Composition:** Iron sulfide (46.5% Fe, 53.5% S). **Tests:** The same as pyrite, except that excess sulfur is freed in the strong nitric acid solution, leaving it cloudy. Some solution takes place in cold dilute nitric acid, indicated by the immediate formation of bubbles on the grains.

Distinguishing characteristics: Likely to be confused only with pyrite, from which it can be distinguished by greater solubility in cold dilute nitric acid. Generally whiter than pyrite on a fresh surface, and, like it, harder than most other sulfide minerals.

Occurrence: The geological conditions that cause iron and sulfur to combine to form the mineral marcasite are critical; normally pyrite is the product. Marcasite is often associated with galena, sphalerite, calcite, and dolomite, as near Joplin, Missouri, and in the Wisconsin lead-zinc region. Marcasite "cockscombs" and spear-shaped intergrowths grow in clays and marls (though many "combs" are often actually distorted pyrite).

Remarks: Marcasite specimens almost invariably oxidize in collections, freeing sulfur to form an acid that attacks the labels and trays, and speeding the disintegration of the specimens. Often it is intergrown with pyrite, but no truly satisfactory method of preventing the decomposition has yet been found. It has been suggested that the breakdown is due to renewed activity of a geologically ancient infection of anaerobic bacteria and that thorough sterilization, as with Lysol, can halt or slow the destruction. It is an interesting suggestion and should be investigated further by collectors. "Sooty" chalcocite, pyrrhotite, and arsenopyrite are other likely prospects for such experimentation.

ARSENOPYRITE FeAsS   Pl. 19

Monoclinic — Monoclinic normal $\dfrac{2}{m}$

Environment: High- and medium-temperature veins, pegmatites; sometimes disseminated in crystalline (igneous) rocks. **Crystal description:** Pseudo-orthorhombic, commonly in distinct crystals, which, like marcasite, are elongated sideways, parallel to a horizontal axis, even appearing prismatic. Often forms solid masses. **Physical properties:** Silver-white. *Luster* metallic; *hardness* $5\frac{1}{2}$–6; *specific gravity* 5.9–6.2; *fracture* uneven; *cleavage* prismatic. Brittle. **Composition:** Iron sulfarsenide (34.3% Fe, 46.0% As, 19.7% S). In veins, often intergrown with loellingite and rammelsbergite. **Tests:** Arsenic (garlic) smell is noted immediately after fracturing with hammer blow. On charcoal gives white fumes and leaves black magnetic mass or, after long blow-piping, a globule. (Make no platinum wire test without extended roasting to free all arsenic.) Decomposed by nitric acid, leaving spongy sulfur mass. A sulfur test can be obtained by fusing with sodium carbonate, crushing to a powder on a silver disk (find an old dime!), and wetting. Tarnished spot proves sulfur's presence.

Distinguishing characteristics: Distinguished from the sulfur-free white nickel arsenides by a sulfur test and by negative results in cobalt-nickel tests. Wedge-topped crystals are common enough to be guides to identification.

Occurrence: Arsenopyrite is an ore of arsenic, usually an unwelcome by-product of other mining operations. Good crystals were common in the Freiberg, Germany, nickel-silver mines; in the Cornwall, England, and tin mines of Bolivia, and in the Iname Mine, Aichi Prefecture, Japan. The Panasqueira, Portugal, arsenopyrites are among the best ever found, 12 in. (30 cm). long. Naillike crystals from Pitkaranta, Finland are unique and remarkable. Typical deposits include a Japanese locality (Obira mine, Kyushu I.); Trepca, in the former Yugoslavia; and a generous Zacatecas, Mexico, mine. A massive vein of arsenopyrite once was mined in Edenville, New York.

Remarks: Found in pegmatites in isolated crystals and associated with garnet and the phosphates. Loellingite sometimes takes the place of arsenopyrite, as at Franklin, New Jersey. A cobaltiferous variety, danaite, in which cobalt may take the place of as much as 9 percent of the iron, is named for J. Freeman Dana of Boston, not for mineralogist James D. Dana.

MOLYBDENITE MoS_2 **Pl. 19**

Hexagonal — Dihexagonal bipyramidal $\frac{6}{m}\frac{2}{m}\frac{2}{m}$

Environment: Disseminated as flakes and tiny crystals in igneous rocks and infrequently in larger crystals in simple pegmatites. **Crystal description:** Crystals are common, sometimes well developed but usually misshapen, since they are tabular and split or bend easily. Also in small irregularly shaped flakes; rarely finely granular. **Physical properties:** Lead gray. *Luster* metallic; *hardness* 1–1^1/$_2$ *specific gravity* 4.7–4.8; *streak* gray on paper; *cleavage* perfect micaceous basal. Flakes flexible, but not elastic; greasy feel; sectile. **Composition:** Molybdenum disulfide (60.0% Mo, 40.0% S). **Tests:** Under the oxidizing flame gives sulfur (rotten-egg) fumes on charcoal and colorful coatings around the assay: red near the assay, yellow cooling to white farther away. The white coating touched by the reducing flame becomes azure blue.

Distinguishing characteristics: Soft and flexible flakes can only be confused with graphite, which is blacker. The blowpipe test is extremely easy and characteristic. Splitting the cleavage, a hint of violet is seen between two slightly separated, mirroring cleavage flakes of molybdenite.

Occurrence: Disseminated flakes of molybdenite became an ore of molybdenum at Climax, Colorado. They are separated with the copper mineral in Bingham Canyon, Utah, where small flakes are abundantly scattered through the porphyry. Large plates (1 in., 3 cm) from Deepwater, New South Wales, associated with quartz are cabinet specimens. Good crystals embedded in pegmatites, coarse granitic rock, or quartz are fairly common. Chelan, Washington, is a notable example for these.

Remarks: Molybdenite, though seldom seen in rocks, may be the primary source of molybdenum, from which secondary molybdenum minerals (molybdates such as powellite) might form as a result of weathering. (See powellite, p. 265.) Although unrecognizable as a mineral, there also appears to be an amorphous, easily oxidized molybdenum sulfide (jordisite, MoS) that decomposes readily to a water-soluble blue dye. On drying, inky blue hues redeposit as the molybdenum oxide called ilsemannite. This oxide tints rocks blue at the Marysvale, Utah, mine and in the ore piled about the wartime Lakeview, Oregon, uranium refinery. Associated with realgar and orpiment, it makes colorful red-yellow-blue hand specimens. Even at Nevada's Getchell Mine, realgar and orpiment have dry-weather blue spots.

CALAVERITE $AuTe_2$ }   **Pl. 19**
SYLVANITE $(Au,Ag)Te_2$ }

Monoclinic — prismatic $\dfrac{2}{m}$

Environment: Rare; in late low-temperature precious metal ore veins. **Crystal description:** Usually in crystals, deeply striated, elongated parallel to a horizontal axis. Commonly twinned and difficult to orient; structurally a real challenge. Also granular and massive. **Physical properties:** Pale brass yellow to silver-white. *Luster* metallic; *hardness* $2\frac{1}{2}$; *specific gravity* 8.2 (sylvanite) to 9.3 (calaverite); *fracture* uneven; *cleavage* none or (sylvanite) a side pinacoid cleavage. Brittle. **Composition:** Inseparable tellurides of gold and of silver (44.03% Au, 55.97% Te). Calaverite becomes sylvanite when 13.4% of its gold is replaced by silver. **Tests:** Gives ice blue tint to flames flaring from bead on charcoal, eventually shrinking into a gold button. A higher silver content of sylvanite makes bead whiter.

Distinguishing characteristics: The deeply striated, elongated, and flat-lying crystals are unmistakable; they are usually the lone metallic glints on specimens. The gold assay bead is easy to obtain and can hardly be misidentified.

Occurrence: Calaverite is a rare mineral, but an important ore of gold in Kalgoorlie, Western Australia; Calaveras Co., California; and Cripple Creek, Colorado. In the veins it is associated only with sylvanite, other tellurides, tellurium, quartz, and fluorite, as a rule with no base metal ores. Cripple Creek was the only really spectacular occurrence of this mineral. Sylvanite is also found with related minerals in Nagyág and Offenbånya in Transylvania. "Blister-gold" specimens, sold long ago in Colorado to tourists as natural gold when Cripple Creek was in production, are actually examples of these two ores that were roasted to drive off the tellurium and bring bubbles of gold to the surface. The structure of these minerals has proved one of the most tantalizing problems that x-ray mineralogists have encountered. Current thinking has classified them as triclinic and twinned.

♦HIGHER ARSENIDES OF COBALT, NICKEL, AND IRON

This group of minerals includes varieties closely related chemically, but divided into two isomorphous series on the basis of their crystal structure. They have been somewhat clarified and their names simplified, so current names no longer match those found in the older literature. Isomorphous is a term appearing frequently in mineralogy; it describes a series of minerals having the same chemical and crystal structure and containing mixtures of two or more of the metallic elements in a chemical combination, any one of which may be more abundant. The pure compounds — salts with only one of the two or more metal elements possible — are called the end-members of the series. The world has few veins of this type; all known ones are fully exploited and deeply dug, so near-surface, open-pocket, well-crystallized specimens are not freely available.

SKUTTERUDITE $(Co,Ni,Fe)As_3$

Cubic — diploidal $\frac{2}{m}\overline{3}$

Environment: This series occurs in medium-temperature veins lining walls, associated with silver and related silver-hued cobalt and nickel minerals, often interlocked and all looking much alike. **Crystal description:** Usually massive and granular. Crystals may develop, particularly on surfaces in contact with a calcite vein filling, but they are dull and uneven. Cube and octahedron faces are most common, sometimes with dodecahedrons and pyritohedrons. **Physical properties:** Tin-white. *Luster* metallic; *hardness* $5\frac{1}{2}$–6; *specific*

gravity 6.1–6.8; *fracture* granular; *cleavage* none. Brittle.
Composition: Triarsenides of cobalt, nickel, and iron. Arsenic amounts to 75% of the weight; the balance is made up by the metals. This series was formerly known under the name smaltite-chloanthite and was considered to be completely isomorphous with a third iron triarsenide. Subsequent studies indicate that only the cobalt triarsenide actually exists in a pure state and cobalt, iron, and nickel are always present in the others. This suggests that skutterudite should be the name for the high-cobalt end-member (formerly smaltite), and the others should be known (depending upon their analyzed composition) as nickelian skutterudite (instead of chloanthite) and ferroan skutterudite (instead of the discredited "arsenoferrite"). **Tests:** Skutterudite fuses on charcoal, giving an arsenic (garlic) odor and forming magnetic ball. A cobalt-rich skutterudite ball dissolves in nitric acid to form a pink solution, though iron and nickel are usually present in sufficient abundance to mask the color. Tests on analyzed samples showed that a nitric acid solution of (cobalt) skutterudite neutralized by ammonia becomes red-violet and a red-violet precipitate settles out. Nickel skutterudite under the same conditions gave a blue-violet solution and a pale green precipitate. Rarer ferroan skutterudite gives a strong brown iron-hydroxide precipitate that will mask either of the other elements.
Distinguishing characteristics: From a collector's standpoint, this series is of marginal significance; distinguishing its specifics requires too-sophisticated tests. Likely to be confused with arsenopyrite, which gives no cobalt or nickel test, and with cobaltite and a series of diarsenides (loellingite and rammelsbergite), which cannot be distinguished by methods available to amateurs.
Occurrence: Valuable ores of cobalt and nickel. In North America this series is abundant and of great economic importance only at Cobalt, Ontario; rare elsewhere. It was important only in minor veins in Germany, France, Spain, Morocco, and Chile. In recent years, the best crystal source of high-cobalt skutterudites has been Bou Azzer, Morocco.
Remarks: Weathering of this triumvirate of minerals results in the formation of pink and green secondary minerals (erythrite and annabergite) on outcrops and near the surface. These colors are good guides to the presence of minerals of this and the related group. They are rarely pure and commonly have closely locked zones with differing compositions so that it is only possible to analyze pure samples with a microprobe.

◆ SULFOSALTS

This is a group of sulfide minerals in which the semimetals antimony, arsenic, or bismuth join with a truly metallic element to form a double salt. For simplicity the formula can be divided into the two sulfide combinations which, with sulfur, make up the mineral. Since there are many combinations of identical elements in different proportions, with each making a different mineral, the collector usually requires some additional data, such as crystal form, to make positive identifications. Often even the qualitative analyses provided by blowpipe and chemical tests will not suffice.

Many of the sulfosalt minerals are relatively rare, so identification is not usually a problem. Crystals are frequent, since all have formed in or near the surface, in relatively low-temperature and low-pressure conditions conducive to crystal pocket development. Usually crystals will confirm a tentative identification. Without crystals, one often cannot make a positive identification, but must turn the specimen over to the x-ray mineralogist.

Some series are more common than others. There are, for instance, several similar lead antimony sulfides, but the lead arsenic sulfides are rarer, fewer, and different in structure. Arsenic can be present in the predominantly antimony-bearing minerals and antimony in the arsenic-bearing minerals, but not to the unlimited extent of an isomorphous series. The near-surface formation means that all of the occurrences in populated areas were found centuries ago. Consequently, notable specimens are now unobtainable for many of the group.

POLYBASITE $(Ag,Cu)_{16}Sb_2S_{11}$ **Pl. 19**

Monoclinic — prismatic $\frac{2}{m}$

Environment: Low-temperature silver-bearing veins. **Crystal description:** Flat pseudohexagonal plates, with pseudorhombohedral faces on the edges. Base commonly triangularly striated parallel to three of the face edges, increasing its resemblance to a rhombohedral mineral. Also massive. **Physical properties:** Iron black; deep red and translucent in thin splinters. *Luster* metallic; *hardness* 2–3; *specific gravity* 6.0–6.2; *streak* blackish red; *fracture* uneven; *cleavage* perfect basal. Brittle. **Composition:** A silver antimony sulfide, in which copper may substitute to the extent of 12%. An average composition might run about 65% Ag, 9% Cu, 10% Sb,

15% S, and about 1% As. **Tests:** Fuses easily, drawing into a shiny, dark metallic globule that dulls on cooling. At first malleable, then crushes to powder. Hot bead is ringed with a white antimony sublimate. Nitric acid solutions respond to the milky silver chloride test.

Distinguishing characteristics: The crystal form is the best guide to this mineral after silver is identified. Crystals might be mistaken for hematite, but softness and the easy fusibility would soon show them to be something different. The reddish streak is dark. Specular hematite would be weakly magnetic with crystals brighter, harder, sharper, and more lustrous.

Occurrence: Polybasite occurs with other silver antimony sulfides. Once abundant in Mexico and fairly common in the German silver districts, it was an important early ore of silver. Outstanding specimens were never found in the U.S., but small quantities occurred in many mines in Colorado, Idaho, Montana, and Nevada. Like all shallow silver vein minerals, practically extinct for collectors.

Remarks: Its mimicry of hexagonal crystals suggests that at some temperature (that of its formation) it inverts to the higher-symmetry group. Little studied now because of rarity.

STEPHANITE Ag_5SbS_4 **Pl. 19**
Orthorhombic — pyramidal m m 2
Environment: Low-temperature silver-bearing veins. **Crystal description:** Usually recognized by its crystals, which are moderately common, well formed, and occasionally several centimeters in size. Short-prismatic to tabular. Sometimes twinned to produce seeming hexagonal shapes. Also massive and disseminated through other ores. **Physical properties:** Iron black, tending to turn dull black in collections. *Luster* metallic; *hardness* 2–2$\frac{1}{2}$; *specific gravity* 6.2–6.3; *streak* black; *fracture* subconchoidal to uneven; *cleavage* 2 poor. Brittle. **Composition:** Silver antimony sulfide (68.5% Ag, 15.2% Sb, 16.3% S). **Tests:** Fuses easily, drawing into a shiny gray globule, which dulls and tarnishes on cooling. White antimony sublimates ring the globule.

Distinguishing characteristics: Identified first as a silver antimony sulfide by blowpiping, and sublimate formation. It then usually can be specifically identified by its good crystal shape.

Occurrence: Stephanite is often associated with more common sulfides (galena, sphalerite, argentite, native silver, tetrahedrite, pyrite), and less often with the ruby-silvers (proustite and pyrargyrite) and the gangue minerals (quartz, barite, siderite, calcite, and fluorite). Fine examples have come from Mexico, where it formed crystals several inches across. It was also found in Germany in Saxony and the Harz; in Cornwall, England; and Bolivia. The chief U.S. occurrence (now exhausted) was as one of the important silver ores of the famous Comstock Lode in Nevada, though few specimens seem to have survived. It is still occasionally found in Colorado and California, and in Canada at Cobalt and South Lorrain, Ontario.

PYRARGYRITE Ag_5SbS_3 **Pl. 20**

Hexagonal — Ditrigonal pyramidal 3 m

Environment: Low-temperature silver veins. **Crystal description:** Often well crystallized; being hemimorphic, the upper faces differ from those of the lower end, although since crystals are seldom doubly terminated, this phenomenon is not usually apparent. Most often truncated at the tip with gently sloping rhombohedron faces above steep scalenohedrons. Also massive. **Physical properties:** Deep red to almost black. *Luster* adamantine; *hardness* $2^1/_2$; *specific gravity* 5.8–5.9; *streak* purplish red; *fracture* conchoidal; *cleavage* 2 rhombohedral (1 good). Brittle. **Composition:** Silver antimony sulfide (59.9% Ag, 22.3% Sb, 17.8% S). Surprisingly low arsenic substitution for antimony, even though it often occurs with proustite. **Tests:** Fuses readily into round shiny globule. Antimony sublimate forms white ring close to assay, best seen immediately after first melting. Continued heating creates a dull gray malleable button, which gives good test for silver (hydrochloric acid added to nitric acid solution).

Distinguishing characteristics: Usually the crystal form and dark red color are a sufficient guide. Pyrargyrite could be confused with dark proustite, but the antimony sublimate around the pyrargyrite button reveals a difference. Cuprite gives copper tests; zincite is infusible. In general, the mineral associations suggest silver minerals whenever we encounter pyrargyrite or proustite.

Occurrence: Pyrargyrite is a late mineral in the silver veins, and probably is also formed secondarily by hot volatile compounds reworking earlier deposits. Specimens are usually discovered only in the early stages of a silver-mining operation, when it is sometimes an important ore of silver. Although fine specimens are often destroyed to quickly obtain their silver value, the specimen value of good crystals is, as a rule, far greater. The best examples have come from Germany, in the Harz and Saxony. In France good crystals were found at Sainte-Marie-aux-Mines, Alsace, and at Chalanches, Isère. Chanarcillo, Chile, better known for its proustite, was a great source, as was Colquechaca, Bolivia. Some Mexican mines, as at Guanajuato, have enough pyrargyrite for it to be an ore. It is not abundant in the U.S. Castrovirreyna, Peru, has lately been a source of respectable examples.

Remarks: Known as dark ruby-silver ore *(dunkles Rotgültigerz)*, distinguished as a rule by its deeper hue from the light ruby-silver ore, proustite *(lichtes Rotgültigerz)*. Both, on exposure to light, have a tendency to darken and develop a dull coating that dims their luster. If the specimen is sturdy enough to stand it, a light brushing with soap and water will remove much of the coating. A quick dip in a silver-polishing solution has been found effective but may be risky to the luster.

PROUSTITE $(Ag_3 \cdot AsS_3)$

Hexagonal — Rhombohedral hemimorphic   3 m

Environment: Near the surface, commonly in vugs (open cavities) in low-temperature silver veins. **Crystal description:** Crystals common, generally more slender with steeper rhombohedrons than those of pyrargyrite, and more often in steep scalenohedrons truncating trigonal prisms. Also massive. Intergrowths of three crystals, trillings, frequent in Chañarcillo (Chile) crystals. **Physical properties:** Light to dark red. *Luster* adamantine; *hardness* $2-2^{1}/_{2}$; *specific gravity* 5.6–5.7; *streak* dark red; *fracture* conchoidal; *cleavage* distinct rhombohedral; Brittle; translucent to transparent. **Composition:** Silver arsenic sulfide $(3Ag2S \cdot As2S3)$. Antimony is sometimes present in about the same amount—to 3%—that arsenic is present in pyrargyrite. **Tests:** Fuses at once into globule on charcoal, giving abundant arsenic (garlic) fumes, coloring flame around assay white, but forming no deposit close to the globule. Malleable dull gray button, formed after long blowing, dissolves in nitric acid and gives silver test when hydrochloric acid is added.

Distinguishing characteristics: Can be mistaken for pyrargyrite, but is usually lighter in color. Other red minerals, with their distinctions, are listed under pyrargyrite (preceding).

Occurrences: Proustite is a late primary or a secondary mineral in the veins. The finest crystals ever found came over a century ago from Chañarcillo, Chile. Some of these are in long crystals, many of which are trillings. They may be over 4 in. (10 cm) long and about $^{1}/_{2}-^{3}/_{4}$ in. (1–2 cm) across, and are dark ruby red. Smaller examples from the little-known Keeley Mine (South Lorrain, Ontario) were also outstanding. Darker but well-developed crystals came from the Harz and Saxony in Germany. It has been an important ore mineral in Mexico, and although occasionally noted in the U.S. it is usually rare. More recently, good crystals have been found only in Niederschlema, near Schneeberg, Germany, an old-time district. Transparent examples have been faceted into small stones. It is close to the top of the list as a mineral collectible.

TETRAHEDRITE	$(Cu,Fe)_{12}Sb_4S_{13}$	**Pl. 19**
TENNANTITE	$(Cu,Fe)_{12}As_4S_{13}$	

Cubic — Tetrahedral $\overline{4}$ 3 m

Environment: Fairly common, usually with gangue, sphalerite, and galena, in medium- and low-temperature ore veins. **Crystal description:** Tetrahedrite commonly well crystallized in sharp, distinct, well-formed tetrahedrons; tennantite usually less well developed, and often richer in forms and more cubic in habit. Also massive. **Physical properties:** Gray to iron black. *Luster* metallic; *hardness* 3–4½ (tennantite harder); *specific gravity* 4.6–5.1 (tetrahedrite denser); *streak* brown to black; *cleavage* none; *fracture* subconchoidal to uneven. Brittle; some specimens of tennantite translucent deep red in thin splinters. **Composition:** Copper, iron antimony, and arsenic sulfide; really a whole series of related minerals (isomorphous series) with antimony and arsenic as end-members. Copper is the predominant metal, but zinc, mercury, silver, and lead can also enter into the composition. Tetrahedrite (the antimony-rich member) is far more common than tennantite. **Tests:** Easily fused, releasing arsenic or antimony fumes, or both, plus sulfur. Fused globule dissolved in nitric acid gives good red-brown precipitate with ammonia (iron), and blue (copper) color to solution. Lead and silver can be shown to be present by adding hydrochloric acid to the nitric acid solution. The blue-green solution turns greener and a white precipitate forms. These tests should suffice; normally the tetrahedral crystals are enough, when visible.

Distinguishing characteristics: When crystals are present they are the best guide. Failing these, the problem becomes more difficult, since there are many gray metallic sulfides with which these two can be confused. Detection of copper, iron, lead, and silver should permit running down tetrahedrite-tennantite by elimination. The subconchoidal, brilliant fracture, lack of cleavage, and comparative hardness are all significant.

Occurrence: Tetrahedrite is one of the most common and economically the most important of the sulfosalts. Often an important ore of copper, it is usually found in typical copper vein associations. Fine glossy crystals, probably the best in the U.S., have come from Bingham Canyon, Utah. It is found in many European localities (in Germany, England, and Czechoslovakia) and in some of the famous South American copper mines (Cerro de Pasco, Casapalca, and Morococha, all in Peru).

Tennantite is much rarer. The best-formed and multifaced crystals have come from the isolated sulfide pocket occurrence at Binnatal, Switzerland. It is also found in many U.S. mines, where it is difficult to distinguish from the tetrahedrite found in other sections of the same veins. Tsumeb, Namibia, has become an important locality with sharp 1-in. (2–3 cm) tennantite tetrahedrons. An occurrence in Zacatecas, Mexico, of like-sized crystals first called tennantite turned out to be a mixture of the two (tennantite and tetrahedrite) grown over crystals of chalcopyrite that are scattered over a crystallized quartz crust.

ENARGITE Cu_3AsS_4 **Pl. 20**
Orthorhombic — pyramidal   m m 2
Environment: Medium-temperature ore veins. **Crystal description:** Smaller crystals fairly common, usually prismatic, with several grooved, almost curving, prisms, and a flat truncating base. Rarely in up to 6-in.-long (15 cm) crystals. Sometimes tabular; also massive and granular. **Physical properties:** Gray-black to iron black. *Luster* metallic; *hardness* 3; *specific gravity* 4.4–4.5; *streak* grayish black; *fracture* uneven; *cleavage* perfect prismatic. Brittle. **Composition:** Copper arsenic sulfide (48.3% Cu, 19.1% As, 32.6% S), but up to 6% antimony can take the place of arsenic. The far rarer tetragonal antimony equivalent, known as famatinite (Cu_3SbS_4), has a reddish tint on a polished surface. Enargite is dimorphous with pinkish, tetragonal luzonite. **Tests:** Fuses on charcoal (with the sublimates and odor of sulfur, antimony, and arsenic), leaving a bead that can produce, with borax fluxes and great care, a copper bead. Touched with hydrochloric acid the melted bead will show a blue copper flame; or in a nitric acid solution plus ammonia will give the copper blue color.

Distinguishing characteristics: The crystals are typical, rather like those of manganite, but the blowpipe response quickly shows the difference. Enargite is difficult to distinguish from many related minerals, though the tests for arsenic and copper separate enargite and luzonite from minerals lacking those elements.

Occurrence: Enargite is an important ore of copper and is usually associated in ore deposits with other copper minerals and sulfides. It is frequently in well-crystallized specimens; individuals once found in Quiruvilca, Peru, were a spectacular 6 in. (15 cm) long.

An abundant ore in the deep sulfide part of the great Chuquimata copper deposit (Chile). Butte, Montana, is the most important locality in the U.S., but it is also found in Colorado, Utah, and California. Microscopic crystals have been found at Picher, Oklahoma, perched on $1/4$-in. (5 mm) chalcopyrite crystals. Good $1^1/_2$-in. (4 cm) crystals are found in Japan at the Kaize-mura Mine, Nagano Prefecture.

Remarks: Enargite was originally thought to be isomorphous with the antimonial equivalent famatinite (antimony present to any amount in place of arsenic). It is now known to be tetragonal. At Morococha, Peru, enargite bands seem to be transformed inward from silvery gray enargite at the base of crystal crusts into a pinkish gray sulfide, seemingly a dimorphous tetragonal equivalent without enargite's distinct cleavage planes known as luzonite. Luzonite crystals have been found at the Teine Mine, Sapporo, Japan, and in Taiwan at the Chinkuashih Mine.

BOURNONITE $PbCuSbS_3$ $(2PbS \cdot Cu_2S \cdot Sb_2S_3)$ **Pl. 20**

Orthorhombic — bipyramidal $\dfrac{2}{m}\dfrac{2}{m}\dfrac{2}{m}$

Environment: In medium-temperature ore veins, full of open cavities. **Crystal description:** A popular mineral among collectors for large interestingly intergrown crystals, which produce a radiating (cogwheel) effect. Usually in short-prismatic, tabular crystals, sometimes several inches across. Also massive. **Physical properties:** Black to grayish black. *Luster* metallic; *hardness* $2^1/_2$–3; *specific gravity* 5.8–5.9; *streak* gray to black; *fracture* subconchoidal to uneven; *cleavage* 1 good, 2 less good at right angles to it. Brittle. **Composition:** Lead and copper sulfantimonide (13.0% Cu, 42.5% Pb, 24.7% Sb, 19.8% S; some As can take the place of Sb). **Tests:** Fuses easily to a silvery, metallic globule with first a white then a yellow ring around the globule. Decomposed by nitric acid, giving a solution that is weak blue-green in color (copper), which becomes cloudy with a white precipitate of sulfur and lead, and a skeletal yellow residue of sulfur.

Distinguishing characteristics: The crystals are very typical, and usually show the intergrowth known as twinning. When crystals are not present, difficult to identify positively.

Occurrence: One of the commonest of the sulfosalt group, and open cavities (vugs) are unusually frequent in bournonite-bearing veins. Its associates are galena, sphalerite, tetrahedrite, chalcopyrite, pyrite, siderite, quartz, and barite. Particularly good, but little twinned, specimens came from Germany, both from Neudorf in the Harz and from Horhausen, Rhine province. Spectacular, fully twinned crystals were found at the Herodsfoot Mine in Cornwall, England, and a few crystals up to 4 in. (10 cm) across have come from Bolivia, where it is found in a number of mines, and from Quiruvilca, Peru. In Japan, the Chichibu Mine, Saitama Prefecture, is a good crystal source. In the U.S., good but unspectacular crystals have been found with pyrite and siderite at Park City, Utah; in Yavapai Co., Arizona; and in Colorado and Montana.

Remarks: Bournonite is known as Radelerz (wheel ore) by German miners and in Cornwall under the equivalent term "cogwheel ore." The striking crystal outline has caught the fancy of miners and collectors alike the world over, and examples of the Cornwall "cogwheels" command premium prices. The finest museum examples will be found in London and Truro, Cornwall.

BOULANGERITE $Pb_5Sb_4S_{11}$

Monoclinic — prismatic $\dfrac{2}{m}$

Environment: Medium- and low-temperature ore deposits.

Crystal description: Long, deeply striated, slender prisms to solid fibrous and feathering masses. **Physical properties:** Bluish lead gray. *Luster* metallic; *hardness* $2\frac{1}{2}$–3; *specific gravity* 5.7–6.3; *cleavage* 1 good, parallel to the elongation (none across, thin fibers flexible, unlike brittle jamesonite needles). Fibrous, splintery. **Composition:** Lead antimony sulfide ($5PbS \cdot 2Sb_2S_3$: 55.4% Pb, 25.7% Sb, 18.9% S). **Tests:** Decrepitates (wear eye protection), then melts easily into flattened bubbly mass that clings to charcoal. Acid reactions are like those of jamesonite, except that solution takes longer.

Distinguishing characteristics: Almost indistinguishable from several similar species of a group known as "feather ores," except by x-ray pattern or by a quantitative analysis. In contrast to jamesonite, boulangerite fuses with decrepitation, forming a spreading, frothing, spongy mass. Jamesonite fibers are more brittle than those of boulangerite. Both tend to alter into a yellow-brown formless mass called bindheimite ($Pb_2Sb_2O_6[O,OH]$).

Occurrence: Boulangerite is associated in veins with other lead sulfosalts, and with stibnite, sphalerite, galena, quartz, and siderite. It occurs at many localities in Europe as well as in Peru and Mexico. In the U.S., solid plumose (feathery) masses are found in Stevens Co., Washington. In Idaho, Colorado, and Nevada similar examples occur with other ores, but it is not abundant in this country. Common in loose hairs resembling the usual jamesonite in Zacatecas, Mexico.

MIARGYRITE $AgSbS_2$ **Pl. 20**

Monoclinic — prismatic $\dfrac{2}{m}$

Environment: Low-temperature silver-bearing veins. **Crystal description:** Usually small black striated crystals of complicated form, very difficult to orient. Also massive with other silver minerals. **Physical properties:** Iron black to steel gray. *Luster* metallic; *hardness* 2–2$\frac{1}{2}$, *specific gravity* 5.1–5.3; *streak* cherry red; *fracture* subconchoidal; *cleavage* 3 poor. Brittle; translucent red in thin splinters. **Composition:** A silver antimony sulfide. Some arsenic may replace the antimony, but the very rare light red (darkening in light) arsenic equivalent (smithite, $AgAsS_2$) has only been found at Binnatal, Switzerland. **Tests:** Fuses easily into elongated, flattened, black globule, with heavy antimony sublimate. On prolonged blowing it "boils" and sinks farther into charcoal. Gives silver test in acids.

Distinguishing characteristics: The red streak and the acid silver test eliminate all minerals but pyrargyrite. Behavior differences before the blowpipe and the often small and complex crystals of miargyrite makes distinction of these two minerals easy.

Occurrence: A rare mineral, never forming large crystals; but with its associates, it is of some silver ore importance in Germany—in Saxony and the Harz—and in Mexico. In silver-bearing veins it is associated with polybasite, stephanite, proustite, and pyrargyrite, as well as with native silver and argentite. Good specimens have been found in the San Juan district of Colorado, in Idaho, and in some quantity in California (Randsberg district).

JAMESONITE $Pb_4FeSb_6S_{14}$ **Pl. 20**

Monoclinic — prismatic $\dfrac{2}{m}$

Environment: Low- to medium-temperature veins. **Crystal description:** Almost always finely fibrous, sometimes in loosely matted hairs. Also in solid feathery masses. **Physical properties:** Dark gray. *Luster* metallic; *hardness* $2\frac{1}{2}$; *specific gravity* 5.5–6.0, *cleavage* across the elongation. Brittle. **Composition:** Lead, antimony, iron, sulfide ($4PbS \cdot FeS \cdot 3Sb_2S_3$: 50.8% Pb, 29.5% Sb, 19.7% S). Also some Zn and Cu, and small percentages of Ag and Bi. **Tests:** Fuses easily and almost disappears into the charcoal, leaving a ring of yellow to white sublimates around the assay that forms a magnetic crust. Pulls together more than boulangerite. Soluble in hot hydrochloric acid, with (rotten-egg) smell of H_2S. A strong solution in hydrochloric acid frees a white flaky precipitate (lead chloride) as the acid cools. Weaker solutions may become only cloudy or even remain clear.

Distinguishing characteristics: Jamesonite is difficult to distinguish from related minerals. Plumosite ($Pb_5Sb_6S_{14}$), meneghinite ($Pb_{13}Sb_7S_{23}$), boulangerite ($Pb_5Sb_4S_{11}$), zinkenite ($Pb_6Sb_{14}S_{27}$) lack the iron but are very similar in appearance, except that jamesonite fibers are more brittle. The Germans call the latter group the flexible "feather ores" (*Federerz*). They might be mistaken for some of the manganese oxides, but the form of occurrence and the blowpipe tests distinguish them.

Occurrence: Jamesonite occurs with lead ores, locally, and is a commercial ore when it is mixed with other metal ores. Pribramins. Bohemia and Baia Sprie (formerly Felsöbanya) in Romania were important sources. Cornwall was a source of good matted-hair specimens. In the U.S., Colorado is an abundant source of feather ores, where felted masses of a mixture of zinkenite and jamesonite were formerly found. Idaho, Utah, Nevada, and California have reported occurrences. Usually it is in solid plumose masses, sometimes in slender hairs on crystal cavity surfaces. However, in Noche Buena, Zacatecas, Mexico, coarse jamesonite resembles tiny stibnites, while boulangerite forms hairy masses.

■ OXIDES

Combinations of metallic elements with oxygen make up this group. Most of the oxides have simple crystal structures and simple chemical compositions. Because of their uncomplicated chemistry, the relationships between them are more obvious than in most groups. Water is a mineral that is often considered with this group but, abundant as it is, it hardly requires further mention.

In general, the oxide minerals are the least consistent in physical properties. Oxides may be very soft or very hard, clear as glass or opaque as coal, flash rainbow hues or look like mud, dissolve in water or stand fast in acid, melt in the sun or resist a fiery furnace. The rarest gems and the most abundant ores are simple oxides. Silver and gold have no affinity for oxygen, and no representation in this group. Lead and zinc oxides are rare, but the oxide of tin is its ore, and the only abundant compound in which that metal is found.

Oxides can be broadly assigned to two categories, primary and secondary, corresponding to anhydrous (lacking water) and hydrous. Many primary anhydrous oxides form deep in the crust, some even in magma when molten rock is cooling; others grow in high-temperature veins. All the really hard oxides are the primary ones. (Quartz was long considered an oxide, but because of its internal crystal structure and its physical properties it is now reassigned to the silicates.) The common, softer, hydrous (water-bearing) oxides, however, are those that form through the atmosphere's destruction of other minerals (such as the sulfides) brought to or near the surface. The softer surface oxides create soil and great rust blankets protecting fresh, unaltered underlying rocks.

CUPRITE Cu_2O Cubic — gyroidal 4 3 2   **Pl. 21**
Environment: Very common in uppermost oxidation zone of copper sulfide ore bodies; usually best developed in desert regions. **Crystal description:** Crystals are commonly cubes and octahedrons and combinations of these forms. Frequently in a lattice of square red needles drawn out into distorted cubes; sheets in parallel growths, lining cavities in limonite (called chalcotrichite). Often scattered throughout limonitic rocks, or forming red films on native copper crystals. **Physical properties:** Red to dark red. *Luster* adamantine; *hardness* $3^1/_2$–4; *specific gravity* 5.8–6.1; *streak* red; *fracture* conchoidal; *cleavage* poor octahedral. Brittle; translucent, transparent. **Composition:** Cuprous oxide (88.8% Cu, 11.2% O). **Tests:** Fuses on charcoal and easily reduced to copper bead. Dissolves in acid, giving a blue copper color, and colors blowpipe flame green.

Distinguishing characteristics: Distinguished by crystal shape and copper tests from the ruby-silvers. The blowpipe tests for copper and sulfur also distinguish it from cinnabar, realgar, and zincite. Rutile is usually too dark and brown and has a hardness of 6–6.5. There are almost invariably blue and/or green copper minerals associated with cuprite.

Occurrence: An important secondary ore of copper. It forms near the surface during the oxidation and enrichment of copper sulfide ore bodies as a result of weathering. Depending on the nature of the original ore body, minerals of similar origin are its usual associates: native copper, malachite, azurite, and limonite. This group reaches its best development in dry regions where the water table is low and oxidation has gone deep. Often it seems to be characteristic of the deepest oxidation zone, with cuprite just above the enriched sulfides. Native copper is often adjacent to the cuprite in such deposits and frequently the cuprite has grown on the copper surface. It is a common mineral of wide distribution. Only a few localities can be mentioned. The most complex crystals came from Cornwall, England. The Chessy, France, malachite-coated octahedrons are common in large collections (see azurite, p. 199). Sw. U.S. has been the chief American source of fine specimens, especially the Copper Queen Mine at Bisbee, and at Clifton, Arizona. Chalcotrichite has been found at Bisbee, Morenci, and Jerome, Arizona. Namibia is a late entrant in the important locality list with some of the largest crystals known, malachite-coated but gemmy and as much as 2 in. (5 cm) across (Ongonja Mine). Australia has had several good occurrences, including Cobar and Broken Hill (New South Wales), Burra-Burra and Wallaroo (South Australia).

Remarks: Cuprite belongs to an uncommon class of the cubic system, and its crystals sometimes show the required rare faces. Since it is invariably a secondary mineral, the best specimens will be found in the early stages of a mine's development.

ZINCITE ZnO **Pl. 21**

Hexagonal — Dihexagonal pyramidal 6 m m

Environment: Essentially a mineral of one locality—a metamorphosed weathered ore deposit in New Jersey. **Crystal description:** Crystals rare, always pyramidal, showing interesting hexagonal hemimorphism, usually lying sideways on a fissure in a calcite vein. Also in solid masses and in calcite in rounded club-shaped masses with distinct partings. **Physi-**

cal properties: Orange-yellow to deep red. *Luster* subadamantine; *hardness* 4; *specific gravity* 5.4–5.7; *streak* orange-yellow; *fracture* conchoidal; *cleavage* prismatic (plus a basal parting). Brittle; translucent to transparent. **Composition:** Zinc oxide (80.3% Zn, 19.7% O). Some Mn present, except in synthetic crystals, which are usually greenish or golden. **Tests:** Infusible on charcoal, but on heating the assay turns black—and with cooling regains the original color. Eventually acquires coating of yellow (hot) or white (cold) zinc oxide, which turns green in oxidizing flame after touch of cobalt nitrate solution. This test is improved by crushing and mixing with sodium carbonate. Soluble in acids.

Distinguishing characteristics: The infusibility, plus the zinc test on charcoal and solubility in nitric or hydrochloric acid, will give a positive identification. The crystals, when present, help; but the most important aspect of all is its invariable association (at Franklin, New Jersey) as a reddish orange mineral with black magnetic franklinite, greenish ultraviolet-fluorescing willemite, and white calcite.

Occurrence: This mineral would not be included here were it not once of considerable economic importance as an ore of zinc at Sterling Hill and Franklin, New Jersey, the only important locality. It occurs there in red grains and masses in a white, highly fluorescent calcite, associated with willemite and franklinite. It is the most abundant red Franklin mineral and so is always easily identified in the ore mixtures that are typical of the Franklin specimens. Minor amounts have been noted in Poland; Tuscany, Italy; Spain; and Tasmania.

Remarks: Manganese is believed to cause its red color. Synthetic crystals are light yellow to colorless to pale blue. Some form accidentally from smelter fumes, and examples were marketed as "willemite from Algeria" and still larger gemmy ones from Poland. They can be grown by hydrothermal methods and from a vapor.

MASSICOT PbO

Orthorhombic — Orthorhombic bipyramidal $\frac{2}{m}\frac{2}{m}\frac{2}{m}$

Environment: Very rare. Oxidized zones of lead deposits. **Crystal description:** Artificial crystals only; natural occurrences are earthy to scaly. **Physical properties:** Sulfur to orpiment yellow, sometimes with reddish tint, due to minium (Pb_3O_4) impurity. *Luster* greasy to dull; *hardness* 2; *specific gravity* 9.7; *cleavage* several; powdery or scaly; scales flexible but not elastic; thin scales transparent. **Composition:** Lead oxide

(82.83% Pb, 7.17% O). **Tests:** Fuses easily to form a yellow glass.

Distinguishing characteristics: Association with galena is the best guide. Its fusibility without burning like sulfur or giving off arsenic fumes like orpiment should identify it.

Occurrence: Massicot is a secondary mineral, forming on the alteration of galena. Two related minor species, litharge and minium, form the same way. Massicot usually forms a scaly coating or crumbly film on corroded cavities in that mineral. Litharge (also PbO) has been described as forming the red edge of the massicot scales. Bright red, earthy minium (Pb_3O_4) almost never forms scattered crusts on galena or on rock a little farther from the immediate vicinity of the fresh lead sulfide.

Possibly far more common than generally supposed, massicot is dismissed by most mineral collectors as a thin dull coating marring the beauty of their galena specimens. It is found in the old slags of the Greek lead workings at Lavrion, Greece. In Sardinia and in Germany and Hungary it is associated with galena. In Mexico it is reported to occur in fumarolic deposits from two great volcanoes. It has been reported from many U.S. localities, especially in Colorado at Leadville (a source of good minium, too) and in Nevada and California. In Missouri near Potosi, it has been found in the galena associated with the barite of the diggings. Bright red masses of minium from Broken Hill, New South Wales, were the result of a fire roasting cerussite and, though of questionable legitimacy as minerals, are the best specimens available to collectors.

CORUNDUM (Ruby, Sapphire) Al_2O_3 Pl. 21

Hexagonal — scalenohedral $\overline{3}\,\frac{2}{m}$

Environment: Common in crystals in plutonic, pegmatitic, and metamorphic rocks, and in placer accumulations. **Crystal description:** Six-sided crystals, sometimes elongated into barrels, tapering bipyramids, or sharp flat-topped prisms, but also in thin 6-sided plates. Massive metamorphic occurrences have large embedded crystals, showing series of parallel striations, like the plagioclase feldspars. May be in fine-grained pepperlike disseminations with magnetite (emery). **Physical properties:** Colorless, brown, black, yellow, red, blue, violet. *Luster* adamantine; *hardness* 9; *specific gravity* 3.9–4.1; *fracture* conchoidal or uneven; *cleavage* none, but has well-developed partings on rhombohedral planes and sometimes on the base. Breaks into sharp fragments (brittle), but often is very tough; transparent to translucent; often triboluminescent, and fluorescent orange, yellow, or red. **Composition:** Aluminum oxide (52.9% Al, 47.1% O). **Tests:** Infusible and insoluble.

Distinguishing characteristics: When opaque and nondescript in form and hue, it is poorly crystallized and resembles many silicate minerals. The fine parallel rulings on parting faces are distinctive and might result in a confusion with some feldspars. It often shows color bands and bronzy luster on basal planes. The great hardness is diagnostic; since it is harder than any other natural mineral except diamond, a hardness test should suffice. Good crystal form and high specific gravity (higher than in most silicates) are also distinctive, when they can be observed or determined. Gemmy crystals, those of ruby and sapphire, are simpler.

Occurrence: Usually characteristic of rocks deficient in silicon oxide, with which presumably the aluminum oxide would otherwise combine to form another mineral. Found in igneous rocks, particularly with nepheline, as an accessory. Also found in pegmatites, in basalt dikes, in schists formed in regional metamorphism of sediments accompanied by an introduction of solutions of aluminum oxide, and in metamorphosed limestones. Associated with spinel, kyanite, garnet, and high-calcium feldspars.

Corundum was long an important industrial abrasive and refractory, but also has many gem varieties. The collector's emphasis will be on gemmy crystals for which there are numerous localities, so only a few of the important ones can be mentioned. The gem gravels of Sri Lanka (Ceylon), perhaps formed from weathered pegmatites, perhaps from solution-eaten marbles, are rich in gemmy corundum. Blocks and crystals of corundum have been mined in Africa, Brazil, and Madagascar for abrasive uses. Some of the South African crystals are particularly well formed and may be very large. The rubies and sapphires of Myanmar (Burma) occur as crystals in a metamorphosed limestone, and many are recovered as residual remnants in the earth resting on top of the fresh rock. Tanzania, along the Umba River, is becoming an important source, where the corundum crystals occur in vermiculite (hydrated mica) dikes and as red plates (ruby) in green zoisite (Longido Hills).

The U.S. occurrences are as large crystals and masses in Georgia and North Carolina, together with a few rubies and sapphires. In Montana it is found near Helena in waterworn pebbles in terrace gravel bars by the Missouri River and at Yogo Gulch as flat, blue, gemmy crystals in a dark-colored fine-grained igneous dike. In California small but well-formed crystals have been found in Riverside, San Bernardino, and San Diego counties. Emery (corundum with magnetite) has been mined at Peekskill, New York, and Chester, Massachusetts.

Remarks: The gem colors are caused by minor metal oxide impurities. Ruby, for example, is colored by chromium oxide. Corundum is often fluorescent, glowing red or orange in ultraviolet light, and some is strongly triboluminescent, giving orange flashes when it is sawed or hammered.

Corundum has proved easy to synthesize (except that temperatures near 2000°C are required), crystallizing instantly on the solidification of the molten aluminum oxide. This has led to the mass production of synthetic jewelry stones by simple melting of a suitably pigmented powder in an oxy-hydrogen flame and allowing the hot rain to build up a stalagmite, known as a boule, which is then cut up into decorative stones. Invented by a French chemist in 1891 who claimed to reconstruct rubies, it is known now as the Verneuil process. Lately, ruby crystals have been grown by hydrothermal methods, crystallized from molten solutions, and "pulled" as rods from pots of fused aluminum oxide, for use as bearings, gems, and lasers.

HEMATITE Fe_2O_3 Pl. 25

Hexagonal — scalenohedral $\overline{3}\ \frac{2}{m}$

Environment: A common substance of general occurrence. Found in compact and friable sedimentary beds, in lava flows, as a volcanic sublimate, and as an accessory in veins. **Crystal description:** A mineral of widely varied appearance, from soft red sludge to black metallic crystals (specular hematite). Thick tabular crystals with rhombohedrons and scalenohedrons sometimes bordering a base. Also thin flat scales, which may be intergrown into "iron roses." Low basal rhombohedrons often merge into a curved surface to make thin lenticular scales. Also in mammillary or reniform radiating growths, sometimes in micaceous black schistlike rocks, and in soft, red earthy masses of "paint ore." **Physical properties:** Red or black. *Luster* earthy or metallic; *hardness* 1–6$\frac{1}{2}$; *specific gravity* 4.9–5.3; *streak* bright to dark red; *fracture* conchoidal to uneven; *cleavage* none, but frequent rhombohedral and sometimes basal parting. Specular varieties brittle; excessively thin plates translucent and red; usually even red grains are slightly magnetic. **Composition:** Iron (ferric) oxide (70.0% Fe, 30.0% O). **Tests:** Infusible on charcoal, but becomes darker and strongly magnetic. Soluble in concentrated hydrochloric acid.

Distinguishing characteristics: The red streak is the most important test in distinguishing dark compact varieties of hematite from limonite. The black metallic crystals of specular varieties (specularite) are similarly differentiated from ilmenite and magnetite. The hardness, infusibility, and magnetism after roasting distinguish it from black sulfide and sulfosalt minerals. Behavior under the blowpipe also distinguishes the soft red varieties from cinnabar, cuprite, minium, and the like. There are some flaky hydrous red iron oxides that are often confused with hematite, of which tiny lepidocrocite (FeO[OH]) is the most important.

Occurrence: The most important ore of iron. It occurs in tremendous beds of sedimentary origin, sometimes hardened, metamorphosed, and enriched by subsequent solutions after being laid down. Small black scales have been found around gas vents on lava flows near volcanoes (Vesuvius and Alaska). Massive black beds and scaly schistose hematite rocks are found in metamorphosed sedimentary formations, and hematite crystals may form in rocks of contact metamorphism. Red hematite commonly forms in the soil as the result of weathering of other iron-bearing minerals, and is responsible for the red coloration of many sedimentary rocks. Hematite has formed important secondary ore deposits after iron sulfides (as in Missouri sinkholes). It is also a primary mineral in veins cutting igneous rocks. It has been suggested that at Los Lagos, Chile, there may have been a lava flow that was pure iron oxide, part of which crystallized as hematite, part as magnetite.

The most spectacular large crystals of hematite—flat plates 6 in. (15 cm) or more across—have been found in metamorphosed Brazilian sediments. Many attractively crystallized specimens of rhombohedral habit, often with an iridescent tarnish, come from the island of Elba, Italy. The famous "iron roses" from crystal-lined pockets in the Alps are unmatched elsewhere, but similar examples have been found near Quartzsite, Ariz. Cumberland, England, produces small specular crystals, and the best examples of the interesting fiber-structured reniform knobs—"kidney ore"—of reddish black splintery ore, which is cut as jewelry material ("Alaska diamonds").

For all of its great iron deposits, the U.S. has not produced many spectacular specimens. The Mesabi Range of Minnesota yields only small crystals, and the softer Clinton Red Beds of Alabama have no crystals. The schistose Michigan hematite is brilliant and typical of that occurrence. In its many varieties hematite is one of the commonest minerals we are likely to encounter.

ILMENITE $FeTiO_3$ Pl. 22

Hexagonal — rhombohedral $\overline{3}$

Environment: In metamorphic and plutonic rocks and in pegmatites. **Crystal description:** Equidimensional to tabular, and down to fine, scaly crystals. Also compact, massive, or granular; and as black sand. **Physical properties:** Black to brownish black (geikielite) and deep red (pyrophanite). *Luster* metallic to submetallic; *hardness* 5–6; *specific gravity* 4.1–4.8; *streak* brown, reddish brown to ocher yellow; *fracture* conchoidal to subconchoidal; *cleavage* none in ilmenite (rhombohedral in geikielite and pyrophanite). Brittle; ilmenite is weakly magnetic. **Composition:** An iron titanium oxide; related to hematite except that half of the iron has been replaced by titanium. Manganese and/or magnesium can also take the place of the remaining iron; then the minerals are known respectively as pyrophanite ($MnTiO_3$) and geikielite ($MgTiO_3$). Normal ilmenite has 36.8% Fe, 31.6% Ti, 31.6% O. **Tests:** Infusible on charcoal, but splinter held in forceps will be slightly rounded on edges in hottest blowpipe flame. Best test is titanium coloration: after fusion in borax and repowdering, the pulverized probe is partially dissolved in hot concentrated hydrochloric acid; the acid is then filtered, leaving a clear yellow solution that, after boiling with real tin, becomes very pale blue or violet. Since this is difficult to observe, it is best to use a very strong solution.
Distinguishing characteristics: Color of the streak distinguishes it from hematite, the lesser magnetism from magnetite, the great hardness from the black sulfosalts, and the magnetism from brookite or rutile. Nonmagnetic columbite and tantalite are much heavier, but may require a chemical or specific gravity test.
Occurrence: Ilmenite is a common accessory grain in basic igneous rocks, and grains often become concentrated in sands resulting from rock destruction by weathering. Fine sharp crystals have been found in a pegmatite at Kragerø, Norway. Flat plates are common in U.S. pegmatites, as at Bedford,

Westchester Co., New York. In the U.S. a formation was mined at Sanford Lake in the Adirondacks, where it forms great masses but no good crystals. Occurrences at Lake Allard, Quebec, are of great economic importance, for titanium has become a valuable commercial metal. The magnesium ilmenite, geikielite, has been found in waterworn pebbles in the gem gravels of Sri Lanka (Ceylon) and in grains in the marble of Riverside, California. The manganese ilmenite, pyrophanite, has been found in small red tabular crystals in Sweden and in a rock in Brazil.

Remarks: Important as a source of white titanium oxide now, the nonhazardous pigment that has replaced lead in white paint. Technological progress has made fabrication of titanium metal a practical and commercial operation, and there are a number of uses for this lightweight yet strong metal. The titanium content that long made ilmenite worthless as an iron ore has now become the more valuable constituent.

BIXBYITE $(Mn,Fe)_2O_3$ **Pl. 23**

Cubic — diploidal $\frac{2}{m}\overline{3}$

Environment: Volcanic (rhyolitic) rocks; also a minor mineral in metamorphic manganese deposits. **Crystal description:** Perfect, shiny, cubic crystals with modified corners; may be half an inch (1 cm) on an edge, or larger. Also granular, mixed with other manganese ores. **Physical properties:** Black. *Luster* metallic; *hardness* 6–6$\frac{1}{2}$; *specific gravity* 4.9–5.1; *streak* black; *fracture* irregular; *cleavage* octahedral (cubic in Patagonian crystals). Brittle. **Composition:** Iron manganese oxide; iron can substitute for the manganese up to about 59% Fe_2O_3, or so little that it is nearly pure Mn_2O_3. **Tests:** Fuses with some difficulty, forming (in the high iron varieties) a magnetic globule. Partly soluble in hydrochloric acid, freeing acrid vapors of chlorine.

Distinguishing characteristics: A rare mineral; the crystals from known localities are easy to identify by their shape. Granular material is identifiable only by x-ray methods. A manganese test would indicate the presence of this element. The associated and similar silicate braunite (Mn_7SiO_{12}) and hausmannite $(MnMn_2O_4)$ are infusible; except for manganite, many of the other manganese minerals are softer, fibrous or columnar, or lack any crystal form.

Occurrence: Bixbyite is of economic importance only when mixed with other manganese ores. The most interesting mineralogical occurrence is that of the Thomas Range,

Utah, where it is found in cavities in a light gray altered rhyolite, associated with topaz, pink beryl, and quartz—the result of deposition from volcanic gases that penetrated and altered the rock. It has been found in Patagonia in larger and more highly modified crystals. Several localities in New Mexico and one in n. Mexico yield small crystals much like those of Utah. Found with other manganese ores in India, Sweden, and South Africa.

Remarks: Though actually too rare to warrant inclusion here, it is nevertheless an often-collected, popular, and desirable mineral because of a famed Utah rhyolite pocket occurrence, associated with topaz, pink beryl, and pseudobrookite needles. It is probably more abundant in manganese ore deposits than generally realized.

RUTILE TiO_2 **Pl. 22**

Tetragonal — Ditetragonal bipyramidal $\dfrac{2}{m}\ \overline{3}$

Environment: In plutonic and metamorphic rocks, often in seams in such rocks. **Crystal description:** Crystals common. In high-temperature almost pegmatitic veins, in alpine pockets with hematite plates, in Brazilian quartz veins, and in rock crystal, it forms hairlike to reticular lattices like bridge girders. Embedded in metamorphic aluminous rocks, crystals are equidimensional and compact, often quite large. Often twinned into 6- or 8-sided forms known as sixlings or eightlings (Fig. 26, p. 66). **Physical properties:** Black. In large crystals, golden to reddish brown in capillary needles or thin, flat crystals. *Luster* metallic adamantine; *hardness* 6–$6\frac{1}{2}$; *specific gravity* 4.2–4.3; *streak* light brown; *fracture* subconchoidal to uneven; *cleavage* basal and prismatic. Brittle; translucent to transparent and deep red-brown in thin pieces. **Composition:** Titanium oxide (60.0% Ti, 40.0% O).

Tests: Infusible and insoluble in acid. Can be made soluble by fusing with borax powder, then tested for Ti by dissolving the mixture in hydrochloric acid, filtering and boiling the yellow solution with real tin to produce faint blue or violet color (see ilmenite, p. 149).

Distinguishing characteristics: Difficult to confuse with other minerals, especially after a test for magnetism (negative) and for Ti. Crystals so common they are easy to identify. The waterworn crystals have an adamantine luster but often a bruised look which gives them a sort of light-colored "skin" that is easy to recognize. Black to reddish brown adamantine crystals may be recognized by their striated prisms or geniculated twins. Distinguished from cassiterite (specific gravity 6.8–7.1) by its lesser heft.

Occurrence: Common in embedded crystals in gneiss or schist, in pegmatites, and free-growing in veins of the alpine type. Since it is also a hard, heavy, and common accessory mineral of primary rocks, it occurs in alluvial concentrations of heavy sands.

Large black shiny crystals, more or less equidimensional, are found in a quartzite at Graves Mountain, Georgia, associated with kyanite and lazulite. Beautiful reticulated growths of slender crystals were found in open seams in North Carolina at Hiddenite. Fine oriented growths of flat reddish rutile needles on hematite plates are common among the Swiss "iron roses." Perfect eightlings and rutile replacements of brookite (TiO_2) crystals (paramorphs) are common at Magnet Cove, Arkansas. Slender red-brown hairs of rutile penetrate quartz crystals—by replacement—to form rutilated quartz, also known as *flèches d'amour* or Venus hairstone. Brazil, Switzerland, and the U.S. (West Hartford, Vermont, and Alexander Co., North Carolina) have produced fine specimens of this growth of rutile and quartz.

Remarks: Rutile is used as an ore of titanium and of purified titanium oxide. It has been synthesized in commercial-size crystals by the Verneuil process (see corundum, p. 145). Color of pure, wholly oxidized material is a pale yellow, almost white; the less oxidized is darker, blue to black. Free titanium may be a partial cause of the dark color of most rutile, though an invariable Fe impurity no doubt shares the responsibility.

Oriented growths of rutile within the crystal network of other minerals are common. Oriented three-dimensional sets of rutile hairs cause the streaks of the stars seen in star quartz and star corundums (star sapphires, star rubies).

PYROLUSITE MnO_2 Pl. 23

Tetragonal — Ditetragonal bipyramidal $\frac{4}{m}\frac{2}{m}\frac{2}{m}$

Environment: Secondary manganese deposits and secondary veins. **Crystal description:** Rarely in prismatic or stubby well-formed crystals. Sometimes in fibrous crystals and usually in fibrous masses that are pseudomorphous after other manganese oxides. Also massive, fibrous; and as black powdery to granular masses. **Physical properties:** Steel gray to iron black. *Luster* metallic; *hardness* 6–6$\frac{1}{2}$ (for crystals) to as little as 2 (for massive material), *specific gravity* 4.4–5.0; *streak* black (soft material blackens the fingers); *fracture* uneven; *cleavage* prismatic. Brittle. **Composition:** Manganese dioxide (63.2% Mn, 36.8% O), often with a small amount of water, heavy metals, phosphorus, and other elements.

Tests: Infusible on charcoal; dissolves in hydrochloric acid with the evolution of acrid chlorine gas. Borax bead test is easy, showing in the oxidizing flame a fine amethystine color. (Avoid getting too much and having a black bead.)

Distinguishing characteristics: The sooty black character of the streak and the manganese tests prove presence of manganese, but it is virtually impossible to tell one manganese oxide mineral from another without distinct crystals, except by x-ray tests. Pyrolusite is a safe name for any fibrous-looking mass of black manganese oxide needles or for the black powdery alterations of other manganese minerals.

Occurrence: Pyrolusite is the most common and most important secondary ore of manganese. It forms under conditions of oxidation, either from primary manganese minerals such as the carbonate rhodochrosite, the silicate rhodonite, and the numerous manganese phosphates or as direct deposits from cold ground water in bogs and on the sea floor. It is usually the mineral responsible for fernlike markings commonly observed along rock fissures. These are known as dendrites and are often mistaken for fossil ferns. The mineral is extremely widespread; good specimens are found in some of the Minnesota and Michigan iron ores.

CASSITERITE SnO_2 **Pl. 23**

Tetragonal — Ditetragonal bipyramidal $\dfrac{4}{m}\dfrac{2}{m}\dfrac{2}{m}$

Environment: Pegmatites and high-temperature veins. **Crystal description:** Commonly in well-formed crystals, sometimes prismatic (Cornwall), even needlelike (Cornwall and Bolivia), but more often bipyramidal. Frequently twinned, showing the characteristic re-entrant angle of a twin crystal. Also in red-brown, fibrous, banded crusts ("wood-tin"), in waterworn gray pebbles with a greasy luster ("stream-tin"), and in granular masses. **Physical properties:** Light yellowish to red-brown to black, usually banded within a single crystal. *Luster* adamantine to greasy; *hardness* 6–7; *specific gravity* 6.8–7.1; *streak* nearly white; *fracture* subconchoidal to uneven; *cleavage* poor prismatic. Brittle; transparent to translucent. **Composition:** Tin oxide (78.6% Sn, 21.4% O); usually with a fair amount of iron and sometimes some tantalum, which substitutes for the tin. **Tests:** Infusible. Grain slowly becomes coated with gray or silvery film of tin metal on standing in cool dilute hydrochloric acid with a strip of zinc (cut from casing of dry-cell battery).

Distinguishing characteristics: The light streak, high gravity, and high hardness rule out most similar minerals. The hydrochloric test for tin then eliminates the rest. Might be confused with black tourmaline (which is much lighter), with rutile or columbite-tantalite (make the tin test), and with magnetite (try for magnetism). Some cassiterite is very black, so tests are sometimes essential. Dark bands across broken crystals and the light true color (despite a black exterior appearance) are very typical.

Occurrence: The only important ore of tin. Occurrence is limited to pegmatites and high-temperature veins, often associated with tungsten ores and with silicate gangue minerals; in pegmatites it is an important dark accessory. Often found in stream placers as waterworn pebbles; in Cornwall these were mined before the veins were. In fumarolic deposits (Durango, Mexico) it has formed with hematite on seams in rhyolite flows.

Good crystals come from Cornwall, where it has been mined since Roman days. Bohemia and Saxony have important high-temperature vein occurrences. Alluvial deposits—which are still worked in China, in West Malaysia, and in Indonesia—are among the most important economic occurrences. In Bolivia beautiful specimens are found in association with a variety of minerals in near-surface and low-pressure but high-temperature veins. In the U.S., cassiterite occurs in pegmatites (of no commercial value), though vein deposits in Virginia and California have been unsuccessfully worked. The small red-brown botryoidal masses of "wood-tin" found attached to rhyolite (and broken loose in placer washings in Durango, Mexico) are very different from the other tin varieties, but once seen they are easily recognized.

ANATASE TiO_2 **Pl. 22**

Tetragonal — Ditetragonal bipyramidal $\dfrac{4}{m}\dfrac{2}{m}\dfrac{2}{m}$

Environment: In seams and silicate veins, probably formed at fairly low temperatures. **Crystal description:** Several habits, but always crystallized. Steeply pyramidal, pseudo-octahedral or tabular, often very complexly modified. **Physical properties:** Blue, light yellow to brown. *Luster* adamantine to submetallic; *hardness* $5^{1}/_{2}$–6; *specific gravity* 3.8–3.9; *streak* white; *fracture* subconchoidal; *cleavage* perfect basal and pyramidal. Brittle; translucent to transparent. **Composition:** Titanium oxide (60.0% Ti, 40.0% O) like rutile, except that its atomic structure, and therefore its crystal form, is different. **Tests:** Same as for rutile (p. 151).

Distinguishing characteristics: Usually the crystal form is sufficient. Brown equidimensional crystals might be confused with an octahedral mineral such as microlite, which is generally far heavier. It is safest to get the titanium coloration test (see ilmenite, p. 149).

Occurrence: Anatase is most frequent in vein- or fissure-type alpine deposits. Of value only to collectors, because of its rarity, but holds great scientific interest. Steep blue-black bipyramids lie on quartz in the French Alpine region and in northern Norway. Modified pseudo-octahedral brown crystals occur on the calcareous gneiss in fissures in the Binnatal area, Switzerland, and at Spissen, where some of the largest known crystals occur: steep ditetragonal bipyramids as much as $1/2$ in. (1 cm) tall. Three-cm crystals have been found at Grieserntal. It is found in Brazil on some of the quartz of the veins of the Diamantina district, often altered to rutile if the crystals were not encased in and protected by the quartz. Waterworn, gemmy, tiny deep blue tabular crystals have come from diamond washing in Minas Gerais, Brazil. Anatase is not common in the U.S. The largest crystals (blue) have been found in Gunnison Co., Colorado. Small steep bipyramids were found in calcite-filled quartz veins in a quarry at Somerville, Massachusetts. Waterworn crystals were found in gold washings in North Carolina, and minute steep bipyramids on mica flakes in Lincoln Co., North Carolina.

Remarks: Anatase is our second of three titanium oxides (with rutile and brookite), all chemically alike but distinguished by their crystal symmetries. Probably rarest of the three, and supposedly the one deposited at the lowest temperature. It is also the most readily altered of the titanium oxides.

BROOKITE TiO_2 Pl. 22

Orthorhombic — Rhombic bipyramidal $\frac{2}{m} \frac{2}{m} \frac{2}{m}$

Environment: Silica-bearing veins deposited by hot solutions.

Crystal description: Always crystallized; usually thinly tabular parallel to a side pinacoid and then elongated and striated vertically. More equidimensional at Magnet Cove, Arkansas.

Physical properties: Red-brown to black. *Luster* adamantine to submetallic; *hardness* $5\frac{1}{2}$–6; *specific gravity* 3.9–4.1; *streak* white to gray or yellowish; *fracture* subconchoidal to uneven; *cleavage* poor prismatic and basal. Brittle; translucent to opaque. **Composition:** Titanium oxide (60.0% Ti, 40.0% O). **Tests:** Same as for rutile (p. 151).

Distinguishing characteristics: The crystals—brown elongated flat plates often variegated in color with black corners—are very typical in their association with quartz in veins. There are not many minerals with which it can be confused, and none of those will give a titanium test.

Occurrence: Brookite is another of the titanium oxide group (with rutile and anatase) forming under special conditions at relatively low temperatures. Found also as detrital grains in sandy sediments—grains reported apparently to have grown larger after their deposition in sand, presumably fed by cool solutions percolating through the rocks.

The Swiss occurrences are among the best, yielding very thin crystals, almost an inch (better than 2 cm) long and clearly showing the red-brown color. A well-known English occurrence is the long-exhausted quartz vein with embedded typical brookite plates at Tremadoc, Wales.

It is not uncommon in similar environments in the U.S., but the outstanding American occurrence is in atypical crystals in the quartzite at Magnet Cove, Arkansas. Abundant, black, more or less equidimensional crystals—1 in. (2 cm) or so across at their best—dot a corroded, rusty quartz at this locality. The more typical thin plates have been found with the quartz at Ellenville, New York, associated with chalcopyrite. Brookite is likely to be encountered in any anatase occurrence, as in Somerville, Massachusetts. Small crystals were in the "sand" in the bottom of an amethyst pocket near Butte, Montana.

URANINITE UO_2 **Pl. 23**

Cubic — hexoctahedral $\quad \frac{4}{m} \, \overline{3} \, \frac{2}{m}$

Environment: Pegmatites and medium-temperature veins. **Crystal description:** Two habits of this material are distinguished: crystals known as uraninite and a botryoidal variety with a radiating structure known as pitchblende. The crystals are cubes, octahedrons, and dodecahedrons. The less pure botryoidal type is more plentiful and significant, but is found at fewer localities. **Physical properties:** Steely to velvety or brownish black. *Luster* submetallic, pitchlike, greasy, or dull; *hardness* 5–6; *specific gravity* 6.4–9.7; *streak* brownish black, grayish, or olive green; *fracture* conchoidal or uneven; *cleavage* none. Brittle; opaque. **Composition:** Uranium dioxide; plus many other elements derived from the spontaneous breakdown of the uranium, the end-products of the series being helium and lead. **Tests:** Infusible. Readily soluble in nitric and sulfuric acids, more slowly in hydrochloric. A drop of concentrated nitric acid left to dry on uraninite (free of calcite) evaporates to leave a fluorescent spot. The powder treated with a drop of nitric acid dries to a brilliantly fluorescent dot. Borax, sodium, and lithium fluoride beads are brilliantly fluorescent in ultraviolet light.

Distinguishing characteristics: Crystal form distinctive, but in rock it might be mistaken for microlite (which gives no fluorescent bead or test), magnetite (magnetic), and spinel (much lighter), among the cubic-system minerals. Other black minerals that might give trouble include tourmaline and cassiterite (light streak), columbite, and tantalite (no uranium test), and a whole series of dark, primary uranium-bearing minerals that would be hard to distinguish. Any of the uranium minerals placed on a photographic film in the dark for about 24 hours (or see your dentist for an x-ray film) would make self photographs.

Occurrence: Uraninite is a constituent of pegmatites; pitchblende is a vein mineral. The pegmatite occurrences are widespread but are economically of little importance. In these it is commonly altered to an orange and yellow, amorphous, greasy material (known as gummite) that sometimes surrounds a residual core of fresh black uraninite.

The important sources of uranium ore are the vein deposits, which have been subdivided into several types. Typical of the best are the silver-pitchblende veins of Jáchymov, Czechoslovakia, and Great Bear Lake, Northwest Territories. Pitchblende in the U.S. has come only from Colorado.

Good crystals and dendrites, altered in part to gummite, have come from the American pegmatites in New England and North Carolina. An unusual calcite pegmatite at Wilberforce, Ontario, has provided the largest known crystals, some of which reach 3 in. (7.5 cm) on a cubic edge. Usually uraninite crystals are small.

Remarks: Once considered almost worthless, pitchblende came into economic consideration first as a source of radium; with the atomic age it became about the most sought-after mineral in the world. Small quantities of uranium are widely distributed.

It has long been used to measure geologic time. Uranium

atom after uranium atom transforms itself to lead, releasing helium. Now that the rate of radioactive decay is known, an analysis of the amount of lead or helium and the amount of remaining uranium immediately gives the time that has elapsed since the mineral came into being in the place where it was found. The only weak point in these analyses, which give the earth an indicated age of nearly five billion years, is an uncertainty about the possibility of a partial escape of some of the elements.

GUMMITE   U oxides, plus H_2O (?)   Amorphous   **Pl. 23**
Environment: Pegmatite veins and pitchblende deposits. **Crystal description:** Appears amorphous and never in crystals, though under the microscope in crossed polarized light it is sometimes doubly refracting (and therefore must be crystallized). **Physical properties:** Orange-red to grayish yellow; *Luster* greasy to waxy; *hardness* $2^1/_2$–5; *specific gravity* 3.9–6.4; *cleavage* none. Brittle. Not really a single mineral but a mixture of several different uranium oxides, silicates, and salts. **Composition:** Uranium oxides plus water, a stage in the alteration of uraninite by oxidation and hydration. All of the fission products of uranium—lead, radon, radium, helium—are present, plus uranium and an assortment of impurities. **Tests:** See uraninite (preceding); the fluorescence test of the evaporated nitric acid solution described there is a good test for some uranium minerals. The fluorescent residue can be obtained with other minerals; absent a Geiger counter, its only value is to prove the presence of uranium.
Distinguishing characteristics: Always in pseudomorphs after uraninite, and the primary mineral is often still present in part. Color and luster both typical and not likely to be confused with any other mineral. Usually not fluorescent (the yellow rim sometimes is), but the whole mass will make self photographs on film.
Occurrence: A secondary mineral; a late stage in the alteration of uraninite by oxidation and hydration. It commonly forms attractive dendritic growths in feldspar, pseudomorphous after uraninite. An intermediate brown stage (noted at Spruce Pine, North Carolina) lies between the colorful gummite and the fresh black uraninite and is known as clarkeite. The whole series of minerals that makes up these crusts of alteration is ill defined and needs further study.

It is common in pegmatites at some localities, though unknown at others. Brilliant red-orange gummite has been found in Rajputana (now approximately Rajasthan and

Ajmer) in India. It is one of the ores in Zaire and is found as a pseudomorph after pitchblende in Bohemia and Saxony. The bright orange part is principally curite (a lead uranate named for the discoverers of radium), together with becquerelite (a calcium uranate), and yellow soddyite (a hydrous uranium silicate).

In the U.S. the best specimens are the large heavy masses found in North Carolina in Mitchell Co., and the brilliant dendrites of the Ruggles Mine at Grafton, New Hampshire. Not common in the weathered ores of Great Bear Lake, Northwest Territories. It is predominantly a denizen of pegmatites, since the uraninite from which it forms is a pegmatite mineral. Black nodules with colorful rims occur in India and Argentina (Angel Mine).

TUNGSTITE $WO_3 \cdot H_2O$ (?) Orthorhombic (?)
Environment: A secondary mineral, derived from the alteration of tungsten minerals. **Crystal description:** Sometimes in small scaly crystals; more often a crumbly yellow coating or film on other tungsten minerals. **Physical properties:** Yellow earth colors; *hardness* $2\frac{1}{2}$; *specific gravity* 5.5 (?); *streak* yellow, powdery; *cleavage* 2 (usually not visible). **Composition:** Probably a simple tungsten oxide with water; analyses have shown about 75% WO_3. **Tests:** Infusible, but blackens before the blowpipe. Insoluble in acids.
Distinguishing characteristics: Could be mistaken for several other earth yellow minerals such as greenockite, some uranium minerals, and limonite, but its insolubility and infusibility will distinguish it from them. Always associated with tungsten minerals, especially huebnerite and wolframite.
Occurrence: Tungstite is very closely associated with, and usually forms coatings on, wolframite and huebnerite. It sometimes colors scheelite yellow or greenish, and is a helpful guide in the recognition of tungsten deposits. Found near the surface wherever tungsten ores occur. Cornwall produced it at one time, and more recently Bolivia has yielded some fine coatings. It can still be found at the old Trumbull occurrence in Connecticut, from which it was first described. Veins of huebnerite in North Carolina (Vance Co.) showed liberal coatings of tungstite. Fine examples come from the Spanish wolframite mines near Ciudad Rodrigo.
Remarks: Though a rare mineral of no commercial value because of its scarcity at most localities, it is important as a good guide to tungsten ore. Such a relationship is frequent in minerals (notably copper [blue and green] and cobalt [pink]

veins) often justifying the inclusion of some rare species even in a limited mineral list.

BRUCITE $Mg(OH)_2$ **Pl. 23**

Hexagonal — scalenohedral $\overline{3}\ \dfrac{2}{m}$

Environment: Veins in serpentine and magnesite. **Crystal description:** Most often in free-standing but ill-defined poor crystal plates; also foliated, massive, and fibrous. **Physical properties:** Pearly white to pale green, yellow, or blue. *Luster* pearly and waxy; *hardness* $2\frac{1}{2}$; *specific gravity* 2.4; *cleavage* micaceous. Plates flexible, nonelastic, and sectile; transparent to pearly translucent; fluoresces blue. **Composition:** Magnesium hydroxide (69.0% MgO, 31.0% H_2O). **Tests:** Infusible but flake glows brightly in the flame. Soluble in acids.
Distinguishing characteristics: Harder than talc but a little softer than mica. The less cleavable plates are inelastic. Gypsum is far less soluble in acids. The fluorescence is probably diagnostic in most cases.
Occurrence: Brucite is derived from the enclosing serpentine through alteration by hot watery solutions and it can be a common constituent of such hydrothermal veins. Also in flakes scattered through marbles, derived from periclase (MgO). The world's outstanding occurrences are American. Large crystals were found in the old Tilly Foster iron mine at Brewster, New York, and comparable specimens came from Texas, Lancaster Co., Pennsylvania, where crystals 7 in. (19 cm) across were found. Long fibers of brucite resembling asbestos are found in the Quebec asbestos mine at Asbestos. Light blue-green veins are occasionally intersected at the Gabbs (Nevada) magnesite mine.

MANGANITE   MnO(OH)   **Pl. 24**

Monoclinic — prismatic $\dfrac{2}{m}$

Environment: In veins and with manganese ores, forming at higher temperatures than the other manganese oxides. **Crystal description:** Usually crystallized, often in well-developed striated prisms commonly terminated by a horizontal base (looks orthorhombic). May be large, an inch (3 cm) or more; usually forms surfaces of closely grown crusts of small crystals. **Physical properties:** Steel gray to iron black. *Luster* submetallic; *hardness* 4; *specific gravity* 4.2–4.4; *streak* reddish brown (nearly black); *fracture* uneven; *cleavage* perfect side, poor prismatic and basal. Brittle; translucent (red-brown) in very thin splinters. **Composition:** Basic manganese oxide

(62.4% Mn, 27.3% O, 10.3% H_2O). **Tests:** Same as for pyrolusite (p. 152).

Distinguishing characteristics: Crystals resemble some entirely different minerals, such as enargite and some black silicates, but can be distinguished from these by the blowpipe reactions solubility, dark streak, and association with pyrolusite. The coarse crystals help to distinguish it from other manganese minerals, but x-ray tests are often necessary. Frequently alters to masses of parallel fibers of pyrolusite; hence, a paramorph.

Occurrence: Since manganite's associations often suggest the presence of low-temperature hot solutions, it is a somewhat different type of occurrence from that of the other secondary manganese minerals. Its associates, along with some other manganese minerals, are barite, calcite, and siderite. It is also found in secondary deposits, and consequently can be associated with pyrolusite, limonite, and psilomelane.

The best crystals are 2–3 in. (4–6 cm) prisms from a long-exhausted but famous occurrence at Ilfeld in the German Harz mining district. Stubbier, but fine, U.S. specimens have come from an iron mine at Negaunee, Michigan, where the crystals line cavities in the iron ore. It is not uncommon elsewhere but is difficult to recognize.

PSILOMELANE $(Ba,H_2O)Mn_{10}O_{20}$ Orthorhombic   **Pl. 24**
  Environment: Secondary manganese oxide deposits. **Crystal description:** Crystals not known; found in stalactitic, reniform, botryoidal, and mammillary masses and crusts, and may also be earthy. **Physical properties:** Iron black to steel gray. *Luster* dull to submetallic; *hardness* 5–6, but often very soft; *specific gravity* 3.3–4.7; *streak* black to brownish black; *fracture* smooth to conchoidal surfaces which may show agate-like banding of brighter and duller layers; *cleavage* none. Brittle to powdery. **Composition:** A basic oxide of barium with 2 valences (2 and 4) of manganese (approximately 16% BaO, 80% MnO and MnO_2, and 4% H_2O, with various other impurities). **Tests:** Same as for pyrolusite (p. 152).
  Distinguishing characteristics: This is the usual "I don't know" name applied to the black, knobby, noncrystalline-looking manganese masses commonly found associated with more definitely crystallized pyrolusite and manganite. Agate-banded black cabochons (highly polished rather than faceted specimens) delight the lapidary.
  Occurrence: Like pyrolusite, a purely secondary mineral. Formerly considered common, but current recognition that true psilomelane is a barium-bearing manganese oxide has

reduced its abundance as a species and narrowed the field of occurrence. The presence of barium is difficult for the amateur to ascertain. "Wad" is the name given to an ill-defined group of hard amorphous-appearing manganese oxides with water. They are mixtures of the barium-bearing psilomelane with other related minerals.

BAUXITE Al(OH)$_3$ plus Al and H$_2$O Amorphous   **Pl. 24**
Environment: Weathered surface deposits. **Crystal description:** Amorphous to microcrystalline. Usually massive; broken surfaces often have a pisolitic texture (a small-scale conglomerate of little spherical brown masses in a lighter matrix); more often like hard clay. Tiny white crystals may lie in the small pisolitic geodes. **Physical properties:** White or gray to dark red-brown. *Luster* dull; *hardness* 1–3, *specific gravity* 2.0–2.5. Crumbly to compact. **Composition:** Bauxite is an omnibus term (like wad, limonite, and gummite), widely accepted and used to describe a mixture of more or less hydrated aluminum oxides, but not used as a proper mineral name. The specific minerals are gibbsite (Al(OH)$_3$), boehmite (AlO(OH)), and diaspore (HAlO$_2$). In the common mixture any crystals will be microscopic and probably indistinguishable; thus the word is still useful. **Tests:** Infusible and insoluble; colored blue when moistened with cobalt nitrate and heated by the blowpipe flame.
Distinguishing characteristics: Much like a clay, though most bauxite is perhaps a little harder than the usual clays. The pisolitic types are easier to spot.
Occurrence: Bauxite is the mined source of aluminum. It is a secondary mineral resulting from the leaching of silica from clay minerals, clayey limestones, or low-silica igneous rocks, commonly under conditions of tropical weathering. This explains the geographical distribution of aluminum ores, most of which are found in the tropics, and some of which (as in Provence, France) are probably residual from earlier geological periods when climates were different. Abundant in Jamaica; in Brazil, Surinam, and French Guiana in South America; in Alabama, Georgia, and Arkansas in the U.S.; and in Europe at Le Baux, France, and in Hungary.

DIASPORE AlO(OH)   **Pl. 24**

Orthorhombic — Rhombic bipyramidal $\dfrac{2}{m}\dfrac{2}{m}\dfrac{2}{m}$
Environment: A constituent of emery, and associated with regionally metamorphosed aluminous rock, recycled perhaps from an earlier bauxite. Occasionally in veins with crystals.

Crystal description: Tiny crystals may be in bauxite pisolites. Good crystals are rare and may cover bladed crusts in worked emery deposits. Large gemmy crystals several inches in size (6–7 cm) have been found in Turkey. **Physical properties:** Colorless, straw-colored, or pale greenish, blue, violet, pink, or reddish (mangandiaspore); pleochroic in several hues. *Luster* glassy to pearly on cleavage face; *hardness* $6\frac{1}{2}$– 7; *specific gravity* 3.3–3.5; *fracture* conchoidal; *cleavage* 1 perfect and 2 minor. Brittle; translucent to transparent. **Composition:** Hydrous aluminum oxide (Al_2O_3 85%, H_2O 15%), with intrusions of Fe and Mn up to about 5% (mangandiaspore). **Tests:** Infusible, but decrepitates strongly into pearly flakes. Then gives aluminum test with cobalt nitrate.

Distinguishing characteristics: The emery environment would suggest diaspore for any colorless orthorhombic crystals found there. It is not at all common.

Occurrence: Although there are many sources, few are noteworthy and until now, diaspore has never delivered on its promise. A new source of spectacular gemmy, straw to violet crystals in Yagatan, Mugla Province, Turkey has inspired this addition. The gemmy Turkish material as been cut into some notable collection stones. Unfortunately the best violet hue lies in the wrong direction for the largest recovery. Good crystals have never been abundant; some of the best came many years ago from Pennsylvania while an emery mine in Chester, Massachusetts, gave crusts of half-inch (1 cm) crystal blades of a pale violet hue. Mangandiaspore is found in coarsely crystalline masses at Postmasburg, South Africa.

GOETHITE HFeO₂   **Pl. 24**

Orthorhombic — Rhombic bipyramidal $\frac{2}{m}\frac{2}{m}\frac{2}{m}$

Environment: Secondary oxidized deposits (with rare exceptions the stuff of rust, the limonite of gossans); sometimes in crystals in low temperature veins. **Crystal description:** Small, black, shiny, equidimensional crystals rare. Commonly in slender flattened plates, velvety surfaces of needles, and occasionally in brilliant rosettes of radiating plates. Also fibrous-massive with reniform surfaces; compact or earthy, even vitreous in the type called Glaskopf. Compare with limonite (following). Golden needles included in quartz. **Physical properties:** Brilliant black to brownish black (crystals) to brown to yellow (fibrous varieties). *Luster* adamantine-metallic, glassy to silky and matte; *hardness* 5–$5\frac{1}{2}$; *specific gravity* 3.3–4.3; *streak* brownish yellow to yellow; *fracture* uneven; *cleavage* side pinacoid of bladed crystals. Brittle to crumbly, sometimes glassy; translucent brown or yellow in thin splinters. **Composition:** Hydrogen iron oxide (62.9% Fe, 27.0% O, 10.1% H_2O). **Tests:** Gives off water in closed tube and turns to hematite and, with time and heat, becomes magnetic. Practically infusible on charcoal.

Distinguishing characteristics: Distinguished from hematite by its streak and from limonite by its structure (silky, fibrous, radiating). The magnetism after heating distinguishes it from most other similar minerals.

Occurrence: After hematite, goethite is the most important ore of iron. Many substances formerly regarded as limonite are now recognized as having a definite goethite structure. In veins it forms crystals in the late stages, and thus becomes an accessory mineral of ore deposits (fluorite, barite, and hematite). Also (and more important economically), it is a secondary mineral formed under weathering conditions from sulfides and siderite. It is deposited as "bog iron ore," and forms residual brown iron ores in the sw. U.S., in Missouri, and in Cuba.

Widespread in Germany, France, and England in crystallized vein specimens and often in pseudomorphs after concretionary pyrite crystals. In the U.S., the best specimens are radiating crystal clusters from pegmatite pockets of the Florissant region of Colorado. Good fibrous specimens are found in the iron mines of Michigan and Minnesota. Often seen as tiny brownish tufts on and in quartz crystals, druse veins, and quartz-crystal-lined geodes.

LIMONITE   FeO(OH)·nH_2O Amorphous   **Pl. 24**
Environment: Secondary deposits resulting from weathering. **Crystal description:** Amorphous, in botryoidal and reniform crusts, stalactites; earthy and powdery; vitreous and without discoverable internal structure. Most of the fibrous-looking material formerly called limonite is now considered goethite, even when cryptocrystalline. **Physical properties:** Brown-black to ocher-yellow. *Luster* glassy to dull; *hardness* to $5^1/_2$; *specific gravity* 2.7–4.3; *streak* brown to yellow; *fracture* conchoidal to earthy; *cleavage* none. Crumbly to brittle. **Composition:** An omnibus name for an assemblage of hydrous ferric oxides; of indefinite composition. **Tests:** Same as for goethite (preceding).

Distinguishing characteristics: Essentially the same as goethite, but it does not show any sort of fibrous or silky appearance on a fresh break. Distinguished from its manganese counter-

part (wad) by the streak, and the magnetism after heating.
Occurrence: Limonite is the coloring matter of soils, forming from iron minerals at surface temperatures as the rocks weather. It stains weathered rock, forms dendrites on rock seams, and colors agate and jasper. Soluble in several acids; oxalic acid is one of the best for cleaning limonite-stained crystals (unlike hydrochloric acid, it leaves no subsequent rusting residue). Alters to hematite quite easily through a loss of water. Soils with slightly higher ambient temperatures are red, not brown (as in U.S. south of Virginia).

Limonite is a usefully ambiguous term, best retained for use when we are speaking of undistinguished hydrous iron oxides or mixtures of several.

◆ MULTIPLE OXIDES

SPINEL $MgAl_2O_4$ **Pl. 25**

Cubic — hexoctahedral $\frac{4}{m} \, \overline{3} \, \frac{2}{m}$

Environment: Plutonic, pegmatitic, and metamorphic rocks.
Crystal description: In octahedrons, with cube and dodecahedron truncations rare. Often two halves are intergrown (twinned), one side rotated 180°, forming a flat triangle and creating re-entrant angles beneath each corner (spinel twins, see Fig. 24). Some large but drab Madagascar crystals show additional forms, but they are very rare. Also in irregular embedded grains, and coarsely granular. **Physical properties:** Multihued: black, dark green, red, blue, violet, orange-brown, lilac, or white. *Luster* glassy; *hardness* $7\frac{1}{2}$–8; *specific gravity* 3.5–4.1; *fracture* conchoidal; *cleavage* none, but poor octahedral parting. Brittle; transparent to opaque; red and lilac varieties fluorescent red or yellow-green. **Composition:** Magnesium aluminum oxide (28.2% MgO, 71.8% Al_2O_3); but in this formula magnesium can be wholly or partly replaced by iron, zinc, or manganese, making a series of related minerals with different names. The zinc spinel (deep green gahnite) is the most common of these; hercynite, the iron spinel, and galaxite, the manganese spinel, are rarer. **Tests:** Infusible, insoluble.
Distinguishing characteristics: Usually distinguished by its crystal shape and hardness, and often by its color and twinning. Magnetite is magnetic, chromite is heavier, garnet is fusible, zircon and microlite are heavier. Most confusion is with ruby rhombohedrons.

Occurrence: Gemmy spinel, like ruby corundum, is a mineral of metamorphosed, generally calcareous gneisses, impure marbles, and low-silica pegmatites, and consequently it is commonly associated with corundum. A significant gemstone, with Myanmar (Burma) and Sri Lanka (Ceylon) almost the sole important sources of gemmy material. Fine large brownish to black crystals with additional forms have come from Madagascar.

The largest American crystals, which are over 4 in. (10 cm) on an edge, came from a lost locality near Amity, New York. Spinel is common in the metamorphosed limestones of the New York–New Jersey highlands belt, with corundum, diopside, graphite, chondrodite, and phlogopite. Fine blue crystals are found near Helena, Montana.

Gahnite, dark green zinc spinel, occurs with garnet at Charlemont, Massachusetts, in good crystals decorated with triangular markings. Also found at Spruce Pine, North Carolina, where it sometimes forms transparent, bright green but very flat crystals in the mica plates. Gahnite is also found at Franklin, New Jersey, and in Brazil's brazilianite pegmatite. Galaxite (iron spinel) forms small black grains with garnets near Galax in North Carolina, on Bald Knob.

Spinel can also separate early from a magma and form phenocrysts in lava. Bronze asteriated octahedrons have been found in northern Mexico.

Remarks: Red spinel, though less famous, is a valuable jewelry stone, often confused with ruby. A famous crown jewel of Great Britain, the Black Prince's Ruby, is such a spinel. Like corundum, the spinel series of minerals melt congruently and recrystallize instantly on cooling, so they are easily synthesized by the Verneuil method. Many common synthetic gemstones are spinels; the spinel lattice seems to accept pigmenting elements more readily to give hues unobtainable in corundum synthesis. Most synthetic "sapphires" are spinel, as are synthetic "aquamarines," "peridots," and "rose zircons."

MAGNETITE $FeFe_2O_4$ Pl. 25

Cubic — hexoctahedral $\frac{4}{m} \bar{3} \frac{2}{m}$

Environment: Plutonic, pegmatitic, and metamorphic rocks, and sands. **Crystal description:** Usually in octahedrons, commonly striated with triangular markings on the octahedron faces. Dodecahedron modifications common. Since these faces are usually built up of heavy octahedron striations, the dodecahedron is striated lengthwise. Cubic habit rare; commonly massive or granular. **Physical properties:** Black. *Luster* metallic; *hardness* 6; *specific gravity* 5.2; *streak* black; *fracture* subconchoidal to uneven; *cleavage* none, but sometimes an octahedral parting. Brittle; magnetic; sometimes a natural magnet (lodestone). **Composition:** Ferrous and ferric iron oxide (72.4% Fe, 27.6% O); also written $FeO \cdot Fe_2O_3$. Other elements—magnesium, zinc, and manganese (rarely nickel)—can substitute in part for the first (the FeO, or ferrous) iron, while small amounts of aluminum, chromium, manganic manganese, and vanadium can replace part of the second (the Fe_2O_3, or ferric) iron. This permits a whole second spinel series of related minerals to which different names have been given, but magnetite is by far the most important. **Tests:** Naturally magnetic; further tests unnecessary. **Distinguishing characteristics:** The magnetism (and frequent polarity) distinguishes it from most other similar minerals. The streak is blacker than that of ilmenite; it is brittle and much lower in gravity than platinum mixed with iron or the native nickel-iron (josefinite) compounds. Zinc-rich magnetite (franklinite) is less magnetic and unique to New Jersey.

Occurrence: An important ore of iron. A widespread accessory mineral forming small grains in igneous rocks, which, after weathering, are often concentrated into black beach sands (once used as ink-blotting sand). Sometimes magnetite is concentrated by magmatic processes into solid ore deposits rich enough to mine. In schistose metamorphic rocks it may form fine phenocrystlike crystals. Also found well crystallized in pegmatites and high-temperature veins.

A very common mineral, so widespread that only a few U.S. localities need be mentioned. Fine crystals have come from French Creek, Pennsylvania, from Port Henry and Brewster, New York, and from the zinc mines at Franklin, New Jersey (franklinite). Sharp octahedrons (2 cm) lie embedded in chlorite schist at Chester, Vermont, with comparable pyrite crystals. Good irregular lodestone masses are found at Magnet Cove, Arkansas, and good clusters of crystals occur in Millard Co., Utah. Crystals of magnetite may be several inches across, but most are smaller; an inch or so (2–3 cm) is the usual size. Balmat, New York has been the source of a number of inch-sized (2.5 cm) rare cubic crystals. Pseudomorphs of hematite after magnetite are common. Many of the best apparent clusters of magnetite crystals, like those from Pelican Point, Salt Lake, Utah, or Durango, Mexico, are now actually composed of hematite, give a red streak, and are only weakly magnetic. They are called martite.

Remarks: Early magnets were made by striking the iron with the natural lodestone magnet, whose properties have intrigued men for generations. Like garnet and spinel, magnetite is often found in thin crystals in mica sheets and can be identified by its color (usually black and opaque, sometimes gray) and by regular partings parallel to the crystal outline that produce tiny cracks in the plate. A light viewed through such a crystal held close to the eye will appear to be surrounded by rays, resembling the asterism described under phlogopite (see p. 304).

CHROMITE $FeCr_2O_4$

Cubic — hexoctahedral $\frac{4}{m} \; \overline{3} \; \frac{2}{m}$

Environment: Magmatic segregations and in basic rocks. **Crystal description:** Octahedral crystals usually small and inconspicuous. Generally massive and granular. **Physical properties:** Black. *Luster* submetallic; *hardness* $5\frac{1}{2}$; *specific gravity* 4.1–4.9; *streak* brown; *fracture* uneven; *cleavage* none. Brittle; sometimes slightly magnetic. **Composition:** A ferrous chromic oxide (68.0% Cr_2O_3, 32.0% FeO). **Tests:** Infusible on charcoal, but gives green color to cooled borax beads.

Distinguishing characteristics: Distinguished from magnetite by its weak magnetism and from spinel by its dark streak and lesser hardness. Commonly associated with green minerals (uvarovite garnet) and the purple chlorite kaemmererite $(H_8[Mg,Fe,Cr]_5Al_2Si_3O_{18})$.

Occurrence: Chromite is the only ore of chromium, and a valuable refractory. Sometimes found as isolated crystals in veins in or scattered through serpentine; but the economically important occurrences are in more or less pure lenses, perhaps magmatic segregation lenses in altered basic rocks. It is also sparsely disseminated through basic rocks as an accessory mineral. Crystals almost 1 in. (2 cm) long have been found in Sierra Leone and lately in Brazil.

Minute crystals are found in the serpentines near New York City (Hoboken and Staten I.), in Maryland, and embedded in pyrrhotite at Outokumpu, Finland, accompanied by the rare (found only there) rhombohedral equivalent of hematite, eskolaite (Cr_2O_3). Small economically workable deposits have been found in Maryland, North Carolina, and California. Russia, India, Africa, Turkey, Brazil, Cuba, and New Caledonia have commercially important deposits that can be worked for ore.

Remarks: Although today the U.S. produces very little chromite, for many years a mine in Maryland was the world's only producing locality. At that time it was used solely as a pigment and for tanning. To date there is no such thing as a really good mineral specimen of chromite, relatively abundant though it is.

CHRYSOBERYL $BeAl_2O_4$ Pl. 26

Orthorhombic — Rhombic bipyramidal $\frac{2}{m} \frac{2}{m} \frac{2}{m}$

Environment: In pegmatite dikes and in the mica along their margins. **Crystal description:** Rarely in simple orthorhombic crystals, elongated prismatically and tabular parallel to the b axis. More often twinned, either two joining in a flat V-shaped pair, or three penetratingly intergrown to produce pseudohexagonal trillings, full of re-entrants, and similar to cerussite trillings. **Physical properties:** Multi-hued: gray, greenish yellow, yellow, brown, blue, blue-green (with the gemstone, alexandrite, becoming violet-red in artificial light. *Luster* glassy; *hardness* $8\frac{1}{2}$; *specific gravity* 3.5–3.8; *fracture* conchoidal to uneven; *cleavage* 3 fair and 1 easy parting along twin boundaries; brittle; translucent to transparent and gemmy; alexandrite fluoresces red. **Composition:** Oxide of beryllium and aluminum (19.8% BeO, 80.2% Al_2O_3). **Tests:** Infusible, insoluble, very hard.

Distinguishing characteristics: Best distinguished by its extreme hardness, just beneath that of corundum. Always in crystals, usually embedded in mica, feldspar, or quartz, but breaking free from the latter and then showing V striations on the broad face. Only beryl, with which it is often associated, presents a likely possibility for confusing the two, but chrysoberyl has a higher luster and is denser. Golden beryl loses its color on heating; chrysoberyl does not.

Occurrence: A relatively rare mineral, but one of considerable importance as a gem mineral. It can occur only in tight pegmatite dikes and (in Russia) in the bordering schists. Near Ekaterinberg it is associated with emerald and phenakite in 4-in. (10 cm), 6-sided flattened twins of the changeable green variety, alexandrite. Golden brown, larger but similar twins with deeper reentrants are found in Brazil. It is also found in single crystals and in gemmy waterworn pebbles in Brazil and Sri Lanka (Ceylon). In Tanzania and at Carnaiba,

Brazil, 1-in. (2 cm), very dark and flat alexandrite-type trillings are associated with emerald in typical mica schist associations. Good but dark alexandrite is found in Fort Victoria, Zimbabwe.

In the U.S., large 7-in. (18 cm) translucent greenish crystals occur in a pegmatite in Boulder Co., Colorado. Found in New England at several localities in Maine—especially Ragged Jack Mountain, Peru—and Haddam Neck, Connecticut. A few crystals were found in Manhattan building excavations.

Remarks: Chrysoberyl frequently contains parallel, needlelike inclusions or tubes of microscopic width, which reflect a streak of light when such a stone is cut in a rounded shape. This is known as chatoyancy, and the resultant gemstone is known as a cat's-eye. Cat's-eye chrysoberyls come from Sri Lanka and Brazil; with alexandrites they are extremely expensive chrysoberyl gems. An almost white "eye" and bright yellow-green color as well as a browner yellow with a colored eye is highly valued. In the clear gem varieties a brilliant greenish yellow is preferred; some Sri Lankan stones are an unattractive brown.

MICROLITE $(Na,Ca)_2Ta_2O_6(O,OH,F)$ $\left.\right\}$ **Pl. 26**
PYROCHLORE $NaCaNb_2O_6F$

Cubic — hexoctahedral $\qquad \dfrac{4}{m}\overline{3}\dfrac{2}{m}$

Environment: Pegmatite dikes and in small crystals disseminated throughout large calcite-rich intrusive masses only recently (around 1940) recognized as magmatic in origin and known as carbonatites. **Crystal description:** Usually octahedral, commonly with corners modified. Pyrochlore crystals darker, rarer, and smaller than those of microlite. Also a light cream color in earthy alterations of simpsonite, $AlTaO_4$. **Physical properties:** Yellow, yellow-brown to almost green-black. *Luster* resinous, *hardness* $5-5^1/_2$; *specific gravity* 4.2–6.4; *streak* white, yellowish or brownish; *fracture* subconchoidal to uneven; *cleavage* none, but octahedral parting (often well developed). Brittle; translucent to transparent. **Composition:** Microlite is a complex oxide of tantalum (with some traces of niobium), with sodium, calcium and oxygen, hydroxyl (OH), and fluorine The niobium equivalent, known as pyrochlore and once thought rare, gives its name to a mineral group, of which microlite is now considered only one member. **Tests:** Usually infusible, sometimes can form with difficulty a slaggy mass. Insoluble in nitric and hydrochloric acids, but decomposes in strong sulfuric acid. Light brown crystals turn almost white after heating and then fluoresce red.

Distinguishing characteristics: Sometimes closely resembles other rare-earth minerals from which it is not easily differentiated. The crystals help when visible. Black varieties may resemble uraninite, but they are lower in density and only slightly radioactive; green varieties resemble small gahnite spinels but are denser. Specimens from the old known localities are easy to tell, but a new find might be difficult to spot.

Occurrence: Microlite is sometimes an ore of tantalum. It was named for the small size of its original (Massachusetts) crystals, but subsequently crystals over 6 in. (15 cm) across were found at Amelia, Virginia. It is quite common in the U.S. but rare in Europe. Good dark octahedral crystals are found in the New England pegmatites (Portland and Haddam Neck, Connecticut, and in Maine). Large yellow-brown or green-brown crystals are common at the Rutherford and Morefield Mines, Amelia, Virginia. It has been mined in Dixon, New Mexico, where light yellow microlite grains are disseminated through violet lepidolite, sometimes in considerable abundance. Green crystals were found at Topsham, Maine, and at Equador, near Parelhas in ne. Brazil. In Minas Gerais, Brazil, brown crystals grew near the base of some Santa Rosa tourmalines. It is reported as a secondary mineral as an alteration product of simpsonite $AlTaO_4$ in Australia, and of tantalite in Brazil.

COLUMBITE $(Fe,Mn)(Nb,Ta)_2O_6$ $\Big\}$ **Pl. 26**
TANTALITE $(Fe,Mn)(Ta,Nb)_2O_6$

Orthorhombic — Rhombic bipyramidal $\dfrac{2}{m}\dfrac{2}{m}\dfrac{2}{m}$

Environment: Pegmatite dikes. **Crystal description:** Always in crystals or crystal aggregates. Sometimes in well-formed rectangular crystals ranging from very thin to almost equidimensional. Parallel (graphic) growths in quartz or feldspar have been noted. **Physical properties:** Black to red-brown and colorless. *Luster* submetallic to resinous; *hardness* 6; *specific gravity* 5.2–8.0; *streak* black to brown to white; *fracture* uneven; *cleavage* front and side pinacoid. Brittle; opaque to translucent or transparent. **Composition:** The two names are applied to the end-members of a continuous mineral series ranging from an almost pure niobate of iron and manganese to an almost pure tantalate of iron and manganese. The niobium or tantalum oxide will range from 78% to 86%. **Tests:** Infusible and insoluble. Some iron-rich varieties weakly magnetic.

Distinguishing characteristics: These minerals are best recognized by the high gravity of the tantalum-rich varieties. The fracture faces are commonly iridescent, bluish. In their occurrence they can be confused with magnetite (but are less magnetic), with uraninite (but are not radioactive), with black tourmaline or cassiterite (but are higher in gravity), and wolframite (which has a more perfect cleavage). Columbite and tantalite are separated on the basis of density; tantalite begins to prevail at about a 6.6 specific gravity.

Occurrence: This pair is found only in pegmatites or in gravels derived from pegmatites. They are the chief ores of niobium and tantalum. The representative in some pegmatites will be high in niobium and in others it will be richer in tantalum. With regional variation, both minerals may even be present in a single pegmatite when there is a long series of stages of rare mineral deposition. In Brazil, however, tantalite is more abundant in Ceará and the north, columbite in Minas Gerais. These are common and widespread minerals, found in commercial quantities in Mozambique, Western Australia, and Brazil. In all of these localities they are also recovered from alluvial deposits, where they have been washed out of decomposing pegmatites. They are commonly associated with cassiterite and with rare-earth minerals.

Fine crystals, up to several inches in length, have been found in the New England pegmatites. Small manganotantalites or manganocolumbites are often associated with the secondary albite feldspar cleavelandite at such pegmatites as Newry, Maine, and Amelia, Virginia. This type is brown and translucent. A white bismuth and antimony-bearing (bismuto/stibio-) tantalite variety, in fragments resembling cerussite in appearance, has been found in Brazil and Mozambique.

Fine columbite crystals have been found in North Carolina around Spruce Pine; New Mexico; the Black Hills, in heavy masses; and the Pikes Peak district of Colorado.

Remarks: Columbite got its name from columbium, the former American name for the element now known universally as niobium. Columbite often forms in parallel crystal growths with a related mineral, samarskite (next). Greater resistance of columbite to alteration makes the columbite areas of these combinations look blacker and fresher than the brown weathered samarskite. Particularly good examples of this association have come from the Divino de Ubá pegmatite in Minas Gerais, Brazil.

SAMARSKITE   Pl. 26

$(Y,Er,Ce,U, Ca,Fe,Pb,Th)(Nb,Ta,Ti,Sn)_2O_6$

Orthorhombic — Rhombic bipyramidal $\frac{2}{m}\frac{2}{m}\frac{2}{m}$

Environment: Tight pegmatite dikes with high concentrations of rare-earth elements, with smoky quartz, biotite, and red-stained feldspars (no aquamarine, topaz, or elbaite). **Crystal description:** Crystals usually embedded in rock and consequently difficult to see. Best obtained when weathered out. Usually prismatic, in quartz or feldspar, showing a rectangular cross section an inch or more (2–3 cm) across. Also massive and partly shattered. **Physical properties:** Velvety black (on a fresh break). *Luster* vitreous to resinous; *hardness* 5–6; *specific gravity* 4.1–6.2; *streak* reddish brown to black; *fracture* conchoidal; *cleavage* 1. Brittle; thin edges translucent. **Composition:** An extremely complex mixture of rare-earth elements with niobium and tantalum oxide. The last two account for about half of the weight. **Tests:** In closed tube it rapidly crumbles to black powder. Splinter edges usually split away, but if preheated in closed tube they will fuse to a black glass on charcoal in the blowpipe flame. Makes a fluorescent bead with sodium fluoride.

Distinguishing characteristics: Rather difficult to tell from related and associated species, but the fracture, color, and gravity mark it as one of the rare-earth minerals. More specific identification requires tests not practical for collectors who do not have access to a mineralogy laboratory.

Occurrence: Like its rare-earth mineral associates, samarskite is exclusively a mineral of pegmatites, usually forming tightly held, roughly crystallized shapes with no free-growing faces. At the few localities where it is abundant, it has some economic value as a source of the rare-earth elements contained. Crumbles with weathering, so ordinarily not found in alluvial deposits.

Originally found in the Urals in a pegmatite rich in rare-earth elements; later it also turned up in Norway and Sweden. The most abundant specimens have come from a deeply weathered pegmatite very rich in rare-earth minerals at Divino de Ubá, Minas Gerais, Brazil, where it formed parallel growths of columbite associated with monazite and euxenite (another black lustrous mineral of about the same composition). Surfaces of these crystals are coated with a yellow-brown oxidation film. Samarskite is not common in the U.S. It is found in Mitchell Co., North Carolina, in large, poorly formed crystals, and in small quantities in Maine, Connecticut, and Colorado.

■ HALIDES

This is a small group of soft minerals, many very soluble in water and some of them of considerable economic importance. The best known is common salt. Some, because of their ready solubility, are very rare; others, like salt, are so abundant that they are common despite their solubility. The water-soluble members of the group are easily recognized by their crystal form and taste. They will be confused only with a few water-soluble sulfates or the very rare nitrates, which will also taste when touched by the tongue but which are very different in crystal form. The water-insoluble ones discussed here crystallize (with but a few exceptions) in the cubic system, and the cube is the prevailing crystal form present.

◆ NORMAL ANHYDROUS HALIDES

HALITE NaCl   **Pl. 27**

Cubic — hexoctahedral $\frac{4}{m} \overline{3} \frac{2}{m}$

Environment: Dried lakes in arid climates; buried sedimentary beds. **Crystal description:** Commonly in cubic crystals, often distorted with hopperlike depressions in each cube face; also massive and granular, like marble; sometimes in large, cleavable, single crystal masses. Sometimes fibrous. **Physical properties:** Colorless, white, sometimes reddish (from impurities), blue or violet (see Remarks). *Luster* glassy; *hardness* 2$\frac{1}{2}$; *specific gravity* 2.1–2.6; *fracture* conchoidal; *cleavage* perfect cubic. Brittle, flows slowly under great pressure; transparent; water-soluble; sometimes red fluorescent. **Composition:** Sodium chloride (39.4% Na, 60.6% Cl). **Tests:** Readily soluble in water, tastes salty. Colors flame yellow (sodium). **Distinguishing characteristics:** The salty taste should be enough. Distinguished from other salty-tasting minerals by the sodium flame (sharper-tasting sylvite is KCl) and from some water-soluble sulfates by the perfect cubic cleavage. **Occurrence:** Halite is sometimes a part of the white crusts around gas vents in volcanic regions, but the important occurrences that would classify it as a one-mineral rock are the sedimentary beds interstratified with other sediments, formed in ancient geological time by the evaporation of closed saltwater basins. These rock salt strata are associated with gypsum and other sedimentary formations. Salt layers may flow under pressure and squeeze up through weak places, making pluglike formations of solid salt (the salt domes of the Gulf Coast). Salt is recovered by mining, or by introducing water to dissolve the salt beds and pumping this brine up through wells from the depths.

Salt formations are worldwide. The best-known European deposits are at Stassfurt, Germany; in Galicia, Poland; near Strasbourg, France; and in the Salzkammergut, Austrian Tyrol. In the U.S., halite is mined in New York State, Michigan, New Mexico, and Louisiana; it is obtained as brine in New York State, Kansas, and elsewhere. Good crystals form on the surface of evaporating dry lakes, as at Great Salt Lake, Utah, and in Death Valley, California. A short-lived pink coloration on halite crystals at Searles Lake, California, is due to an algae that grows in brine. Near Bogota, Colombia, a church has been hewn in a salt mine.

Remarks: Halite (especially in the Stassfurt and New Mexico occurrences) sometimes shows an intense blue to violet color, which forms clouds and irregular patches. This is thought to be attributable to free sodium, or colloidal sodium, combined with natural irradiation and some heat of burial. When such a specimen is dissolved in water, the solution remains colorless, and so is any salt that may be recrystallized from such a brine. With subsequent heat, some irradiation experiments have been successful in creating blue halite, but lake-surface, Bonneville Flats halite crusts only turn black.

SYLVITE KCl   Pl. 27

Cubic — hexoctahedral $\frac{4}{m} \bar{3} \frac{2}{m}$

Environment: Sedimentary salt beds, volcanic fumaroles. **Crystal description:** Like halite, but the cubes are much more frequently modified by octahedron faces, which may even be dominant. Like halite, massive and cleavable. **Physical properties:** Same as halite in color and luster, but not blue or purple. *Hardness* 2; *specific gravity* 2.0; *fracture* uneven; *cleavage* cubic. Brittle; transparent; water-soluble. **Composition:** Potassium chloride (52.4% K, 47.6% Cl). Some Na may be present. **Tests:** More bitter taste than halite. When sodium is not abundant the violet potassium flame is readily seen, but it may be masked by the sodium. More soluble than halite, it can be leached away from sea salt piles by rain.

Distinguishing characteristics: Distinguished from halite by the taste and the flame test. The crystals commonly show octahedral faces (rare in halite). In the mined occurrences, sylvite is frequently colored red by hematite inclusions, though there seems no genetic reason for it.

Occurrence: Sylvite forms layers like halite. Since it is more soluble than that mineral, sylvite beds will usually lie above the halite in the sedimentary deposit series; it is one of the closing minerals to come out of an evaporating salt lake. It is much rarer than halite. Good specimens come from Stassfurt, Germany, and from New Mexico.

Remarks: Both sylvite and halite are said to be very diathermanous, which means being transparent to heat waves; heat acts like light waves penetrating a transparent substance, passing easily through it without being absorbed and without warming the mineral itself. It is of economic importance as a major source of potash for fertilizer.

CHLORARGYRITE	AgCl ⎫	**Pl. 27**
BROMYRITE	AgBr ⎭	

Cubic — hexoctahedral $\frac{4}{m} \overline{3} \frac{2}{m}$

Environment: The weathered, secondary zone of ore deposits.

Crystal description: Cubic crystals fairly common, often embedded in white clayey material. Also in massive crusts, sometimes with a columnar structure. **Physical properties:** Almost colorless to yellowish to greenish gray or gray (darkening to violet-brown in light). *Luster* adamantine; *hardness* 1–$1\frac{1}{2}$; *specific gravity* 5.5; *fracture* conchoidal; *cleavage* none. Very sectile. **Composition:** Silver chloride (60% to 75% Ag; the balance is Cl or Br in varying proportions, making a perfect series). Embolite (Ag[Cl,Br]), is intermediate between the two end members. **Tests:** Fuse easily on charcoal, flattening out in a layer of silver. Gray mass then tested by its malleability or by solution in nitric acid, with a curdy precipitate forming on the addition of hydrochloric acid.

Distinguishing characteristics: Given the weight, waxy look, and high sectility, there are few minerals with which these could be confused other than mercury chloride (calomel, Hg_2Cl_2), which fumes off a probe, so blowpipe production of the metallic silver settles that problem.

Occurrence: Chlorargyrite and bromyrite are secondary silver minerals that form as a result of the surface oxidation of silver ores, most often in regions of deep weathering where there is an abundance of chlorine and bromine as in desert climates. Once an important ore of silver at some localities, as Leadville, Colorado; San Bernardino Co., California, and at Treasure Hill in Nevada. Important elsewhere in Mexico, Peru, and Chile. Like many minerals, these two are practically history, existing only as relics of the past. In populated areas, there are no longer any unexploited ore veins near enough to the surface and rich enough to provide, ever again, good examples of these minerals. Yellow $1/4$-in. (6–7 mm) crystals can still be found in unworked limonite gossan at Broken Hill, New South Wales.

Remarks: Formerly called cerargyrite. The highly sectile character and waxy or hornlike appearance has given this mineral the popular name "horn silver." Specimens should be kept away from light to prevent their darkening.

SAL AMMONIAC NH_4Cl Pl. 28

Cubic — gyroidal (?) 4 3 2 (?)

Environment: Volcanic fumarole deposits. **Crystal description:** Usually in frosty or rounded octahedral, cubic, or dodecahedral crystals, or combinations of these faces. Also in fragile white crystalline crusts. **Physical properties:** White to yellow. *Luster* glassy; *hardness* $1–1\frac{1}{2}$; *specific gravity* 1.5; *fracture* conchoidal; *cleavage* 1 poor. Brittle; transparent; water-soluble. **Composition:** Ammonium chloride (33.7% NH_4, 66.3% Cl). **Tests:** Volatilizes and sublimes on charcoal, and creeps up on walls of closed tube. Soluble in water, tastes bitter. Curdy white precipitate forms (proving chlorine) when silver nitrate crystal is dropped in distilled water solution of sal ammoniac.

Distinguishing characteristics: Its manner of occurrence is typical; a test for chlorine and the volatility, together with the absence of sodium or potassium flame coloration (though unnecessary), are usually sufficient.

Occurrence: Sal ammoniac is of very limited occurrence, since it is a mineral that characteristically is present only between showers at gas vents around active volcanoes or at fissures on fresh lava flows. Ammonium chloride vapor is bluish, and the orifice steam smells like a laundry. The mineral forms without a liquid stage as a sublimate around the vent from which the gas is actually escaping, usually at relatively high temperatures, possibly 400°–500°F (250°–300°C). Vesuvius is one of the oldest and most productive localities, but fine crystals up to $3/8$ in. (1 cm) across formed during the eruption of Parícutin in Mexico in the mid-1940s. Crusts of free-standing crystals were particularly characteristic of the early stages of a cycle of activity, when gas was abundant.

Remarks: Sal ammoniac is made artificially as a vapor by blowing ammonia fumes across hydrochloric acid, and this method is often used to make a dull white coating on objects to be photographed.

CALOMEL   HgCl

Tetragonal — Ditetragonal bipyramidal $\dfrac{4}{m}\dfrac{2}{m}\dfrac{2}{m}$

Environment: Mercury deposits. **Crystal description:** Usually in crystals, often minute and coating other minerals. Most often tabular, sometimes pyramidal. Commonly in skeletal parallel growths rather than good individual crystals. **Physical properties:** White, grayish, or yellowish (darkening on exposure to light). *Luster* adamantine; *hardness* 1–2; *specific gravity* 6.5; *fracture* conchoidal; *cleavage* 2 (1 good). Sectile; translucent; fluorescent red. **Composition:** Mercurous chloride (85.0% Hg, 15.0% Cl). **Tests:** Completely volatilizes on charcoal, without melting.

Distinguishing characteristics: The sectile character and the adamantine luster distinguish it from everything but the silver halides. Silver minerals fume and melt but do not volatilize completely on the charcoal, leaving instead a flattened silver residue. In a mercury association the fluorescence is significant.

Occurrence: A relatively rare mineral, associated with other mercury minerals, probably always secondary and late in the mineral sequence. It will be found in small brilliant crystals in cavities, associated with cinnabar and often perched on crystals of that mercury ore. Found in the U.S. at Terlingua, Texas, and near Murfreesboro, Arkansas; in Europe, at various cinnabar localities.

Two related anhydrous halides are similar in color to calomel even though they contain copper. Rare nantokite (CuCl; copper chloride) and almost as rare marshite (CuI; copper iodide) are the only colorless or white copper minerals. Both are tetrahedral. Marshite forms triangular lustrous tetrahedral crystals at Chuquicamata, Chile, and was formerly found at Broken Hill, New South Wales. In a mine tunnel near Chuquicamata, iron-stained orange incrustations of marshite, catalyzed by iron rails and bolts, form from drainage water.

Marshite is colorless to pale yellow when fresh, as a rule, but seems to turn coppery on exposure to light and air. Iodine vapors emanate when a sealed marshite container is opened, and can be smelled; perhaps copper is freed and remains to give the color noted in older exposed specimens.

FLUORITE CaF_2 **Pl. 27**

Cubic — hexoctahedral $\frac{4}{m} \overline{3} \frac{2}{m}$

Environment: Sedimentary rocks, ore veins, and pegmatites. **Crystal description:** Most commonly in cubes, less often in octahedrons, occasionally in complex combinations. Sometimes forms twin intergrowths with a second individual, whose corners project from each cube face (Fig. 25, p. 66). Also banded, massive, and fine-grained. **Physical properties:** Colorless, black, white, brown, and all spectral and pastel intermediates. *Luster* glassy; *hardness* 4; *specific gravity* 3.0–3.3; *fracture* conchoidal; *cleavage* perfect octahedral. Brittle; translucent to transparent and gemmy; thermoluminescent and often fluorescent. **Composition:** Calcium fluoride (51.1% Ca, 48.9% F). **Tests:** In closed tube or test tube, often becomes phosphorescent on light heating (this thermoluminescence must be observed in the dark). Fuses on charcoal with a little difficulty. Powder mixed with dilute sulfuric acid and boiled in glass test tube etches (frosts) the glass surface to just above the solution.

Distinguishing characteristics: The perfect cleavage and the hardness are distinctive. Often fluorescent (usually blue) under ultraviolet light. Harder than calcite, and commonly more attractively colored (and does not bubble when a drop of hydrochloric acid is placed on it). Much softer than quartz. Its powder does not dissolve in nitric acid, as apatite's does.

Occurrence: A common, often colorful vein or gangue mineral, and a companion of ore minerals. It frequently forms in low-temperature metal deposits; isolated cubic crystals are often found in cavities in limestone quarries with calcite, celestite, and dolomite. The crystal shape (habit) is influenced by the temperature of formation. Octahedral and complex crystals are usually considered characteristic of high-temperature fluorite; cubic crystals prove a low-temperature occurrence. The important and commercial deposits are mainly low-temperature ones; the octahedral high-temperature alpine crevice and pegmatite occurrences are seldom of economic importance. Fluorite is used as a source of fluorine for hydrofluoric acid, for the manufacture of milk glass, as a flux for the steel industry, and in the refining of aluminum.

It is one of the most popular minerals among collectors because of the beauty of specimens. Widespread in occurrence. The most attractive examples are the simple (and penetration twinned), very fluorescent violet cubes from Cumberland, England. Cornwall crystals are often more complex and have greater interest; Germany produces several types of crystals, including vein material of both cubic and octahedral habit. Pink Göschenen (Switzerland) octahedrons are greatly sought after. Though the octahedral face is usually dull, the cubes are often very shiny. Dodecahedral edge truncations on deep purple cubes characterize the La Collada, Asturias, Spain, fluorites.

Fluorite is an abundant and important economic mineral in the U.S. in the Illinois-Kentucky region (cubic crystals replacing sedimentary beds and in veins); at Westmoreland, New Hampshire (beautiful green octahedrons), and in Bingham, New Mexico (pale blue cubes), to mention a few localities. Common in limestone quarries in the Midwest (Ohio-Michigan), as at Clay Center, Ohio (brown crystals fluorescing yellowish). Mexico has become the leading producer of fluorite. Musquis, in Coahuila, has fine light purple specimens; at Naica, it is a gangue mineral, but the exquisite modifications on the light-hued crystals make them the modern equivalents of the 19th-century Cornwall crystals.

Remarks: *Fluorine* and *fluorescence* are two words originating from the name of this mineral. The brilliant colors of some fluorites are attributed to hydrocarbons; they can be removed by heat. Only the softness prevents widespread use for jewelry. The Chinese make many fluorite carvings, which are marketed under the misleading name of "green quartz." Transparent colorless pieces have great value in the manufacture of optics, for which purpose it is now recrystallized synthetically.

ATACAMITE $Cu_2Cl(OH)_3$ Pl. 28

Orthorhombic — bipyramidal $\dfrac{2}{m}\dfrac{2}{m}\dfrac{2}{m}$

Environment: Weathered, secondary ore deposits in arid climates. **Crystal description:** Usually in thin to substantial (1-in., 1–3 cm) prisms. Sometimes in tabular form, when it resembles brochantite or antlerite; also fibrous, massive, granular, and as sand. **Physical properties:** Deep emerald green. *Luster* glassy; *hardness* 3–3$\frac{1}{2}$; *specific gravity* 3.8; *streak* green; *fracture* conchoidal; *cleavage* side pinacoid. Brittle, transparent. **Composition:** Basic copper chloride (74.3% Cu, 13.0% Cl, 12.7% H_2O). **Tests:** Fuses easily, giving continuously a bright blue flame like that normally seen briefly after a touch of hydrochloric acid. Will finally yield copper bead. Easily soluble to a green solution in nitric acid and gives chlorine test (with silver nitrate), leaving a blue solution above the white precipitate.

Distinguishing characteristics: Resembles malachite (but while dissolving does not effervesce) and some copper phosphates and sulfates (which do not so readily—nor for so long—give the blue copper flame without hydrochloric acid, nor do they give a chlorine test).

Occurrence: A rare copper mineral of wholly secondary origin; results from the alteration, through weathering and usually under desert conditions, of copper sulfide minerals. Common under the extreme conditions of continuous dryness of the South American west coast in Chile (the Atacama Desert). The best crystals, nevertheless, came from South Australia. Small needles have been recorded at Vesuvius in a fumarole deposit. The U.S. has produced a few examples at several western localities—including San Manuel, Arizona—but it is probably often unrecognized, being confused with similar-appearing and more common minerals such as brochantite and malachite. Among the popular species sought by competitive collectors, good examples are likely to be high-priced.

Remarks: In South America it is a significant ore when mined with other copper-bearing minerals. Once fashionably elegant as a sand for ink-drying (before blotters); the supplies for this were commonly imported by the British from Chile.

CRYOLITE Na_3AlF_6 **Pl. 27**

Monoclinic — prismatic $\dfrac{2}{m}$

Environment: Extremely rare in pegmatite dikes. **Crystal description:** The monoclinic crystals are usually in subparallel growths on a solid cryolite surface and look like cubes, sometimes with pseudo-octahedral truncations. Also massive. **Physical properties:** White or colorless. *Luster* glassy or greasy; *hardness* $2^1/_2$; *specific gravity* 2.9–3.0; *fracture* uneven; *cleavage* none, but pseudocubic partings. Brittle; translucent. **Composition:** Fluoride of sodium and aluminum (32.8% Na, 12.8% Al, 54.4% F). **Tests:** Fuses very easily on charcoal with a yellow (sodium) coloration of the flame. Bead that forms is clear when hot, white when cold, and fluoresces blue-green in shortwave ultraviolet light.

Distinguishing characteristics: This is practically a one-locality mineral. White massive specimens, with brown siderite, from the one important locality should be easily recognized. Failing that, the fusion test is sufficient.

Occurrence: A strange mineral, surprisingly uncommon in nature. The only important locality was a unique, now worked-out pegmatite in Greenland, where the cryolite formed great solid masses, sometimes with fissures lined with crystals of cryolite or of some other related mineral. Embedded in it, and common in cryolite specimens, are chalcopyrite, siderite, and galena. It was mined for use as the solvent of bauxite aluminum ore, for the electrolytic recovery of aluminum. The insignificant U.S. occurrence is in Creede, Colorado. Cryolite is made artificially from fluorite for aluminum electrolysis.

Remarks: This mineral has a very slight ability to bend light (refraction); it is close to water in that respect. Consequently, cryolite powder put in water comes so close to the liquid in its refraction of light that the powder becomes almost invisible.

■ CARBONATES

These constitute an important and abundant group. Good examples are common, and several are of major economic importance. A single member of the group, calcite, is sufficiently abundant (as limestone) to fulfill that part of a rock definition that says it must "constitute an important part of the earth's crust." Carbonates form in various ways, including some newly recognized primary magmatic intrusions called carbonatites. Carbonates are deposited as primary compounds transported by hot solutions with volatile compounds fresh sprung from earth's depths, from seeping cold solutions on and near the surface, and in the ocean. Carbon dioxide (CO_2) in the air combines with water (H_2O) to form a mild acid—carbonic acid (H_2CO_3)—which attacks surface minerals. As early minerals decay, some of their elements, such as the calcium in feldspar, dissolve, often to reappear in a solid state as carbonates. Corrosion by carbonic acid is one of the principle agents in the weathering destruction of rock. The same foe alters many of the metal ores, the sulfides, whenever they are exposed to the air. When ore veins are in rocks that are predominantly carbonates such as limestone and dolomite (calcium and calcium magnesium carbonates), we often find the metals concentrated and immobilized as carbonates in the upper, weathered, ore levels.

There are two significant, crystallographically similar groups in the carbonates, parallel series in which several elements can mutually replace each other. These form two sets of minerals whose precise identification without crystals may be difficult. One compound, calcium carbonate $CaCO_3$, is common to both; different forms of calcium carbonate (calcite and aragonite) give each series its name. Otherwise the two series mostly do not overlap. The first series, with rhombohedral crystals, is known as the calcite group, and the second, with orthorhombic crystals, as the aragonite group.

Although their structures are different, their chemistry is alike, and as one would expect, they share some properties, like acid solubility.

All of the carbonates are soft, all are light-colored and translucent to transparent, all are soluble in acid (some more reluctantly than others) as bubbles of carbon dioxide escape. Many are predominantly, though not exclusively, secondary in origin.

◆ CALCITE GROUP

Compositions in this group are sometimes depicted with a triangle, the corners of which are labeled respectively $CaCO_3$ (calcite), $MgCO_3$ (magnesite), and $FeCO_3$ (siderite). Mineral names have sometimes also been given to intermediate members, as will be seen. Completely pure calcium, iron, or magnesium carbonates are uncommon, but we can usually say that a specimen is predominantly one or another in composition and therefore give it a name that is close enough. In recent years, accumulated analyses have shown that all possible ratios of these elements with manganese, zinc, and cobalt do not exist in nature, and the old simple (completely isomorphous) explanation is no longer accurate. Although the elements can replace each other to a limited extent, the triangular diagram is somewhat misleading as it implies, that every area of the triangle will have its occupant. More geochemically minded writers call the entire group either calcite or brownspar, including in the latter magnesite, siderite, rhodochrosite, and smithsonite. All of those members of the group belong to the rhombohedral division of the hexagonal system and have excellent rhombohedral cleavage. Crystals and crystalline masses are common. All have strong double refraction (best shown by the doubling of lines or dots seen through a clear cleavage of "Iceland spar" calcite). And of course all dissolve in hydrochloric acid (which sometimes should be warmed), releasing bubbles of carbon dioxide (CO_2) gas.

CALCITE $CaCO_3$ Pl. 28

Hexagonal — Hexagonal scalenohedral $\overline{3}\ \dfrac{2}{m}$

Environment: Every type of occurrence, and associated with all classes of rocks. **Crystal description:** Probably shows the largest number of forms in all mineralogy. Often crystallized, extremely varied in appearance, from tabular (infrequent) to prismatic or needlelike. Scalenohedrons and rhombohedrons most common. Also microcrystalline to coarse, sometimes in banded layers (onyx). **Physical properties:** Colorless, white, pale tints. *Luster* glassy; *hardness* $2^{1}/_{2}$ (base) to 3 (cleavage face); *specific gravity* 2.7; *fracture* conchoidal; *cleavage* rhombohedral. Brittle; transparent to translucent. Often fluorescent, red, pink, yellow; briefly phosphorescent orange-red at Franklin, New Jersey; after pink fluorescence, may also have persistent blue phosphorescent glow; sometimes thermoluminescent. **Composition:** Calcium carbonate (56.0% CaO, 44.0% CO_2; Mn, Fe, and Mg may partially replace Ca). **Tests:** Easily scratched (with fingernail on the uncommon base, but do not deface a friend's specimen trying it). Dissolves in cold dilute hydrochloric acid with effervescence. (Simply place drop of acid on specimen, avoiding good crystal faces, since the acid dulls a lustrous surface.)
Distinguishing characteristics: The bubbles in acid distinguish it from all other minerals with such prominent cleavages, even other carbonates (which mostly do not dissolve so readily in cold acid). Aragonite dissolves as easily but has a different crystal form and no cleavage. When blowpiped, aragonite crumbles to powder and loses its fluorescence. Even when not previously fluorescent, calcite (which holds together better) usually becomes so after such heating.
Occurrence: One of the commonest of minerals. Crystallizes in veins as a gangue mineral of sulfides and precipitates from seawater to build up limestones. Also grows secondarily from solution and redeposition in limestones and other rocks, and hangs as stalactites from the cement of overpasses. Localities are far too numerous to list; crystals may be flat plates 1 ft. (30 cm) across (Palm Wash, California),

steep golden scalenohedrons 2 ft. (61 cm) long (Missouri-Kansas-Oklahoma lead district), or transparent masses a foot (30 cm) through (Iceland—the original Iceland spar). Marble, cave formations, travertine, and onyx are all calcite varieties. An oolitic calcite sand forms the beaches of Great Salt Lake.

Remarks: Calcite is frequently fluorescent; a small amount of manganese is enough to make it glow red under some wavelengths of ultraviolet light. Instead of plastic polarizers, flawless transparent calcite is used in better optical instruments, especially in geological (polarizing) microscopes. Calcite has a well-developed gliding plane—a knife edge can be pressed into the obtuse edge of the cleavage rhombohedron and a section will glide forward to create the effect of a twin crystal. This is easy only with the clear Iceland spar, the optically useful type. Most calcite is white, though various impurities may tint it almost any hue, even black. Since it is a common late-vein overgrowth or filling, the solution of calcite in a weak acid (hydrochloric or acetic—used very weak to avoid damaging anything else) often exposes a wall with well-formed crystals of other minerals.

Calcite is notably softer on the base than on its cleavage face. Though it is on the Mohs scale, it can be scratched with the fingernail on the basal plane (about $2\frac{1}{2}$). The hardness of 3 is found on the rhombohedron cleavage face.

MAGNESITE $MgCO_3$ Pl. 29

Hexagonal — Hexagonal scalenohedral $\bar{3}\ \dfrac{2}{m}$

Environment: Associated with altered and weathered serpentine and in sedimentary beds from which calcium has been completely leached. **Crystal description:** Usually in dull white, sometimes spherical, microcrystalline masses developed in weathering. Small prismatic needles on serpentine; also in large transparent Iceland spar–type crystals and cleavages. Also coarsely granular, like a marble. **Physical properties:** White, colorless, light tints. *Luster* glassy to dull; *hardness* $3\frac{1}{2}$–5, *specific gravity* 3.0–3.2, *fracture* conchoidal to smooth; *cleavage* rhombohedral. Brittle; transparent to translucent. **Composition:** Magnesium carbonate (47.6% MgO, 52.4% CO_2), often with some iron and calcium. **Tests:** The tongue adheres to matte, porcelaneous, massive material. Dissolves with bubbles in hot hydrochloric acid.

Distinguishing characteristics: The white, dull, fine-grained porcelaneous masses can be identified by their behavior in acid. Both the marble-grained and the more recently discovered transparent rhombohedrons can be confused with calcite or dolomite but are heavier and remain little affected in cold hydrochloric acid.

Occurrence: Usually results from a hot-water (hydrothermal) alteration of serpentine, which creates solid white veins in the parent rock. Surface alteration can produce the dull white spheres. Small free-growing crystals were described from serpentine fissures on Staten I., New York. Huge quantities of the dull white material have been mined as sources of magnesia and magnesium in Washington and California. Good crystals (mostly hexagonal, rhombohedron-terminated brownish prisms) have been found associated with strontianite and dolomite at Oberndorf, in Styria, Austria, in a magnesite quarry. Gabbs, Nevada, is the most commercial deposit in the U.S.

The best specimen source is a marblelike variety with very coarse grain, which is being exploited in Brumado, Bahia, Brazil. This deposit has produced hundreds of large Iceland spar–like crystals and cleavages, grown in cavities in the bed accompanied by quartz, topaz, uvite and dravite tourmaline, uranium minerals, and others. This fascinating, perhaps unique, stratified deposit probably represents a final stage after a magnesia-enrichment process changes limestones into dolomites followed, in this case by metamorphic recrystallization into magnesite. A magnesite quarry near Pamplona, Spain, has similar Iceland spar–like rhombohedrons, but all are dolomite.

SIDERITE $FeCO_3$ **Pl. 30**

Hexagonal — Hexagonal scalenohedral $\bar{3}\frac{2}{m}$

Environment: Rarely forms metamorphosed sedimentary strata, commonly in crystals in ore veins, sometimes in pegmatites. **Crystal description:** Most commonly in rhombohedrons, often very acute, sometimes in scalenohedrons. Massive, in granular, crystalline cleavable aggregates, and earthy. Sometimes forms fibrous radial knobs (sphaerosiderite) or saddle-shaped rhombohedron crusts like dolomite. **Physical properties:** Brown, white to gray. *Luster* vitreous to pearly; *hardness* $3\frac{1}{2}$–4; *specific gravity* 3.8–3.9; *fracture* conchoidal; *cleavage* rhombohedral. Brittle; transparent to translucent. **Composition:** Iron carbonate (62.1% FeO, 37.9% CO_2), usually with some magnesium and calcium replacing part of the iron. **Tests:** Fragments become magnetic after being heated on charcoal. Dissolves in hot acid with effervescence.

Distinguishing characteristics: Ease of scratching and the cleavage show it to be a carbonate; usually the brown color, which is often only a thin surface layer, suggests iron carbonate. Magnetism following heating is then sufficient.

Occurrence: Very common in low- and medium-temperature ore veins, in which it is often associated with calcite, barite, and the sulfides. Also characteristic of sedimentary rocks, where it frequently forms concretionary masses ("clay ironstone"). Sometimes used as an ore of iron (France and Germany). Also in pegmatites associated with phosphates.

Some of the best, and usually very dark, crystals came from the Cornwall (England) mines, where they show quite a variety of forms. Allevard, France, and Erzberg, Styria (Austria), are notable as a source of fine clusters of crystals. Panasqueira, Portugal, and the Morro Velho mine at Nova Lima, Minas Gerais, Brazil, are prominent sources of specimen crystals. Large brown embedded cleavages were associated with the Greenland cryolite.

There are no truly notable American examples. Found at many localities in the U.S., including some old mines at Roxbury, Connecticut (where it forms great cleavable masses and free crystals, often altered to limonite), in Vermont, in New York State, in New England pegmatites, and in good crystals in Colorado in ore veins. As a rule, siderite crystals are not large, though very large (if dull) crystals have lately been found at St. Hilaire, near Montreal, Quebec.

Remarks: It is not surprising that siderite, since it is easily altered, is commonly changed to limonite pseudomorphs that preserve the original shape of the crystal.

RHODOCHROSITE $MnCO_3$ Pl. 30

Hexagonal — Hexagonal scalenohedral $\overline{3} \frac{2}{m}$

Environment: Ore veins and metamorphic manganese deposits. **Crystal description:** Most often in rhombohedrons (sometimes very steep), but also in scalenohedrons. Granular, massive, and in rounded spherical and botryoidal crusts. **Physical properties:** Deep rose pink to pale pink, gray, or brown. *Luster* vitreous to pearly; *hardness* $3\frac{1}{2}$–4; *specific gravity* 3.4–3.6; *fracture* conchoidal; *cleavage* perfect rhombohedral. Brittle; transparent to translucent. **Composition:** Manganese carbonate (61.7% MnO, 38.3% CO_2 with any or all of the following present: iron, calcium, magnesium, zinc, and cobalt). **Tests:** Dissolves slowly in cold and rapidly in warm hydrochloric acid with effervescence. Powder colors borax bead violet in oxidizing flame (test for manganese).

Distinguishing characteristics: The cleavage and hardness (and acid test) show it to be a carbonate of this group. The borax bead test shows it to be a manganese mineral and eliminates about everything else. Pink color is the best guide.

Occurrence: Rhodochrosite is usually a gangue mineral of copper and lead ore veins, but sometimes it occurs (like siderite) in pegmatites. At Butte, Montana, it was an ore of manganese. Commonly alters to black manganese oxides on weathering, and the black stains are very apparent on the containing rocks. Good specimens not common. Fine crystals have come from several mines (American Tunnel, Sweet Home) in Colorado, where it forms deep pink rhombohedral crystals up to several inches (10 cm) across, associated with pyrite, fluorite, quartz, and ore sulfides. Butte produced rhombohedral and scalenohedral crystals to 1 in. (2.5 cm) in crusts as well as solid cleavable and granular masses, always paler than the Colorado material, of a milky pink color. Pegmatite rhodochrosite is often grayish or brownish. Botryoidal masses and scalenohedral crystals—secondary in character, for they incrust limonite—have come from Germany (where it has been called Himbeerspat, or "raspberry spar"). Rosinca is a name applied to an Argentine occurrence of banded onyx–like pink crusts used for decorative purposes. Good but often thinly quartz-coated crystals have come from Cananea, Mexico. Hotazell, South Africa, has produced many gemmy, deep red $1/_2$–1 in. (1–2 cm) crystals of an uncommonly transparent nature, which can perhaps be regarded as the most unusual specimens for collectors. Pasta Buena, Peru, has become a source of Colorado-like pink crystals with similar fluorite associations.

SMITHSONITE $ZnCO_3$ **Pl. 30**

Hexagonal — Hexagonal scalenohedral $\overline{3} \frac{2}{m}$

Environment: Secondary (weathered) zone of zinc ore deposits.

Crystal description: Crystals normally indistinct and rounded, usually dull, rounded rhombohedrons, sometimes rounded scalenohedrons. Also thick radiating botryoidal and mammillary crusts, with a crystalline surface (usually blue), brown dull crusts, and earthy masses ("dry-bone ore"). A few larger, steep rhombohedral, almost gemmy crystals have been found in Zambia. **Physical properties:** White, yellow (from cadmium), greenish or bluish (from copper), or pink (from cobalt). *Luster* subadamantine to vitreous; *hardness* 5;

(Text continued on page 191)

PLATES

PLATE 1

PLATE TECTONICS

There may be an untold number of suns that, like ours, have several orbiting planets. As far as we know, only one planet, ours, is fortunate enough to have an orbit salubriously distanced to be both warm enough and cool enough, and to be large enough for its gravity to hold an atmosphere. By lucky chance, that atmosphere is one supportive of life. The air on earth has the oxygen essential for the form of life that has emerged, the carbon essential for organic reactions and exchanges, and most significantly of all, water, whose presence makes everything work. Among water's many unique properties is its behavior of expanding on freezing, which keeps the earth alive and not ringed in ice.

After the Big Bang, matter in considerable abundance formed a series of spherical bodies, the planets, orbiting the Sun. Gravity was the significant force in forming the solar system, pulling gigantic hot masses together into spheres, one of which became Earth. It was also gravity that concentrated the heavier elements like iron and nickel in the Earth's core. Probably in all the planets, and certainly on Earth, each successive layer surrounding the heavy core was richer in lighter elements, the layers forming in onionlike shells. In the outermost layer, however, there was not enough silica, calcium, potassium, and other light elements to complete a continuous shell, so bits and pieces clumped into siliceous islands, a fragmented skin that rested on a dermis of oceanic rock. Though oceans drowned the uneven outermost continuous crust of basalt, they failed to cover the emergent siliceous cratons, embryonic continents that rose above the battering waves, drifting here and there on supporting plates of the uppermost basalt. While the single continents could not migrate, the crustal plates could, and did. With gases still trapped and, to this day, constantly surfacing from inside the cooling Earth, molten magma—lava—finds escape through major fissures in both oceans, spreading out toward fragmented cratons, our present continents.

Rain falls on the elevated siliceous rocks. Water, carbon dioxide, and fluctuating temperatures break down the minerals within them, turning them to clay and sand for rivulets and rivers to bear off to the coasts. Sorted by size and weight, sand and clay pile up on the ocean floor, depressing it with their load. Eventually, the spreading ocean floor of the ancient crust, with an overburden of lighter and more siliceous grains, sinks and is thrust under a craton margin. There, accordioned and mixed with magma, old crust is melted again. Reborn magma of lesser density uplifts the land and, crumpled, it births cordilleras along the continental margins. By this process, continuing since the planet's origin, the Earth has kept mobile; ever renewing, ever presenting a fresh face. Without water, without atmosphere, Mars and the moon are dead, but thanks to its atmosphere, the Earth is perpetually renewed.

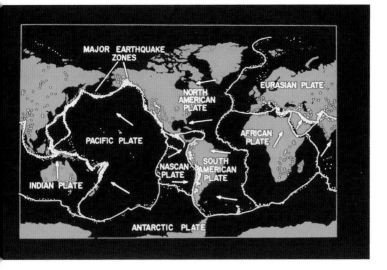

Fractures separate the Earth's crust into plates, whose movement causes continents to migrate, merging and parting over billions of years. The primeval continental mass of 200 million years ago was Pangaea, which 20 million years later split into Laurasia and Gondwana, and about 65 million years ago split further into the present continents, which have since drifted farther apart as the Atlantic Ocean widened from the central rift. The crustal plates are now well defined, and the continents bordering the Atlantic and the Pacific are gradually moving farther apart. Arrows show the direction of crust movement.

Illustration: Science Graphics.

PLATE 2

VOLCANOES

As molten rock and gases rise from the submerged chambers of volcanoes, lava, ash, and rock "bombs" pile up around their vents. These edifices persist, as living, dormant, or dead volcanoes. Some are long-lived, erupting repeatedly — often after prolonged intervals of quiescence that lulled nearby inhabitants into thinking them dead. Eventually, all do die, as the plate on which they've risen drifts off its hot spot. When that happens, a new volcano may spring up in the crust that has moved over the hot spot; the island chain of Hawaii formed this way. Other volcanoes have short lives, spending their lava in a single exuberant effusion and creating a cinder cone. Others pile up into high mountains, some of the tallest being those of the South American Andes and in our own country: Mount Shasta, Mount Hood, Mount Rainier, Mount Lassen, and Mount St. Helens.

A volcano's silhouette reveals much of its history and broadly hints at the composition of the lava of which it is built. The long-lived ones erupt repeatedly for millions of years, piling up a classic conical shape like that of Mount Fuji. These composite cone volcanoes rise to a central crater with leaky slopes from which lava occasionally oozes; a crater from which, from time to time, solid rock bombs explode. Their lava generally is basalt, though slightly more silicic than the oceanic basalts of Hawaii. Thousands of feet of very fluid lava have piled up around a constellation of Hawaiian submarine vents, building the earth's tallest volcanic group. Only the tops of these volcanoes are visible above the sea; the slopes are gentle, but the bulk is enormous.

Very fluid lava may not even produce a cone or anything recognizable as a volcano. On several continents lava has quietly flowed from fissures in the crust and eventually built great plateaus. There may be thousand-year hiatuses between eruptions when forests grow, as in the Columbia River plateau and in India's Deccan Plateau and Brazil's Rio Grande do Sul. Lines of fountains along a fissure in Hawaii and Iceland have produced similar sheets of lava that never even built significant mounds as it flowed over homes and land.

Remelted sediments can lift the silica content of rising lava, reducing its viscosity and making it more explosive. The most dangerous volcanoes, those guilty of causing fatalities, are built of such gas-saturated lava. Such lava is too viscous to allow a quiet and rapid escape of gases, as in Hawaii's watery torrents. Instead, they squeeze out stiff, gas-charged lava that when released explodes into volcanic ash. Tons of thick powder dash downslope at incredible speed, and a billowing incandescent dust cloud is buoyed by hot escaping steam. As Pliny the Younger learned with but few moments for reflection, such was the story of Pompeii, and the scenario was repeated at Mount St. Helens. However, pressure is released by the initial explosion — as when the champagne cork is removed — so for a time afterward, emerging dacite domes usually behave civilly, allowing safe if timid visits.

Photos (except middle left): Frederick H. Pough

Vulcano, in the Lipari Islands of Italy. This quintessential lava edifice, legendary seat of Vulcan's Forge, inspired the name for all such monuments.

Volcanic Isla Isabela, in the Galápagos Islands. Isabela is a low dome volcano with a crater typical of deep-sea basaltic lavas.

Mount Hood, Oregon, is a stratovolcano. A combination of lava and cinder eruptions eventually built a classic cone.
Photo: Breck P. Kent.

A volcano in the making, rich in fluid lava. Cerro Negro, Nicaragua.

The cinder cone Parícutin, in Michoacan, Mexico, was born in 1943 and in six years grew 1,200 feet high before dying.

At Santiaguito, Guatemala, viscous lava slowly pushed up a dome after an ash eruption deposited cubic miles of ash.

PLATE 3
LAVAS, HOODOOS, AND BOMBS

1 Close to its source, very fluid basalt may rush down a slope. As it cools, it slows to an ooze, then hardens into ropy surfaces known in Hawaii and around the world as pahoehoe. Full of bubbles trapped beneath the surface, the brittle basalt is barely crystallized. Each mineral grain is minute, its surface smooth, its interior spongy.

2, 3 As flowing basalt advances and cools, it stiffens into a juggernaut of giant blocks that tumble from the front, each overridden by the advancing flow. Hardened into a solid mass, the basalt cliffs of the fragmented stage may later be exposed by road cuts, the concave-convex surfaces of the blocks as tightly fitted as Inca ruins.

4 Bombs are upflung masses of still-fluid lava; whirling in the air, they take on a football shape. Smaller bombs, hurled up in continuous, small explosions, may pile up around a vent with ash and lava to form a cinder cone.

5 Flows of ignimbrite, or tuff, fill gullies with an unsorted mixture of volcanic products from dust to angular fragments. Unreal landscapes develop when subsequent weathering of such welded tuffs reveals a forest of strange pinnacles known as hoodoos, each capped for a time by an umbrella of rock, a sheltering chunk in the mass of unsorted angular fragments that projects from thick bands of cemented volcanic dust.

6 Basalt magma that fails to surface as a lava flow may squeeze between layers of sediments as a sheet. The thick, bulging sheet may cool into sets of six-sided columns, as at Devil's Postpile. Others raise overlying beds to form lenses known as laccoliths. New Jersey's Palisade is such an intrusive basalt sheet, with hints of columns in its cliffs. Ireland's Giant's Causeway is better developed; its surface is a pavement that looks almost manmade.

Photos: Frederick H. Pough

1 Pahoehoe, or ropy lava, at Kilauea, Hawaii.

2 *Aa* lava blocks at Parícutin in Michoacan, Mexico.

3 Road cut through a flow with typical concave-convex basalt blocks. Route 395 near June Lake, California.

4 Volcanic bombs at Parícutin in Michoacan, Mexico.

5 Hoodoos: pinnacles with protective boulders capping lightly welded pyroclastic ash and rock fragments. Near Chilkoot, California.

6 The hexagonal lava columns of Devil's Postpile, California, were produced by cooling cracks in a basalt flow.

PLATE 4

IGNEOUS ROCKS

1 Scoria, or scorched pieces of crusty lava, occurs in small, shapeless, spongy masses that are ejected with gas-saturated, viscous lava in countless small explosions. They pile up around vents, either the main one of the crater or parasitic ones near the base, and on flows where vents may open from time to time. Fragments falling on escaping lava may be ferried some distance, creating the mounds that often dot old flow surfaces.

2 Irregular black, almost glassy, bubble-filled scoria fragments can pile up around volcanic vents. Mountain-size accumulations make a cinder cone.

3 Wind blowing through Kilauean lava fountains creates the glassy basalt threads and froth called "Pele's hair." The glass threads are often strewn across Hawaiian flows during fiery fountain eruptions.

4 The explosion of viscous, gas-filled lava releases pressure, often resulting in expansion rather like that of rising dough. The stony, spongelike pumice that results is so light it floats on water.

5 Rhyolite, the igneous equivalent of granite, was once a common volcanic product in the West. As the Earth's crust has thickened over time, however, the fluidity of magma has lessened, and today's magma probably originates at a depth where the less siliceous constituents of basalt increase. Outcrops of light-colored rhyolite still characterize the mountains of Nevada, Utah, and Arizona. Rhyolite is generally coarser grained than basalt, and one can often find tiny feldspar and quartz bits in hand specimens ranging in color from almost white through gray to very characteristic reddish and brown hues.

6 Gases remain trapped in chilled rhyolite, which is far more viscous than basalt, creating spongy areas. On weathering, weakened regions develop into contorted pinnacles and caried pockets. With little layering or structure, irregularities in hardness produce imaginary monsters and jagged rhyolite crests, delighting imaginative tourist guides. *Photo: James Cowlin.*

Photos (except bottom right): Frederick H. Pough

Lava fountains on the surface of a flow, with glassy scoria chimneys. Parícutin, Mexico.

2 Scoria with pockets of zeolite. Salmon River, Idaho.

3 "Pele's hair" on pahoehoe. Kilauea, Hawaii.

4 Basalt dikes cutting through granitic rock. Namib Desert, Namibia.

5 A typical rhyolite exposure is light colored, often with small porphyry phenocrysts. Route 93 near Oatman, Arizona.

6 Rhyolite weathers to contorted shapes and jagged peaks. Organ Pipe Cactus National Monument, Arizona.

PLATE 5
IGNEOUS ROCKS: OBSIDIAN

1, 2 Slowly cooled siliceous lavas, which crystallized into rhyolite or granite, were once the dominant volcanic and intrusive magmas in the West. The same magma, quickly cooled and possibly containing fewer gases, produces obsidian, a glass so high in silica that, once flux is fled, no flame of torch or mineral tests can remobilize it. Here and there in the West, however, from Mexico to Canada, there are structures of obsidian that seem to have been intruded in a way that should have allowed crystallization into rhyolite; yet the obsidian has flowed, pooled, and cooled, but stayed glassy. Domed buttes are generally considered to be explosive volcanic vents called diatremes; excavation uncovers a jumble of mostly black obsidian pieces.

3 Obsidian weathers into dull black, often pitted, very opaque surfaces. Since, in time, all glass tends to crystallize into zeolites and other alteration products, none still vitreous is very old in the geological sense. Still-glassy obsidian will be found only in regions of reasonably recent vulcanism, so, if it was ever there, none survives in the eastern U.S.

4 to 8 Native Americans valued obsidian for the ease with which they could flake their points. To them, the common black was good enough. In recent years, however, lapidaries have found undreamed-of variety in obsidian. Obsidian has proved to be full of a number of things that give it a variety of appearances. Four types have long been known: snowflake, with white crystallization centers; mahogany, filled with brick red streaks; and silver- and gold-sheen, with a luster from an alignment of micaceous inclusions or fissures. Lately, rainbow and fire obsidian have further expanded the obsidian menu. Rainbow, or iris, obsidian has streaks of schiller inclusions with a number of rich colors — often so obscured by quite smoky surroundings that they are visible only under bright light. Rainbow obsidian's hues probably vary with the size of the crystallites responsible, its intensity with their abundance. Fire obsidian emits opal-like color flashes from "seams," once cracked then refused, that wind through the mass. Seams intersecting polished surfaces show neither a break in the surface nor a change in luster. *Photo: Bob Mitchell.*

Photos (except bottom right): Frederick H. Pough

1 Obsidian domes; bitterroot blooms on a diatreme. Glass Buttes, Oregon.

2 Obsidian-strewn Oregon ground. Glass Buttes, Oregon.

3 Black volcanic glass with a conchoidal fracture is common throughout western U.S.

4 Mahogany obsidian, streaked red by hematite. Glass Buttes, Oregon.

5 Gold-sheen obsidian. Glass Buttes, Oregon.

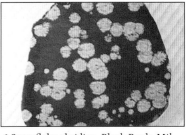

6 Snowflake obsidian. Black Rock, Milford, Utah.

7 Rainbow or iris obsidian, banded blue and purple. Glass Buttes, Oregon.

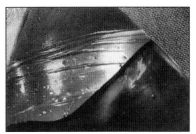

8 Fire obsidian. Glass Buttes, Oregon.

PLATE 6

PLUTONIC ROCKS: GRANITE

1 Granite and quasi-granite make up the basement rock of the lighter continental masses that have cruised the crust for billions of years, riding on plates bottoming in oceanic basalt but buoyed by siliceous crystallines. Much of this continental basement is overlain by sediments, but in Missouri, Texas, Arkansas, and South Dakota granitic hills are uplifted and exposed. Granite — coarse or fine, light or dark — is chiefly potassium feldspar and quartz, with here and there the odd grain of mica, pyroxene, or amphibole.

2 Under mountain chains like the Sierra Nevadas, granitic magma cooled slowly, gases collected, rose, and eventually escaped into overlying formations and finally to the air. The magma crystallized under pressure to a quartz and feldspar porridge subjected to stresses, compression, and thrust. This tended to produce joints and zones of weakness, assisting the passage of escaping gases that further broke down the attachment between grains. Road cuts often show giant boulders protruding from a crumbling slope of almost fresh quartz and feldspar grains.

3 When erosion strips away overlying formations that allowed slow cooling of the magma, the jointing of granite, particularly near the top of a batholithic uplift, produces a landscape strewn with light-hued giant boulders, unmistakable evidence of a batholithic granite basement. Prominent boulder piles are likely the residues of plumes of coarse-textured magma reaching up into now-eroded beds of sediment.

4 On their upward journey, magmas often begin to crystallize while still well below their final site. In the intermediate igneous rock called a porphyry, larger crystals are embedded in a faster-cooled, fine-grained ground mass. *Photo: Jeffrey Scovil.*

5 When gases are more concentrated than usual, the feldspar and the quartz may grow larger, coarser crystals and be accompanied by minerals containing uncommon elements. This more fluid magma may be injected into fissures to crystallize into pegmatitic dikes.

6 Depending on events, a single magma can give birth to several coarsely crystalline granite-textured rocks, as in the labradorite-rich Norwegian gabbro known as norite. Igneous rocks run the gamut from albite-oligoclase diorites to olivine-pyroxene peridotites — rocks with and without quartz, with and without ferromagnesian minerals, even with and without feldspar. To identify a specimen from this family, the petrographer makes a thin section and puts it under a microscope. Depending on the relative abundance of different minerals, to each assemblage he assigns a name like andesite, diorite, or peridotite. It is difficult to attach an unequivocal title to some dark rock picked up by the road; in the field, almost any name is just a guess.

Photos (except middle right): Frederick H. Pough

Coarse pink granite. Roadside near Cheyenne, Wyoming.

2 With bonds weakened, joints often crumble in road cuts, exposing unaffected cores. Granite beside Route 89 in Nevada.

3 Weathering along joints resulted in the landscape of granite boulders at Elephant Rock State Park. Belleview, Missouri.

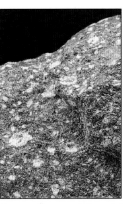

4 Rhyolite porphyry, with large feldspar phenocrysts. Near Wickieup, Arizona.

5 Pegmatitic granite, from magma squeezed into gneiss and schist. Near Idaho Springs, Colorado.

6 Norite, or "Blue Granite," is made principally of bluish feldspars. It is widely used for building facades, including the Chrysler Building.

PLATE 7

SEDIMENTARY ROCKS

1 Air and water, frost and heat create an environment very different from that experienced during magma emplacement. Upon exposure, minerals that were stable under hot magmatic conditions soon alter into substances compatible with the new environment. In general, they break down into sand, clay, and solubles. Water and wind then sort the products: rivers carry the solubles to the sea, spread out the clay in mud flats, and pile the sand on beaches; wind blows it about in valleys. Wind-driven sands are blown into dunes, which march across the land. The cross-bedding pattern laid down by shifting winds remains visible when the dunes become cemented into rock.

2 Water-laid sand beds in road cuts are often massive and formless; others show layering and are friable, made up of individual grains that are easily rubbed off. Consequently, sandstone outcrops are usually rounded, with no sharp edges.

3 The coarse banding of this sandstone is not conspicuous, but the uniform texture of discrete, easily loosed sand grains distinguish it from a fine-grained igneous rock, which would be more compact, harder, and strong enough to retain sharp edges. Sandstones are often interbedded with other sedimentary rocks like shale and limestone.

4 Coal is a sedimentary rock; layers of it can sometimes be seen interstratified with shale and sandstones. Organic accumulations of plants and animals make sedimentary rocks sources of valuable fossil fuels like coal, gas, and oil. *Photo: Stephanie and William Ferguson.*

5 Relatively small formations of rounded pebbles embedded in sand are probably formed on valleys subject to flash floods and torrents. Hardened, they make a rock known as a conglomerate.

6 Conglomerates are formations of rounded gravel cemented in sand. They are usually of limited distribution and sometimes form in valleys subject to flash floods. A trail of spectacular conglomerate reveals the path of the ice sheet from central Massachusetts to the coast south of Boston. *Photo: Gary Gilbert.*

Photos (except middle and bottom right): Frederick H. Pough

1 Ancient wind-blown dunes, now enormous thicknesses of sandstone, are found in several parts of the West. View from U.S. 70 in western Colorado.

2 Rounded outcrops of sandstone near Molina de Aragon, Spain.

3 A strip of cross-bedding indicates desert wind and flash flooding in the history of this formation. Molina de Aragon, Spain.

4 Coal bed in Mesa Verde National Park, Colorado.

5 Pebbles projecting from tightly cemented outcrop of conglomerate. Molina de Aragon, Spain.

6 "Puddingstone" from the Roxbury Conglomerate, near Boston.

PLATE 8
SEDIMENTARY ROCKS

1, 2 Sediments drop out of eroding rivers according to their size; clay particles are ferried farther out than sand, forming great mud flats. The flats teem with clams, snails, and endless sorts of ocean organisms that leave their shells behind when they die. Their preserved, often fossilized remains are evidence of life forms that have come and gone through geologic ages. *Photos: 1, Joy Spurr; 2, Jeffrey Scovil*

3 Shells of brachiopods, extinct clamlike mollusks, are revealed by the erosion of thin, slumping, soft clay sheets. The shells were once aragonite in cartilage-like bonds; the aragonite is now mostly replaced by calcite. Many Paleozoic shale formations are rich in shell remains. *Photo: V.T. King*

4 The still pearly shell of this giant ammonite, a marine mollusk akin to the nautilus, appears to yet be aragonite, though its organic network has long since been replaced by limonite. Compacted, its iridescent layers squeezed closer, the shell probably shines brighter in death than it ever did in life. *Photo: Frederick H. Pough*

5 Insects trapped in amber, or fossilized tree resin, are not themselves fossilized but are often perfectly preserved, even the soft parts. *Photo: Frederick H. Pough.*

6 Fossilization, or petrification, is the replacement of organic material with minerals. The molecule-by-molecule process makes it possible to study extinct species as precisely as if they were still living today. Quartz has replaced wood in these fossilized logs. *Photo: Breck P. Kent*

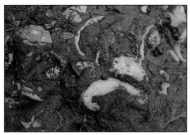

1 Fossil clams from the Eocene Era. Glide, Oregon.

2 Fossilized remains of a trilobite. Pontococ County, Oklahoma.

3 Shells of brachiopods. Rochester Shale, near Rochester, New York.

4 Giant ammonite with brilliantly iridescent aragonite nacre. Lethbridge, Alberta, Canada.

5 Insect preserved in amber. Germany.

6 Fossilized wood, Petrified Forest National Park, Arizona.

PLATE 9
SEDIMENTARY ROCKS

1 Far from land, limey marl chemically precipitated from ocean water and shell remnants falls on sea floors. The thickening sediments are compacted and eventually harden into rock, forming pale beds of limestone and (when subsequently saturated with magnesia) dolostone. Later uplifted, the sedimentary outcrops can be hundreds of feet thick. *Photo: Frederick H. Pough*

2 Because limestone is weakly water soluble, outcrop edges tend to round and may even become fluted where water flows down a cliff. Less compacted, unusually soluble limestones in moist warm climates may develop "sugarloaf" summits in what is known as karst topography. *Photo: Frederick H. Pough*

3, 4 Should shallow continental sea floors rise and fall, shorelines change and sources of sediments move nearer or farther. In roadside cuts, we often find thin-bedded limestones alternating with sheets of sand and beds of shale. Pronounced bedding tells us that the rocks are sedimentary and indicates frequent land level shifts. The slanting beds caused by the twisting and buckling of crustal plates are known as monoclines. An upward arch is called an anticline, one that sinks is a syncline. Large-scale anticlines often serve as traps for oil when capped by an impervious formation. Fractures, or faults, that lift or drop the layers can also seal a pool of oil. *Photos: Breck P. Kent*

5 Limestones range in color from black through buff and gray to chalky white, with a grain too fine to see any texture. They occasionally contain fossils. Very rarely, recrystallization may take place without significant metamorphism, allowing grains to grow enough to provide an architecturally usable and polishable stone that still exhibits fossil remains. *Photo: Frederick H. Pough*

1 Caves leached by ground water can be seen midway up this massive limestone cliff. Pequot Mountain, Nevada.

3 An anticline fold of sedimentary formations. Newfoundland, New Jersey.

2 Karst summits and topography created by solution weathering. Mallorca, Spain.

4 Series of sedimentary beds with a monoclinic plunge. Bighorn Mountains, Wyoming.

5 Weathering has exposed impressions of crinoid stalks in a limestone slab. Central Missouri.

PLATE 10
METAMORPHIC ROCKS

1 As crustal plates slide, crumple, and plunge, grains of sedimentary rocks, eroded on the surface by water, chill, and air, find themselves returned to an earlier environment. With burial, heat, and pressure, it resembles that which produced their igneous ancestors. Squeezed and heated, they begin to reorganize back into igneous minerals. Water-saturated shale is especially susceptible to renewed heat and pressure. It soon hardens into slate, a sheeted rock that tends to split in thin flakes, as small micaceous particles grow at right angles to the pressure.

2 As heat and pressure intensify, slate's mica flakes grow larger. Flat layered slate crumples, and a brighter sheen develops in low-grade metamorphics known as phyllites.

3 Slate outcrops form piles of shiny flakes. The bedding pattern is usually false, induced by the direction of pressure and no longer a reflection of sedimentary bedding.

4 As metamorphic changes reach peak intensity, the clay particles in shale revert to igneous mica, transforming shale to mica schist—the ultimate in recycling. Once again we have an igneous mineral, a born-again mica or amphibole, but the roster has changed. The mica or amphibole finds itself in new company, in different surroundings, and under directional stress. No longer is it scattered here and there through quartz and feldspar grains; it is now a key player. A thoroughly metamorphosed series of sedimentary beds—sandy shale, shaley sand, sandstone, possibly some sheets of limestone—results in an outcrop of densely streaked gneiss and schist formations, the streaks variably rich in mica, amphibole, feldspar, and quartz.

5 Even unweathered granites are not immune to the stress of metamorphism. Granite exposed to compression and a reinvasion of gases assumes some characteristics of gneiss. Responding to directional pressure, flat and elongated micas and dark minerals line up in streaks instead of the random distribution seen in a normal granite.

6 On a miniscale, we can see pegmatite texture here and there where injected magma has crystallized into large grains in some areas of the gneiss. Having become pretty fluid with an abundance of gases, most pegmatites leak into the metamorphics above the batholithic source to form dikes of new minerals with concentrations of rarer elements.

Photos: Frederick H. Pough

1 Slate "tombstone" outcrops near Mariposa, California.

2 Glistening roadside slate outcrop on the Utah-Colorado border.

3 Shiny-surfaced outcrop of a crumpled phyllite. Spain.

4 Richly banded series of gneisses and schists metamorphosed from thin-bedded sediments. Colorado.

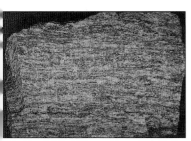

5 Metamorphic specimen, gneiss or schist.

6 Architectural granodiorite gneiss from St. Cloud, Minnesota, on the facade of the Roosevelt Hotel, New York City.

PLATE 11

METAMORPHIC ROCKS

1 Gneisses and schists are composed of the minerals that dominate igneous rocks: micas, feldspars, pyroxenes, amphiboles, and quartz. Such a rock may resemble granite, but the different origin of a metamorphic rock is evidenced by a parallel alignment of flat and elongated grains that is the response to pressure. Some rocks, however, are developed from well-sorted sediments, selectively transported and concentrated in single-mineral deposits. Pure lime can metamorphose only into a rock of pure lime, which we call marble. *Photo: Professor Orlandi of the University of Pisa*

2 Heat, gases, and pressure encourage recrystallization of limestone into coarser grains. With its good cleavage, a broken or cut marble surface sparkles from all the calcite cleavage surfaces. Its grain may equal that of granite, its hues streaked or uniformly white. Many a statue and tombstone has been chiseled from marble. *Photo: Professor Orlandi of the University of Pisa*

3 Since marble, like limestone, is relatively soluble, weathering is often more chemical than mechanical. This type of weathering commonly results in moss-covered marble boulders strewn on the landscape. Marble is much more likely to be covered by vegetation than less permeable and harder igneous rocks or less nutritious and quicker drying sandstone.

4 Like limestone, which under metamorphosis only recrystallizes into coarser units, sandstone is largely unaltered by metamorphism. Sandstone and its metamorphic successor, quartzite, differ little in appearance. Sandstone, however, is always a bit friable, its grains easily rubbed off, especially from weathering surfaces. Quartzite, on the other hand, is truly hard, resistant to all tempests. It reveals larger grains that, thanks to quartz's weak but real cleavage, grasp bits of sand between them.

5, 6 Outcrops that are prominently greenish black and soapy or slippery looking are characteristic of highly altered ferromagnesian rocks such as peridotite. Primarily containing dark minerals, they seem to metamorphose themselves while cooling into soft greenish rock called serpentinite (ser *pent* in ite), a one-mineral formation of serpentine. A belt of serpentinite parallels California Route 49 along the Mother Lode, a formation containing many mercury deposits.

Photos (except top left and right): Frederick H. Pough

1 The peaks at Carrara, Italy, resemble snow-capped mountains.

2 Marble columns in Rome.

3 Moss-covered marble boulders. Columbia State Park, California.

4 Quartzite outcrop. Rajasthan, India.

5 Serpentine outcrop. Mariposa, California.

6 Serpentine, showing characteristic slick greenish surfaces.

PLATE 12

BEST PLACES TO FIND MINERALS: MINES AND QUARRIES

1 Open pit mines using heavy machinery produce much of our copper, gold, and diamonds, often working very low-grade deposits. One of the largest and richest is Chuquicamata, in Chile, where the copper content may run as high as 3%. In most American mines the grade is far lower.

2 Quarries provide rock for architectural uses. Granite and marble are carefully wedged and sawn out for buildings and monuments. From Ohio and Michigan to the Mississippi River, limestone quarries are rich sources of a variety of minerals including calcite, dolomite, and celestite.

3 Gold, tungsten, tin, lead, zinc, fluorspar, barite, and salt are dug from many underground mines. In Illinois, Missouri, and Tennessee lead, zinc, and fluorspar are dug from many underground mines. While the main reason for working them is their product, from the collectors' standpoint, they are rich sources of often spectacular crystals encountered in open pockets. Dumps of waste rock were once great sources of specimens, but in modern mining practices, what once went on dumps is now returned to the mine as backfill. Old dumps are still promising, however, if you dig deeper than your predecessors.

4 Stone quarries blast out rock for use in construction. Basalt, commonly called "traprock," is a prime source of zeolites. The Watchung Mountains in the Paterson, New Jersey, area have long been a famous locality. Many zeolites, with associated species like datolite, apophyllite, and prehnite, have for years provided a bonus for collectors from this utilitarian activity. Elsewhere in the world, in Australia, India, Uruguay, and Brazil, basalt is quarried for fill and construction and for agate and amethyst. Idar-Oberstein, the gem-cutting center of the world, owes its preeminence to the agates once found there. *Photo: Professor Orlandi of the University of Pisa*

5 Third-world mines are often quite simple—unmechanized bucket, pick, and shovel operations. Deep weathering in the tropics commonly destroys all but the toughest minerals. Gem minerals are survivors, but their siblings, quartz and feldspar, have usually succumbed, so collectors can obtain only loose crystals. Escorted tours to such sources generally provide only an opportunity to get closer to a place where the silver pick is the magic tool; anything considered saleable will have been collected before you get there.

6 Placer mines are gravel deposits where heavy minerals like gold, diamonds, or sapphires have been concentrated and can be recovered by panning or sifting. At some gemstone sources, commercial operations have been established where a fee is charged, and finders are keepers.

Photos (except middle right): Frederick H. Pough

1 One of the world's largest mines, famous for minerals formed in desert conditions. Chuquicamata, Chile.

2 Building stone such as marble and granite must be carefully quarried. Seams and pockets may provide crystals. Fantiscritti, Carrara, Italy.

3 Underground mines are usually off limits to collectors, but many miners manage to salvage specimens (at some risk to their jobs). Head frame at Tsumeb, Namibia.

4 Stone quarries blast heavily to produce crushed stone, making for good collecting. Pouchete Quarry, Mount St. Hilaire, Quebec.

5 In third-world mines where picks and shovels are the rule, collectors' finds may be isolated crystals. Topaz mine, Tres Barros, Minas Gerais, Brazil.

6 In U.S. commercial operations, a bucket of gravel can be panned for gems. Some "salting" by management may assure satisfied customers. Gem Mountain Sapphire Mine, Phillipsburg, Montana.

PLATE 13

ELEMENTS

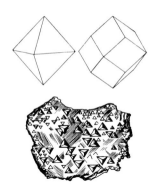

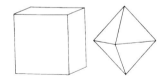

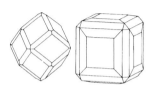

1 GOLD CRYSTALS
Eagle's Nest Mine, Placer Co., CA
Crystal plate of very yellow, very high-karat gold in quartz, typical of the Mother Lode.

2 MERCURY
Socrates Mine, Sonoma Co., CA
Droplets of mercury associated with cinnabar are "quick" to fall from the surface of a fresh ore fracture, hence the name quicksilver.

3 SILVER *Taxco, Guerrero, Mexico*
Wires rising from a catalytically potent galena crystal face. Acanthite also has silver-nourishing properties, when bathed in appropriate solution.

4 PLATINUM NUGGET
Sysert, Ural Mts., Russia
An 8-cm waterworn nugget in the A. E. Fersman Museum of the Russian Academy of Sciences, Moscow.

5 COPPER
Boguslovskiy, N. Urals, Russia
Dendritic growth of native metal, the end product following an enriching series of sulfide reduction.

6 IRON METEORITE
Henbury, Australia
An etched slice showing structural pattern characteristic of meteorites in a medium octahedrite.

PLATE 14

ELEMENTS

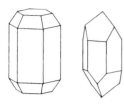

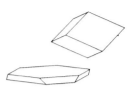

1 TELLURIUM
Cananea, Sonora, Mexico
Tiny needles of this native semi-metal, a low-temperature mineral, can even be found lining hot volcanic fumaroles.

2 ARSENIC
Alden Island, British Columbia
Uncommon in the native state, arsenic crystals are found in low-temperature veins even in hot springs.

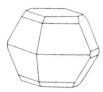

3 SULFUR *Caltanisetta, Sicily*
Orthorhombic low-temperature crystals, probably formed by breakdown of gypsum, are less fragile than monoclinic ones made of volcanic fumarole sublimates.

4 GRAPHITE *Sri Lanka*
Rich veins of graphite are uncommon; more often it forms perfect microcrystals in impure marble.

5 DIAMOND *Mir Mine, Siberia*
With more sources open to us, specimens of diamonds in matrix now may be more readily available.

6 DIAMOND *South Africa*
It is not true that gems of any sort conceal their potential until cut. The identity and value even of rough stones are obvious.

1
⇐

2
⇒

3
⇐

4
⇒

6

PLATE 15

SULFIDES

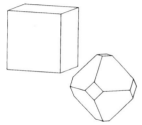

1 ARGENTITE *Zacatecas, Mexico*
Commonly inclined toward skeletal cubes, always inverting to acanthite. Resembles galena but is blacker and lacks the brightness and cleavage.

2 CHALCOCITE *Cornwall, England*
One of the orthorhombics that twin to look hexagonal.

3 GALENA *Picher, OK*
Most galena crystallizes in cubes with faces commonly dulled by oxidation. Literally heavy as lead, the cleavage makes recognition easy.

4 GALENA *Galena, KS*
Galena grows octahedrons under some conditions, possibly related to deposition temperature.

5 SPHALERITE "BLACK JACK"
Carthage, TN
High iron content blackens sphalerite to make it almost resemble the galena with which it is usually associated.

6 SPHALERITE "RUBY JACK"
Oklahoma
In the absence of iron, sphalerite can be greenish golden, red, or even colorless.

1 ⇐

2 ⇒

3 ⇐

4 ⇒

5 ⇐

6 ⇒

PLATE 16

SULFIDES

1 CHALCOPYRITE *Siegen, Germany*
Typical pseudotetrahedral crystals of
this primary copper ore, yellower
than pyrite.

2 BORNITE *Kazakhstan*
Large, well-formed crystal from a
former USSR region.

3 GREENOCKITE *Summit, NJ*
Hemimorphic crystal in traprock
pocket. *Photo: Breck P. Kent*

4 PYRRHOTITE
Sta. Eulalia, Chihuahua, Mexico
Sharp crystal of this sometimes im-
permanent species.

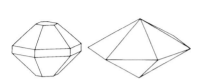

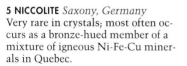

5 NICCOLITE *Saxony, Germany*
Very rare in crystals; most often occurs as a bronze-hued member of a
mixture of igneous Ni-Fe-Cu minerals in Quebec.

6 MILLERITE *Antwerp, NY*
Needle spray in pocket, slightly
more solid than the golden cobwebs
encountered in some Midwest limestone quarries.

1 ⇐
2 ⇒

3 ⇐
4 ⇒

5 ⇐
6 ⇒

PLATE 17

SULFIDES

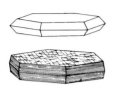

1 COVELLITE
Leonard Mine, Butte, MT
Specimen from the world's best locality for this hexagonal-plate sulfide. More often as solid bluish aggregates of tiny plates.

2 CINNABAR *Hunan, China*
From the best locality for interpenetrating twinned rhombohedral crystals, red to almost black, in a calcite matrix.

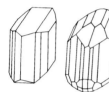

3 REALGAR *Getchell Mine, NV*
Red crystals, accompanied by orpiment's golden hue.

4 ORPIMENT *Peru*
Always associated with realgar, orpiment is slightly more stable and keeps better in collections.

5 STIBNITE *Baia Sprie, Romania*
These slender, often nicely terminated bundles, more typical than the giant Japanese prisms, are abundantly available.

6 BISMUTHINITE *Guangdong, China*
Unlike large and usually altered pegmatite prisms, fresh rods lie embedded in pyrite in complex sulfide ore bodies.

1 ⇐
2 ⇒

3 ⇐
4 ⇒

5 ⇐
6 ⇒

PLATE 18

SULFIDES

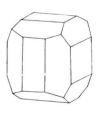

1 PYRITE *Logroño, Spain*
Pyrite crystals are most commonly cubic, the shape they take in sediments and probably the lowest temperature form.

2 PYRITE *Huanca Velica, Peru*
The five-sided face, a form found otherwise only in cobaltite and skutterudite, gives these pentagonal dodecahedral crystals the name pyritohedron.

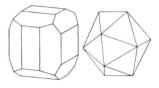

3 PYRITE *Huanca Velica, Peru*
Octahedral crystals are somewhat less common; exactly what causes this form is unknown.

4 COBALTITE
Pele Mine, Riddarhyttan, Norway
The only mineral other than pyrite and skutterudite to form the 12-faced pyritohedron.

5 SKUTTERUDITE *Saxony, Germany*
Localities with good crystals of this mineral are few. Always associated with other Ni-Co species.

6 MARCASITE
Vintirov, Bohemia, Czech Republic
Often unstable and liable to decomposition in collections, possibly victims of anaerobic bacteria.

PLATE 19

SULFIDES

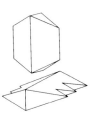

1 ARSENOPYRITE
Parral, Chihuahua, Mexico
Typical silvery crystal with flat tent top, diamond-shaped cross section.

2 MOLYBDENITE *Harp of Erin Mine, Queensland, Australia*
Hexagonal crystal, with the bruising and soft edges inevitable in so soft a mineral.

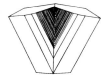

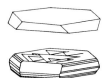

3 CALAVERITE
Cripple Creek, CO
Flat, striated, lathlike crystals of great morphological complexity.
Photo: Sugar White

4 POLYBASITE
Guanajuato, Mexico
Flat crystals with chalcopyrite and quartz.

5 STEPHANITE
Zacatecas, Mexico
Well-developed, shiny crystals on stalactite of quartz.

6 TETRAHEDRITE
Huaron, Peru
Sharp, tetrahedral crystals with triangular surface striations.

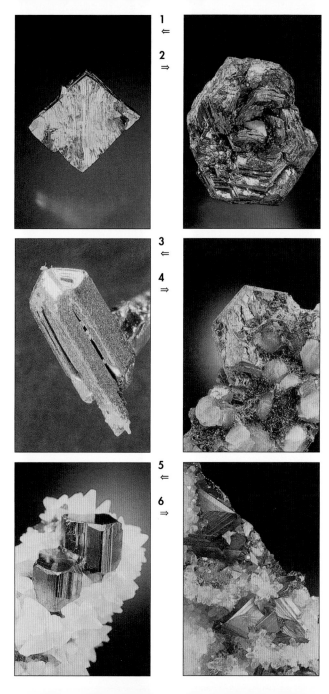

PLATE 20

SULFOSALTS

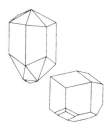

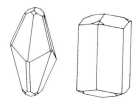

1 PYRARGYRITE *Ancash, Peru*
This often dark silver mineral is usually the latest sulfide in a silver ore sequence. Crystals tend to be blunter and darker than those of its paler mate, proustite.

2 PROUSTITE
Dolores Mine, Chanarcillo, Chile
Steep scalenohedrons characterize this bright arsenical salt; this sample is from the world's most famous source, now deserted and barren.

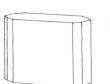

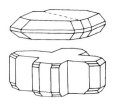

3 ENARGITE *Quiruvilca, Peru*
Bright, flat-ended crystals of this primary copper ore prevalent in western South American mines.

4 BOURNONITE
Pachaqui, Ancash, Peru
The reentrant "cog-wheel ore" teeth are this mineral's key characteristic.

5 MIARGYRITE
San Genaro Mine, Huanca Velica, Peru
A hexagonal crystal outline is the clue to the identity of this rare and usually dull black mineral.

6 JAMESONITE
Sombrete Mine, Zacatecas, Mexico
Often in slender needles, jamesonite sometimes thickens into rods but has no real look-alikes in late silver sequences.

1

2

3 ⇐

4 ⇒

5 ⇐

6 ⇒

PLATE 21

OXIDES

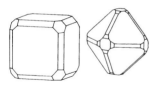

1 CUPRITE
Cornwall, England
The penultimate stage in nature's copper ore enrichment progression from chalcopyrite to native copper.

2 CUPRITE VAR. CHALCOTRICHITE
Arizona
Hairlike crystals of cuprite, actually elongated cubes in a skeletal mat.
Photo: Frederick H. Pough

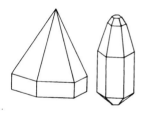

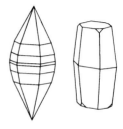

3 ZINCITE
Franklin, NJ
This zinc ore, elsewhere rare to almost unknown, came from a mine near New York City, now open to tours. *Photo: Frederick H. Pough*

4 CORUNDUM VAR. SAPPHIRE
Sri Lanka
Common in low-silica environments and often in marbles, this crystal is typical of Sri Lankan bipyramidal gemmy sapphires.

5 CORUNDUM
Philipsburg, MT
Gem pebbles in a variety of hues from river placer deposits, typical of those found by tourists.

6 CORUNDUM (SYNTHETIC RUBY)
Traditional Verneuil flame fusion boules and flux melt crusts. From Linde Air Products.

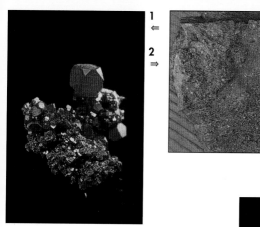

1 ⇐

2 ⇒

3 ⇐

4 ⇒

5 ⇐

6 ⇒

OXIDES

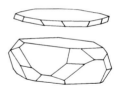

1 CHROMITE
Siskiyou Co., CA
Segregated immiscible droplets in a ferromagnesian igneous intrusion.

2 ILMENITE
Lengenbach, Binntal, Switzerland
Flat crystal from a famed source of uncommon sulphosalt species.

3 RUTILE
Minas Gerais, Brazil
From a kyanite mine, source of possibly the largest known crystals of this mineral. *Photo: Frederick H. Pough*

4 RUTILE
Orissa, India
Rutile needles can pierce solid rock crystal quartz. *Photo: Frederick H. Pough*

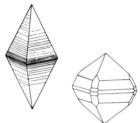

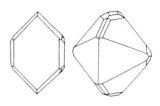

5 ANATASE
Hardeland, Norway
Typical steep, blue-black bipyramids on quartz, a common habit worldwide.

6 BROOKITE ON QUARTZ
Saranpuyva, Polar Urals, Russia
Thin flat crystal on quartz, similar to the original type from Tremadoc, Wales.

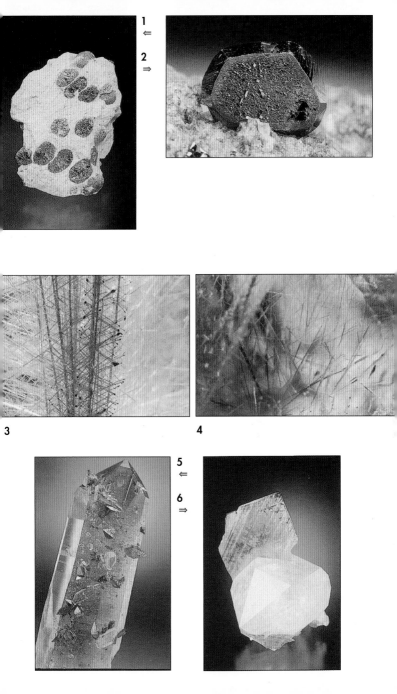

1 ⇐
2 ⇒

3

4

5 ⇐
6 ⇒

PLATE 23

OXIDES

1 BIXBYITE
Thomas Range, UT
Cubic crystal on topaz from a pocket in rhyolite.

2 PYROLUSITE
Negachee, MI
Typical sooty shredding fibers.

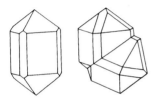

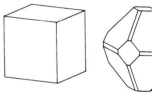

3 CASSITERITE
Cornwall, England
Untwinned single crystal in quartz.

4 URANINITE
Cardiff Uranium Mine, Wilberforce, Ontario
Isolated crystal in carbonatite.

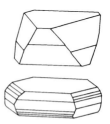

5 GUMMITE
Ruggles Mine, Grafton, NH
Once-black specks of uraninite have altered into secondary species like clarkeite and curite, giving color to omnibus "gummite."

6 BRUCITE
Cedarhill Quarry, Lancaster Co., PA
The flaky blades of this talc-like species resemble a chlorite or a mica.

PLATE 24

OXIDES

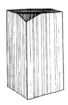

1 MANGANITE
Ilefeld, Harz, Germany
Large crystals from the best locality known for this mineral, in veins cutting a porphyry, with barite and calcite.

2 PSILOMELANE
Montreal Mine, Montreal, WI
Reniform masses.

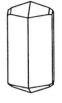
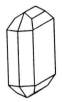

3 BAUXITE
Bauxite, AR
Oolitic masses of several hydrous aluminum oxides in a low-silica rock, leached of SiO_2 in ancient tropical weathering.

4 DIASPORE
Dere, Anatolia, Turkey
Gemmy crystal from an emery mine, the first find of facetable material.

5 GOETHITE
Goethite Hill, Park Co., CO
Crystals surrounding a core of hematite.

6 LIMONITE
Bennington, VT
Stalactitic formation in gossan from the alteration of iron sulfides in a fluorite mine.

1
⇐

2
⇒

3
⇐

4
⇒

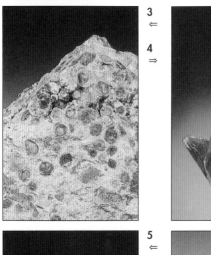

5
⇐

6
⇒

PLATE 25

OXIDES

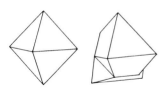

1 SPINEL *Myanmar*
Gemmy red crystal from a marble crust.

2 SPINEL (SYNTHETIC)
Synthetic boules and crystals are easily made by flame fusion of a powder or crystallized from a molten solvent. From Linde Air Products.

3 MAGNETITE *Chester, VT*
Crystal in chlorite.
Photo: Frederick H. Pough

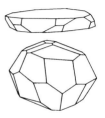

4 MAGNETITE VAR. LODESTONE
Iron Springs, UT
Powder from breakage clings magnetically to polarized examples.

5 HEMATITE
St. Gothard, Switzerland
"Iron rose" cluster of black metallic specular hematite on quartz.

6 HEMATITE
Black Widow Mine, Pima Co., AZ
Mammillary mass of compact black fibrous "pencil ore" that polishes into the beads and cabochons sold as "Alaskan Diamonds."

PLATE 26

OXIDES

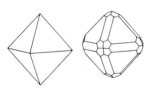

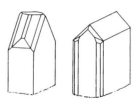

1 MICROLITE
Gillette Quarry, Portland, CT
Original finds were tiny; later specimens are up to a centimeter long.

2 SAMARSKITE
Green Mt., Yancey Co., NC
The crystals of this always black species are invariably dull and altered, often intergrown with other rare earth minerals and biotite.

3 COLUMBITE
Middletown, CT
An unusually large and well-formed example of this exclusively pegmatite species.

4 TANTALITE VAR. MANGANOTANTALITE
Paraiba, Brazil
Isomorphous substitutions of manganese or bismuth in tantalite lighten the color of the Ta end-member of the Nb-Ta series.
Photo: Martha Halleberg

5 CHRYSOBERYL
Minas Gerais, Brazil
Trilling often creates a pseudohexagonal symmetry in orthorhombic species.

6 CHRYSOBERYL VAR. ALEXANDRITE
Malyshevo, Russia
The delicate blue-green hue of this very precious gem mineral is difficult to capture on film.

1
⇐

2
⇒

3
⇐

4
⇒

5
⇐

6
⇒

PLATE 27

HALOIDS

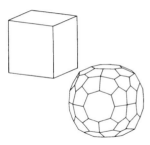

1 FLUORITE
Cave-in-Rock, IL
The commonest habit at all economically significant deposits is the cube, but shiny surfaces are infrequent.

2 FLUORITE
Grant Co., NM
Octahededral crystals are associated with higher-temperature formations.

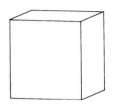

3 CRYOLITE AND SIDERITE
Ivigtut, Greenland
Typical specimen of a unique and now exhausted pegmatite mined for electrolytic aluminum refining.

4 CHLORARGYRITE ON MALACHITE
Bisbee, AZ
Crystals, darkened by exposure to light, on malachite in limonite gossan.

5 HALITE
Neuhoff, Germany
Cubic crystals from a pocket in a salt mine.

6 SYLVITE
Salton Sea, CA
Octahedral crystals are the rule for sylvite, though in this case, the potassium content may be less than in purer mined sylvite.

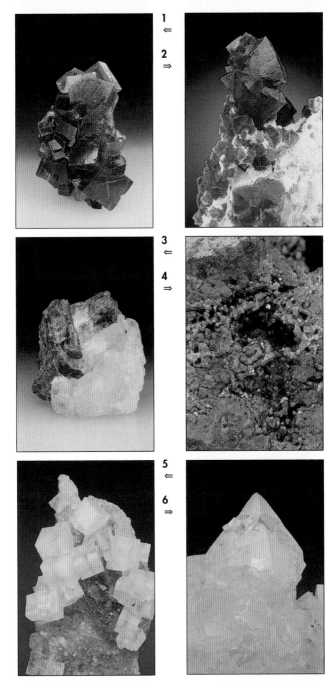

PLATE 28

CARBONATES AND HALOIDS

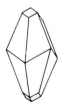
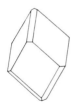

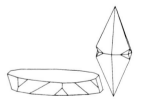

1 CALCITE WITH CELESTITE
Chittenango Falls, NY
Doubly terminated scalenohedral crystals, the most common habit of crystals from mildly warm solutions.

2 CALCITE
Charcas, San Luis Potosí, Mexico
"Poker-chip" flat crystals are indicative of high-temperature formation.

3 CALCITE *Mexico*
Cleavage rhombohedrons of "Iceland spar."

4 CALCITE VAR. ONYX
Spain; Austria
Calcite onyx with cobalt (pink) and copper (green or blue).

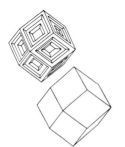

5 SAL AMMONIAC *Parícutin, Mexico*
Sublimated crystals on a fuming vent on lava flow, 1943, initially at about 500°C.
Photo: Frederick H. Pough

6 ATACAMITE
Moonta, N.S.W., Australia
Crystal cluster of stubby rods.

1 ⇐
2 ⇒
3 ⇐
4 ⇒
5 ⇐
6 ⇒

PLATE 29

CARBONATES

1 ARAGONITE
Bisbee, AZ
Spray of crystals on earlier serpentine-coated calcite.

2 ARAGONITE
Molinas de Aragon, Spain
Pseudohexagonal prism trilling from shale bed.

3 ARAGONITE
Styria, Austria
Confused stalactitic overgrowth on iron ore, known as "flos ferri" (iron flowers). *Photo: Frederick H. Pough*

4 ARAGONITE
Forchaim, Jura Mts.
A fossilized ammonite shell, its organic conchiolin foundation replaced by limonite. *Photo: Frederick H. Pough*

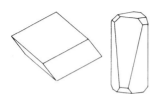

5 MAGNESITE
Brumado, Bahia, Brazil
Transparent "Iceland spar"-type crystals from metamorphism of a magnesia-rich formation.

6 MAGNESITE
Brumado, Bahia, Brazil
White, porcelanous, concretionary mass, formed by surface alteration of a magnesia-rich rock.

1 ⇐

2 ⇒

3

4

5 ⇐

6 ⇒

PLATE 30

CARBONATES

1 RHODOCHROSITE
Emma Mine, Butte, MT
Group of piled rhombohedrons.

2 RHODOCHROSITE
South Africa
Deep red scalenohedral crystals.

3 RHODOCHROSITE ONYX
Catamarca, Argentina
Banded gangue of metal mine, often used in carvings. *Photo: Frederick H. Pough*

4 SMITHSONITE
Kelly Mine, Magdalena, NM
Copper-pigmented rough rhombohedral crystals.

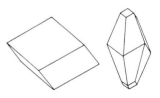

5 SMITHSONITE
Broken Hill, Zambia
Unusual scalenohedral crystal of a mineral that more often forms botryoidal crusts. *Photo: Frederick H. Pough*

6 SIDERITE AND QUARTZ
Allevard, Isere, France
Group of brown rhombohedral crystals from a world-famous source.

1 ⇐

2 ⇒

3

4

5 ⇐

6 ⇒

PLATE 31

CARBONATES

1 DOLOMITE
Ergui, Pamplona, Spain
Interpenetrating rhombohedral twins from magnesite quarry, a habit often found in warm hydrothermal ore veins.

2 DOLOMITE
Galena, KS
Saddle-shaped pink rhombohedra typically line pockets in Midwestern limestone and dolomite quarries.

3 CERUSSITE
Tsumeb, Namibia
Typical trilling of three orthorhombic crystals.

4 CERUSSITE
Tiger, AZ
Reticulated and twinned intergrowth.

5 WITHERITE
Minerva Mine, Cave-in-Rock, IL
Sixlings form a pseudohexagonal bipyramid.

6 STRONTIANITE
Styria, Austria
Another orthorhombic carbonate that frequently forms trillings.

3

4

PLATE 32

CARBONATES

1 HYDROZINCITE
Mina Ojuela, Durango, Mexico
Small feathery crystals coating limonite.

2 AURICHALCITE
Bisbee, AZ
Fragile crystal bundles.

3 PHOSGENITE
Monte Poni, Sardinia, Italy
Typical tetragonal crystal from the world's most generous source of this mineral.

4 LEADHILLITE
Mammoth–St. Anthony Mine, Tiger, AZ
Though copper is a nonessential constituent, pale blue tips seem common to several localities.

5 MALACHITE
Ural Mts., Russia
A shiny, hard, botryoidal mass of a mineral that just as often is soft and crumbling.

6 MALACHITE
China
Compact masses of malachite are raw material for intaglio, intarsia, and figure carving. A carved malachite figure of Kuan-yin, the Bodhisattva of compassion.

1 ⇐

2 ⇒

3 ⇐

4 ⇒

5 ⇐

6 ⇒

PLATE 33

CARBONATES AND NITRATES

1 AZURITE AND MALACHITE
Bisbee, AZ
Surface covered with azurite and malachite, typical of limonitic gossan over an ore body

2 AZURITE AND MALACHITE
Morenci, AZ
Slice of a stalactite showing alternating deposition of malachite and azurite.

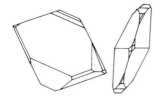

3 AZURITE
Tsumeb, Namibia
Spectacular crystals of azurite from a pocket.

4 AZURITE
Guangdong, China
Spherical mass of crystals grown in fault gouge clay, a frequent phenomenon of copper mines.

5 Nitre-strewn desert floor, Atacamá Desert, Chile. Mostly long since stripped for fertilizer.
Photo: Frederick H. Pough

6 Iodine crystals flow from the fumes freed during purification of fertilizer nitrates.
Photo: Frederick H. Pough

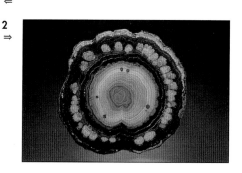

6

PLATE 34

BORATES

1 BORACITE
Friedrichall Mine, Sehnde, Germany
An extremely hard mineral usually found as single crystals in salt beds, although light green scoriaceous masses have been found in England.

2 KERNITE
Boron, CA
A species that is really compressed borax, that is, a borax with water squeezed out by burial and dryness.

3 BORAX
Esmerelda Co., NV
With a loss of water, borax crystals alter to tincalconite.
Photo: Frederick H. Pough

4 ULEXITE
Boron, CA
Fibrous, light-transmitting, transparent crystals; a natural fiber optic ("TV ore").

5 COLEMANITE *Death Valley, CA*
The selectively distributed dust patches on this cabinet specimen suggest piezeoelectric charges and a symmetry less than holohedral.
Photo: Frederick H. Pough

6 HOWLITE *Tick Canyon, San Bernardino Co., CA*
Nodular mass, probably surface recrystallizations of earlier borates.
Photo: Frederick H. Pough

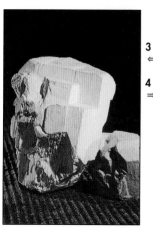

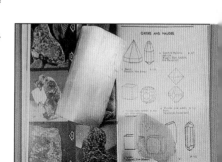

PLATE 35

HALOIDS AND SULFATES

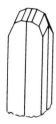

1 POLYHALITE
Carlsbad, NM
Massive chunk from a saline formation above the halite of a salt mine.

2 THENARDITE
Soda Lake, San Luis Obispo Co., CA
Crystals wrested from the mud of a drying saline lake in late summer.

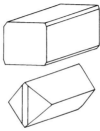

3 BARITE
Wasta, Pennington Co., SD
Crystal growing in crevice in a Badlands shale bed concretion.

4 BARITE
Eagle Mine, Boulder Co., CO
Crystal group from the gangue of a lead-zinc mine.

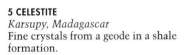

5 CELESTITE
Karsupy, Madagascar
Fine crystals from a geode in a shale formation.

6 ANGLESITE
Mibladen, Morocco
Gemmy crystals from what appears to have been one of the world's best localities.

1 ⇐

2 ⇒

3 ⇐

4 ⇒

5 ⇐

6 ⇒

PLATE 36

SULFATES

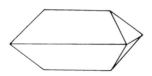

1 ANHYDRITE
Naica, Chihuahua, Mexico
Crystals from the gangue of a lead mine.

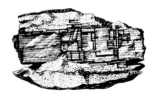

2 ANHYDRITE *Venice, LA*
Residue of insoluble sand from brine production in a salt dome, enhanced with tetrahedra of chambersite and an assortment of other microscopic insolubles.

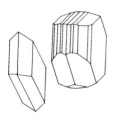

3 GYPSUM
Potosí Mine, Chihuahua, Mexico
Transparent crystals are common in veins, associated with calcite in metal ores.

4 GYPSUM
Many environments foster gypsum growth: clay sediments, alkali lake beds, sand layers (creating "roses"), caverns, and underground pipes.
Photo: Frederick H. Pough

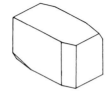

5 CHALCANTHITE *Ely, NV*
Many copper deposits are saturated with blue vitriol solutions; in dry periods, surfaces are tinted with blue.
Photo: Frederick H. Pough

6 CHALCANTHITE *Ely, NV*
Needles of chalcanthite often sprout from evaporating mine waters made acid by still-oxidizing sulfides. Dealers' blue-stained crystals are mostly laboratory grown.
Photo: Frederick H. Pough

1
⇐

2
⇒

3
⇐

4
⇒

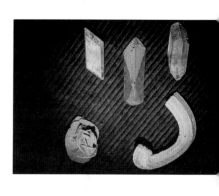

PLATE 37

SULFATES

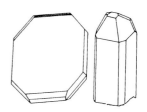

1 CROCOITE
Red Lead Mine, Dundas, Tasmania
Spectacular long, hollow, bright orange prisms from a unique occurrence.

2 LINARITE *Mammoth–St. Anthony Mine, Tiger, AZ*
Though very like azurite, linarite clings closer to the matrix and rarely projects into a pocket.

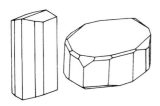

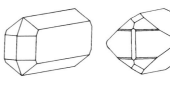

3 BROCHANTITE
*Blanchard Claims,
Bingham, NM*
The green needles, here on quartz with galena and barite, resemble malachite but do not bubble in acid.

4 ANTLERITE
Chuquicamata, Chile
Slender green crystals from Chile are assumed to be antlerite, but the mineral is nearly indistinguishable from brochantite.

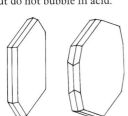

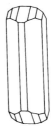

5 COPIAPITE
Mina Quetena, Copiapo, Chile
Found only in extreme deserts; elsewhere, copiapite does not survive the next shower.

6 CALEDONITE
Grand Reef Mine, Graham Co., AZ
Beautiful light blue crystals make this rare species highly regarded by collectors.

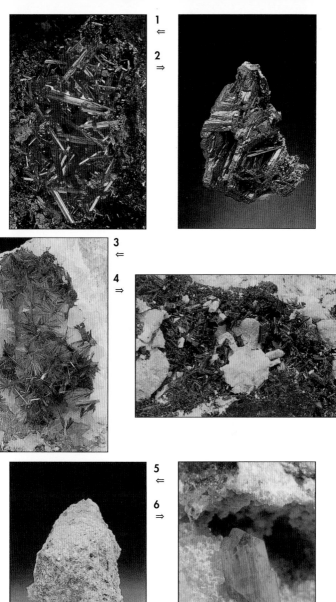

PLATE 38

PHOSPHATES

1 TRIPHYLITE
Chandler's Mills, Sullivan Co., NH
Well-developed dull and embedded blue-gray crystals are uncommon in pegmatites.

2 LITHIOPHILITE
Foote Mine, Kings Mt., NC
Can be olive-brown massive primary pegmatite phosphate, altering into a host of secondary crystals.

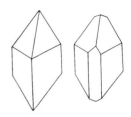

3 HETEROSITE VAR. PURPURITE
Palermo Mine, N. Groton, NH
Treated with HCl, dark brown areas in massive phosphates become sub-metallic purple.

4 HUREAULITE
Mesquitela, Mangualde, Portugal
Typically lilac pink; unlike any other secondary pegmatite phosphate.

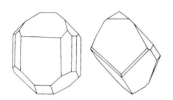

5 MONAZITE *Joaquin Felicia, Minas Gerais, Brazil*
Sharp, and looking very monoclinic, brownish crystals are often twinned in crosses and readily identifed by appearance alone.

6 AMBLYGONITE
Minas Gerais, Brazil
Much like feldspar, amblygonite could easily be mistaken for it in a pegmatite.

1 ⇐

2 ⇒

3 ⇐

4 ⇒

5 ⇐

6 ⇒

PLATE 39

PHOSPHATES AND ARSENATES

1 ROSELITE *Bou Azzer, Morocco*
Cobalt minerals are relatively few, and localites not numerous. Roselite is rich pink in hue, despite its blue coloration of glass and spinel; all cobalt salts are pink.

2 PHOSPHOPHYLLITE
Potosí, Bolivia
Uncommon, and an unlikely find for any amateur, these gemmy crystals cost dearly whenever dealers get one.

 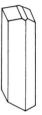

3 VIVIANITE *Morococolla, Bolivia*
Vein vivianite appears to be more stable than crystals associated with fossils. These giants have yet to stand the harshest test, the test of time.

4 ERYTHRITE
Alamos, Mexico
Another pink cobalt mineral, the counterpart of vivianite. More often in fine needles or a pink dusting.

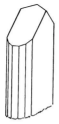

5 ANNABERGITE
Laurium, Greece
Though isomorphous with vivianite, this nickel-tinted arsenate has not been found in giant crystals.

6 BERYLLONITE
Stoneham, ME
A major find of gemmy crystals distinguished this locality; it was an old and until lately unique source.

1 ⇐

2 ⇒

3 ⇐

4 ⇒

5 ⇐

6 ⇒

PLATE 40

PHOSPHATES AND ARSENATES

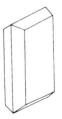

1 DUFRENITE VAR. ROCKBRIDGEITE
Hagendorf, Bavaria, Germany
Feathery fibers of this pegmatitic
lithiophilite form on other minerals.

2 VARISCITE
Fairfield, UT
Nodule from a limey-clay formation
with yellow rind of several uncommon alteration products.

3 STRENGITE
Norbotton, Sweden
One of the more attractive and uncommon mineral species, often in
specular iron mines. Here on rockbridgeite.

4 SCORODITE
Tsumeb, Namibia
A suprisingly rare species, despite
the abundance of its elements.
Tends to crystallize out quickly,
spreading small crystals across the
ore surface.

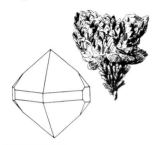

5 DESCLOIZITE
Grootfontein, Namibia
The sharp, many-angled flat crystals
from this source are possibly the
world's best, and relatively obtainable.

6 HERDERITE *Virgem de Lapa, Minas
Gerais, Brazil*
This site is a source of giant crystals
of this uncommon, usually twinned
species (note open-mouthed reentrant in center).

1 ⇐

2 ⇒

3 ⇐

4 ⇒

5 ⇐

6 ⇒

PLATE 41

PHOSPHATES

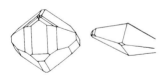

1 BRAZILIANITE *Conselhiero Pena, Minas Gerais, Brazil*
Splayed crystal group, a characteristic growth pattern of the smaller crystals of this find.

2 OLIVENITE
Tsumeb, Namibia
A group of prismatic crystals from the oxidized zone of the Tsumeb Mine.

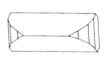

3 ADAMITE *Mina Ojuela, Mapimi, Durango, Mexico*
The compact fan of crystals is a common growth habit of multiple adamite crystals.

4 ADAMITE *Mina Ojuela, Mapimi, Durango, Mexico*
Amethystine-tipped larger adamites, a color phase that tends to form single crystals.

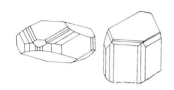

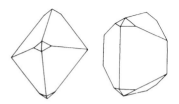

5 AUGELITE *Rapid Creek, Yukon Territory, Canada*
White crystal with other phosphates, unlike the gemmy crystals of Bishop, CA's White Mountain mine of andalusite, used in making spark plugs.

6 LIBETHENITE
Santa Rita Mine, Grant Co., NM
Libethenite is an infrequent secondary copper phosphate, a clue that the primary ore was not arsenical.

PLATE 42

PHOSPHATES

1 APATITE
Vates Mine, Otter Lake, Quebec
Doubly terminated prismatic crystal on calcite.

2 APATITE
Hebron, ME
A highly prized gemmy violet crystal in pegmatite, with quartz crystals.

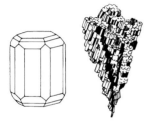

3 PYROMORPHITE
Phoenixville, PA
Hollow-tipped green crystals, associated with limonite.

4 MIMETITE
San Pedro Coralitos, Sonora, Mexico
Rounded masses of ill-formed crystals in limonite gossan.

5 VANADINITE
Old Yuma Mine, Pima Co., AZ
These bright hexagonal crystals coat brecciated vein fragments.

6 LAZULITE
Graves Mt., Lincoln Co., GA
Typical crystal in a granular quartz matrix of rutile and kyanite.

1 ⇐

2 ⇒

3 ⇐

4 ⇒

5 ⇐

6 ⇒

PLATE 43

TUNGSTATES AND PHOSPHATES

1 HUEBNERITE
Adams Mine, Silverton, CO
Manganiferous brown crystals on quartz.

2 LIROCONITE
Cornwall, England
Pseudo-tetragonal crystals of this costly and almost exclusively Cornish mineral.

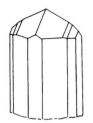

3 EOSPHORITE
Minas Gerais, Brazil
Sprays of dark eosphorites on rose quartz crystals.

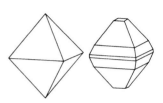

4 WARDITE
Rapid Creek, Yukon Territory, Canada
Tetragonal crystal from phosphate-filled veins.

5 TURQUOISE
Lavender Pit, Bisbee, AZ
Vein of fine-grained jewelry-type turquoise (see also Plate 64).

6 WAVELLITE
Garland Co., AR
Balls and radiating crystals typical of the species.

1 ⇐
2 ⇒

3 ⇐
4 ⇒

5 ⇐
6 ⇒

PLATE 44

URANATES, TUNGSTATES, AND MOLYBDATES

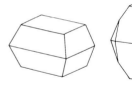

1 AUTUNITE
Trancoso, Portugal
Typical squares, lightly attached to quartz matrix; now dehydrated, they may more properly be called meta-autunite.

2 TORBERNITE
Chinkalobwe, Zaire
Two stages of crystal formation can be seen, the paler ones having lost water and transparency.
Photo: Frederick H. Pough

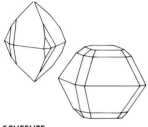

3 SCHEELITE
Nova Lima, Minas Gerais, Brazil
The sample has the characteristic hue and octahedral shape of this pseudo-isometric quartz vein species.

4 POWELLITE
Nasik, India
A moderately common mineral in nonmetallic zeolitic environments; forms on zeolites.

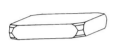

5 WULFENITE
Red Cloud Mine, LaPaz Co., AZ
From a famed source of crystals colored brilliant orange by chromium.

6 WULFENITE
San Francisco Mine, Sonora, Mexico
These thin light yellow crystals frequently line surfaces in breccia veins.

1 ⇐

2 ⇒

3 ⇐

4 ⇒

5 ⇐

6 ⇒

PLATE 45

SILICATES

1 QUARTZ VAR. ROCK CRYSTAL
Mt. Ida, AR
Colorless quartz, or rock crystal, is credited with metaphysical virtues.

2 QUARTZ VAR. AMETHYST
Rio Grande do Sul, Brazil
Crystals line gas pockets in basalt lava flows of southern Brazil and Uruguay.

3 QUARTZ VAR. CITRINE
Charcas, San Luis Potosí, Mexico
Golden crystal from the gangue of a lead mine.

4 SMOKY QUARTZ
Lake George, Park Co., CO
Slender smoky crystal with microcline feldspar.

5 ROSE QUARTZ
Mina de Ilha, Minas Gerais, Brazil
Pink crystals ringing white or smoky quartz crystals seem different from the rose quartz of pegmatite cores.

6 QUARTZ VAR. AGATE
Rio Grande do Sul, Brazil
Agates are formed from row upon row of microscopic crystals lining gas pockets in lava.

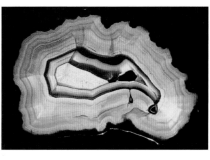

PLATE 46

SILICATES: SILICA

1 AGATE (DYED)
Rio Grande do Sul, Brazil
Agate slab, cut and dyed in various hues.

2 CHRYSOPRASE
Marlborough, N.T., Australia
Chalcedony, naturally colored by nickel.

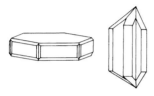

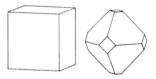

3 TRIDYMITE
Big Luc Mt., Greenlee Co., AZ
Spherical group of twinned crystals in rhyolite.

4 CRISTOBALITE
Coso Hot Springs, Kern Co., CA
White spheres in lithophysae in obsidian.

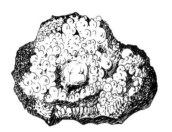

5 OPAL VAR. HYALITE
Valec, Bohemia, Czech Republic
Jellylike clear opal in lava.

6 OPAL
Oregon
Core of precious opal "thunder egg."

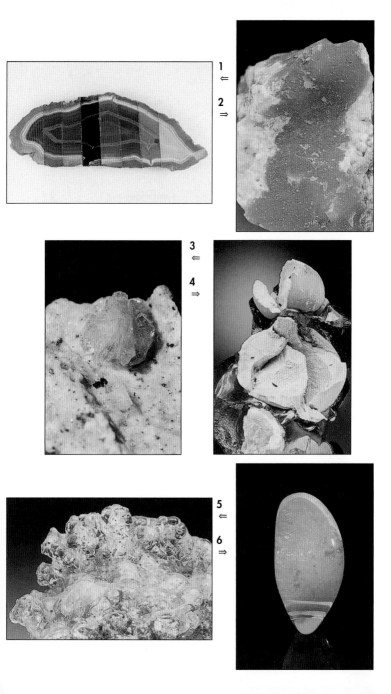

1 ⇐

2 ⇒

3 ⇐

4 ⇒

5 ⇐

6 ⇒

PLATE 47

SILICATES: FELDSPAR

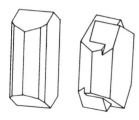

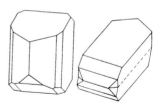

1 ORTHOCLASE
Good Springs, NV
Weathering freed these crystals from a porphyry dike.

2 MICROCLINE
Crystal Peak, St. George, CO
Lead-pigmented green crystal clusters are unique to this Colorado locality. *Photo: Frederick H. Pough*

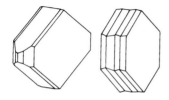

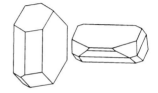

3 ALBITE *Governador Valadares, Minas Gerais, Brazil*
Albite usually grows on microcline or flat blades known as cleavelandite in pegmatites.

4 OLIGOCLASE *Spruce Pine, NC*
Oligoclase specimens are just large feldspar chunks, often showing some moonstone luminescence and usually found in coarse phases of a granitic rock.

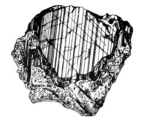

5 LABRADORITE
Finland
The polysynthetic twin planes characteristic of triclinic plagioclases are readily visible in the blue reflections.

6 LABRADORITE VAR. SUNSTONE
Plush, OR
Pebbles with sparkling copper crystals once gleamed in thin lava soil, but today, most remaining feldspar is colorless, making "sunstone" a misnomer for the clear pebbles.

1
⇐

2
⇒

3
⇐

4
⇒

5
⇐

6
⇒

PLATE 48

SILICATES

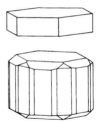

1 LEUCITE
Roccamontina, Casserta, Italy
Small, colorless trapezohedral crystals from low-silica basalt.

2 NEPHELINE
Bancroft, Ontario
Large hexagonal crystals from pegmatitic phase of a nepheline syenite.

3 SODALITE
Bahia, Brazil
Translucent blue massive segregation from nepheline syenite rock.

4 SCAPOLITE
Otter Lake, Quebec
Typical square prisms with pyramidal terminations.

5 LAZURITE
Kakasha Valley, Afghanistan
Isolated blue dodecahedral crystals of an inch and more come from a single Afghanistan occurrence.

6 LAZURITE
Layers of solid lazurite with golden pyrite specks, "lapis lazuli," are popular for carvings.
Photo: Frederick H. Pough

PLATE 49

SILICATES: ZEOLITES

1 HEULANDITE
Garrowilla, N.S.W., Australia
Heulandite is usually pearly and white, but crystals in this locality are reddish.

2 CHABAZITE
Parrsboro, Nova Scotia
Interpenetrating, almost cubic pinkish crystal crusts are common along the shores of the Bay of Fundy.

3 NATROLITE
Horseshoe Dam, Maricopa Co., CA
Natrolite often forms spherical masses of square needles with flat, four-faced terminations.

4 SCOLECITE
Nasik, Maharashtra, India
Resembles natrolite, but scolecite needles are usually coarser and longer.

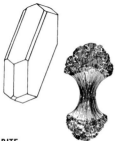

5 STILBITE
Paterson, NJ
Bow-tie crystal clusters are typical of this mineral, which is usually white.

6 ANALCIME
Krashonoyarsky, Russia
A mineral that commonly forms clear trapezohedral crystals.

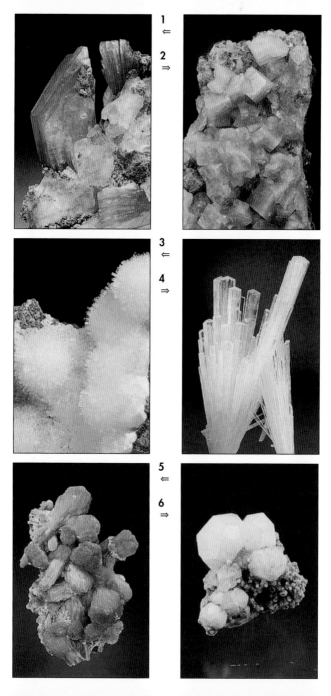

1
⇐

2
⇒

3
⇐

4
⇒

5
⇐

6
⇒

PLATE 50

SILICATES

1 PYROPHYLLITE
Indian Gulch, CA
Radiating mica-like plates are commonly associated with aluminous silicates such as kyanite and andalusite.

2 TALC
Chester, VT
Soft green flakes of crystallized chlorite, here in calcite.

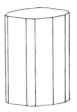

3 CORDIERITE
Timm's Hill, Haddam, CT
Solidly embedded mass typical of a high level of metamorphism.

4 CORDIERITE
Orissa, India
Gemmy fragment on Polaroid, showing the remarkable pleochroism.
Photo: Frederick H. Pough

5 SERPENTINE
Hance Asbestos Mine, Grand Canyon, AZ
Serpentine cut by fibrous asbestos seams.

6 SERPENTINE VAR. WILLIAMSITE
Philippines
This translucent, often carved, serpentine resembles nephrite jade.

1
⇐

2
⇒

3
⇐

4
⇒

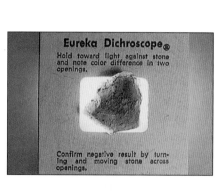

5
⇐

6
⇒

PLATE 51

SILICATES

1 APOPHYLLITE
Poona, India
Pseudocubic crystals with stilbite from typical zeolite pocket.

2 APOPHYLLITE
Maharashtra, India
Green, pyramidally terminated crystal on stilbite.

3 CHLORITE VAR. CLINOCHLORE
Campbell Quarry, Mountsville, VA
Green hexagonal mica-like books, soft and inelastic.

4 KAEMMERERITE
Erzican, East Natolia, Turkey
Red-violet triangular crystals on chromite.

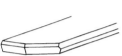

5 MARGARITE
Chester, MA
Often found in veins with emery, also as alteration rims around corundum.

6 PREHNITE
Paterson, NJ

1 ⇐

2 ⇒

3 ⇐

4 ⇒

5 ⇐

6 ⇒

PLATE 52

SILICATES: MICAS

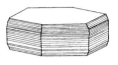

1 MUSCOVITE
Minas Gerais, Brazil

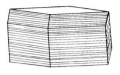

2 MUSCOVITE INCLUSIONS
Governador Valadares, Minas Gerais, Brazil

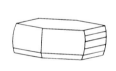

3 PHLOGOPITE
MacFall Lake, Ontario
Triboluminescent crystals in the usual dolomitic marble matrix of this mica.

4 PHLOGOPITE
Madagascar
Inclusions create the hexagonal patterns often noted in phlogopite.
Photo: Frederick H. Pough

5 BIOTITE
Wilberforce, Ontario
An opaque black mica, associated with radioactive and dark minerals, usually in red-stained feldspar.

6 LEPIDOLITE
Auburn, ME, and Minas Gerais, Brazil
Rounded knob, frequent in lithia pegmatites, and a fragment of a large, edge-translucent purple mica book.

1
⇐

2
⇒

3
⇐

4
⇒

5
⇐

6
⇒

PLATE 53

SILICATES: AMPHIBOLES

1 ANTHOPHYLITE
Numma, Greenland
Examples from this locality, known as "nummite," have schiller reflections that give it potential as a jewelry stone.

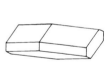

2 ACTINOLITE
Cranston, RI
This example, with tremolite, appears intermediate between the iron and calcium phases.

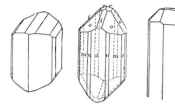

3 TREMOLITE VAR. HEXAGONITE
Fowler, NY
Tremolite, its violet color due to a small percentage of manganese, formed a band in a talc mine.

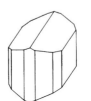

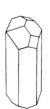

4 HORNBLENDE *Silver Crater Quarry, Bancroft, Ontario*
Stubby giant black crystals punctuate the marble of a quarry wall.
Photo: Frederick H. Pough

5 NEPHRITE
Baikal, Siberia
Translucent slice of typical "spinach jade."

6 NEPHRITE
Tibet, China
Carving of prized white or "mutton fat" jade.

All photos: Frederick H. Pough

1
⇐

2
⇒

3
⇐

4
⇒

5
⇐

6
⇒

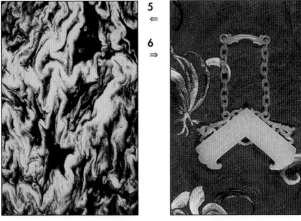

PLATE 54

SILICATES: PYROXENES

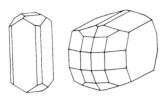

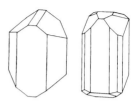

1 ENSTATITE
Telemark, Norway
A single crystal from an unusual dark mineral pegmatite; coarse-grained aggregates of stubby crystals are enstatite's usual form.

2 DIOPSIDE
Val d'Ala, Piemont, Italy
This crystal group is from a metamorphic association of garnet, chlorite, diopside, and vesuvianite.

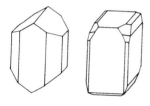

3 AUGITE
Mt. Kenya, Kenya, Africa
Phenocrysts exploded onto volcano slopes during eruptions.

4 AEGERINE (ACMITE)
DeMix Quarry, St. Hilaire, Quebec
Steep acmite-type crystals from a nepheline syenite

5 JADEITE
Myanmar
Waterworn boulder was prepared for auction with a revealing groove ground in its surface.

Photo: Frederick H. Pough

6 JADE
Myanmar and China
The value of this jade carving is enhanced by green areas.

Photo: Frederick H. Pough

1
⇐

2
⇒

3
⇐

4
⇒

5
⇐

6
⇒

PLATE 55

SILICATES

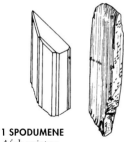

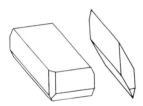

1 SPODUMENE
Afghanistan
Typical feldspar-like massive development. Spodumene may grow in giant crystals; sometimes mined as raw material for lithium.

2 SPODUMENE VAR. KUNZITE
San Diego Co., California
Gemmy lilac crystals were first found in San Diego County, but better ones have been found in Brazil, Madagascar, and the Himalayas.
Photo: Michael Haustad, Houston Museum of Natural Science

3 RHODONITE
Broken Hill, N.S.W., Australia
A crystal from a massive galena vein, an infrequent but favorable matrix for silicate minerals.

4 RHODONITE
Tamworth, N.S.W., Australia
Massive fine-grained rhodonite is used for carvings and mosaics.

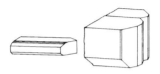

5 PECTOLITE
Paterson, NJ
Typical fine, needle-like crystals were associated with zeolites.
Photo: Peabody Museum, Yale University

6 PECTOLITE
Paterson, NJ

PLATE 56

SILICATES

1 BABINGTONITE
Khandivali, Bombay, India
Black crystals perched on zeolites, as is usual for this mineral.

2 NEPTUNITE
Dallas Mine, San Benito Co., CA
This specimen was embedded with benitoite in a natrolite vein and exposed by an acid solution.

3 CHRYSOCOLLA
Inspiration Mine, AZ
Shiny, botryoidal surface of an opal-like, water-rich silica gel.

4 EUDIALYTE
Chibine, Kola Peninsula, Russia
Solidly embedded crystals are unique to coarse nepheline syenite pegmatites.

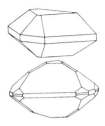

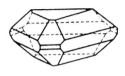

5 BENITOITE
Dallas Mine, San Benito Co., CA
Typical crystal showing the shape characteristic of benitoite's unique symmetry.

6 BENITOITE
Dallas Mine, San Benito Co., CA
Faceted benitoites are the state gem of California, from the only good locality known.

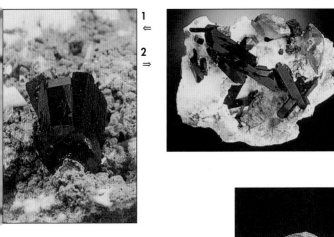

1 ⇐

2 ⇒

3 ⇐

4 ⇒

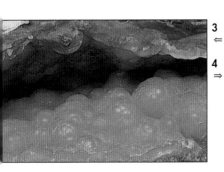

5 ⇐

6 ⇒

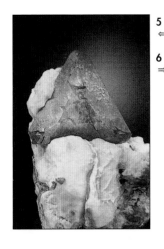

PLATE 57

SILICATES: TOURMALINE GROUP

1 TOURMALINE VAR. SCHORL
Pakistan
The tourmaline commonly found in simple pegmatites, in ore veins and as schist.

2 TOURMALINE VAR. ELBAITE
Cruzeiro Mine, Minas Gerais, Brazil
Most gem tourmaline is lithia-bearing, fortuitously and variously colored.

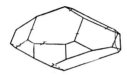

3 TOURMALINE VAR. UVITE
Brumado, Bahia, Brazil
With the recognition that tourmaline should be treated more as a group than a single species, calcium-bearing uvite is more common than once thought.

4 TOURMALINE VAR. DRAVITE
Gujakot, Nepal
Usually brown, black dravite resembles schorl, though its crystals are smoother, shorter, and fatter than schorl's and often resemble dodecahedrons.

5 TOURMALINE VAR. LIDDICOATITE
Madagascar
Famed for its broad prisms, slices of the triangular tips of Madagascar crystals create kaleidoscope patterns.

6 TOURMALINE VAR. BUERGERITE
San Luis Potosí, Mexico
Resembling a sublimate, sprays of this double iron tourmaline coat lava surfaces.

1 ⇐

2 ⇒

3 ⇐

4 ⇒

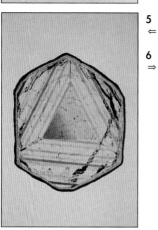

5 ⇐

6 ⇒

PLATE 58

SILICATES

1 BERYL VAR. AQUAMARINE
Pakistan
Typical clean gemmy crystal with feldspar from a pegmatite pocket.

2 BERYL VAR. EMERALD
Muso Mine, Colombia
Gem crystal from the world's best locality, an atypical and unusual calcite vein.

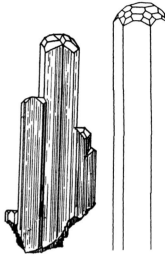

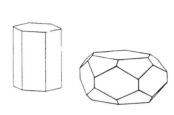

3 BERYL VAR. MORGANITE
Madagascar
A cut gem; the usual habit of these caesium-bearing beryls is short prismatic to flat. *Photo: Frederick H. Pough*

4 BERYL: RED CRYSTAL
Wahwah Mountains, UT
Unknown until recently, truly red beryl crystals are rarer than emeralds.

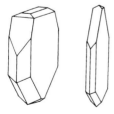

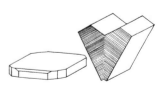

5 HEMIMORPHITE
Chihuahua, Mexico
These bundles show hemimorphism of the crystal bottom.
Photo: Frederick H. Pough

6 BERTRANDITE
Mt. Antero, Chaffee Co., CO
Uncommon single crystals coating smoky quartz (see Plate 64).

PLATE 59

SILICATES

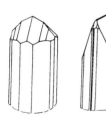

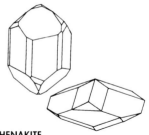

1 DANBURITE
Charcas, San Luis Potosí, Mexico
This uncommon mineral is found in the gangue of boron and high-temperature calcite lead mines.

2 PHENAKITE
São Miguel de Piraçicaba, Minas Gerais, Brazil
Gemmy short prismatic crystal of a species that varies in habit from long crystals to thin scales on microcline.

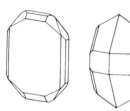

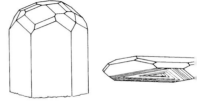

3 OLIVINE VAR. FORSTERITE
Pyaung, Guang, Myanmar
Corroded gem crystal from a metamorphic formation, unlike the usual granular volcanic xenolith bits.

4 WILLEMITE VAR. TROOSTITE
Franklin, NJ
Very typical coarse crystal in a red-fluorescing manganiferous calcite.

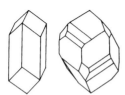

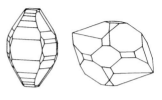

5 DIOPTASE
Tsumeb, Namibia
Dioptase is one of the most popular and costly species for the collector.

6 HUMITE VAR. CHONDRODITE
Tilly Foster Mine, Brewster, NY
A sharp crystal from what was the the best of all localities for this mineral.

1
⇐

2
⇒

3
⇐

4
⇒

5
⇐

6
⇒

PLATE 60

SILICATES: GARNETS

1 PYROPE
Navajo Co., AZ
Occurring as formless grains in volcanic xenoliths, gemmy red pebbles are abundant in three western states and are often gathered by Native Americans.

2 ALMANDINE
Wrangell Island, AK
Perfect examples of porphyoblasts, which can grow sharp crystals despite the surrounding mica.

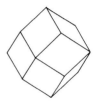

3 GROSSULAR
Coahuila, Mexico
These loose crystals weathered from a vesuvianite-garnet marble.

4 ANDRADITE VAR. DEMANTOID
Sonora, Mexico
Demantoid is the most valuable of all garnets, if rich green. Few are.

5 SPESSARTITE
Little Three Mine, Ramona, CA
The characteristic garnet of granite pegmatites, on albite.

6 UVAROVITE
Sarony, Russia
"Chrome garnet" grows on chromite surfaces.

1 ⇐
2 ⇒
3 ⇐
4 ⇒
5 ⇐
6 ⇒

PLATE 61

SILICATES

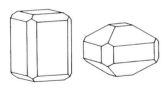

1 VESUVIANITE
Coahuila, Mexico
Sharp crystals weathered free from marble.

2 ZOISITE VAR. TANZANITE
Tanzania
This gemmy crystal has been heated to emphasize the blue-violet hue.

3 EPIDOTE
Untersulzbachtal, Austria
Typical doma bundles of elongated crystals of a classic locality.

4 EPIDOTE VAR. PISTACITE (UNAKITE)
Blue Ridge Parkway, VA
Hydrothermal alteration of this granite's dark minerals has made it a decorative achitectural stone.

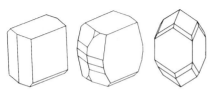

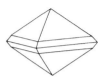

5 ALLANITE
Washington Mine, Washoe Co., NV
Commonly somewhat radioactive and close to epidote in composition, allanite crystals are often embedded in feldspar.

6 ZIRCON
Kipawa Rare Earth Complex, Quebec
One of the best tetragonal species, zircon forms fine, sometimes gemmy, crystals.

1 ⇐

2 ⇒

3 ⇐

4 ⇒

5 ⇐

6 ⇒

PLATE 62

SILICATES

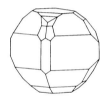

1 DATOLITE
Dal'nygorsk, Russia
These single, multifaced crystals are occasionally found in metal mine gangues.

2 DATOLITE *Delaware Mine, Keweenaw Peninsula, MI*
Fine-grained nodules are found in the U.S. only in Michigan copper mines.

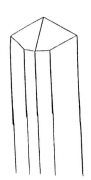

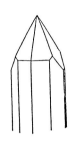

3 TOPAZ
Mursinka, Urals, Russia
A blocky hydroxy-type crystal on a feldspar matrix.

4 TOPAZ
Minas Gerais, Brazil
Though the orange hue known as precious topaz is the most valuable, topaz comes in many hues, most from Brazil. *Photo: Frederick H. Pough*

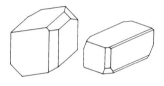

5 EUCLASE
Last Hope Mine, Miami, Zimbabwe
Splotchy blue crystal of an uncommon, probably lower-temperature beryllium silicate species.

6 AXINITE
Melones Lake, Calaveras Co., CA
Sharp-edged crystals typical for the species.

3

4

PLATE 63

SILICATES

1 ANDALUSITE
Arrasuai, Minas Gerais, Brazil
Slightly waterworn gemmy crystals of uncertain origin, indicative of medium-intensity metamorphism.

2 ANDALUSITE VAR. CHIASTOLITE
Bimbowrie, N.S.W., Australia
Cigar-shaped crystals from schist. Sectioned, they show a checkerboard pattern of black impurities.
Photo: Frederick H. Pough

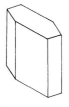

3 SILLIMANITE
Willimantic, CT
The highest-temperature species of the three aluminum silicates that are useful in geological thermometry. *Photo: Frederick H. Pough*

4 KYANITE
Graves Mt., GA
The lowest-temperature and commonest of the three species that give clues to the intensity of metamorphism.

5 STAUROLITE *Cowles, NM*
Staurolite crystals, usually twinned and always embedded in schist. Some examples sold to tourists as "fairy crosses" are altered, freshened, dyed, or fabricated.

6 SPHENE
Gilgit, Pakistan
Typical ax-shaped and twinned crystals with characteristic acute reentrant V-slot.

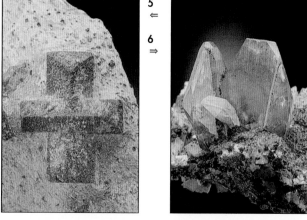

PLATE 64

SILICATES

1 DUMORTIERITE
Los Angeles Co., CA
Most examples are massive and fine-grained, blue and violet in color. Dumortierite may create "blue" quartz when needles saturate SiO_2.

2 URANOPHANE
Terlingua, TX
Tiny needle tufts are typical of many hard-to-identify uranium minerals.

3 DIOPTASE
Kirghese Steppes, former U.S.S.R.
Dioptase is also found in the Western Hemisphere, where tiny crystals seem to be the rule. *Photo: Breck P. Kent*

MICROMOUNTS

Many minerals, in fact most newly recognized ones, exist only as small crystals, measurable in fractions of a millimeter and observable only through a microscope, perhaps even an electron microscope. Even for more common minerals, tiny crystals are usually more perfect than their larger counterparts, and they cost less and take up much less space. Micromounts fit into one-inch (2–3 cm) boxes and are usually viewed through a binocular microscope.
Photomicrographs by Sugar White.

4 MARSHITE
Chuquicamata, Chile
Chloride makes this extremely rare copper species (copper iodide) the only one lacking the blue, green, or red typical of all other copper compounds.

5 GREENOCKITE
Llallagua, Bolivia
Though closely resembling sphalerite in traprock associations, greenockite in veins can be bright orange or yellow. It makes a yellow dust on some Illinois fluorite, and it yellows banded smithsonite ("turkey fat ore") of Sardinia and Missouri.

6 TURQUOISE
Bishop Mine, Lynch Station, VA
In spite of its western abundance, this is one of two or three world localities where crystals, tiny and triclinic, have been found. More often massive, microcrystalline, and blue, a secondary species produced by weathering.

1
⇐

2
⇒

3
⇐

4
⇒

5

6

specific gravity 4.3–4.4; *fracture* conchoidal; *cleavage* rhombohedral, often curving spherically. Brittle; translucent to transparent. **Composition:** Zinc carbonate (64.8% ZnO, 35.2% CO_2), usually with some of the Zn replaced by Fe, Mg, and Ca; Cd, Cu, and Co may be present. **Tests:** Only good test is in closed tube, when the white material is coated with film that is yellow when hot and white when cold. A grain heated on charcoal, then touched with cobalt nitrate and reheated, gives good green (zinc) color. Cleavages and crystal shape show it to be a carbonate, as does its bubbling in hot hydrochloric acid.

Distinguishing characteristics: The hardness is unusual for a carbonate, and the density is high. Crusts sometimes resemble prehnite, which is harder and does not dissolve in acid. Might also be confused with chrysocolla-stained (but much harder) quartz, or with some hemimorphite crusts (Sardinia and Mexico).

Occurrence: In its best development, a mineral of dry climates formed in limestone regions from primary zinc sulfides by weathering. Sometimes an important ore of zinc, as at Leadville, Colorado, where its ore value was overlooked for years.

The most beautiful solid specimens are the thick bluegreen crusts from the Kelly Mine, Magdalena, New Mexico. This material was once marketed for a jewelry stone by the Goodfriend Brothers under the name bonamite. Similar but thinner crusts were found in Lavrion, Greece, and in the Barranca de Cobre, Mexico, where some are pink. Large, translucent, frosty-surfaced, somewhat rounded pale pink, green, and blue crystals were common at Tsumeb, Namibia, but only white ones had flat faces. The largest single crystals are some from the Broken Hill Mine in Zambia, steep, to 2-in. (3–5 cm), clear straw yellow rhombohedrons. Yellow, greenockite-stained "turkey-fat ore" crusts and stalactites come from Arkansas and Sardinia. The most common and easily overlooked type is the hard, porous, dull, bonelike mass known as "dry-bone ore."

Remarks: The mineral was named for James Smithson, an Englishman who willed money for the establishment of a scientific institution in America, now known as the Smithsonian Institution. Smithsonite is often known as calamine in Europe, a name Americans once applied to the zinc silicate but have now dropped in favor of hemimorphite.

◆ ARAGONITE GROUP

This group of structurally and chemically related ortho-rhombic carbonates is also characterized by crystal similarities, particularly by a tendency to intergrow with other individuals into interpenetrating stars of three crystals, assuming a pseudohexagonal appearance. Their cleavage goes from fair to inconspicuous but is never so perfect as that of the calcite group. Like that group, the orthorhombic carbonates have unusually strong double refraction, which may be observed as a conspicuous inner fuzziness in clear members of the family (aragonite and cerussite).

ARAGONITE $CaCO_3$ Pl. 29

Orthorhombic — Rhombic bipyramidal $\dfrac{2}{m}\dfrac{2}{m}\dfrac{2}{m}$

Environment: Deposits around warm and hot springs, some ore veins, and sedimentary formations. Also secreted by mollusks. **Crystal description:** Single crystals, most often long slender needles, also in tabular plates. Trillings (three inter-grown individuals) common, looking like short hexagonal prisms or even hexagonal plates. Re-entrant angle visible in fresh, sharp crystals in the center of each apparent prism of these pseudohexagons. Striations on the apparent base suggest the three individuals. Also in crusts and stalactites. **Physical properties:** Colorless, white, pale violet, light blue, or light yellow. *Luster* vitreous; *hardness* $3\frac{1}{2}$–4; *specific gravity* 2.9–3.0; *fracture* subconchoidal; *cleavage* poor, parallel to prism and side pinacoids. Brittle; translucent to transparent; commonly fluorescent and phosphorescent. **Composition:** Calcium carbonate, like calcite (56.0% CaO, 44.0% CO_2) with strontium (mossottite), lead (tarnowitzite), and sometimes zinc (nicholsonite). **Tests:** Dissolves with bubbles in cold hydrochloric acid, like calcite. Strong solutions give a precipitate of white needles or granules of calcium sulfate when sulfuric acid is added to the hydrochloric acid solution.

Distinguishing characteristics: Recognizable as a carbonate by its effervescence in hydrochloric acid; as the aragonite group by lack of a conspicuous cleavage; as a calcium carbonate by its sulfate precipitate (only in concentrated solutions) and by the weak red-orange coloration of the flame, and aragonite by the pink-violet color it assumes when a powder is boiled in a test tube with a cobalt nitrate solution (calcite stays white). Also, it crumbles more on heating than calcite does and loses its fluorescence, whereas calcite tends to remain intact and to gain fluorescence.

Occurrence: Aragonite is far rarer than calcite, apparently being deposited from warmer solutions than calcite (but not too warm). It is found around hot springs in crusts and thick beds (which are cut as onyx marble). Fine needlelike elongated and pointed crystals were found in the Cumberland (England) iron mines. Good pseudohexagonal trillings common in the Sicilian sulfur mines. Also found as isolated six-sided rods and plates in central Spain, the former in crystal clusters with sulfur, gypsum, and celestite, the latter with gypsum in red and green shale beds often colored by red-stained clay inclusions. Trillings and sandy calcite pseudomorphs of this type have been found at Chaves (near Roswell, New Mexico), in s. France, Spain, Morocco, and at the Matsushiro gypsum mines, Ota City, Shimane Prefecture, Honshu, Japan, in medium to giant spherical crystal balls. Violet pseudohexagonal rods cross gas cavities in basalt at Suzu Gun, Ishikawa Prefecture, in the Noto Peninsula, Japan.

A white coral-like branching growth, called *flos ferri* (iron flowers), has been found in Austrian iron mines (and lesser examples in New Mexico and Mexico).

Remarks: The iridescent inner surfaces of shells (and pearls) are composed of aragonite secreted by mollusks. The light violet cast that is common in some aragonites (in cores of those from green shale in Spain and from Japanese basalt) seems to be due to iron plus a natural irradiation. It fades from crystals exposed on outcrops but can be restored (and the balance made greenish) by irradiation in the laboratory.

WITHERITE $BaCO_3$ Pl. 31

Orthorhombic — Rhombic bipyramidal $\dfrac{2}{m}\dfrac{2}{m}\dfrac{2}{m}$

Environment: Low-temperature lead and fluorite ore veins.
Crystal description: Though orthorhombic, witherite twinned into pseudohexagonal trillings, most often resembling hexagonal bipyramids. Also in crusts with rounded surfaces; columnar and granular. **Physical properties:** White, light yellowish, or gray. *Luster* glassy; *hardness* $3-3\frac{1}{2}$; *specific gravity* 4.3–4.7; *fracture* uneven; *cleavage* 1 good and 2 poor. Brittle; translucent; commonly fluorescent blue. **Composition:** Barium carbonate (77.7% BaO, 22.3% CO_2); may contain some Ca. **Tests:** Dissolves readily in hydrochloric acid with effervescence. Slender white needles form as 2:3 hydrochloric acid solution cools, and dissolve again on heating or dilution. Even dilute solutions form precipitate of barium sulfate crystals when sulfuric acid is added. A strong hydrochlo-

ric acid solution on a platinum wire placed in the flame gives a yellow-green flash (barium flame).

Distinguishing characteristics: Recognized as a carbonate by its hardness and effervescence in acid. Recognized as witherite by the flame coloration and greater-than-average "heft."

Occurrence: Witherite is a surprisingly rare mineral and in its best occurrences accompanies lead ore (galena) in veins. The best specimens, 1-in. (to 3 cm) white pseudobipyramids, have always come from Cumberland and Northumberland, England. Comparable though generally smaller individual trillings, some of a stubbier habit, occur in the s. Illinois fluorite mines. Otherwise it appears to be very rare in the U.S., having been reported only in massive specimens near Yosemite National Park (associated with barite and some rare barium minerals) and at Thunder Bay, Ontario. Possibly it is more common than generally supposed because it is usually not recognized.

Remarks: Its rarity can be accounted for in part by the ease with which it can be altered to the very insoluble sulfate, barite. When commonly associated sulfide minerals alter they produce excess sulfuric acid, which would immediately react with the soluble witherite, reprecipitating it as barite. However, at the Illinois locality, where fluorite is dominant, corroded barite suggests that some of the witherite appears still to be forming at the expense of the calcite rather than forming as barite.

STRONTIANITE $SrCO_3$ Pl. 31

Orthorhombic — Rhombic bipyramidal $\frac{2}{m} \frac{2}{m} \frac{2}{m}$

Environment: Veins or concretions in sedimentary rocks. **Crystal description:** Most common formation is in fibrous veinlets. Also in acicular crystals (long needles), massive, and fine-grained; pseudohexagonal trillings are the rarest of the aragonite group. **Physical properties:** White or colorless, light green, pink, yellowish, brownish, or gray. *Luster* glassy; *hardness* $3\frac{1}{2}$–4; *specific gravity* 3.7; *fracture* uneven; *cleavage* 1 good and 1 poor. Brittle; transparent to translucent. **Composition:** Strontium carbonate (70.1% SrO, 29.9% CO_2) sometimes with a little Ca. **Tests:** Like witherite, readily soluble in warm acid; the concentrated solution forms slender, white, water-soluble crystals on cooling. Precipitates strontium sulfate crystals when sulfuric acid is added to solutions of medium strength. Strong hydrochloric acid solution gives a brilliant red flash (strontium flame) when a platinum wire dipped in it is thrust into the Bunsen burner flame.

Distinguishing characteristics: Recognized as a carbonate by ease of solution in hydrochloric acid with the release of bubbles and by softness, and as a strontium mineral by the brilliant red flame color.

Occurrence: Strontianite locally was an important source of strontium used in the refining of sugar and in making fireworks. It was mined only in Germany at Drensteinfurt, near Hamm, where veins cut shaley limestone beds underlying beet fields.

The narrow veins, up to several inches across, contained frequent crystal-lined cavities. They were the source of the best-known specimens but are now only of historical interest. Also found in fibrous veins in Germany, England, and the U.S. Sometimes forms nodules in limestone, as at Schoharie, New York, in Pennsylvania, and near Barstow, California. Long, pale pink, loosely aggregated needles and compact masses have been found near Cave-in-Rock, Illinois, associated with fluorite and witherite. Brown-tipped, pencil-thick elongated 1-in. (2 cm) trillings found in Oberndorf, Styria, Austria, are the best recently available specimens.

CERUSSITE $PbCO_3$ Pl. 31

Orthorhombic — Rhombic bipyramidal $\dfrac{2}{m}\dfrac{2}{m}\dfrac{2}{m}$

Environment: Secondary (weathered) zone of lead ore deposits.
Crystal description: Flat plates common only in small crystals; larger crystals, up to 6 in. (15 cm), usually intergrown into skeletal lattices, like bridge girders (similar to rutile), or in V's as 2 individuals grown together. Often intergrows in the 6-sided habit of a pseudohexagonal bipyramid, like trillings of chrysoberyl. Also massive, and in fragile sprinkles of loosely consolidated needles. **Physical properties:** Colorless, white, light yellow to gray; some Tsumeb (Namibia) twins are very dichroic in yellow and violet. *Luster* adamantine; *hardness* $3-3\frac{1}{2}$; *specific gravity* 6.5–6.6; *fracture* conchoidal; *cleavage* good prismatic. Brittle; transparent to translucent; often fluorescent yellow. **Composition:** Lead carbonate (83.5% PbO, 16.5% CO_2). **Tests:** One of the most intriguing minerals for blowpiping. Gentle heat turns it yellow to redbrown as it gets hotter and melts. Cools instantly into a faceted crystallized bead. Excessive heat starts rapid reduction to lead. Metal spike is ejected from crystallizing carbonate bead as it solidifies. Make this test; it is one of the most satisfying experiences of blowpipe testing!
Distinguishing characteristics: The luster, high density, and light

color distinguish it from most minerals, and the manner of occurrence distinguishes it from all but anglesite (lead sulfate) and phosgenite (lead chlorocarbonate). The solubility in nitric acid and the fusion behavior distinguish it from the first, the hardness from the latter.

Occurrence: Cerussite is always a secondary mineral that forms from galena through surface alteration, usually when veins of granular and more permeable galena penetrate limestones or dolomites, the carbonate sedimentary rocks. Naturally, its most frequent and best-developed occurrences are where weathering has penetrated deeply, as in desert country. An important ore of lead.

The best and the largest clear crystals have come from Tsumeb, Namibia, associated with malachite, azurite, smithsonite, and anglesite. Good examples were found in the upper levels at the Broken Hill mine, New South Wales. In the U.S., mines in the Organ Mountains, New Mexico, once produced some large V twins, silky white and rust-stained, associated with spectacular wulfenite, anglesite, and vanadinite. Other occurrences are too numerous to list.

◆ OTHER CARBONATES

DOLOMITE $CaMg(CO_3)_2$ **Pl. 31**

Hexagonal — rhombohedral $\overline{3}$

Environment: Sedimentary rocks, ore veins in sediments, and—rarely—in metamorphic rocks in higher-temperature surroundings. **Crystal description:** Crystals rarer and as a rule smaller than calcite, but may range from prismatic to the basic rhombohedron. In limestone or dolomite formations in pockets (often pocket-lining crusts) of pearly, pinkish, subparallel intergrowths of curving saddle-shaped, rhombohedrons. As a bedded rock formation (often called dolostone by today's students), microcrystalline to a coarse marble. **Physical properties:** Colorless, white, pinkish, or light tints. *Luster* glassy to pearly; *hardness* $3\frac{1}{2}$–4; *specific gravity* 2.8; *fracture* conchoidal; *cleavage* rhombohedral. Brittle; transparent to translucent. **Composition:** Calcium magnesium carbonate (30.4% CaO, 21.7% MgO, 47.9% CO_2, if the calcium-magnesium ratio is 1:1). It may vary slightly in either direction from this and still be called dolomite, even when some iron has also intruded. **Tests:** Like calcite, except that it dissolves very slowly in cold acid, unless powdered first and dropped in test tube. Warming the acid speeds up bubbling.

Distinguishing characteristics: The "pearl spar" white to pinkish crystal intergrowths are readily recognizable. Slow effervescence in cold acid distinguishes it from calcite (rapid) and magnesite (only in hot acid). The intermediate specific gravity will help when a pure piece can be obtained. Seems seldom to be fluorescent.

Occurrence: Far less common than calcite; dolomite rock beds probably form by subsequent alteration of a limestone after its deposition. The pearly clusters are especially common in the U.S., in association with galena, sphalerite, and calcite in low-temperature veins (Missouri-Kansas-Oklahoma lead district) and in pockets in limestone or dolomite quarries (Michigan, Ohio, and Rochester, New York).

Large (several inches) and fine crystals have been found in Switzerland, in pegmatitic seams in North Carolina, and in veins in Colorado. Fine clear Iceland spar–type crystals, collected in a magnesite quarry at Ergui, near Pamplona, Spain, have provided excellent specimens for contemporary collectors. Common as white rhombohedrons in Mexican lead ores with fluorite and anhydrite at Naica and Achiles Serdan (Santa Eulalia).

Remarks: Dolomite differs slightly in its crystal form from the other rhombohedral carbonates and does not occur in scalenohedrons. The pink, pearly type is usually early in a mineral series, and directly coats the wall rock, underlying calcite, sphalerite, galena, fluorite, celestite, or gypsum—all of which are likely to be later in the depositional sequence. In Mexico it is more often very late.

HYDROZINCITE $Zn_5(CO_3)_2(OH)_6$ Pl. 32

Monoclinic — prismatic $\dfrac{2}{m}$

Environment: Secondary (weathered) zone of zinc deposits in arid areas. **Crystal description:** Does not occur in crystals; forms snowy crusts that coat limonite and secondary zinc minerals with a fibrous or compact layer. **Physical properties:** White, light gray, or light yellow. *Luster* dull; *hardness* 2–$2\frac{1}{2}$; *specific gravity* 3.6–3.8; *fracture* irregular; *cleavage* none. Earthy; translucent; brilliant blue fluorescence under ultraviolet light. **Composition:** Basic zinc carbonate (75.3% ZnO, 13.6% CO_2, 11.1% H_2O). **Tests:** As with smithsonite, a grain heated on charcoal and touched with cobalt nitrate solution turns green on reheating. Dissolves with bubbles in hot hydrochloric acid.

Distinguishing characteristics: Easy effervescence in hydrochloric acid proves it to be a carbonate. Associations often suggest a zinc mineral, and it is almost always brilliantly fluorescent.

Occurrence: Since hydrozincite only forms as a secondary mineral in weathered zinc deposits, it develops best where weathering is deep and long continued. Its best occurrence was in a mine in Spain, where great thick white crusts were found in a cave. Similarly found elsewhere in adjoining sections of Spain and in Iran. In the U.S. the right conditions are found in the Southwest; it is at its best in New Mexico, in rounded crusts on limonite and hemimorphite. It is popular among collectors for its fluorescence, which is not uncommon on Mexican specimens.

AURICHALCITE $(Zn,Cu)_5(CO_3)_2(OH)_6$ Pl. 32

Orthorhombic   2 2 2

Environment: Secondary (gossan) zone of copper zinc ore deposits. **Crystal description:** Crystals never well defined, usually in delicate crusts of thin, fragile scales. **Physical properties:** Pale greenish blue. *Luster* pearly; *hardness* 2; *specific gravity* 3.5–3.6; *cleavage* micaceous. Flexible; translucent. **Composition:** A basic carbonate of zinc and copper (20.8% CuO, 53.2% ZnO, 16.1% CO_2, 9.9% H_2O). **Tests:** Infusible on charcoal but colors the flame green. Soluble in hydrochloric acid with effervescence, giving green solution, which turns blue on the addition of ammonia.

Distinguishing characteristics: The soft pale blue-green scales, which dissolve so easily in acid, are unlike those of any other mineral. A limonite gossan occurrence is also usual.

Occurrence: Since aurichalcite forms as a result of weathering in ore bodies rather high in zinc, it is a good guide to zinc ore; less conspicuous when copper predominates. Usually forms soft crusts on limonite, often with calcite, smithsonite, and hemimorphite. It is a minor zinc source when smelted with other minerals.

Good specimens have come from several localities in Utah, and it is also found in some of the Arizona, New Mexico, and Mexican copper mines. European localities include the Leadhills locality, Scotland, famous for rare oxide zone minerals; Matlock in Derbyshire; the Altai region of Russia; former Yugoslavia; and Chessy, France.

Remarks: The origin of the name evokes interest, as it is derived from the ancient name for brass (an alloy of copper and zinc). In truth, the mineral can be considered a natural "brass ore," though it is quantitatively so rare that it is unlikely it ever served this purpose.

MALACHITE $Cu_2^{+2}(CO_3)(OH)_2$ **Pl. 32**

Monoclinic $\dfrac{2}{m}$

Environment: Secondary (weathered) zone of copper ore deposits. **Crystal description:** Usually in fibrous and silky crusts and masses; individualized single crystals are rare. When found they are usually silky-appearing twins with a re-entrant angle showing at the top. Also massive and earthy, often as thin films staining rock. **Physical properties:** Light to dark green. *Luster* usually silky, crystals vitreous; *hardness* $3\frac{1}{2}$–4; *specific gravity* 3.9–4.0; *streak* green; *fracture* usually splintery; *cleavage* basal, visible in the rare single crystals and sometimes across crusts. Brittle; opaque to translucent. **Composition:** Copper carbonate (71.9% CuO, 19.9% CO_2, 8.2% H_2O). **Tests:** Dissolves readily in hydrochloric acid with the release of bubbles. Gives all copper tests: solution color, bead test, copper bead on charcoal, and flame color.
Distinguishing characteristics: Its intense green color shows it to be a copper mineral, but, in case of any doubt, a test could be made to make sure that it is not a chromium or nickel green. Likely to be confused with numerous copper sulfates, arsenates, and phosphates, but the effervescence as it dissolves in the hydrochloric acid eliminates them and proves it to be a carbonate.
Occurrence: The most common and most stable of the secondary ores of copper, always forming as a consequence of the weathering of primary copper sulfides. In its environment, it is so abundant that it constitutes an important ore, frequently appearing in the capping over a copper deposit, together with azurite, cuprite, and native copper.

Malachite usually forms fibrous crusts and masses. In a very compact form it was extensively used in Russia for carvings and mosaics. Since it varies considerably in hardness and may be poorly consolidated, only the hardest masses are suitable for this use. Several African countries still produce this dense lapidary material. Some years ago specimens were abundant at the famous Copper Queen Mine at Bisbee, Arizona, though most Arizona occurrences are soft, almost velvety crusts of slender needles, stalactites, and stalagmites, layered masses frequently alternating with bands of azurite, a constant associate.

Crystals of malachite are rare and usually small; few are over $\frac{1}{16}$ in. (2 mm) across. The best have come from Germany, Russia, Namibia, Zaire, and sw. U.S. Large pseudomorphs composed of radiating velvety malachite needles, which seem to start from several centers on each surface, result from the alteration of dark blue crystals of azurite. Most recently the largest malachite crystals have come from the Ongonja Mine, Namibia, but previously they came from other localities, particularly Arizona and Morocco. A few large pseudomorphs after giant azurites like those of Tsumeb have been found in Michoacán, Mexico.

PHOSGENITE $Pb_2(CO_3)Cl_2$ **Pl. 32**

Tetragonal — Tetragonal trapezohedral   4 2 2

Environment: Secondary (weathered) zones of galena deposits. **Crystal description:** Always in crystals; tiny ones as long and slender prisms, but giants of several inches are shorter and squarer. May be up to 6 in. (15 cm) in length and several inches across. **Physical properties:** Colorless, white, yellowish brown to gray. *Luster* adamantine; *hardness* $2^1/_4$–$2^3/_4$; *specific gravity* 6.0–6.1; *fracture* conchoidal; *cleavage* good prismatic, poor basal. Slightly sectile; transparent to translucent; fluoresces a brilliant orange-yellow. **Composition:** A chlorocarbonate of lead (81.9% PbO, and about 13% Cl and 8% CO_2). **Tests:** In reducing flame, blackens, bubbles, and spreads thinly, fuming and sinking into charcoal and leaving lead bead.

Distinguishing characteristics: Recognized as a carbonate by its bubbles in acid, as a lead mineral by its gravity and the blowpipe tests. Distinguished from cerussite by its tetragonal crystal form and blowpipe behavior. Hardness varies with crystal direction; the prism face or prism cleavage surface may be scratched by the fingernail parallel to the long (vertical) axis (hardness $2^1/_2$), but not across it. (Do not damage a good crystal demonstrating this; find a broken surface.)

Occurrence: A rare secondary lead mineral, particularly popular among collectors for its rarity and fluorescence, and sometimes found in good crystals. It forms as a result of the weathering of primary lead ores. Good crystals were found with related secondary minerals at Matlock, England, but the finest locality has proved to be Monteponi in Sardinia, where crystals many centimeters across have been found, derived with anglesite and cerussite from the alteration of a granular galena. More recently obtained at the Mammoth Mine, Tiger, Arizona, and in a few giant examples at Tsumeb, Namibia.

Remarks: Phosgenite is one of the secondary, tiny-crystal lead minerals that formed in gas holes in slag dumped into the Mediterranean by the ancient Greeks in their operation of the mines at Lavrion, Greece.

AZURITE $Cu_3(CO_3)_2(OH)_2$ Pl. 33

Monoclinic — prismatic $\dfrac{2}{m}$

Environment: Secondary (weathered) zone of copper ore deposits. **Crystal description:** Commonly crystallized, often in large, well-formed, equidimensional, deep blue crystals and in rosette aggregates. Also in slender blue needles or even hairs. Frequently altered completely or in part to malachite. Commonly forms botryoidal growths like (and interlayered with) malachite, in crusts, stalactites, or stalagmites; also massive and earthy. **Physical properties:** Light blue to almost black. *Luster* glassy; *hardness* $3\frac{1}{2}$–4; *specific gravity* 3.8; *streak* blue; *fracture* conchoidal; *cleavage* 1 good and 2 poor. Brittle; transparent in very thin flakes. **Composition:** Copper carbonate (69.2% CuO, 25.6% CO_2, 5.2% H_2O). **Tests:** Copper blue color is distinctive. Fuses on charcoal, and with careful treatment will give copper bead in reducing flame. Dissolves in hydrochloric acid with effervescence. Drop of solution on platinum wire gives fine blue copper flame; green acid solution turns blue with addition of ammonia.

Distinguishing characteristics: Most other blue, disseminated minerals are harder. Its effervescence in acid distinguishes it from other secondary copper compounds for which it might be mistaken (relatively rare linarite is the most likely).

Occurrence: One of the very desirable mineral collectibles. Azurite forms under conditions that are identical with those of malachite, with which it is always associated. Although azurite is rarer than malachite, and apparently less stable, fine occurrences are common and much too numerous to list. Morocco has provided some good crystals, and several Arizona and Utah mines still have good crystals. Azurite and malachite stains on the rocks have served as valuable prospecting guides. Found in fine crystals at Chessy, France, from which it received its British name chessylite. South Australia and New South Wales gave comparable examples. Sharp brilliant crystals, the finest known and up to 6 in. (15 cm) long, were found at Tsumeb, Namibia. Clifton and Bisbee, Arizona, were noted for fine azurite crystals in their early days. Fine malachite pseudomorphs have come from Tsumeb and from Arizona.

A common habit at many mines is crystallized masses which seem to grow freely and uniformly, like the aragonite balls described above. Very lustrous and almost black groups from Guangdong, China, are notable. In Northern Territory, near Alice Springs, Australia, there are flat discs of very blue azurite, a similar habit apparently grown in a thin clayey layer. Azurite also grows in hollow concretionary masses with crystal-linings, a habit for which Chessy was perhaps the best example, with an occasional malachite-coated cuprite octahedron.

LEADHILLITE $Pb_4(SO_4)(CO_3)_2(OH)_2$ **Pl. 32**

Monoclinic — prismatic $\dfrac{2}{m}$

Environment: Secondary (weathered) zone of lead deposits.
Crystal description: Usually in plates, which look hexagonal because of a twinning. The base has a pearly luster and on more prismatic crystals may be concave. Blue or green tints on the summits usually fade downward to white. **Physical properties:** White, often tinged with light yellow, blue, or green. *Luster* pearly on the prominent cleavage surface, resinous to adamantine on the others; *hardness* 2.5; *specific gravity* 6.3–6.4; *fracture* conchoidal; *cleavage* 1 perfect, almost micaceous; slightly sectile; translucent to transparent; fluoresces orange. **Composition:** Sulfate and carbonate of lead (82.7% PbO, 7.4% SO_3, 8.2% CO_2, 17% H_2O) **Tests:** Fuses easily on charcoal and is yellow when hot, white when cool (a sign of lead). Dissolves in nitric acid, forming bubbles, but leaves a residue of white insoluble lead sulfate.
Distinguishing characteristics: It is likely to be confused with other oxidized lead minerals such as phosgenite and cerussite (which dissolve in nitric acid without a sulfate residue) and anglesite (which does not dissolve).
Occurrence: This rare but attractive mineral usually forms crystals, but occurs at few localities. Delicate blue crystals were found in the Mammoth Mine, Tiger, Arizona, associated with malachite, cerussite, willemite, dioptase, and wulfenite. Fine platy crystals were found in cavities from which galena had been leached at the Beer Cellar Mine, Granby, Missouri. The original occurrence was in the lead district on the northern border of England, and was first described from Leadhills, Scotland, to which it owes its name.

■NITRATES

This is a small, mineralogically insignificant group of minerals. Because of their extreme solubility in water and deliquescence (a tendency to absorb water from the air and melt or dissolve), they cannot be found in ordinary climatic regions. The arid west coast of Chile and some of the dry-lake deposits of California and Nevada are virtually the only occurrences; sometimes occurs as efflorescences in bat caves. All are soft; only one appears to be insoluble in water, and that one is very rare.

SODA NITER $NaNO_3$

Hexagonal — Hexagonal scalenohedral $\bar{3}\,\dfrac{2}{m}$

Environment: Residual water-soluble surface deposits in deserts, primarily in Chile. **Crystal description:** Usually in white masses; cavities sometimes have rhombohedral crystals, resembling calcite. **Physical properties:** Colorless, white, soil tinted red-brown, or yellow. *Luster* glassy; *hardness* $1\frac{1}{2}$–2; *specific gravity*: 2.2–2.3; *fracture* conchoidal; *cleavage* perfect rhombohedral. Slightly sectile; transparent to translucent. **Composition:** Sodium nitrate (36.5% Na_2O, 63.5% N_2O_3). **Tests:** Burns, with spurt of yellow flame when dropped on glowing spot in charcoal. Dissolves in water, tastes cooling to the tongue. Heated in closed tube with potassium disulfate, gives off brown fumes (nitric oxide, NO).

Distinguishing characteristics: The deflagration on coals shows it to be a nitrate, and the yellow flame color shows the sodium. Could only be confused with halite, which only melts on the hot charcoal.

Occurrence: Once abundant on the desert surface in beds—composed principally of gypsum, halite, soda niter, some iodides, and other related minerals—in the world's driest region, the Atacama desert, Chile, just west of the Andes. Small quantities of nitrates are reported in some of the dry California lake beds and in Humboldt Co., Nevada. Small amounts are still scavenged in Chile for use in fertilizers, but the once-rich layers from the heyday of nitrate mining are now only to be seen sealed up in museum jars. At the Chilean refinery, a violet iodine vapor floats from the retort.

Remarks: Its crystal network is identical in character and dimensions with that of calcite. Soda niter crystals in exact parallel position can be grown on the surface of calcite rhombohedrons from saturated solutions of soda niter. Discarded specimens of this mineral tossed in a monastery garden led to the discovery of the importance of nitrogen to plant growth.

NITER KNO_3

Orthorhombic — Rhombic bipyramidal $\dfrac{2}{m}\dfrac{2}{m}\dfrac{2}{m}$

Environment: Cavern walls, as an efflorescence. Also in dry soils in the floor of bat caves but recovered only by dissolving in water, titrating, and recrystallizing. **Crystal description:** Occurs as thin crusts and as silky short fibers on rock surfaces, cavern walls, etc. Never in well-formed crystals (but crystals easily produced in the laboratory; hence, data on cleavage, fracture, and tenacity are available). **Physical properties:** White. *Luster* glassy; *hardness* 2; *specific gravity* 2.1; *cleavage* good. Fragile, slightly sectile. **Composition:** Potassium nitrate—"saltpeter" (46.5% K_2O, 53.5% N_2O_5). **Tests:** Like soda niter, but burns and explodes on hot coals, with violet flame.

Distinguishing characteristics: Behavior on coals distinguishes it from other salts, and the violet flame characterizes it as a potassium mineral.

Occurrence: Niter is found only as an efflorescence that forms on surfaces protected from rain, as in caves and along cliffs, from solutions percolating down through the rocks. Probably of organic origin. Rarer than soda niter but sometimes useful as a fertilizer, for which caves have been mined. Found in the dirt floor of caves in Kentucky and Tennessee, and sometimes in efflorescences along the limestone cliffs.

■ BORATES

These compounds form an important class of minerals that can be divided into two groups: (1) anhydrous—free or almost free of water—in high-temperature veins and pegmatites, of primary origin from plutonic hydrothermal sources and (2) the hydrous borates, forming in arid climates from surface—possibly hot-spring—solutions. Although collectibles, the anhydrous borates are relatively rare, with crystals of mostly modest dimensions. Hydrous borates are locally abundant and commercial sources of borax; they may be associated with halite, gypsum, and related sulfates. Some borates are extremely hard, like the almost legendary pegmatitic jeremejevite, $Al_6B_5O_{15}(OH)_3$, which was recently found (in blue crystals) for only the second time (in Namibia); the original occurrence was a 19th-century discovery in Siberia. Although the hardness of water-free borates can reach $7\frac{1}{2}$, the hydrous borates are soft. Some of the artificial water-free boron compounds are among the hardest substances known.

BORACITE $(Mg,Fe,Mn)_3B_7O_{13}Cl$ **Pl. 34**
Orthorhombic tetrahedral (pseudo-cubic) $\overline{4}$ 3 m
Environment: Salt and gypsum formations as isolated single crystals. **Crystal description:** Dodecahedrons and tetrahedrons to $^1/_2$ in. (1 cm). **Physical properties:** Pale green to colorless (boracite), deep violet to amethystine (chambersite, Mn), red (ericaite, Fe). *Luster* glassy; *hardness* $7-7^1/_2$; *specific gravity* 2.95; streak white; *fracture* irregular; *cleavage* octahedral. Brittle; transparent to translucent; weak greenish fluorescence (shortwave). **Composition:** Boracite is in an isomorphous series with three end members. Boracite is high in calcium, ericaite is at the iron end, and chambersite is at the manganese end of the series. (Mg,Fe,Mn 31.4%, B_2O_3 62.5% and ClO_2 6.1%). **Tests:** The crystals and occurrence are so distinctive that no tests are needed. Massive material would be hard to identify without x-rays. Melts readily to a pearly crystalline bead, tinting the flame green. Moistened with cobalt nitrate, becomes deep pink on refiring.
Occurrence: The blue-green, transparent, dodecahedral crystals and gray cubes of Stassfurt and vicinity in Germany—found in salt beds and in associated Luneburg salt and gypsum formations—are widely known. Boracite is rare in the U.S.; small and unexciting greenish crystals have been found in the insoluble anhydrite sand residues at Choctaw Dome and in a bedded formation in Louisiana. A few small red tetrahedrons of the iron member of the series are now named ericaite (formerly eisenstassfurtite). Chambersite tetrahedra to about $^1/_2$ in (15 mm) were found in some abundance in Barbers Hill in Texas and in a dome in Venice, Louisiana. All the larger purple Venice crystals had trapped pressurized bubbles and exploded on the way to the surface, though pinkish dodecahedrons survived the rise intact. Most recently, layers of greenish crystals have been found in a mine in Loftus, England.

◆HYDROUS BORATES

KERNITE $Na_2B_4O_6(OH)_2 \cdot 3H_2O$ **Pl. 34**
Monoclinic — prismatic $\dfrac{2}{m}$
Environment: In strata buried beneath an ancient dry lake bed at Boron, California. **Crystal description:** Forms solid veins of

large embedded crystals. Specimens are usually elongated fragments, parts of a single crystal, bounded by the cleavage planes of the base and the front faces. **Physical properties:** Colorless, but turns white on long exposure to dry air (forming tincalconite, $Na_2B_4O_5[OH]_4 \cdot 3H_2O$). *Luster* glassy, but dulls as the surface alters; *hardness* 3; *specific gravity* 1.9; *fracture* conchoidal (difficult to see because of the good cleavage); *cleavage* perfect basal and front pinacoid, producing long splinters. Brittle (splintery); transparent when fresh. **Composition:** Hydrous sodium borate (51.0% B_2O_3, 22.7% Na_2O, 26.3% H_2O). **Tests:** Under the blowpipe reacts like borax, but with less swelling.

Distinguishing characteristics: The blowpipe reaction is characteristic, and only resembles that of borax itself. Distinguished from borax ($Na_2B_4O_5(OH)_4 \cdot 8H_2O$) by greater hardness, its cleavage, and greater resistance to the chalky alteration.

Occurrence: Kernite was found in a drill hole several hundred feet beneath the surface at Boron, Kern Co., California, in a great concealed bed, associated with borax and believed to have been derived from borax by the pressure and temperature resulting from the deep burial. It probably occurs elsewhere in many yet-undrilled borax deposits, that formed in the same way. A little has been found near the surface on the floor of Death Valley, an indication of the summer temperatures there. Also found in Argentina.

Remarks: New minerals discovered today usually occur in small quantities and are of no commercial importance. This startling exception was found in 1926 in the process of drilling some prospecting holes at the Kern Co. locality, and it almost immediately became the leading ore of borax. Specimens do not keep well in collections since they usually exchange moisture with the air, which dulls the surface or penetrates cracks and makes the specimen cloudy. It is also an ideal and remarkably generous ore because the crystallization of a water solution yields 1.59 times as much of the desired product—borax—as would borax itself.

BORAX $Na_2B_4O_5(OH)_4 \cdot 8H_2O$ **Pl. 34**

Monoclinic — prismatic $\dfrac{2}{m}$

Environment: Dry lake beds in desert country. **Crystal description:** Usually (especially with human assistance) forms crystals, often very large and well formed. Unfortunately they whiten and crumble to powder in the mineral cabinet. Also mixed with other compounds in crusts of various minerals in salt lake beds. **Physical properties:** White, colorless but often stained by impurities; *Luster* glassy; *hardness* 2–2$\frac{1}{2}$; *specific gravity* 1.7; *fracture* conchoidal; *cleavage* 3, 1 good. Brittle; starts transparent to translucent, but crystals lose water and turn white. **Composition:** Hydrous sodium borate (36.6% B_2O_3, 16.2% Na_2O, 47.2% H_2O) **Tests:** Swells and fuses easily to a clear glass sphere that clings to the charcoal, coloring the flame yellow (this is the same borax bead used to test for metals in minerals). Water-soluble; tastes sweetish but astringent.

Distinguishing characteristics: Not likely to be confused with any other mineral; characteristic fusion behavior will distinguish it from most minerals. Rapid whitening of the crystals confirms other tests.

Occurrence: Used from ancient times, and brought to Europe by caravan from the dry lake bed in Tibet where it was found. Extensive deposits of this type are, or have been, worked in California and Nevada. The crystals are loose, fully developed, and often quite large; single crystals to 6 or 7 in. (15 or 20 cm) long and as much as a pound (0.5 kg) in weight have been recorded. Many are natural, as at Searles Lake, California; better ones are formed in sumps during mining operations, as at Boron, California. It is used as a flux, an antiseptic, as a water softener—and in mineralogy for borax beads. Its ancient name, tincal, is now applied to the unpurified state of sodium borate (tincalconite).

ULEXITE $NaCaB_5O_6(OH)_6 \cdot 5H_2O$ **Pl. 34**

Triclinic — pinacoidal $\overline{1}$

Environment: Desert borax deposits. **Crystal description:** Usually, near-surface forms are soft white cottony masses of loosely intergrown fibrous crystals commonly known as cotton balls or sheet cotton. A deeper form, at Boron, California, is solid veins of parallel fibers, the so-called television ore. **Physical properties:** White. *Luster* silky; *hardness* 2$\frac{1}{2}$; *specific gravity* 1.6. Soft and cottony or firm and fibrous; translucent fibers in tight asbestos-like seams. **Composition:** Hydrous sodium calcium borate (43.0% B_2O_3, 7.7% Na_2O, 13.8% CaO, 35.5% H_2O). **Tests:** Fuses easily to a clear glass, coloring the flame yellow (sodium). Glass fluoresces white in longwave ultraviolet; phosphoresces yellow. Slightly soluble in hot water.

Distinguishing characteristics: Fusibility distinguishes it from fibrous asbestos varieties; relative insolubility in water will distinguish it from capillary sulfates or salt. Associations are important.

Occurrence: Ulexite forms in borax deposits and salt beds in loose fragile balls or crusts, often mixed with salt, gypsum, or glauberite. Found in 3–4 in. (7–10 cm) balls in the Mojave Desert of s. Nevada and California. Similar occurrences are found in Chile and Argentina.

Remarks: The fibrous compact-vein parallel-fiber ulexite appears to be limited to the deep Boron deposit. It transmits light and images along each fiber and presaged the invention of fiber optics by transmitting images along a bundle of such threadlike crystals, seemingly shifting the underlying image to the upper surface.

COLEMANITE $Ca_2B_6O_{11} \cdot 5H_2O$ Pl. 34

Monoclinic — prismatic $\dfrac{2}{m}$ (?)

Environment: Desert borax deposits. **Crystal description:** Commonly in distinct crystals; sometimes thin, platy and razor-sharp; more often well developed more or less equidimensional, and several inches in size. Also in granular masses, and lining geodes in beautiful druses. **Physical properties:** White or colorless. *Luster* glassy; *hardness* 4–4$^1/_2$; *specific gravity* 2.4; *fracture* subconchoidal to uneven; *cleavage* perfect side pinacoid. Brittle; transparent; sometimes fluorescent yellowish white or bluish. **Composition:** Hydrous calcium borate (50.9% B_2O_3, 27.2% CaO, 21.9% H_2O) **Tests:** Decrepitates so violently that it is difficult to fuse on charcoal. Very thin grain in forceps decrepitates but melts with protrusions a little like borax. Colors flame green. Soluble in hot hydrochloric acid, with the precipitation of floating "snowflakes" of boric acid upon cooling.

Distinguishing characteristics: Resembles many colorless minerals, but its manner of occurrence is a good guide. Then the blowpipe test should prove the identity, for it does not resemble many other borates.

Occurrence: Another of the borate minerals to form in association with borax, ulexite (from which it is believed to have formed), and Tertiary clays in old lake beds in s. California. The most important ore of borax until kernite was discovered. Good specimens have been found in Death Valley at Ryan, California, and in several other borax mining areas in San Bernardino Co., California. Comparable crystals have been obtained in Turkey. Realgar needles are often associated, suggesting that volcanic sources were involved in its formation.

Remarks: Colemanite specimens in collections have a tendency to collect dust on certain face junctions on crystal surfaces. Though the reputed crystal symmetry does not permit the compound to be pyroelectric (showing positive and negative charges with temperature changes), like tourmaline and quartz, it needs explaining and suggests that some lack of structural symmetry must be responsible for this. Most specimens in mineral cabinets show conspicuous dustiness in particular areas; it is sufficiently prevalent to be a distinguishing characteristic in infrequently tended collections.

HOWLITE $Ca_2B_5SiO_9(OH)_5$ **Pl. 34**

Monoclinic — prismatic $\dfrac{2}{m}$

Environment: Desert borax deposits and related formations; commonly a near-surface secondary after other borates. **Crystal description:** Only tiny crystals visible in its w. U.S. occurrence, which is in the form of white rounded nodules. They make solid compact masses, without marked structure, with surfaces looking like small cauliflower heads. In Nova Scotia crystal overgrowths have been noted on the surfaces of similar nodules. **Physical properties:** White; gray streaks in masses. *Luster* subvitreous or bone dull; *hardness* $3\frac{1}{2}$; *specific gravity* 2.5–2.6; *fracture* even; *cleavage* none. Chalky to compact; crystals clear, masses opaque; sometimes fluorescent. **Composition:** Basic silicoborate of calcium (44.6% B_2O_3, 28.6% CaO, 15.3% SiO_2, 11.5% H_2O). **Tests:** Fuses to a clear glass sphere under the blowpipe, though less readily than borax and kernite. Soluble in hydrochloric acid, and with careful evaporation will be found to leave a silica gel on walls of test tube.

Distinguishing characteristics: Fusion behavior under the blowpipe reveals its boron roots; in hydrochloric acid, solubility and softness distinguish it from a chemically similar mineral (bakerite, $Ca_4B_4(BO_4)(SiO4)_3 \cdot H_2O$, hardness $4\frac{1}{2}$) and from datolite (hardness $5\frac{1}{2}$), which is very different in occurrence. Distinguished from the sodium borates by the green (boron) flame coloration and insolubility in water.

Occurrence: Found as nodules embedded in clay of borax deposits in California. Nova Scotia has similar but smaller nodules in gypsum and anhydrite beds.

■ SULFATES

This is a widespread and abundant group of minerals that have a few properties in common, making them, as a rule, easy to classify. All are translucent to transparent. Many are very light in color; those with the few pigmenting metals are colorful. A few of the sulfates of the common metals are very soluble in water, a number are insoluble in water but soluble in acid, and one important group is rather insoluble. None is hard, but several are fairly high in specific gravity.

To test for the group: The powdered mineral is fused with soda on charcoal into a gray mass. This mass is placed on a silver sheet (once it was a coin, but now only old coins are true silver) crushed, and moistened. Presence of sulfur is proved by appearance of a black stain on the silver when the assay is washed off. Water-soluble sulfates form a precipitate of white calcium sulfate needles when a calcium solution (hydrochloric acid in which calcite has been dissolved, forming calcium chloride), is added to the sulfate solution. The fluorescence of the cooled whitened portion of blowpiped minerals of the barite-celestite-anhydrite series is an original test that investigation-minded collectors should check out. The induced fluorescence does not show while the grain is still hot.

THENARDITE Na_2SO_4 Pl. 35

Orthorhombic — Rhombic bipyramidal $\frac{2}{m}\frac{2}{m}\frac{2}{m}$

Environment: Crusts of dry salt-lake beds in desert climates. **Crystal description:** Commonly in intergrown, poorly defined crystal clusters, and difficult to recognize. When distinct: tabular, short-prismatic, or pyramidal. Sometimes in sharp crossed-twin crystals. Also forming beds of solid material. Unstable in humidity, unsatisfactory for collections. **Physical properties:** Colorless to light yellowish or brownish, often clay-filled and gray. *Luster* glassy; *hardness* $2\frac{1}{2}$–3; *specific gravity* 2.7; *fracture* uneven; *cleavage* good basal. Brittle; transparent to translucent; weakly fluorescent (yellow-green under longwave ultraviolet) and phosphorescent. **Composition:** Sodium sulfate (56.3% Na_2O, 43.7% SO_3). **Tests:** Fuses easily, at first to clear glass (which becomes cloudy on cooling and nonfluorescent); then bubbles, spreads flat, fluoresces white in shortwave ultraviolet light. Dissolves readily in water; tastes salty. Water solution precipitates calcium sulfate out of the calcium chloride solution made when calcite is dissolved in hydrochloric acid.

Distinguishing characteristics: Recognized by the flame coloration (sodium), a sulfur test, and ease of solution in water. Confused with other water-soluble minerals like halite, but distinguished from them by sulfur test. Distinguished from glauberite by being very soluble in very little water.

Occurrence: Thenardite has formed very frequently as the result of evaporation of a salt lake. Known from such occurrences in Spain, Siberia, and the Caucasus. Also found in Africa and in numerous deposits in Chile. Likely U.S. lake beds are in Arizona, Nevada, and in California at Searles Lake, San Bernardino Co., and Soda Lake, San Luis Obispo Co.

BARITE $BaSO_4$ Pl. 35

Orthorhombic — Rhombic bipyramidal $\dfrac{2}{m}\dfrac{2}{m}\dfrac{2}{m}$

Environment: A very common mineral of greatly varying habit and a variety of parageneses; in sedimentary rocks and a frequent late gangue mineral in ore veins. **Crystal description:** Crystals commonly tabular, often very large. Also prismatic, equidimensional, in featherlike and crested groups, concretionary masses, "desert roses," even stalactitic, fine-grained, massive, and rocklike. **Physical properties:** Crystals colorless to bluish, yellow, reddish brown, also fine-grained and earthy. *Luster* glassy; *hardness* 3–3$\frac{1}{2}$; *specific gravity* 4.3–4.6; *fracture* uneven; *cleavage* several perfect basal and prismatic, and a fair side pinacoid. Brittle; transparent to translucent; sometimes fluorescent (see tests). **Composition:** Barium sulfate (65.7% BaO, 34.3% SO_3). **Tests:** Decrepitates, whitens, but fuses only with some difficulty. After intense heating, whitened assay fluoresces, usually bright orange. Gives sulfur test with sodium carbonate flux.

Distinguishing characteristics: The unusually high gravity in such a light-colored mineral is usually sufficiently significant. Distinguished from calcite by insolubility in acid; from feldspar by its softness; from celestite and anhydrite by orange fluorescence after firing and the green flame color; and from fluorite by lack of typical fluorite fluorescence, cleavages, and crystal shape.

Occurrence: Although barite often is an accompanying mineral in a sulfide ore vein, it is even more common in sedimentary rocks, where it forms concretionary nodules and free-growing crystals in open spaces. Veins of almost pure barite have been mined in several localities. The finest large barite crystals have come from Cumberland, England; single many-faced free-growing crystals were as much as 8 in. (20 cm) long. The British occurrences are notable for delicate coloring and well-formed crystals. There are many other fine localities, however. In Baia Sprie (Felsöbanya), Romania, it is intimately associated with stibnite needles, usually in flat colorless or yellowish crystals. In Morocco and Egypt it is found in unattractive but giant, foot-long (30 cm) crystals. Other occurrences abroad are too numerous to mention.

In the U.S. it is mined in the Midwest, as in Missouri. There white-bladed masses are found where the soil contacts the undecomposed limestone—the barite having settled as the enclosing rock weathered away. Good white to clear crystals, some a foot (30 cm) long, have also been found in Missouri. It is found in perfect imitative "roses" of a red-brown color and sandy texture near Norman, Oklahoma. Fine crusts of blue crystals are found in veins in soft sediments near Stoneham, Colorado. Great concretions, known as septarian nodules, found in the badlands of South Dakota, contain up to 4-in. (10 cm) fluorescent, transparent, amber-colored crystals in the cracks.

Remarks: An important commercial mineral; widely used as a pigment, in the preparation of lithopone (a pigment also known as zinc sulfide white), and as a filler for paper and cloth. Barite "mud" is poured into deep oil wells to buoy up the drilling tools. Several hundred years ago, a massive, concretionary variety of barite from Italy was found to phosphoresce on light heating, and was called Bologna stone from its locale of discovery. It was, of course, of great interest to the alchemists, the founders of chemistry, who were trying to make gold from the base metals.

CELESTITE $SrSO_4$ **Pl. 35**

Orthorhombic — Rhombic bipyramidal $\dfrac{2}{m}\dfrac{2}{m}\dfrac{2}{m}$

Environment: Sedimentary rocks; rather rarely a gangue mineral of ore veins. **Crystal description:** Usually in crystals, commonly tabular, resembling barite; also granular and in fibrous veins. **Physical properties:** Pale blue to deep and splotchy blue, white, colorless, red-brown, orange. *Luster* glassy; *hardness* 3–3$\frac{1}{2}$; *specific gravity* 3.9–4.0; *fracture* uneven; *cleavage* like barite, perfect basal and prismatic and poor pinacoidal. Brittle; transparent to translucent; sometimes fluorescent. **Composition:** Strontium sulfate (56.4% SrO, 43.6% SO_3). **Tests:** Cracks, fuses with difficulty on charcoal. After firing, with whitening of the surface, fluoresces and phosphoresces bright green. Gives sulfur test with silver.

Distinguishing characteristics: Light blue color, which often tints only part of the otherwise white crystal, is the best diagnostic point. The flame test can only be confused with that from anhydrite (but calcium much less red than strontium). Similar minerals of other groups can be distinguished by the softness and acid insolubility of the celestite, and the greenish fluorescence after heating.

Occurrence: Only rarely an accessory mineral of ore veins that were formed from warm solutions (Cripple Creek, Colorado). Usually found in sedimentary rocks; the best occurrences are in cavities in sandstone or limestone, associated with fluorite, calcite, gypsum, dolomite, galena, and sphalerite. Its color in these occurrences very often is the characteristic blue.

Fine, white, elongated, square crystals, an inch (2–3 cm) or so in length, were abundant in the Sicilian sulfur mines, associated with sulfur. Small blue crystals of similar habit were found on a white calcite at Herrengrund (now Spania Dolina, Czechoslovakia). Large flat white blades are found in England at Yate, Gloucestershire.

There are many occurrences in the U.S. Tremendous crystals were found on Kelleys I., Lake Erie, in a large limestone quarry. Some of these crystals were 6–8 in. (15–20 cm) across. A more recent outstanding locality from the standpoint of abundance is Clay Center, Ohio (another limestone quarry), in which pockets are filled with fine blue-to-white bladed celestite, associated with a brown fluorite and yellowish calcite. Some of the white crystals are very thin and fragile; others are thicker, blue, and resemble barite. Other quarries in that area are known for their celestite. Good crystals have also been found at Chittenango Falls, New York.

Geodes with large blue crystals much like those from Kelleys I. are found at Lampasas, Texas. Colorless transparent crystals occur with the colemanite in geodes of the Death Valley area. Orange cloudy crystals are found near Hamilton, Ontario, and near Colorado Springs, Colorado, though in neither locality are they free-standing. Fine blue crystals are found near Manitou Springs, Colorado, and blue radiating columnar crystal intergrowths (a rare hydrothermal occurrence) were found in the gold mines at Cripple Creek, Colorado. A blue fibrous vein material from Bellwood, Blair Co., Pennsylvania, described in 1791, was the original celestite, the first discovery of this mineral, which is named for its color. Brilliant geodes lined with gemmy blue crystals are found near Sakoony, Bombetoka Bay, Madagascar, and are now available in great abundance.

Remarks: The blue of celestite has been attributed to the presence of minute amounts of gold, but irradiation also turns some crystals a persistent blue.

ANGLESITE $PbSO_4$ Pl. 35

Orthorhombic — Rhombic bipyramidal $\frac{2}{m}\frac{2}{m}\frac{2}{m}$

Environment: Secondary (weathered) deposits of lead ore in generally siliceous formations. **Crystal description:** Tabular to prismatic crystals, may be elongated in any of the axial directions. Also massive, fine grained, granular to very compact. **Physical properties:** Colorless to white or grayish, or tinted with impurities (red or green); surface turns golden in bleach. *Luster* adamantine; *hardness* $2^3/_4$–3; *specific gravity* 6.4; *fracture* conchoidal; *cleavage* basal and prismatic. Brittle; transparent to translucent; often fluorescent (yellow-orange). **Composition:** Lead sulfate (73.6% PbO, 26.4% SO_3) **Tests:** Fuses very easily, forming white enamel, which is briefly yellow while still very hot. With continued blowpiping in the reducing flame, it boils away in spurts and finally yields lead bead.

Distinguishing characteristics: Easily recognized as a lead mineral by blowpipe reactions. Distinguished from cerussite and phosgenite by lack of effervescence in acids and its behavior on charcoal.

Occurrence: Anglesite forms during the alteration by weathering of lead sulfide. The best crystals appear to be associated with granular lead ores rather than ores with large well-formed galena crystals, perhaps because the permeable galena is more porous and more readily attacked, letting the anglesite crystals grow faster. Usually associated with other lead minerals such as phosgenite and cerussite, and with other oxidized-zone minerals such as malachite and azurite (which may have preempted the available carbon dioxide). Far rarer than cerussite.

Fine, transparent, well-developed isolated crystals an inch (2–3 cm) or so in size are found in small cavities in the granular galena of Monteponi, Sardinia. Large crystals have been found at Tsumeb, Namibia (with a secondary copper ore), and with galena and cerussite at Broken Hill, New South Wales, and at Coeur d'Alene, Idaho. Fine crystals were once found with wulfenite, pyromorphite, and cerussite at the old Wheatley Mine, Phoenixville, Pennsylvania. Small crystals are common in holes in altering solid galena accompanied by tiny yellow sulfur crystals. Sometimes massive and nondescript sulfate rims will be found forming concentric gray to black bands enclosing a nucleus of unaltered galena. Good pseudomorphs of anglesite after cubes of galena have been found in the Joplin (Missouri) District and Bingham, New Mexico. In an interesting Mexican occurrence, yellowish tabular anglesite crystals are embedded in sulfur. There are numerous other good occurrences, too many to list.

ANHYDRITE CaSO$_4$ Pl. 36

Orthorhombic — Rhombic bipyramidal $\frac{2}{m}\frac{2}{m}\frac{2}{m}$

Environment: Sedimentary beds, gangue in ore veins, in traprock zeolite occurrences, and as insoluble sand from halite brines. **Crystal description:** Larger crystals relatively rare, rectangular pinacoidal, or elongated parallel to domes. Also coarse to fine-grained, granular formations capping salt domes. **Physical properties:** Colorless, white, gray, blue, lilac. *Luster* glassy to pearly; *hardness* 3–3^1/$_2$; *specific gravity* 3.0; *fracture* uneven to splintery; *cleavage* 3 good, pinacoidal. Transparent to translucent; sometimes fluorescent. **Composition:** Calcium sulfate (41.2% CaO, 58.8% SO$_3$). **Tests:** Cracks, decrepitates mildly, and fuses with difficulty on charcoal. Gives good sulfur test with silver. Fluoresces various colors after roasting: pink (Balmat, New York), yellow-green (Paterson, New Jersey), or blue-white (Switzerland).

Distinguishing characteristics: The cubic aspect of its cleavage and the sulfur test, coupled with the low specific gravity, make its identification easy. Often associated with gypsum in same specimen.

Occurrence: Anhydrite is surprisingly rare in good mineral specimens, probably because it is easily altered to gypsum through hydration. It can be deposited directly from seawater. It is found most abundantly in sedimentary rocks, especially associated with salt beds. The metamorphic rock occurrences were probably derived from recrystallized gypsum. For a long time, the best occurrences were European. Highly prized, attractive lilac crystals and cleavages were encountered in drilling the Simplon Tunnel in Switzerland. It is abundant in Poland in the salt mines near Kraków, and in Germany at the Stassfurt mine. In these occurrences it is usually massive, as well as in small crystals all through the water-soluble salt.

A most interesting U.S. occurrence has little anhydrite today. It is only a silica skeleton preserved in the form of hollow 3-faced (sides and top) pseudomorphs of quartz and zeolites, after what must have been long blades of anhydrite, preserved in zeolite pockets in the West Paterson (New Jersey) traprock area. Some residual anhydrite, altered in part to white gypsum, has been found; the discovery solved a controversy about the origin of the rectangular voids. Countless numbers of tiny clear crystals have been found in salt-well insoluble residues in Louisiana and Texas. Equally tiny colorless crystals of anhydrite were recovered from halite that was caught up in a pegmatitic intrusion encountered in the zinc mine at Balmat, New York, and a violet anhydrite is associated with it in the bounding dike. Anhydrite is an important gangue mineral in some ore veins. It is found in lilac masses in Peru and Chile and is abundant in giant 12-in. (30 cm) crystals in the gangue of the Faraday Mine, Bancroft, Ontario. Freestanding, jagged-ended, Mayan-arch-tipped, 6-in. (15–25 cm) blue crystals are found with the Naica, Mexico lead ores in great abundance, making it now probably the world's richest specimen source.

Anhydrite beds once occurred in Nova Scotia, but they are now largely altered to gypsum; hydration swelling caused a beautiful crumpling of the weak layers, providing very graphic small-scale illustrations of the geologic process of the folding of stratified beds under compression. Pressure or elevated temperatures, or both, seem essential to anhydrite formation.

GLAUBERITE $Na_2Ca(SO_4)_2$

Monoclinic — prismatic $\dfrac{2}{m}$

Environment: Dry salt-lake beds and alkaline lake shores in desert climates. **Crystal description:** The steeply pointed, inclined bipyramidal crystals are very characteristic. May also be tabular to the base. **Physical properties:** White or light yellow to a mud-filled gray or buff. *Luster* glassy; *hardness* $2^1/_2$–3; *specific gravity* 2.7–2.8; *fracture* conchoidal; *cleavage* perfect basal. Brittle; transparent to translucent; salt taste; may phosphoresce. **Composition:** Sodium calcium sulfate (22.3% NaO, 20.2% CaO, 57.5% SO_3). **Tests:** Decrepitates, then fuses easily to a white enamel, coloring the flame yellow (sodium). In water it turns white and partially dissolves, leaving a residue of calcium sulfate. Bitter taste.

Distinguishing characteristics: Its crystals are distinctive. It can be recognized as a sulfate by a chemical sulfate test with calcite in a hydrochloric acid solution. It is distinguished in this way from the water-soluble halides. Can be told from thenardite by its slow solubility and the residue of calcium sulfate left after its solution in a little water.

Occurrence: Glauberite commonly forms in and with salt beds upon the evaporation of salt lakes, occurring thus in Germany (at Stassfurt), Russia, Kenya (on a lake shore), Chile, India, Spain, and Austria. It is found in the U.S. in San Bernardino Co. at Searles Lake (California) and in Arizona at Camp Verde, where it has largely altered to calcite or gypsum. Existing crystals pulled from Searles Lake are usually small, normally only a few centimeters. Once more widespread, since casts of other minerals and sediments around glauberite-crystal-shaped cavities are fairly common. Great opal masses (known as pineapples in Australia) are thought to be opal pseudomorphs after this mineral. Perfect, sharp, empty glauberite crystal casts in sandstone have been found in New Jersey. In the trap quarries of Paterson, one of the unknown minerals that are commemorated by the well-known quartz casts may have been glauberite.

◆HYDRATED SULFATES

POLYHALITE $K_2Ca_2Mg(SO_4)_4 \cdot 2H_2O$ **Pl. 35**

Triclinic — pinacoidal $\overline{1}$

Environment: Sedimentary beds associated with (overlying) other remnants of an evaporated sea. **Crystal description:** Usually occurs in massive, granular beds, or in fibrous or lamellar masses. Crystals simple, small, and rather rare. **Physical properties:** If pure, colorless to white, but often pale cloudy red to brick red. *Luster* resinous; *hardness* $3^1/_2$; *specific gravity* 2.8 (but water-soluble so not usually determined); *fracture* usually fibrous or splintery; *cleavage* 1 good. **Composition:** Hydrous sulfate of potassium, calcium, and magnesium (15.6% K_2O, 18.6% CaO, 6.7% MgO, 53.1% SO_3, 6.0% H_2O). **Tests:** Bitter taste. Colors flame purple (potassium) and fuses easily. Dissolved in a small quantity of water, it frees an insoluble residue of calcium sulfate.

Distinguishing characteristics: Much like some of the other bedded salts, and often impure. Likely to be confused with sylvite but distinguishable by its incomplete solubility.

Occurrence: Likely to be found in commercial bedded-salt deposits where the several layers are being mined for rock salt (halite) and sylvite. More soluble than the chlorides, it is at the top of the beds. In the U.S. it has been found in the salt beds near Carlsbad, New Mexico, and w. Texas. Also found in the salt deposits near Hallstatt, Austria; in Galicia, Poland; and at Stassfurt, Germany.

Remarks: The name at first glance may lead one to expect a haloid, but refers to the Greek for "many" (poly) "salts" (hal), in reference to the large number of salts that compose it.

GYPSUM $CaSO_4 \cdot 2H_2O$ **Pl. 36**

Monoclinic — prismatic $\dfrac{2}{m}$

Environment: Sedimentary rocks as massive beds, in free crystals in clay beds, alkaline lake muds, and crystallized in cavities in limestone. Often in opaque, sand-filled crystal clusters. Crystals constantly grow and clog various contrivances of human making: water pipes, mines, and dumps. **Crystal description:** Crystals are common, often assuming a tabular habit: model-like, backward-slanting, monoclinic plates, with the horizontal axis the shortest. "Fishtail" twins are frequent. The most common crystals—which may be large ill-formed sheets—are found loose and free-growing in clay beds and cover outcrops in mica-like sheets; glassy gypsum known as selenite. Stony bands of massive Italian gypsum, known as alabaster, are carved and dyed in Florence; fibrous warm-hued chatoyant veins known as satin spar are Russian sculptors' grist. **Physical properties:** Colorless, white, and pale tints. *Luster* glassy, pearly (on cleavage face), and silky (avoid washing very lustrous surfaces, for even water has been found to dull them); *hardness* 2; *specific gravity* 2.3; *fracture* conchoidal and splintery; *cleavage* 2, 1 perfect and micaceous. Sectile; often fluoresces yellow in an hourglass pattern within crystal; also phosphorescent. **Composition:** Hydrous calcium sulfate (32.6% CaO, 46.5% SO_3, 20.9% H_2O). **Tests:** Soluble in hot dilute hydrochloric acid; the addition of barium chloride solution makes a white precipitate. After firing, fluorescent and phosphorescent in longwave ultraviolet light.

Distinguishing characteristics: With its low hardness, and flakes that are easily scratched by a fingernail, no other test is needed. The clear plates bend but lack the elastic rebound of mica; they are softer than uncommon brucite. Massive alabaster is softer than anhydrite or marble, and gypsum will not bubble in acid like the latter.

Occurrence: A widespread, commercially important mineral. The massive material is quarried, or mined, for the manufacture of plaster of Paris and various plaster products. The most abundant deposits are the sedimentary beds, some of which have formed from the alteration of the water-free variety, anhydrite. It is such beds that are mined for economic applications in New York, Michigan, Texas, Iowa, and California. Nova Scotia has great beds of altered anhydrite that show interesting crumpling of the layers as they swelled with the addition of water—metamorphic structures on a very small scale.

Good crystals are found in clay beds of Ohio and Maryland, and interesting cave rosettes of spreading fibers (gypsum flowers) come from Kentucky. The most beautiful gypsum (selenite) crystals are foreign in origin, though the largest probably came from a cave in Utah. The large water-clear crystals from the Sicilian sulfur mines, often with inclusions of sulfur, are classics of all collections. In Naica, Chihuahua, Mexico, a cavern in the mine (Cave of the Swords) contains meter-long, slender, slightly milky needles with tubular water-filled cavities and movable bubbles.

Remarks: The name *plaster of Paris* comes from its early source in the Montmartre quarries of Paris. The name *gypsum* comes from the Greek word for the calcined (or "burned") material. *Selenite* comes from a Greek comparison of the pearly luster of a cleavage plate to moonlight. Decomposed gypsum is considered a source of sulfur in the Sicilian mines.

CHALCANTHITE $CuSO_4 \cdot 5H_2O$ Pl. 36

Triclinic — pinacoidal $\overline{1}$

Environment: Always a secondary mineral that forms during copper sulfide mineral oxidation; likely to persist only in arid environments because of its high solubility in water. Regrows in some copper mines after every rain. **Crystal description:** Usually forms botryoidal or stalactitic masses, and rarely rising in blue fibers from earthy ore. Sharp model-like crystals are easily grown in the laboratory and are so exceptional in nature as to be unbelievable when offered for sale. **Physical properties:** Sky blue. *Luster* vitreous; *hardness* $2\frac{1}{2}$; gravity 2.3; streak pale blue; *fracture* conchoidal; *cleavage* 3 poor. Brittle; translucent to transparent; sweetish metallic taste. **Composition:** Hydrous copper sulfate (31.9% CuO, 32.1% SO_3, 36.1% H_2O). **Tests:** None necessary as a rule; the taste and color are enough to identify it. *Poisonous.* Limit taste testing!

Distinguishing characteristics: Not likely to be mistaken for any other water-soluble salt except the related iron sulfate melanterite, $FeSO_4 \cdot 7H_2O$) or iron copper sulfate (pisanite, $(Cu,Fe)SO_4 \cdot 7H_2O$), which are greener. Chalcanthite is sufficiently abundant in fibrous veins as at Chuquicamata and El Teniente (Sewell), Chile, to form an important ore of copper. Elsewhere it is too rare to have any value alone, though copper can be recovered from leach-water solutions of copper sulfate by exchanging the copper in the solution for scrap iron, which goes into solution as a sulfate and then breaks down into limonite rust. This is a valuable source of copper at Minas de Río Tinto, Spain.

Occurrence: Aside from its occurrence in actual veins in rock in Chile, it usually forms on mine timbers and on the walls of tunnels as a result of the exposure of wet sulfide ores to air as the mine is worked. Fine blue stalactites have formed in many mines, notably at Bingham, Utah; Ducktown, Tennessee; and the Arizona copper mines. Almost without exception, the dealers' fine crystals perched on matrix are artificial, and should be regarded as fakes. When pure, with no iron, as in chemically pure man-made crystals, copper sulfate seems to be pretty stable, but when some iron is present, it will not keep in open collection drawers. Chalcanthite comes from Greek for "flower of copper." Used as a fungicide.

EPSOMITE $MgSO_4 \cdot 7H_2O$

Orthorhombic — Rhombic bisphenoidal 2 2 2

Environment: Cave walls, as a white efflorescence deposited by salt springs. **Crystal description:** Usually not in crystals but in white hairlike or cottony efflorescences. Also in botryoidal masses and small prismatic crystals. **Physical properties:** White. *Luster* silky, glassy to earthy; *hardness* 2–2$^1/_2$; *specific gravity* 1.7 (but water-soluble, so not readily determined); *fracture* conchoidal; *cleavage* 1 perfect and 2 less perfect. Brittle (artificial crystals) to cottony; translucent to transparent; bitter taste. **Composition:** Hydrous magnesium sulfate (16.3% MgO, 32.5% SO_3, 51.2% H_2O). **Tests:** Rapidly and completely water-soluble. Melts readily to a liquid in its own water of crystallization.

Distinguishing characteristics: Its taste and ready solubility, together with its occurrence, are usually distinctive. Tests for sulfate (p. 171) tarnish silver.

Occurrence: In the U.S., epsomite's principle occurrences are as white efflorescences on the walls of limestone caves, where they are protected from solution by rain or much dampness. During droughts it has been found in large crystals in a lake-bed deposit on Kruger Mountain, Oroville, Washington. In some very dry localities, as in South Africa, it may form beds of considerable thickness, but in general it can be considered rare. It has also been found around fumaroles on Vesuvius lavas. The name is derived from its occurrence in the solution from a medicinal mineral spring at Epsom, England.

BROCHANTITE $Cu_4(SO_4)(OH)_6$ Pl. 37

Monoclinic — prismatic $\dfrac{2}{m}$

Environment: Oxidized (weathered) zones of copper deposits, particularly in rocks low in carbonates. **Crystal description:** Small, prismatic to short-prismatic or tabular crystals; also soft masses like malachite. Commonly twinned to look orthorhombic, with terminal faces that are characteristically rounded, lacking the even surfaces and sharp definition usual in the prism and pinacoid faces. The observed smooth shiny face will always lie in the prism zone, making orientation easy. **Physical properties:** Bright to dark green. *Luster* glassy (slightly pearly on the cleavage faces); *hardness* $3^1/_2$– 4; *specific gravity* 4.0; *streak* light green; *fracture* conchoidal; *cleavage* perfect side pinacoidal. Splintery or flaky fragments form on crushing; translucent to transparent. **Composition:** A sulfate of copper (70.4% CuO, 17.7% SO_3, 11.9% H_2O). **Tests:** Same as for antlerite (see next).
Distinguishing characteristics: See antlerite.
Occurrence: A common mineral of deeply altered copper deposits, especially in rocks other than limestone; consequently it has been found in many of the western copper localities. Especially well crystallized specimens have come from Nevada, but it is also found in Arizona, New Mexico, Utah, and California. It was abundant in the old European localities, in Russia, Romania, Italy, and England. It was named for a French geologist, Brochant de Villiers.

ANTLERITE $Cu_3(SO_4)(OH)_4$ Pl. 37

Orthorhombic — Rhombic bipyramidal $\dfrac{2}{m}\dfrac{2}{m}\dfrac{2}{m}$

Environment: Like brochantite, in secondary (weathered) zone of copper deposits, perhaps in environments more arid than its counterpart. **Crystal description:** Forms small tabular to short-prismatic green crystals; also occurs in soft, fibrous, green masses resembling malachite and in brittle, hazardous, skin-penetrating needles. **Physical properties:** Bright to dark green. *Luster* glassy; *hardness* $3^1/_2$–4, *specific gravity* 3.9; *streak* bright green; *fracture* uneven; *cleavage* pinacoidal, perfect side, poor front. Splintery; translucent to transparent. **Composition:** Alkaline sulfate of copper (67.3% CuO, 22.6% SO_3, 10.1% H_2O). **Tests:** Dissolves in hydrochloric acid without carbonate's effervescence; a chip of calcite added to the solution causes white needles (of calcium sulfate) to form.

Distinguishing characteristics: Distinguished from malachite by lack of bubbling in acid and from copper phosphates and arsenates by the sulfate test. Antlerite is chemically indistinguishable from brochantite, though dome faces are flatter and more even than the base (pseudodomes) of brochantite.

Occurrence: Antlerite, like brochantite, is a mineral of the oxidized zones of copper deposits in siliceous rocks that cannot supply an abundance of the carbon dioxide needed by the carbonate group of copper minerals. It was thought rare, but since its recognition as the principal secondary ore of copper at Chuquicamata, Chile, its greater abundance and more widespread distribution has been recognized. It has often been confused with brochantite, from which it is nearly indistinguishable by simple tests, and is probably far more common than thought. It was named from the Antler Mine in Arizona and is probably fairly common in copper deposits in the West.

LINARITE $PbCu(SO_4)(OH)_2$ **Pl. 37**

Monoclinic — prismatic $\dfrac{2}{m}$

Environment: Secondary (weathered) zone of carbonate deficient ore deposits, and highly regarded by collectors. **Crystal description:** Slender prismatic blades to tabular, parallel to a base. Typically smaller, more lustrous, and less erect than azurite. **Physical properties:** Deep blue. *Luster* glassy to adamantine; *hardness* $2^1/_2$; *specific gravity* 5.3–5.4; streak bright blue; *fracture* conchoidal; *cleavage* 1 perfect and 1 fair. Brittle; translucent to transparent in thin blades. **Composition:** Alkaline sulfate of lead and copper (19.8% CuO, 55.7% PbO, 20.0% SO_3, 4.5% H_2O). **Tests:** Decomposed and partially dissolved by 1:1 nitric acid, leaving a white insoluble residue of lead sulfate, and forming a green solution that turns blue with the addition of ammonia copper test.

Distinguishing characteristics: Among the common minerals, it could only be confused with azurite and can be distinguished from that by its lack of effervescence and its incomplete solubility in acid. Blue diaboleite ($Pb_2CuCl_2[OH]_4$), a rare tetragonal associate at the Mammoth Mine, Tiger, Arizona, is a chloride so will not give the sulfate precipitate. Another chloride, boleite ($Pb_{26}Ag_{10}Cu_{24}Cl_{62}[OH]_{48}\cdot3H_2O$) comes in deep blue 1-cm edged cubes, essentially only from Baja California, Mexico.

Occurrence: The blue masses and crystals of linarite are probably more common than is generally thought, but they are so similar to azurite in appearance that they are usually mistaken for those of the commoner mineral. Large crystals are rare; perhaps the best yet, 4 in. (10 cm) or more long, were found at the Mammoth Mine. Elsewhere it is usually in small crystals, as at Tintic, Utah; Eureka, Nevada; and Cerro Gordo, Inyo Co., California. Better-than-average 2-in. (2–3 cm) crystals come from Graham Co., Arizona. The richest U.S. locality is Bingham, New Mexico. Named for Linares, Spain, where it was first recognized; also found in Great Britain in Cornwall, Cumberland, and Scotland's Leadhills, and in Germany, Siberia, Chile, Argentina, and Namibia.

ALUNITE $KAl_3(SO_4)_2(OH)_6$

Hexagonal — Ditrigonal pyramidal   3 m

Environment: A secondary rock-making mineral where acid, often ore-bearing, solutions altered orthoclase feldspar-rich rocks such as rhyolite. **Crystal description:** Usually massive; crystals are rare and most often pseudocubic rhombohedrons. When seen they are likely to be coating the walls of a fissure in massive alunite. **Physical properties:** White, light gray, or flesh red. *Luster* vitreous to pearly; *hardness* $3\frac{1}{2}$–4; *specific gravity* 2.6–2.9; *fracture* flat conchoidal to uneven; *cleavage* fair basal and poor rhombohedral. Brittle; translucent to transparent; sometimes fluorescent orange in longwave ultraviolet light. **Composition:** Alkaline hydrous sulfate of aluminum and potassium (11.4% K_2O, 36.9% Al_2O_3, 38.7% SO_3, 13.0% H_2O). **Tests:** High heating in closed tube gives water that tests acid with litmus paper (a blue paper that turns pink in acid). Colors flame purple (potassium). Infusible, but after blowpiping becomes soluble in nitric acid. **Distinguishing characteristics:** Closely resembles, in its massive form, limestone and dolomite. A test is essential for identification if alunite is suspected. Its eventual solubility, without effervescence, is a favorable sign. **Occurrence:** A great mountain of alunite is to be found at

Marysvale, Utah, as well as elsewhere in the West, where hydrothermal alteration has alunitized rhyolitic formations. Several attempts, so far unsuccessful, have been made to work the Utah deposit commercially, to extract potash for fertilizer and use the balance as an ore of aluminum. Similar large alunite deposits are known in Colorado, at Red Mountain, and associated with the ores at Goldfield, Nevada. Although uninteresting from the specimen standpoint, it is potentially valuable as a raw material. White and colorless crystals are found in Civatavecchia, Italy and elsewhere.

JAROSITE $KFe_3(SO_4)_2(OH)_6$

Hexagonal — Ditrigonal pyramidal   3 m

Environment: A secondary mineral, forming from predominantly gold-pyrite veins under weathering conditions in arid climates. **Crystal description:** Microscopic to less than 1 mm, as a rule, crystals of hexagonal or, more commonly, triangular habit; also in fibrous crusts, granular and massive ocherous aggregates. **Physical properties:** Glistening surface crusts of triangular faces ocher-yellow to clove brown. *Luster* vitreous to subadamantine; *hardness* $2^1/_2$–$3^1/_2$; *specific gravity* 2.9–3.3; *fracture* uneven; *cleavage* perfect basal. Brittle to sectile; translucent and transparent. **Composition:** Alkaline hydrous sulfate of iron and potassium (9.4% K_2O, 47.8% Fe_2O_3, 32.0% SO_3, 10.8% H_2O). **Tests:** On charcoal, with the blowpipe, gives black magnetic bead, colors flame purple (best seen by touching fused grain with drop of nitric acid and noting first flash of color). A partially fused mass gives the blackening test for sulfur obtained by crushing and moistening on silver disk.

Distinguishing characteristics: The crystallized specimens are easily recognized by the hexagonal and rhombohedral shapes. The massive material normally dismissed as typical gossan resembles limonite but can be distinguished by the blowpipe tests listed above. In routine testing, potassium and sulfur are good indications of jarosite, but it is not an easy mineral to identify without crystals.

Occurrence: Most frequently found near western ore veins in rocks that are rich in silica, supposedly formed by alteration of pyrite in the vein. Good specimens have been found in Chaffee Co., Colorado; Maricopa Co., Arizona; and Tintic, Utah. Jarosite has been found in nodules with iron phosphates in Midvale, Virginia.

COPIAPITE $(Fe,Mg)Fe_4(SO_4)_6(OH)_2 \cdot 20H_2O$ **Pl. 37**

Triclinic — pinacoidal $\overline{1}$

Environment: Limited to oxidized iron sulfide deposits in desert climates. **Crystal description:** Usually occurs as loose masses of crystalline scales, also in compact granular crusts. No good crystals. **Physical properties:** Ocher to sulfur yellow. *Luster* pearly; *hardness* $2\frac{1}{2}$–3; *specific gravity* 2.1; *cleavage* micaceous. Piles of shiny flakes; translucent; astringent metallic taste. **Composition:** Alkaline ferric sulfate (about 25.6% Fe_2O_3, 38.5% SO_3, 30.3% H_2O, often with some MgO, CuO, and Al_2O_3). **Tests:** Water-soluble; clear, cold solution becomes and remains cloudy on boiling. Gives magnetic bead on charcoal before the blowpipe.

Distinguishing characteristics: Difficult to distinguish, without extensive tests, from several similar iron sulfates that resemble it in appearance and occurrence. However, the taste and the water solubility distinguish them from similar appearing minerals of unrelated species. It is also less brilliantly yellow than several oxides of uranium minerals, most of which are brilliantly fluorescent. Becomes magnetic as a roasted bead.

Occurrence: Copiapite is the most common of the ferric sulfates and is selected here as representative of a large group of similar and related species, all of which form in the same fashion. The only reliable method of distinguishing between them is with x-rays. Copiapite is likely to be found in the U.S. wherever pyrite is oxidizing rapidly, as on coal mine refuse piles, or at a burning copper mine in Jerome, Arizona. It has also been noted at Sulphur Bank, California, and in some of the California mercury mines, such as Mt. Diablo. It, or a substitute, continuously formed yellow gobs of gunk in some of the Missouri sinkhole iron sulfide deposits as soon as their pyrite was exposed to the air.

CALEDONITE $Cu_2Pb_5(SO_4)_3(CO_3)(OH)_6$ **Pl. 37**

Orthorhombic — Rhombic bipyramidal $\frac{2}{m}\frac{2}{m}\frac{2}{m}$

Environment: Secondary (weathered) zone of lead and copper ores. **Crystal description:** Usually in small, nice, well-formed prismatic crystals, often with several prisms and a series of parallel truncating faces. Though small they make very attractive specimens, especially for micromounts. **Physical properties:** Turquoise blue to light blue-green. *Luster* resinous; *hardness* $2\frac{1}{2}$–3; *specific gravity* 5.8; *fracture* uneven;

cleavage 1 good and 2 poor. Brittle; translucent. **Composition:** Alkaline carbonate sulfate of lead and copper (9.9% CuO, 69.2% PbO, 14.9% SO_3, 2.7% CO_2, 3.3% H_2O). **Tests:** Fuses easily to a metal bead on charcoal. The bead dissolves easily in nitric acid to give a green solution, which turns blue with ammonia (copper). Added hydrochloric acid makes a milky (lead) solution.

Distinguishing characteristics: There are few similar species of this turquoise hue. The mineral is quite rare. Its prismatic crystals and color (both of which are very characteristic), together with its occurrence and associates, make its recognition very easy.

Occurrence: Probably the world's finest examples of caledonite were the $1/_2$-in. (1–1.5 cm) crystals from the Mammoth Mine at Tiger, Arizona. Also found in crusts of small crystals in lead-copper mines at Cerro Gordo, Inyo Co., California; Beaver Creek, Utah; and Dona Ana Co., New Mexico. It is not a common mineral, even in Scotland, where it was first found (whence the name), nor in Cornwall, Sardinia, Chile, or other potential occurrences. Good specimens are very desirable.

CROCOITE $PbCrO_4$ **Pl. 37**

Monoclinic — prismatic $\dfrac{2}{m}$

Environment: Oxidized lead-chromium veins, as a secondary mineral. **Crystal description:** Almost always in prismatic crystals, up to several inches long and striated parallel to their length. Terminations may be hollow with deep-pitted depressions. **Physical properties:** Brilliant orange. *Luster* adamantine; *hardness* $2^1/_2$–3; *specific gravity* 5.9–6.1; *fracture* uneven; *cleavage* poor prismatic. Very brittle and fragile; almost transparent to translucent. **Composition:** Lead chromate (69.1% PbO, 30.9% CrO_3). **Tests:** Fuses very easily to black bead. In borax bead gives the green (chromium) color. Darkens in closed tube and flies apart (decrepitates), but upon cooling regains its orange color.

Distinguishing characteristics: Distinguished from wulfenite by the prismatic crystal habit and the borax bead and closed-tube tests (plus its lower specific gravity). Realgar volatilizes completely in white fumes on charcoal.

Occurrence: A very rare but very spectacular mineral that was first found in Russia. Its finest development was reached in Tasmania as crystals several inches (10–20 cm) long. It appears to form under the unusual condition of chromium-bearing solutions altering lead deposits. Small examples have been reported from the Mammoth Mine, Tiger, Arizona, and in California at the Darwin Mine, Inyo Co., and the Eldorado Mine, Indio, Riverside Co., but never in noteworthy specimens. Also reported from Brazil and the Philippines.

Crocoite is among the most showy and colorful of mineral species. The supply of truly elongated and sturdy Tasmanian specimens seems to have been exhausted many years ago; specimens from a recent reopening are much smaller and rather fragile. A Russian source, the first find, had stockier and sounder crystals on a black matrix with green vauquelinite, $Pb_2Cu(CrO_4)PO_4(OH)$.

■PHOSPHATES, ARSENATES, VANADATES, AND URANATES

Some of these are primary minerals (one in particular, apatite) but most are secondary, forming during surface alterations from ore minerals. This is especially true of the vanadates and the arsenates, which are mostly secondary (weathered) zone minerals. None is hard; the maximum hardness is about 6. Since many contain heavy elements, specific gravity is relatively high. The nickel, copper, cobalt, vanadium, and chromium ore alterations are often highly colored. Many of the uranates are brilliantly fluorescent as well.

There are some chemical tests for the different elements which will prove useful. Phosphorus makes a yellow precipitate in a solution of ammonium molybdate when a few drops of a nitric acid solution of the phosphate compound is added to it. The precipitate may take a few minutes to appear. Arsenates can usually be detected by the garlic smell when they are blowpiped on the charcoal, though arsenic in this form is not as easily volatilized as in the sulfides. With the common vanadates and uranates, it usually is quite unnecessary to test, since most of the former are distinctively crystallized and unmistakable; the latter are likely to be fluorescent.

| **TRIPHYLITE** | $LiFePO_4$ | **Pl. 38** |
| **LITHIOPHILITE** | $LiMnPO_4$ | |

Orthorhombic — Rhombic bipyramidal $\dfrac{2}{m}\dfrac{2}{m}\dfrac{2}{m}$

Environment: A primary phosphate of complex pegmatite dikes, giving birth through alteration to a panoply of secondary phosphates. **Crystal description:** Crystals rare, usually embedded and simple, commonly in solid masses of large crystal units without external faces. Triphylite is usually smaller, sharper, and more isolated; lithiophilite forms larger, cruder knots with altered rims and numerous secondary species. **Physical properties:** Gray-blue to gray-blue-green (triphylite) or pinkish to greenish brown (lithiophilite). *Luster* glassy; *hardness*: $4^{1}/_{2}$–5; *specific gravity* 3.4–3.6; *streak* white; *fracture* uneven to numerous small conchoidal patches; *cleavage* 1 fair and 2 imperfect. Brittle; transparent to barely translucent. **Composition:** An isomorphous series of lithium, iron, and manganese phosphate (about 9.5% Li_2O, about 45% Fe_2O_3 plus Mn_2O_3—both are always present—and about 45% P_2O_5). **Tests:** Fuse on charcoal to black bead, with lithiophilite fusing more readily than triphylite. Triphylite bead is magnetic. Crushed powder moistened with hydrochloric acid gives red lithium flame color. Moistened with sulfuric acid gives red lithium flash and then the continued blue-green flame of phosphorus.

Distinguishing characteristics: The lithium flame coloration, with the dark color and the easy fusibility, distinguishes these from similar minerals. Their geological associations (pegmatite mineral) eliminate most other substances that might be confusing. In case of doubt, the chemical phosphorus test would be helpful.

Occurrence: Triphylite and lithiophilite are comparatively rare minerals, but are found in a number of pegmatites, which are in consequence called phosphate pegmatites. They may form tremendous irregular masses, often with secondary alteration products around their margins. Good crystals (triphylite) have been found at Chandler's Mill, Newport, New Hampshire. Great masses of both varieties are found at the Palermo quarry, North Groton, New Hampshire. Reported from Custer, South Dakota, and Pala, San Diego Co., California, in similar masses; some now-exhausted quarries and one active quarry (at Hagendorf) in Bavaria; from Rajasthan, India, and Mangualde, Portugal; and from several quarries in Rio Grande do Norte, Brazil, in great abundance.

Remarks: Wherever these minerals occur, but especially with the manganese-rich variety lithiophilite, one may expect to find whole series of interesting phosphates derived from the alteration of the primary phosphate. Cracks and fissures in the fresh mineral are often lined with microscopic crystals of secondary phosphates. Branchville, Connecticut, became famous as a mineral locality because of the secondary phosphates formed from the lithiophilite found there (and its proximity to Yale geologists). The final stage in the alteration of lithiophilite is a black manganese oxide. This substance is likely to stain heavily such other species in phosphate-rich pegmatite and serve as a good guide to pegmatites of this makeup. Lithium-phosphate pegmatites are among the most rewarding localities for mineral collectors because the altering lithiophilite yields a wealth of colorful species.

| **HETEROSITE** | $(Fe,Mn)PO_4$ | **Pl. 38** |
| **PURPURITE** | $(Mn,Fe)PO_4$ | |

Orthorhombic — Rhombic bipyramidal $\dfrac{2}{m}\dfrac{2}{m}\dfrac{2}{m}$

Environment: In complex pegmatites closest to the parent lithiophilite, often ringed with solution cavities lined with several secondary phosphate minerals. **Crystal description:** Neither takes the form of pocket-grown, free-standing crystals, growing instead on the margins of large quartz- or feldspar-encased lithiophilite units, often with other secondary phosphates rimming a single crystal unit. Submetallic violet (purpurite) or black cleavage surface reflections come from the same plane over a large area rimming and replacing lithiophilite. **Physical properties:** Dark violet-brown to bright purple (hue generally enhanced by a short acid treatment). *Luster of* heterosite dull, purpurite pearly, submetallic; *hardness* 4–4$\frac{1}{2}$; *specific gravity* 3.2–3.4; *streak* brown-black (or violet); *fracture* uneven; *cleavage* good basal and fair side pinacoid, sometimes crinkly and discontinuous. Brittle; almost opaque. **Composition:** Iron and manganese phosphates (about 53% Mn_2O_3 and Fe_2O_3, with 47.0% P_2O_5). **Tests:** None usually necessary, but both fuse easily.

Distinguishing characteristics: Purpurite is identified by its bright purple color, and by its invariable occurrence and associations with other phosphates. Heterosite is less distinctive.

Occurrence: Heterosite-purpurite is always an alteration product that forms on the surface of altered masses of triphylite-lithiophilite. It is relatively rare because its parent mineral is relatively rare, but when that mineral does form, it is a very frequent alteration. Appears to be more likely to form around the manganese phosphate, and seldom from triphylite alone.

Purpurite was first described from Kings Mountain, North Carolina, but subsequently was recognized as isomorphous with heterosite and is an abundant mineral in some of the New England pegmatites, particularly in Maine and New Hampshire. Also found in the Black Hills of South Dakota, in the Pala district in California, and abroad in Hagendorf, Germany, and Mangualde, Portugal.

Remarks: To bring out their real beauty, most specimens of purpurite require a short immersion in weak acid. Originally dark brown cleavage surfaces cleaned by the acid become pearly in luster, bright purple in hue. Such specimens are attractive, but since this is not the natural state of the mineral, purists may frown on the practice.

BERYLLONITE $NaBePO_4$ **Pl. 39**

Monoclinic — prismatic $\dfrac{2}{m}$

Environment: Pegmatite dikes. **Crystal description:** Loose, well-formed, transparent, slightly frosted and very complex crystals an inch (2–3 cm) or more across were the first found in the residue of a deeply weathered pegmatite. Subsequently found in rosettes and in larger embedded white masses with columnar cleavage in intact dikes. **Physical properties:** Colorless or white. *Luster* glassy; *hardness* $5^1/_2$–6; *specific gravity* 2.8; *fracture* conchoidal; *cleavage* good basal and several less good cleavages. Brittle; transparent to translucent. **Composition:** Sodium beryllium phosphate (19.7% BeO, 24.4% Na_2O, 55.9% P_2O_5). **Tests:** Fuses with difficulty to a cloudy glass. Wet on the charcoal with sulfuric acid, the powdered mineral boils and froths, coloring the flame yellow (sodium), succeeded later by a greenish phosphorus flame.

Distinguishing characteristics: Gemmy crystals might be confused with many minerals of pegmatites, but the low fusibility, the flame colorations, and the solubility would be very significant. More easily fusible than herderite, and neither phosphorescent nor fluorescent.

Occurrence: A rare beryllium mineral found in remarkably perfect crystals at the only good locality, a decomposed pegmatite dike on Harnden Peak, Stoneham, Maine, where the loose colorless crystals were associated with quartz, feldspar, beryl, and columbite.

Large white crystals, breaking with a vertically striated surface, have been found at Newry, Maine, in a complex pegmatite in the usual associations of cleavelandite, lithium tourmaline, and the like. In Brazil it has been found with rose quartz crystals and amblygonite at the Sapucaia pegmatite in Minas Gerais. Most recently it has been found, with at least one giant crystal, in Afghanistan.

MONAZITE (Ce,La,Y,Th)(PO$_4$)   **Pl. 38**

Monoclinic — prismatic $\dfrac{2}{m}$

Environment: Pegmatites, specks in plutonic rocks, and concentrated in heavy-sand placers. **Crystal description:** Usually in small, red-brown, embedded, opaque, flattened crystals whose skewed monoclinic symmetry is obvious. Also found in sand, in light yellow-brown, transparent, rolled grains. **Physical properties:** Yellow to reddish brown. *Luster* subadamantine to resinous; *hardness* 5–5$\frac{1}{2}$; *specific gravity* 4.9–5.3; *streak* light yellow-brown; *fracture* conchoidal to uneven; *cleavage* 1 good, several poor, with well-developed basal parting (especially in stressed embedded crystals). Brittle; transparent to translucent; strong absorption lines in the spectrum (use spectroscope). **Composition:** Phosphate of cerium, lanthanum—usually with some yttrium, a little uranium, and considerable amounts of thorium and silica (about 35% Ce$_2$O$_3$, 35% La$_2$O$_3$, and 30% P$_2$O$_5$). **Tests:** On charcoal infusible, but turns gray. After fired grain is moistened with sulfuric acid and reheated, a bluish green flash (phosphorous) can be seen around the assay.

Distinguishing characteristics: This is a potential future gem, when a locality is found. In color and occurrence, monazite resembles some zircons and some sphenes but is not fluorescent, and the crystal shape is very different. The oblique cleavages and parting make it break into splinters (red-brown fragments) that are rather characteristic. Difficult to identify in sand (use a spectroscope).

Occurrence: Monazite forms small primary grains that are disseminated through many gneisses and granites. Since it is heavy and more resistant to weathering than the rock-making minerals, it frequently persists, along with quartz and other heavy grains, in beach or river sand. Deposits of monazite-rich sands are dug and separated for the recovery of several valuable minerals. The thorium oxide content is high enough to make the monazite valuable as an ore of that substance. Once in strong demand for the manufacture of Welsbach gaslight mantles, where it still has a small role.

Commercial deposits of monazite occur in Travancore, India, in Brazil, and along the North Carolina and Florida coasts.

Monazite forms larger crystals in pegmatites, units that may be several inches (10 cm) across. Both Pomba and Divino de Uba, Minas Gerais, Brazil, and some pegmatites in northern Brazil are particularly rich in the mineral, associated with black euxenite, (with all the rare earth elements), polycrase, samarskite, and columbite (see samarskite, p. 173). Similar large brick red crystals are found in Norwegian biotite pegmatites, rich in rare earths, xenotime, fergusonite, and black mica. In the U.S. it has been found in pegmatites in Maine (Standpipe Hill), Connecticut (Norwich), Virginia (Amelia), Colorado (Boulder Co.), and New Mexico (Petaca district). Monazite sands are found from North Carolina to Florida, and in Idaho and California. Small greenish, changeable (alexandritic pinkish) crystals have been found in Llallagua, Bolivia tin mines.

Alpine crystal cavities sometimes contain small, clear, golden crystals perched on clear quartz, a type that was described under the name of turnerite. This type of monazite is widespread in France, Switzerland, and Austria.

HUREAULITE $H_2Mn_5(PO_4)_4 \cdot 4H_2O$ **Pl. 38**

Monoclinic — prismatic $\frac{2}{m}$

Environment: A secondary pegmatite phosphate, often within the confines of an altering lithiophilite crystal. **Crystal description:** Commonly in attractive pink crystals, representative of the many tertiary phosphates spawned by lithiophilite alteration. Relatively small crystals, usually subparallel bundles and sheaves of obvious monoclinic symmetry (steep slanted summits). **Physical properties:** Predominantly pink, to grayish, yellowish, or reddish brown. *Luster* glassy; *hardness* $3\frac{1}{2}$; *specific gravity* 3.2; *fracture* uneven; *cleavage* frontal, good. Brittle; translucent to almost transparent. **Composition:** Hydrous manganese (with some iron substituting for the Mn) phosphate (about 48% MnO, 38% PO_4, and 12% H_2O). **Tests:** Melts quietly, with a few bubbles, drawing into a fine spherical bead that is dull black while hot, turning red-brown to golden and shinier on cooling. Gives water in a closed tube. Succumbs reluctantly to acid: only slowly soluble in hydrochloric acid or oxalic acid, but luster dulls.
Distinguishing characteristics: Invariably associated with other secondary pegmatite phosphates, usually distinctively pink

and often in good bow-tie-type crystal clusters. Does not bubble in hydrochloric acid like rhodochrosite and lacks the rhombohedral cleavage of that mineral. There are few similar possibilities with this association.

Occurrence: The finest specimens of this very attractive phosphate have come from Hagendorf, Bavaria, where crystal sheaves to $1^1/_2$ in. (4 cm) have been found in phosphate-crystal-lined pockets. The largest crystal masses are clinkerlike, with crystal pockets, found at Mesquitela quarry, Mangualde, Portugal. Small brownish crystals deck the surfaces of openings in lithiophilite from several pegmatites in the Rio Grande do Norte-Paraíba region of Brazil.

The best American localities are the old ones of New England: Branchville, Connecticut, and the Palermo Mine, North Groton, New Hampshire. It was observed in San Diego Co., California, with other secondary phosphates in tourmaline pegmatites.

Remarks: The name comes from a locality in France, Huréaux; hence the anglicized pronunciation should be *hoo RAY o lite.*

ROSELITE $Ca_2(Co,Mg)(AsO_4)_2 \cdot 2H_2O$ **Pl. 39**

Monoclinic — prismatic $\dfrac{2}{m}$

Environment: Oxidized zone of cobalt arsenide-rich ore veins.
Crystal description: Small, ill-formed crystals and crystallized crusts. Largest crystals about $1/_4$ in. (6 mm). **Physical properties:** Depending on cobalt content, deep rose to pink. *Luster* glassy; *hardness* $3^1/_2$; *specific gravity* 3.5–3.7 (darker is heavier); *streak* pink; *fracture* uneven; *cleavage* side pinacoid and easy. Translucent to transparent. **Composition:** Hydrous calcium cobalt magnesium arsenate (CoO content variable, from 8.6 to almost 16%; CaO about 30%, MgO about 4%, As_2O_5 about 50%, and H_2O about 10%). **Tests:** Fusible with difficulty, giving arsenic fumes. Heated crystals turn blue (and remain so after cooling). Gives fine cobalt blue bead (use thoroughly roasted assay; any remaining arsenic will spoil the platinum wire).
Distinguishing characteristics: The association with cobalt ores and the rich blue-red color are sufficient to alert collectors to the possibility of finding roselite. Very cleavable foliaceous erythrite is similar in hue but makes needles or micaceous flakes; turns blue on the surface at even lesser temperatures. Sphaerocobaltite is very rare, has rhombohedral cleavage, and bubbles in warm hydrochloric acid. Contrary to

Dana, the rose hue does not return to heated crystals after cooling.

Occurrence: First found in Schneeberg, Saxony, but always in tiny crystals and very rare. Named not for its hue but for a German mineralogist, Gustav Rose (1798–1873). The complex twinning characteristic of the small crystals made it difficult to solve the structure in the days before x-rays.

Larger and more abundant crystals have been found in the upper secondary mineral levels of the two Moroccan cobalt mines, particularly at Bou Azzer, where it is commonly associated with erythrite. Since roselite is so colorful, it is popular among collectors; almost all specimens available to them come from Morocco.

A triclinic, dimorphous mineral of the same composition, very similar in appearance and superficially indistinguishable has been called beta-roselite. Examples from Morocco seem to be deep rose overgrowths bordering an isomorphous zinc arsenate. Beta-roselite is like the darker roselite examples in hue, and is essentially free of MgO. In Schneeberg it was in granular masses, with no distinct crystals. The original describers supposed both of these arsenates to be of primary hydrothermal origin, but this is not a likelihood for the Moroccan occurrence which is clearly an oxidized upper level of the mine. Free-standing crystals of beta-roselite have been found with roselite in Morocco.

PHOSPHOPHYLLITE $Zn_2(Fe,Mn)(PO_4)_2 \cdot 4H_2O$ **Pl. 39**

Monoclinic — prismatic $\frac{2}{m}$

Environment: Only three occurrences: two pegmatitic, the third in a tin vein; all probably late hydrothermal and primary. **Crystal description:** Well-developed isolated crystals, more or less equidimensional, often paired in fishtail-type contact twins. **Physical properties:** Light blue-green when clear, to gray or black (inclusions?). *Luster* glassy; *hardness* $3^{1}/_{2}$; *specific gravity* 3.1; *streak* white; *fracture* conchoidal; *cleavage* frontal and perfect. Transparent to translucent. **Composition:** Fundamentally a hydrous phosphate of zinc, with iron and manganese (ZnO about 35%, FeO about 12%, MnO about 5%, P_2O_5 about 32%, and H_2O 16%). **Tests:** Swells and exfoliates under the flame, becomes (cooled) chalky and pale yellow-brown; with continued heating finally fuses. Soluble in acids.

Distinguishing characteristics: Few minerals have this color: some apophyllites, which will only be in zeolite associations; and euclase, which is very much harder ($7^1/_2$). Environment probably the best guide. We might expect it in other vein occurrences where Zn and P_2O_5 are present, such as Zacatecas, Mexico, and Trepca, in the former Yugoslavia.

Occurrence: First found in pockets in mica masses, and in proximity to triphylite in the Hagendorf (Bavaria) pegmatite. It has not been found there lately, despite an abundance of secondary phosphates, so may be primary and not one of the triphylite-lithiophilite alteration products so well developed at that locality. Also, similarly, at the Palermo Mine in North Groton, New Hampshire.

Beautiful gemmy crystals to 4 in. (10 cm) long, mostly twinned, have been found in the Potosí (Bolivia) tin mine. Their beauty has made them important; despite great rarity, collectors vie for them. Fortunately, unlike vivianite (another Bolivian phosphate of great charm) phosphophyllite seems not to deteriorate with time.

Pronounced *fos fo FILL ite* (the name refers to its composition and ready cleavage). It seems possible that further localities will be discovered in time.

VIVIANITE $Fe_3(PO_4)_2 \cdot 8H_2O$ Pl. 39

Monoclinic — prismatic $\dfrac{2}{m}$

Environment: Late or secondary mineral in ore veins and phosphate pegmatites and in sedimentary clays as a concretion. **Crystal description:** Usually in small tabular crystals with a prominent cleavage parallel to the plates, and a conspicuous pearly luster on those faces. May be crumbly and earthy, then bright blue in color. Also forms fibrous crusts. **Physical properties:** Nearly colorless to light blue-green, indigo blue, and violet. *Luster* glassy to pearly, *hardness* $1^1/_2$–2; *specific gravity* 2.6–2.7; *streak* white, turns blue on exposure to light; *fracture* subconchoidal with striations; *cleavage* micaceous, parallel to side pinacoid. Flexible laminae; transparent to translucent; gliding plane across elongations makes bent crystals customary. **Composition:** Hydrous iron phosphate (43.0% FeO, 28.3% P_2O_5, 28.7% H_2O). **Tests:** Fuses readily to a dull black magnetic globule. Dissolved in nitric acid it makes a yellow (phosphorous test) precipitate when added to a solution of ammonium molybdate.

Distinguishing characteristics: Not likely to be confused with other minerals; its streak, bright blue color, and soft, micaceous, tabular crystals are distinctive.

Occurrence: The best specimens of vivianite are late deposits in ore veins, as in Idaho, Utah, and Colorado. Particularly fine Bolivian specimens—the crystals are several inches (10 cm) long and light blue-green in color—have been found in cavities in the tin ore veins. Good clusters have been found in Trepça, in the former Yugoslavia. Crusts of rounded tabular crystals were found in the Ibex Mine in Leadville, Colorado. In time these crystals have a tendency to darken and crack parallel to their cleavage direction. Crystals comparable to the Bolivian ones were found many years ago in Cornwall, England. Fine crystals have been found at Bingham, Utah, and Cobalt, Idaho.

Smaller and less showy crystals are often found in fossils in sedimentary rocks, as at Mullica Hill, New Jersey, where dark blue crystals line cavities formed by fossil casts in a brown sandstone. Vivianite has been found in a mammoth skull in Mexico, in a fossil tusk in Idaho, and adjacent to whale bones in Richmond, Virginia. The largest crystals ever found, yard-long (meter-long) "broadswords," were of similar origin, having been dug from a tropical swamp in Anloua, N'Gaoundéré, Cameroon. Small crystals and powdery blue coatings are found as alterations of other phosphates in pegmatites. Slender crystals often coat such minerals as triphylite; in fact, much of the blue stain in slightly altered pegmatite phosphates (triphylite) may be this mineral. In highly oxidized pegmatites, it will form bright blue spots on the black manganese oxides, which were derived through the surface weathering of the pegmatite phosphates.

Remarks: Vivianite usually is an unwise purchase for the collector, since it tends to dry out, darken, and cleave apart in time. Primary (vein) vivianite persists better than that from secondary formations.

ERYTHRITE $(Co,Ni)_3(AsO_4)_2 \cdot 8H_2O$ **Pl. 39**

Monoclinic — prismatic $\frac{2}{m}$

Environment: Secondary (weathered) portions of cobalt ore deposits. **Crystal description:** Usually forms pink earthy crusts and coatings, sometimes in slender prisms, and rarely in clusters of long flat needles. **Physical properties:** Bluish pink to deep raspberry red. *Luster* glassy to pearly; *hardness* $1\frac{1}{2}$–$2\frac{1}{2}$; *specific gravity* 2.9; *fracture* not significant; *cleavage* perfect micaceous, parallel to the side pinacoid. Laminae flexible; sectile; transparent to translucent. **Composition:** Hydrous cobalt arsenate (37.5% CoO, 38.4% As_2O_5, 24.1% H_2O, with some nickel in place of the cobalt). Actually forms a continuous series with annabergite, the nickel equivalent (see next mineral), but much more common. **Tests:** Fuses into flattened gray mass with arsenic (garlic) smell. Borax added to a fragment of this mass turns deep blue (cobalt). (Do not put on platinum wire, because of the arsenic.) Lightly heated crystal flake (on hot plate) turns blue on surface.

Distinguishing characteristics: No mineral resembles this except a rare cobalt carbonate (sphaerocobaltite, which effervesces in acid) and a rare related arsenate (roselite, p. 231). Kaemmererite, a violet-red chlorite, does not give the cobalt bead.

Occurrence: Erythrite forms as a result of the surface alteration of primary cobalt arsenides. It is known as cobalt bloom and is the most significant guide to cobalt ore. It is found almost everywhere that cobalt ores occur but rarely makes attractive specimens. Among the finest crystals are the 4-in. (10 cm) radiating blades in cavities in quartz from Schneeberg, Saxony, that were found in the early days of mining in the area. Outstanding specimens are provided by the Bou Azzer, Morocco, skutterudite occurrence, where it is associated with equally fine examples of the rare roselite pair. Solid crusts of slender interpenetrating needles have come from Queensland, Australia, and Alamos, Mexico. Found in Cobalt, Ontario, in pinkish crusts and small crystals. Good specimens are not at all common in the U.S., although erythrite "bloom" has been noted in Nevada, Idaho, Arizona, New Mexico, and California.

ANNABERGITE $(Ni,Co)_3(AsO_4)_2 \cdot 8H_2O$ **Pl. 39**

Monoclinic — prismatic $\dfrac{2}{m}$

Environment: Secondary (weathered) portion of nickel ore deposits. **Crystal description:** Usually in light green earthy crusts and films; crystals slender capillary needles, always small. **Physical properties:** Light apple green to pale pink. *Luster* silky or glassy; *hardness* $2\frac{1}{2}$–3; *specific gravity* 3.0; never solid enough to show a *fracture*; *cleavage* side pinacoid, usually not visible. Earthy; translucent. **Composition:** Hydrous nickel arsenate (35.5% NiO, 38.4% As_2O_5, and 24.1% H_2O, usually with cobalt replacing part of the Ni). See erythrite (preceding). From its ability to impart color, Co appears to dominate the Ni, and examples that are actually higher in Ni than in Co can still be pink in hue. **Tests:** Fuses, and with strong heating in reducing flame can be fused into a magnetic metallic bead. If doubt remains, the chemical test for nickel can be made: the mineral dissolved in nitric acid neutralized with ammonia (NH_4OH), and a little dimethylglyoxime solution added. Boiling makes a bright pink solution. **Distinguishing characteristics:** The green nickel color might be confused with a copper color, but the magnetic bead would prove nickel. Green minerals owing their color to chromium do not reduce to a magnetic bead under the blowpipe.

Occurrence: A rare mineral, forming near the surfaces of cobalt nickel-silver arsenide sulfide veins, usually just a greenish film, as in Cobalt, Ontario, and Saxony, Germany. Good small crystals are almost restricted to a Lavrion, Greece, occurrence, where it is known as cabrerite (from a Spanish occurrence in the Sierra Cabrera). Unlike erythrite, has never been found in really outstanding specimens. The best U.S. occurrence is in Humboldt Co., Nevada. Like erythrite, the green annabergite coating also has a prospector's name, "nickel bloom," and has served as a good guide to ore.

VARISCITE	$Al(PO_4) \cdot 2H_2O$	**Pl. 40**
STRENGITE	$Fe(PO_4) \cdot 2H_2O$	

Orthorhombic — Rhombic bipyramidal $\dfrac{2}{m} \dfrac{2}{m} \dfrac{2}{m}$

Environment: Really of two very different origins (parageneses). Variscite forms in secondary deposits near the surface in clay-rich rocks sometimes associated with other secondary phosphates. Strengite is generally a secondary phosphate of pegmatite associations. **Crystal description:** Variscite usually massive, sometimes in thin crusts of small crystals of pyramidal habit. Strengite in crystals and botryoidal crusts. **Physical properties:** Light green or emerald green (variscite); deep pink or amethyst (strengite). *Luster* porcelaneous; *hardness* $3\frac{1}{2}$–$4\frac{1}{2}$; *specific gravity* 2.2–2.8; *fracture* smooth to conchoidal; *cleavage* not obtainable as a rule. Brittle; translucent in thin splinters to transparent in crystals. **Composition:** Hydrous aluminum iron phosphates (variscite about 32.3% Al_2O_3, 44.9% P_2O_5, and 22.8% H_2O). Variscite forms an isomorphous series with strengite, the iron phosphate equivalent. **Tests:** Infusible, but most variscite specimens turn violet and brittle on light heating. Decompose, but insoluble in dilute hydrochloric acid before heating; become soluble afterward. Will then give phosphorus test with ammonium molybdate. Strengite crystals turn ocherous and cleave up on heating.

Distinguishing characteristics: The green color, acid insolubility, and lack of copper or nickel tests eliminate any minerals of those metals. Variscite resembles turquoise but is greener and contains no copper. Strengite can be distinguished from amethyst by its softness and by blowpipe reactions, and from other substances by the phosphorous test.

Occurrence: Both minerals appear to be secondary. Like turquoise, their ingredients are derived from the breakdown of minerals in the surrounding rock. Variscite may form veins, crystallized crusts, and nodular masses; the best occurrence is the rounded nodules, up to a foot (30 cm) across, that are embedded in a soft rock at Fairfield, Utah. The cores of these nodules vary in color from dark green to pale green, though the darker pieces have a tendency in time to become paler, probably through the evaporation of moisture. The nodules of this locality are framed with rims of other phosphates, minerals derived from the alteration of the variscite with some shrinkage, so that an open space is commonly found between the differently colored rims and remaining variscite. In Lucin, Utah, variscite forms in greenish veins. Both localities have produced material used in jewelry. An interesting occurrence of thin crystallized greenish crusts of variscite has been noted in Montgomery Co., Arkansas. Also found in Pontevedra, Spain, and in large masses at Pannecé (Loire-Atlantique), France, and Freiberg, Germany.

Strengite is very different in occurrence. It is found in iron mines as a late mineral, in crusts and small crystals. However, the best crystals came from altered phosphates in an old German pegmatite at Pleystein. Radiating pink rosettes and coatings of an intermediate variscite-strengite are found in a phosphate-bearing pegmatite in Rio Grande do Norte, Brazil. Good strengite or dimorphous phosphosiderite crystals have been found in altered triphylite at the Bull Moose Mine, Custer, South Dakota. Attractive microrosettes of strengite were found at Indian Mountain, Alabama, associated with a number of other phosphates.

SCORODITE   Fe(AsO$_4$)·2H$_2$O   Pl. 40

Orthorhombic — Rhombic bipyramidal $\dfrac{2}{m}\dfrac{2}{m}\dfrac{2}{m}$

Environment: Oxidized, weathered zone of ore deposits. **Crystal description:** Short-prismatic to pyramidal (octahedral-appearing) crystals, which are very typical; also banded and scoriaceous gray-green masses. **Physical properties:** Light green, greenish brown, blue, violet. *Luster* glassy to subadamantine; *hardness* 3$\frac{1}{2}$–4; *specific gravity* 3.1–3.3; *fracture* uneven; *cleavage* several poor. Brittle; transparent to translucent. **Composition:** Hydrous ferric arsenate (34.6% Fe_2O_3, 49.8% As_2O_5, 15.6% H_2O, although aluminum can replace most of the iron). **Tests:** On charcoal it gives arsenic (garlic) fumes and melts more or less readily to a gray magnetic globule. Soluble in hydrochloric acid.

Distinguishing characteristics: Its crystals resemble zircon, but scorodite is much softer and is fusible and nonfluorescent. The massive varieties resemble a number of minerals, especially fine-grained rocks that have been impregnated and stained with iron sulfate solutions from pyrite alteration, but scorodite's fusibility, fumes, and acid solubility eliminate them.

Occurrence: Scorodite is virtually always a secondary mineral, forming in the oxidized upper portions of an ore vein that contains arsenic minerals, especially arsenopyrite. It also occurs as a thin deposit from hot springs, very rarely found in primary veins, and (like vivianite) may be late primary in genesis.

Among the best crystals are some light green ones that have come from a Brazilian occurrence, near Ouro Preto in Minas Gerais, where they have reached about $3/8$ in. (1 cm) across. Small crystals have been found at several places, with other oxidized minerals: Carinthia, Austria; Cornwall, England; and Lavrion, Greece. It is common in the U.S. at Gold Hill, Utah, and was in the Tintic district; in New York at Carmel in a gray-green vein of crystalline material with arsenopyrite; and at many other localities, but nowhere in attractive specimens. There are two outstanding specimen localities. Clusters of 1-in. (2–3 cm) crystals have been found in Tsumeb, Namibia. In the Noche Buena Mine, Zacatecas, Mexico, beautifully developed, deep blue crystals are scattered on white quartz crusts. They are strongly dichroic in blue and violet and reach about 1 in. (2.5 cm) in size. Smaller blue crystals can be numbered among the great variety of Mapimi (Mexico) species.

DESCLOIZITE	$(Zn,Cu)Pb(VO_4)(OH)$	
MOTTRAMITE	$(Cu,Zn)Pb(VO_4)(OH)$	**Pl. 40**

Orthorhombic — Rhombic bipyramidal $\dfrac{2}{m}\dfrac{2}{m}\dfrac{2}{m}$

Environment: Secondary (weathered) zone of ore deposits. **Crystal description:** Usually in small to very small, transparent, yellow-brown, short spearlike blades, or in velvety black druses of microscopic crystals. Large solid crystals at one locality. Also stalactitic as mammillary crusts. **Physical proper-**

ties: Cherry red to yellow-brown, chestnut brown, green, or black. *Luster* greasy; *hardness* $3^1/_2$; *specific gravity* 5.9 (mottramite) to 6.2 (descloizite); streak yellowish orange to brownish red; *fracture* small conchoidal areas; *cleavage* none. Brittle; transparent to translucent. **Composition:** Alkaline lead, zinc-copper, vanadates of variable composition making a series (approximately 55.4% PbO, 22.7% V_2O_5, 2.2% H_2O, and about 20% divided between Cu and Zn); the Zn member is descloizite, but when copper is more abundant it is mottramite. **Tests:** Fuse readily on charcoal, boiling at first, even after flame is removed, eventually making a ball of lead surrounded by a black slag. The powder is dissolved by hydrochloric acid and makes a yellow-green solution. A piece of pure zinc added to this solution turns it blue, then violet (vanadium test).

Distinguishing characteristics: They are usually recognized by their color, crystal form, and associations, and do not greatly resemble any other mineral in their kind of associations.

Occurrence: The descloizite-mottramite series is commonly associated with wulfenite and vanadinite, in the usual secondary mineral suites from oxidized areas of ore deposits. It is especially widespread in both Arizona and New Mexico, and is commonly found crusting the rock matrix of specimens of wulfenite and vanadinite. Black velvety crusts of descloizite came from Sierra Co., New Mexico, and also from Bisbee and Tombstone, Arizona. The most remarkable occurrence known was in Otavi, Namibia, where some mammoth crystals of mottramite—over an inch (3 cm) in size, dark brown in color, and resembling sphalerite—were found, forming great crystal clusters. Unfortunately, they are not as aesthetically appealing as the small brown or green "trees" from Berg Aukas, Grootfontein, Namibia.

HERDERITE $CaBe(PO_4)(OH,F)$ **Pl. 40**

Monoclinic — prismatic $\dfrac{2}{m}$

Environment: Pegmatite dikes. **Crystal description:** Found in well-formed crystals several inches (10cm) long at best, often very complex, with many forms. Prism-zone faces commonly rounded, not really flat. Monoclinic symmetry usually visible, but sometimes symmetrically intergrown with a second crystal (twinned) so that it looks orthorhombic (Topsham, Maine). Also in rounded nodules, radiating fibrous aggregates, and scattered grains. **Physical properties:** Colorless, lilac, white, yellowish, or light bluish green. *Luster* greasy to glassy; *hardness* 5–5$^1/_2$; *specific gravity* 2.9–3.0; *fracture* sub-conchoidal; *cleavage* interrupted prismatic. Brittle; transparent to translucent; sometimes fluoresces deep blue in longwave ultraviolet light. **Composition:** Fluophosphate of beryllium and calcium (15.5% BeO, 34.8% CaO, 44.0% P_2O_5, and 5.6% H_2O—except that some of the OH is always replaced by fluorine). **Tests:** Thermoluminescent, glowing briefly with a blue-white phosphorescence on the charcoal just before becoming incandescent. After light heating (enough only to crack and slightly whiten the specimen) it is usually fluorescent in longwave ultraviolet light. Fuses with difficulty, becoming white and opaque. Dissolves slowly in acid, giving phosphorus test.

Distinguishing characteristics: The crystals are usually slightly etched and, if large enough, have a distinctive and recognizable rounded, greasy look. The fluorescence and thermoluminescence are usually obtainable.

Occurrence: Herderite was first described from some high-temperature tin veins in Germany, but it turned out to be very rare there and was later found to be fairly common in some of the New England pegmatites. Topsham, Maine, has produced a great many white and pale blue crystals, twinned so that they look something like barite. Probably some of the largest crystals are those from Stoneham, Maine, of a light yellow-brown color, slightly etched but well formed. Not uncommon at several other Maine localities, and nearby at the Fletcher Mine, Alexandria, New Hampshire, in crystals that equal the best from Maine. Small crystals have turned up in San Diego Co., California. Large crystals have been found at the Golconda Mine, and Virginia de Lapa near Governador Valadares, Minas Gerais, Brazil. Most are twinned like "fishtail" gypsum.

AMBLYGONITE   LiAl(PO_4)(F,OH)   **Pl. 38**

Triclinic — pinacoidal $\overline{1}$

Environment: Lithium-bearing pegmatite dikes. **Crystal description:** In its usual occurrence it forms medium to large embedded crystals with rough, irregular outlines. Now, however, being found in fine white and transparent crystals with numerous forms, several inches (to 20 cm) in length.

Physical properties: Colorless, yellow to white, light gray-green, lilac, or gray-blue. *Luster* glassy; *hardness* 5$^1/_2$–6; *specific gravity* 3.0–3.1; *fracture* uneven to subconchoidal; *cleavage* perfect basal, and interrupted cleavages on other planes. Brittle; transparent to translucent; often fluorescent, weakly orange in longwave ultraviolet light. **Composition:** Basic lithium aluminum fluophosphate (10.1% Li_2O, 34.5% Al_2O_3, 48.0% P_2O_5, 12.8% F, but some of the F replaces O, 5.4% of O equals F). **Tests:** Fuses easily to white porcelaneous sphere that fluoresces white in shortwave ultraviolet light. Acid on powder gives red lithium flame. Dissolves in acid to give a good phosphorus test.

Distinguishing characteristics: In pegmatites it might be confused with feldspar, from which it is easily distinguished by its fusibility. A difference in luster is apparent to the trained eye.

Occurrence: Amblygonite is a mineral of complex pegmatites and may be abundant locally, occurring in large masses embedded in quartz or feldspar. Such masses are found in Ceara, Brazil, where it almost seems to substitute for the feldspar of a dike. It is found similarly in pegmatites in Sweden, Western Australia, the Black Hills of South Dakota, California (Pala), and Maine. Although a potential source of lithium, it is not now used for that purpose to any extent. The Newry (Maine) occurrence of well-formed, colorless, and transparent to milky white crystals is apparently a late stage of pegmatite formation—later than is usually the case with this mineral. In normal occurrences the amblygonite is embedded in other minerals and is only crudely formed into crystals. Brazil appears to have at least two good occurrences in Minas Gerais, near Governador Valadares. Gemmy yellow crystals as much as 4 in. (10 cm) across characterize one source; elongated, flattened twins as much as 6 in. long, 1 in. wide, and $1/4$ in. thick (15 x 2 x 0.5 cm) come from the other locality (Mendes Pimentel).

BRAZILIANITE $NaAl_3(PO_4)_2(OH)_4$ **Pl. 41**

Monoclinic — prismatic $\dfrac{2}{m}$

Environment: A primary pegmatite phosphate. **Crystal description:** Well-developed crystals, sometimes very large. Single crystals on mica and divergent as aggregates of somewhat elongated (on the a axis) points. **Physical properties:** Yellow to greenish yellow, sometimes gemmy. *Luster* glassy; *hardness* $5^1/_2$; *specific gravity* 2.98; *streak* white; *fracture* conchoidal; *cleavage* perfect side, 1 direction. Brittle, translucent to transparent. **Composition:** Alkaline sodium aluminum phosphate (8.6% Na_2O, 42.5% Al_2O_3, 39.0% P_2O_5, and 9.9% H_2O). **Tests:** Soon turns white on heating; on charcoal it swells slightly and finally fuses on edges. Yellow hue fades while the chip is still intact and glass clear. Some white gemstones of brazilianite have been sold that owe their lack of color to mild heating, perhaps during dopping (mounting for cutting). Nonfluorescent at any time.

Distinguishing characteristics: Since brazilianite is always yellow and always crystallized, few minerals resemble it. Most of the gemmy minerals such as chrysoberyl are harder, apatite does not have its ready side cleavage, and amblygonite is usually orange fluorescent and gives a red coloration to the flame as it melts into a small white bubble on the edge of the chip. The blowpipe differentiation is very simple.

Occurrence: This was a remarkable mineral to turn up in a pegmatite so late in time. Seldom do new minerals first appear in conventional deposits in 6-in. (15 cm) gemmy and well-formed crystals. The first examples were of uncertain origin; Conselheiro Pena in Minas Gerais was reported to have been their source. It has subsequently been found in several other Minas Gerais pegmatites (Córrego Feio, Galileia; Mendes Pimentel and Gramados, Conselheiro Pena) and, strangely enough, in New Hampshire in the already well-studied Palermo Mine, North Groton, and the G. E. Smith Mine at Chandler's Mill, Newport. The early Brazilian crystals were mainly equidimensional, with a readily recognizable prism zone, but the later finds, in both Brazil and New Hampshire, have shown that an elongation parallel to the front and back axis, the a axis, is more usual.

OLIVENITE $Cu_2(AsO_4)(OH)$ **Pl. 41**

Orthorhombic — Rhombic bipyramidal $\frac{2}{m}\frac{2}{m}\frac{2}{m}$

Environment: Secondary (weathered) zone of ore deposits. **Crystal description:** Small prismatic crystals, with few faces. Also commonly in long slender prisms, and in silky crusts of slender fibers, with color bands, sometimes very pale. **Physical properties:** Pistachio green to greenish black. *Luster* adamantine or silky; *hardness* 3; *specific gravity* 3.9–4.4; *fracture* conchoidal to uneven; *cleavage* 2 indistinct. Brittle; translucent to opaque. **Composition:** Alkaline copper arsenate (56.2% CuO, 40.6% As_2O_5, 3.2% H_2O). **Tests:** After slowly melting on charcoal, it suddenly boils and volatilizes with arsenic fumes. Dissolves readily in nitric acid with the typical copper blue-green, becoming intense blue when ammonia is added.

Distinguishing characteristics: Can be separated from similar-appearing sulfates and phosphates by the arsenic (garlicky) smell and unusual behavior on the charcoal. It can be proved to contain copper by the chemical color tests. Resembles several other green minerals—like epidote, which has identical coloration—but none of these is so fusible or so easily tested for copper.

Occurrence: A descriptively named but rather rare secondary mineral that forms in the upper zone of copper deposits, where it is associated with malachite, azurite, cerussite, and cuprite, and often coats limonite. Once found on mine dumps in some quantity in Cornwall, England, in crusts of vertical needles, but color-banded in various tints (deepest near the top) that gave it the local name "wood-copper." Good specimens of stubby crystals have been found at Tsumeb, Namibia. In the U.S. good crystals were once found in the old Arizona copper mines; particularly good examples of both crystallized and "wood-copper" olivenite at Tintic, Utah.

LIBETHENITE $Cu_2(OH)PO_4$ **Pl. 41**

Orthorhombic — Rhombic bipyramidal $\dfrac{2}{m}\dfrac{2}{m}\dfrac{2}{m}$

Environment: Secondary (weathered) zone of copper ore deposits. **Crystal description:** Crystals common, solid layers (druses) of usually short-prismatic crystals, diamond-shaped in cross section. Also in globular crusts. **Physical properties:** Dark olive green. *Luster* resinous; *hardness* 4; *specific gravity* 3.6–3.8; *fracture* subconchoidal to uneven; *cleavage* 2 good. Brittle; translucent. **Composition:** An alkaline copper phosphate (66.4% CuO, 29.8% P_2O_5, 3.8% H_2O). **Tests:** Fuses easily with boiling, eventually drawing into black spherical bead. Gives copper and phosphorus tests in solutions. **Distinguishing characteristics:** Distinguished from malachite by lack of effervescence in acid; from brochantite and olivenite by the phosphorus test; and from other green minerals by the fusibility and solubility. There are, however, a number of other related minerals with similar associations, too rare to list here, with which it might be confused. They require further tests for certain identification.

Occurrence: Libethenite, like olivenite, brochantite, and malachite—all of which are likely associations—is one of the secondary minerals formed in the alteration through weathering of sulfide ore minerals. Usually best developed where weathering is deep and concentrations high.

Originally found with many of the normally associated minerals at Libethen, Romania (now Lubetová, Czechoslovakia), where it formed typical crystals. Those of Cornwall formed in similar associations. The best U.S. occurrence of this group of minerals has been in the Tintic region (Utah) and occasionally in Arizona and Nevada.

ADAMITE $Zn_2(AsO_4)(OH)$ **Pl. 41**

Orthorhombic — Rhombic bipyramidal $\frac{2}{m}\frac{2}{m}\frac{2}{m}$

Environment: Secondary (weathered) zone of ore deposits. **Crystal description:** Drusy crusts of short-prismatic or horizontally elongated crystals. **Physical properties:** Light yellow, greenish, rose, or violet. *Luster* glassy; *hardness* $3\frac{1}{2}$; *specific gravity* 4.3–4.4; *fracture* uneven; *cleavage* domal. Brittle; transparent to translucent; often brilliantly fluorescent yellow-green. **Composition:** Alkaline zinc arsenate (56.7% ZnO, 40.2% As_2O_5, 3.1% H_2O). **Tests:** Fuses reluctantly, with slight decrepitation. Loses fluorescence on first heating, as it whitens and becomes opaque. Slight arsenic (garlic) smell. Becomes less fusible as water bubbles away. Green zinc color appears after cobalt nitrate drop on fusion is heated.

Distinguishing characteristics: The light yellow to white varieties (free of copper, which "poisons" fluorescence) can be identified by their brilliant fluorescence. Nonfluorescent green crusts can be distinguished from smithsonite by the lack of carbon dioxide bubbles on solution in hydrochloric acid. The cobalt nitrate test shows zinc. **Occurrence:** A secondary mineral found in the oxidized portion of metal ore veins at a few localities. The pink and green colorations are caused by cobalt and copper impurities, and both are found at Cap Garonne, France. Fine fluorescent specimens have long been known from the ancient mines at Lavrion, Greece, which also yield attractive copper-green specimens. Similar specimens may be collected at Gold Hill, Utah, and magnificent yellow fluorescent specimens in considerable abundance at the Ojuela Mine, Mapimí, Durango, Mexico. At all these localities, except Cap Garonne, the crystals line cavities in limonite. In Mexico, where it assumes an infinite variety of hues from white to brick red, yellow-green, blue-green, and violet, it is associated with hemimorphite; austinite $CaZn(AsO_4)(OH)$; rare legrandite $Zn_2(AsO_4)(OH) \cdot H_2O$ in elongated yellow straws and sprays; still rarer triclinic dimorphous paradamite, $Zn_2(AsO_4)(OH)$; and with aurichalcite, wulfenite, and mimetite.

AUGELITE $Al_2(PO_4) \cdot (OH)_3$ **Pl. 41**

Monoclinic — prismatic $\dfrac{2}{m}$

Environment: Hydrothermal deposits; a late mineral. **Crystal description:** Microscopic tabular crystals in most occurrences; in one occurrence transparent and colorless, up to an inch (2.5 cm) across, and about equidimensional. **Physical properties:** Colorless to white, yellowish, or rose. *Luster* glassy; *hardness* $4\frac{1}{2}$–5; *specific gravity* 2.7; *fracture* conchoidal; *cleavage* 2 good. Brittle; transparent to translucent. **Composition:** Basic aluminum phosphate (51.0% Al_2O_3, 35.5% P_2O_5, 13.5% H_2O). **Tests:** Swells and whitens, retaining angular shape under blowpipe. Cobalt nitrate drop added to mass gives good blue color on second firing. Can be dissolved in acid after sodium carbonate fusion, to give chemical phosphorus test.

Distinguishing characteristics: It would be difficult for the amateur to recognize the small crystals, since any colorless substance resembles many minerals; tests above are significant. **Occurrence:** Originally described from a Swedish occurrence where it forms no crystals. Later it was recognized as a scattering of small crystals on ore minerals in tin mines at Oruro and near Potosí, Bolivia. Became interesting when found as large (over 1 in.; 2.5 cm), well-formed, transparent, gemmy crystals at White Mountain, California, associated with other phosphates in a metamorphic andalusite deposit, and in New Hampshire pegmatites at North Groton and Newport (G.E. Smith Mine, Chandler's Mill). Most recently in Canada in the Yukon Territory (Rapid Creek) with lazulite and other phosphates.

DUFRENITE $Fe_5(PO_4)_3(OH)_5 \cdot 2H_2O$ **Pl. 40**

Monoclinic — prismatic $\dfrac{2}{m}$

Environment: Weathered ore deposits; with pegmatite phosphates; and limonite formations. **Crystal description:** Most commonly as dull green powdery films coating other minerals. Sometimes in rounded nodules or crusts with a fibrous radiating structure. **Physical properties:** Dull olive green to green-black. *Luster* earthy (pulverulent) to silky; *hardness* $3\frac{1}{2}$–$4\frac{1}{2}$; *specific gravity* 3.2–3.4; streak yellow-green; no *fracture* visible as a rule; *cleavage* side and front pinacoid. Brittle to earthy; translucent. **Composition:** Alkaline hydrous iron phosphate (57.1% Fe_2O_3 and FeO, 31.1% P_2O_5, 11.8% H_2O). Related species of very similar composition have been named rockbridgeite and frondelite. **Tests:** Turns brown, then fuses with a little difficulty to a dull black, slightly magnetic bead. As glowing bead cools, a new wave of light passes over it, caused by heat release with crystallization, and a dimple forms simultaneously on the surface.

Distinguishing characteristics: The green-yellow film might resemble greenockite; the best test is to make the phosphorus test of dropping a few drops of the acid solution into ammonium molybdate, producing the yellow precipitate that indicates phosphorous. The radiating spheres resemble several phosphates, but none that would become magnetic under the blowpipe.

Occurrence: Usually found as a thin, dull green film on other minerals, especially in iron mines and sometimes in pegmatites. Also (the best specimens) in thick, botryoidal, black fibrous crusts without any crystal faces. Good specimens are uncommon. Most old dufrenite specimens are actually now called frondelite or rockbridgeite; the distinction of manganiferous varieties would be difficult without the tests available to specialists. Rockbridgeite forms rich masses at Midvale, Rockbridge Co., Virginia, and in Sevier Co., Arkansas. It fills geodes in a sandstone at Greenbelt, Maryland. Often found associated with primary phosphates in pegmatites, as at the old and new Palermo Mine in North Groton, New Hampshire, in radiating rosettes associated with other phosphates. Crusts of appreciable thickness coat fresh, colorless rhombohedral whitlockite (a calcium magnesium phosphate). Also found in Cornwall, England, and Westphalia, Germany. Fine solid crusts have been found at Hagendorf, Bavaria, with other secondary pegmatite phosphates.

PHOSPHURANYLITE $(UO_2)(PO_4)_2 \cdot 6H_2O$

Orthorhombic — Rhombic bipyramidal $\frac{2}{m}\frac{2}{m}\frac{2}{m}$

Environment: Secondary mineral of uranium-bearing rocks. **Crystal description:** Forms crusts of thin tabular crystals of microscopic dimensions. **Physical properties:** Straw to golden yellow. *Luster* glassy; *hardness* soft; *specific gravity* undetermined; *fracture* undeterminable; *cleavage* basal. Brittle; transparent; not fluorescent. **Composition:** Basic hydrous calcium uranium phosphate of uncertain composition. **Tests:** Blackens, but not easily fusible. Makes fluorescent bead with sodium fluoride. Readily soluble in nitric acid, drying to leave fluorescent residue. The nitric acid solution dropped into solution of ammonium molybdate forms a yellow (phosphorous test) precipitate.

Distinguishing characteristics: This is one of a dozen similar minerals that form yellow, nonfluorescent or weakly fluorescent crusts and are difficult to determine accurately. Absence of vanadium is shown by failure of flake to turn red in the acid. Usually associated with autunite, a highly fluorescent mineral making the uranium content of such crusts at once apparent.

Occurrence: Considered rare but probably a very common mineral, forming nonfluorescent yellow films on seams in rocks containing radioactive minerals. Originally described from Spruce Pine, North Carolina. Since then it has been found in Spain, Zaïre, Bavaria (Wölsendorf), Brazil (Rio Grande do Norte), and in New Hampshire at the Ruggles Mine, Grafton, and the Palermo Mine, North Groton.

APATITE $Ca_5(Cl,F)(PO_4)_3$ **Pl. 42**

Hexagonal — Hexagonal bipyramidal $\dfrac{6}{m}$

Environment: Plutonic rocks, pegmatite dikes, ore veins, bedded sedimentary deposits. **Crystal description:** Often crystallized, with considerable variation in crystal habit: long-prismatic, short-prismatic, to tabular. Also in botryoidal crusts and in great massive beds. **Physical properties:** Colorless, white, brown, green, violet, blue, or yellow. *Luster* glassy; *hardness* 5; *specific gravity* 3.1–3.2; *fracture* conchoidal; *cleavage* inconspicuous basal and prism. Brittle; transparent to translucent; sometimes fluorescent yellow-orange (manganapatite—to 10.5% Mn replacing Ca), and thermoluminescent blue-white; usually becomes fluorescent orange (longwave ultraviolet light) after strong heating. **Composition:** Calcium fluophosphate or calcium chlorophosphate, or an intermediate (about 54.5% Ca, 41.5% P_2O_5, and about 4% F and Cl). There is so large a range of composition in the various apatites that they are labeled a group by some authorities. However, the examples usually called apatite are relatively constant in appearance and associations, and the mere fact that some vanadates, arsenates, or metallic phosphates have a like structure does not make them apatites. Ordinary apatite is not isomorphous with the far-afield species such as pyromorphite and mimetite. **Tests:** Does not fuse, but chip held in the Bunsen burner flame melts on the edges, coloring the flame reddish yellow (calcium). Crushed and moistened with sulfuric acid gives green-white flame (phosphorus). Soluble in acids; fluorescent after heating (if not already so).

Distinguishing characteristics: Crystals resemble beryl but can be distinguished by the hardness. Manganapatite resembles green tourmaline, but also is softer than that mineral, and is usually fluorescent. Herderite and beryllonite fuse.

Occurrence: Apatite is a common minor constituent of rocks, and is the source of the phosphorus required by plants. Specimens come from crystallized concentrations in pegmatites, in some ore veins, and in the form of the occasional rich masses of igneous segregations. Green manganapatite is a common mineral of the early stages of mineral formation in pegmatites; it occurs embedded in feldspar and quartz. Colorful short-prismatic and tabular apatite crystals form in cavities in cleavelandite in the late replacement phases of complex pegmatite formation. Apatite also forms good crystals in some ore veins, such as the violet crystals in the Ehrenfriedersdorf tin veins in Germany, and the gemmy yellow crystals associated with the Durango iron deposits, Mexico. Among the most abundant crystals are the yellow ones from Durango, Mexico, which can be 3 in. long (8 cm) and are often gemmy. Giant crystals of this type have been found near Copiapó, Chile, and in Brazil. The colorless, brilliant plates in the Austrian Tyrol reflect an alpine assemblage.

Entirely different in occurrence are the indigo blue apatites of Campo Formosa, Bahia, Brazil, and the large brown and green corroded crystals found in Ontario, embedded in flesh-colored calcite. These crystals are to 18 in. (40 cm) or more in length and may be several inches deep. Clear, gemmy, violet crystals to 1 in. (2.5 cm) across have been collected in some New England pegmatites, especially at Mt. Apatite, Maine. Granular beds of apatite that can be mined for fertilizer use are found in the Russian Kola Peninsula, and in Brazil. The apatites of Panasqueira, Portugal, are among the most attractive ones of open pockets. Bolivia yields fine colorless to violet crystals.

Remarks: Bone has essentially an apatite composition and structure. Apatite has an interesting crystal symmetry often revealed in the smaller, shiny crystals by faces to the right or left of the horizontal axis unpaired with a corresponding face on the other side. These are known as third-order faces.

PYROMORPHITE $Pb_5(PO_4,AsO_4)_3Cl$ **Pl. 42**

Hexagonal — Hexagonal bipyramidal $\dfrac{6}{m}$

Environment: Secondary (weathered) zone of lead ore deposits.
Crystal description: Short hexagonal prisms up to $\frac{1}{2}$ in. (1 cm) across and twice as long. However, coarse crystals are nearly always cavernous; good terminations will be found only

on slender needles. **Physical properties:** Dark green, yellow-green, light gray, brown. *Luster* resinous; *hardness* $3^1/_2$–4; *specific gravity* 6.5–7.1; *fracture* subconchoidal to uneven; *cleavage* prismatic. Brittle; translucent. **Composition:** Lead chlorophosphate (81.2% PbO, 2.5% Cl, 16.3% P_2O_5, but the phosphorus is usually replaced in part by arsenic, which grades into mimetite (see below). **Tests:** Fuses easily on charcoal to a globule, which on cooling assumes an angular shape with shiny faces, like a crystal.

Distinguishing characteristics: The cavernous crystals and color are very characteristic. They can be confused only with others of the same group, and are distinguished from mimetite and vanadinite by the blowpipe test.

Occurrence: A secondary mineral forming in oxidized lead deposits, the phosphorus presumably coming from the apatite of neighboring rocks. Not common, and for this reason not an important ore of lead. Good brown crystals were found in Germany; some had been altered back to galena in pseudomorphs. Fine specimens have come from Phoenixville, Pennsylvania (which in the 19th century was one of the world's best localities, yielding fine crusts of large green crystals), and Davidson Co., North Carolina, which produced thinner crusts of small yellow-green crystals. Not abundant in the West except in the Coeur D'Alene district of Idaho, since it does not appear to be (in spite of what one might expect) a compound best developed by desert climates. Some of the finest ever found came from El Horcajo, central Spain.

Remarks: The name means "fire form" in Greek, and refers to the unique behavior of a grain under the blowpipe. Compare with cerussite (p. 193). Green crystals are invariably characteristic of more highly altered ore levels, and limonite is generally visible in the matrix. White to brown crystals can actually grow on galena, far below an oxidation level that would result in the development of limonite.

MIMETITE $Pb_5(AsO_4,PO_4)_3Cl$ **Pl. 42**

Hexagonal — Hexagonal bipyramidal $\dfrac{6}{m}$

Environment: Secondary (weathered) zone of lead ore deposits.
Crystal description: Slender to thick needles, sometimes in yellowish mammillary crusts. Orange-yellow rounded crystals (melon-shaped) called campylite. **Physical properties:** White, yellow, yellow-orange to brown. *Luster* resinous; *hardness* $3^1/_2$; *specific gravity* 7.0–7.3; *fracture* uneven; *cleavage* pyramidal. Brittle; transparent to translucent. **Composition:** Lead

chloroarsenate (74.6% PbO, 23.2% As_2O 2.4% Cl). **Tests:** Fuses readily on charcoal; suddenly boils, giving off arsenic fumes (garlic odor), and reduces to a lead bead.

Distinguishing characteristics: Appearance, associations, and occurrence show it to be a member of this group. Distinguished from pyromorphite and vanadinite by arsenic smell.

Occurrence: Like pyromorphite and vanadinite, mimetite is a secondary mineral. It is rather rare, being far less common than the other two, and only occasionally is it of importance as an ore of lead. Best distributed in collections are the old campylite specimens. Campylite occurs in small (to $3/8$ in.; 1 cm) crystals at several British localities. Mimetite is rare in the U.S. Most frequent occurrence is across the border in Durango, Mexico, where it formed orange-yellow botryoidal coatings of great charm at San Pedro Corralitos. Brilliant orange blobs illuminate thin yellow wulfenites at Cerro Prieto, Sonora, Mexico, and at the Rowley and 79 Mines in Theba and Hayden, Arizona. It has been found at Eureka, Utah. The best and largest isolated crystals of former times were found in the old mine visited by Goethe at Johanngeorgenstadt, Saxony. Remarkable, gemmy, pale yellow, beautifully terminated 2-in. (4–5 cm) crystals have lately been found at Tsumeb, Namibia, and provide what is probably the all-time great for this mineral.

VANADINITE $Pb_5(VO_4)_3Cl$ **Pl. 42**

Hexagonal — Hexagonal bipyramidal $\dfrac{6}{m}$

Environment: Secondary (weathered) zone of lead ore deposits.

Crystal description: Small 6-sided prisms, and often in larger crystals in built-up masses that are cavernous in the center. Pyramidal terminations only on slender crystals. **Physical properties:** Bright red-brown-orange to yellow-brown, or brown. *Luster* resinous; *hardness* $2^3/4$–3; *specific gravity* 6.7–7.1; *fracture* uneven; *cleavage* none. Brittle; transparent to translucent. **Composition:** Lead chlorovanadate (78.7% PbO, 19.4% V_2O_5, 2.5% Cl; As sometimes substitutes for the V; a 1:1 ratio of V to As is known as endlichite). **Tests:** Fuses to a black mass with a shiny, slightly angular surface. After continued blowing, little beads of lead eventually appear (like the yolk in a frying egg) and the slag slowly goes away.

Distinguishing characteristics: Separated from pyromorphite and mimetite by its blowpipe reactions.

Occurrence: A secondary mineral forming in desert country as a result of the alteration, by weathering, of lead ores. Associated with descloizite, wulfenite, cerussite, and other secondary ore minerals. A unique occurrence of very large crystals completely coated with descloizite was found in Namibia. There are numerous U.S. localities in Arizona and New Mexico, among which the bright orange-red crystals from the old Yuma Mine near Tucson, Arizona, are especially well known. The orange skeletal crystals from Stein's Pass, New Mexico, are also popular. The clear, light yellow arsenic variety called endlichite is found at Hillsboro and Lake Valley, New Mexico. Flat, bright orange, hexagonal, platy crystals characterize the Mibladen, Morocco, occurrence, which seems to be about the best for this mineral.

Remarks: Though apparently abundant, vanadinite did not prove to be rich enough in any southwestern occurrence to be workable as an ore during World War II, when vanadium was much sought after. Since bright mahogany red crystals have a tendency to darken and dull on prolonged exposure to light, museum displays may be disappointing.

LAZULITE $(Mg,Fe)Al_2(PO_4)_2(OH)$ **Pl. 42**
SCORZALITE $(Fe,Mg)Al_2(PO_4)_2(OH)_2$

Monoclinic — prismatic $\dfrac{2}{m}$

Environment: Pegmatite dikes, metamorphic rocks, and quartz veins in metamorphics. **Crystal description:** Good crystals uncommon; when found, they are wedge-shaped and embedded as a rule. Also in small solid masses without external crystal forms. **Physical properties:** Bright blue to dark blue (scorzalite). *Luster* glassy; *hardness* $5\frac{1}{2}$–6; *specific gravity* 3.1–3.4; *fracture* uneven; *cleavage* poor prismatic. Brittle; transparent to translucent. **Composition:** These two comprise an isomorphous series from an alkaline high-magnesium phosphate (lazulite) to a high-iron phosphate (scorzalite); (about 32% Al_2O_3, 45% P_2O_5, and 5.5% H_2O, with the remainder divided between MgO and FeO). **Tests:** Only slowly soluble in hot acids. In the blowpipe flame they turn white to dark brown (depending on iron content), crack open, swell up, and the pieces blow away.

Distinguishing characteristics: The light to deep blue color is rather distinctive. Blue vesuvianite fuses readily to a glass, sodalite and lazurite whiten and fuse with some difficulty to a glass, blue spinels are infusible. The copper-blue minerals are readily soluble in acid and easily fused.

Occurrence: Lazulite and scorzalite are high-temperature hydrothermal minerals of limited occurrence. Crystals have been found at very few localities. In Zermatt, Switzerland, and in w. Austria, lazulite forms good blue crystals with shiny faces in quartz veins. In Brazil it forms rich masses in veins cutting the sandstone near Diamantina. The very dark blue high-iron variety, scorzalite, from a phosphate-bearing pegmatite in e. Minas Gerais, is a recent breakdown from a series once lumped as lazulite, a mineral of variable composition. A few truly gemmy bits of the lazulite type have been found in Minas Gerais pegmatite detritus. They are strongly pleochroic: when turned, they change from yellowish to nearly colorless to sapphire blue. The largest is about hazelnut size.

In the U.S. it forms in nodules in a vein near Death Valley, California, which cuts a light-colored schist. Scattered grains may be found in a phosphate-rich pegmatite at North Groton, New Hampshire. The best U.S. crystals are the slightly sandy ones, often slightly altered on the surface, which are found embedded in a quartzite at Graves Mountain, Georgia, associated with rutile and kyanite. There is a similar formation, with the same paragenesis, near Copiapó, Chile. In a remarkable find, crusts of 1-in. (2.5 cm) deep blue crystals have been collected from phosphate-rich veins in the Yukon Territory, Canada. Associated minerals are wardite, brazilianite, and siderite, on quartz.

LIROCONITE $Cu_2Al(AsO_4)(OH)_4 \cdot 4H_2O$ **Pl. 43**

Monoclinic — prismatic $\dfrac{2}{m}$

Environment: Secondary mineralized zone of copper arsenide deposits. **Crystal description:** Usually individually crystallized, occasional crusts with crystals on edge. Isolated single crystals are pseudotetragonal bipyramids, though the faces present are actually 4 prism faces and 4 clinodomes (inclined only 1°27'). In specimens the crystals are usually attached on one side and give the impression of 4-faced low pyramids. The largest known crystal (Truro Museum, Cornwall) is about $^3/_4$ in. (almost 2 cm); most are only about $^1/_4$ in. (0.5 cm). **Physical properties:** Rich sky blue to slightly greenish blue. *Luster* glassy; *hardness* 2–2$^1/_2$; *specific gravity* 3.0; streak pale blue (giving it its name from the Greek for "pale powder"); *fracture* uneven; *cleavage* 2, poor, paralleling the usual faces. Brittle; translucent. **Composition:** Hydrated alkaline copper aluminum arsenate (CuO about 37%, Al_2O_3 11%, As_2O_5 [plus P_2O_5] 27%, and H_2O 25%). **Tests:** In the blowpipe it turns deep blue, then blackens, fusing to a black bead. Soluble in acid.

Distinguishing characteristics: No testing needed as a rule; the color, crystals, and specimen's character usually suffice. The few other similarly hued minerals have entirely different associations. Crystals are very distinctive and localities few.

Occurrence: From a practical standpoint, liroconite (pronounced with emphasis on *roc*), is an English (Cornwall) mineral, for it was found there in good specimens at three different mines and, so far, nowhere else as more than a few small crystals. The Cerro Gordo Mine, Inyo Co., California, is said to have yielded some liroconite, associated with caledonite and linarite. Wheal Gorland, Gwennap, is most often listed as a source. Microscopic crystals have been reported from Germany, Czechoslovakia, and Russia. No specimens have been found recently, though any surrounding Gwennap dumps might still yield a few. Collectors, who greatly admire the mineral, have to content themselves with the old-timers gleaned from private collections and museum duplicates.

CHILDRENITE $(Fe,Mn)Al(PO_4)(OH)_2 \cdot H_2O$ **Pl. 43**
EOSPHORITE $(Mn,Fe)Al(PO_4)(OH)_2 \cdot H_2O$

Orthorhombic — bipyramidal $\frac{2}{m}\frac{2}{m}\frac{2}{m}$

Environment: Late-mineral ore veins and a pegmatite phosphate (probably primary). **Crystal description:** Two completely distinct types; one consisting of large, pink, well-formed (though usually corroded or altered) crystals; the other sheaves of subparallel crystals and radiating sprays of the bundles, with rough, very dark terminations. Vein crystals sharper, but usually small and dark. **Physical properties:** Salmon pink, light to dark brown, gray, and almost black. *Luster* glassy (to pearly on the front face of the brown bundles); *hardness* $4\frac{1}{2}$; *specific gravity* 3.06–3.25; *fracture* conchoidal; *cleavage* front and side pinacoid. Brittle; translucent to transparent. **Composition:** Hydrous alkaline iron and manganese aluminum phosphate, forming an isomorphous series (MnO-FeO 31%, Al_2O 22%, P_2O_5 31%, and H_2O 16%). In my experience, though they form an isomorphous series, the pegmatite occurrences are wholly unlike the small crystals in the ore veins, and the large pink eosphorites bear little superficial resemblance to the much more frequent dark brown ones. **Tests:** On heating, both types swell and lose weight and are easily crushed to powder. Brown material turns black and becomes magnetic. Pink variety turns buff color and is but weakly magnetic.

Distinguishing characteristics: The brown sprays are distinctive in a pegmatite environment, though they resemble some stilbites in appearance. The pink crystals resemble nothing else in such an environment but hureaulite, which fuses easily into an orange-brown sphere.

Occurrence: This series has come due for restudy since the discovery of unique large salmon pink (but corroded, or even altered completely to limonite) crystals in Minas Gerais, Brazil. Brown sprays—like some from Branchville, Connecticut, and several of the New Hampshire and Maine pegmatites—contain more iron. Perhaps the proper name for the browner material should be childrenite rather than the eosphorite it has always been called. The Brazilian rose quartz crystal locality, Taquaral, has fine sprays of the brown crystals, some even on the rose quartz itself. They seem fresher, later, and perhaps more of a secondary mineral than the larger corroded pink crystals. On simple inspection one would not suspect the two types to belong to the same species, for they seem so very different. Bolivian childrenite crystal crusts are made up of very small individual crystals and are dark gray. Childrenite from Cornwall occurs as sparsely scattered, small, bright brown, rather equidimensional crystals. With so tremendous a habit variation in this series—almost too unlike for members of one series—it seems difficult to believe that they are truly completely isomorphous.

The brown crystals and sprays of Taquaral can be $1\frac{1}{4}$ in. (about 3 cm) long, whereas the pink crystals are as much as 2–$2\frac{1}{2}$ in. (5–7.5 cm) long and $\frac{1}{2}$ in. (1 cm) across.

WARDITE $NaAl_3(PO_4)_2(OH)_4 \cdot 2H_2O$ **Pl. 43**
Tetragonal — Tetragonal pyramidal   4

Environment: Fairly uncommon secondary mineral with aluminum phosphates. Rare late mineral in pegmatite dikes. **Crystal description:** Small, light blue-green bipyramidal crystals in phosphate nodules or white coarser crystals and crusts; also granular masses. **Physical properties:** Bluish green to white. *Luster* glassy; *hardness* 5; *specific gravity* 2.8–2.9; *fracture* conchoidal; *cleavage* good basal. Brittle; translucent to transparent. **Composition:** Hydrous alkaline sodium calcium aluminum phosphate (7.6% Na_2O 3.4%, CaO 37.5%, Al_2O_3 34.8%, P_2O_5 16.6%). **Tests:** Before the blowpipe it whitens and swells. Cobalt nitrate drop gives, after refiring, the blue aluminum test. Chemical tests show phosphorus.

Distinguishing characteristics: The appearance and occurrence at the principal American locality are unique, but the white, pseudo-octahedral crystals of the infrequent pegmatitic occurrences look like several other minerals, and would be difficult for the amateur to recognize when crystals are not present.

Occurrence: Wardite in its best-known American occurrence forms a blue-green innermost mineral border around altering variscite cores in the nodules from Fairfield, Utah. Striated white $3/8$-in. (7 mm) crystals have lately been found in lazulite veins in Canada (Yukon Territory). It was first described from a French pegmatite occurrence at Montebras as a secondary mineral under another name, soumansite, when it was not recognized as the same substance. Also found in a New Hampshire pegmatite at Beryl Mountain, South Acworth, and in a German pegmatite in $1/4$-in. (5 mm) unimpressive white tetragonal bipyramids. Larger crystals of like hue were found on feldspar and on the rose quartz crystals at the Mina de Ilha, Taquaral, Minas Gerais, Brazil.

Remarks: Named for Professor Henry A. Ward, the founder of Ward's Natural Science Establishment.

TURQUOISE $CuAl_6(PO_4)_4(OH)_8 \cdot 4H_2O$ **Pl. 43**

Triclinic — pinacoidal $\overline{1}$

Environment: A secondary near-surface mineral, forming veins in weathering copper and alumina-rich rocks of desert regions. **Crystal description:** Usually in fine-grained solid veins. Crystals very rare and tiny, until recently believed unique to a quartz-veined schist surface in Virginia, where they formed thin crusts and small rosettes of microscopic short-prismatic crystals. Now also found in one or two localities in the West. **Physical properties:** Sky blue to light greenish blue. *Luster* porcelaneous; *hardness* 5-6, *specific gravity* 2.6-2.8, *streak* white; *fracture* smooth. Brittle; translucent on thin edges, crystals transparent. **Composition:** Hydrous alkaline aluminum phosphate plus copper (about 9.8% CuO, 37.6% Al_2O_3, 34.9% P_2O_5, 17.7% H_2O). **Tests:** Decrepitates (flies to pieces) violently and will not stay on the charcoal. In closed tube, turning brown, it also flies to pieces. Gives chemical phosphorus and copper tests.

Distinguishing characteristics: Not likely to be confused with many other minerals. Turquoise can be distinguished from more glassy chrysocolla by the phosphorus test, from fine grained quartz (with copper stain) by its solubility in acid, and from similar, but green, variscite by the color shift with heat. Hard to tell from prosopite and ceruleite without a phosphorus test.

Occurrence: Turquoise veinlets and masses appear to be almost invariably products of arid climates. It is commonly found where copper-bearing formations have been deeply altered, usually filling veins in shattered igneous rocks. Its phosphorus probably came from apatite in the fresh rock, the alumina from the feldspar, and the copper from chalcopyrite grains.

New Mexico, Nevada, and Colorado are all important turquoise states. More expensive turquoise comes from Iran and Tibet, where the matrix often is black. The American matrix is commonly brown to white. Large veins have been found in Chuquicamata, Chile.

At the crystallized occurrence in Virginia, the turquoise is not in solid veins but forms druses of small crystals on a schist in a copper mining prospect. The tiny pointed crystals are light blue to greenish blue, and scattered singly or in clusters over the surface of seams, the more spectacular crystals coating white quartz. The new western finds seem identical in nature and in size.

Remarks: Iron-stained fossil bones called "bone turquoise" or odontolite have often been confused with and sometimes used in the same way as true turquoise. Can be distinguished by testing for copper, which is absent in fossil bone.

WAVELLITE $Al_3(OH)_3(PO_4)_2 \cdot 5H_2O$ **Pl. 43**

Orthorhombic-rhombic bipyramidal $\frac{2}{m} \frac{2}{m} \frac{2}{m}$

Environment: Late low-temperature mineral in hydrothermal veins. **Crystal description:** Usually in crusted assemblages of stars of needle-like crystals, late fillings of what would be hemispheres, were the fissure wide enough. Also in half-greenish domes with crystalline surfaces. Can be knobby coatings, late overgrowths on other minerals in mesothermal ore veins, with poorly defined crystals. More often in spherulitic masses with a radiating structure, sometimes filling a seam surface with stellate discs when the fissure is split open and — if thick enough — yellowish or greenish. **Physical properties:** White to gray, yellow, green, brown, or black. *Luster* glassy to silky; *hardness* $3\frac{1}{2}$–4; *specific gravity*

2.4; *fracture* uneven to subconchoidal or splinters; *cleavage* basal so that it exposes depths of the dome, and side pinacoid. Brittle; transparent to translucent. **Composition:** Hydrous alkaline aluminum phosphate (37.1% Al_2O_3, 34.5% P_2O_5, 28.4% H_2O) **Tests:** The fine fibers glow whitely and exfoliate. A needle bundle can be kept intact by gently heating only the one end. Touched with cobalt nitrate and refired, it gives the blue aluminum test. A chemical test will show phosphorus.

Distinguishing characteristics: Except for one occurrence, not a striking mineral and one that could be confused with several others. The two tests given above are very useful for minerals answering this general description. A botryoidal crust may resemble chalcedony, but wavellite is softer and slowly soluble in acid.

Occurrence: Wavellite is a late mineral when on the surface of hydrothermal veins, usually encrusting earlier crystals. Seams can be scattered through somewhat fragmented sedimentary formations like sandy gray limestones. The most attractive U.S. examples are the approximately 1-in. (2–3 cm) radiating spherules of a yellow-green color found in veins in a gray rock in the area of Dug Hill, Avant, Garland Co., Arkansas. Small crystal faces may be seen truncating the radiating crystals that build the spheres. Considerable quantities of a pale, botryoidal, compact wavellite have been found at Llallagua, Bolivia, where it forms overgrowths on the earlier (and more attractive) vein minerals of the tin mines. Black shale surfaces are coated with greenish sunbursts at Ronneburg, Germany. Arkansas-like hemispherical balls, many coated with variscite crystals, have been found at Pannece (Loire-Atlantique), France.

TORBERNITE $Cu(UO_2)(PO_4)_2 \cdot 8-12(H_2O)$ **Pl. 44**

Tetragonal — Ditetragonal bipyramidal $\frac{4}{m} \frac{2}{m} \frac{2}{m}$

Environment: A secondary mineral on seams in granite and pegmatites. **Crystal description:** Usually in thin square plates, sometimes in small bipyramids. Also micaceous flakes with indefinite outlines. **Physical properties:** Emerald- to yellow-green. *Luster* glistening on base, vitreous in prism directions; *hardness* soft, perhaps 2–2½; *specific gravity* 3.2–3.6; *fracture* not visible as a rule; *cleavage* perfect basal and good frontal pinacoidal. Fragile and brittle; transparent (when fresh and 12 H_2O) to translucent (when 8 H_2O, metatorbernite). **Composition:** Hydrous copper uranium phosphate

(56.6% UO_3, 7.9% CuO, 14.1% P_2O_5, 21.4% H_2O, but part of the water is likely to evaporate spontaneously; metatorbernite has 8% H_2O). In a collection, one can assume that all crystals are dehydrated and should probably be labeled metatorbernite for nitpicking accuracy. (Very fragile when desiccated; try not to touch.) **Tests:** Fuses easily to a black sphere. Gives copper flame in acid solution, and a fluorescent bead with sodium fluoride.

Distinguishing characteristics: Can be confused with some rare copper phosphates and arsenates, though none has the square outline characteristic of torbernite. Resembles others of its group (autunite), but torbernite is not fluorescent and the others are. Zeunerite, the arsenic equivalent, resembles it closely, but would give arsenic fumes on charcoal and is more often bipyramidal.

Occurrence: Appears to be a late mineral, and its most frequent appearance is in thin green micaceous plates and small square crystals very lightly attached to the matrix, coating fissures in pegmatites and granite joints. It has also been found in some ore veins associated with other uranium minerals. Large and remarkably stable, thin, concave crystals over 1 in. (3 cm) across were found at Gunnislake, near Calstock, Cornwall. Next in size are the large crystals from Mt. Painter, South Australia. It also occurred in Portugal at Trancoso, in the Bois Noir, France, and in Saxony and Bohemia. It constitutes an ore of uranium only at Shaba (Katanga) in Zaïre, where it forms magnificent, giant specimen crusts and is associated with the world's most colorful and remarkable uranium mineral suite. In French, tobernite may be known as chalcolite.

U.S. occurrences are infrequent; the best are well-formed $1/4$–$3/8$ in. (5–10mm) plates coating a gray quartz in a quarry at Little Switzerland, North Carolina. Scattered crystals are found at many localities, but it is far rarer than autunite (next). Small bipyramidal crystals have been found at the Kinkel Quarry in Bedford, New York.

Remarks: This mineral, autunite, and other high-water hydrates of their like, tend to dry and crumble in collections. *Caution:* Washing old specimens will probably result in their total destruction. While colorful, they are really not very satisfactory subjects to collect. Since uranium is radioactive, excessive exposure to its rays and dust is not recommended, and such actions as blowing on and breathing in its dust are hardly wise.

AUTUNITE $Ca(UO_2)_2(O_4)_2 \cdot 10–12H_2O$ **Pl. 44**

Tetragonal — Ditetragonal bipyramidal $\dfrac{4}{m}\dfrac{2}{m}\dfrac{2}{m}$

Environment: Secondary mineral in weathered zones of uraninite and metal-ore deposits; also as scales on joints and
seams in pegmatites and in granite quarries. **Crystal description:** Square plates, also scattered thin flakes and solid micaceous crusts, with crystals standing on the edge. Swelling
sheaves on edge in crusts tend to exfoliate as desiccation
proceeds. **Physical properties:** Greenish yellow to lemon yellow. *Luster* glistening on cleavages, to glassy; *hardness* fragile and not significant, 2–2½; *specific gravity* 3.1; *fracture*
not notable; *cleavage* micaceous basal and prismatic. Fragile and brittle; transparent fresh, translucent dry (see torbernite); probably the most brilliantly fluorescent (green) of all
minerals in ultraviolet light (longwave or shortwave). **Composition:** Hydrous calcium uranium phosphate (58.0% UO_3,
5.7% CaO, 14.4% P_2O_5, 21.9% H_2O), but usually loses water after capture and becomes metaautunite (see torbernite,
preceding). **Tests:** The brilliant fluorescence makes all other
testing unnecessary.

Distinguishing characteristics: The fluorescence and the square
plates distinguish it from all other minerals except rare
members of the same group. The presence of calcium can be
confirmed by obtaining the calcium sulfate precipitate, produced when sulfuric acid is added to the nitric acid solution.

Occurrence: Autunite is probably always a secondary mineral
that forms as a result of the surface alteration of uranium
ores. In daylight it may be almost invisible on a rock face,
but at night with ultraviolet, can form a fluorescent "eye"
around a center of less-altered, nonfluorescent uranium minerals in a pegmatite. Ultraviolet light examination of rocks
with altered uraninite usually shows an unexpected abundance of autunite in flakes so thin that they were not noted
in ordinary light.

Very abundant in and near uranium-bearing pegmatites all
over the world. Especially rich masses have been found at
Spruce Pine, North Carolina. In Portugal at Urgeiriça and
Trancoso, and in South Australia at Mt. Painter, it has
formed veins that were rich enough to be mined, those of
Mt. Painter being up to 9–12 in. thick (20–30 cm). Rich
greenish yellow crusts and some of the largest, 1-inch (2.5
cm) square crystals were found in France, at Saône-et-Loire,
or Margnac, Haute-Vienne.

Like torbernite, it tends to crumble in collections. Many

of the finest U.S. specimens, very rich crusts of pure mineral from the Daybreak Mine, near Spokane, Washington, have to be lacquered or otherwise treated to preserve them intact.

CARNOTITE $K_2(UO_2)_2V_2O_5 \cdot 3H_2O$

Monoclinic — prismatic $\dfrac{2}{m}$

Environment: Yellow concentrations, coatings, and disseminations in sandstone and limestone sediments. May replace fossil wood, etc. in such sedimentary beds. **Crystal description:** Few recognizable crystals; microscopic plates sometimes visible. Usually forms powdery disseminations or films. **Physical properties:** Bright yellow. *Luster* earthy; *hardness* indeterminate (soft); *specific gravity* 4.1; crystal plates said to have a basal *cleavage,* but would not be visible. Powdery and crumbling; opaque like an ocher; not fluorescent. **Composition:** Hydrous potassium uranium vanadate (10.4% K_2O, 63.4% UO_3, 20.2% V_2O_5, 6.0% H_2O). **Tests:** Infusible. Powder turns red-brown when dropped in boiling nitric acid, and dissolves for green solution. Cold borax bead is fluorescent green. Residue of evaporation of acid is fluorescent.

Distinguishing characteristics: The bright yellow uranium color without the normal uranium fluorescence is significant. A bead test with ultraviolet light will prove uranium.

Occurrence: The only important deposits are in sandstones in w. Colorado and e. Utah, with some in Arizona and New Mexico. Its exact origin is uncertain; presumably it has formed from the alteration of pre-existing uranium and vanadium minerals. It is disseminated through a red-brown sandstone, often replacing fossil wood, then making rich masses of relatively pure carnotite. Yellow stains of carnotite have been found in a conglomerate along a railroad cut at Mauch Chunk, Pennsylvania. It has been found in n. Mexico, at Radium Hill, South Australia, and with the uranium ores at Shaba (Katanga), Zaire. The only actual U.S. crystals seem to be those of small limestone pockets at Grants, New Mexico.

Remarks: For some years, before the discovery of the Zaire uranium ores, the U.S. carnotite deposits were the world's chief source of radium. The Curies obtained their experimental material from Colorado. These deposits were closed when the development of richer African ores reduced the price of radium. When radioactive interest shifted to uranium they became an important U.S. source of that metal.

TUNGSTATES (WOLFRAMATES) AND MOLYBDATES

This small group of ore minerals is colorful and interesting. Wulfenite belongs to a rare tetragonal crystal class characterized by third-order faces. Scheelite and powellite are both desirable collectibles for their fluorescence, and belong to the same crystal class as wulfenite. The wolframite pair of minerals are important tungsten (wolfram) ores.

Tungsten and molybdenum can replace each other in some minerals to a limited extent. The blue color of molybdenum oxide noted in an evaporated acid solution residue is conspicuous and helps in the distinction between powellite and scheelite. The yellow fluorescence of powellite, an indication of the presence of molybdenum, helps differentiate it from scheelite.

WOLFRAMITE $(Fe,Mn)WO_4$ **Pl. 43**

Ferberite $FeWO_4$ ⎫ Monoclinic-prismatic $\dfrac{2}{m}$
Huebnerite $MnWO_4$ ⎭

Environment: High-temperature and medium-temperature quartz veins, occasionally in granitic pegmatites. **Crystal description:** Wolframite usually occurs in fair-sized 1–6-in. (3–15 cm) black blades commonly embedded in or surrounded by quartz crystals, the edges revealing the perfect cleavage on the fracture face. More often than not the crystals are twinned on the front face so the termination has a V-shaped notch. Ferberite can also form crusts of small stubby black blades on rock surfaces in open cavities (Colorado); also massive granular. Ferberite is dead black and completely opaque; huebnerite tends toward reddish brown, usually showing color through clinging translucent cleavage flakes over inner cracks. **Physical properties:** Black to red-brown. *Luster* submetallic; *hardness* 4–4$\frac{1}{2}$; *specific gravity* 7.1–7.5; *streak* black to red-brown; *fracture* uneven; *cleavage* perfect side pinacoid. Extremely brittle; ferberite is opaque, huebnerite translucent in thin flakes. **Composition:** Tungstates of iron and manganese, the two elements form a continuous series with end members known as ferberite (with 23.7% FeO and 76.3% WO_3) and huebnerite (with 23.4% MnO and 76.6% WO_3). **Tests:** Decrepitates (flies apart), then fuses to a globule that assumes, on solidifying, a slightly faceted (crystalline) surface (that from ferberite is magnetic). The best tungsten test is to fuse the material on the charcoal under sodium carbonate, dissolve the slaggy mixture in strong hydrochloric acid, and add pure tin, which imparts a blue color to the solution. It's best to try out this test several times with known tungsten-bearing ores, to acquire the technique. Exaggerated heat sensitivity makes crystals vulnerable to damage if too intensely illuminated, as in the mineral-show display cases.

Distinguishing characteristics: The tungsten test is the best guide and may be essential. Manganese-rich huebnerite can resemble goethite, which is magnetic (huebnerite is not magnetic after fusion) and will give no tungsten test. It also resembles columbite, tantalite, and manganotantalite, and again the tungsten test is the one to apply, although tungsten sometimes can be found in these minerals; then the problem may become complicated.

Occurrence: Wolframite is a widely distributed mineral most often found in deep-seated quartz veins. Frequently shows embedded blades extending in from the wall, so perfect that they could serve as textbook vein illustrations. The perfect cleavage is very pronounced and helps to distinguish it from the interrupted surface of columbite. However, though pegmatitic occurrences of wolframite are rare, they are the customary environment of columbite-tantalite, so with knowledge of the formation on which you are hammering, laboratory distinction is largely only of academic interest. Ferberite, on the other hand, can also form drusy crusts of small, free-growing, brilliant black crystals over rock surfaces in open low-pressure but high-temperature veins, like those of Nederland, Boulder Co., Colorado, and Llallagua, Bolivia. The finest large crystals come from Panasqueira, Portugal, from n. Peru, and from Tong Wha, South Korea.

Specimens have been found in quartz veins at Frederick, Missouri; Ouray Co., Colorado; Lincoln Co., New Mexico; Nye Co., Nevada; and Townsville, North Carolina. Ferberite is best developed in Colorado with similar specimens in Bolivia. Colorado huebnerite veins form brown quartz-coated sprays. Daredevil dealers dissolve the quartz with hydrofluoric acid — a risky, not recommended procedure — to obtain fragile specimens of the crystals.

Remarks: An important ore of tungsten. Its name refers to the early name for tungsten, which, in an ore mixture with tin ore, reduced the recovery of that metal by "wolfing" the ore.

SCHEELITE CaWO$_4$ Pl. 44

Tetragonal — Tetragonal bipyramidal $\dfrac{4}{m}$

Environment: Contact-metamorphic deposits, high-temperature quartz veins, and, rarely, in pegmatites. **Crystal description:** Often occurs in well-formed bipyramidal crystals, often with a sliver of asymmetrical truncation (third-order form) on the left side of the pyramid. The crystals may be small and brilliant or fairly large, even to 3 or 4 in. (15 cm). Transparent white and amber crystals suitable for cutting into gemstones have been found. Also in grains embedded in rock, without regular external form. **Physical properties:** White, clove brown, light green (cuproscheelite). *Luster* adamantine; *hardness* $4\frac{1}{2}$–5; *specific gravity* 5.9–6.1; *streak* white; fracture uneven; *cleavage* 3, pyramidal best. Translucent to transparent; most specimens are fluorescent (shortwave ultraviolet) blue, from high tungsten, to white or yellow (depending upon molybdenum content). **Composition:** Calcium tungstate, usually with some of the tungsten replaced by molybdenum (19.5% CaO, 80.5% WO$_3$). **Tests:** Tests are rarely necessary, since the fluorescence in ultraviolet light is the recognized method of prospecting. A gravity test and the blue tungsten test mentioned under wolframite (preceding) may be given, but yellow precipitate and coating obtained by simply boiling a powder in hydrochloric acid are usually sufficient.

Distinguishing characteristics: The fluorescence may be confusing, especially when it becomes whitish or yellow from molybdenum substitution, but density and hardness differentiate it from fluorescent fluorite and the crystals are so common that they will often be seen.

Occurrence: Most frequently found in contact-metamorphic deposits, where granitic rocks have intruded an impure limestone and the heat and gases have caused the typical minerals of this occurrence to form. Associates will be garnet, epidote, and vesuvianite. Scheelite should always be considered likely under these circumstances; check with shortwave ultraviolet. It will also be found in high-temperature quartz veins, often in crystals associated with cassiterite, topaz, fluorite, wolframite, and apatite.

Good crystals have been found at many localities, particularly at Bishop and Atolia, California, and in Mohave and Cochise Cos., Arizona. Interesting crystals and replacements of wolframite after scheelite crystals have been found at Trumbull, Connecticut. Most of the once commercially important Mill City, Nevada, scheelite was in grains embedded in a very compact rock. Gemmy, orange-brown crystals have been found in Sonora, Mexico, with black tourmaline (dravite) and elongated white apatite prisms.

Foreign localities of note include Malaga, Spain; Slavkov (Schlaggenwald, Bohemia), Czechoslovakia; and Tong Wha, South Korea. It was abundant in n. Brazil in metamorphic formations with vesuvianite. A seemingly secondary cool-water type of deposit has been found in a n. Mexico source where the scheelite is later than chrysocolla.

Remarks: An important ore of tungsten and, as a result of prospecting with ultraviolet light, has been discovered at many localities where it was not previously recognized. Resembles quartz when seen in the rock and probably has often not been recognized. Readily synthesized, melting congruently.

POWELLITE $CaMoO_4$ **Pl. 44**

Tetragonal — Tetragonal bipyramidal $\dfrac{4}{m}$

Environment: May form, like scheelite, in medium-temperature quartz veins, usually from hydrothermal alteration of molybdenite. Rarely it is a companion of zeolites. **Crystal description:** Crystals mostly small and rare, but resemble those of scheelite in development. Apparently not an alteration product of molybdenite without hydrothermal intervention. **Physical properties:** White, yellowish brown, light blue. *Luster* adamantine; *hardness* $3\frac{1}{2}$–4; *specific gravity* 4.2; *fracture* uneven; *cleavage* pyramidal. Brittle; transparent to translucent; fluorescent yellow (shortwave ultraviolet). **Composition:** Calcium molybdate with some tungsten replacing the molybdenum (28.0% CaO, 72.0% MoO_3, with up to 10.0% WO_3 replacing the latter in part). **Tests:** Distinguished from scheelite by its yellow fluorescence and lesser density. Chemical tests rarely necessary, but it is decomposed by hydrochloric acid to give yellow solution; a drop of solution evaporated on streak plate leaves an inky residue (molybdenum).

Distinguishing characteristics: The crystals are much like those of scheelite, which is far more common.

Occurrence: Good specimens are excessively rare, and all present collection specimens are from the Deccan basalts of India. The original material, in microscopic crystals from a mine in Utah, was named for Major John Wesley Powell, once a director of the U.S. Geological Survey, who led the first group to descend the Colorado River through the Grand Canyon. Magnificent greenish crystals, the best known, were found in the Michigan copper district at the Isle Royale and South Hecla mines, in what we now recognize may be the preferred association, zeolitic. Brown $1/4$-in. (3 mm) crystal crusts have been found at Goldfield, Nevada.

Colorless, brilliant crystals occur with zeolites in basalt at the Clayton Quarry, Panama. Has been described in a similar paragenesis in Scotland and now noted in 1-in. (2.5 cm) crystals in a Poona, India, zeolite mixture.

The identification of the alteration of molybdenite into powellite, often in earthy and crumbling pseudomorphs after flaky crystals of molybdenite, was only recognized after it was known as a crystallized mineral. It could be a common occurrence and should always be looked for in any altered or weathered specimen of molybdenite-bearing rock. However, at Superior, Arizona, it was noted that crystallized powellite (made visible only with ultraviolet light) is always very close to obvious small seams in the specimen, with corroded molybdenite and a green scaly copper molybdate, lindgrenite, $Cu_3(MoO_4)_2(OH)_2$.

WULFENITE $PbMoO_4$ Pl. 44

Tetragonal — Tetragonal pyramidal   4

Environment: A secondary mineral forming near the surface in lead veins. **Crystal description:** Almost always in crystals, usually tabular, often very thin and fragile. Basal plane well developed; occasional third-order pyramid faces make base appear interestingly skewed in relation to the crystal outline. Prismatic and pyramidal habits less frequent. On the large thin plates the prism faces are often irregularly developed so that the crystals are not sharply bounded. **Physical properties:** Yellow, orange, brown, gray, almost white and matching streaks. *Luster* adamantine; *hardness* $2^3/4$–3; *specific gravity* 6.8; *fracture* subconchoidal; *cleavage* pyramidal good, 2 poor. Very fragile and brittle; transparent to translucent. **Composition:** Lead molybdate (60.7% PbO, 39.3% MoO_3). **Test:** The brilliant color, high luster, and platy habit make most tests unnecessary. Fuses easily to slag that is yellow when hot, gray when cold. Shiny fragment under a drop of hot hydrochloric acid becomes frosted on the surface, turns blue when rubbed with steel needle while wet.

Distinguishing characteristics: The brilliant colors characteristic of this mineral, together with the tabular development of the crystals, make it one of the easiest minerals to recognize. There is almost nothing with which there is any danger of confusing it except stolzite, the rare tungsten equivalent ($PbWO_4$).

Occurrence: Best developed in dry climates where weathering has extended fairly deep. The American Southwest and Mexico are particularly notable for their occurrences of wulfenite. (See comment under molybdenite, p. 128, about the fugitive character of Mo solutions.) Solutions bearing ilsemannite could be the source of the molybdenum needed for the wulfenite formation, the origin of which has always been something of a mystery. The most brilliant orange crystals, the hue said to be due to chromium, are still found at the Red Cloud Mine, Yuma Co., Arizona, and at Chah-Kharbose in Iran. There are many occurrences in the Southwest however, far too many to list. The orange to caramel crystals of Los Lamentos, Chihuahua, Mexico, tend to be more prismatic in habit than is common. Rare and unusual e. U.S. occurrences were at a lead mine in Southampton, Massachusetts; and at Phoenixville, Pennsylvania, with the pyromorphite. The thickest crystals of wulfenite are almost colorless (within) 2-in. (5 cm) square ones from M'fouati, Congo Republic, usually coated with quartz, which adheres tightly to the base face (it chips easily from the pyramid faces). Spectacular thin yellow crystals, with orange mimetite, come from the San Francisco Mine in Sonora, Mexico. Cerro Prieto has smaller but similar crystals. Scheelite-like crystals from Broken Hill, New South Wales, will be stolzite.

The first occurrence, in Carinthia, Austria, was described by Xavier Wulfen in 1785, who made recognizable pictures of many prismatic and pyramidal crystals a decade before the importance of the shape of crystals was widely recognized.

■ SILICATES

This final group of minerals is the largest and includes the most common. Because silicates resist destruction (chemical, atmospheric, and physical), its members are the most difficult to identify individually. Recognition of the group in general is easy, since most of the silicates are completely or relatively insoluble in our troika of acceptable acids. They are translucent — at least in their splinters, giving a pale or white streak — and average higher in hardness and lower in specific gravity than most minerals. Their resistance to acids, and in many cases to fusion, makes them more difficult to identify by the tests in vogue among amateurs than minerals of other groups. In some cases a series of negative test results are about all that can be obtained.

The sequence of this group was originally changed in anticipation of the seventh edition of *Dana's System of Mineralogy*, which has yet to be published in its entirety. Since that work is the accepted international reference work of all professionals, and the sequence will be that of most museum collections, it seems desirable to follow that arrangement here. Beginners should then not have to rearrange what they have learned as they advance their knowledge and expand their libraries.

The determination of the atomic arrangements within crystals, briefly discussed in the section on crystallography, has led to the present classification of the silicates. It is based upon the recognition that all of the silicate minerals are characterized by groups of four oxygen atoms equidistant in space from a central silicon atom. This four-cornered, imagined solid is called a tetrahedron, and the tetrahedrons are linked together by sharing corners or edges in one way or another to create six different sorts of arrangements (or structures). The structures are responsible for some of the properties.

A sheet structure, for example, is revealed by unusually good cleavage in one plane; chain structures encourage good cleavages in two planes, and so on. For this reason it is both logical and convenient to group them in this fashion, even though it results in the separation of some minerals that occur naturally together in the same environment and are chemically somewhat similar.

The silicate section is subdivided into the following types:

Silica	SiO_2	Framework structure
Disilicate	Si_2O_5	Sheet structure
Metasilicate	Si_3O_8 Si_4O_{11} SiO_3	Chain structures
	Si_nO_{3n}	Ring structure
Pyrosilicate	Si_2O_7	Isolated groups of tetrahedrons
Orthosilicate	SiO_4	Isolated single tetrahedrons
Subsilicate	SiO_5	Isolated tetrahedrons with additional O

◆Silica Type Si:O = 1:2

Mainly sodium, calcium, and potassium aluminum silicates, sometimes with water, in an open network. This arrangement gives its members a low specific gravity and is responsible for a tendency toward an equidimensional crystal habit.

●Silica Group

QUARTZ SiO_2 **Pl. 45**
Hexagonal — Trigonal trapezohedral   3   2
Environment: Commonest of minerals, found in every class of rocks and forming in every conceivable condition. **Crystal description:** Quartz can be divided into two groups on the basis of its appearance: crystallized and microcrystalline. The microcrystalline group can in turn be subdivided into a parallel, fibrous crystal arrangement and a heterogeneous, finely granular type.

1. Crystallized quartz often occurs in large, well-formed, colorless crystals or crystal crusts, often transparent and gemmy. Colorless crystals are known as rock crystal. Violet crystals are known as amethyst. Yellow-brown crystals are known as citrine. Gray to black crystals are known as smoky quartz. Also forms veins or central cores in pegmatites of coarsely crystallized material, which may be milky quartz or rose quartz.
2a. Chalcedony is a microscopically crystallized, translucent variety of the same mineral, in which layers of microscopic individual crystals have arranged themselves as layers of slender upright fibers arranged in parallel bands. The upper surface of a chalcedony-lined pocket tends to be botryoidal or mammillary, and is often uniformly smooth. White or cloudy banding irregularities commonly develop on cross-fractured weathering surfaces. In agate, the banding is colored and penetrating, often making a series of concentric rings lining geodes.
2b. The chert, flint, and jasper group are also tight and hard, microscopically grained quartz, but in these there is no definite banding nor translucency. They form dull-surfaced opaque masses. Usually chert and jasper have appreciable quantities of impurities, with lusters ranging from earthy to sub-glassy (flint) to matte. Jasper is often colorful, tinted by ocher or hematite.

Massive white quartz chunks, sometimes with gold, can originate in solid veins that slash older rocks. Massive quartz, quartz sand, and disseminated grains of quartz in other rocks, or in pebbles of quartz or quartzite, are very common, and usually are the most important constituents of any gravel or sand beach.

Free-growing quartz crystals vary in habit from long slender prisms to crusts or "points." Prism faces are usually horizontally striated; six terminal faces usually exhibit alternating development of larger and smaller faces (indicating the rhombohedral rather than a hexagonal symmetry). More than a thousand differently indexed faces have been described (on alphaquartz, see below).

Because of the composition, quartz and the other SiO_2 minerals, cristobalite, tridymite, and coesite were long grouped with the oxides, but their physical properties and crystal structure are more in accord with those of the silicate group, so it now seems appropriate to group them as silicates. Quartz itself has several crystal-class modifications, and although it has only right- or left-hand rhombohedral symmetry at normal temperatures, it is fully developed or paired rhombohedral at temperatures above 573°C. This higher symmetry form is known as beta-quartz (ß-quartz), and only forms when quartz crystallizes from truly hot solutions. However, after crystallizing — as its surroundings cool below 573°C — the structure then changes to alpha-quartz (∂-quartz), and all quartz that we find in our temperate surroundings is of course ∂-quartz. Quartz has been useful as a geological thermometer, because the habit it assumes sometimes indicates whether it formed above or below 573°C.

Two chemically identical minerals to be described following quartz carry geological thermometry higher. SiO_2 crystallizing above 870°C forms platy orthorhombic crystals of a mineral known as tridymite *(TRID ih mite)*. Crystallizing above 1470°C, SiO_2 forms in white cubic-system crystals and is known as cristobalite. Hence, from the series of differently crystallizing compounds of this fortunately common substance, we can deduce the temperature of the formation of many rocks. The two high-temperature SiO_2 compounds are rarer than might be expected, for in solidifying, cooling rocks stay liquid down to far lower temperatures expected if we were to judge by the heat that is required to remelt them, once they have recrystallized. Under some conditions it is thought that tridymite and cristobalite can form at temperatures slightly lower than those at which they are really stable. **Physical properties:** Colorless, white, smoky, rose, violet, green, yellow and brown; also translucent and tinted any hue by impurities. *Luster* glassy; *hardness* 7; *specific gravity* 2.6; *fracture* conchoidal (irregular for microcrystalline); *cleavage* rhombohedral, sometimes observable. Large crystals brittle, microcrystalline varieties tough to very tough; transparent to subtranslucent from impurities. Rock crystal often triboluminescent; electrically responsive to pressure (piezoelectric) and current; irradiation will make aluminous rock crystal smoky, and subsequent heating will then turn some examples yellow. **Composition:** Silicon dioxide (46.7% Si, 53.3% O). **Tests:** Infusible (before the blowpipe; it melts at 1720°C), insoluble. The hardness of 7 is important. Powder mixed with sodium carbonate fuses to a clear glass.

Distinguishing characteristics: The luster and fracture are typical, together with a hardness greater than that of most similar minerals. Crystals are easy to recognize if the hexagonal pattern (of usually alternating larger and smaller triangular faces) or the typical points can be seen. Horizontal striations on the prism are very helpful. Specific gravity is a useful test for this mineral. A crystal flake held in gas flame flies to pieces (as soon as it reaches 573°C). White beryl just frosts but stays intact, white topaz has a ready cleavage. On a diamond saw, a groove being cut in rock crystal shows an orange glow of constant sparking.

Occurrence: Quartz can occur almost anywhere. High-temperature veins are usually coarsely crystallized, whereas low-temperature veins and geodes in sedimentary rocks may be lined with crystals or show one of the finer-grained varieties.

Veins with colorless crystals of "rock crystal" are abundant everywhere: in Arkansas in the Hot Springs area; at Little Falls, New York, in small, brilliant, doubly terminated crystals ("Herkimer diamonds"); in Ontario near Lyndhurst. The smoky crystals of the Pikes Peak area of Colorado are often spectacular, and some fine crystals have come from the Maine and the California pegmatite areas. Foreign localities include the famous Alpine crystal-lined pocket occurrences (it seems that the higher their discovery elevation, the smokier their crystals) and the commercially important Madagascar and Brazilian rock crystals.

Beautiful amethyst is just too common to be in the precious category. It is found in Maine, Pennsylvania, Virginia, North Carolina, along the north shore of Lake Superior (Thunder Bay), Arizona, and elsewhere in the U.S. The purple variety is more often in points than in tall prismatic crystals, but Mexico is the home of two fine prismatic sources, one in Guerrero (veins) with steep rhombohedron faces, and a second at Las Vegas, in the state of Vera Cruz (pockets in andesitic lava). Bahia and Rio Grande do Sul are the two important amethyst-producing states in Brazil; also in neighboring Uruguay and Bolivia. For many years an occurrence in Kapnik, Hungary, was about the only known site for elongated amethysts; almost all the South American specimens were groups of points.

Citrine quartz is naturally yellow, but rather uncommon. An occurrence of internally gemmy, though superficially ugly, frosted prisms in veins in granite at Villasbuenos, Salamanca, Spain was the original site for "Spanish Topaz," long a popular jewelers' name for citrine. With heat of around 400–500°C, Brazilian amethysts bleach, and above 500°C (but under 573°C) turn golden to brown; others show green after such treatment. A combination, now called ametrine, which has citrine and amethyst sections in the same crystal, has been found in southern Bolivia. Irradiation turns heated amethyst-citrines back to amethyst, but ametrine appears to be natural.

Slightly cloudy rose quartz, perhaps with microcrystalline rutile, is a pegmatite mineral often occupying the quartz core of a pegmatite. Pink crystals are scarce; token ones were found long ago at Newry, Maine, and more spectacular ones at two Brazilian localities. The failure to find large, well-formed crystals of rose quartz is a geological mystery, and even now there seem to be some possibly basic differences between the common solid rose quartz of pegmatite cores and the three occurrences of pink-hued, slightly cloudy, late-formed crystals often associated with pink chalcedony. Sapucaia and Taquaral in Minas Gerais, Brazil, have produced some beautiful specimens of pink crystals. Glass-clear pink bands have been noted in some Brazilian rock crystals but have not yet been studied.

Smoky quartz appears to have been naturally irradiated aluminum-bearing material. It is common in the Alps; there seems a relationship between the elevation of the source and the blackness of the crystals.

The best agate forms in cavities in basaltic rock, as in the w. U.S., northern Mexico, and in Rio Grande do Sul, Brazil, the chief source of commercial agate. The famous Idar gem-cutting industry of Germany owes its start to the occurrence there of agate concretions in neighboring lava flows.

Queensland, Australia has fine small agate nodules and much of the jadelike green chalcedony called chrysoprase.

While we prefer to designate as agate the abundant Brazilian banded material, the word is loosely used and often applied to nonbanded material, as in the dendritic black-stained chalcedony known as Montana agate, the green and red "moss"-saturated chalcedony known as moss agate, and the jasperized (inappropriately called agatized) Arizona petrified wood. There are various opaque microcrystalline examples. Bloodstone, for example, seems to be a moss agate so full of green and hematite specks, that it approaches jasper's opacity. Microcrystalline quartz that forms pseudomorphs after asbestos fibers can be cut into chatoyant stones known as "tiger eye." Similar material rich in red hematite is found in Australia and sold as "tiger iron."

Whole books have been written on quartz and its relatives. Volume 3 of the seventh edition of Dana is devoted to SiO_2.

Remarks: An important industrial material from many standpoints. Sand is used in glass manufacture or to make fused silica. The clear rock crystal is of great value in electronic equipment, as in oscillators for controlling radio frequencies and in watches. The beautifully colored varieties have gem value. Rose quartz often shows asterism when cut in a sphere or hemisphere. White quartz veins are common guides to gold in some regions. Chalcedony and agate, which can be dyed in rainbow hues for decorative use, are also of value for bearings and in mortars. Flint, for which the Dover Cliffs are famous, is a gray to black, subvitreous and compact variety once valued for the sparks it gave when struck by steel. Chrysoprase is a natural, nickel-stained green chalcedony but it is perfectly duplicated with dyes in Idar Oberstein, Germany. Simple "onyx" is a dyed-black chalcedony (not to be confused with banded calcite onyx of cave and hot spring deposits). There is a rainbow of other dyed chalcedony-onyxes. Chert, the common light-colored nodule quartz in Midwest limestones, was used for arrowheads. Jasper is usually darker and more opaque and may contain as much as 20 percent impurities such as hematite and goethite. When fairly pure it can be very, very tough and has been used in ball mills for crushing sulfide ores. Cryptocrystalline (microcrystalline) quartz is a favorite medium for the gem carvers of Idar Oberstein, which owes its preeminence to the once-abundant agate mined in the hills and contained in stream cobbles.

TRIDYMITE SiO_2 Pl. 46

Orthorhombic — Rhombic bipyramidal $\frac{2}{m}\frac{2}{m}\frac{2}{m}$ (pseudohexagonal)

Environment: Rare mineral of volcanic rocks. **Crystal description:** Usually seen in thin rock slices when they are examined under the microscope, but may sometimes be observed in small cavities in volcanic rocks. They appear as thin tabular crystals, often developed so that they look hexagonal, but commonly grouped into sheaves of three crystal plates (reminiscent of a half-opened book on its side), or in intergrowths of three snow-crystal-like shapes in the commonly pseudohexagonal twinning. **Physical properties:** White or colorless. *Luster* glassy; *hardness* 7; *specific gravity* 2.3; *fracture* conchoidal; *cleavage* prismatic. Fragile plates; transparent to translucent. **Composition:** Silicon dioxide; like quartz, but commonly contains a significant percentage of sodium aluminum silicate. **Tests:** Test behavior same as for quartz (p. 269), but the amateur collector will have to recognize it by its crystal form and manner of occurrence. Might resemble a zeolite in poor developments, but the tip of a flame would make the latter froth and boil, while tridymite just sits there.

Distinguishing characteristics: The tabular crystals, especially when grouped into sheaves, and the rock associations are typical.

Occurrence: Significant as a high-temperature silicate mineral, forming only in rocks solidifying at high temperatures. Quartz, tridymite, and cristobalite (next) all have the same composition but form under different conditions. Tridymite undoubtedly sometimes forms at temperatures below its theoretically stable limit, 870°C, as does cristobalite. Then it often changes to quartz, and many specimens are really quartz pseudomorphs after tridymite.

Crystals of tridymite are usually microscopic; the largest are under $\frac{1}{2}$ in. (1 cm) long and very thin. Good crystals have been found in gas cavities in the lavas of the San Juan Mountains of Colorado and on the flanks of Mt. Lassen in California. Reported in the crystallizing nuclei (lithophysae) of the Yellowstone National Park obsidian, with quartz, feldspar, and fayalite.

Remarks: The name refers to its usual habit of crystallizing in booklike trillings, or groups of three individuals.

CRISTOBALITE SiO_2 **Pl. 46**

Tetragonal — trapezohedral (pseudo-isometric) 4 2 2

Environment: A high-temperature mineral of volcanic rocks. **Crystal description:** Forms small white crystals, normally pseudo-octahedrons and twinned intergrowths. Crystal faces rarely smooth and crystals always microscopic. Commonly in little spherical masses. **Physical properties:** White. *Luster* glassy; *hardness* 5–7; *specific gravity* 2.3. Translucent; often fluorescent. **Composition:** Silicon dioxide; like quartz, with various impurities. **Tests:** The white milky look disappears on heating to about 175°C without otherwise affecting the crystal, which, on cooling, resumes its white, frosty appearance. **Distinguishing characteristics:** There are, of course, many minerals with which cristobalite might be confused, but the manner of occurrence, like that of tridymite — with which it is, indeed, often associated — is all that is needed for identification.

Occurrence: In small cavities (as lithophysae) in volcanic rocks. One of the best occurrences is in small (under $^1/_{16}$ in; 1 mm) crystals in the shrinkage cracks in lithophysae of Inyo Co. (Little Lake, Coso Hot Springs), California, obsidian, associated with small green-black blades of fayalite. Also in the lavas of San Juan Mountains of Colorado, and at the Cerro San Cristobal (from which it got its name) near Pachuca, Mexico.

COESITE SiO_2 Monoclinic prismatic $\dfrac{2}{m}$

Environment: Found only as a very fine powder, often seeming amorphous, in meteor craters, a product of heat and impact on sandstone. **Crystal description:** Crystals resembling a common gypsum shape are known from synthetic manufacture. All the following data came from them, rather than the natural white dust or glassy cement around quartz sand grains in the several meteor craters where it has been found. **Physical properties:** Colorless. *Luster* glassy; *hardness* $7^1/_2$ (estimated); *specific gravity* 2.93. Transparent. **Composition:** Silicon dioxide, like quartz.

Occurrence: It was first made synthetically (and named for the maker) before being found as an almost singly refracting powder with embedded sand grains in the Barringer Meteor Crater, Arizona. Since then it has been found in the Riesskessel meteorite impact crater in Bavaria, the Wabar crater in Al Hadida, Arabia, and in two ancient craters in Ohio (Sinking Springs) and Indiana (Kentland, Newton Co.)

Remarks: This is relatively recently recognized (1960) as a natural variant of silica, though it was known to have been synthetically made many years earlier.

OPAL $SiO_2 \cdot nH_2O$ Amorphous   **Pl. 46**
Environment: In gas holes in fresh volcanics, deposits from hot springs, and in sediments, as poikilitic units enclosing sand or replacing fossils. **Crystal description:** There are two types, common opal and precious opal. Common opal is amorphous, therefore not in crystals except as pseudo-morphs of others. Can be colorless (hyalite) or colored blue, green, red, or yellow by impurities; in amygdules, veins, and seams; also botryoidal, reniform, stalactitic. Commonly pseudomorphous after wood, shells, or bone. Precious opal is transparent material with a play of color. Electron micro-scope photographs of precious opal reveal a regimented structure that explains the fire. Silica, having flocculated into tiny, uniformly sized and perfectly aligned spheres, cre-ates a microgrooved effect, like that on a compact disc, and the rulings in a diffraction grating, to create a color play of reflected light. **Physical properties:** Colorless or with all light tints; also with rainbow play of color. *Luster* glassy to resin-ous; *hardness* 5–6; *specific gravity* 1.9–2.2; *fracture* con-choidal. Rather fragile and brittle; tending to lose water and crack; transparent to translucent; often highly fluorescent (yellow-green), from uranium impurities. **Composition:** Silicon dioxide, like quartz, but with water to 10%. **Tests:** Infusible and insoluble, but gives water in closed tube upon intense ignition; usually decrepitates in flame, may whiten. Distin-guished from chalcedony by the shiny fracture surface.
Distinguishing characteristics: Broken fragment might be con-fused with quartz, but opal's lesser hardness is a good guide. Fluorescence frequent (when uranium is present).
Occurrence: One of the varieties of opal, the variety character-ized by a play of rainbow colors in what is essentially clear material, is known as precious opal and is a valuable jewelry stone. Fire opal is the name given red-orange transparent common opal, often faceted and associated with precious opal in Mexico. Common opal has no particular value, though it is often highly fluorescent and collected for that reason.

There are many occurrences of opal deposited from hot water, as in the hot spring terraces and steaming geyser chimneys of Yellowstone National Park. A light yellow al-tered wood occurs in Virgin Valley, Nevada, together with precious opal log replacements. Diatomaceous earth is made from the fossil external skeletons of microscopic plants. Precious opal was found in volcanic rocks in the first known occurrence, in Czechoslovakia, and later in Idaho and California, and preeminently in the Querétaro district of Mexico. Of greater value, however, are the opals of the sedimentary rocks of e. Australia, which at many different places yield numerous types of precious opal. It is found in concretions and in cracks and crevices in soft sediments, and often in Queensland as opalized fossils. It occurs on seams in clay-iron stone boulder opal. An opal-cemented white quartzite from Australia is commonly dyed to resemble black opal. Similar material has lately been found at some depth in Louisiana. There is an occurrence of a fairly hard white precious opal in Brazil, at Dom Pedro II, Ceará. Colorless to blue hyalite is common on seams in pegmatites in the Spruce Pine district, North Carolina. Glassy hyalite droplets in Oregon and Mexican rhyolite pockets resemble masses of frog eggs, as do oolitic opal concretions around a hot spring in Japan, each enclosing a tiny central speck.

●Feldspars

This group of minerals might, with some justification, be regarded as varieties of a single mineral species. On this premise feldspar, rather than quartz, could be considered the most abundant of all minerals. Feldspars are igneous and plutonic rock-making minerals. All are aluminum silicates of soda, potash, or lime (with a few rarer varieties) and are closely related in structure and composition. Soda and lime can replace each other in one triclinic series with very gradual differences so different names are arbitrarily assigned, depending on the relative abundance of sodium and/or calcium.

Potash feldspars include monoclinic orthoclase and twinned triclinic microcline; the triclinic Na:Ca plagioclases are albite, oligoclase, andesine, labradorite, bytownite, and anorthite.

ORTHOCLASE $KAlSi_3O_8$ Monoclinic — prismatic $\frac{2}{m}$ **Pl. 47**

Environment: A mineral of igneous, plutonic, and metamorphic rocks, and occasionally of high-temperature veins. **Crystal description:** Isolated, 1-in. (3–4 cm) sharp white singles sometimes weather from porphyry dikes (Good Springs, Nevada, etc.) where they can be collected on the outcrop of a

are found in the Swiss and Austrian Alps. Moonstone, a variety with bluish schiller reflections, is found in Sri Lanka (Ceylon), Madagascar, and rarely (not commercially) in the U.S.

Oligoclase is mostly translucent and white but sometimes, when gemmy, has a bluish cast; clear, pale blue and colorless pleochroic masses are found in North Carolina and Tanzania. Much of the feldspar in coarse-grained Manhattan Island schist is oligoclase; rounded crystals weathered from a marble can be found in St. Lawrence Co., New York. Reddish golden iron oxide inclusions in Norwegian and Canadian oligoclase reflect brilliantly in one plane to produce the original "sunstone" (calcic labradorite "sunstone" is discussed below).

Andesine is a white feldspar of fine-grained common andesite lavas (named from the Andes), but is rare in mineral specimens.

Labradorite makes up rock masses, often very coarsely crystalline — as in Labrador. It is used as a decorative stone for carvings and building facades, where it is valued for the beautiful bluish reflections, often resembling a Brazilian butterfly's wing. (Take a field trip to New York City's Chrysler Building, then step over for a look at the gneissic Minnesota granite of the Roosevelt Hotel.) Little of the Adirondack labradorite shows this schiller. Most gleaming architectural "blue granite" comes from Norway, though the brightest of all is Finnish "spectrolite." Clear, glassy labradorite occurs as phenocrysts in basalt flows in Oregon (Plush), near Milford, Utah, and in n. Mexico. Sometimes the Oregon crystals are sunstone-like, with tiny copper microlite reflections; a few are tinted red and green and are faceted for colorful transparent gemstones also called "sunstones."

Bytownite, if it exists, is a rare feldspar forming grains in lime-rich igneous rocks. It would be another step toward anorthite in this series, but the original Canadian source credited to Bytown has now been discredited, and this calcium-to-sodium ratio may not exist in nature.

Anorthite is very rare, but forms small crystals in lava-marinated limestone blocks ejected from Monte Somma (pre-Vesuvius) and in some lavas as glassy phenocrysts with basalt skins and altered surfaces, as in Miyake-jima, Japan. Rough greenish crystals have been described from a Franklin, New Jersey, marble quarry.

●Feldspathoids

Members of this group of quasi-feldspars form in lava and/or magma when the available silica is insufficient to completely balance the alkalis present: the potash, lime, or soda. The common feldspathoids are leucite and nepheline. Since feldspars would have formed in their place if there had been an abundance of silica, quartz (SiO_2) will not be found as a primary mineral in association with them.

LEUCITE $KA Si_2O_6$ **Pl. 48**

Tetragona — trapezohedral (pseudo-isometric)   4 2 2
Environme t: Fresh low-silica lavas. **Crystal description:** Found as dull-s rfaced, embedded crystals to about 1 in. (2 cm). Usually rapezohedral; rarely in pseudocubes. **Physical properties:** Gr to white to colorless. *Luster* glassy (altering in older exar ples to dull as silica freed by weathering of the surround gs breaks down the leucite into a feldspar); *hardness* $5^1/_2$–€ pecific gravity 2.4–2.5; *fracture* conchoidal; *cleavage* impe ct. Brittle; transparent to translucent. **Composition:** A pota um aluminum silicate (21.5% K_2O, 23.5% Al_2O_3, 55.(SiO_2). **Tests:** None necessary; the garnet-like white cry ls are characteristic.

Dist juishing characteristics: The crystals resemble only those of net, which is fusible (and usually dark), and analcime, w h is fusible and gives water in a closed glass tube.

C rrence: The best examples of leucite are fresh crystals edded in Vesuvius lavas. It alters readily to pseudoleu- (a chalky-white mixture of nepheline, orthoclase, and lcime) and then to clay. Very large white crystals of this be are found in Poços de Caldas, Brazil. Good embedded ystals are found at Magnet Cove, Arkansas, in boulders on e shores of Vancouver Island, British Columbia, and in the eucite Hills of Wyoming.

Has been used in Italy as a source of potassium for fertiliz- rs, and an effort was made to recover aluminum from it.

EPHELINE $(Na,K)(Al,Si)_2O_4$ **Pl. 48**

Hexagonal — hexagonal pyramidal   6
Environment: Low-silica plutonic rocks and igneous rocks. **Crystal description:** Flat hexagonal prisms; the volcanic crystals are very small and clear, with few modifications. Larger, coarse six-sided crystals with corroded surfaces have been found in pegmatitic nepheline syenite dikes. Usually as white grains in rock. **Physical properties:** Colorless, white,

gray, reddish, smoky. *Luster* greasy; *hardness* $5^1/_2$–6, *specific gravity* 2.5–2.65; *fracture* subconchoidal; *cleavage* good prismatic. Brittle; transparent to translucent; often fluorescent orange-red in portions of the crystal. **Composition:** Sodium, potassium, aluminum silicate (21.8% Na_2O, very little K_2O, 35.9% Al_2O_3, 42.3% SiO_3). **Tests:** Splinter rounds to a clear glass droplet, with a brilliant yellow sodium flame. A powder is easily soluble in hydrochloric acid, evaporating to make a silica gel.

Distinguishing characteristics: The easy fusibility, usual associates, and unusual luster distinguish it from all minerals except the even more fusible cryolite, which it resembles. It is softer than feldspar and quartz. The somewhat similar scapolite melts to a white glass with small bubbles. Old exposed surfaces of nepheline-bearing rocks always show pits where the nepheline has been dissolved out; feldspar seams cutting through such outcrops stand out in relief.

Occurrence: Crystals are found in the cavities in the limestone block thrown out by the volcano (Monte Somma) that preceded Vesuvius. Nepheline forms grains in plutonic rocks in Karelia (now Karelskaya), Russia, and at Bancroft, Ontario. Small glassy crystals may line cavities in uncommon low-silica volcanic rocks. Large coarse crystals are found in pegmatitic segregations in the Bancroft area where crystals to 6 in. (15 cm) or more across have been noted.

In recent years, nepheline has become an important glass and ceramic raw material. Nepheline-bearing rocks will not contain quartz and melt well. If enough silica were present, feldspar would have formed in place of the nepheline.

● Sodalite Group

SODALITE $Na_4Al_3Si_3O_{12}Cl$ **Pl. 48**

Cubic — hexoctahedral $\frac{4}{m} \overline{3} \frac{2}{m}$

Environment: A mineral of alkaline igneous and plutonic rocks, low in silica. **Crystal description:** Crystals primarily small in cavities of volcanic rocks, or in Monte Somma (Italy) or Laacher See (Germany) bombs, commonly dodecahedrons. Usually in massive nepheline-syenite formations in considerable concentrations. Specimens are primarily blue rocks, rather than crystals. Often used as a decorative architectural stone. **Physical properties:** Colorless, white, blue, violet, and pink (hackmanite). *Luster* glassy; *hardness* $5^1/_2$–6;

specific gravity 2.2–2.3; *fracture* conchoidal to uneven; *cleavage* poor dodecahedral. Brittle; transparent to translucent; frequently yellow to orange in longwave ultraviolet light. **Composition:** Sodium aluminum silicate with chlorine (25.6% Na_2O, 31.65% Al_2O_3, 37.2% SiO_2; up to 7.3% Cl replacing some O). Hackmanite contains S in place of chlorine. **Tests:** Soon loses color and eventually fuses to a white glass with a yellow (sodium) flame coloration. After being roasted, the heated specimen fluoresces a brilliant orange in longwave ultraviolet, and the melted end fluoresces blue in shortwave ultraviolet.

Distinguishing characteristics: The blue hue is very typical and likely to be confused only with lazulite and lazurite (see next). Blue grains in rock may not originally be fluorescent, but the pink variety (hackmanite) is brilliantly fluorescent and reversibly sensitive to light, fading to white in daylight and becoming again deep pink on exposure to ultraviolet. Surfaces of sodalite-rich nepheline syenite always seem to contain some fluorescent (longwave) areas. On weathered surfaces, sodalite appears to be somewhat soluble and likely to develop a pitted surface with feldspar grains standing out in relief.

Occurrences: Rich blue masses are found near Bancroft, Ontario, and nearby along the York River there are several massive occurrences of hackmanite. Thinner veins of blue sodalite are found in nepheline rocks on the Ice River, British Columbia. Litchfield, Maine, has sodalite in smaller masses of moderate richness, with a translucent orange associate, cancrinite ([Na, K, Ca]$_{6-8}$[Al,Si]$_{12}O_{24}$ [CO_3,SO_4,Cl]$_{1-2}$·nH_2O). Hackmanite, some perpetually pink, occurs in coarse rock areas at St. Hilaire, Quebec. Transparent crystals of appreciable size (large enough to provide some small faceted gemstones) were found in the St Hilaire quarry. Large sodalite formations are quarried as decorative stone in Bahia, Brazil, and in South Africa. Colorless crystals are found in the altered limestone blocks thrown out by the eruptions of Vesuvius.

LAZURITE   (NaCa)$_{7\bullet8}$(AlSi)$_{12}$(O,S)$_{24}$[(SO$_4$)Cl$_2$(OH)$_2$]   **Pl. 48**

Cubic — hexoctahedral $\frac{4}{m}\overline{3}\frac{2}{m}$

Environment: A mineral of metamorphosed limestones. **Crystal description:** Dodecahedral crystals to 1 in. (2.5 cm) in size, but rare. Usually granular, massive, disseminated in limestone. **Physical properties:** Blue, violet-blue, or greenish blue. *Luster* glassy; *hardness* 5–5$\frac{1}{2}$; *specific gravity* 2.4–2.5; *streak* sky blue; *fracture* uneven; *cleavage* poor dodecahedral. Brittle; translucent to opaque. **Composition:** Sodium aluminum silicate, with sulfur and some admixture of related minerals such as sodalite (approximately 23.1% Na_2O, 30.7% Al_2O_3, 39.3% SiO_2, 8.4% S). **Tests:** Retains color even after heating to incandescence. Fuses with difficulty.

Distinguishing characteristics: Almost invariably associated with pyrite and so distinguishable from the similar blue minerals lazulite and sodalite. On heating does not swell as lazulite does; usually is deeper in color, more opaque, and finergrained than sodalite. Commonly associated with calcite, which dissolves with effervescence in the hydrochloric acid. Not associated with copper minerals; the hue is attributed to sulfur, not iron, cobalt or copper.

Occurrence: A rather rare mineral; significant amounts in the U.S. found only in Colorado, where it occurs as small grains in a dark rock. The best occurrence of fairly large rich masses and scattered crystals is in Afghanistan; the dull-surfaced crystals are embedded in white marble and range to 2 in. (5 cm) or more in diameter. Found in disseminated grains near Lake Baikal, Siberia, and high in the Andes at Ovalle, Chile.

Lazurite forms a decorative and jewelry stone known as lapis lazuli; it is the "sapphire" of the ancients. Selected crushed grains of lapis lazuli formed the "ultramarine" pigment of the old masters. A synthetic lazurite has now replaced it in paint.

●Scapolite (Wernerite) Series

MARIALITE $Na_4Al_3(Al,Si)_3Si_6O_{24}(Cl,CO_3,SO_4)$ ⎫ **Pl. 48**
MEIONITE $Ca_4Al_3(Al,Si)_3SiO_{24}(Cl,CO_3,SO_4)$ ⎭

Tetragonal — Ditetragonal bipyramidal $\dfrac{4}{m}\dfrac{2}{m}\dfrac{2}{m}$

Environment: Metamorphic rocks, especially metamorphosed impure limestones, and calcic pegmatites. **Crystal description:** Commonly in prismatic crystals, often large and usually milky, with dull surfaces; also in great, massive, single crystals or in aggregates of coarse crystals. **Physical properties:** Colorless, white, violet, yellow, pink, gray. *Luster* glassy; *hardness* 5½–6; *specific gravity* 2.5–2.7; *fracture* subconchoidal; *cleavage* poor prismatic. Transparent to translucent; often fluorescent in longwave ultraviolet, orange to bright yellow, less often red. **Composition:** Sodium and calcium aluminum silicate, with chlorine, carbonate, and sulfate. Sodium and calcium mutually replace each other to any amount, making a series named marialite for the NaCl-rich end-member and meionite for the $CaCO_3$ end. The average composition is 7.15% Na_2O, 12.9% CaO, 26.5% Al_2O_3, 51.9% SiO_2, and about 2% Cl, etc. **Tests:** Fuses to a white bubbly glass, coloring the flame yellow (sodium). After heating (without fusion), fluorescence is yellower and brighter; better in long-wave ultraviolet light.

Distinguishing characteristics: The color and the frequent fluorescence suggest scapolite; the fusibility, flame color, and solubility distinguish it from feldspar. Prismatic crystals are common. The cleavage surface has a typical, interrupted, irregularly striated character. Irradiation turns it violet.

Occurrence: The largest and purest masses are found in impure limestones that have been altered by igneous intrusions, forming large and dull-surfaced crystals. Good crystals of this type are found at Rossie and Pierrepont in St. Lawrence Co., New York, and in Bedford and Renfrew, Ontario. Pegmatitic crystals are found in unusual calcite-rich pegmatites with pyroxene and apatite in Arendal, Norway, and Madagascar. Crystals of the pegmatite type are sometimes transparent and suitable for cutting, as in Madagascar (yellow-brown), Minas Gerais, Brazil, and Tremorgio, Switzerland (pale yellow). Gemmy pink and naturally violet scapolite has come from Myanmar and central Africa. Weak cat's-eyes can be produced from some of the needle-filled bits.

●Zeolite Family

This is a large family of related minerals related in composition, in occurrence, and — many of them — in appearance. There are several other minerals (including apophyllite, pectolite, datolite, and prehnite), described later, that are usually associated with zeolites in occurrence but differ a little too much in composition to belong to this family. The group includes over 50 members. Many of the individuals are not easily distinguished without tests too complicated for the beginner. Only the most common are included here. In their compositions sodium and calcium readily substitute for each other, and each can actually replace the other in the solid mineral. This easy substitution of elements is utilized in zeolite water softeners. Calcium in solution makes water "hard," but the calcium is removed and replaced by sodium from the synthetic zeolite linings of the water-softener containers. Water with sodium substituted for calcium is far better for washing. Reversal takes place, the softening effect renewed, by occasional rinsings with a concentrated brine that drives out the calcium and replaces it in the zeolite structure with sodium. The name zeolite is a Greek reference to the ease with which these minerals boil during fusion under the blowpipe flame.

All the zeolites are very late minerals, forming best in cavities in lava flows, probably as late deposits either from water dissolved in the lava itself or from later solutions working over lavas that have been preconditioned for such alteration and deposition by the water originally present in the lava. Also, sometimes, occurs as late deposits in plutonic rock crevices during the last stages of pegmatite formation and rarely in veins and alpine fissures.

The following members of the group are described here: heulandite, stilbite, chabazite, natrolite, and analcime.

HEULANDITE $(Ca,Na,K)_6Al_{10}(Al,Si)Si_{29}O_{80}\cdot25H_2O$ Pl. 49

Monoclinic — prismatic $\dfrac{2}{m}$

Environment: Typical zeolite associations. **Crystal description:** Always in elongated tabular crystals, to 1 in. (2.5 cm) in length but usually smaller. Shape characteristic, widest at center, like an old-fashioned coffin; hence, in older books, called "coffin-shaped." **Physical properties:** White, reddish, yellowish. *Luster* pearly on the often slightly concave cleavage face and glassy otherwise; *hardness* $3^1/_2$–4; *specific gravity* 2.2, *streak* white; *fracture* subconchoidal to uneven; *cleavage* perfect side pinacoid. Brittle and flaky; transparent to translucent. **Composition:** Hydrous sodium, calcium, potassium aluminum silicate (9.2% CaO, 16.8% Al_2O3, 59.2% SiO_2, 14.8% H_2O). **Tests:** On fusion swells and writhes, finally melting at ends to white droplets; fused mass often has a stringy look.

Distinguishing characteristics: Crystal form very typical and usually suffices, when considered in its associations as a zeolite. Stilbite and apophyllite also have a pearly look in one direction but usually the crystal form is distinctive. Stilbite fuses in more splintery fragments; apophyllite fuses with bubbling but much less swelling.

Occurrence: Perhaps the most common zeolite. Beautifully developed in the traprock quarries of the Paterson, New Jersey, region near New York City. Also in fine crystals in Nova Scotia in the Partridge I. area. Good crystals were found years ago in Berufjördhur, Iceland, and it was named for an early English mineral dealer, H. Heuland, who went there to collect specimens. Very common, but usually small, amygdular pocket linings. Common, but usually small in many Idaho, Oregon, and Washington traprock localities. Larger (2 in., 5 cm) red crystals are found at Gunnedah, New South Wales; and eastern Russia.

STILBITE $(Ca,Na)_3Al_5(Al,Si)Si_{14}O_{40} \cdot 15H_2O$ **Pl. 49**

Monoclinic — prismatic $\dfrac{2}{m}$

Environment: Typical zeolite associations and very common. **Crystal description:** In tabular crystals, commonly intergrown to give an orthorhombic symmetry, and often in bundles spreading slightly at either end to give the impression of wheat sheaves or bow ties Sometimes in dull-surfaced 1 in. (2–4 cm) rounded knobs with radiating structures. **Physical properties:** Yellow, brown, reddish, white. *Luster* glassy, pearly on cleavage face; *hardness* $3\frac{1}{2}$–4; *specific gravity* 2.1– 2.2; *fracture* irregular; *cleavage* 1 perfect. Brittle; transparent (small crystals) to translucent. **Composition:** Hydrous calcium, sodium, aluminum silicate (1.4% Na_2O, 7.7% CaO, 16.3% Al_2O_3, 57.4% SiO_2, 17.2% H_2O). **Tests:** On fusion swells and writhes like heulandite, but the protuberances are more wormlike.

Distinguishing characteristics: The larger, sheaflike crystals are sufficiently typical to distinguish stilbite from the other common zeolites. In fusing, the worms are more splintery than in heulandite. Apophyllite boils and melts to droplets with less swelling.

Occurrence: Excellent specimens come from the Paterson, New Jersey, district and from Nova Scotia around the Bay of Fundy. Bright orange crystals have been found at Great Notch, New Jersey; Victoria, Australia; and Kilpatrick, Scotland (at the latter, $1\frac{1}{2}$ in. [4 cm] long). There are numerous other localities for stilbite; it may be encountered in many types of occurrences, including ore veins and late pegmatite stages. The crystals of Iceland, of Rio Grande do Sul, Brazil, and Poonah, India, are notable. Probably the most common of the zeolites to occur in atypical zeolite surroundings (seams in granite and the like).

CHABAZITE $(Ca,Na,K)_7Al_{12}(Al,Si)_2Si_{20}O_{80} \cdot 40H_2O$ **Pl. 49**

Hexagonal — Hexagonal scalenohedral $\overline{3}\,\dfrac{2}{m}$

Environment: Typical zeolite associations. **Crystal description:** Flesh-hued rhombohedral crystal crusts that look like slightly distorted cubes are the rule. Frequently penetration-twinned like fluorite, with triangular points of a smaller individual projecting from each face of the larger. May be an inch (2.5 cm) or more across. Faces usually show crackled appearance just beneath a glazed surface. White penetration twins are known as phacolite. **Physical properties:** Colorless, white, pink. *Luster* glassy; *hardness* 4–5; *specific gravity* 2.1–2.2; *cleavage* good rhombohedral. Brittle; transparent to translucent. **Composition:** Hydrous calcium, sodium, aluminum silicate, usually with potassium, and in varying proportions (averaging about 47% SiO_2, 20% Al_2O_3, 5.5% CaO, 6% Na_2O, and 21% H_2O). **Tests:** Fuses with less swelling than many zeolites, retaining more of the original shape. Often fluorescent blue after heating, particularly the area in contact with the charcoal.

Distinguishing characteristics: The melting behavior under the blowpipe identifies it at once as zeolite. With the rhombohedral (pseudocubic) outline and without a pearly cleavage surface, it can be distinguished from all the other zeolites or zeolite associates.

Occurrence: The localities are in general the same as for the other zeolites: Paterson, New Jersey, and along the Bay of Fundy in Nova Scotia being particularly good. Also Goble, Oregon, and Richmond, Victoria, Australia.

NATROLITE $Na_2Al_2Si_3O_{10} \cdot 2H_2O$ **Pl. 49**
Orthorhombic — Rhombic pyramidal   m m 2
Environment: Typical zeolite associations. **Crystal description:** Slender needles make sprays of long, prismatic, often very slender, square needle crystals, ending in what resembles the low four-faced pyramid expected on a tetragonal crystal. Also white radiating nodules, compact masses in nepheline syenite class rocks, and in gemmy singles, sometimes immense (Russia). **Physical properties:** Colorless or white. *Luster* glassy; *hardness* 5–5$^1/_2$; *specific gravity* 2.2; *fracture* uneven across the prism; *cleavage* good prismatic. Very brittle (needles fall off on every inversion; don't touch); transparent to translucent; often fluorescent orange. **Composition:** Hydrous sodium aluminum silicate (16.3% NaO, 26.8% Al_2O_3, 47.4% SiO_2, 9.5% H_2O). **Tests:** Melts rather quietly to a bubbly but colorless glass. Heated needles and glass fluoresce greenish white or blue. Partially melted crystals fluoresce brightest.

Distinguishing characteristics: Its ready fusibility distinguishes it from most acicular crystals, and the crystal form is characteristic among the zeolites. The hardness distinguishes it from prismatic gypsum; its fluorescence is a help when it is a rock constituent, as in Magnet Cove, Arkansas.

Natrolite is one of three minerals very similar in habit. Scolecite, a calcium equivalent $(Ca[Al_2Si_3]O_{10}\cdot3H_2O)$, forms comparable sprays and in many zeolite occurrences of the volcanic type substitutes for natrolite. It fuses with wormlike extrusions; hence the name, which is derived from the Greek for "worm." Mesolite is intermediate in composition, having both calcium and sodium $(Na_2Ca_2[Al_6Si_9]O_{30}\cdot8H_2O)$. The sodium-bearing pair are structurally monoclinic in symmetry, but with no inclination of the front axis. Usually twinned on the front face, they appear to be as orthorhombic (and tetragonal) as natrolite. As a rule (one known exception), mesolite crystals are very slender. Scolecite, on the other hand, tends to be sturdier than natrolite in filling its volcanic pockets.

Occurrence: Natrolite can form part of the groundmass of igneous rocks and can occur in large individual crystals in pegmatitic phases of such rock, as at St. Hilaire, Quebec, and in the Kola Peninsula, Russia. More often it forms crystal sprays in vesicles in lavas. Scolecite and mesolite occur in the same way and are not usually rock constituents; they are slightly less frequent. Natrolite is found in New Jersey traprock quarries, on Table Mountain, Golden, Colorado, and in Oregon traprock areas. Large crystals to 8 in. (12 cm) in length have been found mainly as loose and sometimes doubly terminated singles in Bound Brook, New Jersey. Crystals 1–2 in. (2.5–5 cm) long were found in California in an asbestos quarry near Coalinga.

Many old European localities such as Ustí nad Labem (Aussig), Bohemia; County Antrim, Ireland; and the Faroe Is. are famous. Very large crystals, far bigger than those of Bound Brook, New Jersey, Montana, or Coalinga, California, have been found in Russia.

Tight veins of white natrolite cut other rocks. In San Benito Co., California, such natrolite is noteworthy because it fills seams in serpentine walls that are lined with neptunite and benitoite; these can be exposed by dissolving away the natrolite with hydrochloric acid.

Scolecite has turned out to be relatively abundant in many important localities, such as Theigerhorn and Berufjördhur, Iceland; Poona, India; and Santa Catarina, Brazil. In each of these deposits it forms long sprays, those of Brazil and India being as much as 6 in. (15 cm) long.

Mesolite is usually in thinner needles, but in the building of a dam at Skookumchuck, Washington, crystals of a size comparable to the normal ones of scolecite were found in what appears to have been a unique occurrence. Mesolite is common in the Oregon-Washington traprock, but is usually hairlike in dimension.

ANALCIME (Analcite) $NaAlSi_2O_6 \cdot H_2O$ Pl. 49

Cubic — hexoctahedral $\frac{4}{m} \, \overline{3} \, \frac{2}{m}$

Environment: Typical zeolite associations. **Crystal description:** This, with garnet and leucite, is a classic example of a tetragonal trisoctahedron (translated, this means three four-sided faces on each octahedron face, making 24 in all), perhaps better known as a trapezohedron. Rarely in cubes with trapezohedron faces on the corners. May be 1 in. (2.5 cm) or more, smaller ones glassy. **Physical properties:** Colorless, white, greenish, or reddish. *Luster* glassy; *hardness* 5–5$\frac{1}{2}$; *specific gravity* 2.3; *fracture* subconchoidal; *cleavage* traces of cubic. Brittle; gemmy to milky. Often enclosing pyrite or copper (Beech Creek, Ore). **Composition:** Hydrous sodium aluminum silicate (14.1% Na_2O 23.2% Al_2O_3, 54.5% SiO_2, 8.2% H_2O). **Tests:** Clear crystals become cloudy, then clear again as they start to melt. When cooled at this point, they fluoresce yellow-green, sometimes quite brightly.
Distinguishing characteristics: Its crystals are free-growing in cavities, and usually transparent and shiny, in contrast with the embedded dull-surfaced crystals of leucite. Softer than the rare light-colored garnet, fuses more easily, and becomes fluorescent.
Occurrence: Analcime crystals will be found in the same traprock cavities in which other zeolites grow. Therefore it will be found in association with them in the New Jersey and Nova Scotia zeolite areas. Very good examples have been found in the copper mines of the Upper Peninsula of Michigan, in the Table Mountain traprock near Golden, Colorado, and near the Owyhee Dam and elsewhere in Oregon. The largest crystals have come from Fassatal, in the Austrian Tyrol. It can form in the microscopic groundmass of basalts as a rock-making mineral constituent. Very large white crystals have been found at St. Hilaire, Quebec. Often encloses pyrite or copper (Beech Creek, Oregon).

CORDIERITE $(Mg,Fe)_2Mg_2Al_4Si_5O_{18}$ **Pl. 50**

Orthorhombic — Rhombic bipyramidal $\dfrac{2}{m}\dfrac{2}{m}\dfrac{2}{m}$

Environment: Usually a mineral of metamorphic rocks, considered indicators of intense heat and pressure. **Crystal description:** Crystals rare, and embedded, often more or less altered to a mica or chlorite. Usually in grains or masses embedded in rock without crystal outlines. **Physical properties:** Gray and blue in the same grain. *Luster* glassy; *hardness* 7–7¹/₂; *specific gravity* 2.6–2.7; *fracture* subconchoidal; *cleavage* poor pinacoidal (side pinacoid best). Brittle; gemmy to translucent; strong transformation of hue in different crystal directions, changing from violet-blue to grayish as it is turned (the inspiration for one of its alternate names, "dichroite"). **Composition:** Magnesium, aluminum silicate; plus iron, calcium, and hydroxyl (OH): 10.2% MgO, 33.6% Al_2O_3, 49.4% SiO_2, perhaps 5.3% FeO, and 15% H_2O. **Tests:** No blowpipe test is necessary. The color change from blue to gray, which will be seen through most flakes, is sufficiently distinctive. In case of doubt, look through chip at light reflecting from a polished table top or glass sheet and turn it to see the two colors.

Distinguishing characteristics: Color and dichroism (directional change in color) are very characteristic; there is no other very common violet-blue schist mineral with this appearance.

Occurrence: The largest (altered) crystals have been found in Bodenmais, Germany. Good embedded glassy masses are found at Orijärvi, Finland; Kragerø, Norway; and Mt. Tsilaizina, Madagascar. Gemmy waterworn pebbles are found in the Sri Lanka (Ceylon) gem gravels and in India. Recently found in Yellowknife, Northwest Territories.

In the U.S. it is found near Haddam, Connecticut, on the w. side of the Connecticut River.

Also known as iolite for its violet color and as dichroite because of the remarkable directional color change. It has been used as a jewelry stone but is lacking in brilliance, since it is rarely really clear and usually too dark. Valued as a geological thermometer and used as a guide to the grade of metamorphism. It has been suggested that this mineral was used in the Norsemen's Atlantic navigation to locate the sun's position in cloudy weather (the strongest polarization of sky light, and the bluest hue in the iolite, is at 90° from the sun).

◆ Disilicate Type Si:O = 2:5

This group of silicates is characterized by an arrangement of the SiO_4 tetrahedrons in a way that makes their closest grouping in a horizontal plane, closely locked sheets, giving the crystals a hexagonal or pseudohexagonal symmetry. Hydroxyl (OH) and fluorine are commonly present. In the members of this group the structure reveals itself by the pronounced basal cleavage; mica is a classic example of the sheet-structure type. The structure also creates other considerable directional differences in properties; differences in hardness and in transparency are two of the more obvious ones. It will be noted that one or several of these pronounced directional characteristics are typical of the group.

PYROPHYLLITE $Al_2Si_4O_{10}(OH)_2$ **Pl. 50**

Monoclinic — prismatic $\frac{2}{m}$

Environment: A mineral of metamorphosed rocks. **Crystal description:** Sometimes in radiating bundles of small micaceous crystals attached to quartz crystals or embedded in a quartzite rock. Also occurs in compact, fine-grained, soapstone-like refractive masses. **Physical properties:** White, silvery, pale green, or stained black and brown. *Luster* pearly to greasy; *hardness* 1–2; *specific gravity* 2.8–2.9; *cleavage* perfect micaceous. Flexible flakes; translucent to opaque. **Composition:** Alkaline aluminum silicate (28.3% Al_2O_3; 66.7% SiO_2; 5.0% H_2O). **Tests:** Micaceous or radiating clusters (quartz overgrowths) writhe, exfoliate, and glow whitely when heated on charcoal, without fusing (whence the name pyrophyllite: *pyro*, "fire," and *phyl*, "leaf"). Compact material also whitens and gives blue color on moistening with drop of cobalt nitrate solution and heating (aluminum test).

Distinguishing characteristics: Before heating, more silvery and lighter in color than vermiculite (a hydrated micaceous silicate). Heated material is very white. Talc becomes violet rather than blue from cobalt nitrate. The fine-grained micas are harder.

Occurrence: The best U.S. specimens are the coarse crystalline masses on quartz crystals from Lincoln Co., Georgia; almost identical specimens are found in Quartzsite, Arizona, and near Copiapo, Chile. Radiating masses are found in Montgomery Co., North Carolina, in the Chesterfield district of South Carolina, and at Indian Gulch, California.

Remarks: The "agalmatolite" of Chinese "soapstone" carvings is a fine-grained pyrophyllite. In its massive state, it is valued as a carrier for insecticide dusts. The compression chambers for the tetrahedral anvil press, used in early diamond synthesis, were cut from it.

KAOLIN $Al_2Si_2O_5(OH)_4$

Monoclinic — prismatic $\dfrac{2}{m}$

Environment: Representative of a number of clays. A secondary mineral, derived from fresh aluminum silicates in soils, and in place in rock from simple hydrothermal alteration of feldspar in granite and pegmatite. **Crystal description:** Crystals microscopic and in compact masses, the individuals usually indistinguishable. The electron microscope has produced interesting pictures of kaolin plates with the shape of gypsum crystals. Kaolin forms dull earthy masses, sometimes pseudomorphic after feldspar. Many similar clay minerals are identical in appearance. **Physical properties:** White, may be stained red, brown, or black. *Luster* dull; *hardness* 2–2¹/₂ (undeterminable because it simply breaks up); *specific gravity* 2.6 (also not ascertainable by ordinary means); *cleavage* micaceous. Can be cut or shaped; opaque. **Composition:** Alkaline aluminum silicate (39.5% Al_2O_3, 46.5% SiO_2, 14.0% H_2O). **Tests:** Earthy odor when breathed upon. Gives bright blue color from heating, after being touched with cobalt nitrate.

Distinguishing characteristics: The amateur cannot distinguish the clay minerals (which the professional identifies by heat absorption, x-ray, or electron microscope methods). It is more friable than pyrophyllite.

Occurrence: Clay beds, stream-sorted and derived from the alteration of earlier rocks, are everywhere and are widely exploited in the northern states. Farther south, pegmatites have been worked for the kaolin formed from the feldspar. In Cornwall, England, a high-quality china clay is extracted from the altered potassium feldspar of a granite.

Remarks: Widely used in ceramics, and with other clays is the important constituent of soil.

TALC $Mg_3Si_4O_{10}(OH)_2$ **Pl. 50**

Monoclinic — prismatic $\dfrac{2}{m}$

Environment: Secondary mineral formed by the alteration of magnesium silicates, interbedded with other metamorphics. **Crystal description:** Rarely in free crystals, usually in embedded micaceous flakes and masses, white or apple-green color; most commonly fine-grained, massive (soapstone or steatite). **Physical properties:** White, greenish, gray, almost black. *Luster* greasy to pearly; *hardness* 1; *specific gravity* 2.7–2.8; *cleavage* micaceous. Easily cut; greasy feel; translucent to opaque. **Composition:** Alkaline magnesium silicate (31.7% MgO, 63.5% SiO_2, 4.8% H_2O). **Tests:** Very soft; fuses only with difficulty. Micaceous masses swell, whiten, and give violet color with cobalt nitrate solution after blowpiping.

Distinguishing characteristics: Greasier and softer than brucite, mica, or chlorite. The violet color of the cobalt nitrate test distinguishes it from pyrophyllite, which turns blue. Harder brucite fluoresces blue.

Occurrence: In the metamorphosed rocks of the Appalachian Mountains, talc appears mainly in the massive (soapstone) form. It has been quarried in Vermont, Connecticut, New York, Virginia, and other states along the mountain line. Collectible talc in light green micaceous blades is found in Staten I. and St. Lawrence Co., New York; Chester Co., Pennsylvania; Disentis, Switzerland; the Austrian Tyrol; and many other places. Interbedded and mined with tremolite and magnesite in Brumado, Bahia, Brazil.

Remarks: Ground talc makes talcum powder. The massive variety (soapstone) is used for sinks, table tops, etc. Soapstone found a use in Babylonian days when signature cylinder seals were often carved from it. The Egyptians also used it as a base for some of their blue faience figurines, which were then fired to fuse the glaze. California Indians also used it as sculpture material.

SERPENTINE $Mg_3Si_2O_5(OH)_4$ Pl. 50

Monoclinic — prismatic $\dfrac{2}{m}$

Environment: A secondary mineral, resulting from non-simple hydrothermal alteration of magnesium silicates. Serpentinizing solutions tend to be very pervasive, attacking any rock in the area, so we find alterations and coatings on quite unrelated species, such as quartz crystals. **Crystal description:** Crystals unknown, except as the parallel fibers called chrysotile asbestos. Also massive, sometimes with a botryoidal surface as if it had been amorphous when formed. **Physical properties:** White, green, brown, yellow, red, black. *Luster* silky, waxy to greasy; *hardness* 2–5; *specific gravity* 2.2–2.6; *cleavage* none to fibrous. Reasonably compact to flaky and slickensided; translucent to opaque; yellowish varieties often fluorescent cream-yellow. **Composition:** Alkaline magnesium silicate (43.0% MgO, 44.1% SiO_2, 12.9% H_2O, plus some iron and possibly nickel). **Tests:** Infusible, but tends to decrepitate (fly apart) very badly. Light-colored material blackens, gives water, and then lightens in closed tube. Decomposed by hydrochloric acid, the freed silica separating as gel.

Distinguishing characteristics: Both a rock and a mineral. A very common mineral in regions of metamorphism (see also in the rock section). Always suspect it in a rock with a greasy feel. Usually relatively soft and dark greenish. White varieties are not common and typically are associated with other serpentines. The serpentine asbestos (chrysotile) varieties are softer and more flexible than the amphibole asbestoses. The blackening and the water released in the closed tube also distinguish it from amphibole asbestos. Ease with which the green massive material can be scratched distinguishes it from nephrite jade; it is harder than chlorite, however.

Occurrence: Since serpentine seems frequently to form by the alteration of primary magnesium silicates taking up the water originally present in the magma, they are found wherever dark-colored magnesium silicate rocks occur. Great serpentine formations, as in the California Coast Ranges, give it rock status as well as mineralogical identity. Readily identifiable in highway cuts by the shiny, concave-convex greenish, slickensided surfaces.

Serpentinization seems commonly to invade mineralized areas, altering quite unrelated minerals to serpentine. In this way we find at the famous Tilly Foster Mine (Brewster, New York) that serpentine is pseudomorphous after numerous minerals, and also forms botryoidal coatings and films ranging from white to black. Large masses of serpentine result from the alteration of the dark intrusives, as at Hoboken, New Jersey; Staten I., New York; Eden Mills, Vermont; Thetford and Asbestos, Quebec. Veins of fibrous asbestos cut through such bodies; there are quarries or mines for chrysotile asbestos in those regions near Coalinga, California, and in Arizona.

Varieties:
Fibrous and silky: chrysotile
Columnar: picrolite
Waxy: retinalite
Platy: antigorite

Micaceous: marmolite
Massive and mottled: ophiolite
Translucent (often black-specked) light green: williamsite

Remarks: Chrysotile is considered the safer asbestos (crocidolite, a bluish amphibole, is the alternative). Serpentine marbles make the popular verd antique (dark green with white calcite veins). Closely related nickel-bearing serpentines are important ores of that metal (garnierite) and are mined in New Caledonia. Closely resembling nephrite jade and commonly used in decorative Chinese carvings. Nephrite boulders are associated with serpentine and may be a result of metamorphic creation of excessively hot knots, dehydrated into nephrite.

APOPHYLLITE $(K,Na)Ca_4Si_8O_{20}(F,OH)\cdot 8H_2O$ **Pl. 51**

Tetragonal — Ditetragonal bipyramidal $\dfrac{4}{m}\dfrac{2}{m}\dfrac{2}{m}$

Environment: Though technically not a zeolite, associated with them in traprocks and in some ore veins. **Crystal description:** Practically always in crystals, frequently distinct individuals, varying from the common, short-prismatic habit with a more or less well-formed pyramidal truncation to simple, blunt, square prisms, pseudocubes. Tabular habit rare. Often over an inch or two (3–5 cm or more) across, or in 2-in.-long (5 cm) prisms. Prism faces have parallel vertical lines; base has a very pearly look. **Physical properties:** Colorless, white, pale pink, pale to emerald green. *Luster* glassy and pearly; *hardness* $4\frac{1}{2}$–5; *specific gravity* 2.3–2.4; *fracture* uneven; *cleavage* perfect basal. Brittle and a bit fragile from the ready cleavage; transparent to translucent. **Composition:** Alkaline calcium, potassium fluosilicate (5.2% K_2O, 25.0% CaO, 53.7% SiO_2, 16.1% H_2O, with the fluorine replacing some of the oxygen). Sometimes variants are given the subspecies names hydroxyapophyllite, fluorapophyllite, and natroapophyllite. **Tests:** Fuses easily, bubbling and swelling to a white vesicular enamel. The depths of the mass fluoresce weak greenish white after heating.
Distinguishing characteristics: The different (pearly) luster on the basal (cleavage) face distinguishes apophyllite from some cubic minerals such as fluorite that it might otherwise suggest. The typical square pyramid and prism combination with the two lusters is easy to recognize. In case of doubt, the basal cleavage makes the identity certain. Distinguished from stilbite and heulandite by less exuberant swelling, quicker

melting with boiling, and the fluorescence usual after heating.
Occurrence: Found in typical, well-formed white crystals in
the traprocks of Paterson, New Jersey, and Bay of Fundy,
Nova Scotia, beaches. Beautiful 2–3-in. (5–8 cm) crystals on
prehnite were found near Washington, D.C., at Fairfax, Virginia. It is also sometimes found in cavities in pegmatitic
dikes, where it is one of the last minerals to form, and in ore
veins. Two notable occurrences of the latter are the delicate
pink prismatic crystals at Guanajuato, Mexico, and once in
the Harz Mountains of Germany. Excellent tabular crystal
clusters and "roses" were found at French Creek and Cornwall, Pennsylvania. Unusually clear, tabular crystals occur
in the Michigan Upper Peninsula copper mines, with analcime and datolite. Particularly large, fine, pale green crystals were found in a railway cut (and now in numerous quarries) in Santa Catarina, Brazil. Very clear ones have come
from Iceland.

CHLORITE $(Mg,Fe,Al)_6(Si,Al)_4O_{10}(OH)_8$ **Pl. 51**

Monoclinic — prismatic $\dfrac{2}{m}$

Environment: Commonly a secondary, and often pervasive,
mineral like serpentine, but usually affecting localized
spots of primary iron, magnesium, aluminum silicates in the
rock rather than the entire mass, as is the behavior of serpentines. **Crystal description:** Two types form distinct crystals:
penninite, though monoclinic, is pseudorhombohedral and
forms thick (often triangular) crystals; clinochlore usually
grows in broader thinner crystals and is hexagonal in outline. Also fine-grained, in masses, blades, and fibers, or in little rounded knobs and green surfaces defacing nicer crystals
(adularia). **Physical properties:** Green, black, also brown, red-
purple, yellow, and even white. *Luster* glassy to pearly; *hardness* 2–2$\frac{1}{2}$; *specific gravity* 2.6–3.0; *cleavage* perfect micaceous. Foliaceous and flexible, but not elastic like mica;
transparent to opaque. **Composition:** Chlorite actually is a
group name, but it is not practical for the amateur to distinguish between varieties. At best, one can usually assign
names only on the basis of appearance, when other tests cannot be given. The chlorites are basic iron, magnesium, aluminum silicates with about 36.1% MgO, 18.4% Al_2O_3,
32.5% SiO_2, and 13.0% H_2O. The reddish varieties contain
chromium in place of the aluminum, and the reddish brown
varieties contain manganese. **Tests:** Whitens, but fuses only

with great difficulty; gives water in the closed tube.

Distinguishing characteristics: Very flaky. Usually the larger chlorites can easily be distinguished from the micas by their color and the lack of elasticity in the cleavage flakes, and from talc by its greater hardness.

Occurrence: Most commonly as a spot of green alteration of an earlier pyroxene or amphibole in rock; also in chlorite-rich to almost pure chlorite schists, which may enclose pyrite and/or magnetite crystals. Occasionally crystallized in triangular wedges (penninite) in cavities, as in the alpine crevices or in rocks altered by hot-water solutions. Also in good crystals in Lancaster Co., Pennsylvania. Some of the best crystal (to 2 in.; 5 cm) clinochlore plates were found with magnetite and chondrodite on the surfaces of a serpentinized rock at the old Tilly Foster Mine, Brewster, New York. Also found with talc in Chester Co., Pennsylvania, and in fissures in California serpentine formations with melanite garnet and brown-black, adamantine $1/4$-in. (2–3 mm) crystals of perovskite ($CaTiO_3$) near the benitoite locality. The red-purple chromiferous variety (kaemmererite) is well developed in small crystals at Texas, Lancaster Co., Pennsylvania, in some of the chromite mines in California, and in showy $1/2$-in. (1 cm) crystals in Erzincan, East Anatolia, Turkey.

MARGARITE $CaAl_4Si_2O_{10}(OH)_2$ Pl. 51

Monoclinic — prismatic $\dfrac{2}{m}$

Environment: Commonly associated with corundum in emery deposits, and as alteration rims around corundum crystals. **Crystal description:** Rarely in very thin distinct crystals standing on edge and resembling mica. Usually in foliated micaceous aggregates, often with fairly coarse individual cleavage surfaces. **Physical properties:** Light violet, pink, white, gray. *Luster* pearly on cleavage face; *hardness* $3^1/2$ (cleavage face) to 5 (prism face); *specific gravity* 3.0–3.1; *cleavage* perfect micaceous. Brittle; translucent to transparent. **Composition:** Alkaline calcium, aluminum silicate (14.0% CaO, 51.3% Al_2O_3, 30.2% SiO_2, 4 5% H_2O). **Tests:** Fuses with some difficulty, swelling and turning white on edges of the plates. Cobalt nitrate gives this edge a blue color after strong heating. **Distinguishing characteristics:** Resembles muscovite mica but is harder, less fusible, and the flakes are more brittle. A corundum or emery association is a clue.

Occurrence: Margarite is probably usually a product of the alteration of corundum, and it may ultimately become a pseudomorph of the original corundum crystal. Commonly there is a residual core of unaltered corundum, as in Madison Co., North Carolina, and Unionville, Pennsylvania. Good specimens of the pinkish bladed masses are found in the emery deposit at Chester, Massachusetts, associated with diaspore, emery, and chlorite. The best American specimens are the veins of light lilac plates standing on edge. Also found in a similar associations in the emery deposits of Asia Minor and Greece.

PREHNITE $Ca_2Al_2Si_3O_{10}(OH)_2$ Pl.51
Orthorhombic — Rhombic pyramidal m m 2
Environment: A mineral of hot-water rock alteration origin, almost invariably associated with zeolites. In traprocks, it is a first lining of a cavity. **Crystal description:** Many early specimens were rough-surfaced, green, botryoidal, inch-thick cavity linings (mostly from Paterson, N.J.). Isolated well-formed crystals of this mineral are very rare. Sometimes it occurs in dull, cloudy, elongated, almost square crystals with a blunt top. Sometimes it projects from knobs as little square platforms, or in South Africa, sometimes in pseudomorphs after amethystine quartz. Slender, pointed, colorless crystal clusters, wholly unlike the prehnite, have been found associated with remarkably large, flat pectolite blades at Asbestos and St. Hilaire, Quebec. **Physical properties:** White, light green and green to green-yellow. *Luster* glassy; *hardness* 6–6$^1/_2$; *specific gravity* 2.8–2.9; *fracture* uneven; *cleavage* poor basal (commonly concave, following a curved crystal-growth habit). Brittle; translucent to almost transparent. **Composition:** Hydrous calcium aluminum silicate (27.1% CaO, 24.8% Al_2O_3, 43.7% SiO_2, 4.4% H_2O, often with some iron replacing of part of the Al and imparting color). **Tests:** Fuses, with swelling and bubbling, to a dirty yellowish or greenish glass. After this fusion, dissolves in hydrochloric acid to form a gelatinous mass.
Distinguishing characteristics: Crusts resemble hemimorphite and some smithsonite (though usually rougher surfaced and lower in luster and lighter in gravity than either). Fuses more readily than hemimorphite and does not dissolve in hydrochloric acid with bubbles like smithsonite. Its zeolite associates are often characteristic.
Occurrence: The occurrence in zeolitic traprock is the key. Prehnite is a common mineral found in many localities with zeolites: Paterson, New Jersey; Farmington, Connecti-

cut (yellowish); and Westfield, Massachusetts (bright green). The white and colorless, sharp, $\frac{1}{2}$-in. (1 cm) prehnite crystals from the Jeffrey Quarry, Asbestos, Quebec, together with some stubbier and larger ones seem almost unique. Good specimens were found with the axinite in the Dauphiné province of France, sometimes almost like gray-green marbles. Some South African examples are almost clear enough to facet.

Remarks: Named for the explorer Colonel Prehn, the first mineral to be named for a person.

●Mica Group

This is a group of often rock-making minerals similar in structure and physical properties and related in chemical composition. They do not, however, form a complete series, with elements substituting for each other in any percentages. All have perfect basal cleavage, permitting the removal of elastic sheets of infinite thinness. The inclination of the base to the prism is so near to 90° that crystals look hexagonal or orthorhombic, as the case may be. A cleaved sheet develops an interesting six-rayed set of cracks around the point of impact of a sharp point (called a "percussion figure"), the strongest ray of which parallels the side pinacoid faces. The micas to be described are muscovite, biotite, phlogopite, and lepidolite.

MUSCOVITE $KAl_3Si_3O_{10}(OH)_2$ Pl. 52

Monoclinic — prismatic $\frac{2}{m}$

Environment: One of the common rock-forming minerals, an important constituent of granite and the main constituent of some schists, but best developed in pegmatite dikes. **Crystal description:** Crystals are common in occurrences of mineralogical interest, though rare in relation to the abundance of rock-forming muscovite in general. Usually tabular parallel to the cleavage, often hexagonal in outline. Also finegrained, sometimes so granular and compact as not to resemble a mica at all. May have inclusions between the sheets: flat, opaque black magnetite and/or hematite crystals that develop sets of crystallographically aligned cracks, red hematite, and flattened almandine garnets. **Physical properties:** White, light yellow, colorless, amber, bright rose, green. *Luster* glassy to pearly; *hardness* 2–2½, *specific gravity* 2.8–3.0;

cleavage perfect basal. Easily peeled plates flexible; translucent to transparent (thick crystals pearly and opaque on the cleavage face, but, through the sides, often very transparent, brown or emerald green). **Composition:** Alkaline potassium, aluminum silicate, often with impurities of many other elements (11.8% K_2O 38.5% Al_2O_3, 45.2% SiO_2, 4.5% H_2O). **Tests:** Variable fusibility, sometimes almost infusible, rounding and whitening a little on the edges of the flakes; sometimes actually melting and bubbling slightly. Insoluble in acid.

Distinguishing characteristics: The thin, flexible, and elastic cleavage flakes distinguish it from most other minerals except other micas. Greater flexibility distinguishes it from margarite. Sharpness of the prism faces and elasticity of the basal plates distinguish even green crystals from the chlorites. Selenite gypsum has been mistaken for muscovite, but it cannot be split into the thin, flexible, elastic sheets obtainable from muscovite. Pink muscovite resembles lepidolite but is far less fusible and does not color the flame red. The fine-grained, compact type is nondescript, difficult or impossible to recognize without microscopic tests. Phlogopite is darker and is decomposed by sulfuric acid. Biotite is very dark to black.

Occurrences: Muscovite is found wherever igneous and metamorphic rocks are found. The best crystals are in pegmatites and may be free-growing or embedded. The largest crystals are always embedded, and are mined in pegmatite areas in New England, North Carolina, the Black Hills of South Dakota, and in Colorado. India and Brazil are commercial sources. Beautifully zoned green crystals have been found near Salt Lake City, Utah, and small, bright "green-edged" crystal aggregates are found in Lincoln Co., North Carolina. Rose muscovite has been found in Goshen, Massachusetts, Amelia, Virginia, and in abundance in Dixon, New Mexico.

Other minerals are often trapped between the plates of the muscovite and grow in characteristic patterns of flattened crystals. The flat garnets of Spruce Pine, North Carolina, are particularly fine in this respect.

Remarks: It was once valued as window-making material, derived from Russia — whence the name muscovite — and is still used in iron-stove windows. More important as an insulator for electrical equipment (screw-in fuses with mica windows, older electric toasters). Large clear sheets were once of great commercial value. Scrap mica has many uses, from lubricant to Christmas-tree "snow." A fluorine-bearing muscovite is synthesized in medium-sized crystal plates and is used in a crushed ceramic aggregate form, not in sheets like natural micas.

BIOTITE $K(Mg,Fe)_3AlSi_3O_{10}(OH)_2$ Pl. 52

Monoclinic — domatic m

Environment: Like muscovite, one of the rock-making minerals of igneous and metamorphic rocks, but rarer than muscovite and associated with less alkalic pegmatites; no show specimens. **Crystal description:** Good crystals common in pegmatites and in some metamorphosed, impure limestones; usually tabular, sometimes somewhat barrel-shaped. Most often in embedded grains, sometimes intergrown with muscovite, but it does not form platy groups like muscovite. **Physical properties:** Dark brown to black, rarely (in Vesuvian bombs) light yellow. *Luster* glassy; *hardness* $2\frac{1}{2}$–3; *specific gravity* 2.8–3.4; *cleavage* perfect basal. Peels, yielding thin flexible and elastic sheets; very opaque as a rule. **Composition:** Alkaline potassium, magnesium, iron, aluminum silicate (averaging about 8.5% K_2O, 21.0% MgO, 13.0% FeO plus Fe2O3, 16.0% Al_2O_3, 38.0% SiO_2, and 3.5% H_2O). **Tests:** Fuses easily on thin edges to a dull, black magnetic glass.

Distinguishing characteristics: Distinguished from the other micas by the dark color; in its rare (Vesuvian) light phases, by its sulfuric acid reaction (forming milky solution on boiling in strong acid).

Occurrence: A common mineral of pegmatites, often taking the place of muscovite in pegmatites bearing rare-earth minerals; hence, a useful hint of that type of pegmatite. Associated feldspar likely to be brick red. Good crystals are found in New England and elsewhere. Commonly found in sections of the same occurrences as muscovite. Small, complex, light-colored crystals occur in cavities in the Vesuvius limestone blocks. Often in dark volcanic rocks as larger crystals (porphyry phenocrysts).

PHLOGOPITE $K(Mg,Fe)_3(AlSi_3)O_{10},(F,OH)_2$ Pl. 52

Monoclinic — prismatic $\frac{2}{m}$

Environment: Usually a mineral of metamorphosed dolomite (dolostone), sometimes in serpentines and igneous rocks. **Crystal description:** Good crystals not uncommon, generally embedded in crystalline dolomite. Often prismatic (elongated, for a mica); sometimes very large. **Physical properties:** Light to dark brown. *Luster* often pearly or submetallic on cleavage face; *hardness* $2\frac{1}{2}$–3; *specific gravity* 2.7; *cleavage* perfect basal, yielding thin, flexible, and elastic plates. Easily cleaved; translucent, especially marked through the prism faces; commonly asteriated (6- or 12-rayed star visible around a small and distant light source when viewed through a thin cleavage sheet). May be triboluminescent, glowing in the dark at the line of separation when sheets are pulled from a "book." **Composition:** Alkaline potassium, magnesium, aluminum silicate (about 8% K_2O, 28% MgO, 16% Al_2O_3, 42% SiO_2, and 6% H_2O, F, and Fe). **Tests:** Reacts much like muscovite but sometimes can be found to make a cloudy solution like biotite if boiled in strong sulfuric acid. **Distinguishing characteristics:** Best told from muscovite by association with crystalline marbles and its golden brown color (lighter than biotite). Usually less transparent than muscovite, with innumerable microscopic inclusions very apparent. The asterism is a useful guide, also a deepening change of color as the sheet is turned to view at a slant instead of directly through it. Sometimes twinned sheets of phlogopite show a distinct color break across their face as this color change is observed, one side showing the deeper hue. **Occurrence:** Can occur in large sheets, and Canadian and Madagascar phlogopite is in good demand for electrical purposes. For some uses phlogopite mica is preferable to muscovite. Large sheets are obtained in the Burgess area, Ontario. Well-formed several-inch (decimeter-sized) crystals of phlogopite have been found in abundance at Franklin, New Jersey, and in St. Lawrence Co., New York.

LEPIDOLITE $K_2Li_3Al_4Si_7O_{21}(OH,F)_3$ Pl. 52
Monoclinic — domatic   m
Environment: A mica mineral of the core area of lithium-bearing pegmatites. **Crystal description:** Commonly occurs in medium- to fine-grained aggregates; well-developed crystals of sharp hexagonal outline less common. Sometimes in late growths bordering ordinary muscovite mica, but the cleavage flakes show a slight marginal break and are not quite continuous. Crystals 1–2 in. (2.5–5 cm), tapering down to a slender point and more prismatic than tabular, occur at some localities. Elsewhere often in curving convex hemispheres embedded in feldspar. **Physical properties:** Lilac, gray-green, pale yellow. *Luster* pearly and vitreous; *hardness* directional variable $2\frac{1}{2}$ and 4; *specific gravity* 2.8–3.3; *cleavage* perfect basal (micaceous), making elastic plates. Micaceous; translucent to transparent; can be gorgeous amethyst-

ine hue through the side, reminiscent of kunzite spodumene. **Composition:** Alkaline fluosilicate of lithium, potassium, and aluminum (about 5% Li_2O, 12% K_2O, 26% Al_2O_3, 51% SiO_2, 1.5% H_2O, and 4.5% F). **Tests:** Fuses easily to a bubbly fluorescent glass (blue and pinkish fluorescence). Colors the flame red.

Distinguishing characteristics: Since lepidolite colors can be confusing, a melting and flame test is desirable if there is any reason (such as the presence of elbaite tourmalines or of other lithium minerals) to suspect a mica is lepidolite, rather than the more common muscovite. The fluorescence and flame tests will also distinguish it from the more intensely colored chromium chlorites, dumortierite, and similar hydrous silicates.

Occurrence: Once, before alkali lake brines proved better, an important ore of lithium. Relatively rare, since it is only found in the complex pegmatites that have a history of a long series of replacements by successive elements; always an associate with lithium minerals. Only found in regions where dikes of this type are exposed, as in New England, particularly in Maine, and at Portland, Connecticut, and San Diego Co., California.

Well-formed crystals up to an inch (2.5 cm) or more across are found at Auburn, Maine. Fine-grained aggregates are common in many Maine localities, and are associated with microlite at Dixon, New Mexico. The coarsest crystals form bladed aggregates at Ohio City, Colorado. Foreign localities include Afghanistan and Pakistan; Minas Gerais, Brazil; Madagascar; Varutrask, Sweden; Namibia; Western Australia (where there are sheets as much as 6 in. [15 cm] across in the Londonderry pegmatite); Russia; and Germany. The Alto Ligonha pegmatite in Mozambique had abundant notable lepidolite knobs to 12 in. high and 6 in. across (30 × 15 cm).

◆Metasilicate Types

Chain Structures

Si:O = 3:8	(triple chains)
Si:O = 4:11	(double chains)
Si:O = 1:3	(single chains)

The structural crystallographer pictures the SiO_4 tetrahedrons in this subtype of the metasilicates as linked together

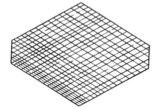

Amphibole cross section and cleavage planes (56° & 124°)

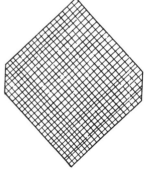

Pyroxene cleavage (87° & 93°)

in single or multiple chains. The important additional elements in their compositions are Mg, Fe^{+2}, Ca, Mn, Al, and Fe^{+3}. The crystals are all distinctly prismatic and may even be fibrous. Pronounced prismatic cleavages and strong directional differences in properties such as color and hardness are normal to these structures.

● Amphiboles

This large group of minerals has been subdivided into several series; optical mineralogists can distinguish the individuals by their refractive indices under the microscope and x-ray physicists by scanning lines in an x-ray powder pattern. The average collector with neither the training nor the instrumentation for these identifications will find a positive distinction most impractical. The more prominent amphiboles do show some consistency in color and occurrence, aspects that are about the only practical guides for the purposes of this book. In general, amphiboles are major members of the rock-making group of silicates, and they will often be found as significant rock constituents. Amphibole (mainly hornblende) schist is responsible for the dark bands in almost any striped gneiss/schist outcrop series.

A second problem for the collector is differentiating members of the amphibole group from those of a parallel pyroxene series. That rock-making series (described on p. 312) is similar in appearance, origin, and occurrence. The pyroxene series, too, includes a number of calcium, iron, magnesium, aluminum silicates in which there are also isomorphous series and overlapping relationships.

The anhydrous pyroxene series can be distinguished from the oxygen- and hydroxyl- (OH) bearing amphibole series by the angles at which the prismatic cleavage planes meet. The prism cleavage planes of the amphibole series meet at 56° and 124° to each other, giving a wedge-shaped cross section to the cleavage splinters. The prisms of the pyroxene series cross at 87° and 93°, so that cleavage needles of this group have almost square or rectangular cross sections. Recognition is aided by a tendency for the amphiboles to form longer, more slender, and more crumbly crystals than the pyroxenes. Any massive specimen made up of elongated splintering crystals should be suspected of being an amphibole. Tremolite and actinolite are particularly conspicuous in this respect.

ANTHOPHYLLITE $(Mg,Fe)_7Si_8O_{22}(OH)_2$ **Pl. 53**

Orthorhombic — Rhombic bipyramidal $\frac{2}{m} \frac{2}{m} \frac{2}{m}$

Environment: An uncommon mineral of metamorphic rocks, one usually associated with ore minerals emplaced during metamorphism. **Crystal description:** Individual crystals not likely, usually in compactly intergrown masses with a fibrous structure. **Physical properties:** Generally brown to black, sometimes with grayish or greenish tints. *Luster* glassy; *hardness* $5\frac{1}{2}$–6 (but usually splinters and appears softer); *specific gravity* 2.9–3.4; *cleavage* prismatic. Slivers translucent; polished surfaces sometimes exhibit blue, golden or yellow schiller reflections. **Composition:** Alkaline magnesium iron silicate (27.8% MgO, 16.6% FeO, 55.6% SiO_2, plus water). **Tests:** Fuses with some difficulty to a black magnetic glass ball. Insoluble in acid.

Distinguishing characteristics: Though not easily confirmed, it is a good guess for a compact, felted brown silicate mineral with the proper cleavage, hardness, and field associations.

Occurrence: Anthophyllite is thought to be a secondary mineral forming from olivine under conditions of moisture and pressure. Since more moisture and, perhaps, less pressure would have produced serpentine, the two should not be associated.

Well developed in the U.S. in the metamorphic rocks of Franklin Co., North Carolina, and in feathery masses in Delaware Co., Pennsylvania. Fairly common in schists. A closely related species, cummingtonite, forms brown fibrous "starsprays" at Cummington, Massachusetts. Beautiful blue schiller reflections reminiscent of labradorite characterize an unusual anthophyllite amphibolite from near Butte, Montana. Anthophyllite with a similarly coarsely felted mass of yellow and brown blades was brought to the U.S. from Greenland under the name nummite, as a possible decorative stone; it has also been found in Wyoming, Norway, and Finland.

TREMOLITE	$Ca_2Mg_5Si_8O_{22}(OH)_2$	**Pl. 53**
ACTINOLITE	$Ca_2(Mg,Fe)_5Si_8O_{22}(OH)_2$	

Monoclinic — prismatic $\dfrac{2}{m}$

Environment: An isomorphous pair resulting from the metamorphism of impure limestones or dolomites. Also in green schists and gneisses (actinolite) possibly derived from pyroxenes. The ultra-compact, fine-needled jade variety called nephrite seems to develop large nodular masses in hot-spot nodes of more intense alteration in serpentine during regional metamorphism. **Crystal description:** Single crystals of amphiboles tend toward elongation. In a marble, single tremolite or actinolite crystals may be a bit stubby but can also be long, large, and well formed. Deeper-hued actinolite crystals often form coarse splintery bundles of dark green, almost black crystals. Fine, very tough and tightly bonded, interlocked masses of needles make nephrite jade, which ranges from white through green to black. Soft, loose, and light bundles of white fibers make amphibole asbestos, bysssolite, and "mountain leather." **Physical properties:** White, light green, violet (hexagonite), and dark green. *Luster* glassy; *hardness* 5–6; *specific gravity* 3.0–3.3; *fracture* subconchoidal to uneven; *cleavage* perfect prismatic. Transparent to translucent; sometimes fluorescent yellow-orange (tremolite). **Composition:** Alkaline calcium magnesium (and iron) silicate. When free of iron it is light in color, or white, and is called tremolite. Iron replacing 2% or more of the magnesium makes it green and changes the name to actinolite. Other than color, there is no simple nor logical way of identifying intermediate examples (CaO, MgO, and FeO total about 42%; and SiO_2, about 57%). **Tests:** Thin splinters of tremolite and actinolite fuse to a black or white glass, the more iron-rich varieties fusing more easily. Insoluble in acid. **Distinguishing characteristics:** This series of minerals is most likely to be confused with some of the related series, the pyroxenes. The well-crystallized varieties can be recognized by their prismatic habit and the characteristic cleavage angles. Wollastonite is commonly fluorescent (lost after heating without fusing), and is decomposed by hydrochloric acid. Scapolite melts more easily and is (or on heating becomes) fluorescent in longwave ultraviolet light. Tourmaline has no cleavage. Epidote melts more readily to black magnetic slag.

Occurrence: Tremolite and actinolite are minerals that have formed through metamorphism of impure limestones and serpentine under conditions of moderately high temperature and pressure, in the presence of some water. They will therefore be found in marbleized limestones, and in gneisses and schists with serpentines. Locally they may form considerable formations of rock, when they tend to be in compact masses of rather slender crystals. The best crystals are found piercing coarsely crystalline calcite, from which they are readily freed by careful chiseling or by acid solution of the host calcite.

Good greenish or white tremolite crystals are found in the calcite of Canaan, Connecticut. Coarse green or gray crystals are abundant at many localities in St. Lawrence Co., New York, and in Ontario. An attractive lilac variety known as hexagonite occurs in masses, sometimes shot with more robust and gemmy 1-cm-broad blades, at Fowler, St. Lawrence Co., New York. Gemmy chrome-tremolite, an emerald green variety, has been found in Ontario, Brazil, Finland, and Tanzania. A gray-brown variety in splendid crystals is known as fluo-richterite, found in a coarse marble near Wilberforce, Ontario.

Actinolite also forms solid masses of elongated slender intergrowing crystals and is quite common in this form. Chester, Vermont, is a typical locality, but there are hundreds of others. Actinolite sometimes fills quartz crystals with finely fibrous green "byssolite" hairs, notably at French Creek, Pennsylvania; it appears to influence a steeper crystal shape when included in quartz in Greece and in Plumas County, California. In the form of loose bundles, byssolite mulches the roots of the famed epidote blades of Untersulzbachtal in Austria.

Remarks: Nephrite jade is also actinolite or tremolite, but earns its title by being very compact and massive. It is one of two mineral species called jade (the other, jadeite, is a pyroxene). Amianthus is the ancient name for a white amphibole asbestos. It melts more easily and its dust has been said to be more dangerous to human health than serpentine asbestos.

A related sodium iron silicate known as crocidolite *(crow-SID o lite)* forms the economically worked blue asbestos veins of South Africa where, after alteration to quartz, it is known as "tiger eye." Mountain leather is a natural mat of soft and flexible light-colored interlocking amphibole asbestos fibers.

HORNBLENDE $CaNa(Mg,Fe)_4(Al,Fe,Ti)_3Si_6O_{22}(O, OH)_2$ **Pl. 53**

Monoclinic — prismatic $\dfrac{2}{m}$

Environment: Like tremolite and actinolite, a mineral of metamorphic and igneous rocks, often pseudomorphously replacing pyroxene (uralite). **Crystal description:** Commonly crystallized, short to long prismatic, in calcite and/or quartz. Often several inches (1 dm) in length. Also solid schistose crystalline aggregates. **Physical properties:** Rarely pale, even white or yellow as microcrystalline, occasionally green (edenite), bluish green (pargasite), to black. *Luster* glassy; *hardness* 5–6; *specific gravity* 3.0–3.4; *fracture* subconchoidal to uneven; *cleavage* prismatic. Microcrystalline form may be transparent to translucent on splinter edges, mostly opaque black. **Composition:** With several interchangeable elements, the hornblendes have been subdivided into a whole series of aluminous amphiboles (some authorities even throw in nonaluminous tremolite and actinolite) with numerous ideal — but possibly nonexistent — end-members, difficult even for the professional to name. The collector can and should usually only make a good guess on identity and regard hornblende as almost a group name. (Alkaline calcium, sodium, magnesium, iron, aluminum silicate; with about 15% Al_2O_3, and 40% SiO_2). **Tests:** Fusible with some difficulty to a black glass. Gives water in a closed tube.
Distinguishing characteristics: Identified as an amphibole by its sharper cleavage angles of 56° and 124° in contrast to the squarer cross section of pyroxenes. The individuals are recognized by their color; any readily cleavable black amphibole is probably hornblende. Tourmaline lacks the cleavage and splintery fracture, though readily breaking unevenly.
Occurrence: Hornblende is a common dark igneous or plutonic rock constituent. It sometimes forms schistose masses known as amphibolite or hornblende schists that are made up of black, thin, parallel crystals. Amphibole also commonly forms by pseudomorphic alteration of pyroxenes in the late stages of the cooling of igneous rock, when they may be bathed in hot water. Fibrous amphibole grains are common-

ly seen in pyroxene-suggestive shapes in thin sections of rock. Large — and stubby for hornblende — crystals were found at Franklin, New Jersey, embedded in calcite. Similar large crystals are found in St. Lawrence Co., New York, and Renfrew Co., Ontario, where in carbonatite pegmatites they attain giant dimensions. Tiny yellow crystals may be seen in Vesuvius bombs and in Murcia, Spain, volcanics.

●Pyroxenes

This group parallels the amphibole series, as water-free (and/or hydroxyl- (OH) free) equivalents of that group, with relatives on the Moon. Pyroxenes are similar in composition with the same rock-building propensity of the hydrous series. The compositions are far simpler, however, and as a group they are well understood since their relationships have been the subject of exhaustive investigations. Pyroxenes crystallize in both the orthorhombic and monoclinic systems but, in contrast with the amphiboles, tend toward stubbier prism shape. The prism cleavages meet almost at right angles (see illustration, p. 308), making a distinction from the amphiboles easy. The cleavage angle is most easily observed on a small splinter, broken across its length and viewed through a hand lens from above. It is then quite apparent whether the cross section is wedge-shaped or rectangular.

ENSTATITE $\quad$ $MgSiO_3$ $\Big\}$ $\qquad$ **Pl. 54**
HYPERSTHENE $(Mg,Fe)SiO_3$ $\qquad$ 312

Orthorhombic — Rhombic bipyramidal $\dfrac{2}{m}\dfrac{2}{m}\dfrac{2}{m}$

Environment: Minerals of igneous rocks, often forming phenocrysts with olivine in ultrabasic rocks, and in plutonic rocks. Common constituents of meteorites and of the rocks of the lunar highlands. **Crystal description:** Usually in short grains and coarsely crystalline aggregates, sometimes in free individuals. Crystals well formed at only a few localities, and then with few faces. **Physical properties:** Colorless, grayish, greenish, yellowish, bronze-brown to almost black. *Luster* glassy to silky, or submetallic (bronzite); *hardness* $5^{1}/_{2}$–6; *specific gravity* 3.2–3.9; *fracture* uneven; *cleavage* perfect prismatic. Transparent to translucent in splinters. **Composition:** Magnesium and magnesium iron silicates (about 40% [MgO, FeO] and 60% SiO_2). **Tests:** Practically infusible, except on the thinnest edges, but increasingly fusible with more iron. Hypersthene is decomposed by hot hydrochloric acid.

Distinguishing characteristics: Most likely to be confused with the amphiboles, from which they may easily be distinguished by the 87° and 93° cleavage angles of the prism faces. Difficult to tell from other members of the pyroxene family, such as augite, with tests suitable for the amateur. Weather-freed phenocrysts are commonly altered to amphibole.

Occurrence: Embedded crystals of enstatite and hypersthene can be found in fine-grained igneous rocks, porphyries, and in coarser plutonics. Enstatite is the more common variety. At times it forms coarse granular aggregates with the individuals about $1/2$ in. (1 cm) across. Such green-black masses have been common at the Tilly Foster Mine in Brewster, New York. Similar masses are found in Boulder Co., Colorado; in Lancaster Co., Pennsylvania; and at Bare Hills, Maryland. Weathering often changes the surfaces of such masses to a bronze-hued serpentine with schiller reflections characteristic of the bronzite (also called bastite) variety. A greenish amphibolitic alteration is known as uralite. Hypersthene is rarer than enstatite and is found in the dark plutonic rocks of the Adirondack Mountains region of New York, especially well developed in North Creek garnet occurrences. Emerald green, chromium-rich, enstatite gravel bits have been found in Arizona's volcanic peridot-olivine areas, associated with black spinel. Black four-ray starred cabochons (possibly shaped from freed phenocryst pebbles) are abundant at Jaipur lapidaries in India. Lately a colorless, gem-clear enstatite has been found in Sri Lanka. Unattractive transparent dark brown hypersthene is an occasional gemstone in India and Tanzania; Finland is a source of clove-brown cat's-eye rough.

Remarks: Enstatite has several structural variations at elevated temperatures and pressures, becoming unstable at high temperatures (1140°C to below 955°C). Depending upon the iron content, enstatite and hypersthene are transformed to a monoclinic crystal form and are known as clinoenstatite and clinohypersthene. These phases are not common in plutonic rocks but are well known in meteorites and probably common on lunar peaks.

DIOPSIDE $CaMgSi_2O_6$
HEDENBERGITE $Ca(Fe,Mg)Si_2O_6$

Pl. 54

Monoclinic — prismatic $\dfrac{2}{m}$

Environment: Minerals of contact metamorphism and of regional metamorphism of dolomitic limestones. Less frequently in rarer types of pegmatites. **Crystal description:** Crystals embedded in marbles are common and may be large. Grayish crystals making free-growing crusts, as at Asbestos, Quebec, are much smaller. Fine ones may be embedded in a crystalline marble matrix, from which they are easily freed. Although such crystals commonly have rough terminal faces, they preserve well-developed and lustrous prism surfaces. Can also form coarsely granular aggregates. **Physical properties:** Colorless, white, light green, emerald to dark green, brown, black. *Luster* glassy; *hardness* 5–6; *specific gravity* 3.3–3.5; *fracture* conchoidal; *cleavage* perfect prismatic, frequently exhibiting a cleavage-like basal parting (a pseudo-cleavage) due to twinning. Translucent to transparent; light-colored varieties in dolomitic marble may fluoresce blue or yellow. **Composition:** Calcium magnesium silicate (25.9% CaO, 18.5% MgO, 55.6% SiO_2). Iron may replace some, often much, of the magnesium, darkening the crystal and forming the variety hedenbergite, a less common calcium iron silicate. The diopside series is the pyroxene equivalent of the tremolite-actinolite series in the amphiboles. Both are common and important groups. **Tests:** Splinters fuse with a little difficulty to a darker glass. Insoluble in hydrochloric acid, but etched-out crystals often have a brittle, luster-dimming silica scum on their surfaces.

Distinguishing characteristics: The common light green color cleavage angles of 87° and 93° and the associations are usually a sufficient guide.

Occurrences: The best American diopside occurrence was in De Kalb, St. Lawrence Co., New York, where large, light green, transparent to translucent, short-prismatic crystals 2–3 in. (5-8 cm) long were found. There are numerous localities in the West, including several California counties, particularly Riverside Co. at Crestmore. Almost white, fluorescent crystals are found in and near New York City (Ossining) in a dolomite marble, and locally called malacolite. Gemmy light smoky brown, medium-large crystals with prominent basal partings were found in a pegmatite at Laurel, Quebec, associated with brownish gemmy idocrase.

Except for New York State, foreign localities have produced better-formed crystals. Some approximately 2-cm, simple and free-growing crystals in a pyroxene rich enough in iron and dark enough to be considered hedenbergite are found at Nordmark, Sweden. Hedenbergite is also one of the silicates scattered through the galena of Broken Hill, New South Wales, intermixed with spessartite garnets, pinkish red chatoyant bustamite, transparent deep red pyroxmangite, and rhodonite. Fine light-colored diopside crystals have been found in the Italian, Swiss, and Austrian Alps. Many of these are much lighter, to almost white and chatoyant at one end and green at the other. In the Tyrol, diopside lies in a chlorite schist; in Ala, Italy, it rises in cavities above perfect brown essonite garnet crystals. Large, green, and transparent diopside crystals have been found in an unusual pegmatite in Madagascar and in a North Korean pegmatite near the 38th parallel. Dark and well-formed 2-cm crystals have been found in Afghanistan.

Some jewelry-quality, gemmy emerald green chrome-diopside has been mined in Outokumpu, Finland, with still better fragments coming in some quantity from Russia. Diopside can form in some ultrabasic rocks, with olivine and garnet and microcrystals it has been found as inclusions in diamond.

Remarks: Sometimes cut as a collector's gemstone, either as clear faceted dark green gems or in rounded shapes (cabochons) to show a streak of light ("cat's-eye diopsides").

AUGITE $(Ca,Na)(Mg,Fe,Al)(Si,Al)_2O_6$ **Pl. 54**

Monoclinic — prismatic $\frac{2}{m}$

Environment: A rock-making mineral, the most abundant pyroxene and an essential dark component of many of the darker plutonic rocks. A major constituent grain of basalt and traprock, and common as larger porphyritic crystals in fine-grained igneous rocks and in volcanic ejecta. **Crystal description:** The best crystals, loose or weakly cemented in andesite and basalt porphyries, usually are not over an inch (2 cm or so) in size. They are commonly very perfect, however. Granular, massive augite is frequent in other rocks — including pyroxenites, which are almost wholly augite. **Physical properties:** Black, yellow-brown in microcrystalline forms. *Luster* glassy; *hardness* 5–6; *specific gravity* 3.2-3.4; *fracture* uneven; *cleavage* perfect prismatic at 87°–93°. Black crystals translucent only on the thinnest splinter edges. **Composition:** Actually a whole series of minerals with different names, from aluminum substitutions for both magnesium and silicon. The Al_2O_3 ranges from 3% to 9%. Magnesium and iron percentages also vary, as do calcium and sodium. **Tests:** Fusible with some difficulty; insoluble in hydrochloric acid.

Distinguishing characteristics: Free crystals are very typical and easily recognized. Massive material is distinguished from amphibole by its acute cleavage angle, and from tourmaline by prismatic cleavage. Acmite-aegirine crystals are more elongated with a very different (alkali) paragenesis; diopside-hedenbergite is lighter in color.

Occurrence: Common as a rock constituent in the U.S., but well-formed crystals freed from volcanic rocks are not common. At Vesuvius, when the crater had a floor, $1/2$-inch (1–2 cm) crystals were abundant in the rotted lava that filled it. Similar crystals are found in the ancient lavas of the German Eifel, Bohemia, and near Barcelona, Spain. Loose, perfect crystals of Vesuvian size, exploded, sharp, and free of adhering lava, all formed during the recurrent paroxysms of the Stromboli volcano in Italy. Tiny crystals, with olivine, form a sandy layer on the summit rim of Haliakala, Maui.

Large crystals are found in the marble of St. Lawrence Co., New York, and in calcite-rich deposits in Renfrew Co., Ontario. A black pyroxene is also one of the once-abundant minerals from Franklin, New Jersey.

ACMITE $NaFeSi_2O_6$ **Pl. 54**
AEGIRINE

Monoclinic — prismatic $\dfrac{2}{m}$

Environment: Minerals of plutonic rocks so low in silica that they are in part made from a low-silica equivalent of feldspar — the feldspathoids, minerals such as nepheline and leucite, and called nepheline syenites. **Crystal description:** Visually recognizable only when crystallized; the pyroxene cleavage angles and a steep termination then become diagnostic. Usually in prismatic, embedded crystals, several inches (10 cm) long, terminated by steep points. Also in fibrous masses. **Physical properties:** Black, brown, or green on thin edges. *Luster* glassy; *hardness* 6–6$^1/_2$; *specific gravity* 3.4–3.5; *fracture* uneven; *cleavage* easy prismatic. Brittle; translucent on thin edges. **Composition:** Sodium iron silicate (13.4% Na_2O, 34.6% Fe_2O_3, 52.0% SiO_2). Acmite has almost exactly this composition and probably would not be separately recognizable; in any case aegirine is the acceptable identification for the mineral when it is found, since species tailored to exact theoretical compositions are not usual in nature. Only the steep-tipped crystals should be called acmite. **Tests:** Fuses easily to shiny, black magnetic bead, giving a yellow sodium color to the flame.

Distinguishing characteristics: These are the common dark minerals of their particular alkaline (low-silica feldspathoid) group of rocks; therefore, the crystal habit and associates are the usual guides to the identity. They are more fusible than most other black silicates they resemble.

Occurrence: Aegirine is common in high-soda, low-silica rocks: the nepheline syenites (very black biotite, albite, and occasional natrolite, nepheline, and red eudialyte) in the fine-grained equivalents. This entire family of high-soda, low-silica rocks, however, is not common. The best U.S. occurrence is at Magnet Cove, Arkansas, where slender crystals several inches (10 cm or more) long are abundant. In Canada, St. Hilaire in Quebec has become famous for its feldspathoid group of hundreds of nepheline syenite associates. In Russia, the Kola Peninsula is equally famed for a like assemblage, commonly with rare-earth, zirconium, and titanium minerals. Acmite needles are set in a dark-hued dike of this material at Beemerville, New Jersey. Mid-size crystals are found in low-silica rocks in the Bear Paw and Highwood mountains in Montana and near Colorado Springs. The same sort of rock is found in Greenland; at Langesundfjord, Norway; and near Poços de Caldas, Brazil.

JADEITE $Na(Al,Fe)Si_2O_6$ **Pl. 54**

Monoclinic — prismatic $\dfrac{2}{m}$

Environment: Little known in place, usually in waterworn boulders; freed by weathering from masses formed in serpentine by alteration of a soda-rich rock (nepheline and albite can be altered to jadeite). **Crystal description:** Free (pocket) crystals are known only from California. Usually in distinctly granular masses of somewhat elongated blades, which give thin slices strength (but coarser and less tough than the finer-textured nephrite masses). Individual Mexican crystals, commonly associated with albite, are coarser (to $1/4$ in., 1–2 mm across), and less uniformly translucent than high-quality Myanmar material. Polished slabs sometimes show a silky luster from parallel cleavage cracks. **Physical properties:** Emerald to light green, white, violet, lilac, malachite green. (Boulder surfaces weather to yellow, orange, or red-brown, and skins of this hue are often left on Chinese artifacts). *Luster* glassy to silky; *hardness* $6^1/_2$–7; *specific gravity* 3.3-3.5; *fracture* difficult, splintery; *cleavage* prismatic. Translucent to opaque. **Composition:** Sodium aluminum silicate (15.4% Na_2O, 25.2% Al_2O_3, 59.4% SiO_2; some varieties, particularly that of Mexican artifacts, quite high in CaO and mixed with albite). **Tests:** Fuses easily to a bubbly white glass, with a yellow sodium flame coloration.

Distinguishing characteristics: Differs from far more common nephrite by its easy fusion and yellow flame coloration. Distinguished in worked objects by its gravity, which also separates it from idocrase and massive grossular. Hardness tests readily distinguish jade from soft-mineral (serpentine, agalmatolite, fluorite) carvings without any need for gravity tests, which can be complicated for large objects.

Occurrence: Until recent years jadeite has been something of a mystery mineral, but we now know of primary sources in Guatemala as well as several California occurrences of white or grayish jadeite. Boulders in which a few small freestanding crystals have been seen occur in San Benito Co., California, with additional finds in Clear Creek, between New Idria and Hernandez. All Mexican jadeite is in artifacts, from unknown sources. Little of the Guatemalan rough resembles the fine bluish Olmec or richly green Mayan material; the sources for these are yet undiscovered (probably gathered as stream boulders, so now unrecognized). "Chinese" jadeite is mostly found as boulders in streambeds in Myanmar and traded to the Chinese carving centers. Low-quality rough has been found in place at one locality in Japan.

Remarks: A valuable material for gem purposes (almost transparent emerald green stones are very valuable); the larger, less translucent and colorful masses are widely used for carvings in China. Color is often spotty, and sometimes present only as thin green seams in paler material with a spotty color pattern that can encourage a carver to excise detracting grains in favor of holes. Jadeite can be dyed and/or bleached, and buyers should observe caution, especially with violet jadeite.

SPODUMENE $LiAlSi_2O_6$ Pl. 55

Monoclinic — prismatic $\dfrac{2}{m}$

Environment: Almost exclusively a pegmatite mineral. **Crystal description:** Usually in elongated, embedded feldspar-like crystals, commonly well developed. Free-growing examples are characterized by striated prism and pinacoid faces and steep terminations. Very large (40 ft.; 10 m) crystals have

been described in South Dakota. Networks of intergrowing crystals may not show any terminations. Very susceptible to attack by late-phase alkaline solutions and commonly deeply etched and pitted. Also smaller and gemmy in lithium pegmatite pockets. **Physical properties:** Opaque varieties buff, white, lavender, greenish; transparent varieties colorless, lilac, (kunzite), yellow (triphane), pale green (Brazil), and — in North Carolina only — emerald green (hiddenite). *Luster* glassy; *hardness* 6½–7; *specific gravity* 3.1–3.2; *fracture* uneven, rather tough and splintery across prism directions; *cleavage* perfect prismatic 87° and 93° good partings parallel to front pinacoid. Transparent to translucent; thermoluminescent, often fluorescent under ultraviolet followed by a brilliant and persistent phosphorescence in orange.
Composition: Lithium aluminum silicate (8.0% Li_2O, 27.4% Al_2O_3, 64.6% SiO_2). **Tests:** Fuses to a clear glass after developing small zeolite-like protuberances, while coloring the flame bright red (lithium). On initial heating will show marked thermoluminescence. Fluoresces orange, seen best in longwave ultraviolet or in x-rays; fused material fluoresces blue in shortwave ultraviolet. Fresh from the mine and kept in the dark it may be bluish or greenish, but heat or exposure to light changes it to a normal kunzite violet, which seems to be the stable hue (though inclined to fade a little in time). Brilliantly phosphorescent after irradiation, giving in daylight to a careless observer the illusion of a short-lived brownish color, before showing its normal greenish irradiation hue which eventually reverts to lilac.
Distinguishing characteristics: The pegmatitic occurrence, the common association with other lithium minerals, such as lepidolite mica and elbaite tourmalines, is usually sufficient. A tough splintery fracture distinguishes opaque cleavages from feldspar. Distinctive in many ways, including its luminescent qualities.
Occurrence: Found only where there are lithium-rich pegmatites, and it is usually, though not always, associated with lepidolite, bright-hued elbaite tourmaline, cesium beryl, amblygonite, and/or herderite.

The transparent colored varieties have value as gems; the ordinary material was an important ore of lithium. Lithium pegmatites are found in New England — notably in Maine, Connecticut, and Massachusetts. The usual lithium mineral associates are absent at the commercially mined deposit of Kings Mountain, North Carolina. The Hiddenite (Alexander Co., North Carolina) locality is unusual because the small green gem (hiddenite) crystals occur in alpine-type seams in gneiss and must have been deposited largely from solutions, rather than from magma.

Good crystals are found at Dixon, New Mexico and in the Black Hills of South Dakota, especially at the Etta Mine, where the mammoth crystals mentioned above were mined. Gemmy lilac crystals (kunzite) are found in several San Diego Co. pegmatites in the vicinity of Pala, California. Elsewhere in the world spodumene is found in Minas Gerais, Paraíba, and Rio Grande do Norte, Brazil; Madagascar; Namibia; and Varütrask, Sweden. Kunzite in abundance has also come from Urupuca, Minas Gerais, Brazil. In this decade, Pakistan and Afghanistan have flooded the market with the freshest, least etched, and most spectacular crystals to date.

Remarks: The massive ore-type of spodumene alters easily to greenish mica pseudomorphs ("pinite") or to clay pseudomorphs after the crystals. Gemmy crystals are frequently traversed by long curving slender tubes that start from the bottom of etch pits on the crystal surface, ending in like and opposite pits. Except for the abundant Afghanistan finds, clear spodumene from other sources is invariably so etched so that the original surface of the faces has been lost.

●Pyroxenoids

RHODONITE (Mn,Mg,Fe)SiO$_3$ **Pl. 55**

Triclinic — pinacoidal $\overline{1}$

Environment: A mineral of metamorphic rocks, related to manganese occurrences; rarely associated with ore veins.

Crystal description: Usually massive, sometimes in fine-grained masses. Good several-cm, equidimensional crystals were found embedded in calcite, in the early days of Franklin, New Jersey. Smaller, flattened, acute-angled crystals of deeper hue are also found there. Similar rich-hued, very cleavable material has been found in Congonhas, Brazil. However, the most significant crystal occurrence of rhodonite is one of large, gemmy, chunky red crystals embedded in galena, at Broken Hill, New South Wales, Australia, with very similar pyroxmangite (MnSiO$_3$) and bustamite ([Mn,Ca]$_3$Si$_3$O$_9$). **Physical properties:** Pink to grayish, blackening rapidly on the surface through weathering. *Luster glassy; hardness* 5^1/$_2$–6; *specific gravity* 3.4–3.7; *fracture* splintery, very tough in massive state; *cleavage* prismatic at about 88° and 92°. Crystals brittle; transparent to translucent. **Composition:** Manganese silicate (54.1% MnO, 45.9% SiO_2, with Ca partially replacing Mn). **Tests:** Fuses to a brown glass. Gives manganese test in borax bead.

Distinguishing characteristics: The pink material is likely to be mistaken only for rhodochrosite (but it is much harder than the manganese carbonate) and for feldspar, which gives no manganese test or easy fusion. The gemmy red crystals are practically indistinguishable from the similar, closely related iron-bearing pyroxmangite. Bustamite is less intensely red. A black stain quickly develops on exposed internally pinkish boulders and is really diagnostic.

Occurrence: The world's leading specimen locality for large crystal masses is Franklin, New Jersey, a mine from which have come specimens that add luster to museums of the world; the crystals were worked out by careful excavation from a matrix of enclosing calcite. Massive rhodonite is found at Plainfield, Massachusetts, and at numerous western and foreign localities — California, Brazil (Minas Gerais), Siberia, Australia (Tamworth, New South Wales), and Tanzania, to name a few.

Good and sometimes transparent red crystals are found with other silicates distributed through sulfide ores at Broken Hill, New South Wales (in Japanese manganese mines, pyroxmangite predominates). Masses suitable for carving are found in the Ural Mountains. Small late Franklin-type wedge crystals are found at Pajsberg and Langban, Sweden.

WOLLASTONITE $CaSiO_3$
Triclinic — pedial 1
Environment: A mineral of contact-metamorphic deposits in limestones and in ringing intrusive stocks. **Crystal description:** Usually in fibrous, somewhat splintery masses of elongated crystals flattened parallel to the base and to the front pinacoid, giving the impression of slender prismatic needles. Also, but infrequently, as single crystals, often coarsely granular, compact, and massive. **Physical properties:** White to colorless, pink, or gray. *Luster* glassy to silky; *hardness* $4^1/_2$–5; *specific gravity* 2.8–2.9; *fracture* splintery; *cleavage* perfect pinacoidal (pseudoprismatic) on base and front pinacoid at 84° and 96° to each other. Translucent; often fluorescent in yellow and orange. **Composition:** Calcium silicate (48.3% CaO, 51.7% SiO_2). **Tests:** Fuses to a white globule. Dissolves in hydrochloric acid, with a separation of shreds of silica.

Distinguishing characteristics: Distinguished from tremolite by greater fusibility and its cleavage angles, which are near those of the pyroxenes and far from the 56° and 124° of the amphiboles. Distinguished from diopside and prismatic topaz (pycnite) by its fusibility and solubility in acid. Fluorescence is commonly an aid to quick identification.

Occurrence: Common where limestones have been strongly metamorphosed, as in Llano Co., Texas, and Riverside Co. (at Crestmore) and San Diego Co., California. Good examples of distinct crystals come from Natural Bridge, St. Lawrence Co., New York. Richly fluorescent specimens were found at Franklin, New Jersey. As might be expected, crystals are found in the altered limestone blocks thrown out by the eruptions of Monte Somma on Vesuvius. Typical fibrous masses come from Perheniemi, Finland, and crystals from Banat, Romania, and in the marble of Tremorgio, Switzerland. A small amount is mined for use in ceramics.

PECTOLITE $NaCa_2Si_3O_8(OH)$ **Pl. 55**

Triclinic — pinacoidal $\dfrac{1}{m}$

Environment: Usually an associate of the zeolites in traprocks; sometimes a secondary mineral or vein in coarser rocks such as nepheline syenites. **Crystal description:** For many years known primarily in mammillary, pin-cushion needle masses with fibrous structures lining or filling cavities in traprocks. Rarely, a thin top of an occasional coarser blade may protrude, exposing traces of side pinacoids. Also along vein surfaces in successive domes, the needle sprays radiating from successive centers along each wall and hazardous to the finger. New developments of this decade, however, include two occurrences of slightly conchoidal flat plates almost 1 in. (2 cm) long and about $\frac{1}{2}$ in. (0.75 cm) across, in addition to pale blue compact masses of radiating needles.

Physical properties: White to gray to pale blue, often stained yellowish or reddish. *Luster* silky; *hardness* 5 (but since most is easily separated into fibers it appears softer); *specific gravity* 2.7–2.8; *fracture* splintery; *cleavage* the common type crumbles into fibers from perfect basal and front pinacoid (pseudoprismatic) planes. Translucent; usually weakly fluorescent yellowish to orange in longwave ultraviolet.

Composition: Hydrous calcium sodium silicate (33.8% CaO, 9.3% NaO, 54.2% SiO_2, 27% H_2O). **Tests:** Fuses easily to a white glass, coloring flame yellow (sodium). Fused mass fluoresces weakly white in shortwave ultraviolet, losing its longwave ultraviolet fluorescence.

Distinguishing characteristics: Usually the zeolite companionship is characteristic enough. If tests are necessary it can be distinguished from the amphiboles by greater fusibility and from wollastonite by the water that escapes in the closed tube. Distinguished from fibrous zeolites by lack of a blue color (aluminum) in the cobalt nitrate test.

Occurrence: Very abundant in domes and in the described hemispherical crusts and bundles at Paterson, New Jersey, and nearby zeolite occurrences. Warning: The easily separated slender needles of New Jersey zeolite pocket pectolites readily penetrate the skin and are difficult to remove because they are so brittle. Avoid handling as much as possible. Fluorescent pectolite is a component of the nepheline syenite found in the Magnet Cove, Arkansas, nepheline syenite (readily noted with ultraviolet illumination). Massive white pectolite is found in Tehama Co., California, and as waterworn pink amygdular masses on Isle Royale beaches in Lake Superior. The first occurrence of distinct and well-formed crystals was the Jeffrey Quarry, Asbestos, Quebec. The long (up to $1\frac{1}{2}$ in.; 3 cm), bluish white blades with good slanting "terminations" (they are probably elongated on the b-axis), partly crusted here and there with white tacharanite $[(Ca,Mg,Al)[Si,Al]O_3 \cdot H_2O)$, are really unusual and entirely unlike any pectolite previously found. Subsequently, similar pectolite blades have been found in St. Hilaire, Quebec. Yet more unusual is a deep buried gem material find in the Dominican Republic; the delicately blue compact radiating needle masses are cut into cabochon stones and sold as Larimar, nearly identical in appearance to a crystallized Japanese Iimori phosphate "glass" called "Victoria Stone." Nondestructively distinguishable by longwave fluorescence.

BABINGTONITE $Ca(Fe^4,Mn)Fe^3Si_5O_{14}(OH)$ **Pl. 56**

Triclinic — pinacoidal $\overline{1}$

Environment: A late, probably hydrothermal (hot-water), secondary mineral, commonly associated in traprock with the zeolites, and on joint surfaces in dark plutonics or gneiss. **Crystal description:** Tiny crystals usually very brilliant. Roughly equidimensional, with zeolite-surrounded faces striated. Always in crystals. **Physical properties:** Black. *Luster* glassy; *hardness* $5\frac{1}{2}$–6; *specific gravity* 3.4; *fracture* conchoidal; *cleavage* 2 pinacoidal (1 good) at 87° and 93°. Translucent as thin splinters. Grains under the polarizing microscope are colorful and beautifully pleochroic. **Composition:** Alkaline calcium iron silicate (about 19% CaO, 29% FeO plus Fe_2O_3,

51.5% SiO_2, and 0.5% H_2O, often with some manganese).
Tests: Fuses easily to a black magnetic globule. Insoluble in hydrochloric acid.

Distinguishing characteristics: In appearance and in the hand, it might be rather difficult to distinguish from some of the black pyroxenes, but is less prismatic than the amphiboles usually are. The easy melting and the magnetism are helpful; but most of all, one relies on the mineral associates and the paragenesis. Typically perched on prehnite.

Occurrence: An attractive but uncommon mineral of seams and silicate veins, found best at several quarry localities in Massachusetts. Once, at a quarry in Blueberry Hill, Woburn, Massachusetts, in crevices in a diorite, with sphene, calcite and thin-bladed crystals of prehnite. Small ones uncovered by dissolving away the calcite are very brilliant and unmistakable. Larger crystals at a Westfield, Massachusetts, traprock quarry seem contemporaneous with green prehnite. Thin-bladed and often partially altered (to a bronze amphibole) crystals at Paterson and Great Notch, New Jersey, and in Poona, India, specimens.

Good crystals coat feldspar in pegmatites in granite at Baveno, Italy, and Arendal, Norway. Similarly in Devonshire, England. Actually too uncommon to justify inclusion here, but attractive and collectible with trophy satisfaction for collectors, especially those in Massachusetts.

NEPTUNITE $(Na,K)_2(Fe,Mn)TiSi_4O_{12}$ **Pl. 56**

Monoclinic — prismatic $\frac{2}{m}$

Environment: In pegmatitic nepheline syenite cavities and on one serpentine surface with natrolite and benitoite. **Crystal description:** Always in crystals, the best from California over 1 in. (3 cm) long, distinctly prismatic in habit, and about $3/8$–$1/4$ in. (4-6 mm) across. Often forms crossed × twins. **Physical properties:** Black with reddish reflections from surface cracks *Luster* glassy; *hardness* 5–6; *specific gravity* 3.2; *fracture* splintery (conchoidal across splinters); *cleavage* perfect prismatic. Translucent red brown on thin edges. **Composition:** A sodium and potassium, iron manganese titanosilicate (17.8% TiO_2, 9.8% Na_2O, 5.1% K_2O, 11.6% FeO, 3.8% MnO, 51.9% SiO). **Tests:** Fuses readily to a black nonmagnetic shiny glass sphere that crushes to a brown powder.

Distinguishing characteristic: The perfect cleavages at about 80° and 100° distinguish it from the amphiboles, and it is more fusible than most similar pyroxenes. The red-brown translucency and streak are very characteristic. The Coalinga, San Benito Co., California serpentine surface with its benitoite association is unique.

Occurrence: A rare mineral but of special interest to the American collector because of the lone occurrence in San Benito Co., California, where it has formed on walls bordering natrolite veins and accompanied by well-crystallized benitoite in a green serpentine. Dealers have usually exposed both minerals in specimens from under a white natrolite coating with a hydrochloric acid bath. Smaller and duller crystals were found in Narsarssuak, Greenland, in pockets in a nepheline syenite along the coast. Similar crystals have been found in the Kola Peninsula, Russia.

CHRYSOCOLLA $Cu_2H_2Si_2O_5(OH)_4$ **Pl. 56**
Monoclinic

Environment: In the oxidized zone of copper deposits, mainly in arid climates. **Crystal description:** Microcrystalline, usually in solid vein-filling or botryoidal masses, from dull to glassy and opal-like in appearance. Convincingly crystal-like needles were only found at one locality (Mackay, Idaho). **Physical properties:** Sky blue to greenish blue and green, often streaked with black. *Luster* glassy, dull, or earthy; *hardness* 2–4; *specific gravity* 2.0–2.4; *fracture* conchoidal. Physically unstable, sectile to brittle. **Composition:** Basic copper silicate (45.2% CuO, 34.3% SiO_2, 20.5% H_2O). **Tests:** Tongue usually clings to specimen. Blackens and gives water in closed tube. Practically infusible, but decomposed by hydrochloric acid with a separation of silica. Desiccated material, glassy or matte and long in a collection, tends to take up water and crumble when immersed, so never wash. Breaks apart violently in a flame.

Distinguishing characteristics: Only likely to be confused with much harder turquoise (6, so not scratched by a knife and it does not stick to the tongue) and with chrysocolla-impregnated chalcedony which has, of course, the quartz hardness of 7.

Occurrence: Chrysocolla occurs very widely in the Southwest in copper deposits. Blue chrysocolla-impregnated quartz, covered by sparkling little crystals of white quartz, from the Globe Mine, Gila Co., Arizona, and Mexico are frequent in collections. Elsewhere, as in Superior, Arizona, the chrysocolla is spread through the chalcedony to color a hard and attractive chrysoprase-like gem material (which amateur lapidaries loosely tend to call chrysocolla, too). Fine massive specimens were found, in the early stages, in most of the w.

U.S. copper mines. Still found in abundance in Africa and Chile. Russia and England (Cornwall and Cumberland) once produced good specimens. Glassy-luster specimens are uncommon.

Remarks: It is an ore of copper when associated with other secondary copper minerals. In the West it often occurs impregnating and tinting otherwise worthless rock with associated copper minerals, as in Israel (Elat stone), and used like turquoise for jewelry. True chrysocolla, free of quartz, is fragile and likely to crack as it loses water in dry cabinet environments.

◆Metasilicate Types   Si:O = n:3n

Ring Structures

The silica tetrahedrons in this type of structure form a closed ring. There are two ring structures: one of three tetrahedrons forming a trigonal pattern, the other of six forming a hexagonal pattern. As would be expected, the minerals with these patterns reveal their structure as trigonal or hexagonal crystals.

BENITOITE $BaTiSi_3O_9$ **Pl. 56**
Hexagonal — Ditrigonal bipyramidal   6 m 2
Environment: At San Benito Co., California (practically the only occurrence), crystals have grown on the sides of natrolite veins cutting a schistose serpentinite, and associated with black neptunite. **Crystal description:** Good tabular triangular crystals, to $2\frac{1}{2}$ in. (5 cm) across, usually unevenly colored blue and white. The triangular base is likely to be duller in luster and whiter than the pyramids and prisms. **Physical properties:** Blue to white (rarely pink). *Luster* glassy; *hardness* 6–$6\frac{1}{2}$; *specific gravity* 3.6; *fracture* conchoidal; *cleavage* poor pyramidal. Transparent to translucent; fluorescent blue in shortwave ultraviolet light. **Composition:** Barium titanium silicate (36.3% BaO, 20.2% TiO_2, 43.5% SiO_2). **Tests:** All specimens are crystals with a shape so distinctive that tests are unnecessary.
Distinguishing characteristics: Since there is but one significant occurrence, with constant associates and appearance, it has never been necessary to test specimens; it resembles no other mineral.
Occurrence: Mainly known from a limited deposit of compact granular natrolite veins cutting a gray-green fibrous schist

interlayered with serpentine. Collectors might eventually turn up other occurrences of this attractive mineral. Small pinkish "roses" of benitoite have been found near the California occurrence, and it has been reported in six-sided blue crystals at Omi Machi Nishi-kubiki Gun, Niigata Prefecture, Japan.

Remarks: Until this mineral was found in 1907, the mineral world had no naturally occurring representative of this crystal class. Even now it is the only mineral example. The official California gemstone, it is expensive when transparent, free of flaws, and of good color. One carat is fine; anything over five carats can be regarded as very special.

EUDIALYTE $Na_4(Ca,Ce,Fe)_2ZrSi_6O_{17}(OH,Cl)_2$ **Pl. 56**

Hexagonal — Hexagonal scalenohedral $\overline{3}\ \dfrac{2}{m}$

Environment: A species restricted to the coarse or pegmatitic phases of nepheline syenite. **Crystal description:** Usually embedded, with the grains occasionally showing a few unidentifiable crystal faces; always associated with the mineral assembly usual for this infrequent environment, as its multi-element composition would suggest. Crystals to 2 in. (5 cm) have been found. **Physical properties:** Garnet red; pink, brown. *Luster* dull; *hardness* 5–6; *specific gravity* 2.9–3.0; *fracture* uneven; *cleavage* poor basal. Almost gemmy to translucent. **Composition:** A complex silicate of calcium, sodium, zirconium, cerium, iron, and manganese, with hydroxyl and chlorine (about 50% SiO_2, 14% ZrO_2, and 2% to 3% Ce_2O_3). **Tests:** Fuses fairly easily to a shiny green glass.

Distinguishing characteristics: The unique associations of feldspar and nepheline, usually with aegirine, are sufficiently characteristic. In most cases, collectors in such a quarry knows where they are and of the plethora of uncommon species to be found. The fusibility of the eudialyte would distinguish examples from zircon, garnet, and from the varieties of the more common minerals. The rare red sodium fluoride villaumite (NaF), has cubic cleavage and rhodochrosite (usually brown in this environment) is rhombohedral.

Occurrence: Eudialyte is attractive and popular with serious collectors despite its rarity. In the U.S. it is found in good crystals in the coarse phases of the Magnet Cove, Arkansas, nepheline syenite where it has a good pink-red color. In Greenland, disseminated grains are so abundant in outcrops that they can be seen offshore; they sometimes form rich red bands. Also found on the Kola Peninsula in Russia, in Norway, and Madagascar. An often mentioned quarry near Quebec, St. Hilaire, has been a rich source of nepheline syenite rarities in the last decade.

TOURMALINE GROUP   Pl. 57
Hexagonal — Ditrigonal pyramidal   3 m

Schorl	black	$NaFe_3B_3Al_3(Al_3Si_6O_{27})(OH)_4$
Dravite	green, brown, reddish	$NaMg_3B_3Al_3(Al_3Si_6O_{27})(OH)_4$
Uvite	black, white	$CaMg_3Al_3(Al_3Si_6O_{27})(O,OH)_4$
Elbaite	the spectrum	$(Na)(Al,Fe,Li,Mg)_3B_3Al_3(Al_3Si_6O_{27})(O,OH,F)_4$

Environment: Primarily a mineral of high temperatures and pressures forming in igneous and metamorphic rocks, and best developed in granitic pegmatites. Tourmaline grains in sand have been shown to have been overgrown in sedimentary environments by new tourmaline, restoring crystal surfaces to rounded grains. Brown-black fibrous crystals, probably all schorl, commonly accompany copper veinlet disseminations in Mexico, Peru, and Chile. **Crystal description:** Commonly in prismatic crystals, sometimes very large and up to a yard (1 m) long and several inches wide. Frequently with a three-face rhombohedral or flat-plane top, with a different set of surfaces on the bottom (demonstrating hemimorphism). Clusters sometimes form stellate radiations. Cross sections usually nearly triangular, but multiply-striated prism faces merge to create a bulging cross section. Squat, tabular schorl crystals are rare enough to be notable. Colored crystals of elbaite are always prismatic, with hues that changed as growth progressed from one end to the other or from the center outward. Also in hair-thin veins of fine needles or in meter-thick black masses. Brown crystals (dravite) differ, are not elongated nor rounded prismatically, solid crystals from Australia are commonly so sharp and equidimensional that they could easily be mistaken for dodecahedrons. **Physical properties:** Any color in the spectrum plus colorless, brown, and black. *Luster* glassy; *hardness* 7–7$\frac{1}{2}$; *specific gravity* 3.0-3.3; *fracture* very easy across the crystal (almost a cleavage), lengthwise, uneven to conchoidal; *cleavage* poor prismatic and rhombohedral. Opaque to transparent; pyroelectric (becomes strongly charged electrically on heating and cooling) and piezoelectric (rapidly becomes charged in response to pressure). Light brown magnesium (dravite) varieties often fluorescent yellow in shortwave ultraviolet light. **Composition:** A complex series of compounds with varying amounts and ratios of sodium, calcium, magnesium, lithium, aluminum, and iron but with a constant overall structure and content of the critical elements: boron, aluminum, silica, and the volatile compounds. (B_2O_3 averages about 10%; the Li_2O responsible for elbaite, the polychromatic variety, is only 1.0 to 1.5%.) **Tests:** Fusibility depends upon the composition; the brown magnesium varieties are most easily fused, while the lithium varieties are infusible. Some form a crust of brownish powder. Crystals will magnetically attract dust, ashes, or bits of paper to their ends when warmed and cooled. Prize subject for a demonstration of the red lead-sulfur electrical response test (see Chapter 3).

Distinguishing characteristics: The bulging triangular cross section of most crystals is usually all that is required. The poor cleavage separates it from the pyroxenes and amphiboles.

Occurrence: Tourmaline is found in the U.S. wherever coarse granitic rocks and their related pegmatite dikes come to the surface. New England — particularly the vicinity of West Paris, Maine — and San Diego Co., California, are famous for their colored tourmalines. Black tourmalines are found in pegmatites in many states, and tourmaline-bearing schists are also found in Maine and California. The usually brown magnesium dravite tourmalines in St. Lawrence Co., New York, are formed in a metamorphosed limestone, as are the sharp black dravites (long considered schorl) at Pierpont, New York. Small brown crystals have been found in the Inwood dolomite along the Harlem River in New York City, and giant ones are numerous at Yinniethara, Western Australia. Brumado, a magnesite mine at Bahia, Brazil, has also given up some fine dravite specimens.

Morphologically, dravite seems to be alike at both ends. The prism faces are sharp, there is no rounding, and the Australian crystals could easily be taken for slightly elongated dodecahedrons. A colorless "dravite" from Gouverneur, New York, suggests a possibility of collecting the uvite variety in St. Lawrence County. An odd brown variety found in sprays on rhyolite surfaces in Mexico, with iron replacing calcium or potassium, has been called buergerite.

Since tourmaline is valued as a gem mineral, all known foreign localities have been sought out and worked for jewelry stones. The state of Minas Gerais, Brazil, is presently the major source of gem material, including some unique brilliant blue-green stones colored by copper (Paraíba). Several localities in Madagascar have yielded crystals up to 20 in. long by 6 in. (50 cm × 15 cm), with slices showing interesting color zoning of triangular patterns memorializing growth stages in changing termination hues. Some of these with more calcium than sodium are known as liddicoatite. Namibia yields fine blue, red and green crystals. The island of Elba, off the Italian coast, has been celebrated for its pink crystals, often tipped with black; it provides the name of the lithium subdivision, elbaite. The Urals once produced some fine deep reds. Chainpur, Nepal, produces small light-hued elbaite of gemstone quality, and the hundreds of pegmatites of Afghanistan, with their abundance of largely pastel-hued elbaites accompanying beryl, topaz, and kunzite, has become the latest treasure chest.

Remarks: For generations tourmaline was treated as a single species with an enormous composition range but basically one general formula. It is now treated as a mineral group with numerous theoretical series and end members.

The colored tourmaline varieties make valuable gems, and these as well as the more glassy black varieties are used for electrical apparatus that utilizes their pressure-stimulated electrically responsive (piezoelectricity) characteristic. Jewelers give gem varieties special names, with red known as rubellite, blue as indicolite, while simple tourmaline indicates the green variety to the gem trade.

BERYL $Be_3Al_2Si_6O_{18}$ **Pl. 58**

Hexagonal — Dihexagonal bipyramidal $\frac{6}{m}\frac{2}{m}\frac{2}{m}$

Environment: Almost exclusively a pegmatite mineral, rarely in high-temperature veins and in rhyolite seams and pockets where it has formed from beryllium-bearing gases or very hot solutions. **Crystal description:** One of the most beautifully crystallized minerals, usually in prismatic hexagons, sometimes several feet long and weighing many pounds (kilos). Rarely in tabular crystals; the pink cesium-bearing beryls are more likely to develop this flat habit. Also massive and embedded as grains or columnar masses. **Physical properties:** White, blue, yellow, green, pink, red. *Luster* glassy; *hardness* 8; *specific gravity* 2.6–2.8; *fracture* conchoidal; *cleavage* poor basal; *clarity* gemmy and transparent, to translucent; sometimes weakly fluorescent yellow (emerald may fluoresce pink to deep red also, especially as a synthetic). **Composition:** Beryllium aluminum silicate (14.0% BeO, 19.0% Al_2O_3, 67.0% SiO_2; sodium, lithium, and cesium may replace part of the beryllium, thus reducing the BeO content and lowering its value as an ore of beryllium). Impurities create many of the characteristic colors; iron is responsible for aquamarine, chromium and/or vanadium for emerald, and manganese for red beryl. **Tests:** Glows white, but does not decrepitate violently like quartz, instead remaining whitened but intact in the flame. Edges fuse with great difficulty to a white glass. Insoluble in the common acids.

Distinguishing characteristics: The pegmatitic occurrence and six-sided crystal outline are very characteristic. Only likely to be confused with apatite (which is much softer, often fluorescent, and soluble in acid), with white, massive topaz (wholly infusible and with a good cleavage), and with quartz (which, before attaining near-red heat, decrepitates violently).

Occurrence: Ordinary beryl is the chief ore of beryllium. Transparent varieties have gem value and are called aquamarine (blue and blue-green), emerald (green), golden beryl (yellow-brown), morganite (pink), and ruby (red). Since as a rule it is a mineral of once deeply buried rocks, it will be found primarily on gneiss and schist roofs above batholiths, where pegmatites have been exposed on the surface as weathering has removed overlying formations. New England has many pegmatite localities; their beryls, sometimes enormous, usually appear as well-formed crystals in quartz and feldspar pegmatites. Crystals ordinarily break free of their matrix without much difficulty. Farther south, North Carolina pegmatites are also sources of common beryl, with emeralds from the chromium-colored variety occurring at several localities in the state. Tabular beryl crystals (generally thought to indicate a high cesium content) have been found in some abundance in New Mexico at Dixon. Large crystals are found in the Black Hills of South Dakota, though gem material is unlikely. Short-prismatic pink (morganite) beryls occur with the aquamarine, kunzite, and colored tourmaline in San Diego Co., California. An unusual occurrence for beryl is that of ruby red crystals in the Wha Wha Mountains, Utah. where they are more or less embedded in a white rhyolite, $1-1\frac{1}{2}$ in. (2-3 cm) long. Smaller, flatter, and paler raspberry-pink crystals and rose-colored clusters have been found in the gas cavity in the Thomas Range (Utah) rhyolite, best known for its topaz and bixbyite.

In a freak paragenesis, emeralds are found in calcite veins in a black limestone at Muso, and in almost-pegmatite veins at Chivor, and Gachala, Colombia. Biotite schists bordering a pegmatite are considered the source of the chromium coloring emeralds in the Ekaterinberg, (Sverdlovsk) Russia district, accompanied there by alexandrite, chrysoberyl, and phenakite. Large crystals of aquamarine and fine morganites come from Madagascar. Brazil has long been the chief source of aquamarine, and crystals weighing several hundred pounds (100–150 kg) have been recovered from streambeds and dikes, principally in Minas Gerais, Brazil. In a tin mine of South Africa, clusters of slender needles are unusual gangue minerals in an unusual vein deposit. Numerous pegmatites have lately been worked in the mountainous Afghanistan-Pakistan border area; large numbers of splendid aquamarine crystals have been found, though most are too pale to have other than specimen value.

◆Pyrosilicate Type   Si:O = Si2O7

Silicates of this structure group contain cells with two SiO4 tetrahedrons sharing one of the oxygens. Aluminum is usually not present. They have no special characteristics to give them distinction. Crystals are often tabular, and because of a frequent presence of heavy elements, the minerals may be high in specific gravity.

HEMIMORPHITE $Zn_4Si_2O_7(OH)_2 \cdot 2(H_2O)$ **Pl. 58**
Orthorhombic — Rhombic pyramidal   m m 2
Environment: The oxidized zone of zinc deposits. **Crystal description:** Commonly crystallized in flattened prismatic plates up to an inch (2–3 cm) in length, attached at the base so that the unlike array of the lower end (indicative of its hemimorphism) is not apparent. Also in mammillary rounded groups with convexly crystallized surfaces (Franklin, New Jersey) and in smoother botryoidal knobs, granular, massive, and earthy. **Physical properties:** White, sometimes slightly stained with iron or copper (brown and blue or green). *Luster* glassy; *hardness* $4\frac{1}{2}$–5; *specific gravity* 3.4–3.5; *fracture* uneven to poor conchoidal; *cleavage* prismatic. Transparent to translucent. Strongly susceptible to electrical charges with changing temperature (pyroelectric); often fluorescent pale orange in longwave ultraviolet light. **Composition:** Alkaline hydrated zinc silicate (67.5% ZnO, 25.0%

SiO_2, 7.5% H_2O). **Tests:** Decrepitates, and readily becomes frosted; develops a coating, yellow when hot, turning white when cold. Following roasting, fluoresces bright orange in longwave ultraviolet, white in shortwave ultraviolet.

Distinguishing characteristics: Distinguished from smithsonite by its lack of bubbling in acid; recognized as a zinc mineral by its colored coating after blowpiping. Heavier than prehnite, not found in basalts, and not associated with the similar zeolites.

Occurrence: No longer a significant American mineral. The best U.S. specimens were found in the Stone Mine, Leadville, Colorado, and at Elkhorn, Montana. Solid masses of white, giant crawling-caterpillar-like crystalline surfaces were obtained in the early days at Franklin, New Jersey. Excellent bladed examples now come from Mapimi, Durango, Mexico, with crystals 1 in. (2.5 cm) and more in length standing up in limonitic gossan pockets. Crusts of upstanding, flat, and well-terminated crystals $^1\!/_2$ to 4 in. (1–7 cm) long and $^1\!/_8$–$^1\!/_4$ in. (1-3 mm) broad, have likewise been found at Santa Eulalia, Chihuahua, Mexico, many smaller ones protruding like hedgehog spines from white dolomite rhombohedrons and more delicate than most hemimorphites. Any remaining crystals from the Joplin, Missouri, district are small, on cavernous ocher hemimorphite masses mixed with a brown and earthy smithsonite ("dry-bone ore").

Remarks: The old name, calamine, was once widely used but has been changed by international consent to hemimorphite, which describes the asymmetrical crystal class (no center of symmetry) to which it belongs. The current name eliminates centuries of confusion resulting from the European miner's use of "calamine" for both carbonate and silicate.

BERTRANDITE $Be_4Si_2O_7(OH)_2$ **Pl. 58**
Orthorhombic — Rhombic pyramidal   m m 2

Environment: A secondary mineral mostly formed from late post-deposition hydrothermal attack on pegmatitic beryl. Can also be primary from lower-temperature gas deposition (sublimate) causing rock alteration. **Crystal description:** Recognizable only when in distinct crystals, mostly small, and commonly tabular parallel to the base. The pearly luster of the base is quite characteristic and is probably due to a lamellar, parallel growth of individual crystals, possibly in a polysynthetic twinning sequence. Often twinned into "heart-shaped" twins, which then are not tabular in habit but very typical of the mineral. **Physical properties:** Colorless, flesh color. *Luster* pearly on base, glassy otherwise; *hardness* 6; *specific gravity* 2.6; *fracture* flaky; *cleavage* perfect basal, good prismatic. Transparent to translucent; strongly responsive electrically to temperature changes. **Composition:** Alkaline beryllium silicate (42.1% BeO, 50.3% SiO_2, 7.6% H_2O). **Tests:** Whitens but will hardly fuse on charcoal, insoluble in acid. Turns blue with cobalt nitrate test.

Distinguishing characteristics: Specimens found almost exclusively in complex pegmatites with corrosion-pitted beryls, eliminating any similar mineral. It is less fusible than the feldspars, but untwinned crystals may be difficult to distinguish from later albite feldspar growths in pockets. Usually the later albite will have grown on an earlier feldspar surface and aligned with them so that a group of prominences will reflect light simultaneously, in contrast to randomly oriented bertrandites that each reflect as individuals. The distinctive twins are easily recognized. Similar zeolites (resembling stilbite) fuse easily.

Occurrence: Bertrandite is usually considered rare, but actually is far more common than realized. It is likely to be encountered in any beryl pegmatite that hints of a history of secondary mineral formation, such as etching of the beryl, the growth of albite — especially the cleavelandite variety — or sulfide, fluorite, and calcite deposition in late cavities. Until recently, the best crystals came from Mt. Antero, Colorado, up to $1/2$ in. (1 cm) long. Excellent small crystals are found in pockets in the cleavelandite feldspar at Portland, Connecticut. Small crystals were found coating beryl of Bedford, Westchester Co., New York. It is associated with apatite at Stoneham, Maine.

Pseudomorphs of masses of bertrandite plates after beryl are found in a pegmatite in Jefferson Co., Colorado, and similarly in the state of Rio Grande do Norte in Brazil. Small primary crystals have been found on cassiterite-mica seams in Portugal and on beryl at Raade, Norway. Most European examples are inconspicuous, occupying cavities where beryl once grew. Simultaneously, in 1993, 1-in. (2.5-cm), slightly concave, and flattened stilbite-like, pectolite-like betrandite crystal bundles turned up with dealers from sources as distant as Pakistan and Brazil.

Remarks: Though hemimorphic, like hemimorphite, the low symmetry is less apparent in this mineral because the crystals are so commonly flattened parallel to the basal pinacoid. Hence, the slight difference in truncations on upper and lower edges is not especially noticeable, and, as suggested, it seems likely that there may be repetitive twinning.

DANBURITE $CaB_2Si_2O_8$ **Pl. 59**

Orthorhombic — Rhombic bipyramidal $\frac{2}{m}\frac{2}{m}\frac{2}{m}$

Environment: Has a remarkable variety of parageneses. Typically in high-temperature deposits, either in veins with sulfide ore or in contact-metamorphosed rocks. Also in pegmatites and in regional metamorphic environments. Also in salt-dome anhydrite-gypsum assembles. May be more common than supposed. **Crystal description:** Usually vertically striated prismatic crystals, often resembling topaz. May be very small and slender, or as much as 12 in. (30 cm) long and 4 in. (10 cm) across. Sometimes corroded so groups separate easily. Free-growing in pockets or embedded in matrix. **Physical properties:** Colorless, white, pale pink, gray, brownish, straw yellow. *Luster* glassy; *hardness* 7; *specific gravity* 3.0; fracture uneven to conchoidal; *cleavage* poor basal. Transparent to translucent. **Composition:** Calcium borosilicate (22.8% CaO, 28.4% B_2O_3, 48.8% SiO_2). **Tests:** Fuses with little difficulty to a milky glass that fluoresces bright blue in shortwave ultraviolet.

Distinguishing characteristics: The crystal form of danburite is similar to that of barite and topaz; its hardness distinguishes it from the barite group, and the lack of cleavage and fusibility distinguish it from the topaz group.

Occurrence: Once the most desirable danburite crystals were those from the Toruku and Obira Mines in Miyazaki and Oita Prefectures, Kyushu I., Japan, Some are clear at the summit and may grade down to milky. Others are sand-filled but may be as much as 4 in. (10 cm) long and in part implanted on axinite. The original occurrence at Danbury, Connecticut, consisted of corroded groups of brownish crystals with dolomite in white feldspar, but the locality appears to have been lost. A somewhat similar occurrence is at Russell, St. Lawrence Co., New York. At De Kalb, New York, corroded embedded grains are scattered in a white pegmatite quartz.

Thousands of slender, colorless prismatic crystals associated with chlorite once lined a fissure at Skopi, Switzerland. Accompanying rubies, danburite occurs in Myanmar as isolated crystals in the dolomitic marble matrix, often in fair-sized straw yellow, gemmy masses. In Bolivia, cloudy 1-in. (2 cm), gray to white doubly terminated crystals have been found embedded in a dolomite with gypsum (and tiny boracites), colored by inclusions of foreign matter. Abundant, spectacular, 3-in. (8 cm) and larger white and palest pink prism clusters are part of the gangue from La Aurora and

San Bartolo lead mines in Charcas, San Luis Potosí, Mexico. Large milky crystals to 4 in. (10 cm) long and half as broad have been found in a pegmatite in Baja California. Giant crystals, milky white and well formed, have been found at Vostochnaya, Siberia, some as much as 10 or 12 in. (25–30 cm) long. Microscopic crystals have been found in the insoluble salt-dome residues in the Gulf states.

Remarks: Sometimes it is cut as a colorless or straw-colored gem for collectors.

◆Orthosilicate Type Si:O = 1:4

The silicates of this type have the highest ratio of O to Si, which means that the tetrahedrons are independent and not interlocked. Chemically they differ greatly and there is no notable tendency for any elements to be present or absent. The packing is close, with the heavier elements dominant over silica, so the members are fairly high in specific gravity, and hard. Crystals tend to be equidimensional in their development, with little tendency toward elongation or flattening.

●Olivine Series

OLIVINE $(Mg,Fe)_2SiO_4$ **Pl. 59**

Orthorhombic — Rhombic bipyramidal $\dfrac{2}{m}\dfrac{2}{m}\dfrac{2}{m}$

Environment: A common rock-forming mineral of the darker rocks, never found with free quartz. Common in meteorites. **Crystal description:** Usually in embedded grains, rarely in free-growing crystals; commonly any free crystals that are found will be altered to serpentine. Solid sandy masses of olivine are known (making a rock called dunite). **Physical properties:** Green, light gray, brown. *Luster* glassy; *hardness* $6\frac{1}{2}$–7; *specific gravity* 3.3–3.4; *fracture* conchoidal; *cleavage* 1 fair and 1 poor. Transparent to translucent. **Composition:** Olivine is really a series of minerals of slightly varying compositions, ranging from the pure magnesium silicate (forsterite) through the magnesium iron silicate, chrysolite, to fayalite, the iron silicate (SiO_2 will average about 36.1% for a 1:1 Mg:Fe ratio). **Tests:** Infusible but slowly soluble in hydrochloric acid. Higher-iron examples fuse to a dark magnetic globule; but even if unfused, roasted powder may still become slightly magnetic, when high enough in iron.

Distinguishing characteristics: It is usually identified by color and occurrence. No similar mineral of this hardness and color is likely to be encountered in the same environment. Apatite is usually fluorescent and softer; green tourmaline comes in granite pegmatites where olivine could not form; garnet is easily fusible. A green glass produced by assayers is often confused with olivine, but it is unstable, and an efflorescence forms on the surface.

Occurrence: Solid, granular masses are found in basalt bombs in Arizona, near volcanic cinder cones, and in the Hawaiian lavas. A bed of slightly finer granular material is found near Webster, Jackson Co., North Carolina. Isolated crystals will be found in many porphyries of the Southwest, and fair-sized rounded grains may be found on anthills, with garnets, near Holbrook, Arizona. Common in the Italian volcanic bombs and in the old German volcanoes of the Eifel district. Large crystals formed near Møre and Snarum, Norway, but most were then altered to serpentine. A vein of shattered and serpentinized chrysolite that cements a number of fresh unaltered crystals cuts serpentine on St. John's I. (Zebirget) in the Red Sea. It is the chief source of jewelry peridots, but large corroded crystals have also been found in Burma. The crystals may be $2\frac{1}{2}$–3 in. (7–8 cm) long and about the same across and through. Similar crystals have been found in Pakistan.

Remarks: Dunite sand has been used for cast-iron molds and considered as a source of magnesium. The gem peridot is the chrysolite variety of olivine; facetable rough has come from the Southwest, Norway, Myanmar, and St. John's I. (Zebirget).

PHENAKITE Be_2SiO_4 **Pl. 59**
Hexagonal — Rhombohedral   3
Environment: A mineral of pegmatites and high-temperature veins. **Crystal description:** Almost always in free, well-developed crystals, which range from wedge-edged rhombohedral scales (usually on feldspar), to short, or even long, prisms (with quartz and beryl). Usually small, commonly only a fraction of an inch (0.5 cm) across. Elongated crystals often penetration-twinned, with re-entrants in the tips. **Physical properties:** Colorless and white. *Luster* glassy; *hardness* $7\frac{1}{2}$–8; *specific gravity* 3.0; *fracture* conchoidal; *cleavage* poor prismatic. Transparent to translucent. **Composition:** Beryllium silicate (45.6% BeO, 54.4% SiO_2). **Tests:** Infusible and insoluble in acids. Unlike quartz, usually does not decrepitate in the flame.

Distinguishing characteristics: Crystals provide the best clues; the rhombohedral scales can only be confused with one of the carbonates, which will be acid-soluble and soft. The prismatic crystals often resemble those of quartz, but quartz is striated horizontally on the prisms, whereas phenakite is striated vertically. Topaz has a basal, and better, cleavage. Quartz decrepitates, preventing any effort to fuse it; sturdier beryl whitens and fuses only on thinnest edges.

Occurrence: The best U.S. specimens are from Mt. Antero, Colorado, in pegmatitic pockets in short-prismatic, commonly penetration-twinned crystals, associated with beryl, fluorite, and quartz. Also near Colorado Springs at several localities in the Cheyenne Mountains district in rhombohedral-habit crystals often perched on microcline feldspar, with smoky quartz. Similar crystals are found on Baldface Mountain in New Hampshire on the Maine border; not far away, at Lord's Hill, Maine, prismatic crystals to $3/4$ in. (1.5 cm) long grow on smoky quartz. The most attractive specimens are flat crystals up to 2 in. (5 cm) across, with short-prism zones, sometimes grouped in great clusters at São Miguel de Piraçicaba, Minas Gerais, Brazil. The largest crystals are prisms embedded in cleavelandite feldspar or white quartz at Kragerø, Norway. They attain 6 or 8 in. (15–20 cm) in length and are an inch or more (2–3 cm) thick. The original discovery was of 2–3 in. (5–8 cm) crystals in mica, companions of the emeralds of (Sverdlovsk) Ekaterinburg in Russia.

Remarks: Named from a Greek word for "to deceive," because it was long confused with quartz. A crystal was pictured in a British mineralogical work in 1811 (J. Sowerby) and designated as white tourmaline 20 years before it was recognized as a new mineral.

WILLEMITE Zn_2SiO_4 Pl. 59

Hexagonal — Rhombohedral 3

Environment: Secondary, in oxidized portions of commonly arid-region zinc veins, and in one unique post-oxidization metamorphosed zinc deposit. **Crystal description:** Usually small and simple, short-prismatic or rhombohedral. The freak Franklin, New Jersey, occurrence has produced very large embedded crystals (troostite) in white calcite and, in cavities, well-formed small and highly fluorescent ones, sometimes with steep terminations on slender prisms. Also massive, fibrous, radiating. **Physical properties:** White, colorless, or steel blue, commonly stained reddish brown by iron (Belgian occurrence), or pale blue by copper (w. U.S. occurrences); also (N.J.) reddish, green, yellow-green, yellow, orange, black. *Luster* resinous to glassy; *hardness* $5\frac{1}{2}$; *specific gravity* 3.9–4.2; *fracture* uneven to conchoidal; *cleavage* basal. Transparent to translucent; often strongly fluorescent and sometimes phosphorescent and triboluminescent (giving flash of light when struck with metal point). **Composition:** Zinc silicate (73.0% ZnO, 27.0% SiO_2, with manganese replacing up to 12% of the Zn at Franklin, New Jersey, where it may be in large, dull, reddish or grayish crystals, a guise known as troostite). **Tests:** Ordinary willemite is nearly infusible, but the Franklin version fuses with difficulty. A chip dipped in sodium carbonate fuses to a dark brown enamel, a small tip of which is colored green after reheating with a drop of cobalt nitrate placed on it. Soluble in hydrochloric acid.

Distinguishing characteristics: A mineral recognized as a zinc mineral by the cobalt nitrate test can be distinguished from hemimorphite by the failure to give off moisture in the closed tube. It would be distinguished from smithsonite by a greater hardness and by slow, quiet solution in hydrochloric acid (smithsonite bubbles). Recognized in Franklin specimens usually by its brilliant green fluorescence and by association with zincite and franklinite. Fluorescence is also frequent in the other occurrences.

Occurrence: The world's preeminent willemite occurrence is at Franklin, New Jersey, where, with franklinite and zincite in a green, black, and red mixture, it is a principal zinc ore. At this locality it has had several stages of formation. Small free crystals may line cavity walls while coarse and unattractive crystals lie embedded in crystalline limestone. It has been suggested that the Franklin deposit, with its unique mineralogy, is the result of the metamorphism of an earlier oxidized zinc-sulfide ore body that commenced as the usual hemimorphite and smithsonite. Willemite is generally recognized as an important secondary zinc ore in African occurrences, where at Tsumeb it forms blue and green crystal crusts, and at Grootfontein, in Namibia, where it forms almost gemmy light brown crystal clusters. The American Southwest is now known to have a number of willemite occurrences; some of the best white and pale bluish crusts came from the Mammoth Mine at Tiger, Arizona. Small, colorless, platy crystals are embedded in a greenish serpentine rock at Balmat, New York. Pale blue gemmy crystals found in nepheline syenites in Greenland and at St. Hilaire, Quebec, seem to be primary in origin.

The original occurrence was at Altenberg, Moresnet, Belgium, in small reddish brown crystals. It was named for William I of Belgium in 1830, even though the mineral was described before that from the Franklin occurrence, without having been given a name at the time.

DIOPTASE H_2CuSiO_4 **Pls. 59, 64**
Hexagonal — Rhombohedral 3

Environment: Oxidized zones of copper ores, particularly in arid climates. **Crystal description:** Usually crystallized, with the crystals generally quite small; short-prismatic to rhombohedral habit; long-prismatic habit rare. **Physical properties:** Bluish emerald green. *Luster* glassy; *hardness* 5, *specific gravity* 3.3–3.4; *fracture* uneven to conchoidal; *cleavage* perfect rhombohedral. Transparent to translucent. **Composition:** Hydrous silicate of copper (50.4% CuO, 38.2% SiO_2, 11.4% H_2O). **Tests:** Crystals dull in hydrochloric acid; decrepitate, blacken, and give water in closed tube; turn brown on charcoal, without fusing.

Distinguishing characteristics: It is harder than similar green minerals — the copper sulfates, carbonates, and phosphates. The rhombohedral termination is invariable and very typical. Brochantite is softer and crushes easily to a green powder. Malachite dissolves in hydrochloric acid with effervescence. The bluish look of dioptase's green is very distinctive; experienced collectors can spot this typical shade at some distance. Once seen it becomes unmistakable.

Occurrence: There is no outstanding U.S. occurrence. Rich crusts of very slender, short, upright and bundled green needles associated with willemite and wulfenite were found at Tiger, Arizona, in the Mammoth Mine. Other Arizona localities include the Christmas Mine and Salome, always as crusts of tiny crystals. Because of the similarity to brochantite and malachite, it is probably more common than generally realized at many of the western copper mines. Copiapó, Chile, has two mines where the thin U.S.-type crystals have been found. Mexico has small crystals too, but Western Hemisphere examples take second place to those of the Eastern Hemisphere.

Tsumeb, Namibia, is remarkable as the source of the largest dioptase crystals, which may be as much as 1 in. (2.5 cm) long. More slender, gemmy prismatic crystals to 2 in. (5 cm) long have been found at Mindouli in the Congo Republic. The classic locality, given as the Kirghiz Steppe, Ural Mountains (now labeled Altyn-Tuba, Karaganda Oblast, Kazakhstan) was of seams in a limestone, on brownish quartz with some quite respectable specimens. Though rare, dioptase has always been one of the most popular and desirable minerals in the eyes of the general collector. Good specimens are usually expensive.

●Humite Group   Pl. 59

This is a group of closely related minerals that chemically can be considered a mixture of forsterite (Mg_2SiO_4) with brucite ($Mg[OH]_2$), the layer of brucite alternating or lying between two, three, or four layers of forsterite. The members of the group and the formulas are:

NORBERGITE	$Mg_2SiO_4 \cdot Mg(OH,F)_2$	or	$Mg_3(SiO_4)(F,OH)_2$
CHONDRODITE	$2Mg_2SiO_4 \cdot Mg(OH,F)_2$	or	$Mg_5(SiO_4)_2(F,OH)_2$
HUMITE	$3Mg_2SiO_4 \cdot Mg(OH,F)_2$	or	$Mg_7(SiO_4)_3(F,OH)_2$
CLINOHUMITE	$4Mg_2SiO_4 \cdot Mg(OH,F)_2$	or	$Mg_9(SiO_4)_4(F,OH)_2$

Humite and norbergite: orthorhombic $\dfrac{2}{m} \dfrac{2}{m} \dfrac{2}{m}$

Clinohumite and chondrodite: monoclinic $\dfrac{2}{m}$

The relative length of the vertical axis varies, depending on the composition; the two other axes remain constant. Consequently, the general appearance, as well as the blowpipe responses, are about the same in all, and the amateur collector cannot distinguish between members of the group. Chondrodite, found in metamorphic iron deposits, is the most frequent and the most spectacular member of the group. With the others, it is also found in contact and regionally metamorphosed dolomitic marbles. Iron is usually present, replacing some of the magnesium. Formulas are often written thus: humite $(Mg,Fe)_7Si_3O_{12}(F,OH)_2$. **Crystal description:** Commonly in embedded, shapeless or nearly shapeless grains in crystalline limestones. Well-formed crystals with smooth and shiny faces (but rather numerous, making orientation difficult) are found in a few places: Tilly Foster Mine, Brewster, New York, and Kafveltorp, Sweden. Italian crystals are smaller. **Physical properties:** Red-brown to yellow. *Luster* glassy; *hardness* 6–6½; *specific gravity* 3.1–3.2; *fracture* subconchoidal; *cleavage* basal, not always easy to observe. Transparent to translucent; sometimes yellow fluorescence. **Composition:** Alkaline magnesium fluorosilicates (see above; about 57% MgO, several percent of FeO, and 35% SiO_2). **Tests:** Infusible, but give water in closed tube.

Distinguishing characteristics: None of the similar minerals give water in the closed tube. Likely to be confused with garnet (which, however, is fusible), with brown tourmaline (usually fusible), and with staurolite (which is heavier and unlikely to be found in the same environment).

Occurrence: The world's finest locality for chondrodite is the famous Tilly Foster Mine, at Brewster, New York, where free-growing crystals up to 2 in. (5 cm) across were found in a serpentine, associated with magnetite and equally remarkable clinochlore crystals. The finest are deep red-brown, shiny, and transparent, but many are more or less altered to serpentine. Smaller yellower brown and less well-formed crystals are distributed through metal sulfides at Kafveltorp, Sweden. Yellow-brown grains of chondrodite are common in the crystalline limestones of n. New Jersey, associated with dark gray spinel octahedrons.

All members of the humite group have been reported in paler crystals in the altered limestone blocks thrown out on the flanks of Vesuvius (Monte Somma). Facetable clinohumite has been found in Russia.

●Garnets Pl. 60

On the basis of chemical analyses, the members of this common group have been divided into two series that mix with each other to a limited extent, but within each group they appear to grade into each other without sharp lines of demarcation. The amateur can only approximate identities from color, gravity, and associations. One series has been christened the "pyralspite" series, from the names pyrope, almandine, and spessartine; the other series, the "ugrandite," from uvarovite, grossular, and andradite.

PYROPE	$Mg_3Al_2Si_3O_{12}$	
ALMANDINE	$Fe_3Al_2Si_3O_{12}$	
SPESSARTINE	$Mn_3Al_2Si_3O_{12}$	Cubic — hexoctahedral
UVAROVITE	$Ca_3Cr_2Si_3O_{12}$	
GROSSULAR	$Ca_3Al_2Si_3O_{12}$	$\frac{4}{m}\,\overline{3}\,\frac{2}{m}$
ANDRADITE	$Ca_3Fe_2Si_3O_{12}$	

In detail they are as follows:

Name	Color	Principal occurrence	Specific gravity
Pyrope	Deep yellow-red	In igneous rocks	3.5
Almandine	Deep violet-red	Metamorphic rocks	4.3
Spessartine	Brown, with a reddish or pinkish tone	Rhyolite pockets, pegmatites and in metamorphic rocks with Mn	4.2
Uvarovite	Emerald-green	In chromium deposits	3.8
Grossular	Various, usually pale tints to orange-red	Metamorphosed limestones	3.5
Andradite	Pale tints to brown and black, not reds	Igneous and metamorphics; on seams and in crusts on serpentines but not in mica schists	3.8

Crystal description: Crystals are very common, especially in some varieties, depending in part on the type of their usual occurrence. Pyropes usually embedded in volcanic rocks are not in sharp and well-formed crystals. Almandine, growing in mica schists, usually shows faces of the dodecahedron or the trapezohedron, as does spessartine, which commonly forms in open cavities. Uvarovite commonly coats seams in chromite and so is free to form good dodecahedral crystals. Grossular forms on seams and shows smooth trapezohedral and dodecahedral faces, crystallizes in pockets in pegmatite (essonite or "cinnamon stone," light brown in color), or is embedded in limestone, where it is usually in good dodecahedrons. Andradite commonly coats seams and forms small lustrous crystals, unless embedded in asbestos (as in Val Malenco, Italy, and the demantoids of the Urals), when it may be rounded. Occasionally in sandy aggregates of fine grains, or in massive white, pink, or green veins (grossular, particularly: "South African jade"). **Physical properties:** Red, brown, black, green, yellow, white. *Luster* glassy; *hardness* 6–7^1/$_2$; *specific gravity* 3.5–4.3; *fracture* conchoidal to uneven; *cleavage* none; but occasional partings. Transparent to translucent; almandine weakly magnetic. **Composition:** A series of aluminum silicates with magnesium, iron, and manganese; and a second series of calcium silicates with chromium, aluminum, and iron in which the SiO_2 amounts to about 35%. **Tests:** Theoretically, distinguished by their variation in color, fusibility, and behavior:

Pyrope	Fuses with slight difficulty to black non-magnetic globule
Almandine	Fuses to black magnetic globule
Spessartine	Fuses with boiling to gray or black non-magnetic globule
Uvarovite	Almost infusible, but always bright green
Grossular	Fuses easily to light-colored nonmagnetic globule that colors blue when a cobalt nitrate drop is added and it is remelted
Andradite	Darkens and then fuses to black magnetic globule

However, enough iron is present in many garnets to make the globule magnetic anyway.

Distinguishing characteristics: The garnet varieties are so generally crystallized and so typical in their occurrence that the group is very easily recognized. Red grains seen embedded in metamorphic and igneous rocks are most likely to be garnets. Apatite is softer and does not melt. Altered pyrite gives a limonite streak; zircons often fluoresce and will not fuse. Short tourmalines can look like dodecahedrons, but tourmaline will not fuse like garnet.

Occurrence: Garnet is one of the commonest of all minerals, and ordinary localities are far too numerous to list. Special localities might be worth mentioning. Pyrope is found in transparent grains in Arizona and New Mexico, in Bohemia, and in the South African diamond pipes. Large almandine crystals are found in the Adirondacks at North Creek, New York, where it is mined for garnet paper. Almandine is the most widely used of the jewelry stones and comes, for this use, from Madagascar and India. Spessartine is less common; it is usually pegmatitic or associated with metamorphic manganese deposits. It is sometimes gemmy, a bright orange has been found in Brazil (Golconda Mine and Fortaleza Brazil) and in Namibia. At Nathrop, Colorado, and in the Thomas Range, Utah, it occurs in brown-black crystals in gas cavities in a light-colored rhyolitic lava flow.

Uvarovite occurs mainly as green crusts often associated with other minerals of chromium, usually on seams and in fissures in that mineral. The largest crystals, to 1 in. (2 cm), have been found at a Finnish copper mine — an untypical occurrence. Grossular has been found in light-colored crystals most often in contact-metamorphic deposits, as in Morelos and Lake Jaco, Mexico, where it forms pale greenish, light pink, and white crystals associated with vesuvianite.

Massive white grossular has been found with jade in Myanmar and has been carved by the Chinese. Green grossular garnet occurs in Africa in a solid vein, and some has been carved and sold as "South African jade." A Tanzanian emerald green chrome grossular rivals demantoid as a gemstone though it lacks fire (tsavorite). Andradite is probably the rarest of the garnets, and may form on metamorphic rock crevices as crusts of lustrous crystals; yellow-green topazolite and emerald green demantoid are varieties. Black melanite andradite is found in San Benito Co., California.

Remarks: Some varieties are important gemstones; pyrope is used in garnet paper, a variety of sandpaper esteemed for its better cutting qualities.

VESUVIANITE $Ca_{10}Mg_2Al_4(SiO_4)_5(Si_2O_7)_2(OH)_4$ **Pl. 61**
(IDOCRASE)

Tetragonal — Ditetragonal bipyramidal $\frac{4}{m}\frac{2}{m}\frac{2}{m}$

Environment: Contact-metamorphic deposits in impure limestones, associated with garnet, diopside, and wollastonite; rare in pegmatite. **Crystal description:** Almost always in crystals, either free growing and prismatic in habit with shiny faces, or totally embedded in crystalline calcite and tending toward a stubby or bipyramidal habit. Also massive. **Physical properties:** Green, brown, yellow, blue ("cyprine"), violet. *Luster* glassy; *hardness* $6\frac{1}{2}$; *specific gravity* 3.4–3.5; *fracture* conchoidal to uneven; *cleavage* poor prismatic. Transparent to translucent. **Composition:** Alkaline calcium, iron, magnesium silicate (about 36% CaO, often 5% FeO, plus Fe_2O_3, about 3% MgO, and 16.5% Al_2O_3, 36.5% SiO_2, 3.0% H_2O). BeO has been reported in a brown idocrase from Franklin, New Jersey, and a little F is often recorded. **Tests:** Fuses easily, with large bubbles, to a shiny, brownish, glassy nonmagnetic sphere.

Distinguishing characteristics: Recognized by square cross sections and very typical crystals. Zircon is infusible and usually fluorescent. The massive but readily broken material (californite) resembles jade, but jadeite jade fuses even more easily and colors the flame yellow, and nephrite jade is much harder to fuse, eventually making a black glass. Epidote and garnet are magnetic after fusion; tourmaline fuses with great difficulty or not at all.

Occurrence: The finest U.S. vesuvianite crystals have come from an asbestos quarry at Eden Mills, Vermont, embedded in quartz, where they form green, brilliant, prismatic crystals terminated by a pyramid. At the Jeffrey Mine, Asbestos,

Quebec, vesuvianite forms loose agregates of pale green crystals — rarely tipped with violet. Large, brown, corroded but shiny crystals with rounded edges and consisting of a base and prisms are found near Olmstedville, New York, where they have been freed from crystalline calcite by weathering. Large, green, corroded, short-prismatic, and bipyramidal crystals have been uncovered in the fields at Magnet Cove, Arkansas and in Luning, Nevada. Limestone quarries at Crestmore, California, were once famous for their green-brown bipyramidal crystals in blue calcite. Small emerald green prismatic crystals of gem quality have been found at Georgetown, California. The massive green vesuvianite known as californite has been found in Butte and Fresno counties, and along Indian Creek in Siskiyou Co. in California. In Mexico it is associated with the grossular crystals.

Vesuvianite is also common abroad and was first recognized as a distinct mineral in Italy, where it was found on the slopes of Vesuvius (Monte Somma) in metamorphosed limestone blocks expelled from the crater; thus the name vesuvianite (though the International Mineralogical Association briefly called it idocrase). At Pitkäranta (Russia, but formerly Finland) the light brown vesuvianite crystals are long and thin, like a bundle of cut nails. Steep, gemmy pyramidal crystals are found in Pakistan. Cuttable yellow-brown crystals come from Quebec and Tanzania.

●Epidote Group

This is a rather complex group with several members, most of which are rare and not merging into more common varieties as a continuous series. There may be considerable substitution of iron and manganese for aluminum. The varieties discussed here are relatively common and sufficiently distinctive in some of their properties to be easily recognizable from the description, with tests. Crystals are mainly monoclinic, usually elongated on the horizontal *(b)* axis, so technically, not prismatic.

ZOISITE $Ca_2Al_3(SiO_4)_3(OH)$ **Pl. 61**

Orthorhombic — Rhombic bipyramidal $\frac{2}{m} \frac{2}{m} \frac{2}{m}$

Environment: Metamorphic rocks; also in quartz veins, pegmatites, and some ore deposits. **Crystal description:** Usually as isolated prismatic single crystals, sometimes to 4 in. (10 cm) long, but with tips generally poorly developed. Best crystal shapes are found when zoisite is embedded in quartz or metal sulfides, from either of which it breaks cleanly. Also in interlocking masses of needles. **Physical properties:** Almost colorless, gray, brown, pink (thulite), blue, violet (tanzanite hues), and green (smaragdite). *Luster* glassy; *hardness* 6; *specific gravity* 3.3–3.4; *fracture* subconchoidal to uneven; *cleavage* perfect side pinacoid. Translucent to transparent. Pink thulite may fluoresce yellow-orange in longwave ultraviolet. Tanzanite is very pleochroic in three directions: yellow-orange, blue, and purple when it has not been heated. Heating destroys the yellow-orange color direction. **Composition:** Alkaline calcium aluminum silicate (24.6% CaO, 33.7% Al_2O_3, 39.7% SiO_2, 2.0% H_2O). Some Fe may replace the Ca, and when enough is present — over 5% Fe_2O_3 — it lowers the symmetry, and examples grade into clinozoisite and epidote. **Tests:** Grows "worms," swells, and fuses in a dark bubbly mass that then does not easily melt down to a sphere. Light-colored varieties color blue on second melting after touch with drop of cobalt nitrate solution.

Distinguishing characteristics: Differing from the amphiboles by the single plane of cleavage (and often a pearly luster on the cleavage face). Tourmaline has no cleavage. Zoisite is much paler in hue than other members of group. Pink tourmaline is not fluorescent like some thulite, which is seldom in crystals of any appreciable size. Strong directional coloring differences (pleochroic), especially tanzanite.

Occurrence: Not uncommon in metamorphic rock areas in the U.S., as in New England, and most easily recognized as gray prismatic crystals in quartz veins. The fluorescent pink variety, thulite, is found in Mitchell Co., North Carolina, in a pegmatite with albite feldspar. Good brown crystals are found embedded in the sulfide ores at Ducktown, Tennessee. In California, zoisite occurs in green schists near Sulphur Bank.

Remarks: With the discovery of a vanadium-pigmented and very pleochroic blue phase in an impure, high-lime-content micaceous gneissic rock in Tanzania, promoted in the gem trade as tanzanite, zoisite has assumed much more importance as a species. It is also the green matrix material that often accompanies ruby corundum. Thulite derives its name from the ancient one for Norway (Thule), where it occurs associated with blue cyprine at Telemark in attractive specimens. The transparent, now costly, gemmy variety from Tanzania has been profitably promoted as tanzanite into popularity. It is a vanadium-pigmented and very pleochroic blue phase in an impure, high-lime-content, micaceous gneissic rock. Its ready cleavage makes it far less wearable than the sapphires it resembles, but it has given zoisite much more importance as a species. Zoisite is also the green matrix material that often accompanies ruby corundum. A gemmy green has been found in Pakistan.

EPIDOTE $Ca_2(Al,Fe)_3(SiO_4)_3(OH)$ **Pl. 61**

Monoclinic — prismatic $\dfrac{2}{m}$

Environment: Metamorphic rocks, contact-metamorphosed limestones, altered igneous rocks, pegmatites, and in traprock amygdules with zeolites. Tiny pistachio green crystals common on shrinkage seams in granite, formed from the last gases or solutions to escape, often accompanied by albite and fluorite. **Crystal description:** Often crystallized in greenblack surfaces or as long, slender, grooved prisms, crystals actually stretched out along a horizontal (b-axis) direction and giving an impression that the side faces are slanting, if we follow our normal inclination to stand the crystals upright. Also in very thin crusts of small paler green crystals, and in greenish films thickening to crusts of massive or fine-grained "pistacite" (suggestive of the color). **Physical properties:** Pistachio green, green, blackish green, brown, light yellow-brown. *Luster* glassy (pearly on cleavage); *hardness* 6–7; *specific gravity* 3.4–3.5; *fracture* uneven; *cleavage* perfect basal (remember the base is usually a face paralleling the elongation of the crystal). Transparent to translucent; strongly pleochroic, two different colors coming through as a translucent prism is rotated, usually green and dark brown. **Composition:** Alkaline calcium iron silicate (averaging about 23.5% CaO, 11.5% Fe_2O_3, 25.0% Al_2O_3, 38.0% SiO_2, and just under 2% H_2O). **Tests:** Fuses with bubbling to a usually magnetic dull black scoriaceous glass. Since it is insoluble in dilute hydrochloric acid, epidote walling calcite veins is readily exposed by an acid soaking (dilute hydrochloric acid) of the specimen.

Distinguishing characteristics: The color and the general appearance of epidote are so characteristic that tests are rarely necessary. Splintery actinolite, the green amphibole, has two cleavages, and single crystals do not show any pronounced color change as a prism is rotated. Viewed from the side, tourmaline, with no cleavage, also shows no color change.

Occurrence: This mineral is extremely common. Notable localities include Sulzer, Prince of Wales I., Alaska, with crystals remarkable for their size (to 3 in., 7–8 cm), and a short prismatic, almost tablet, shape. Slender prisms are found stretched across pegmatite feldspar in the Mitchell Co. area of North Carolina. Epidote and garnet are abundant at several localities in California, where in one locality they sometimes form alternating bands shaped by the garnet crystal outline.

The world's leading epidote locality is Untersulzbachtal, in the Austrian Tyrol, where magnificent, dark, lustrous crystals up to a foot long (30 cm) and an inch (3 cm) or more across were found in a notable pocket in a chlorite-actinolite schist, with colorless apatite crystals and byssolite bundles. Small sprays of crystals and large singles and crusts have been found in Baja California and on Guadalupe I. in the Gulf. Some very black crystals come from Guerrero, Mexico. Larger sprays, up to 3 in. (7–8 cm) long, have been found in Minas Gerais, Brazil, in pegmatites. Most recently crystals of Austrian quality have turned up in Namibia and in Afghanistan, though from neither land have we seen the numbers that came in Untersulzbachtal.

ALLANITE (Orthite)   Pl. 61

$(Ca,Ce,La,Na)_2(Al,Fe,Be,Mn,Mg)_3(SiO_4)_3(OH)$

Monoclinic — prismatic $\dfrac{2}{m}$

Environment: In pegmatites, and as a minor black grain in igneous rocks. **Crystal description:** Usually in elongated, dull-surfaced crystal grains, embedded in feldspar but so shattered that it is difficult to remove them intact. Large crystals are often thin, dull-surfaced plates. Some similar to epidote but paler in hue. **Physical properties:** Black to medium brown. *Luster* pitchy or resinous; *hardness* $5\frac{1}{2}$–6; *specific gravity* 2.7-4.2; *fracture* subconchoidal to uneven; *cleavage* several poor, not conspicuous. Transparent and rarely gemmy to translucent to opaque; radioactive and showing staining dark red haloes cut by radiating cracks in the feldspar enclosing the grain. **Composition:** An extremely variable catch-all silicate containing rare-earth elements including thorium, cerium, disprosium, lanthanum, yttrium, and erbium, which may total — as oxides — as much as 20% of the weight. **Tests:** Fuses quickly with bubbling to a dull, black magnetic glass. Weakly affects photographic film by its radioactivity. Readily attacked by acid.

Distinguishing characteristics: When embedded it is immediately noted as a radioactive mineral from its effect on the enclosing feldspar. Magnetism after fusion distinguishes it from uraninite. Similar-looking radioactive minerals, which will also have halos of alteration around them in the rock, react very differently under the blowpipe. Magnetite is magnetic without fusion.

Occurrence: Fairly common as small black grains in coarse granite pegmatite. Also in Geiger counter–determinable concentrations in some black magnetite and apatite veins, as in Essex and Orange Counties, New York. Large flat black crystals from Madawaska, Ontario. Small crystals are common in Manhattan rocks; many specimens were found in the excavations for the Brooklyn-Battery tunnel. Larger crystals have come from Llano Co., Texas; Chester Co., Pennsylvania; and Warwick, New York. Very large crystals have been found in Oaxaca, Mexico, and in San Diego Co., California. Also common in Europe; particularly good crystals have been collected at Arendal, Norway, where it is called orthite.

ZIRCON $ZrSiO_4$ Pl. 61

Tetragonal — Ditetragonal bipyramidal $\dfrac{4}{m}\dfrac{2}{m}\dfrac{2}{m}$

Environment: Common minor accessory of granitic rocks, occasionally in metamorphosed limestones, also in veins in fine-grained nepheline-rich rocks and in pegmatites. Frequently found as a residual heavy mineral in sands and gravels. **Crystal description:** Always in crystals, which may be 1 in. (2 cm) or more across; in Canada, Norway, Russia, and Australia even larger ones have been found. Usually short-prismatic, sometimes bipyramidal or with narrow prism zones. **Physical properties:** Brown, colorless, gray, green, reddish, bluish, violet. *Luster* adamantine; *hardness* $6\frac{1}{2}$–$7\frac{1}{2}$; *specific gravity* 4.0–4.7; *fracture* conchoidal; *cleavage* 2, usually poor. Transparent to translucent; gemstones commonly fluorescent yellow-orange. **Composition:** Zirconium silicate (67.2% ZrO_2 with up to 4.0% of hafnium oxide and, often, rare earths, which make it weakly radioactive, 32.8% SiO_2). **Tests:** Infusible, but colored varieties may whiten and some varieties glow intensely for a moment (thermoluminescent), although only once. Fluorescent frequently enough for this to be a good test for the diamond look-alikes in jewelry (fluorescent diamonds show a variety of hues, not just yellow-orange).

Distinguishing characteristics: The tetragonal shape is very typical. The only common similarly shaped mineral is vesuvianite, which is much lighter in weight and readily fusible.

Occurrence: Well-formed sharp crystals are often found loose in the soil near Henderson Co., North Carolina. Bluish-skinned brown crystals are embedded in the marble of Limecrest Quarry, Sparta, New Jersey, and very long slender crystals occurred similarly at Natural Bridge, New York. Brown crystals accompany magnetite at an iron mine in Pricetown, Pennsylvania. Small grains are common in heavy sands in North Carolina and south to Florida. Often they are sharp, colorless, perfect crystals.

Very large crystals are found in Renfrew, Ontario. Smaller good crystals come from Tory Hill, Wilberforce, Ontario. Isolated crystals and crusts are common on Cheyenne Mountain, near Colorado Springs, Colorado, with a neighboring occurrence of violet-brown bipyramids in white quartz. In Brazil it is found in the Poços de Caldas district of Minas Gerais as isolated large crystals in the coarse nepheline syenite. Similar crystals have come from Madagascar and near Alice Springs in central Australia. Most of the gemstones occur as brown crystals in Thailand and are heated to change them to colorless, golden, or blue.

Remarks: The presence of radioactive elements is indicated by the frequency of radioactive halos around zircon grains embedded in mica. Often the mineral has broken down after geological ages of radioactive attack and no longer has the internal structure indicated by the crystal shape. Heating encourages it to revert to the original structure (when it glows) and raises the specific gravity to the upper level of its range. It may also change the color; all the blue and many golden Thailand zircons of jewelry commerce are heated brown stones. These often tend to revert to brown, a process hastened by a triggering exposure to sunlight. Readily chipped, they do not wear well; fine large stones are spectacular, but are unsuitable for daily wear. Tiffany used to sell them as "starlites."

Cyrtolite is a radioactive zircon easy to recognize by an identical, but modified, crystal shape, dull convex pyramid faces becoming rounded and convex. Analysis shows it to contain uranium and yttrium. It is abundant in some pegmatites, particularly in Norway, and masses from Bedford, Westchester Co., New York, have actually been used for the recovery of rare-earth elements. Cyrtolite in pegmatites tends to aggregate more than the isolated zircon crystals of the coarse granitic rocks do, and to form rows of crystals, all with rounded faces, usually red-brown in hue.

DATOLITE $Ca_2B_2(SiO_4)_2(OH)$ **Pl. 62**

Monoclinic — prismatic $\dfrac{2}{m}$

Environment: Though not a zeolite, it is often associated with zeolites, in cavities in traprock. Rarely occurs as gangue in ore veins in Michigan, Mexico, and Russia. **Crystal description:** Usually in crystals, which may be 2 in. (5 cm) across. Often well formed, more or less equidimensional, but all faces not equally lustrous; some usually dull. Also (in Michigan) in white porcelaneous opaque nodules, round masses of microscopically granular material, commonly stained reddish by iron. **Physical properties:** Colorless, light yellow-green, white; fine-grained examples stained reddish. *Luster* glassy and porcelaneous; *hardness* $5–5^1/_2$; *specific gravity* 2.8–3.0; *fracture* conchoidal to uneven, *cleavage* none. Transparent to translucent. **Composition:** Alkaline calcium boron silicate (35.0% CaO, 21.8% B_2O_3, 37.6% SiO_2, 5.6% H_2O). **Tests:** Fuses very easily with bubbling to form a viscous, clear glass ball that fluoresces blue in shortwave ultraviolet. Gives green (boron) flame.

Distinguishing characteristics: In appearance datolite resembles a zeolite, but the green boron flame, with the easy fusibility and moderate swelling (zeolites might be called immoderate), is a certain test.

Occurrence: Fine examples are found in the traprocks of the New England coast, with the sharpest examples coming from the Lane Quarry at Westfield, Massachusetts, in an association with prehnite, babingtonite, and epidote. The best of the Paterson, New Jersey, specimens, from a similar occurrence, are almost as good.

The cluster of small crystals and the spherical gas-cavity fillings of fine-grained material in the Lake Superior copper mines are also good. The fine-grained porcelaneous Michigan datolite, the original find responsible for its name, appears not to be found elsewhere now. Good crystals are found in Andreasberg in the German Harz, in the Italian and Austrian Alps, and in Tasmania. Remarkably large greenish crystals, closely intergrown and poorly individualized, are frequent in the Charcas, Mexico, danburite locality. Clear, pseudo-orthorhombic crystals to 1 in. (2 cm) have been found in the uranium mine near Bancroft, Ontario.

EUCLASE $BeAlSiO_4(OH)$ Pl. 62

Monoclinic — prismatic $\dfrac{2}{m}$

Environment: Almost exclusively a pegmatite mineral, though it has been reported from a Tyrolean locality in crystals to $^1/_2$ in. (1 cm) and with emerald in veins. **Crystal description:** Probably always in more or less well-formed crystals. Generally late in a depositional sequence, so its crystals lie on top of the earlier species such as muscovite, microcline, topaz, and beryl. Usually prismatic and very evidently monoclinic, with well-developed down-slanted front faces. Only rarely flat enough on the sides to give crystals a blockier outline, but caution is urged, since a good cleavage often amputates a crystal's edge. The prettiest crystals, colorful Brazilian ones, are unfortunately grown in solid quartz vein material with precious topaz, rather than in pocket-prone pegmatites, where uncommon euclase is commonly colorless. **Physical properties:** Colorless, light blue, green-blue, pale yellow, pale amethyst, light green and splotchy ink blue. *Luster* glassy; *hardness* $7\frac{1}{2}$; *specific gravity* 3.09–3.11; *fracture* shelly (conchoidal); *cleavage* perfect side, front and back domes poor. Transparent, often gemmy. **Composition:** Alkaline aluminum silicate (with about 17.2% BeO, 35.2% Al_2O_3, 41.4% SiO_2, 6.2% H_2O). **Tests:** Testing seldom necessary, as environment and crystal shape are so typical. One does not find barite or celestite, (quasi-look-alikes) in pegmatite pockets (usual homes of euclase) nor in Brazilian topaz veins, where it is equally obvious from its color. Nonfluorescent, holds together in heat, but edges of splinter whiten and finally fuse with little points of white incandescence.

Distinguishing characteristics: In its associations, euclase might be confused with topaz, but the cleavage is parallel to the prism instead of across it, as in topaz. The easy cleavage, which gives it its name, is very distinctive. The color is likely to be irregularly distributed in the crystal.

Occurrence: One of the popular rare minerals for collectors. It has been cut as an unusual gem, and the green and blue examples command a high price. It is associated in Brazil with the topaz seams in the Ouro Preto region of Minas Gerais, and has recently been found in São Sebastião de Maranhão in Minas Gerais and in another pegmatite, Alto Santino, in Rio Grande do Norte. In Russia, crystals were found in gold placers with pink topaz in the Sanarka River; surprisingly, considering their cleavability, the lovely blue-green Russian crystals were intact though a little waterworn. Perhaps the largest crystal found to date is a light blue milky one from Kenya, now in the British Museum (Natural History) and about 6 in. (15 cm) tall. Large colorless cleavages have been found in Brazil, splinters that indicate originally still bigger crystals. Some fine, blue, side pinacoid-flattened, 1 in. or more (3 cm) crystals have been found with emeralds in Gachala, Colombia. In some abundance in inky crystals in Zimbabwe.

TOPAZ $Al_2SiO_4(F,OH)_2$ **Pl. 62**

Orthorhombic — Rhombic bipyramidal $\dfrac{2}{m} \dfrac{2}{m} \dfrac{2}{m}$

Environment: In pegmatites, seams in granitic rock, high-temperature veins and replacement impregnations, and gas cavities in rhyolite. **Crystal description:** Commonly crystallized, often in free-growing transparent crystals, sometimes very large. The c-face, the base, may be conspicuous or may be entirely missing; it is usually present. Also in parallel columnar growths (pycnite); in pseudomorphs after feldspar crystals; and in granular masses. When doubly terminated, "precious" (golden) crystals may appear hemimorphic, for the terminal faces at the two ends of the Brazilian precious topaz are usually unlike. **Physical properties:** Colorless, white, pale blue, light yellow, yellow-brown, pinkish brown, pink, and ruby red. *Luster* glassy; *hardness* 8; *specific gravity* 3.5–3.6; *fracture* conchoidal; *cleavage* perfect basal. Transparent to translucent. **Composition:** Aluminum fluohydroxysilicate (56.5% Al_2O_3, 33.3% SiO_2, and about 10% F and OH). The paragenetical habit differences are great enough to suggest major structural differences, perhaps related to the F and OH content. **Tests:** Infusible, and insoluble in all but hydrofluoric acid. The powder turns blue (aluminum test) when moistened with cobalt nitrate and heated.

Distinguishing characteristics: Great hardness and its good cleavage are excellent indications, along with its crystal form and typical occurrence and pegmatitic associations. Beryl fuses on thin edges; quartz decrepitates more violently and easily.

Occurrence: A valuable jewelry stone, especially in the pink, red, and brown hues. Not to be confused with the brown quartz commonly sold in Brazil and other lands (under the name topaz, as in "smoky topaz."

Large topaz crystals are not common in the U.S.; the biggest are probably some crudely shaped white ones found in the pegmatite at Amelia, Virginia, associated with microcline. Clear crystals, to 4–5 in. (10 cm) across and somewhat etched, from Devils Head and Pikes Peak, Colorado; smaller crystals have come from other Colorado localities. Large and deeply etched blue crystals were found at Topsham, Maine, and many 1–2 in. (2–5 cm) crystals were found in small miarolitic cavities in granite with smoky quartz, feldspar, and phenakite at Baldface Mountain, New Hampshire. Less etched, pale blue crystals are found in Mason Co., Texas. Also important in San Diego Co., California, dikes associated with beryl and tourmaline.

Rhyolite extrusions of the Thomas Range, Utah (and, less

conspicuously, of Nathrop, Colorado, and New Mexico) contain many gas cavities in which there are 1-in. (3 cm) light brown crystals, which soon fade to colorless on exposure to light. Larger but sandy crystals within the rhyolite, mostly filled with quartz and opaque, are always simpler in their terminations. It is associated in Utah with black bixbyite ([Mn,F]$_2$O$_3$) cubes, rosy beryl (not morganite), and in Colorado with spessartine garnet. In San Luis Potosí, Mexico, similar and sometimes larger topaz appears to occur alone or perhaps with cassiterite in the rhyolite seams.

Brazilian topaz is outstanding and comes in pegmatitic colorless and blue crystals, as well as in a series of quartz veins in rich brown gemmy crystals known as "precious topaz." Pink crystals of this type have also been found in nearby hematite mines and lately in Pakistan. Small natural pink Russian topazes from the valley of the Sanarka River resemble some of the brown Brazilian gemstones, with the same crystal habit. Fine blue topaz crystals (and sherry-hued fading to blue) were found years ago in pegmatites in the Ural Mountains; lately large numbers of pale brown crystals, fading to white, have been found in Pakistan.

Though like pegmatite crystals in habit, the small crystals cut for the Saxon crown jewels were straw-hued topazes from veins in and near the "Schneckenstein" (snail stone, from its shape) in the Erzgebirge near the Czechoslovakian border.

Remarks: Golden Brazilian "precious" topaz turns pink on heating, and most pink jewelry topaz has been heated, though recent finds in Pakistan are naturally pink. Topaz is a very attractive and abundant species, characterized by beautiful crystals, placing it among the more popular gemstones with collectors. The common deep blue topaz now so abundant in the jewelry trade is largely irradiated white material; no naturally blue topaz ever reaches such a rich hue.

AXINITE   H(Ca,Mn,Fe)$_3$Al$_2$B(SiO$_4$)$_4$ **Pl. 62**

Triclinic — pinacoidal $\overline{1}$

Environment: Veins in slate and/or granitic rock and in contact metamorphic deposits near granite intrusions. **Crystal description:** Always in sharp and flat crystals or crystalline bladed aggregates with many parallel lines on the crystal surfaces, shapes which inspired its name. Crystals are extremely characteristic; they often reach 2 in. (5 cm) or more in size, and for collectors are the preeminent examples of the triclinic system. **Physical properties:** Violet-brown, gray, and yellow-orange. *Luster* glassy; *hardness* $6\frac{1}{2}$–7; *specific gravity* 3.3–3.4; *fracture* conchoidal; *cleavage* 1 good and several poor. Transparent to translucent; very dichroic with an amethystine direction. **Composition:** Hydrous calcium, manganese, and iron aluminum borosilicate (about 21% CaO, 3.5% MnO, 9% FeO plus Fe_2O_3, 17.5% Al_2O_3, 5% B_2O_3, 42.5% SiO_2, and 1.5% H_2O; but subject to considerable minor substitutions). **Tests:** Fuses easily all over the grain to a frothy glass, and remains frothy on cooling. Insoluble in hydrochloric acid.

Distinguishing characteristics: Color and crystal form are both distinctive and not likely to be mistaken for any other mineral. Titanite is usually not striated, fuses much less easily, and any fusion froth collapses upon cooling.

Occurrence: Large crystals have been found in a contact metamorphic deposit with epidote at Luning, Nevada. Outstanding crystals have been found by a dam in New Melones and Riverside County, California. The Franklin, New Jersey, occurrence of a red-fluorescing, manganese-rich variety is most unusual for color; the light orange-yellow crystals are small but very attractive. Other U.S. occurrences are not rare, but except for several isolated sites in California none is outstanding in quality. N. Baja California has been a good source, in scheelite pits. The Le Bourg-d'Oisans occurrence, in s. France, with epidote, prehnite, and quartz is one of the world's best, though Russia's Polar Urals have lately produced spectacular, very transparent crystals. Axinite veins are very abundant in the granite and the altered slates of Cornwall, England. Robust, less flattened crystals from Obira, Japan, are browner and build up into aggregates of parallel crystals, rather than single individuals; they are associated with danburite. Bahia, Brazil, has yielded the largest known complete crystal, 9 in. (22 cm) from point to point.

◆Subsilicate Type Si:O = 1:5

Like the orthosilicates, this structure has independent SiO_4 tetrahedrons, but its minerals contain additional oxygen, which is not bonded into the silica tetrahedra. In this way we get ratios of Si:O in their formulas that can be as low as 2:27, with silicates merging into titanates, borates, and rare-earth minerals. They might be considered a subtype of the orthosilicate group, since they have the isolated SiO_4 tetrahedrons. They have no consistent diagnostic or distinctive characteristics.

ANDALUSITE Al_2SiO_5 **Pl. 63**

Orthorhombic — Rhombic bipyramidal $\frac{2}{m}\frac{2}{m}\frac{2}{m}$

Environment: Metamorphic rocks and in contact-metamorphic zones near granite intrusions; grossly different in different parageneses. **Crystal description:** Coarse, embedded crystal masses, usually dull-surfaced with blunt box-like terminations, and generally slightly altered on the surface so any original luster is lost. A variety known as chiastolite forms rounded fossil or cigar shapes, bulges wrapped in dark schist. In cross section, each rod displays a pattern of light and dark areas, apparently created as the growing crystal thrust dark foreign particles into definite areas. The pattern of checkerboard squares changes in successive slices through the length of the crystal. Smaller gemmy, waterworn andalusite crystals have been found in Brazil and Sri Lanka (Ceylon), but their parent is unsure; no such crystals have been collected from a matrix. **Physical properties:** Gray, pink, brown, white, and emerald green. *Luster* glassy; *hardness* 7^{1}/$_{2}$; *specific gravity* 3.1–3.2; *fracture* conchoidal; *cleavage* fair to good prismatic. Transparent to translucent. Uncommon green andalusite, known as viridine, is strongly dichroic in yellow and green; gemmy white varieties are very dichroic in green and brown. **Composition:** Aluminum silicate (63.2% Al_2O_3, 36.8% SiO_2). **Tests:** Infusible and insoluble, but powder is slightly colored blue by strong firing after it is moistened with cobalt nitrate (aluminum test).

Distinguishing characteristics: The variety chiastolite is easily recognized. The altered, mica-wrapped cigar shape and dull surface with the square cross section (dominant prisms are virtually at right angles to each other) are very distinctive. The bluish cobalt nitrate coloration test is more easily obtained with kyanite and sillimanite powders than with andalusite.

Occurrence: Like the next two aluminum silicates, andalusite can be used in spark plugs and other porcelains requiring high heat resistance. The clear material makes an interesting gem because of its two-color effect. Chiastolite is found in Fresno, Kern, and Mariposa counties, California, and in boulders in farmers' stone walls near Lancaster, Massachusetts. Gemmy pinkish andalusite grains from shattered small crystals are found in the mica schist of Mt. Washington, New Hampshire. Great gray to white masses were mined at White Mountain, Laws, Inyo Co., California. Good opaque crystals have come from Standish, Maine, and

Delaware Co., Pennsylvania. The viridine Brazilian variety is said to be manganiferous.

Gemmy andalusite, in somewhat waterworn pebbles and crystals, comes from Minas Gerais in Brazil and from Sri Lanka (Ceylon). As a gemstone, it is distinctive because of the two colors it shows in the sides and ends of the cut stone: grayish green sides and reddish brown ends in cushion-cut stones, their best shape.

SILLIMANITE Al_2SiO_5 Pl. 63

Orthorhombic — Rhombic bipyramidal $\dfrac{2}{m}\dfrac{2}{m}\dfrac{2}{m}$

Environment: Mica schists and gneisses, and in contact metamorphic deposits. **Crystal description:** Usually in finely fibrous gray or brownish masses, embedded in rock. Very fine needles can form a compact rock (Brazil and New Mexico) that streams wear into interesting shapes (Brazil). Distinct pale blue prismatic crystals, clear and transparent, with good side pinacoidal cleavage in the rare gemmy variety. **Physical properties:** Usually white, sometimes brownish or greenish (gem variety light blue). *Luster* satiny (glassy when gemmy); *hardness* 6–7 (but splinters and is difficult to determine; gemmy examples are $7\frac{1}{2}$); *specific gravity* 3.2–3.3; *fracture* splinters lengthwise, but conchoidal breaks across elongation; *cleavage* perfect pinacoid, but usually fibrous. Translucent to transparent. **Composition:** Aluminum silicate (63.2% Al_2O_3, 36.8% SiO_2). **Tests:** Infusible and insoluble, but the crushed mineral, or a bundle of fibers, turns blue when heated with cobalt nitrate solution (aluminum test).

Distinguishing characteristics: Infusibility distinguishes it from fibrous anthophyllite, which it may resemble (anthophyllite fuses to a black magnetic bead). Hardness and brittleness of the fibers distinguish them from those of asbestos.

Occurrence: Relatively rare, in fibrous, more or less parallel masses in schist, and often altered in part to mica; therefore lacking in normal hardness. Interesting because its Myanmar and Sri Lanka occurrences (where it is found in waterworn, clear, blue, gemmy pebbles) are so unlike the fibrous embedded masses of New England at Worcester, Massachusetts, and Norwich and Willimantic, Connecticut. Also in New York and Pennsylvania. Sometimes, as in North Carolina and Brazil, it is compact enough to form tough waterworn pebbles that may be cut to resemble a cat's-eye. Lately in some abundance in Orissa, India. Pebbles of the compact fibers can water-wear into smooth and shiny surfaces, even more lustrous than waterworn jade masses. Another (historical) name, fibrolite, comes from its appearance; the official name sillimanite was given in honor of Yale's first professor of mineralogy, Benjamin Silliman. New Mexican Indians fashioned many tools from sillimanite masses.

KYANITE Al_2SiO_5 **Pl. 63**

Triclinic — pinacoidal $\overline{1}$

Environment: Schists and gneisses formed from clay-rich rocks. **Crystal description:** Always in embedded bladed crystals, sometimes packed in solid aggregates, sometimes singles isolated in a mica schist. May be up to a foot (30 cm) or more long; usually shorter. **Physical properties:** Bluish, greenish, to colorless, with the color distributed centrally and in splotches; also in black sprays (Brazil). *Luster* glassy; *hardness* 5 parallel to the prism, 7 across; *specific gravity* 3.6–3.7; *fracture* splintery but cuts straight across crystals; *cleavage* perfect pinacoidal. Transparent to translucent. **Composition:** Aluminum silicate (63.2% Al_2O_3, 36.8% SiO_2). **Tests:** Infusible and insoluble. Best tested by the unique hardness difference, which permits a knife to scratch it parallel to the crystal length but not across.

Distinguishing characteristics: Very distinctive in appearance; in case of doubt the hardness test should settle it. The black sprays of Brazil are very atypical and unlike any other specimens.

Occurrence: Like its companions andalusite and sillimanite, kyanite is an important refractory for porcelains, high-temperature bricks, and spark plugs. It is common in the New England schists and gneisses, and is found in some of the building excavations of New York City. Minable masses occur in Virginia, North Carolina, and Georgia. Typical crystals occur at Graves Mountain, Georgia, associated with giant rutiles and lazulite.

The Swiss Pizzo Forno occurrence (a white mica schist with brown staurolite) is a classic locality. In recent years mining operations in Kenya, East Africa, have produced some of the largest, clearest crystals. Clear waterworn pebbles have been found in Sao Paulo, Brazil. Also spelled "cyanite" and known in some countries as disthene (France).

STAUROLITE $FeAl_4Si_2O_{10}(OH)_2$ **Pl. 63**

Monoclinic — prismatic (pseudo-orthorhombic) $\dfrac{2}{m}$

Environment: Embedded "pressure" mineral which, like almandine garnet, grows as regional metamorphism forms schist and gneiss. **Crystal description:** Always crystallized, commonly with two individuals intergrown at right angles (twinned) so as to produce a cross; they may also intergrow at other angles. To 2 in. (5 cm) in length. **Physical properties:** Dark brown. *Luster* glassy; *hardness* 7–7$\frac{1}{2}$; *specific gravity* 3.6–3.7; *fracture* subconchoidal; *cleavage* fair pinacoidal. Translucent to almost transparent. **Composition:** Iron aluminum silicate; can be regarded chemically as a mixture of kyanite with iron hydroxide (15.8% FeO, 55.9% Al_2O_3, 26.3% SiO_2, 2.0% H_2O). **Tests:** Infusible and insoluble, but after flame roasting, grain crushes easily to a brown, weakly magnetic powder.

Distinguishing characteristics: Since staurolite is always in schist in typical brown crystals, with some individuals commonly twinned, it presents no special recognition problem. Andalusite appears to be unaffected by the blowpiping; dravite tourmaline of this color would fuse.

Occurrence: Large and well-formed crystals are found in Fannin and Cherokee counties, Georgia, and near Taos, New Mexico. Smaller ones are commercially exploited in Fairfax Co., Virginia, as good luck charms. However, many of the twins one sees appear to have been carved from a soft clay, probably dyed brown, and are not the real mineral, though some may be pseudomorphs.

Untwinned, lustrous crystals of more than usual translucency are associated with the blue kyanite of Pizzo Forno, Switzerland, and make attractive specimens, lying in their matrix of fine-grained white mica. Still larger ones, likewise more often untwinned, are found in Bahia and in Minas Gerais, Brazil.

TITANITE (SPHENE)   CaTiSiO$_5$ Pl. 63

Monoclinic — prismatic $\frac{2}{m}$

Environment: Best developed in metamorphic rocks, in marbles, schists, and gneisses; also common in small crystals in lighter-colored coarse igneous rocks and in some pegmatites in an epidote and albite association in dioritic and gabbroic rocks. **Crystal description:** Usually crystallized, in brown "envelope-shaped" crystals in granitic igneous rocks, but forming larger and more complex crystals when growing free in cavities in gneisses and schists. Commonly twinned so that the crystal edge shows a sharp re-entrant angle. Crystals may be 2–6 in. (10 cm) across. **Physical properties:** Brown, yellow, green, gray. *Luster* adamantine; *hardness* 5–5$\frac{1}{2}$; *specific gravity* 3.4–3.5; *fracture* conchoidal; *cleavage* fair prismatic, with several others, and commonly also a parting. Transparent to translucent, often gemmy. **Composition:** Calcium titanium silicate (28.6% CaO, 40.8% TiO_2, 30.6% SiO_2). **Tests:** Fuses, with bubbling only on hottest places, to a dark mass. Brown (Canadian) specimens turn lighter, even gemmy, and are frosted on the surface if heated without fusion. Practically insoluble in hydrochloric acid.

Distinguishing characteristics: The high luster, color, and typical wedge-shaped crystal cross section are very characteristic. Brown type distinguished from staurolite by the ease of melting under blowpipe, the greenish yellow type from sphalerite by its ease of fusion and greater hardness. Axinite melts readily, producing abundant froth.

Occurrence: Gemmy examples have been cut for collectors; gem titanite has great brilliance and, with strong dispersion, more fire than diamonds.

The best known North American specimens are large dark brown crystals from Renfrew, Ontario, where it occurs in a coarse marble. Good, clear, yellow-brown crystals were once found in the Tilly Foster Mine at Brewster, New York, and in Bridgewater, Pennsylvania. Gemmy brown crystals were found in a pegmatite near Butte, Montana. Large wedge-shaped chocolate-colored embedded crystals occurred in the pegmatites at the babingtonite locality near Woburn, Massachusetts, and smaller crystals like the Canadian ones are common in St. Lawrence Co., New York. Brick-hued, envelope-type $1/4$-in. (5 mm) crystals are found in a gneiss in the Odenwald, near Heidelberg, Germany.

The most beautiful and the clearest titanite crystals have come from the Alps and the Tyrol, associated with transparent or white albite feldspar crystals and often more or less coated, even saturated, with chlorite. The largest crystals (from n. Baja California) are etched, flat, brown-yellow ones, more significant for their 6-in. (15 cm) size than for their beauty. Similar giants have been found in Madagascar and India. A pegmatite at Capelinha in Minas Gerais, Brazil, is an abundant source of typical twinned greenish yellow, gemmy crystals, associated with small albites and chlorite. Similar, though unremarkable, crystals have been found in Pakistan.

DUMORTIERITE $Al_8BSi_3O_{19}(OH)$ **Pl. 64**

Orthorhombic — Rhombic bipyramidal $\dfrac{2}{m}\dfrac{2}{m}\dfrac{2}{m}$

Environment: Scattered single crystals in pegmatites, in quartz concentrations in metamorphic rocks, and in gneisses and schists; also in solid, economically minable crystal masses. **Crystal description:** Rarely in small embedded distinct crystals; usually in very finely fibrous compact masses. **Physical properties:** Violet, pink-violet, or blue. *Luster* glassy to pearly *hardness* 7; *specific gravity* 3.3–3.4 (but usually impure); *fracture* conchoidal; *cleavage* poor pinacoidal. Translucent to transparent gemmy (very rare). **Composition:** Alkaline aluminum borosilicate (64.6% Al_2O_3, 55% B_2O_3, 28.5% SiO_2, 14% H_2O). **Tests:** On the charcoal under the blowpipe, it whitens, but with cooling, the color partially (or entirely) returns. Sometimes fluorescent blue after firing, sometimes naturally purple fluorescent.

Distinguishing characteristics: Bright color and fibrous appearance are distinctive, and distinguish it from nonfibrous-looking lazulite and lazurite (which usually have yellow to orange fluorescent associates). The great hardness distinguishes the purple variety from similar-appearing rare species or lepidolite.

Occurrence: In the U.S., dumortierite is most common in the West and has been mined in Oreana, Nevada, for spark plug ceramics. The blue is found in Los Angeles Co., California, with a gray quartz, and has been carved as an imitation lapis lazuli in China. Scattered needles through quartz are found in many localities and are recognized by their color. New York City building excavations produce fair dumortierite needles. Alpine, San Diego Co., California, dumortierite has a purple fluorescence. Blue "knots" in white quartz occur near Karibib, Namibia. A light "blue quartz" quartzite (comparable to green mica-saturated aventurine) from Brazil is colored by dumortierite. Several carat-sized gemstones, strongly dichroic in blue and white, have been found as waterworn Brazilian pebbles.

URANOPHANE $CaU_2Si_2O_{11}\cdot^7H_2O$ Pl. 64

Orthorhombic — Rhombic bipyramidal (?) $\frac{2}{m}\frac{2}{m}\frac{2}{m}$

Environment: Secondary mineral associated with uraninite or pitchblende. **Crystal description:** Usually in minute sprays of light yellow crystals in crevices or on open fracture surfaces. Uranotile is probably about the same, but is thought to be triclinic and to occur in thicker crystals. **Physical properties:** Yellow, orange-yellow. *Luster* glassy to pearly; *hardness* 2-3 (undeterminable as a rule); *specific gravity* 3.8–3.9; *fracture* undeterminable; *cleavage* probably pinacoidal. Translucent; weakly fluorescent yellow-green. **Composition:** Hydrated calcium uranium silicate (about 6.5% CaO, 67%

UO_3, 13.9% SiO_2, 12.6% H_2O). **Tests:** Soluble, quietly, in warm hydrochloric acid, without effervescence and with a separation of silica gel. Drop of nitric acid solution, allowed to dry on a streak plate, is very fluorescent.

Distinguishing characteristics: Likely to be confused with other uranium compounds, some of which may be carbonates that dissolve with bubbling in cold acid. Distinguished from yellow iron compounds by its fluorescence and by the fluorescence of the evaporated drop.

Occurrence: Not rare as an alteration product of pitchblende, and often found in cavities or on seams in pegmatites from which uraninite may have been leached. Coarser uranotile needles of this type occur at Bedford, Westchester Co., New York, and the more slender uranophane is found in Mitchell Co., North Carolina; at Stone Mountain, Georgia; Avondale, Pennsylvania; Marysvale, Utah; and Grants, New Mexico. The most notable foreign occurrence is the Zaire uranium mines, where velvety uranophane coats other uranium alteration minerals. Also found in Schneeberg (Saxony, Germany), and elsewhere in the Jáchymov (Czechoslovakia) uranium district.

Occurs mixed with other secondary uranium salts, as in the "gummite" borders around altering uraninite. There are a tremendous number of associated secondary uranium minerals, all jumbled together in a colorful array of tiny crystals, mostly characterized by fluorescence and strong orange, yellow, and green colors. Many are fluorescent. For those that are not, but are suspected of being uraniferous anyway, try the dried nitric acid residue described above for fluorescence. Or set on a piece of unexposed film (a dentist's film pack) for a week.

GLOSSARY
REFERENCES
INDEX

GLOSSARY

Acicular. Needlelike; refers to the growth of a mineral in long and slender crystals.

Adamantine. The word used to describe a very high luster, like the luster of a diamond. It is a submetallic luster on a translucent material.

Adularescence. A bluish reflection coming from a definite plane in a mineral. Comes from the feldspar variety adularia and is best known in the gemstone "moonstone."

Amygdule. A rounded mass of mineral formed in a gas cavity in a volcanic rock, a rock that solidified before all the gas bubbled out.

Andesite. Very fine crystalline extrusive rock of volcanic origin composed largely of plagioclase feldspar (oligoclase or andesine) with smaller amounts of dark-colored mineral (hornblende, biotite, or pyroxene). The extrusive equivalent of diorite.

Anticline. An arch in sedimentary rocks.

Asterism. A starlike figure, as in star sapphire (corundum).

BB. An abbreviation for "before blowpipe. "

Botryoidal. Describing a mineral surface that is rounded, like the surface of a compact mass of grapes.

Boule. The name given to the form of synthetic ruby or sapphire grown from molten drops in a furnace. The word is French for "ball" and persists from the round pea-sized shapes of the first synthetic rubies and sapphires.

Caliche. Calcareous deposit in arid areas from leaching and desiccation on rock surfaces and forming earthy crusts.

Chatoyancy. Having the property of changing luster or color by reflecting a narrow band or streak of light, like a cat's eye.

Conchoidal. Describing the smoothly curved, glasslike (literally, shell-like) character of a fracture (broken surface) common to many minerals.

Country rock. The underlying basic geological formation of an area.

Craton. Name given to lighter-weight crust rock that generally rode above sea level, drifting about to make and remake islands and continents in the Earth's early history.

Crystallite. A small, rudimentary form of crystal of unknown mineralogic composition that does not polarize light.

Dacite. A fine-grained volcanic rock with slightly more calcium feldspar than an andesite.

Decrepitation. The explosive shattering of mineral grains on heating, commonly observed during blowpipe testing or in the open- and closed-tube tests.

Dendrite. The fernlike (literally, treelike), branching markings commonly observed along rock fissures, resulting from a branching crystal growth pattern (as in moss agates).

Detrital. Describing a form of occurrence for minerals, in gravels that came from a mineral deposit. Hard or heavy minerals, like diamonds and gold, are often found in detrital deposits (see *placer*).

Diabasic. A rock texture that is a common traprock type, characterized by lathlike feldspar crystals, around which grains or crystals of dark minerals (pyroxene) have filled in.

Dichroism. Literally, "two colors." It refers to mineral crystals whose color is disparate in different crystal directions. Tourmaline is the most common example: in one direction it may be green and in the other brown to almost black (see *pleochroism*).

Dike. An intrusive, cross-cutting, thin sheet of igneous rock.

Dolostone. Alternate name for dolomite rock. Coined to avoid confusion, as dolomite, like serpentine, can be both a mineral and a rock.

Double refraction. The property possessed by minerals crystallizing in anything but the cubic system of bending (refracting) light differently in different crystal directions. Very pronounced in some minerals, such as calcite, and related to *dichroism* and *pleochroism*, which will be seen, of course, only in the colored minerals.

Druse. A crystal-coated surface of rock, commonly used interchangeably (but erroneously) with *vug*.

Ductile. Able to be drawn into a wire; a characteristic of some of the metals.

Extrusive. Describing lava that reached the earth's surface or igneous rock formed from such lava, characterized by a glassy or fine crystalline texture.

Fluorescence. A luminescence originating in substances while being irradiated by rays of invisible light, such as ultraviolet light or x-rays, but stopping with the cessation of the stimulus.

Foliated. Made up of thin leaves, like a mica schist.

Fumarole. A hole in a volcanic region through which hot gases escape.

Gangue. The minerals of no value associated in veins with ore minerals.

Geniculated. Describing "kneelike" intergrowths of crystals; especially common in rutile and cassiterite.

Geode. A rounded concretionary rock mass, often hollow and lined with crystals.

Gliding plane. A crystal direction along which the atoms within a crystal can slip a definite distance without destroying the coherence of the crystal. Best noted in stibnite and vivianite.

Gossan. A weathered, residual rock deposit capping a sulfide deposit, from which minerals have been leached, leaving behind reddish iron oxide.

Graben. A down-dropped crust segment, such as the Rhine Valley in Europe, the Great Rift in central Africa, and Owens Valley in the U.S.

Groundmass. The finer-grained body of material containing larger grains, as in porphyry rock. Also sometimes used for *matrix*.

Habit. The general shape of a crystal, sometimes long and thin, other times short and flat. Often an indication of the temperature and pressure conditions under which a crystal formed.

Hackly. The fracture characteristic of metals in rock, such as gold and copper. Drawn to points as the rock breaks, the metal grains catch the skin as the finger is scraped across a hackly surface.

Hemimorphic. "Half-formed"; describing crystals in which the faces that grow on one end are different in angle and position from the faces to be found on the other end.

Hydrothermal. A self-explanatory word, "hydro" meaning water and "thermal" meaning heat. Hydrothermal solutions, from which so many minerals are deposited, are solutions of hot water escaping from subterranean sources, possibly of molten rock. Hydrothermal solutions may have the temperatures of superheated steam or be as cool as bath water.

Intrusive. Describing magma (molten rock) or rock formed from magma that hardened before reaching the surface, forced into cracks or layers between existing rock and characterized by larger crystals than extrusive rock.

Isomorphous. "Iso" means equal and "morph" means form—minerals in which two or more elements can replace each other to any extent without notably changing the appearance of the crystal. (See dufrenite, p. 245, or lazulite, p. 251).

Karst. Topography that develops over very soluble limestones and dolomites, characterized by sinkholes and fluted limestone remnants.

Laccolith. Domed sill-like intrusions of lava.

Lapilli. Rounded volcanic "hail" of small diameter, from pyroclastic eruptions. Singular is *lapillus.*

Lithophysae. Rounded nodular areas in obsidian that represent centers where crystallization of the molten rock began before it cooled into glass. Usually contracted and cracked, creating crystal-coated surfaces.

Litmus paper. Colored paper (pale blue) used in chemistry to show whether a solution is acid (turns pink) or alkaline.

Magma. The name given to molten rock under the surface of the earth. Magma becomes lava if it escapes on the surface at a volcano.

Magmatic. Describes changes in the rocks or minerals that form as a result of magma movements. *Magmatic segregations* are mineral deposits created directly as a result of the separation of one part of a mass of molten rock in one spot. Some iron deposits are thought to have formed in this way, by a separation and concentration of magnetite crystals from a mass of magma.

Malleable. Can be flattened out by pounding, a characteristic of the native metals and of the metals freed from ores in blowpipe testing.

Mammillary. Descriptive of some mineral surfaces, rounded like botryoidal and reniform but larger.

Matrix. The fine-grained background material that surrounds larger crystals, pebbles, or fossils in rock, especially sedimentary rock. (See also *groundmass.*)

Metamorphism. Changes in the rocks brought about, in the general usage of the word, by heat and pressure acting in the rocks below the immediate surface. *Contact metamorphism* is the result of heat and hydrothermal solutions accompanying and preceding intrusions of magma, with pressure playing no important part.

Monocline. A tilted succession of sediments.

Native. Uncombined with other elements; native metals are those found as minerals, such as gold, silver, and copper.

Ore. A mineral occurring in sufficient quantity and containing enough metal to permit its recovery and extraction at a profit. The term is also applied to rock containing such a mineral or metal, as "gold ore" and "copper ore."

Orientation. Applied to crystals, this means visualizing the disposition of the principal directions (top and bottom, front and back, side to side) within the crystal. It is essential to the recognition of the crystal system to which a crystal belongs, and soon becomes automatic.

Outcrop. A place where bedrock is exposed on the surface without any soil capping to conceal it.

Paleontology. The study of prehistoric life and the fossilized remains of that life found in the rocks.

Pangaea. A supercontinent of merged strata, of about 200 million years ago, that broke up into Gondwanaland and Laurasia.

Paragenesis. The sequence in time in which a mineral crystallizes with respect to the other minerals. Important for what it tells us of the requirements for each mineral's formation in pressure, temperature, and geological environment.

Paramorph. A crystal that is chemically identical to the original crystal, but the atoms have been rearranged so that they no longer conform to the original outline (see *pseudomorph*). The change of brookite to rutile or of aragonite to calcite is this type of paramorph.

Parting. A smooth fracture in minerals that looks like a cleavage but takes place only in certain planes in the crystal, not between any set of atoms, like cleavage. The planes along which parting takes place seem to be planes along which a row of atoms lie in a twinned position, and for this reason the bonding along that particular plane is weaker. Parting that looks like cleavage is particularly common in corundum.

Pegmatite. A very coarse plutonic rock, generally granitic in composition. Usually forming dikes that cut granite or the gneisses and schists that border granite masses. They represent the last liquid portion of the crystallizing magma. They are coarse because the liquid residue at the time of their crystallization contained a high percentage of water and other volatile elements that did not go into the makeup of the common minerals of granite, and which were for that reason concentrated in the residue. They are interesting mineralogically because minerals of the rarer elements are found with the coarse quartz, feldspar, and mica that principally compose them.

Percussion figure. The six-rayed starlike cracks that radiate outward in a sheet of mica from the point of impact of a sharp, hard-driven needle.

Petrography. The study of the mineral makeup of rocks. It is usually carried on with the assistance of the "petrographic microscope" and thin, transparent slices of rock, known as "thin sections," ground to $3/1000$ in. (0.07 mm) thickness.

Petrology. The study of the origin of rocks, trying to understand and explain some of the unusual mineral combinations that have been found as rock masses of considerable volume.

Phenocryst. Any crystal embedded in a rock such as porphyry and large enough to be conspicuous.

Phosphorescence. A luminescence emanating from substances that have been irradiated with ultraviolet light or x-rays, but persisting after the source of the stimulation has been removed (see *fluorescence*).

Piezoelectric. Describes a substance that becomes electrically charged by pressure; it can only occur in certain crystals belonging to classes of low symmetry. Always associated with pyroelectrlclty.

Pinacoid. A plane face (or pair) intersecting one axis and paralleling the plane of the other two (three).

Pisolitic. Describing a rock texture characterized by a small-scale conglomeration of tiny ($1/16$–$1/2$ in., 2–10 mm) spherical (literally, pealike) brown masses in a lighter-colored matrix.

Placer. A deposit of heavy minerals in streambeds, in which the valuable substances have been concentrated as the lighter-weight minerals have been carried away by the stream.

Pleochroism. Like dichroism except that it is applied to minerals with three instead of two different colors.

Plumose. Describes a feathery mineral growth, composed of a compact mass of slender branching crystals. A common appearance of some of the sulfosalt minerals.

Poikilitic. Describes a grain texture in which a larger grain includes a number of smaller, disoriented grains.

Polarized light. Light that has been forced to vibrate in a single plane rather than in all planes. Limited polarization takes place when light is reflected from polished nonmetallic surfaces. Light escaping from a Nicol prism (made from calcite) or coming through a green tourmaline or a sheet of Polaroid is almost completely polarized.

Polysynthetic twinning. A term that has been applied to multiple intergrowths of a mineral in twinned positions, giving the effect of many narrow striations on a cleavage or fracture surface. It is best observed in the triclinic feldspars and aids in their recognition, since it is almost invariably present.

Primary. Refers to a mineral deposit that formed directly from hot-water solutions or from molten rocks.

Pseudomorph. A substance with the crystal form of some other mineral, forming as the result of the alteration of the original mineral without losing the original shape. Pseudomorphs may form by a breakdown and rearrangement of the same atoms (a paramorph), by a slight change in composition, by a coating over another crystal, or by a complete replacement by an entirely different mineral.

Pyroclastic. Ash flow of exploded lava that became pulverized as it came down a slope to form a deposit of fragmented rocks and dust. Common in the western U.S. (See also *tephra.*)

Pyroelectric. Describes a substance that becomes electrically charged by temperature changes (see *piezoelectric*).

Rare-earth minerals. Those containing a high concentration of one or more of the group of elements called the rare earths: cerium, praesodymium, samarium, europium, gadolinium, terbium, dysprosium, neodymium, promethium, holmium, erbium, thulium, ytterbium, and lutetium. (They are no longer considered rare.)

Re-entrant angle. An angular depression, bounded by crystal faces, that characterizes twinned crystal intergrowths.

Refraction. The bending of light as it passes from air into transparent substances. Each mineral has a very definite ability to bend light differently in different crystal directions as a rule (making "double refraction"), and the determination of the "indices of refraction" is a method of mineral identification. A petrographic microscope and considerable training are required to make this a useful tool for mineral recognition.

Reniform. A descriptive term for rounded mineral surfaces, meaning kidney-like. It is coarser than botryoidal and finer than mammillary.

Scalenohedral. A crystal whose faces are scalene triangles, e.g., triangles whose three sides are unequal in length.

Schiller. A German term, from the name of a turbid German wine, for the almost metallic, sometimes bronzy, reflections that come from certain planes in some minerals. They are due to minute platy particles within the crystals, forced into a parallel arrangement by the atomic pattern of the host.

Secondary enrichment. A mineral deposit that has been altered and enriched in valuable metals such as copper as a result of the weathering of the surface portion of the vein. The dissolved metals seep downward and reach the fresh unweathered section of the vein, where they react chemically with the lower-grade minerals to form new compounds richer in copper.

Sectile. Can be cut by a knife, with a shaving curling away, like cerargyrite ("horn silver") and some of the softer metals.

Sheet. See *sill.*

Sill. An intrusive shet of lava that squeezed into sedimentary strata. The Palisades across the Hudson River from New York City are a good example. Also called a sheet.

Slickenside. A smooth, often striated, gliding or fault-rock surface. Very common in serpentinous rock outcroppings.

Sphenoidal. An incomplete type of crystal growth, in which upper and lower pyramid faces develop alternately. A simple sphenoidal crystal will look like a wedge with four flat faces. See chalcopyrite (p. 113).

Stock. A small magma intrusion rising through overlying formations and often enriching the surroundings with ore precipitated from the volatile solutions accompanying the intrusive dome.

Sublimate. A deposit that has grown from a vapor rather than from a solution. Sublimates are often seen in blowpipe testing, and some minerals around volcanoes form this way.

Syncline. Basined, sunken series of sedimentary formations; the opposite of anticline.

Tephra. Deposit of variously sized fragments ejected by a volcano.

Thermoluminescence. A glow of light resulting from the mild heating of a substance, released and visible well below the point of incandescence. Best observed in fluorite.

Till. Glacial deposit of boulders and clay left when the ice sheet of a glacier melted.

Traprock. General term for dark-colored, fine-grained, extrusive igneous rock, especially partially altered, coarse basalt. Often called simply trap.

Triboluminescence. A production of light taking the appearance of tiny sparks observed in the dark in some minerals (sphalerite, corundum) when a hard point is dragged across the surface of the mineral.

Trilling. An intergrowth of three separate orthorhombic crystals, crossing at a center and giving the effect of a six-sided (hexagonal) crystal.

Tufa. Calcarious lime deposits from springs.

Tuff. Also called welded tuff. A cemented mass of tephra with up to 50 percent sediments mixed.

Twin. Two (or more) crystals intergrown with a definite relationship between the crystal structures, so that one or more of the faces of one are parallel to unlike faces on the other. Twinning is sometimes difficult to recognize, and amateurs are likely to confuse true twinning with parallel growths, in which like faces are parallel (instead of unlike faces), or with random intergrowths, in which no consistent angular relationship is to be seen.

UV. An abbreviation for ultraviolet light.

Valence. The relative combining capacity of an atom in relation to hydrogen, which has a valence of 1. Some ele-

ments, such as iron, sometimes have more than one valence (ferrous, Fe^{+2}, and ferric, Fe^{+3}), so that you can get
either FeO, or Fe_2O_3.

Vein. A more or less upright sheet deposit of minerals, cutting other rocks and formed from solutions rather than
from a molten magma like a dike.

Vermiculite. A hydrated mica that swells and writhes in
wormlike fashion when heated, used as a moisture re-
tainer in potting soils and for an insulating plaster.

Volatilize. To change into a gaseous state, sometimes without
melting (as with ammonium chloride).

Vug. Open cavity in rocks, often lined with druses of crystals.

Vulcanism. The phenomena associated with volcanoes: fumaroles, hot springs, and lava flows.

Weathering. In the broadest sense, any of the destructive effects of the atmosphere and the exposure of rocks to the
temperature extremes of the surface. More specifically,
the chemical effects of water, carbon dioxide, and oxygen attacking and destroying the minerals that are near
the surface of the earth. Minerals that formed deep in
the earth, at high temperatures and pressures, become
unstable under surface conditions and alter to form new
compounds.

X-ray pattern. The arrangement of spots or lines revealed in a
photographic negative that has been exposed behind a
crystal or the powder of crystals at the time a slender
beam of x-rays is directed at it. Such photographs are
used for the determination of the crystal structures of
minerals, and by comparison with known minerals, for
identification.

REFERENCES

Mineralogy has reached peaks far beyond the knowledge and abilities of the average amateur. During the latter half of the twentieth century, a schism has grown between mineral lovers and today's university assemblage of laboratory technicians, who, using sophisticated equipment and a variety of specialized skills, determine all manner of details of structure and behavior. Although described species have leapt past 3,700, most of today's additions are microscopic. Basically, our grandfathers knew practically all any amateur wants to know about the handful of minerals, barely a hundred, that the amateur will find and be able to recognize. For this reason, the older texts are not outdated and often contain information unnoted in more recent publications, citing sources, history, and facts of which recent specialists are ignorant. Americans, and much of the world, still honor the work of the science's great pioneer, James D. Dana, whose first significant work, *A System of Mineralogy*, was published in 1837, starting a tradition furthered by his son, Edward Salisbury Dana, in his final effort of 1892 .

For beginners and those ready to advance beyond this work, we recommend:

Anthony, Bideaux, Bladh, and Nichols. 1990–. *Handbook of Mineralogy*. 2 vols to date. Tucson, Ariz.: Mineral Data Publishing Co. An ambitious and current project containing the modern data on minerals absent from the works of the last century. Vol. 1, dated 1990, discusses in alphabetical sequence the Elements, Sulfides, and Sulfosalts. Vol. 2, Silica and Silicates, Parts 1 and 2, were published in 1995. Further volumes are expected to appear soon. One page is devoted to each mineral (in most cases), with the headings Occurrence, Associations, Distribution, Names, (Location of) Type Material, and References.

Dana, Edward Salisbury. *Minerals and How to Study Them,* 3rd ed., revised by Cornelius S. Hurlbut, Jr., 1971. New York: John Wiley and Sons. An introductory version of the more advanced *Manual of Mineralogy,* and although excellent, not to be preferred to it except for youngsters.

——. *A Textbook of Mineralogy,* 5th ed., revised and enlarged by William E. Ford, 1954. New York: John Wiley and Sons. This oldie-but-goodie one-volume work lists practically all the significant minerals to its date, giving some descriptive data on each. For the average collector, this is the ultimate; buy it in a second-hand book shop. The now seldom-used introductory material on testing and crystallography is noteworthy, but of college level. If you can find one, this is still and will remain the best all-around advanced textbook. A new and perhaps excessively reworked edition is in the offing (rewritten by Skinner, Foord, and Gaines) and will soon be available. However, since it is reported that the introductory class/laboratory information on crystallogrphy and testing is being omitted, the earlier Ford version will remain ever desirable.

Dana, James Dwight. *Manual of Mineralogy,* 20th ed., revised by Cornelius Hurlbut, Jr. and Cornelius Klein, 1985. (21st ed. by Cornelius Klein, 1993). New York: John Wiley and Sons. Probably the best college-level textbook in any language, giving considerable space to the properties of minerals and their identification, together with descriptions of the most common and important varieties.

——, and Edward Salisbury Dana. *The System of Mineralogy,* 7th ed. 3 vols. Rewritten and enlarged by Charles Palache, Harry Berman, and Clifford Frondel, 1944–62. New York: John Wiley and Sons. This is the English-language standard international reference work on minerals, a revision and the latest update of the original work begun by James Dwight Dana in 1837 and brought up to date in 1892 by his son Edward Salisbury Dana. It is usually referred to as *Dana's System of Mineralogy.* No serious mineralogist should be without these works. The 1892, 6th edition of the *System* is still essential for serious collectors. Copies can be found in second-hand book shops.

Fleischer, Michael, and Joseph A. Mandarino. 1991. *Glossary of Mineral Species.* The Mineral Record, Tucson., Ariz. Brief listings of most minerals to its date with many references to publication sources. It would not take the place of the Dana and Anthony books; it is only supplemental as a quick alphabetical reference, but it is authoritative, convenient, and the reference used by judges of competitive case labels.

Roberts, Willard L. , George R. Rapp, Jr., and Julius Weber. 1974. *Encyclopedia of Minerals.* New York: Van Nostrand Reinhold Company. A nearly complete, beautifully illustrated compendium of the most recent data on a great many of the known species. Although costly because of the numerous color photographs (the work of Julius Weber), it is indispensable for the advanced collector and a very convenient one-volume reference work for professionals. A second, far less desirable, edition, in which the Weber illustrations are replaced with ill chosen though artistic coffee table–type illustrations appeared in 1989 and may be all that is available, but the wise will try to find the first edition.

Sinkankas, John. 1989. *Emerald and Other Beryls.* Phoenix, Ariz.: Geoscience Press (and abbreviated by Peter Read, Beryl Butterworth, New York and London, 1986).
———. 1984. *Gem Cutting,* 3rd ed. New York: Chapman & Hall.
———. 1988. *Gemstone and Mineral Data Book.* New York: Geoscience Press.
———. 1959. *Gemstones of North America.* Princeton: Van Nostrand Reinhold.
———. 1976. *Gemstones of North America,* vol 2. New York: Van Nostrand Reinhold.
———. 1964. *Mineralogy for Amateurs.* Princeton: Van Nostrand Reinhold.
———. 1970. *Prospecting for Gemstones and Minerals.* New York: Van Nostrand Reinhold.
All of the John Sinkankas books are authoritative and readable and are highly recommended.

For university-level investigations:

Short, M.N. 1931. *Microscopic Determination of the Ore Minerals.* Washington, D.C., U.S. Geological Survey Bulletin 825. Intended for the student of polished-ore specimens as seen under the microscope, but the latter half of the book has an excellent set of tests, some of which need not be microscopic in dimension, for the identification of the metals in those minerals.

Smith, Orsino C. 1953. *Identification and Qualitative Chemical Determination of Minerals*, 2nd ed. Princeton: Van Nostrand Reinhold. Out of print but very useful if obtainable. A series of tables listing all minerals to 1946 by hardness and specific gravity, and suggesting chemical confirmatory tests. Good section on qualitative analysis precedes tables, with all the data required to begin this type of testing. Highly recommended as a reference and a guide, but only to supplement other books. Can replace the laboratory testing type works common early in the century.

Winchell, Alexander N., and Newton Horace Winchell. 1951. *Elements of Optical Mineralogy.* New York: John Wiley and Sons. 3 vols: Part I, *Principles and Methods;* Part II, *Description of Minerals;* Part III, *Determinative Tables.* A standard reference work on optical mineralogy and the identification of non-opaque minerals under the microscope. This is a college-level text and will be useful only to the advanced amateur with petrographic microscope equipment. The first volume is the best source of information on the discussion of optical principles. Newer books add little to Winchell, which is now out of print.

The technical journal of professional mineralogists is *The American Mineralogist*, Suite 330, 1130 17th Street, N.W., Washington, D.C. 20036.

For serious hobby collectors, the indispensable American journal is *The Mineralogical Record*, 7413 North Mowry Place, Tucson, AZ 85741.

Good international publications:
Lapis, a German publication, Christian Weise Verlag, AG, Gmbh, Orleansstrasse 69, D-81667, Munich, Germany.

Journal of the Russell Society, journal of British Topographical Mineralogy 83 Hollywood Lane, Frindsbury, Rochester, Kent, ME3 8AT, England.

Mup Kamhs World of Stones, a promising new English language Russian journal is now available for foreign subscribers , though it is likely new subscripotion arrangements are in the making.

Less serious American amateur journals are numerous and specialize in different aspects of the hobby. They include:

Gems and Minerals, P. 0. Box 687, Mentone, CA. 92359.

The Lapidary Journal, P. O Box 1100, Devon, PA 19333-0905.

Rocks and Gems, 16001 Ventura Blvd., Encino, CA. 91316.

Rocks and Minerals, 1319 18th St. N.W., Washington, D.C. 20036-1802.

For those who wish to study rock types:

Maley, Terry. 1994. *Field Geology Illustrated.* Mineral Land Publications, P.O. Box 1186, Boise, ID 83701.

The reasonably priced Roadside Geology series, for 16 states (with more in preparation), is available from the Mountain Press Publishing Co., P. O. Box 2399, Missoula, MT 59806.

INDEX

THIS INDEX covers rock and mineral descriptions and selected important subjects. Rock and mineral names are capitalized, and those that refer to main text entries are in boldface type, as are all plate numbers. The abbreviation "(sp.)" follows mineral species that are briefly described in the main-entry texts of other minerals. Other rock and mineral names include varieties, synonyms, and alternate names; popular, foreign, and vernacular names are in quotation marks.

IGNEOUS AND
PLUTONIC INTRUSIONS
    Quartz
    Feldspar
    Mica
    Dark minerals

PEGMATITE DIKES AND
MIAROLITIC CAVITIES
    Granite minerals
    Topaz
    Beryl
    Tourmaline
    Garnet
    Apatite

ORE VEINS
    Sulfides
    Gold, Tellurides

CONTACT-METAMORPHIC ORES
    Sulfides
    Scheelite
    Garnet
    Vesuvianite
    Epidote

WEATHERED VEINS
    Malachite
    Azurite
    Copper
    Anglesite
    Cerussite
    Wulfenite
    Smithsonite

FUMAROLES
    Sal Ammoniac
    Sulfur
    Sulfates, Hematite

CONTACT-
METAMORPHIC
ZONE

ORE VEINS

WEATHERING ALL ALONG THIS SURFACE

FUMAROLES

LAVA FLOW

STOCK

METAMOR

DIKE

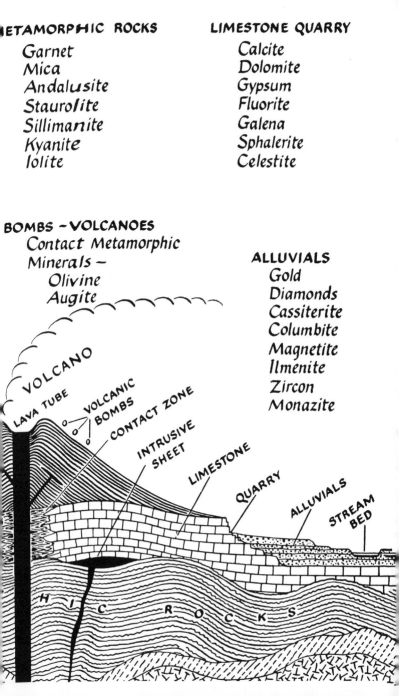